AF838117

Assuring Continuous Compliance with Joint Commission™ Standards: A Pharmacy Guide

Seventh Edition

Charles P. Coe, R.Ph.
President
Eagle Rx
Health System Pharmacy Services

John P. Uselton, R.Ph.
Vice President
Center for Safety and Clinical Excellence
Cardinal Health

American Society of Health-System Pharmacists®
Bethesda, Maryland

Any correspondence regarding this publication should be sent to the publisher, American Society of Health-System Pharmacists, 7272 Wisconsin Avenue, Bethesda, MD 20814, attention: Special Publishing.

The information presented herein reflects the opinions of the contributors and advisors. It should not be interpreted as an official policy of ASHP or as an endorsement of any product.

Because of ongoing research and improvements in technology, the information and its applications contained in this text are constantly evolving and are subject to the professional judgment and interpretation of the practitioner due to the uniqueness of a clinical situation. The editors, contributors, and ASHP have made reasonable efforts to ensure the accuracy and appropriateness of the information presented in this document. However, any user of this information is advised that the editors, contributors, advisors, and ASHP are not responsible for the continued currency of the information, for any errors or omissions, and/or for any consequences arising from the use of the information in the document in any and all practice settings. Any reader of this document is cautioned that ASHP makes no representation, guarantee, or warranty, express or implied, as to the accuracy and appropriateness of the information contained in this document and specifically disclaims any liability to any party for the accuracy and/or completeness of the material or for any damages arising out of the use or non-use of any of the information contained in this document.

Director, Acquisitions and Special Publishing: Jack Bruggeman
Senior Editorial Project Manager: Dana Battaglia
Project Editor: Kristin Eckles
Design Manager: David Wade

Library of Congress Cataloging-in-Publication Data

Coe, Charles P.

Assuring continuous compliance with Joint Commission standards : a pharmacy guide / Charles P. Coe, John P. Uselton. -- 7th ed.

p. ; cm.

Rev. ed. of: Continuous compliance with Joint Commission standards. 6th ed. 2006.

Includes bibliographical references and index.

ISBN 978-1-58528-171-8 (alk. paper)

1. Hospital pharmacies--Quality control. 2. Hospital pharmacies--Standards--United States. I. Uselton, John P. II. Coe, Charles P. Continuous compliance with Joint Commission standards. III. Joint Commission. IV. American Society of Health-System Pharmacists. V. Title.

[DNLM: 1. Pharmacy Service, Hospital. 2. Accreditation--standards. 3. Guideline Adherence. 4. Quality Control. WX 179 C672c 2008]

RA975.5.P5C54 2008
362.17'820685--dc22

2007035146

©2008, American Society of Health-System Pharmacists, Inc. All rights reserved.

No part of this publication may be reproduced or transmitted in any form or by any means, electronic or mechanical, including photocopying, microfilming, and recording, or by any information storage and retrieval system, without written permission from the American Society of Health-System Pharmacists.

ASHP® is a service mark of the American Society of Health-System Pharmacists, Inc.; registered in the U.S. Patent and Trademark Office. The Joint Commission™ is a trademark of The Joint Commission, Oakbrook Terrace, IL. The Joint Commission does not endorse or sponsor this project.

ISBN: 978-1-58528-171-8

Table of Contents

Example Forms and Documents

Appendices

Dedication

To Lynnette, Deborah, Elizabeth, Kathryn, and Stephen

To Susan, Sarah, and Brian

About the Authors

The authors have helped hundreds of health-system pharmacies comply with Joint Commission standards. This book reflects their experiences in guiding pharmacies through more than 2,000 Joint Commission surveys since 1980.

About the Contributors

Robert Jordin, R.Ph.
Director, Accreditation and Medication Safety
Center for Safety and Clinical Excellence
Cardinal Health

Patricia C. Kienle, R.Ph., MPA, FASHP
Director, Accreditation and Medication Safety
Center for Safety and Clinical Excellence
Cardinal Health

Lee B. Murdaugh, R.Ph., Ph.D.
Director, Accreditation and Medication Safety
Center for Safety and Clinical Excellence
Cardinal Health

The contributors are actively involved in helping health-system pharmacies incorporate Joint Commission standards into their everyday practice. They participated in the planning, writing, review, and critique of this edition and their contributions, experiences, and suggestions are reflected in every chapter.

Acknowledgments

As with past editions, many Cardinal Health Pharmacy Management pharmacists provided survey-related information that is reflected in this edition. Their criticisms, comments, and suggestions are reflected in the text, checklists, and examples. We are also grateful to Dana Battaglia, Kristin Eckles, and other ASHP staff who reviewed and edited the manuscript and ensured the timely completion of the project.

Reviewers

Chapter 25—Reviewed by American Osteopathic Association (AOA).

Introduction and How to Use This Book

There have been a number of changes in the Joint Commission's accreditation process since the sixth edition of this book was published in 2005. Among these are the increased emphasis on periodic self-assessments, reduced emphasis on preparing for surveys, and a requirement that health care organizations be in continuous compliance with standards. Since 2006, preparing for surveys has been impractical as surveys evolved into unannounced evaluations of how organizations continuously comply with the standards and improve care, treatment, and services. Also, since the sixth edition was published, The Joint Commission™ approved additional medication management standards, expanded its National Patient Safety Goals (NPSGs), and continued the integration of its standards and the NPSGs into the accreditation process.

The evolving title of this book reflects the Joint Commission's decreased emphasis on survey preparation and its increased emphasis on continuous compliance with standards. To that end, it aims to help pharmacies comply with the standards and NPSGs and incorporate them into their everyday practice.

Every section of the seventh edition has been completely reviewed and, when necessary, updated and expanded to reflect current standards, requirements, expectations, and interpretations. Standards and requirements effective from January 2008 are addressed to the extent they are known. New standards, requirements, expectations, and interpretations can be announced at any time. Chapter 1 lists services and resources to help pharmacists stay current. Readers are encouraged to review the literature and monitor Joint Commission and other Internet Web sites regularly.

Although some of the changes are significant, for most pharmacies, continuous compliance with the current standards is not much more difficult than compliance with previous standards. Compliance may be even easier in some cases if the pharmacy's services have been improved since the last survey.

Improvements to the Seventh Edition

A significant improvement in the seventh edition is the companion CD that, for the first time, includes many example forms and documents in a Microsoft® Word format. Now readers can easily customize the forms and documents for their organization.

A number of changes aim at improving readability and ease of locating items. The checklists clearly distinguish the authors' notes from the "check-off" items. Chapter titles are at the tops of pages throughout each chapter. Contact information is in a new appendix instead of scattered throughout the book. References are numbered consecutively within each chapter but, for convenience, are grouped in a references and resources section at the end of the book. These format improvements and the expanded index should make it easier for the reader to navigate through the book.

Overview of This Book

This book provides a guide for progressing toward continuous compliance with Joint Commission standards relating to pharmacy and medication use. It reflects onsite experiences and survey reports from hundreds of hospitals.

- ***Chapter 1*** is a general discussion of the Joint Commission and the role of accreditation in improving care, treatment, and services.
- ***Chapter 2*** describes the Joint Commission's survey process and includes updated examples of survey agendas.
- ***Chapter 3*** provides an organized approach to progressing toward continuous compliance with Joint Commission standards.
- ***Chapter 4*** is a checklist for compliance with medication management standards.
- ***Chapter 5*** describes the medication management individual-based system tracer.

- *Chapters 6 through 11* are checklists that address human resources standards; education and training of patients and family; infection control; safety, security, and storage; policies and procedures; and frequently requested documents.
- *Chapters 12 through 14* address pharmacy and therapeutics activities, competence assessment, and performance improvement activities.
- *Chapters 15 through 18* provide overviews of the Joint Commission's ORYX initiative, the Occupational Safety and Health Administration's Hazard Communication Standard, the National Institute for Occupational Safety and Health Recommendations for Handling Hazardous Drugs, and the United States Pharmacopeia Chapter <797>: Pharmaceutical Compounding—Sterile Preparations.
- *Chapter 19* describes the Joint Commission's NPSGs and the Joint Commission's compliance expectations.
- *Chapter 20* presents each 2008 NPSG requirement for hospitals in a checklist format.
- *Chapters 21 through 23* are devoted to medication safety, adverse drug reactions, and the FDA MedWatch program.
- *Chapters 24 and 25* summarize current pharmacy-related standards of the Centers for Medicare and Medicaid Services and the Healthcare Facilities Accreditation Program (HFAP) of the American Osteopathic Association.
- *Appendix A* contains contact information (e.g., names, addresses, telephone numbers, and Internet Web sites) for the organizations mentioned in the book.
- *References and Resources* contains the references grouped by chapter as well as suggested resource materials for selected chapters.
- *Example Forms and Documents* may be useful in pharmacy practice and for documenting continuous compliance with the standards. You may use them as they are or customize them to meet your needs.

How to Use this Book

Begin by Reading—Begin by reading the first three chapters of this book. Read the other chapters as you address the standards to which they pertain.

Determine Whether Standards in Other Accreditation Manuals Apply—Determine whether standards in other Joint Commission manuals of standards apply to your organization. (*See* Chapter 1.)

Complete the Checklists—Complete the checklists in this book (i.e., Chapter 4, Chapters 6 through 11, and Chapter 20).

Identify Current Deficiencies—Use the checklists to identify current deficiencies, and develop an action plan for progressing toward continuous compliance. (*See* Develop an Action Plan in Chapter 3.)

Work with the Organization's Leaders—Work closely with the organization's leaders. Perform a Periodic Performance Review (PPR) as described in Chapter 2 and share information with the organization as described in Chapter 3.

Focus on Problematic Areas—Give special attention to the problematic areas described in Chapter 3.

Follow the Suggestions in Chapter 3—Chapter 3 contains additional suggestions for using this book. These include organizing documents and conducting mock surveys and tracers. Attention to these suggestions provides an organized approach to progressing toward continuous compliance.

Charles P. Coe

John P. Uselton

September 2007

CHAPTER 1

The Joint Commission™

The Joint Commission (formerly known as The Joint Commission on Accreditation of Healthcare Organizations® or JCAHO®) is a nonprofit, private (i.e., independent, nongovernmental) organization. Its mission "is to continuously improve the safety and quality of care provided to the public through the provision of health care accreditation and related services that support performance improvement in health care organizations." "The Joint Commission's corporate members are the American College of Physicians, the American College of Surgeons, the American Dental Association, the American Hospital Association, and the American Medical Association." The Joint Commission maintains "state-of-the-art standards that focus on improving the quality and safety of care provided by health care organizations."[1]

Compliance with Joint Commission standards is voluntary; any health care organization may request a survey (i.e., an evaluation) to determine its level of compliance. (*See* Chapter 2.) Health care organizations request a survey by completing an application for accreditation. To ensure accuracy, the organization may ask pharmacy representatives to provide information to administrative staff who are responsible for completing the application.

Accreditation

The Joint Commission accredits acute care hospitals and other health care organizations (e.g., long-term, ambulatory, home, and behavioral health care organizations). To be accredited, organizations must provide evidence that they are in continuous compliance with the standards applicable to their organization. They must also comply with the Joint Commission's National Patient Safety Goals (NPSGs). (*See* Chapter 19.) Organizations can provide evidence that they comply with the standards and NPSGs by doing the following:

- Performing self-assessments of compliance
- Providing corrective action plans to the Joint Commission
- Providing data and information for assessment by the Joint Commission
- Undergoing on-site surveys by Joint Commission representatives (i.e., surveyors). (*See* Chapter 2.)

The director of pharmacy must ensure that the pharmacy department complies continuously with relevant standards (e.g., medication management and infection control) and the NPSGs. However, note that the Joint Commission accredits health care organizations—not pharmacies or other individual departments and services.

The Joint Commission provides a certificate of accreditation to organizations that comply with its standards and accreditation requirements. Accreditation is valid until the next full survey (which may occur at any time) and is not renewed automatically. To continue their accreditation beyond this period, organizations must undergo another full survey and comply with the standards, NPSGs, and other requirements in effect at that time.

Why Organizations Seek Accreditation

Organizations seek accreditation to be assured that they are providing safe, high-quality patient care on a continuous basis. Although Joint Commission accreditation is voluntary, failure to meet Joint Commission standards or the loss of accreditation may signal substandard patient care. Patients may be at risk, organizations may find it difficult to attract qualified practitioners, and the adverse publicity may cause patients to go elsewhere for medical care. Some states may consider Joint Commission accreditation in their state licensure process and/or exempt accredited organizations from some inspections.

Medicare Participation—Organizations must be certified by the Centers for Medicare and Medicaid Services (CMS) to participate in the federal Medicare program. CMS confers "deemed status" on a health care organization when that organization is in compliance with relevant CMS requirements because it has been accredited by an organization whose standards are determined by CMS to be equivalent to those of the Medicare program. Joint Commission-accredited organizations are eligible automatically for reimbursement in the Medicare program. Without accreditation, organizations must undergo a CMS survey and demonstrate compliance with CMS Conditions of Participation. (*See* Chapter 24.) Organizations accredited by the Healthcare Facilities Accreditation Program (HFAP) of the American Osteopathic Association (AOA) are also eligible for reimbursement in the federal Medicare program. (*See* Chapter 25.) Note that the Joint Commission and HFAP accredit; CMS certifies.

Legal Status of Standards

The Joint Commission provides uniform, nationally recognized standards on which many accredited and nonaccredited organizations base their bylaws, rules, regulations, policies, and procedures. Also, Joint Commission standards may be used to define the expected legal standards of care and failure to comply with Joint Commission standards might present legal difficulties for an organization. Furthermore, Joint Commission standards are consistent with guidelines and standards published by other organizations (e.g., the Life Safety Code® of the National Fire Protection Association). Organizations must be aware that legal requirements take precedence when Joint Commission standards conflict with laws, rules, regulations, and the guidelines and standards of other organizations.

Using Joint Commission Standards to Support Improved Services

The Joint Commission may be the pharmacy's best ally in its efforts to improve pharmacy services. Because compliance with Joint Commission standards is important to patients, leaders, and the medical staff, standards can often be used to support proposals for additional personnel and equipment needed to expand and improve services. Proposals should clearly indicate the following:

- Specific standards that will be met
- Quality of care and patient safety improvements that will be made
- Problems that will be avoided
- Legal liability for failure to meet the standards

Comprehensive Accreditation Manual for Hospitals: The Official Handbook

The Joint Commission publishes its standards in the *Comprehensive Accreditation Manual for Hospitals: The Official Handbook (CAMH)*.[2] The *CAMH* includes accreditation policies and procedures, accreditation participation requirements, the latest standards, compliance information, how to gauge compliance, and a glossary of terms. The *CAMH* divides an organization's important functions into three sections. Table 1-1 lists the sections, the functions included in each section, and examples of topics for each function.

Note: The Joint Commission also publishes its standards in the *Hospital Accreditation Standards (HAS)*. It is smaller and more compact than the *CAMH* and is intended to be a quick reference to the standards. Although the *HAS* is published annually, it may not be as current as an up-to-date *CAMH*.

The *CAMH* is available as a subscription service with twice a year updates published in March and September. The updates ensure that organizations have new standards and current information. The Joint Commission provides a current *CAMH* to all accredited organizations and to organizations seeking accreditation. Organizations may order additional copies of the *CAMH* from the Joint Commission.

An annual software product, *Accreditation Manager Plus—An Interactive Tool Kit for Continuous Compliance*, is also available from the Joint Commission. *Accreditation Manager Plus* contains all the information in the *CAMH* and has project management, documentation, and performance tracking capabilities.

Other Joint Commission Manuals of Standards

In addition to the manual of standards for acute care hospitals, the Joint Commission publishes other manuals of standards. A complete list is on the Joint Commission's Internet Web site. (*See* Joint Commission Internet Web site in this chapter.) These manuals include the following:

- *Comprehensive Accreditation Manual for Ambulatory Care (CAMAC)*
- *Comprehensive Accreditation Manual for Laboratory and Point of Care Testing (CAMLAB)*
- *Comprehensive Accreditation Manual for Long-Term Care (CAMLTC)*
- *Comprehensive Accreditation Manual for Behavioral Health Care (CAMBHC)*
- *Comprehensive Accreditation Manual for Home Care (CAMHC)*
- *Comprehensive Accreditation Manual for Critical Access Hospitals (CAMCAH)*
- *Comprehensive Accreditation Manual for Office-Based Surgery Practices (CAMOBS)*

Pharmacists should check with their organization's leaders to determine whether any areas or services (e.g., long-term care and behavioral health units) will be surveyed under standards in these manuals. If necessary, they should review the standards for these services and modify the process for assuring compliance accordingly.

Additional Joint Commission Services and Resources

The Joint Commission provides several services and resources to help organizations comply continuously with standards and improve services. Organizations may inquire about services, order Joint Commission publications and periodicals, and subscribe to free Joint Commission e-mail newsletters and information by telephoning Joint Commission Customer Service or through the Joint Commission's Internet Web site. (*See* Joint Commission Internet Web site in this chapter and Appendix A.)

Joint Commission Internet Web Site—The Joint Commission's Internet Web site offers information about the Joint Commission and its affiliated organizations. It also provides information about Joint Commission educational programs and services, proposed standards and standards undergoing field reviews, and how to order publications. (*See* Appendix A.)

Interpretation of Standards—The Joint Commission will provide official interpretation of its standards and information on how to comply with standards upon request. Requests must be submitted to the Joint Commission's Standards Interpretation Group. Organizations can also submit requests by using the standards online question submission form on the Joint Commission's Internet Web site. (*See* Appendix A.) Although oral advice may be sufficient, a written response will be provided if requested.

Standards Clarifications/Frequently Asked Questions—The Joint Commission's Standards Interpretation Group develops standards clarifications when a significant number of organizations have questions about standards that are not clearly addressed in an accreditation manual. Frequently asked questions (FAQs) relating to standards are available on the Joint Commission's Internet Web site. (*See* Appendix A.) Organizations should be aware that surveyor interpretations of the standards might not be consistent with the FAQs and other Joint Commission clarification and interpretation resources.

Accreditation Process Guide for Hospitals—The Joint Commission's annual publication *Accreditation Process Guide for Hospitals* helps organizations understand the Joint Commission's accreditation process, how to apply for accreditation, and what to expect during a survey. It contains sample survey agendas and other information needed to ensure a smooth survey experience. Although the guide does not focus on the pharmacy, pharmacies will probably find it a useful supplement to the material in this book.

Joint Commission Perspectives®—The Joint Commission's official monthly newsletter, *Joint Commission Perspectives*, is the primary source of information on changes to standards, accreditation requirements (e.g., the survey process), and Joint Commission initiatives. *Joint Commission* Perspectives is available on-line to subscribers. (*See* Joint Commission Internet Web site in Appendix A.) Pharmacy managers should read the newsletter.

Joint Commission Perspectives on Patient Safety™—The Joint Commission's monthly newsletter *Joint Commission Perspectives on Patient Safety* provides information on preventing errors and improving patient safety. Topics include strategies for meeting the Joint Commission's NPSGs (*see* Chapter 19), creating a culture of safety, risk management, and specific patient safety issues (e.g., falls and suicide prevention). *Joint Commission Perspectives on Patient* Safety is available on-line to subscribers. (*See* Joint Commission Internet Web site in Appendix A.) Pharmacy managers should read the newsletter.

Sentinel Event Alert—The Joint Commission's *Sentinel Event Alert* newsletter provides information for chief executive officers, chief medical officers, chief nursing officers, and other organization leaders (e.g., pharmacy directors) about the occurrence, cause, and management of sentinel events. (*See* Chapter 14.) It includes information relating to sentinel event policies and procedures, describes specific types of sentinel events, and offers suggestions for preventing sentinel events. The newsletter is currently distributed by e-mail and is available on the Joint Commission's Internet Web site. (*See* Appendix A.) Organizations are expected to forward the newsletter to appropriate staff. Pharmacy managers should read the newsletter.

Other Joint Commission Patient Safety Publications—The Joint Commission publishes other patient safety publications. A complete list is available on the Joint Commission's Internet Web site. (*See* Appendix A.) These publications include the following:

- *Preventing Medication Errors: Strategies for Pharmacists*
- *Medication Reconciliation Handbook*
- *Medication Use: A Systems Approach to Reducing Errors*
- *Sentinel Events: Evaluating Cause and Planning Improvement*
- *Root Cause Analysis in Health Care: Tools and Techniques*
- *Failure Mode and Effects Analysis in Health Care: Proactive Risk Reduction*
- *Front Line of Defense: The Role of Nurses in Preventing Sentinel Events*
- *Patient Safety Essentials for Healthcare*

Joint Commission Resources Consulting—The Joint Commission, through Joint Commission Resources (JCR) Consulting, offers consulting and educational services to hospitals, long-term care facilities, and other types of health care organizations. JCR Consulting can provide a thorough assessment of an organization and offer clear suggestions for improving compliance. JCR Consulting is entirely separate from the Joint Commission. Organizations that retain JCR Consulting will not receive special treatment from the Joint Commission. Organizations can obtain information about JCR Consulting on the JCR Internet Web site or by telephone. (*See* Appendix A.)

JCR Seminars—JCR offers seminars on standards compliance, performance improvement, and other survey-related topics. However, these programs tend to focus on organizationwide standards and are rarely specific to pharmacy. Organizations can obtain information about the seminars through the JCR Internet Web site or by telephoning JCR Customer Service. (*See* Appendix A.)

American Society of Health-System Pharmacists Resources

The American Society of Health-System Pharmacists (ASHP) has several resources to help pharmacists keep current and comply continuously with Joint Commission standards. Organizations can obtain information about ASHP resources through the ASHP Internet Web site or by telephone. (*See* ASHP Internet Web site in this chapter and Appendix A.)

ASHP Internet Web Site—ASHP's Internet Web site offers resources that help pharmacists stay current on standards, laws, and how to comply continuously with Joint Commission standards. (*See* Appendix A.) These include the following:

- Sections and Forums (e.g., Clinical Specialists and Scientists; Home, Ambulatory, and Chronic Care Practitioners; Inpatient Care Practitioners; and Pharmacy Practice Managers)
- Resource Centers (e.g., Compounding, Emergency Preparedness, and Patient Safety)
- Continuing Education (e.g., courses and publications)

American Journal of Health-System Pharmacy—The *American Journal of Health-System Pharmacy (AJHP)* is a source of timely information on standards and laws pertaining to health-system pharmacy practice. Articles in the *AJHP* may include suggestions for compliance and are often accompanied by editorial comment.

ASHP Meetings—Educational programming at ASHP's Summer Meeting and Midyear Clinical Meeting includes topics relevant to Joint Commission standards. Joint Commission representatives often make presentations at these meetings. Expert pharmacy practitioners share their experiences and offer advice on how to ensure continuous compliance. Information about ASHP meetings is available on ASHP's Internet Web site and in the *AJHP*. (*See* ASHP Internet Web site in this chapter and Appendix A.)

ASHP Policy Positions, Statements, and Guidelines—ASHP has established best practices for pharmacy services. Since these are often more stringent, more explicit, and less subject to misinterpretation than some Joint Commission standards, they can help an organization meet or exceed Joint Commission requirements. ASHP's best practices are contained in its professional policy positions, statements, and guidelines, published in the *AJHP* and compiled in *Best Practices for Hospital & Health-System Pharmacy: Guidance Documents of ASHP*. They are also available on ASHP's Internet Web site. (*See* Appendix A.)

ASHP Publications—Many ASHP publications address specific Joint Commission related topics. For example, ASHP's *Competence Assessment Tools for Health-System Pharmacies* contains job descriptions, performance evaluations, study materials, tests, skills assessment checklists, and guidelines for assessing the competence of pharmacists and support staff. ASHP's *Handbook of Institutional Pharmacy Practice* contains material on investigational drugs, controlled substances management, sterile preparations, medication safety, and many other topics relating to Joint Commission standards. ASHP's *Medication Teaching Manual: The Guide to Patient Drug Information* contains easy-to-photocopy drug monographs to help comply with the Joint Commission's patient and family education requirements. Pharmacists can obtain these publications and other ASHP publications by telephoning ASHP Customer Service or through ASHP's Internet Web site. (*See* Appendix A.)

Other Resources

In addition to Joint Commission and ASHP resources, the following may be helpful:

Hospital Pharmacy—*Hospital Pharmacy* focuses on topics of interest to pharmacists in a variety of practice environments. Topics include preventing medication errors, reducing adverse drug reactions, and compliance with Joint Commission standards. Subscription information and issues of *Hospital Pharmacy* are available on the Internet. (*See* Appendix A.)

Medication Errors—*Medication Errors* edited by Michael R. Cohen provides an examination of some of the causes of medication errors and suggestions to prevent them. Information in this publication can help organizations meet the intent of the Joint Commission's patient safety standards. The American Pharmacists Association (APhA) publishes *Medication Errors*. It is available through ASHP's Customer Service or ASHP's Internet Web site. (*See* Appendix A.)

ISMP Medication Safety Alert!—The Acute Care Edition of the *ISMP Medication Safety Alert!* is a biweekly publication of the Institute for Safe Medication Practices (ISMP). Issues contain vital, potentially life-saving information about medication and device errors and adverse drug reactions that can help organizations meet the intent of the Joint Commission's patient safety standards. Similar publications for nurses and community/ambulatory practitioners are also available. ISMP sends the Acute Care Edition of the *ISMP Medication Safety Alert!* to subscribers by e-mail. ISMP also provides a Medication Safety Self Assessment® for hospitals. Subscription information about the *ISMP Medication Safety Alert!* and the Medication Safety Self Assessment is available on ISMP's Internet Web site. (*See* Appendix A.)

Independent Publications That Focus on Compliance with Joint Commission Standards—Health care organizations often subscribe to independent publications that focus on compliance with Joint Commission standards. Some of them are easily confused with official Joint Commission publications. Although they may be helpful, they are sometimes inaccurate and misleading. Often they focus on impressing surveyors and passing surveys instead of using the standards to improve patient safety and the quality of patient care. The Joint Commission makes it clear that it has no relationship with these publications. The Joint Commission is the best source for accurate information related to standards and surveys.

Independent Consultants—Health care organizations often employ independent consultants to assess their survey readiness and help them prepare for a survey. Many are excellent; some are questionable. JCR Consulting is likely to be more current and reliable than independent consultants. Organizations can obtain information about independent consultants from other organizations, health care journals, and the Internet (e.g., by searching for "joint commission consultants" or "jcaho consultants").

Table 1-1. *CAMH* Functions and Example Topics

Section 1: Patient-Focused Functions	Example Topics
Ethics, Rights, and Responsibilities (RI)	Relationships with patients, providing adequate information to patients, involving patient and family in decisions, research, informing patients and families about outcomes of care, privacy, and confidentiality
Provision of Care, Treatment, and Services (PC)	Assessing patient needs; planning care, treatment, and services; providing the care, treatment, and services the patient needs; and coordinating care, treatment, and services
Medication Management (MM)	Patient specific information; selecting and procuring medications; storing medications; ordering medications and transcribing medication orders; preparing and dispensing medications; administering medications; and monitoring the effects of medications
Surveillance, Prevention, and Control of Infection (IC)	Reducing the risk of acquiring and transmitting infections
Section 2: Organization Functions	**Example Topics**
Improving Organization Performance (PI)	Improving patient outcomes by improving patient-related processes
Leadership (LD)	Governance; managing; planning, designing, and providing services; improving safety and quality of care; using clinical practice guidelines; and teaching and coaching staff
Management of the Environment of Care (EC)	Reducing risks and hazards, preventing accidents and injuries, maintaining safe and secure conditions, emergency procedures, hazardous materials, look and feel of spaces, and the patient's social environment
Management of Human Resources (HR)	Providing adequate competent staff; orienting, training, and educating staff; and assessing, maintaining, and improving competence
Management of Information (IM)	Capturing, analyzing, comparing, transmitting, and using data and information
Section 3: Structures with Functions	**Example Topics**
Medical Staff (MS)	Medical staff organization, bylaws, rules, regulations, credentialing, medical education, and role in performance improvement activities
Nursing (NR)	Responsibilities of the nurse executive and nursing leaders, establishing standards of nursing practice, and role in performance improvement activities

CHAPTER 2

Joint Commission™ Surveys

The Joint Commission's accreditation process includes undergoing an on-site survey by Joint Commission representatives. (*See* Accreditation in Chapter 1.) Joint Commission surveys focus on assessing the quality of care, continuous operational improvement, and continuous compliance with all standards and National Patient Safety Goals (NPSGs). (*See* Chapter 19.) An understanding of the standards and the survey process is essential to demonstrating continuous compliance. This chapter provides an overview of the standards; self-assessments of compliance; types of surveys; and what to expect before, during, and after a survey.

Standards

The Joint Commission assigns a two-letter prefix to each standard. The following prefixes are used:

EC	=	Management of the environment of care
HR	=	Management of human resources
IM	=	Management of information
IC	=	Surveillance, prevention, and control of infection
LD	=	Leadership
MM	=	Medication management
MS	=	Medical staff
NR	=	Nursing
PC	=	Provision of care, treatment, and services
PI	=	Improving organization performance
RI	=	Ethics, rights, and responsibilities

Numbering of Standards—The Joint Commission assigns a number to each standard. For example, MM.2.40 is medication management standard number 2.40.

Notes, Rationales, and Elements of Performance—A rationale for the standard follows some, but not all, standards. One or more elements of performance (EPs) are provided for each standard and the EPs for each standard are numbered consecutively. Notes and footnotes clarify some standards and EPs.

Example Standard, Rationale, and EPs—An example medication management standard with its rationale and EPs follows[1]:

> "Standard MM.2.40
>
> A process is established to safely manage medications brought into the hospital by patients or their families.
>
> Rationale for MM.2.40
>
> A number of valid reasons exist for allowing patients to use their own medications in a hospital, including the need for continuous therapy; a patient's use of a nonformulary medication; or a lack of alternatives to a patient's personal medication. The hospital defines its responsibilities for the safe use of these medications.
>
> Elements of Performance for MM.2.40
>
> The hospital addresses the use of medications brought into the hospital by patients or their families, including the following:
>
> 1. Defining when such medications can be used or administered.
> 2. Identifying the medication and visually evaluating its integrity, when medications brought in by the patient or family are allowed.
> 3. Informing the prescriber and patient if medications brought into the hospital by patients or their families are not permitted."

Scoring EPs and Judging Compliance with Standards

The Joint Commission uses a simple process for scoring EPs and judging compliance with standards.

Scoring of EPs—Scoring of the EPs determines the organization's compliance with a standard. A compliance track record for an initial survey or a full survey must be achieved. Most EPs are scored on the following scale:

Score		Initial Surveys	Full Surveys
0	Insufficient compliance	4 months or more	12 months or more
1	Partial compliance	2 to 3 months	6 to 11 months
2	Satisfactory compliance	Fewer than 2 months	Fewer than 6 months
NA	Not applicable		

Each EP is assigned to a scoring criterion category (i.e., A, B, or C). Scoring of EPs varies by category. The Joint Commission's *Comprehensive Accreditation Manual for Hospitals (CAMH)* contains detailed information on scoring criterion categories and scoring of EPs.[1]

Judging Compliance with Standards—Standards are not scored. They are judged as either compliant or not compliant. An organization is *compliant* with a standard if 65% or more of its EPs are scored 2. An organization is *not compliant* with a standard if *any* of its EPs are scored 0. The *CAMH* contains more information on judging compliance with standards.

Periodic Performance Review (PPR)

A PPR is a mandatory annual assessment of compliance with all applicable standards and EPs, all NPSGs, and all Accreditation Participation Requirements (APRs). Organizations use the Joint Commission's extranet to obtain an electronic PPR tool and to submit the completed PPR to the Joint Commission.

Organizations must complete and submit the PPR, submit corrective action plans for standards that are not in full compliance, and identify how they will evaluate the success of the plans. Although PPR results will not affect the accreditation decision, failure to complete a PPR could affect the decision. More information on completing the PPR is in the *CAMH*.

PPR Options—There are alternatives to participating in the full PPR self-assessment described above. After legal counseling, an organization may choose one of the options described below. More information on PPR options is in the *CAMH*.

Option 1—Complete, but not submit, a PPR, plan of action, and Measures of Success (MOS) for deficiencies identified during the assessment. (*See* Measures of Success Report in this chapter.) The organization *may* elect to participate in a conference call with the Joint Commission to discuss issues relating to the standards. During the next full survey, surveyors validate that MOS data show that performance was achieved and sustained.

Option 2—Undergo a limited survey and submit a plan of action and MOS for deficiencies cited at the survey. The organization also may elect to participate in a conference call with the Joint Commission to discuss the plan of action and MOS. During the full survey, surveyors validate that MOS data show that performance was sustained.

Option 3—Undergo a limited survey and *not* submit a plan of action and MOS for deficiencies cited at the survey. The organization *may* elect to participate in a conference call with the Joint Commission to discuss issues relating to the standards.

Types of Surveys

There are several types of Joint Commission surveys. The *Accreditation Process Guide for Hospitals* provides a full description of each type. (*See Accreditation Process Guide for Hospitals* in Chapter 1.) Brief descriptions of some types of surveys follow:

Unannounced Surveys—The Joint Commission conducts unannounced surveys of acute care organizations. In the past these were about every three years. Currently, these surveys can occur at any time. In these full on-site surveys, surveyors look for 12 months of implementation of the standards and continuous compliance. Since regular unannounced surveys are the most common, they are the focus of this book.

Initial Surveys—Organizations that are operating and are seeking an initial accreditation must undergo a full survey. However, they will need to show only a four-month record of ongoing satisfactory compliance with the standards (instead of a 12-month record required for a regular unannounced survey). All initial surveys are unannounced.

Early Surveys—A new organization may choose to be surveyed before it begins operating. The Joint Commission provides a limited survey option and a full survey option to organizations that desire an early survey.

Multiorganization Surveys—Systems that include two or more organizations may undergo a multiorganization survey. A multiorganization survey includes a corporate orientation and a survey of each of the organizations within the system. Accreditation is awarded to the individual organizations (i.e., not the system).

Complex Organization Surveys—Organizations that provide more than one level or type of care in more than one type of setting may undergo a complex organization survey. These organizations will be surveyed under standards and EPs from two or more accreditation manuals.

Unscheduled and Unannounced for Cause Surveys—An unscheduled and unannounced for cause survey is usually performed when there is reason to believe that a serious situation is present (e.g., a threat to patient care or safety) or credible reason to believe that an organization has falsified accreditation information. No advance notice is provided for these surveys. These surveys can include all of an organization's services or address only those areas where serious concerns exist. The results may prompt follow-up activities and alter an organization's accreditation status (e.g., from "accredited" to "accreditation denied").

Random Unannounced Surveys—Each year, the Joint Commission performs random, unannounced surveys of about 5% of its accredited organizations. Organizations should be prepared for a random, unannounced survey from 9 to 30 months after the date of their last full survey. However, the Joint Commission may perform these surveys at any time.

Random, unannounced surveys are conducted for one day by one surveyor. The surveyor assesses compliance with both *fixed* and *variable* components. *Fixed* components are based on selected program-specific Priority Focus Areas (PFAs) and the NPSGs applicable to the organization. *Variable* components are organization-specific PFAs identified through a Priority Focus Process (PFP).

The focus of a random, unannounced survey may change from year to year. PFAs and NPSGs are updated annually and published in *Joint Commission Perspectives*®. (*See* Chapter 1.) Organizations may contact the Joint Commission for a current list of fixed components. (*See* Appendix A.) (*See* Pre-Survey Activities in this chapter for more information on PFAs and the PFPs. *See* Chapters 19 and 20 for more information on NPSGs.)

Survey Length

The number of days required for a survey is based on information in the organization's application for accreditation (e.g., size and patient populations). (*See* Chapter 1.) Most surveys last three or four days. However, surveys of very small organizations may be shorter, and those of very large organizations may be longer. Tables 2-1 and 2-2 are examples of survey agendas.

Note: If necessary, surveyors may conduct "off-shift visits" (i.e., evenings, nights, and weekends). These visits will not be scheduled in advance and may occur at anytime during a survey.

The Survey Team

The composition of the survey team is based on information in the organization's application for accreditation. (*See* Chapter 1.) Teams usually consist of two or three members (e.g., a physician and registered nurse, or a physician, registered nurse, and administrator). One surveyor conducts some surveys. Survey teams also include a *Life Safety Code*® Specialist who conducts a one or two-day review of life safety and physical plant requirements. Surveys of large organizations or multiple-site facilities, or organizations with specialized services may require additional team members (e.g., long-term care, home health, behavioral health, or pharmacist surveyors). A medical technologist may inspect the laboratory at another time (e.g., three to four weeks before the survey). Occasionally, surveyors or inspectors from other agencies (e.g., the state health department or a licensing entity) accompany Joint Commission surveyors.

Pre-Survey Activities

The Joint Commission must conduct several activities before surveying an organization. The Joint Commission's pre-survey activities include:

Priority Focus Process—The Joint Commission uses data from the organization's application for accreditation, previous survey findings, ORYX data (*see* Chapter 15), other data provided by the organization, and data from external sources (e.g., state inspection reports) to prepare a Priority Focus Process (PFP) for the survey. PFP information is available to surveyors before an on-site survey. It is available to an organization on the morning of its unannounced survey.

Priority Focus Areas and Clinical/Service Groups—The Joint Commission analyzes pre-survey data and identifies the organization's Priority Focus Areas (PFAs) and Clinical/Service Groups (CSGs). PFAs are an organization's processes, systems, or structures that have a significant affect on the quality and safety of care. Examples of PFAs are medication management, infection control, and patient safety. CSGs are categories of patients or services. CSGs vary by organization. Examples of CSGs are general surgery and pediatrics. PFAs and CSGs help surveyors set their focus for the survey, identify potential processes and relevant standards to assess, and schedule on-site survey activities.

Opening Survey Sessions and Activities

Organizations can expect their survey to begin with the following sessions and activities:

Opening Conference and Orientation to the Organization—The morning of the first survey day begins with an Opening Conference and Orientation to the Organization. During the Opening Conference, surveyors explain how the survey will be conducted and the organization's senior leaders and key staff ask questions about the survey. During the Orientation to the Organization, the organization's senior leaders and key staff explain and describe the organization to the surveyors.

Surveyor Preliminary Planning Session—Surveyors hold a Surveyor Preliminary Planning Session immediately after the Opening Conference and Orientation to the Organization. Surveyors use this session to look at PFAs, CSGs, and other information about the organization; plan the survey agenda; select the initial individual tracers to use in the survey; and identify representative CSGs.

Tracer Activities

Much of a survey consists of visits to care and service areas (e.g., patient care units and pharmacy) and the use of tracers to assess continuous compliance with relevant standards (including implementation of NPSGs) and determine how well the organization provides care, treatment, and services. Tracer methodology is used in the building assessment, visits to patient care areas, chart reviews, and staff and patient interviews. In addition, surveyors use tracers to validate the organization's self-assessment and implementation of its corrective action plan. (*See* Periodic Performance Review in this chapter.)

Individual Tracers—Individual tracers follow a specific individual (e.g., patient, resident, or client) from preadmission to postdischarge (i.e., all areas associated with the individual's care). Surveyors review output from the PFP to identify individual tracers based on the organization's top CSGs. During the Surveyor Preliminary Planning Session, surveyors and the organization select initial individual tracers from a list of active patients, residents, or clients. Individual tracer activities begin where the selected individuals are currently located and may lead surveyors to the pharmacy and other departments. Pharmacy personnel must be ready to respond to questions relating to medications.

Individual-Based System Tracers—Individual-based system tracers focus on important organizationwide high-risk processes or functions and are used in visits to departments or areas involved in a process or function. Individual-based system tracers for medication management, infection control, and data use are described below.

Medication Management System Tracer—The medication management system tracer includes a review of medical records to identify high-risk patients and/or patients on high-risk/high-alert and other specified medications. The activity traces the path of medications through the organization and addresses medication processes (i.e., selection and procurement, storage, ordering and transcribing, preparing and dispensing, administering, and monitoring). It includes area visits and an evaluation of the organization's medication management process; processes for reporting errors, system breakdowns, near misses; other issues relating to safe and effective use of medications; and implementation of NPSGs relating to medication management. (*See* Chapter 5.)

Infection Control System Tracer—The infection control system tracer evaluates the organization's infection control processes. It includes a review of a patient record followed by a review of the patient's progress through the organization to determine how staff follows infection control processes (including processes that reduce the risk of health care–associated infections). Staff can expect surveyors to observe and discuss processes relating to the NPSGs (e.g., continuous compliance with CDC hand-hygiene guidelines and managing as sentinel events all identified cases of unanticipated death or major permanent loss of function associated with a health care–associated infection). Infection control system tracer activities may lead surveyors to the pharmacy and other departments. Pharmacy personnel must be ready to respond to questions relating to infection control (e.g., procedures for compounding sterile preparations, risk points in the process for compounding sterile preparations, education and training in compounding sterile preparations, and environmental monitoring of sterile preparation compounding areas). (*See* Chapter 8.)

Data Use System Tracer—The data use system tracer evaluates how the organization uses data to improve patient safety and patient care. Surveyors may review data relating to medication errors, adverse drug events, staffing effectiveness, and infection control. Staff can expect surveyors to discuss and evaluate how the organization uses data associated with the NPSGs (e.g., accurate patient identification, effective communication, safe use of medications, reduced risk of health care–associated infections, reconciliation of medications, and reduced risk of patient falls.) Organizations must be able to show how they use data to monitor adherence to CDC hand-hygiene guidelines. Pharmacy personnel must be ready to respond to questions relating to data use (e.g., ensuring data security and integrity, methods for tracking pharmacy interventions, methods for monitoring overrides of automated medication storage and distribution devices, and methods for tracking adverse drug events).

Program-Specific Tracers—Program-specific tracers may be conducted in some organizations that have unique characteristics. These tracers aim to identify safety concerns within different levels and types of care. The *CAMH* contains additional information about the applicability of program-specific tracers to specific organizations.

Other Survey Sessions and Activities

Other survey sessions and activities include the following as applicable:

Life Safety Code® Building Tour—During the *Life Safety Code* Building Tour, a surveyor will tour the facilities and determine how the organization complies with fire protection requirements of the National Fire Protection Association. The surveyor might visit the pharmacy during this tour. (*See* The Survey Team in this chapter.) Pharmacy personnel must be ready to respond to questions pertaining to fire safety (e.g., fire evacuation routes and location of fire extinguishers).

Environment of Care Session—The Environment of Care Session includes a group discussion of the organization's environment of care (EC) management plans, emergency management, and EC issues identified during the survey. A surveyor asks questions pertaining to the organization's EC management process. The surveyor may observe how the organization implements specific EC processes or trace how the organization addresses a specific risk.

Competence Assessment Process—The Competence Assessment Process focuses on how the organization determines that staff is qualified and competent. A surveyor uses data from tracer activities to guide the discussion. Topics pertain to determining compliance with policies and procedures, staffing adequacy, orientation and education, and competence assessment for contract staff.

Medical Staff Credentialing and Privileging—During the Medical Staff Credentialing and Privileging activity, a surveyor facilitates a discussion of the organization's process for credentialing and privileging medical staff members and licensed individual practitioners (LIPs). The surveyor reviews credentials files of selected medical staff members and LIPs

Credentialing and Assigning of Clinical Responsibilities—During the Credentialing and Assigning of Clinical Responsibilities activity, the organization and surveyors identify issues relating to credentialing and the assignment of clinical responsibilities. It includes determining if practitioners practice within their scope of assigned clinical responsibilities.

Clinical Leadership and Staff Discussion Session—The Clinical Leadership and Staff Discussion Session is a group discussion relating to the involvement of leaders and staff in providing care. It addresses the continuum of care and the interrelationships and communication between and among staff, disciplines, and services.

Governance Discussion Session—The Governance Discussion Session examines the structure and function of the organization's governing body. It includes how the governing body communicates, its knowledge of laws and regulations, its understanding of performance improvement approaches and methods, and its understanding of leadership standards relating to its role in the organization.

Special Issue Resolution—Surveyors reserve about 30 minutes in the late afternoon to resolve issues that may have arisen during the day or to devote extra time to some areas.

Surveyor Team Meeting—The survey day ends with a Surveyor Team Meeting. Surveyors use this meeting to share their findings and plan for the remainder of the survey.

Daily Briefings—The second and subsequent survey days (except for the last day) begin with a briefing for the organization's leaders. During the daily briefings, surveyors discuss general observations from the previous day and, give staff an opportunity to note important information that may have been missed on previous days. Surveyors also review the agenda for the upcoming day.

Leadership Session—At the start of the last day of the survey, surveyors meet with the organization's leaders to discuss issues relating to their findings at the system level and identify opportunities for improving the system.

Closing Survey Sessions and Activities

Surveys close with the following sessions and activities:

Surveyor Report Preparation—On the final day of the survey, surveyors meet to integrate their findings and prepare a report that reflects the organization's compliance with the standards. Surveyors also use this session to prepare for the CEO Exit Briefing and the Organization Exit Conference.

Accreditation Survey Findings Report—The Accreditation Survey Findings Report includes the surveyors' findings, requirements for improvement (RFIs) for any noncompliant standards, follow-up requirements, and supplemental findings that are less serious and do not affect the accreditation decision. Reports do not include numerical scores.

Surveyors base their accreditation decision recommendations on the number of standards judged "not compliant" at the time of the survey. If there are no RFIs, the organization is accredited as of the day after completing the survey. If there are RFIs, the Accreditation Survey Findings Reports reflects one of the following accreditation decision recommendations: accredited with RFIs, conditional accreditation, or preliminary denial of accreditation.

CEO Exit Briefing—At the conclusion of the survey, the survey team presents its Accreditation Survey Findings Report to the organization's chief executive officer (CEO). The surveyors and CEO discuss the report and decide if it will be shared with the organization's staff at the Organization Exit Conference.

Organization Exit Conference—Immediately after the CEO Exit Briefing, surveyors hold an Organization Exit Conference with the organization's leaders and staff. The surveyors present the survey findings and distribute a copy of the report if authorized by the CEO. Leaders and staff may ask questions and make comments during this session. They may also question the findings and submit additional evidence of compliance.

Post-Survey Activities

After the Organization Exit Conference, the survey team leaves the Accreditation Survey Findings Report with the organization and transmits the results to the Joint Commission's Central Office. Post-survey activities vary with the accreditation decision recommendation reflected in the report.

Evidence of Standards Compliance (ESC) Report—If the Accreditation Survey Findings Report indicates that an organization is accredited *with no RFIs*, no further action is required of the organization. Organizations that are accredited *with RFIs* must submit a corrective and/or clarifying Evidence of Standards Compliance (ESC) Report within 45 days of the survey. Organizations that receive conditional accreditation or preliminary denial of accreditation must submit an ESC Report *and undergo an on-site survey*. The complete requirements are in the *CAMH*.

The ESC Report is *not* a plan that describes how the organization will meet the RFI. Rather, it must state how the organization currently complies with the standards or clarify how the organization believes it was compliant at the time of the survey. The ESC Report must include, when applicable, a measure of success (MOS) used to assess sustained compliance with an EP. (*See* Measures of Success Report in this chapter.)

Measures of Success Report—An *M* in the left margin of the *CAMH* next to some EPs is an MOS icon. Organizations must develop an MOS for these EPs when a standard is judged to be out of compliance through an on-site survey or a PPR. An MOS usually relates to an audit that shows that actions taken were successful and sustained. (*See* the *CAMH* for more on developing an MOS.) A Measures of Success Report is due to the Joint Commission four months after the Joint Commission approves the ESC Report.

Accreditation Decisions—The Joint Commission bases its accreditation decision on its review of the ESC Report and the findings of any follow-up on-site survey. Accreditation decision categories are described below. They are described more fully in the *CAMH*. There is a process for appealing the Joint Commission's decisions.

Accredited—The organization meets the Joint Commission's accreditation requirements.

Provisional Accreditation—The organization does not address all requirements for improvement in the ESC Report or the organization's Measures of Success Report does not show that actions taken were successful and sustained.

Conditional Accreditation—The organization's number of not-compliant standards is equal to or greater than a threshold number that triggers further scrutiny. The Joint Commission may render an alternative accreditation decision. Thresholds may change. Information about the current threshold for Conditional Accreditation is on the Joint Commission's Internet Web site. (*See* Appendix A.)

Preliminary Denial of Accreditation—The organization's number of not-compliant standards is equal to or greater than a threshold number that triggers further scrutiny. The Joint Commission may render an alternative accreditation decision. Thresholds may change. Information about the current threshold for Preliminary Denial of Accreditation is on the Joint Commission's Internet Web site. (*See* Appendix A.)

Denial of Accreditation—The organization is not compliant with the standards and has no more review and appeal opportunities.

Preliminary Accreditation—The organization is compliant with selected standards in the first of two surveys in an early survey option. (*See* Types of Surveys in this chapter.)

Quality Reports

The Joint Commission publishes Quality Reports on its Quality Check® Internet Web site. (*See* Appendix A.) Quality Reports provide meaningful, comparative performance information about the quality and safety of accredited organizations. Information in Quality Reports pertains to an organization's accreditation status, implementation of the Joint Commission's NPSGs, and other measures and indicators of quality. Quality Reports do not contain scores for the standards.

Table 2-1. Example Three Day/Two Surveyor Agenda

Day 1

Time	Physician	Nurse
8:00–8:30 A.M.	Opening Conference and Orientation to Organization	
8:30–11:00 A.M.	Preliminary Planning Session	
11:00–12:30 P.M.	Individual Tracer Activity	Individual Tracer Activity
12:30–1:00 P.M.	Surveyor Lunch	
1:00–1:30 P.M.	Individual Tracer Activity	Individual Tracer Activity
1:30–3:00 P.M.		*Life Safety Code®* Building Tour[a]
3:00–4:00 P.M.	Special Issue Resolution	
4:00–4:30 P.M.	Surveyor Team Meeting/Planning Meeting	

Day 2

Time	Physician	Nurse
8:00–8:30 A.M.	Daily Briefing	
8:30–9:30 A.M.	Individual Tracer Activity	System Tracer—Data Use
9:30–12:00 P.M.		Individual Tracer Activity
12:00–12:30 P.M.	Surveyor Lunch	
12:30–1:00 P.M.	Surveyor Team Meeting/Planning Meeting	
1:00–1:30 P.M.	Individual Tracer Activity	System Tracer—Infection Control
1:30–2:00 P.M.		
2:00–2:30 P.M.		Individual Tracer Activity
2:30–3:00 P.M.	System Tracer—Medication	
3:00–3:30 P.M.	Management	
3:30–4:00 P.M.	Special Issue Resolution	
4:00–4:30 P.M.	Surveyor Team Meeting/Planning Meeting	

Day 3

Time	Physician	Nurse
8:00–9:00 A.M.	Leadership Session	
9:00–9:30 A.M.	Individual Tracer Activity	Competence Assessment Process
9:30–10:00 A.M.		
10:00–10:30 A.M.		Environment of Care Session[b]
10:30–11:00 A.M.		
11:00–11:30 A.M.	Medical Staff Credentialing	
11:30–12:00 P.M.	and Privileging	Individual Tracer Activity
12:00–1:00 P.M.	Surveyor Lunch	
1:00–3:30 P.M.	Surveyor Report Preparation	
3:30–4:30 P.M.	CEO Exit Briefing and Organization Exit Conference	

[a]Survey teams include a *Life Safety Code®* Specialist who conducts a one- or two-day review of life safety and physical plant requirements.

[b]The Environment of Care (EC) Session includes a 1½ hour Emergency Management Interview.

Table 2-2. Example Three Day/Three Surveyor Agenda

Day 1

Time	Physician	Nurse	Administrator
8:00–9:00 A.M.	Opening Conference and Orientation to Organization		
9:00–11:00 A.M.	Preliminary Planning Session		
11:00–12:30 P.M.	Individual Tracer Activity	Individual Tracer Activity	*Life Safety Code®* Building Tour[a]
12:30–1:00 P.M.	Surveyor Lunch		
1:00–3:30 P.M.	Individual Tracer Activity	Individual Tracer Activity	Individual Tracer Activity
3:30–4:00 P.M.	Special Issue Resolution		
4:00–4:30 P.M.	Surveyor Team Meeting/Planning Meeting		

Day 2

Time	Physician	Nurse	Administrator
8:00–8:30 A.M.	Daily Briefing		
8:30–9:30 P.M.	Individual Tracer Activity		System Tracer—Data Use
9:30–12:00 P.M.			Individual Tracer Activity
12:00–12:30 P.M.	Surveyor Lunch		
12:30–1:00 P.M.	Surveyor Team Meeting/Planning Meeting		
1:00–2:30 P.M.	Individual Tracer Activity	Individual Tracer Activity	Individual Tracer Activity
2:30–3:30 P.M.	System Tracer—Medication Management		
3:30–4:00 P.M.	Special Issue Resolution		
4:00–4:30 P.M.	Surveyor Team Meeting/Planning Meeting		

Day 3

Time	Physician	Nurse	Administrator
8:00–9:00 A.M.	Leadership Session		
9:00–9:30 A.M.	Individual Tracer Activity	Competence Assessment	Environment of Care Session[b]
9:30–10:00 A.M.		Process	
10:00–10:30 A.M.		System Tracer—Infection	
10:30–11:00 A.M.		Control	Individual Tracer Activity
11:00–11:30 A.M.		Individual Tracer Activity	
11:30–12:00 P.M.			
12:00–12:30 P.M.	Surveyor Lunch		
12:30–1:30 P.M.	Medical Staff Credentialing and Privileging	Individual Tracer Activity	Individual Tracer Activity[c]
1:30–3:30 P.M.	Surveyor Report Preparation		
3:30–4:30 P.M.	CEO Exit Briefing and Organization Exit Conference		

[a]Survey teams include a *Life Safety Code®* Specialist who conducts a one- or two-day review of life safety and physical plant requirements.

[b]The Environment of Care (EC) Session includes a 1½ hour Emergency Management Interview.

[c]Three-day surveys are distinguished from one- or two-day surveys by the increase in the number of Individual Tracer Activities performed.

CHAPTER 3

Assuring Continuous Compliance with Joint Commission™ Standards

Organizations must comply continuously with Joint Commission standards. Start preparing now. This chapter provides an organized approach to progressing toward continuous compliance.

Begin by Reading—Begin by reading the first three chapters of this book. Read the other chapters as you address the standards to which they pertain.

Determine Whether Standards in Other Accreditation Manuals Apply—Check with the organization's leaders to determine whether any areas or services (e.g., long-term care and behavioral health units) will be surveyed under standards in other Joint Commission manuals of standards. (*See* Chapter 1.)

Complete the Checklists—Complete the checklists in this book (i.e., Chapter 4, Chapters 6 through 11, and Chapter 20). If necessary, read the standards in context in the *Comprehensive Accreditation Manual for Hospitals (CAMH)*. Also read the medication management (MM) standards and pharmacy-related standards in other Joint Commission manuals that are applicable to the organization. (*See* Chapter 1.) Modify the process for assuring compliance accordingly.

Identify Current Deficiencies—The checklists include the MM standards, other standards that affect pharmacy, and notes and suggestions for compliance. Use the checklists to identify current deficiencies, assess the pharmacy's compliance status, and develop an action plan for progressing toward continuous compliance. (*See* Develop an Action Plan in this chapter.)

Perform a Periodic Performance Review (PPR)—Assist the organization in performing a PPR. (*See* Chapter 2.)

Provide Information to the Organization—The Joint Commission uses information provided by an organization to determine the length of the survey and the numbers and types of surveyors. The pharmacy may need to supply some of this information to the organization's administrative staff for inclusion in the application for accreditation (e.g., provision of pharmacy services to home care and long-term care patients). Be sure the information is accurate. Inaccurate information may result in additional costs to the organization and/or delay the Joint Commission's accreditation decision.

Obtain Information from the Organization—Obtain information about the next survey from the organization. Examples include areas to be surveyed, type of survey, and expected format for the survey (e.g., length and composition of the survey team). The organization should also update the pharmacy on the status of previous deficiencies relating to medications (e.g., the organization's failure to meet National Patient Safety Goals [NPSGs]).

Focus on Problematic Areas—Some standards are problematic in many organizations. Give special attention to the following problematic areas:

- Failure to secure and control access to medications in all areas of the organization. (*See* EP 5 for MM.2.20 in Chapter 4.)
- Failure to ensure medication orders are written clearly and transcribed accurately. (*See* MM.3.20 in Chapter 4.)
- Failure to accurately and completely reconcile medications across the continuum of care. (*See* NPSG 8 in Chapters 19 and 20.)
- Failure of a pharmacist to review medication orders prior to administration of the drug. (*See* MM.4.10 in Chapter 4.)
- Failure to prevent the use of unapproved abbreviations as defined by the organization. (*See* NPSG 2B in Chapters 19 and 20.)
- Failure to remove all expired medications in the pharmacy and patient-care areas. (*See* EP 7 for MM.2.20 in Chapter 4.)
- Failure to control the handling of contrast media and other medications in the Imaging department. (*See* MM.2.20, MM.4.10, and MM.4.20 in Chapter 4.)
- Failure to control the handling of respiratory medications throughout the organization. (*See* MM.2.20, MM.4.10, and MM.4.20 in Chapter 4.)
- Failure to ensure that emergency medications are secure and controlled. (*See* MM.2.30 in Chapter 4.)
- Failure to provide medications in a safe manner when the pharmacy is closed. (*See* MM.4.50 in Chapter 4.)

- Failure to identify a list of look-alike/sound-alike drugs and implement processes to prevent errors involving the interchange of those drugs. (*See* NPSG 3C in Chapters 19 and 20.)
- Failure to develop processes for managing high-risk/high-alert medications. (*See* MM.7.10 in Chapter 4.)
- Failure to secure and account for controlled substances. (*See* EP 6 for MM.2.20 in Chapter 4 and Examples 4-9 through 4-12.)
- Failure to implement a standardized approach to "hand-off" communications relating to medications. (*See* NPSG 2E in Chapters 19 and 20.)
- Failure to remove concentrated electrolytes (e.g., potassium chloride, potassium phosphate, and sodium chloride greater than 0.9%) and other high-risk/high-alert medications specified by the organization from patient care areas. (*See* EP 11 for MM.2.20 in Chapter 4.)
- Failure to prepare sterile preparations properly. (*See* EP 6 for MM.4.20 and Chapter 18.)
- Failure to inspect *all* medication areas (e.g., emergency medications) or failure to inspect the areas routinely (e.g., monthly). (*See* EP 15 for MM.2.20 in Chapter 4 and Examples 4-14 through 4-16.)
- Failure to completely document medication refrigerator and freezer temperature checks. (*See* EP 2 for MM.2.20 in Chapter 4 and Examples 4-5 through 4-7.)
- Failure to assess the competence of staff (e.g., age-specific, sterile preparation compounding, and medication safety competencies). (*See* Competence Assessment in Chapter 6, Chapter 13, and Examples 6-5 through 6-8.)

Develop an Action Plan—Although the time needed to prepare an action plan for progressing toward continuous compliance may be substantial, the benefits of a plan are worth the effort. Make the plan easy to update. Table 3-1 is an example of an action plan. The following approach is suggested:

1. List each deficiency on a form with four columns labeled *What*, *When*, *Who,* and *Status*:

   What—Break each deficiency down into the steps required for its resolution. Then list the steps in the order that they should be completed. Several drafts may be needed to develop a satisfactory listing.

   When—Assign target dates for the completion of each step. Steps with the highest priorities should have the earliest target dates.

   Who—List the names of the individuals responsible for the completion of each step. Consider their capabilities as well as their experience and interests. Divide responsibilities so that no one is overloaded.

   Status—Track progress in correcting deficiencies.

2. Check off the steps as they are completed.

3. Refer to the checklists in this book and move the check marks from "No" to "Yes" as deficiencies are corrected.

Organize Documents—Improvements in pharmacy services and patient care are fostered and pharmacy management is enhanced if files and records are organized and thinned of unneeded materials. The Joint Commission does not specify a length of time for retaining documents. However, organizations must retain documents for the period required by law.

During a survey, surveyors may ask for documents (e.g., specific policies and procedures). Only documents that surveyors request are necessary. Documents for the previous 12 months should be sufficient.

Chapter 11 is a checklist of frequently requested documents. Record the document locations on the checklist (especially if they are kept outside the pharmacy). If necessary, identify (e.g., highlight or underline), statements or areas of the documents that show compliance with standards (e.g., entries in pharmacy and therapeutics [P&T] committee minutes).

Update Policies and Procedures—Ensure that all policies and procedures are updated regularly, reflect current practices, and do not conflict with policies and procedures of other departments. Chapter 10 is a checklist of suggested policies and procedures. Some pharmacies organize their policies and procedures according to the Joint Commission's functions. (*See* Table 1-1 in Chapter 1 and Policies and Procedures in Chapter 12.)

Check with Other Pharmacies—Check with other directors of pharmacies to determine how they ensure continuous compliance. In addition, their experiences may help you understand how they demonstrate continuous compliance. Determine whether their surveyors had special interests. Surveyors, who are interested in continuing education (CE), may want to see instructional materials, CE records, and evidence that the pharmacy used CE activities to address its problems. Surveyors who are interested in infection control may want to see records pertaining to compounding sterile preparations (including assurance of competence for persons who compound sterile preparations).

Conduct Mock Surveys and Tracers—Mock surveys and tracers—conducted by the organization's administration, performance improvement (PI) staff, the pharmacy director, another organization, or an outside consultant—help to ensure continuous compliance. (*See* Chapter 2.) Because in-house staff may be biased or reluctant to criticize, some organizations look to outside consultants for an objective and unbiased approach. Surprise mock surveys may help increase the likelihood of continuous compliance. Persons who normally staff patient care areas as well as part time and temporary staff should be included in mock surveys. Plan carefully for the survey sessions and be prepared to respond to questions that surveyors might ask. (*See* Chapter 5.)

Prepare Staff and Cooperate with Other Departments/Services—Involve pharmacy staff in preparing for continuous compliance and keep them informed of how the pharmacy and organization are progressing. Discuss patient care and safety-related topics (e.g., new or revised policies and procedures) during staff meetings and in-service education presentations. Regular meetings with representatives from other departments (especially nursing service) can identify mutual problems and help departments work together to resolve them.

Emphasize Continuous Readiness—A survey may be conducted at any time; there is no advance notice. Keep policies and procedures up-to-date. Keep documents in order and materials well organized. Concentrate on the list of problematic areas in this chapter, but do not neglect other areas. Inspect areas often. Open refrigerators, medication cabinets, and drawers to inspect them as a surveyor would. Examine seals on emergency medication boxes and carts. Look under sinks and behind linen. Be alert for infection control and safety violations and risks. (*See* Chapters 8 and 9.) Keep the pharmacy clean and ensure that areas for compounding sterile preparations meet current requirements. Aim for continuous compliance. Example 3-1 is a list of pharmacy activities with suggested frequencies for performing them.

Be Prepared to Interact with Surveyors—Surveyors understand that people are often apprehensive about surveys and they try to make them as painless as possible. Experienced surveyors do not embarrass staff before their peers and superiors. So relax and be courteous and attentive. Answers must be honest and complete but concise. Staff should be advised to be patient and ask questions if they become confused. Surveyors like to explain new standards and offer suggestions. It is not true that surveyors "always find something!" Some organizations finish the survey with no deficiencies.

There is no substitute for documented compliance with the standards. However, the following suggestions may be helpful when interacting with surveyors:

- *Show and Tell*—Convert data into pictures, graphs, tables, and charts that tell a story better than words and lend credibility to responses. Posters or storyboards displaying PI activities remind staff of projects and showcase improvements.
- *Emphasize Measurements*—Quantify problems in terms of time, numbers, and cost (e.g., how long it took, how many errors were made, and how much it cost).
- *Emphasize Action Taken*—State what has been done to improve patient care (e.g., processes revised, forms revised, orientation and education provided, and staffing and organization changes made).
- *Emphasize Improvements*—Describe improvements as a result of actions taken. State how current measurements compare with initial measurements (e.g., faster, more accurate, safer, and less costly).
- *Emphasize Medication Safety*—Give specific examples of actions that resulted in safer medication processes.
- *Emphasize Teamwork*—Stress how the department works with other departments, patients, and the community to improve safety and patient care.
- *Stress Competence*—Show that individuals demonstrate their competence prior to assuming their duties.
- *Discuss Differences*—Discuss differences in interpretation of a standard or a legal requirement. Surveyors may reverse their opinions if an organization can demonstrate that it meets the standard or legal requirement.
- *Do Not Panic*—If a policy, procedure, or other document cannot be located, continue to look for it. If surveyors see the document before the exit conference, they may change the finding.
- *Relax*—Surveyors' comments and suggestions are not meant to be critical and will not necessarily be reflected in a deficiency.

Provide Truthful and Accurate Information—Information, whether verbal, written, or electronic, provided to the Joint Commission must be truthful and accurate. Never provide surveyors with falsified or misleading information (including redrafted or reformatted documents or documents that have had contents deleted) at any time. If the Joint Commission determines that an organization has falsified information, it may deny or remove accreditation and prohibit the organization from being surveyed for a period of one year.

Look Ahead—Continue to emphasize continuous compliance between surveys. Keep up with changes in contemporary pharmacy practice and address new Joint Commission standards and NPSGs promptly. Continuous compliance fosters safe, high-quality care and ensures readiness for an unannounced survey at any time.

Table 3-1. Action Plan Example

Action Plan for Continuous Compliance

Page _____ of _____

What	When	Who	Status
2008 NPSG Requirement 2A: Improve the effectiveness of communication among caregivers: For verbal or telephone orders or for telephonic reporting of critical test results, verify the complete order or test result by having the person receiving the information record and "read-back" the complete order or test result. Some staff can not verbalize the correct process for taking verbal orders. Actions needed:			
1. Provide staff with copy of verbal order policy and procedure.	Week 1	Administrative Assistant	Administrative Assistant provided verbal order policy to all pharmacists June 2nd and 3rd.
2. Make verbal order presentation to staff on each shift.	Week 2	Shift Supervisors	Presentation made to all pharmacists on all three shifts.
3. Audit medical records containing verbal orders to verify compliance.	Weeks 3 and 4	Quality Improvement Manager	30 medical records (containing verbal orders) reviewed on Week 3 with 95% compliance. 30 medical records reviewed on Week 4 with a 100% compliance rate. Will continue to audit medical records monthly for compliance.
MM.2.20 Medications are properly and safely stored. EP7: All expired, damaged and /or contaminated medications are segregated until they are removed from the hospital. Expired medications are in patient care areas. Actions needed:			
1. Remove all expired medications from patient care areas during monthly unit inspections.	Monthly	Pharmacists and Technicians	In progress.
2. Audit areas for compliance.	July 1st	Quality Improvement Manager	To be determined.

CHAPTER 4

Medication Management Standards Checklist

The Joint Commission's medication management (MM) standards address critical MM processes and support compliance with the National Patient Safety Goals (NPSGs). (*See* Chapters 19 and 20.) Organizations surveyed under the *Comprehensive Accreditation Manual for Hospitals (CAMH)* must comply with the MM standards that are applicable to them. Chapter 5 provides an overview of the MM individual-based system tracer and a strategy for demonstrating compliance with the MM standards.

When pharmacy services are provided through a contract, the contract should address responsibility for meeting the MM standards. Organizations must ensure that contracted pharmacy services comply with the standards.

The Joint Commission's Definition of Medication

The Joint Commission™ defines *medication* broadly and includes items that in the past may not have been considered to be medications. In a footnote to the overview of the MM chapter, the Joint Commission states, "For the purpose of these standards, *medication* includes prescription medications, sample medications, herbal remedies, vitamins, nutraceuticals, over-the-counter drugs, vaccines, diagnostic and contrast agents used on or administered to persons to diagnose, treat, or prevent disease or other abnormal conditions; radioactive medications; respiratory therapy treatments; parenteral nutrition; blood derivatives; intravenous solutions (plain, with electrolytes and/or drugs); and any product designated by the Food and Drug Administration (FDA) as a drug. The definition of *medication* does not include enteral nutrition solutions (which are considered food products), oxygen, and other medical gases."[1] The MM standards apply to *all* medications included in the definition.

Organization of the Checklist

This chapter presents the MM standards, rationales, and elements of performance (EPs) for hospitals in a checklist format. Their sequence follows their arrangement in the *CAMH* (i.e., patient-specific information, selection and procurement, storage, ordering and transcribing, preparing and dispensing, administering, and monitoring). The checklist quotes the standards, notes, rationales, and EPs. "Not applicable" standards and EPs are reserved for behavioral health care, long-term care, and other specialty organizations. The text for these standards and EPs are not included in this chapter. Organizations that are surveyed under the *CAMH* are not required to comply with "not applicable" standards and EPs.

The authors' comments, experiences, and suggestions are italicized and follow the EPs. They are based on the authors' personal experiences, reports from surveyed organizations, and surveyors' statements. Some reflect legal requirements, previous Joint Commission standards, or commonly accepted standards of practice. Others note variations in interpretation of the standards.

Using the Checklist

To assess compliance, use the checklist and proceed systematically. Mark the element and standard "Yes" if you are currently compliant and are sure you will continue to be compliant. Mark the element and standard "No" if you are currently not compliant (even if you are sure you will be compliant later). If you are not sure of your answer, leave a blank response. A few items may be not applicable ("NA"). Answer honestly, use a pencil (so you can change your answers), and make notes on the pages (e.g., reasons for noncompliance). Concentrate your efforts on resolving all "No" and blank responses.

Joint Commission Medication Management Standards, Rationales, and Elements of Performance

Yes **NA** **No**

PATIENT-SPECIFIC INFORMATION

Standard MM.1.10

Patient-specific information is readily accessible to those involved in the medication management system. ___ ___ ___

Rationale for MM.1.10

A major cause of medication-related sentinel events and medication errors is a lack of information. Licensed independent practitioners and health care staff who participate in the medication management system need access to important information about each patient in order to do the following:

- Facilitate continuity of care, treatment, and services.
- Create an accurate medication history and a current list of medications (also known as a *drug profile*).
- Safely order, prepare, dispense, administer, and monitor medications, as appropriate.

Elements of Performance for MM.1.10

Element 1 for MM.1.10

A written policy describes the minimum amount of information about the patient that is to be available to those involved in medication management. ___ ___ ___

Note: The hospital defines who has access to this information. (*See* Standard IM.2.10.)

Authors' Comments, Experiences, and Suggestions

The information must be in the patient's medical record and on the medication administration record (MAR).

Patient-specific information may be manual and/or electronic.

Surveyors like to see a computerized or electronic medication administration record that is provided by the pharmacy and reconciled by nursing.

In addition to patient-specific information in the medical record, the pharmacy should maintain a profile of important information for each patient (i.e., a pharmacy patient profile).

Pharmacists should verify the accuracy of entries in pharmacy patient profiles (e.g., by initials or a computer code).

	Yes	NA	No

The pharmacy must maintain the privacy and confidentiality of information. Disclosure of personal information must be limited and access must be restricted "to individuals who have need, reason, and permission for such access." (IM.2.10 and definitions associated with IM.2.10 in the CAMH, EPs 1 and 2 for RI.2.130 in the CAMH.)

Discussions relating to patients must be out of the hearing range of staff, visitors, other patients, and individuals who do not have a need or reason to know the information. Staff should not discuss patient-care issues in elevators, food service areas, and other public places.

Medication orders, pharmacy patient profiles, labels, meeting minutes, and other patient-related documents (i.e., those that contain patients' names or identifying numbers, or information relating to patients' status, treatment, diagnosis, and medications) must be securely stored and access restricted to those who have a legitimate need or reason to know and use the information therein. Some hospitals require staff to sign a confidentiality of patient information agreement. (See Example 4-1.) However, surveyors rarely ask to review this.

Disposal of patient-related documents must guarantee confidentiality. These documents must not be placed in regular trash for disposal. Complete destruction (e.g., by shredding) is usually required.

Staff must be aware that communication technology presents additional confidentiality problems. For example, patient information (and other confidential information) contained in e-mail messages can be inadvertently disseminated inside and outside the organization. Also, measures should be taken to prevent unauthorized individuals from viewing facsimile transmissions, computer screens containing patient information, and screens of automated medication storage and distribution devices.

Element 2 for MM.1.10

At a minimum, the information includes the following:

- The patient's age ____ ____ ____
- The patient's sex ____ ____ ____
- The patient's current medications ____ ____ ____
- The patient's diagnoses, comorbidities, and concurrently occurring conditions ____ ____ ____
- The patient's relevant laboratory values ____ ____ ____
- The patient's allergies and past sensitivities ____ ____ ____

As appropriate to the patient, the hospital also includes information regarding the following:

- Weight and height ____ ____ ____

	Yes	NA	No
• Pregnancy and lactation status	____	____	____
• Any other information required by the hospital for safe medication management	____	____	____

Authors' Comments, Experiences, and Suggestions

The information may include the date of birth instead of patient's age.

Current medications should include nonprescription (i.e., over-the-counter) drugs, herbal remedies, blood derivatives, and all other medications included in the Joint Commission's definition. (See The Joint Commission's Definition of Medication in the chapter.)

Known problems should be documented when diagnoses are not known.

Weight, height, or both weight and height must be available when one or the other or both are needed to determine the dose for the patient.

A current list of medications for each patient must be included in the patient's record in accordance with the organization's medication reconciliation policy.

Other information required for safe medication management may include the patient's use of illegal drugs; misuse of prescription and nonprescription medications; use of investigational medications; potential medication-food interactions; creatinine clearance (especially for patients 65 years of age and older); drug levels; hemoglobin; hematocrit; and body surface area for patients undergoing chemotherapeutic regimens.

Standard IM.6.20 requires each patient medical record to contain the following:

- *"Allergies to foods and medicines*
- *Every medication ordered or prescribed*
- *Every dose of medication administered, including the strength, dose, or rate of administration, administration devices used, access site or route, known drug allergies, and any adverse drug reaction*
- *Every medication dispensed or prescribed on discharge*
- *All relevant diagnoses/conditions established during the course of care, treatment, and services." (EP 1 for IM.6.20 in the CAMH.)*

Surveyors may look at medical records to ensure that administration is documented for contrast agents, blood derivatives, respiratory therapy treatments, and other medications included in the Joint Commission's definition of medication. (See The Joint Commission's Definition of Medication in this chapter.)

	Yes	NA	No

Standard IM.6.20 requires each patient medical record to contain "the patient's name, sex, address, date of birth, and authorized representative, if any." (EP 2 for IM.6.20 in the CAMH.)

The medical record of patients who receive continuing ambulatory care services must contain the following:

- *"Known adverse and allergic drug reactions*
- *Known long-term medications, including current prescriptions, over-the-counter drugs, and herbal preparations." (EP 3 for IM.6.40 in the CAMH.)*

Element 3 for MM.1.10

The information is accessible when needed (except in emergency situations when time does not permit) to licensed independent practitioners, and other health care staff. ____ ____ ____

Authors' Comments, Experiences, and Suggestions

The element does not define the term "accessible." Surveyors will determine if care providers can access relevant patient-specific information when they need it, where they need it, and in time to be of value. There should be no undue difficulty or delay in accessing the information.

Information in the pharmacy's patient profiles should be accessible to other care providers (directly or indirectly). Care providers may obtain after-hours access to the pharmacy's patient profiles by contacting an on-call pharmacist who can make the profile information available.

There should be procedures in place to protect patient records and prevent their loss and destruction. (EP 6 for IM.2.20 in the CAMH.)

There should be a process for the recovery of electronic records in the event of an interruption, unforeseen occurrence, or disaster. (EP 3 for IM.2.30 in the CAMH.)

Data must be protected from accidental or unauthorized intentional changes (Definition associated with IM.2.20 in the CAMH.)

Surveyors may ask pharmacy staff how they protect patient information data (e.g., data on billing documents, pharmacy patient profiles, medication labels, copies of physicians' orders, and other documents that can be linked by name or number to a patient).

The organization must retain patient-related data and information for a length of time that complies with laws and regulations. The Centers for Medicare and Medicaid Services (CMS) requires retention for five years. Many organizations require a much longer retention period.

Yes NA No

The pharmacy must make patient-related data and information available for analysis and decision making. (IM.4.10 in the CAMH.)

SELECTION AND PROCUREMENT

Standard MM.2.10

Medications available for dispensing or administration (including stock medications) are selected, listed, and procured based on criteria. ___ ___ ___

> ***Note:*** The formulary is synonymous with the list of medications available for use.

Elements of Performance for MM.2.10

Element 1 for MM.2.10

Members of the medical staff, licensed independent practitioners, and health care staff involved in ordering, dispensing, administering, and/or monitoring effects of medications develop written criteria for determining what medications are available for dispensing or administration. ___ ___ ___

Authors' Comments, Experiences, and Suggestions

In many organizations, the P&T committee or its equivalent develops and maintains the list. However, any collaborative, multidisciplinary mechanism may be used provided the medical staff approves the medications on the list. (See Formularies in Chapter 12.)

Appropriate health care professionals often include representatives from nursing services, administration, nutrition services, infection control, quality assurance/performance improvement, and laboratory.

Staff involved in ordering, dispensing, administering, and/or monitoring medications include physicians, nurses, respiratory therapists, imaging technologists, physical therapists, and pharmacists.

Element 2 for MM.2.10

At a minimum, the criteria include the indication for use, effectiveness, risks (including propensity for medication errors, abuse potential, and sentinel events), and costs. ___ ___ ___

Authors' Comments, Experiences, and Suggestions

Organizations should document their criteria and ensure that they include the minimum stipulated in the element.

	Yes	NA	No

Risks include look-alike/sound-alike names, packaging and labeling, known incidence of adverse drug reactions, and other factors that affect patient safety. The organization should review "black box warnings" to ensure it is prepared to use the medications appropriately and safely (e.g., perform laboratory tests and monitor patients). FDA Safety Alerts are available on the FDA MedWatch Internet Web site. (See Appendix A.)

Organizations should review the Institute for Safe Medication Practices (ISMP) Medication Safety Alerts that are available on the ISMP Internet Web site. (See Appendix A.)

Some organizations require a failure mode and effects analysis (FMEA) to identify the risks associated with medications proposed for inclusion on the list. (See Chapter 14.)

Evidence of approval by the medical staff (e.g., documentation in P&T committee minutes) should show that the criteria were considered when selecting medications for inclusion on the list.

Element 3 for MM.2.10

A list of medications for dispensing or administration (including strength and dosage form) is maintained and readily available. ____ ____ ____

Note: Sample medications are not required to be on this list.

Authors' Comments, Experiences, and Suggestions

A simple alphabetical listing meets the standard (because only the medication names, strengths, and dosage forms are required). Organizations may include other information.

The list must include all medications available for dispensing or administration (e.g., herbal remedies, diagnostic and contrast agents, and blood derivatives). (See The Joint Commission's Definition of Medication in this chapter.)

The list must include all medications used in clinics and off-site facilities.

The Joint Commission does not require sample medications to be on the list. However, many organizations choose to include them.

If the organization regularly dispenses and administers samples of medications (e.g., from ambulatory clinics) the medications should be approved.

A current list must be available to all prescribers, nurses, pharmacists, and other care providers who may need it.

Yes **NA** **No**

Electronic lists are easy to update. However, if the list is maintained electronically, ensure that it us accessible to those who need it (e.g., prescribers, nurses, pharmacists, and other care providers). There should also be a process for accessing the list if there is a computer failure.

Element 4 for MM.2.10

Processes and mechanisms are established to monitor patient responses to a newly added medication before the medication is made available for dispensing or administration within the hospital. ____ ____ ____

Authors' Comments, Experiences, and Suggestions

The process should be written and approved by the medical staff (e.g., by the P&T committee).

If the labeling for a newly added medication requires specific monitoring or tests, the organization must ensure that it is prepared to perform them and report the results in a timely manner.

Before a newly added medication is dispensed or administered, pharmacists, nurses, physicians and other care providers must be educated about the expected side effects of the medication and must know how to monitor patient responses. Information on the medication and monitoring guidelines should be readily available to care providers.

Element 5 for MM.2.10

Medications designated as available for dispensing or administration are reviewed at least annually based on emerging safety and efficacy information. ____ ____ ____

Authors' Comments, Experiences, and Suggestions

Formulary review and updating should reflect new knowledge about medications currently on the list, availability of new medications, and cost changes. Although the standards require a review at least annually, many organizations conduct more frequent (e.g., quarterly or continuous) reviews. Whatever the mechanism, each medication on the formulary must be reviewed at least once in a 12-month period.

Annual reviews should determine if medications should be added or deleted based on the medical staff's written criteria.

The medical staff's review and revision of the list should be documented (e.g., in P&T committee minutes and on a dated cover page with the list). Some organizations require a signed cover page.

Yes NA No

Some organizations require the completion of a formulary addition request form for adding medications to the formulary. (See Example 4-2.) The Joint Commission does not require such a form.

A formulary addition request form, if used, should include the criteria for selection and an assessment of safety. Some organizations monitor package insert changes and/or black box warnings to ensure that these issues are presented to the P&T committee when the medication is considered for addition to the formulary.

Physicians and other staff who prescribe medications should be kept informed of additions, deletions, and changes to the formulary (usually through P&T committee reports, letters, newsletters, memoranda, etc.).

Outdated editions of formularies should be destroyed or archived and labeled so that it is clear that an updated edition replaced them. Outdated editions should not be available to care providers.

Element 6 for MM.2.10

The hospital has processes to approve and procure medications that are not on the hospital's medication list. ____ ____ ____

Authors' Comments, Experiences, and Suggestions

The process should be written and approved by the medical staff (e.g., by the P&T committee).

The element requires all nonformulary medications to be approved prior to procurement.

The process for procuring nonformulary medications should require justification for the procurement.

The process does not require a complete review and approval of a nonformulary medication prior to procuring it. However, there must be written criteria to guide the pharmacy in procuring the nonformulary medication (e.g., review of safety concerns, need to educate staff who will dispense and administer the medication, cost of the medication, and amount to procure).

Organizations often require procurement of nonformulary medications to be approved by one or two designated, qualified individuals (e.g., director of pharmacy and/or chairman of the P&T committee).

Organizations should periodically (e.g., quarterly) aggregate and analyze requests for nonformulary medications and use the findings to improve their formulary review process.

	Yes	NA	No

Some organizations require a nonformulary medication request form for ordering nonformulary medications. (See Example 4-3.) The Joint Commission does not require such a form.

Although the Joint Commission does not require documentation, some organizations document approval on a nonformulary medication request form.

Some organizations maintain a list of nonformulary medications in stock that are awaiting approval for inclusion in the formulary and nonformulary medications that have been procured to meet patients' needs. (See Example 4-4.)

Element 7 for MM.2.10

The hospital has processes to address medication shortages and outages, including the following:

	Yes	NA	No
• Communicating with prescribers and staff who participate in the medication management system	____	____	____
• Developing approved substitution protocols	____	____	____
• Educating licensed independent practitioners, and health care staff who participate in the medication management system about these protocols	____	____	____
• Obtaining medications in the event of a disaster	____	____	____

Authors' Comments, Experiences, and Suggestions

Processes should be written and approved by the medical staff (e.g., by the P&T committee).

Processes should address shortages that occur repeatedly or can be anticipated as well as unexpected shortages.

Substitution protocols should be reviewed and approved by the medical staff (e.g., by the P&T committee).

Education about these protocols may be through P&T committee reports, letters, newsletters, memoranda, etc.

The organization must ensure the availability of medications for prophylaxis and treatment in the event of a disaster. Because stockpiling of adequate supplies of medications locally may not be practical, there must be a mechanism for obtaining additional supplies from vendors and emergency supply depots (e.g., the Strategic National Stockpile).

Yes NA No

STORAGE

Standard MM.2.20

Medications are properly and safely stored. ___ ___ ___

Rationale for MM.2.20

Appropriate medication storage increases patient safety. Medication storage is designed to assist in maintaining medication integrity, promote the availability of medications when needed, minimize the risk of medication diversion, and reduce potential dispensing errors.

> *Note:* The following elements of performance also apply to emergency medications. Additional requirements for emergency medications are addressed at standard MM.2.30.

Elements of Performance for MM.2.20

Element 1 for MM.2.20

Only approved medications are routinely stocked or stored. ___ ___ ___

> *Note: See* standard MM.2.40 for the exception to this element of performance. The hospital has a process to safely manage medications brought in to the hospital by the patient or the patient's family.

Authors' Comments, Experiences, and Suggestions

Although Element 1 states that only approved medications are routinely stocked or stored, the Joint Commission does not prohibit the pharmacy from stocking nonformulary medications that are awaiting evaluation and approval and nonformulary medications that have been procured to meet patients' needs.

Pharmacies should inspect their medication stocks and remove medications that are not approved for inclusion on the formulary (except medications awaiting evaluation and approval and nonformulary medications that have been procured to meet patients' needs).

Although the standard does not explicitly require on-site storage, the Joint Commission expects all medications on the formulary to be stored in the organization. Some surveyors say quick availability (e.g., within an hour) from another source is acceptable. There should never be undue difficulty or delay in patient care because a medication is stored off-site.

Element 2 for MM.2.20

Medications are stored under conditions suitable for product stability. ___ ___ ___

Yes **NA** **No**

Authors' Comments, Experiences, and Suggestions

Temperatures in the pharmacy and sterile preparations area must be monitored to ensure that medications therein are stored at temperatures appropriate for the medications.

Repackaged medications must be in light-resistant containers to ensure their stability.

Organizations must ensure that medication refrigerators, freezers, and warmers contain an accurate and reliable thermometer.

In areas that are not open every day, organizations should consider using thermometers that show high and low temperatures reached.

Refrigerator temperatures for medications must be maintained between 36°F and 46°F (2°C and 8°C).

Freezer temperatures for medications must be maintained between –4°F and 14°F (–20°C and –10°C). The appropriate temperature must be maintained in freezers in the pharmacy, patient care areas, and clinics. Freezers in some small (i.e., dormitory type) refrigerators will not maintain the required temperature range. Some medications must be maintained at temperatures below this range. For example, commercially available dinoprostone vaginal suppositories must be stored at temperatures not exceeding –4°F (–20°C).

There is no standard temperature range for warmers. Warmer temperatures vary with the product stored. Different warmer temperatures are required for irrigation solutions in surgical areas, contrast media in imaging, and mannitol in pharmacy.

The stability of the product is shortened when the overwrap is removed from a parenteral solution bag. If the overwrap is removed, the pharmacy must assign a new beyond-use date in accordance with the manufacturers' recommendations.

New beyond-use dates must be assigned when succinylcholine, atracurium, insulin, lorazepam and other medications that are usually refrigerated are stored at room temperature.

The Joint Commission does not require organizations to perform temperature checks or maintain a log of temperature checks. However, it requires evidence that refrigerators, freezers, and warmers maintain the appropriate temperature range for medication storage. If the organization requires temperature checks, the organization must specify the frequency. Many organizations require daily monitoring and recording of temperatures. Other mechanisms may be used (e.g., self-recording temperature devices, wireless remote thermometers, and temperature alarms). (See Chapter 9 and Examples 4-5 through 4-7.)

	Yes	NA	No

If temperatures are not within the appropriate range, the temperature log (or other record) must describe the action taken.

Most surveyors expect medications to be stored in separate refrigerators and freezers designated solely for medications. Organizations should prohibit storage of medications in refrigerators and freezers that contain food, chemicals, reagents, and patient specimens. If storage of medications in refrigerators and freezers with these items is unavoidable (e.g., due to space constraints), they should be in separate, well-marked containers or compartments. Every effort must be taken to prevent contamination (e.g., if appropriate, sealing the containers). Some organizations designate compartments or containers on uppermost shelves for medications and compartments or containers on lower shelves for nonmedications. When medications and nonmedications are stored in the same refrigerator or freezer, the unit must be kept at a temperature range that is suitable for all of the items in the unit.

Organizations must ensure temperatures in receiving areas and storerooms are appropriate for the medications stored therein. These areas are more likely to be subject to temperature extremes. Medications that are not stored in refrigerators or freezers may require storage at a controlled room temperature (maintained between 68°F and 77°F [20°C and 25°C] with occasional fluctuations to 59°F and 86°F [15°C and 30°C]) permitted).

Medications must also be stored safely. Agents for external use should be stored separately from agents for internal use. Flexible collodion, acetone, ethyl chloride spray, and other extremely flammable products must be stored in a cabinet designed for the storage of flammable products. They must never be stored in refrigerators.

Element 3 for MM.2.20

There is a written policy addressing the storage of medication between receipt of a medication by an individual health care provider and medication administration. At a minimum, the policy addresses the following:

	Yes	NA	No
• Safe storage	____	____	____
• Safe handling	____	____	____
• Security	____	____	____
• Disposition of these medications (including return to the pharmacy medication storage area) at the end of the individual's shift	____	____	____

Authors' Comments, Experiences, and Suggestions

Organizations must develop a written policy for how medications are handled from the time the health care provider receives the medication (or removes the medication from an automated medication storage and distribution device) until the time it is administered.

	Yes	NA	No

The organization must have written guidelines for the disposition of the remaining medication if the entire dose of the medication is not administered to a patient during a single shift.

The policy must address the disposition of medications at the end of the individual's shift.

The security of these medications must meet or exceed the minimum levels defined by the Centers for Medicare and Medicaid Services (CMS), Joint Commission, federal and state laws and regulations, and the organization's policy.

Element 4 for MM.2.20

The policy addressing the storage of medication between receipt of a medication by an individual health care provider and medication administration is implemented. ___ ___ ___

Authors' Comments, Experiences, and Suggestions

Individual doses of medications should be removed from automated medication storage and distribution devices (or floor stock) and administered immediately to patients.

Medications must not be stored in a fanny pack or the pocket of a health care provider.

Medications must be properly labeled until administered to a patient.

Element 5 for MM.2.20

Unauthorized persons, in accordance with the hospital's policy and law or regulation, cannot obtain access to medications. ___ ___ ___

Authors' Comments, Experiences, and Suggestions

CMS's definition of "secured" requires (1) that all drugs and biologicals be kept in a secure area, and locked when appropriate (2) drugs listed in Schedules II, III, IV, and V of the Comprehensive Drug Abuse Prevention and Control Act of 1970 must be kept locked within a secure area (3) only authorized personnel may have access to locked areas. *(See Chapter 24.)*

All drugs and biologicals must be stored in a manner to prevent access by nonauthorized individuals.

Persons without legal access to drugs and biologicals cannot have unmonitored access to drugs and biologicals.

Yes **NA** **No**

Persons without legal access to drugs or biologicals cannot have keys to medication storage rooms, carts, cabinets or containers. Whenever persons without legal access to the drugs or biologicals have unmonitored access to or could gain access to the drugs or biologicals stored in an area, the hospital is not in compliance with the requirement to store all drugs and biologicals in a locked storage area."[2] (See Chapter 24.)

All Schedule II through V controlled substances must be locked in a secure area wherever they are stored throughout the organization.

Locked storage may be necessary for some medications and some areas. Constant observation may be sufficient for other medications and other areas. Security must be sufficient to prevent diversion or tampering.

Individuals who access automated medication storage and distribution devices should be able to obtain only the medications they are permitted to use. For example, respiratory therapists should be able to obtain only respiratory therapy medications and imaging technologists should be able to obtain only medications they are authorized to administer (e.g., contrast agents).

The element does not stipulate that all medications must be stored in the pharmacy. Some medications (e.g., contrast agents and intravenous solutions without added medications) may be stored in other areas (e.g., central supply/materials management) provided they are secure and their stability ensured.

Keys to medication storage areas must be in the possession of authorized staff. They must not be left in a drawer or other area. Where combination locks are used, only authorized staff members are allowed to have knowledge of the codes. (Most surveyors do not consider housekeeping personnel, dietary personnel, orderlies, unit clerks, etc., to be authorized staff.)

Time-outs set on electronic locking mechanisms of medication carts and automated medication storage and distribution devices must not allow for the possibility of accessing medications after authorized staff members have left the device.

Anesthesia Medications

- *Security, control, and accountability for controlled substances, inhalation gases, and other medications in anesthetizing areas are often problematic. They should never be left unattended on the tops of anesthesia carts, in unsecured cart drawers, or in anesthesia workrooms. All controlled substances in these areas should be locked in an automated medication storage and distribution device, substantially constructed cabinet, or anesthesia cart.*
- *Anesthesia carts and workrooms must be secure (e.g., locked) when not in use.*

Yes **NA** **No**

- *Inhalation gases (e.g., desflurane and sevoflurane) should be stored to reduce the potential for diversion and abuse.*

Medication Samples

- *Surveyors expect to see a control system (e.g., a perpetual log) that tracks the receipt and distribution of each medication sample. Although the Joint Commission does not require a log, many organizations find that a log is the best way to demonstrate adequate control. (See Example 4-8.)*
- *Each medical record (e.g., patient chart) must contain all medications ordered or prescribed and every medication dispensed or prescribed on discharge. This includes sample medications. (EP 1 for IM.6.20 in the CAMH.)*
- *There should be an order for all medication samples dispensed and all samples dispensed should be properly labeled for patient use (including patient name, clear instructions for use, and any applicable cautionary statements).*
- *Samples must not be repackaged.*
- *Surveyors expect medication samples to be in locked storage or under constant surveillance throughout the organization (including the emergency department, physicians' offices, and ambulatory clinics). If patients, visitors, manufacturers' representatives, and unauthorized staff can remove samples, the storage is not secure.*
- *The Prescription Drug Marketing Act of 1987 prohibits charging patients for medication samples.*

Element 6 for MM.2.20

Controlled substances are stored to prevent diversion and according to state and federal laws and regulations. ___ ___ ___

Authors' Comments, Experiences, and Suggestions

Locked storage for controlled substances in the pharmacy and throughout the organization is required. CMS regulations require locked storage in a secure area for all controlled substances. A few states specify double-locked storage; a locked pharmacy door is counted as the second lock in many, but not all, of these states.

Keys to controlled substances storage areas must be in the possession of authorized staff. They must not be left unattended in a drawer or other area.

Many organizations use automated medication storage and distribution devices to store controlled substances. Organizations should choose models that provide a high degree of security and control, and are capable of documenting accountability for the medications.

	Yes	NA	No

There must be adequate security for lorazepam and other controlled substances in patient care area refrigerators (e.g., locked refrigerators, locked boxes in refrigerators, or locked doors to rooms in which refrigerators are located).

Organizations should be particularly attentive to controlled substances stored in anesthesia areas (especially Schedule II controlled substances, thiopental, midazolam, and ketamine).

Expired, recalled, or otherwise unusable controlled substances must be stored securely in a manner that prevents their distribution and diversion and ensures that they are disposed of safely and properly. Periodic inventories should be performed.

Inventories of controlled substances (including expired items) must be in accordance with state and federal regulations and the organization's policy. (See Examples 4-9 and 4-10.)

Wastage and destruction of controlled substances must be witnessed and properly documented in accordance with state and federal regulations and the organization's policy. Organizations should be particularly attentive to documentation of wastage and destruction of controlled substances patches, PCAs, epidurals, and other controlled substances infusions.

Surrender, loss, and theft of controlled substances must be properly documented in accordance with state and federal regulations and the organization's policy. (See Examples 4-11 and 4-12.)

Element 7 for MM.2.20

All expired, damaged, and/or contaminated medications are segregated until they are removed from the hospital. ____ ____ ____

Authors' Comments, Experiences, and Suggestions

This element should also apply to damaged and defective devices (e.g., insulin devices, infusion pumps, and IV administration sets).

Periodic inspections of medication storage, administration, and dispensing areas can identify most unusable medications and devices.

Unusable medications include those with broken packages or seals; those that are mislabeled, illegibly labeled, or whose labels are worn or missing; deteriorated medications; defective medications (e.g., improperly packaged medications, discolored medications, and medications whose integrity, effectiveness, and stability are questionable).

Yes NA No

Containers or cabinets that contain expired and unusable medications should be clearly labeled "Outdated and Unusable. Do Not Dispense, Administer, or Use" (or a similar warning). The containers should be segregated from usable medications.

Defective devices should be clearly identified with a distinctive label or tag stating "Defective. Do Not Use" (or a similar warning).

If expired and unusable medications are stored outside the main pharmacy, the storage area must be locked to prevent access by unauthorized individuals.

Element 8 for MM.2.20

Identify and, at a minimum, annually review a list of look-alike/sound-alike drugs used in the organization, and take action to prevent errors involving the interchange of these drugs. ___ ___ ___

Note: The preceding requirement is not scored here. It is scored at National Patient Safety Goal 3, Requirement 3C.

Authors' Comments, Experiences, and Suggestions

See Requirement 3C for NPSG 3 in Chapter 20.

Organizations should use distinctive packaging and labeling to the extent practical. The use of combinations of upper and lower case (e.g., "Tall Man") letters on medication labels can reduce errors due to look-alike names. For example, labeling medications as HydrOXYzine or HydrALAzine can help prevent mistaking one medication for the other. Some manufacturers include these combinations on their labels. Organizations may also use these combinations on their internally created labels.

External medications should be stored separately from medications intended for internal use.

High-risk or high-alert medications should be stored only in patient care areas where they are clinically necessary and clearly marked as high-risk or high-alert medications. (See Standard MM.7.10.)

In addition to segregation from other medications, limited access to high-risk or high-alert medications and conspicuous warning labels also help to reduce the potential for errors.

Organizations should consider using different color medication storage bins in pharmacy, patient care area, and clinic refrigerators to separate and distinguish insulin products with look-alike and sound-alike names (i.e., Humulin and Humalog, Novolog and Novolin, etc.).

	Yes	NA	No

Organizations should consider purchasing medications from different manufacturers to avoid packages that are visually similar.

Element 9 for MM.2.20

Medications and chemicals used to prepare medications are accurately labeled with contents, expiration dates, and warnings. ____ ____ ____

Authors' Comments, Experiences, and Suggestions

Organizations must assign expiration (beyond-use) dates to chemicals that do not have expiration dates (e.g., one year from date of receipt).

Some chemicals (e.g., phenol, Monsel's solution, and Lugol's solution) are available in unit-of-use containers that are labeled appropriately (including beyond-use dates).

Element 10 for MM.2.20

Standardize and limit the number of drug concentrations available in the organization. ____ ____ ____

Authors' Comments, Experiences, and Suggestions

Surveyors state that the requirement for standardizing and limiting the number of drug concentrations applies to all medications (not just concentrated electrolytes and other "high-alert" medications).

All areas (including interventional procedure areas) must use standardized concentrations approved by the organization. The organization's formulary must document that drug concentrations are standardized and the number of drug concentrations is limited.

Surveyors suggest limiting the number of concentrations to the minimum required to meet patient needs.

Surveyors are aware that some specialty areas may require more than one concentration of a drug. However, they expect the organization to demonstrate why multiple concentrations are required and have precautions in place to avoid errors.

Organizations should require prescribers to order only standard concentrations. Nurses must be prepared to administer a standard concentration and vary the rate if needed.

Surveyors state that the "Rule of Six," which results in individualized concen-

Yes **NA** **No**

trations, does not meet the standard. However, some surveyors will allow the organization to use the Rule of Six for a limited time while transitioning to standardized drug concentrations.

All written protocols (including those used in critical care) should reflect that standardization and limits on the number of drug concentrations are implemented.

To avoid dosing errors, special precautions should be taken when multiple concentrations of a drug are clinically necessary (e.g., on a pediatric unit). For example, the order should specify actual drug dose (not volume). The dose calculation including specific data elements (e.g., the patient's weight, dose per unit weight, and rate of administration) should be documented.

Surveyors state that organizations can have a limited set of standard concentrations for routine use and another limited set of standard concentrations for patients with special requirements (e.g., fluid-restricted patients and pediatric patients). Accurate drip charts using standardized concentrations for critical care infusions and infusions used in pediatric emergencies should be developed.

If Broselow Pediatric Emergency Tape™ is used for emergencies, organizations must modify its use so it is used only with the standardized drug concentrations available in the organization. The tape must be the current edition and same edition must be used throughout the organization. Surveyors will determine if the tape is used only for standardized concentrations available in the area.

Surveyors state that the Joint Commission permits the use of nonstandard concentrations, when it is not possible to use a standard concentration to administer the dose needed for a specific patient. Nonstandard concentrations must be used infrequently and must be mixed in the pharmacy and stored in the pharmacy to minimize the risk for error. Organizations must take precautions to ensure that nonstandard concentrations are not used inadvertently.

Organizations should purchase commercially-available premixed concentrations when possible (including dopamine and dobutamine for crash carts). Organizations should review their records for evidence of purchase and preparation of nonstandard drug concentrations.

The organization should limit concentrations of high-risk oral liquid medications (e.g., morphine, antipsychotic drugs, and pediatric formulations).

Stocking medications with tenfold differences in concentration (e.g., morphine 0.1 mg/mL and morphine 1 mg/mL) can be confusing and lead to underdoses or overdoses. This is a particular concern when multiple concentrations are stored on nursing units and there is no independent check prior to their use. Using standardized concentrations for PCA and infusion pumps introduces an additional measure of safety.

	Yes	NA	No
Element 11 for MM.2.20			
Concentrated electrolytes are removed from care units or areas, (unless patient safety is at risk if the concentrated electrolyte is not immediately available on a specific care unit or area, in such situations, specific precautions are taken to prevent inadvertent administration).	___	___	___

Authors' Comments, Experiences, and Suggestions

Concentrated electrolytes must be stored in the pharmacy and controlled and monitored by the pharmacy. (Exceptions are noted below.)

Unless clinically necessary, concentrated electrolytes must not be stored in patient care areas. It may be acceptable to store concentrated electrolytes in patient care areas providing the organization has an alternative approach (that has been approved by the Joint commission) and precautions are taken to minimize the risk of errors.

When it is necessary for a concentrated electrolyte to be stored in a patient care area (e.g., concentrated potassium for heart surgery or concentrated sodium chloride for dialysis) access to the drug must be strictly restricted and controlled and special precautions taken to avoid inadvertent misuse. Precautions should include explicit warning labels, limited quantities and sizes, restricted access, separation (segregation) from all other drugs, and education, training and competence testing of staff.

Concentrated potassium chloride includes strengths of 20 mEq/10 mL and greater. Surveyors state that 10 mEq/50 mL piggyback bags are not concentrated and thus not within the scope of this requirement.

Vials of concentrated magnesium sulfate in obstetrics can be replaced with premixed solutions.

Magnesium sulfate 10 mL syringes are concentrated forms that must be diluted before injection to prevent inadvertent IV administration.

Staff should monitor patient care areas to ensure that concentrated electrolytes are not inadvertently brought to the areas from areas where their storage may be permitted (e.g., a dialysis unit) or from outside services (e.g., a contract dialysis service).

Electrolytes in emergency drug containers (e.g., emergency drug trays or crash carts) should be in a ready-to-use form (i.e., already diluted). If an undiluted form (e.g., calcium chloride and calcium gluconate) must be stored, there must be special protections against misuse. Protections against misuse include limiting the quantity stored, size of vials, separated storage, and the application of warning labels.

If nonpharmacy personnel enter the pharmacy after hours, concentrated electrolytes must be secured (i.e., in locked storage) and not accessible.

	Yes	NA	No
Element 12 for MM.2.20 Medications in care areas are maintained in the most ready-to-administer forms available from the manufacturer or if feasible, in unit doses that have been repackaged by the pharmacy or a licensed repackager.	___	___	___

Authors' Comments, Experiences, and Suggestions

Pharmacies should avoid providing medications in bulk containers to care areas.

Repackaging must comply with FDA and USP requirements (e.g., maintaining appropriate records and the use of beyond-use dates that are suitable for the medication and the packaging materials used). (See Example 4-13.)

Amber prescription vials and plastic bags are not acceptable containers for repackaging medications.

Element 13 for MM.2.20

Not applicable.

Element 14 for MM.2.20

Not applicable.

	Yes	NA	No
Element 15 for MM.2.20 All medication storage areas are periodically inspected according to the hospital's policy to make sure medications are stored properly.	___	___	___

Authors' Comments, Experiences, and Suggestions

Inspections should focus on storage conditions (e.g., refrigeration and protection from light), security (especially for controlled substances), removal of expired and other unusable medications and devices, identification of hazardous conditions, and labeling.

Inspections should include all areas where medications are stored, dispensed, or administered (e.g., patient care units, ambulatory clinics, automated medication storage and distribution devices, emergency medication carts and containers, anesthesia, emergency department, imaging, surgery and recovery areas, respiratory care, after-hours stocks, and areas where procedures are performed [e.g., endoscopy and cardiac catheterization]). (See The Joint Commission's Definition of Medication in this chapter.)

A few surveyors state that only a pharmacist is qualified to make these inspections and some state regulations may require a pharmacist to perform the in-

Yes NA No

spections. However, most surveyors allow inspections by other professionals (e.g., nurses and pharmacy support staff) provided they are qualified. Surveyors often ask for evidence that individuals who perform inspections are qualified (e.g., competence assessment documentation). There should be evidence that a pharmacist has overall responsibility for the inspection and reviews the inspection findings.

Current standards do not specify an inspection frequency. The organization must define the frequency. However, many surveyors expect inspections to be performed at least monthly and some state regulations may require monthly inspections. Surveyors expect organizations to comply with their policies and state requirements.

If the organization permits inspections to be less than monthly (e.g., quarterly) medications that are due to expire before the next scheduled inspection must be removed.

Inspections must be documented. Any reasonable form may be used to document inspections. Inspection forms should include the criteria used in the inspections. Most surveyors prefer a separate form for each area (rather than a single form for multiple areas). Deficiencies should be noted and corrective actions should be documented. Many surveyors like inspection forms that provide spaces to document corrective action taken. Surveyors like to see evidence that inspection findings were shared with staff in the area (e.g., signature of the individual in charge of the area). (See Examples 4-14 through 4-16.)

Organizations must show compliance with their inspection policy for 12 continuous months (e.g., every month for the last 12 consecutive months or, if the organization requires quarterly inspections, every quarter for the last four consecutive quarters).

Standard MM.2.30

Emergency medications and/or supplies, if any, are consistently available, controlled, and secured. ___ ___ ___

Note: The following requirements for emergency medications are in addition to the requirements at standard MM.2.20, which are also applicable to emergency medications.

Elements of Performance for MM.2.30

Element 1 for MM.2.30

Not applicable.

	Yes	NA	No

Element 2 for MM.2.30

Hospital leadership, in conjunction with members of the medical staff and licensed independent practitioners, decides which emergency medications and/or supplies will be readily available in patient care areas. ___ ___ ___

Authors' Comments, Experiences, and Suggestions

Joint Commission standards do not require specific emergency medications to be available in patient care areas. Although surveyors seldom contest the items stocked, they frequently determine if the kinds and quantities on hand agree with the list of approved emergency medications. The list of emergency medications should be reviewed regularly (e.g., annually) to ensure the needs of patients seen by the organization are continually met and to meet professional practice standards (e.g., Advanced Cardiac Life Support [ACLS] guidelines).

Emergency medications may be kept in emergency carts and other containers (e.g., cabinets, boxes, and kits) and include all supplies of medications used in emergency situations (e.g., malignant hyperthermia carts, thrombolytic boxes, rapid sequence intubation boxes, and toxemia kits).

The organization should limit the strengths and sizes of medications available in emergency carts and containers. Multiple strengths and sizes increase the potential for error. If multiple strengths and sizes are needed, there should be provisions (e.g., distinctive packaging, warning labels, and segregated storage) to decrease the potential for error.

Emergency carts and containers should be standardized to the extent practical (e.g., standard concentrations of medications, standard sizes of medications, and standardized arrangement of medications and supplies).

Emergency medications should be stocked at nursing and special care units (especially critical care units) and in emergency department or service areas, ambulatory care areas, and other designated areas. Pediatric emergency medications and equipment should be available in areas where they may be needed.

Common antidotes and medications used for the management of poisoned patients should be kept where needed (e.g., the emergency department).

The imaging department should have an emergency medication supply for treating reactions caused by radiographic contrast media (diagnostic agents).

Element 3 for MM.2.30

Emergency medications are available in unit-dose, age-specific, and ready-to-administer forms whenever possible. ___ ___ ___

Yes NA No

Authors' Comments, Experiences, and Suggestions

Dobutamine, dopamine, heparin, magnesium sulfate, nitroglycerine and lidocaine should be in commercially available ready-to-administer forms provided by the manufacturer.

If Broselow Pediatric Emergency Tapes™ are used with carts or containers for pediatric emergencies, they should be the most current edition available and the same edition must be used throughout the organization. The required strengths on the tapes must be available in the carts or containers. If commercial preparations are not available, there must be clear directions for dilution.

Element 4 for MM.2.30

Not applicable.

Element 5 for MM.2.30

Not applicable.

Element 6 for MM.2.30

Emergency medications are stored in sealed or locked containers; in a locked room; or under constant supervision in accordance with law or regulation. ___ ___ ___

Authors' Comments, Experiences, and Suggestions

See Element 3 for MM.2.20 in this chapter.

Emergency medication carts and containers must be secure (i.e., locked, in a locked room, or stored so that unauthorized individuals [e.g., patients, visitors, and staff] do not have access to them). Emergency medication carts and containers that are not secure must be under constant observation.

Although plastic seals are permitted, they are not as secure as a lock and do not prevent theft or tampering. If seals are used, numbered seals are preferred. A numbered seal may provide a higher degree of control and accountability if personnel record the number each time they inspect the emergency cart or container. The organization must use seals that cannot be removed and reattached without evidence of tampering.

Surveyors expect the pharmacy to control the seals. Other mechanisms are permitted providing the security and integrity of the cart or container is assured.

Yes **NA** **No**

It may not be feasible for the pharmacy to have strict control over seals for emergency medications in remote locations (e.g., off-site clinics). However, surveyors expect to see a process that ensures that emergency medications are readily available and their integrity maintained. Some pharmacists train individuals at remote locations in replacement procedures and how to control the seals. Pharmacy staff should visit the sites periodically (e.g., monthly or quarterly) to verify that the process works.

Surveyors expect all controlled substances (e.g., diazepam, midazolam, and phenobarbital) stocked in emergency carts and containers to be locked. They state that an unsealed cart or container or a cart or container with a breakable seal provides less control and accountability than areas where controlled substances are stored using a "real" lock.

All emergency medication carts, kits, etc., throughout the organization must be included in the periodic inspection of medication storage areas. (See MM.2.20 in this chapter.) The inspection must be documented.

Many surveyors expect periodic inspections of emergency medications and supplies to occur at least monthly. At a minimum, the inspection must ensure that all required medications are present and usable. Tags or stickers on the outside of carts or containers that indicate the expiration dates of the contents are helpful but are not sufficient to ensure that all required medications are present and usable (e.g., unbroken and not deteriorated).

Responsible health care professionals (e.g., nurses, respiratory therapists, and imaging technologists) should observe sealed carts and containers frequently to ensure that the seals are present and unbroken. They must also inspect sealed carts and containers regularly. The inspection frequency and process should be consistent throughout the organization. Most organizations require daily inspections. At a minimum, most surveyors expect to see documentation that the seal was inspected and was not broken. Other ways to ensure the integrity of emergency medications are acceptable to the Joint Commission provided they ensure that when emergency medications, supplies, and equipment are needed for a patient's care, all are present and in usable condition. (See Example 4-17.)

Element 7 for MM.2.30

Emergency medications and supplies are replaced as soon as possible after their use in accordance with the hospital's policies and procedures. ____ ____ ____

Authors' Comments, Experiences, and Suggestions

The replacement process should ensure that emergency medication carts or containers are restocked in a timely manner. The organization should define the time period for replacing medications and supplies and monitor the process to ensure compliance with the policies and procedures.

Yes NA No

Emergency medication carts or containers that have been used and are waiting restocking must be secure (e.g., removed from the patient care area and stored in central supply, pharmacy, or other secure area until they are restocked). Many organizations require a complete cart replacement (i.e., after the cart is used, the entire cart is replaced).

Although current standards do not prohibit nurses from restocking, checking, and sealing emergency medication carts or containers, many surveyors insist that pharmacy personnel perform these functions. Some states regard restocking as dispensing and restrict restocking to pharmacists or pharmacy personnel under the supervision of a pharmacist.

Standard MM.2.40

A process is established to safely manage medications brought into the hospital by patients or their families.

Rationale for MM.2.40

A number of valid reasons exist for allowing patients to use their own medications in a hospital, including the need for continuous therapy; a patient's use of a nonformulary medication; or a lack of alternatives to a patient's personal medication. The hospital defines its responsibilities for the safe use of these medications.

Elements of Performance for MM.2.40

The hospital addresses the use of medications brought into the hospital by patients or their families, including the following:

Element 1 for MM.2.40

Defining when such medications can be used or administered. ___ ___ ___

Authors' Comments, Experiences, and Suggestions

Each organization must determine if patients' own medications may be used and how they are stored, controlled, and administered.

Some organizations prohibit the use of medications brought into the organization by patients or their families if the medication is on the organization's formulary and is available for use.

Medications brought into the organization by patients or their families must be administered only in response to orders that permit their administration.

The organization's policies must address the administration of investigational

Yes **NA** **No**

medications brought into the organization by patients or their families. (See Orders for Investigational Medications under Element 6 for MM.3.20 in this chapter.)

Element 2 for MM.2.40

Identifying the medication and visually evaluating its integrity, when medications brought in by the patient or family are allowed. ____ ____ ____

Authors' Comments, Experiences, and Suggestions

Medications brought into the organization by patients or their families must not be administered until identified. Although not required by the Joint Commission, a pharmacist should identify the medications. If physicians, nurses, or others identify medications that belong to patients, there should be a process to ensure the accuracy of the identification (including the availability of current references to aid in identification). The competence of individuals who identify medications should be documented.

There should be a mechanism to alert nursing staff that patients' own medications have been identified and are suitable for administration. Some organizations attach a sticker that indicates that the pharmacy identified the medication and the initials of the pharmacist who identified it.

Element 3 for MM.2.40

Informing the prescriber and patient if medications brought into the hospital by patients or their families are not permitted. ____ ____ ____

Authors' Comments, Experiences, and Suggestions

If the medications are not to be used during the patient's stay in the facility, they should be packaged and sealed and either given to the patient's family or stored and returned to the patient or patient's family at discharge.

Storage may be at the nursing unit, in the pharmacy, or at a central location (e.g., a valuables vault). Storage must be secure. Organizations often require the medications to be counted and sealed in the presence of the patient or the patient's family. They also document the process (e.g., record the kind and quantity of the medications on a log or other record). (See Examples 4-18 and 4-19.)

If the medication is a controlled substance, it must be in locked storage in a secure area to prevent diversion.

	Yes	NA	No

Some organizations require an organization representative (e.g., a nurse) to witness the counting and sealing of controlled substances and ensure that they are stored securely.

Patients' own medications that are not claimed by the patient should be disposed of according to policy. Disposal after 30 days is suggested.

ORDERING AND TRANSCRIBING

Standard MM.3.10

Only medications needed to treat the patient's condition are ordered, provided, or administered. ____ ____ ____

Element of Performance for MM.3.10

Element 1 for MM.3.10

There is a documented diagnosis, condition, or indication-for-use for each medication ordered. ____ ____ ____

Authors' Comments, Experiences, and Suggestions

The diagnosis, condition, or indication for each medication must be in the patient's medical record—not necessarily on the medication order. The information could be in admission notes, care plan, progress notes, or other areas of the patient's record. (See Element 3 for MM.3.20 in this chapter.)

When the organization reviews and revises its preprinted orders, it should consider adding an indication or condition for each medication listed. Note, however, that adding the indication or condition is not required and might not be feasible for all medications.

Having this information only in the records of other departments (e.g., pharmacy patient profiles or imaging film jackets) does not comply with the element. The information must be contained in the patient's medical record.

This element applies to all medications (including herbal remedies, vitamins, and over-the-counter drugs) ordered in any setting in the organization. There must be an indication (or reason) for each medication ordered. (See The Joint Commission's Definition of Medication in this chapter.)

Yes NA No

The organization should review patients' records to determine compliance with this element. Medical records personnel often perform this function when they review patients' medical records.

Standard MM.3.20

Medication orders are written clearly and transcribed accurately. ____ ____ ____

Rationale for MM.3.20

Many medication errors occur while communicating or transcribing medication orders. The hospital is responsible for taking steps to reduce the potential for error or misinterpretation when orders are written or verbally communicated. The required elements of all orders must be specified. To reinforce the skills and judgments needed for safe medication ordering, the organization offers education to care providers. Clear understanding and communication between staff involved in the medication process is essential. Best practices, external and internal data, and medication risks are considered when the organization develops medication policies and procedures.

Elements of Performance for MM.3.20

Written policy(ies) address the following:

Element 1 for MM.3.20

The required elements of a complete medication order. ____ ____ ____

Authors' Comments, Experiences, and Suggestions

Organizations as well as some laws and regulations often require medication orders to include the patient's name, medication, strength, route, rate, and frequency. They may require an indication for use or limit on the number of doses or duration of administration for some medications.

Medication orders should clearly state administration times or time intervals between doses.

Terms such as "prn" and "on call" must be qualified so that there is no question as to the prescriber's intent (e.g., "q4h prn pain scale of 5–7" and "on call to OR").

Prohibited abbreviations, symbols, acronyms, and dose designation units must not be used. (See Requirement 2B for NPSG 2 in Chapter 20.)

The metric system should be used for ordering medications (as well as labeling, and recording administration of medications).

	Yes	NA	No

Element 2 for MM.3.20

When generic or brand names are acceptable or required as part of a medication order. ____ ____ ____

Authors' Comments, Experiences, and Suggestions

The element does not require medication orders to contain the brand name, the generic name, or both the brand and generic names. The organization's policies must address this issue.

Many organizations state that the generic name is preferred but the trade name is acceptable.

Element 3 for MM.3.20

Whether or when indication for use is required on a medication order. ____ ____ ____

Authors' Comments, Experiences, and Suggestions

The element does not require the diagnosis, condition, or indication for use to be on a medication order. However, this information must be contained in the patient's medical record.

The organization must determine when the diagnosis, condition, or indication for use must be on a medication order.

Some organizations require an indication for use on all as needed (prn) medication orders and for specified confusing medications, or high-risk or high-alert medications (e.g., medications with look-alike, sound-alike names). (See Element 4 for MM.3.20 in this chapter.)

Although not required by the element, some organizations provide a place on the medication order to record the diagnosis, condition, or indication for use for each medication ordered.

Element 4 for MM.3.20

Special precautions or procedures for ordering drugs with look-alike or sound-alike names. ____ ____ ____

Authors' Comments, Experiences, and Suggestions

See Requirement 3C for NPSG 3 in Chapter 20.

	Yes	NA	No
Element 5 for MM.3.20			
Actions to take when medication orders are incomplete, illegible, or unclear.	___	___	___

Authors' Comments, Experiences, and Suggestions

To be considered complete, medication orders must contain all elements required by the organization's written policy (e.g., drug, strength, dosage form, and route). All missing elements should be clarified.

Pharmacists, nurses, and other qualified individuals must contact the prescriber to clarify medication orders that are incomplete, illegible, or unclear.

Medication orders that are incomplete, illegible, or unclear cannot be carried out until clarified by the prescriber.

Organizations should not permit orders for multiple medications with the same indication without guidelines for which medication to use and when to use it.

The organization's policies should state the actions to be taken if medication orders must be clarified.

The clarification should be entered in the patient's medical record as a new order.

Staff members who make entries (e.g., clarifications of orders) in patients' medical records must be authorized by the organization to do so. (EP 1 for IM.6.10 in the CAMH).

The organization must define which entries require countersigning and/or authentication. (EP 2 and EP 4 for IM.6.10 in the CAMH).

Medical record entries must be dated and the author identified. (EP 4 for IM.6.10 in the CAMH).

Element 6 for MM.3.20

The hospital specifies the required elements of the following types of orders that it deems acceptable for use:

	Yes	NA	No
• "As needed" (PRN) orders—orders acted upon based on the occurrence of a specific indication or symptom	___	___	___
• Standing orders—written instruction to administer a medication to a person in circumstances specified in instructions without a prescription	___	___	___
• Hold orders—instruction to temporarily suspend (place medication orders on hold) under specified conditions and to alert users at specified times while a medication is on hold	___	___	___

	Yes	NA	No
• Automatic stop orders—a date or time to discontinue a medication	____	____	____
• Resume orders*—restart an order that was previously held	____	____	____
Note: See EP 9. A blanket reinstatement of previous orders for medications is not acceptable.			
• Titrating orders—orders in which the dose is either progressively increased or decreased in response to the patient's status	____	____	____
• Taper orders—orders in which the dose is decreased by a particular amount with each dosing interval	____	____	____
• Range orders—orders in which the dose or dosing interval varies over a prescribed range, depending on the situation or patient's status	____	____	____
• Orders for compounded drugs or drug mixtures not commercially available	____	____	____
• Orders for medication-related devices (for example, nebulizers and catheters)	____	____	____
• Orders for investigational medications	____	____	____
• Orders for herbal products	____	____	____
• Orders for medications at discharge or transfer	____	____	____

Authors' Comments, Experiences, and Suggestions

"As Needed" PRN Orders

- *PRN orders for medications must be qualified to include the symptom or indication for use. There should be no question as to the prescriber's intent. For example, prn for nausea for 3 days, prn at bedtime for sleep, every 4 hours prn for pain scale of 5–7, and prn for temperature over 100°F.*

Standing Orders

- *Some organizations refer to "standing" orders as "standard" orders, "protocols," or other names.*
- *Organizations may limit standing orders to specific indications, specific medications, specific prescribers, or specific settings.*
- *Standing orders should be reviewed and approved periodically (e.g., annually) by the appropriate committee (e.g., a P&T committee), printed, and be available to physicians, nurses, pharmacists, and other staff who need them.*
- *Versions of standing orders that are no longer current should be destroyed or not available.*

Hold Orders

- *Hold orders must include the time, situation, or circumstance for initiating the hold and the time, situation, or circumstance for ending the hold.*
- *Some organizations consider hold orders to be discontinued orders unless a specific parameter is indicated (e.g., hold digoxin for one dose).*

Yes **NA** **No**

Automatic Stop Orders

- *The Joint Commission does not require organizations to have an automatic stop order policy. Some state regulations may require an automatic stop order policy. Organizations that adopt an automatic stop order policy should consider the following:*
    - *Automatic stop orders should define when all or some of a patient's medication orders must be canceled. There should also be a mechanism for notifying the prescriber when these orders are about to expire (e.g., an electronic or printed notification or a stamp or sticker on the patient's chart).*
    - *Blanket reinstatement of previous orders (including automatic stop orders) is not acceptable. (See Element 9 for MM.3.20 in this chapter.)*
- *The Joint Commission does not specify medications that must be included in an automatic stop order policy. However, some states specify the medications. Medications frequently included in automatic stop order policies include antibiotics, anticoagulants, controlled substances, corticosteroid medications, chemotherapeutic medications, hypnotic and sedative medications, and oxytocic medications.*
- *The Joint Commission does not specify time limits for automatic stop orders. However, some states do. Time limits vary with the medication and type of organization. Policies often specify time limits ranging from 24 hours to 10 days. The trend is toward shorter time limits (e.g., 48–72 hours). Long-term care facilities and facilities with long-term care units often assign up to 30-day limits for medications.*
- *The CMS regulations stipulate that unless a specific time or number of doses is indicated, medication orders must be automatically stopped after a reasonable time that is predetermined by the medical staff.*[2] *(See Chapter 24.)*

Resume Orders

- *Organizations must require a "resume medications" order to list the previous orders (including medication name, strength, dose, route, frequency, and other basic elements of a medication order). Prescribers may write the orders or sign orders that are prepared for their signature. (See Element 1 for MM.3.20 in this chapter.)*

Titrating Orders

- *Titrating orders should include the amount of dose increase or decrease for each step in response to the patient's status, the titrating interval or frequency, and the maximum allowable dose.*
- *The order must include an objective parameter (e.g., a specific blood pressure, level on a pain scale, or level on a sedation scale) used to titrate the medication including the endpoint.*
- *Some organizations establish titrating protocols for specific medications and require orders to state that the medications be given according to the protocol.*

Yes NA No

Taper Orders

- *Taper orders should address the tapering steps, the amount of dose decrease for each step, and the tapering interval or frequency.*
- *Some organizations establish taper protocols for specific medications and require orders to state that medication be given according to the protocol.*

Range Orders

- *Range orders contain doses or dosing time intervals (i.e., time between doses) that vary over a prescribed range, depending on the situation or the patient's status.*
- *Range orders should be limited and avoided entirely when possible.*
- *The organization should specify how ranges should be expressed and how nurses should interpret the order.*
- *Some organizations place a limit on the upper range of the order. For example, the American Pain Society (see Appendix A) states that the maximum dose within the range should not be greater than four times the minimum dose.*
- *Range order policies should guide health care personnel in selecting the appropriate dose and time for administering medications.*
- *The organization should identify how health care providers should select the starting dose and starting time interval between doses. For example, orders for 1 or 2 tablets will start at 1 tablet and, if needed, increase to 2 tablets. Orders for every 4 to 6 hours will start as every 6 hours and, if needed, decrease the time interval between doses to every 4 hours. Surveyors look for consistent interpretation of range orders.*
- *Some surveyors state that organizations should not permit prescribers to include both a dose range and a time range in the same order.*
- *Organizations may use their pain measurement scale to manage pain medications if this process is permitted and described in their policies.*

Orders for Compounded Medications or Medication Mixtures

- *The organization should require the order to include the formula or refer to a standardized, approved formula that is on file in the pharmacy. The formula must be available to prescribers and care providers.*
- *Formulas for commonly used compounded medications or medication mixtures should be reviewed and approved by the medical staff (e.g., P&T committee).*
- *If compounding is performed by an outside entity (e.g., a nuclear pharmacy or a pharmacy that compounds total parenteral nutrition preparations) the administration must approve the entity and the medical staff must be aware that the compounding is performed by an outside entity.*

Yes **NA** **No**

Orders for Medication-Related Devices

- *Orders for medication-related devices should specify the device and include all the information needed to ensure they are used appropriately and safely.*

Orders for Investigational Medications

- *Standard RI.2.180 states that "The hospital protects research subjects and respects their rights during research, investigation, and clinical trials involving human subjects." See the CAMH for additional requirements relating to this topic.*
- *Orders for an investigational medication must be limited to prescribers authorized to order the investigational medication.*
- *Orders for investigational medications shall be subject to the provisions of the investigational medication protocol.*
- *See Element 1 for MM.2.40 in this chapter.*

Orders for Off-Label Use of Medications

- *Although orders for the use of approved medications for unlabeled indications (i.e., off-label use) may be legal and commonplace, it may, in some cases, be inappropriate and potentially dangerous. The organization's rules, regulations, or policies should provide guidelines for controlling the off-label use of medications and the organization should obtain legal advice if the safe use of these medications is in doubt.*

Orders for Herbal Products

- *The organization must control the use of herbal products (remedies) and other alternative therapies. They are medications and are subject to all of the provisions of the MM standards. (See The Joint Commission's Definition of Medication in this chapter.)*
- *There must be a documented indication or reason for use for orders for herbal products.*

Orders for Medications at Discharge

- *Medications may be dispensed to discharged patients only on written order of an authorized prescribing practitioner.*
- *Medications ordered for discharged patients should be included on the medication reconciliation form. The complete current list must be provided to the patient or the patient's family at discharge.*
- *Medications ordered for discharged patients must be indicated in the patient's medical record.*
- *Discharged patients should not be permitted to take the remainder of their*

	Yes	NA	No
inpatient medications home unless permitted by organization policy and they are dispensed in an appropriate container and labeled appropriately for outpatient use.			

Element 7 for MM.3.20

In addition, the hospital minimizes the use of verbal and telephone medication orders.	___	___	___

Authors' Comments, Experiences, and Suggestions

See Requirement 2A for NPSG 2 in Chapter 20.

Verbal, as used in this element, refers to spoken (orally transmitted) orders rather than written orders. A telephone order is a specific type of orally transmitted order.

Some organizations differentiate between verbal and telephone orders. They will not allow verbal orders (except in emergencies, such as codes, or perioperatively from the surgeon) because the prescriber is present and could write the order.

Some organizations prohibit telephone orders for nonurgent, high-risk or high-alert medications (e.g., oncology medications) or high-risk patients (e.g., neonatal and pediatric patients).

Medical staff rules and regulations or hospital policy should identify, by title or category, personnel who are qualified and authorized to accept (receive) and transcribe (record) verbal orders (e.g., nurses and pharmacists). This process must be in accordance with state and federal law. (EP 1 for IM.6.50 in the CAMH.)

Verbal orders must reflect authentication as specified in the organization's policy and state or federal law or regulation (e.g., dated and authenticated with the names and signatures of the individuals who gave and received the orders. The records must indicate the individuals who implemented the orders. (EP 2 for IM.6.50 in the CAMH.)

Verbal orders must be authenticated within the specified time frame and in accordance with state and federal law. (EP 3 for IM.6.50 in the CAMH.)

The process for taking verbal or telephone orders must require a verification "read-back" of the complete order by the person receiving the order. (EP 4 for IM.6.50 in the CAMH.)

Staff must be prepared to discuss the steps the organization takes to minimize the use of verbal and telephone orders. (See Requirement 2A for NPSG 2 in Chapter 20.)

	Yes	NA	No

Some organizations require documentation that verbal orders were read back to the prescriber (e.g., writing "read back" or "RBV" on patients' medical records). Not all organizations require documentation of the read back. Individuals who receive verbal orders must comply with their organization's policy.

Element 8 for MM.3.20

In addition, the hospital reviews and updates preprinted order sheets as needed to support clarity, accuracy, and safety. ___ ___ ___

Authors' Comments, Experiences, and Suggestions

The P&T committee often reviews preprinted orders. Other mechanisms for review and updating are permitted.

There should be an initial review and periodic (e.g., annual) reviews thereafter. Reviews should ensure that preprinted orders are clear, contain all required elements, and reflect appropriate and safe medication usage. For example, terms on the organization's "Do Not Use" list must not appear on preprinted orders. (See Requirement 2B for NPSG 2 in Chapter 20.)

Preprinted orders must comply with all medication management standards (e.g., not specify blanket reinstatement of orders). (See Element 9 for MM.3.20 in this chapter.)

Element 9 for MM.3.20

In addition, the hospital specifies that blanket reinstatement of previous orders—a summary order to resume all previous orders—for medications are not acceptable. ___ ___ ___

Authors' Comments, Experiences, and Suggestions

This element applies to "continue preoperative medications" orders, "continue home medications" orders, automatic stop orders, and all other orders. The organization cannot exempt specific medications or types of orders from this element.

The reinstated orders must include all of the required elements of a medication order (including medication name, strength, dose, route, and frequency). That is, the order must be rewritten.

Some organizations use a function of their MAR program to create a list of current medications for the physician to continue or discontinue after invasive procedures.

	Yes	NA	No
Element 10 for MM.3.20			
In addition, the hospital defines in writing when weight-based dosing for pediatric populations is required.	___	___	___

Authors' Comments, Experiences, and Suggestions

Organizations often require weight-based dosing for aminoglycosides, other antibiotics, and specific high-risk or high-alert medications, and for children less than a specific age or weight. The decision is up to the organization.

Element 11 for MM.3.20

Not applicable.

Element 12 for MM.3.20

Not applicable.

	Yes	NA	No
Element 13 for MM.3.20			
Policies and procedures regarding medication orders are implemented.	___	___	___
Element 14 for MM.3.20			
Influenza and pneumococcal polysaccharide vaccines are administered according to a physician order, or, as permitted by law and regulation, according to physician-approved, organization-specific protocol(s).	___	___	___

Authors' Comments, Experiences, and Suggestions

The element corresponds with CMS requirements and allows for appropriate staff, other than physicians, to administer these vaccines without an individual physician order.

Element 15 for MM.3.20

Not applicable.

Yes **NA** **No**

PREPARING AND DISPENSING

Standard MM.4.10

All prescriptions or medication orders are reviewed for appropriateness. ___ ___ ___

Elements of Performance for MM.4.10

Element 1 for MM.4.10

Before dispensing, removal from floor stock, or removal from an automated storage and distribution device, a pharmacist reviews all prescription or medication orders unless a licensed independent practitioner controls the ordering, preparation, and administration of the medication; or in urgent situations when the resulting delay would harm the patient, including situations in which the patient experiences a sudden change in clinical status (for example, new onset of nausea). ___ ___ ___

Authors' Comments, Experiences, and Suggestions

The Joint Commission defines a licensed independent practitioner (LIP) as "Any individual permitted by law and by the organization to provide care, treatment, and services, without direction or supervision, within the scope of the individual's license and consistent with individually granted clinical privileges."[1]

A licensed independent practitioner (LIP) is not required to be at a patient's bedside when medications are administered in the emergency department or the imaging department. Organizations are encouraged to develop policies that define the role of LIPs within the two departments. When medications are administered, policies must require the LIP to be available within the department to intervene immediately if there is an adverse medication event.

This element applies to all medications and all patient care areas. No medication or patient care area is specifically exempt from this requirement. For example, the element applies to preprinted labor and delivery orders, orders for respiratory therapy medications, orders for emergency department patients who are waiting for transfer to an inpatient room, orders for preoperative patients in an ambulatory surgery unit, and orders for patients in a 23-hour observation unit.

Nurses are not permitted to administer medications they obtain from floor stock or automated medication storage and distribution devices if a pharmacist has not reviewed the order. (See Element 1 of this standard for exceptions.)

Cardiopulmonary arrest is an example of a situation in which the resulting delay would harm the patient.

Yes NA No

The Joint Commission does not define a time for "delay that would harm the patient." Organizations must determine this.

The name of the pharmacist who reviewed and entered the medication order should be recorded electronically or manually.

Element 2 for MM.4.10

Not applicable.

Element 3 for MM.4.10

When an on-site licensed pharmacy is not open 24 hours a day, 7 days a week, a health care professional determined to be qualified by the hospital reviews the medication order in the pharmacist's absence. ____ ____ ____

Authors' Comments, Experiences, and Suggestions

Organizations should develop a policy and procedure specifying when nurses and other care providers are allowed to obtain medications (e.g., from floor stock or an automated medication storage and distribution device) prior to a pharmacist review of the medication order. (See MM.4.50 in this chapter.)

There must be a process that minimizes the potential for error when a prospective review by a pharmacist is not performed.

The prospective review by a nonpharmacist should include the items specified in Element 5 for this standard.

Qualified health care professionals include nurses and physicians. Other health care professionals may be designated provided they are qualified. The organization should assess the competence of all health care professionals who review medication orders in the absence of a pharmacist.

Element 4 for MM.4.10

When the pharmacy is not open 24 hours a day, 7 days a week, a pharmacist conducts a retrospective review of all orders during this period as soon as a pharmacist is available or the pharmacy opens. ____ ____ ____

Authors' Comments, Experiences, and Suggestions

Many organizations require a pharmacist to conduct the retrospective review within 24 hours. The review should be documented (e.g., in a night log).

	Yes	NA	No

Element 5 for MM.4.10

The hospital has a process to review all prescriptions for the following:

	Yes	NA	No
• The appropriateness of the drug, dose, frequency, and route of administration	____	____	____
• Therapeutic duplication	____	____	____
• Real or potential allergies or sensitivities	____	____	____
• Real or potential interactions between the prescription and other medications or food	____	____	____
• Current or potential impact as evidenced by laboratory values	____	____	____
• Other contraindications	____	____	____
• Variation from organizational criteria for use	____	____	____
• Other relevant medication-related issues or concerns	____	____	____

Authors' Comments, Experiences, and Suggestions

Other relevant issues or concerns could include incompatibilities and problems specific to the organization.

The review should be documented on the medication order and, if applicable, in a night log.

Element 6 for MM.4.10

All concerns, issues, or questions are clarified with the individual prescriber before dispensing the medication. ____ ____ ____

Authors' Comments, Experiences, and Suggestions

The clarification of concerns, issues, or questions with the individual prescriber should be documented. (See Example 4-20.)

Standard MM.4.20

Medications are prepared safely. ____ ____ ____

Elements of Performance for MM.4.20

Element 1 for MM.4.20

When an on-site, licensed pharmacy is available, only the pharmacy compounds or admixes all sterile medications, intravenous admixtures, or other drugs except in emergencies or when not feasible (for example, when the product's stability is short). ____ ____ ____

	Yes	NA	No

Authors' Comments, Experiences, and Suggestions

If there is no organized pharmacy, the organization should obtain pharmacy services from outside source(s) (e.g., a hospital or community pharmacy) that can provide pharmacy services. The organization must ensure the quality and integrity of medications obtained from outside sources and provide for their appropriate storage and safe use.

Organizations should review all sterile medications prepared and compounded outside the pharmacy and ensure that they are prepared and compounded in the pharmacy to the extent possible.

The use of commercially available, premixed sterile medications as well as commercially available, closed-system, parenteral solution bag and medication vial combinations may eliminate the need for preparing many sterile preparations outside the pharmacy.

The pharmacy should provide premixed oxytocin infusions.

Routine preparation of epidural medications by anesthesia providers should be discouraged.

If the organization uses an outside pharmacy for any compounding, the organization should obtain a written statement that the compounding pharmacy meets or exceeds the requirements of USP <795> (for nonsterile compounding) and/or USP <797> (for sterile compounding).

Element 2 for MM.4.20

The hospital has a written policy that addresses the safety and use of medications acquired by a practitioner from sources other than the hospital for use in patient care in that hospital. The policy addresses the following:

	Yes	NA	No
• Whether such medications are allowed to be used	___	___	___
• If allowed, a process to evaluate the integrity of medications brought in by a practitioner prior to use in patient care	___	___	___

Authors' Comments, Experiences, and Suggestions

Organizations should develop written policies that discourage physicians from using medications that are acquired from sources other than the organization.

Organizations should develop written policies that define the procedure that a physician must follow to acquire and use medications from sources other than the organization.

	Yes	NA	No

The process should comply with the requirements of MM.2.10 (the formulary process).

If practitioners are allowed to bring in medications from other sources, the process to evaluate their integrity should include verification of identity, appropriate labeling, evidence that they have been stored under appropriate conditions (e.g., proper temperature), and are procured from a reputable source (i.e., they are not counterfeit or adulterated).

Element 3 for MM.4.20

The written policy that addresses the safety and use of medications acquired by a practitioner from sources other than the organization for use in patient care is implemented. ___ ___ ___

Authors' Comments, Experiences, and Suggestions

A committee that includes representatives from the medical staff and leadership should approve each instance where medications from outside sources are requested for use in the organization.

Element 4 for MM.4.20

Whenever medications are prepared, staff uses safety materials and equipment while preparing hazardous medications. ___ ___ ___

Authors' Comments, Experiences, and Suggestions

See Chapters 9, 16, and 17.

Safety materials and equipment include personal protective apparel (e.g., gowns, gloves, eyewear, and face protection).

Clearly labeled spill kits should be readily available to staff in areas where hazardous medications and materials are received, stored, or handled.

There must be provisions for safe disposal of hazardous trash and waste, contaminated apparel, and contaminated work equipment (e.g., vials, ampuls, syringes, and needles) in accordance with laws and regulations.

Antineoplastic and other hazardous materials must be prepared in a biological safety cabinet (BSC) or compounding aseptic containment isolator (CACI) specifically designed for the preparation of hazardous medications.

	Yes	NA	No
BSCs or CACIs used for preparing hazardous medications cannot be used also for preparing nonhazardous medications.			

Element 5 for MM.4.20

Whenever medications are prepared, staff uses techniques to assure accuracy in medication preparation.	____	____	____

Authors' Comments, Experiences, and Suggestions

Techniques to assure accuracy in medication preparation include the use of dilution charts, standardized concentrations and formulas, and double-checking calculations and quantities used in preparing medications.

Assurance of accuracy of equipment (e.g., burettes, repeater pumps, and compounders) is also necessary.

Element 6 for MM.4.20

Whenever medications are prepared, staff follow techniques to avoid contamination during medication preparation, including but not limited to the following:

• Using clean or sterile techniques	____	____	____
• Maintaining clean, uncluttered, and functionally separate areas for product preparation to minimize the possibility of contamination	____	____	____
• Using a laminar airflow hood or other class 100 environment while preparing any intravenous (IV) admixture in the pharmacy, any sterile product made from nonsterile ingredients, or any sterile product that will not be used within 24 hours	____	____	____
• Visually inspecting the integrity of the medications	____	____	____

Authors' Comments, Experiences, and Suggestions

See Chapter 9 and NPSG 7 in Chapter 20.

A class 100 environment is equivalent to an ISO-5 environment.

Compliance with the requirements of USP <797> will help ensure the sterility of parenteral medications and thus reduce the risk of health care–acquired infections.[3] (See Chapter 18.)

Staff who compound or prepare these products must be educated, trained, and competent to do so.

	Yes	NA	No

There must be evidence that laminar airflow workbenches, biological safety cabinets, and compounding aseptic isolators are maintained and cleaned according to the organization's policy (e.g., through certification records and cleaning logs).

Intravenous admixtures and other products addressed in this element must not be prepared on a medication cart in a patient care area as these are not functionally separate.

When appropriate, filter needles/straws are used to withdraw medications from glass ampuls.

When parenteral nutrition services are provided, there must be mechanisms to assure safe preparation and dispensing of parenteral nutrition preparations (e.g., calibration of automatic compounders, verification of fluids and additives attached to automatic compounders, and testing of the final product at the end of the process).

Standard MM.4.30

Medications are labeled. ___ ___ ___

Rationale for MM.4.30

A standardized method for labeling all medications will minimize errors.

Elements of Performance for MM.4.30

Element 1 for MM.4.30

Medications are labeled in a standardized manner according to law or regulation and standards of practice. ___ ___ ___

Authors' Comments, Experiences, and Suggestions

There should be evidence that medications are labeled in a standardized manner.

All medications (including inpatient medications, metered dose inhalers, parenteral nutrition products, diagnostic and contrast agents, floor stock, sample medications, medications obtained from other pharmacies, and medications dispensed to ambulatory care and home care patients) must be labeled appropriately and safely and include accessory or cautionary statements and beyond-use dates.

Medications dispensed to discharged and ambulatory care patients must be

Yes NA No

labeled for outpatient use in appropriate child-resistant containers. Instructions for storage and administration of the medication must be clear.

Medication cart drawers should be labeled with patients' names and locations.

Although not included in the Joint Commission's definition of medication, disinfectants and cleaning products should be labeled appropriately and safely and include accessory and cautionary statements. (See The Joint Commission's Definition of Medication in this chapter.)

Check FDA, USP, and state regulations for assigning beyond-use dates to repackaged medications (e.g., unit-dose packages).

Element 2 for MM.4.30

Any time one or more medications are prepared but are not administered immediately, the medication container* must be labeled. ___ ___ ___

Note: A container can be any storage device such as a plastic bag, syringe, bottle, box, medicine cup, or basin.

Authors' Comments, Experiences, and Suggestions

All reconstituted and mixed medications (including oral liquid antibiotics, respiratory therapy treatments, oral contrast media, and diagnostic agents) must be labeled with the reconstitution date and/or date beyond which the medication should not be used. The concentrations of reconstituted medications must be noted on labels.

The organization must not allow unlabeled containers of medications in any area of the organization (e.g., unlabeled medication cups and unlabeled syringes that are prefilled for later use).

The organization must not allow empty medication containers that are prelabeled for future use (e.g., prelabeled empty syringes) to be stored in any area of the organization.

The American Organization of PeriOperative Registered Nurses (AORN) practice guidelines includes information on appropriate labeling of medications on and off the sterile field. (See Appendix A.)

Element 3 for MM.4.30

At a minimum, all medications prepared in the hospital are labeled with the following:

	Yes	NA	No
• Drug name, strength, amount (if not apparent from the container)	____	____	____
• Expiration date when not used within 24 hours*	____	____	____
****Note:** Expiration date, also called the *beyond-use date,* refers to the last date that the product should be used by the patient.*			
• Expiration time when expiration occurs in less than 24 hours	____	____	____
• The date prepared and the diluent for all compounded IV admixtures and parenteral nutrition solutions	____	____	____

Authors' Comments, Experiences, and Suggestions

Organizations should check manufacturers' recommendations; USP, FDA, and state requirements for assigning beyond-use dates to repackaged and compounded preparations.

See Element 4 for this standard for labeling medications prepared and dispensed by the pharmacy.

Element 4 for MM.4.30

When preparing individualized medications for multiple specific patients or when the person preparing the individualized medications is not the person administering the medication, the label also includes the following:

	Yes	NA	No
• Patient name	____	____	____
• Patient location	____	____	____
• Directions for use and any applicable cautionary statements either on the label or attached as an accessory label (for example, "requires refrigeration," "for IM use only")	____	____	____

Authors' Comments, Experiences, and Suggestions

This element applies to medications prepared and dispensed by the pharmacy, as well as all other medications prepared in advance (e.g., vaccine syringes in clinics, anesthesia medication syringes in anesthesia areas, and oral contrast agents in the imaging department).

The Joint Commission does not provide complete guidelines for labeling medications. The following is typical in many organizations:

- *Patient's name and location, if applicable*
- *Medication name, strength, and dosage form*
- *Appropriate accessory or cautionary statements (e.g., shake well)*
- *Beyond-use date, when applicable*

Yes NA No

- *Manufacturer (if not clearly apparent from the brand name)*
- *Manufacturer's lot number or pharmacy control number*

The Joint Commission does not provide complete guidelines for labeling parenteral and sterile preparations. The following is typical in many organizations:

- *Patient's name and location, if applicable*
- *Generic medication name (and trade name or manufacturer, if applicable) and amount added*
- *Name and volume of the parenteral solution (i.e., the diluent)*
- *Name or identifying code (e.g., initials) of the individual who prepared the solution*
- *Name or identifying code (e.g., initials) of the individual who checked the final preparation*
- *Rate of administration*
- *Date and time prepared*
- *Date and time to be administered*
- *Beyond-use date and time*
- *Supplemental instructions (e.g., storage information)*

Standard MM.4.40

Medications are dispensed safely. ____ ____ ____

Elements of Performance for MM.4.40

Element 1 for MM.4.40

Quantities of medications are dispensed and minimize diversion and yet are still consistent with the patient's needs. ____ ____ ____

Authors' Comments, Experiences, and Suggestions

The pharmacy should not dispense bulk quantities of medications.

The organization should determine the quantities of medications to dispense. Many organizations limit quantities to a 24-hour supply.

Element 2 for MM.4.40

Dispensing adheres to law, regulation, licensure, and professional standards of practice, including record keeping. ____ ____ ____

Yes **NA** **No**

Authors' Comments, Experiences, and Suggestions

A licensed pharmacist must prepare and dispense all medications and monitor all medication preparation and dispensing performed by nonpharmacists.

The Joint Commission expects pharmacies to meet state requirements for the use of nonpharmacists.

Medications must be dispensed only on the order of a legally authorized prescriber who has been granted clinical privileges to write such orders. (See EP 14 for MM.3.20 for an exception to this.)

The pharmacy should have a mechanism to determine whether medication orders are written by individuals who are currently authorized to prescribe (e.g., a written or electronic list of authorized prescribers).

Pharmacy staff should be aware of state laws and regulations and organizational policies concerning practitioners other than physicians who can prescribe medications (e.g., dentists, podiatrists, optometrists, advanced practice nurse practitioners, and physician assistants).

Pharmacy staff should be able to describe how they verify that individuals are permitted to prescribe medications and their prescribing restrictions, if any.

Pharmacy staff should have a mechanism to verify that individuals who prescribe controlled substances are legally permitted to do so (e.g., have a current DEA number).

Medications dispensed to a discharged patient must be recorded in the patient's medical record.

Medication Containers

- *Medications must be dispensed in clean containers that are appropriate for the contents and do not interact physically with the medication or otherwise absorb, adsorb, or deleteriously affect the contents. Containers must protect the contents from light, moisture, temperature, air, and handling, as required.*
- *Medications dispensed to outpatients must be in child-resistant containers.*
- *Medications dispensed from the emergency department (if such dispensing is permitted) must be in appropriate containers that comply with the state's dispensing regulations.*

Element 3 for MM.4.40

Medications are dispensed in a timely* manner to meet patient needs. ___ ___ ___

	Yes	NA	No
****Note:*** Timely is defined by organization policy and based on the intended use of the information.			

Authors' Comments, Experiences, and Suggestions

The Joint Commission does not define a time frame for "timely manner."

Many organizations define specific time expectations for STAT, as soon as possible (ASAP), and routine orders.

Element 4 for MM.4.40

Medications are dispensed in the most ready-to-administer forms available from the manufacturer or if feasible, in unit doses that have been repackaged by the pharmacy or licensed repackager. ____ ____ ____

Authors' Comments, Experiences, and Suggestions

The organization should purchase all medications (including liquid oral medications and topical medications) in unit-dose and ready-to-use forms to the extent practical. The organization should avoid dispensing or providing medications in bulk containers.

The pharmacy should repackage bulk medications in appropriate, tamper-evident, unit-dose packages when unit-dose forms are not available from the manufacturer or licensed repackager.

The organization should purchase premixed IV medications when available (e.g., premixed dobutamine, dopamine, heparin, magnesium sulfate, nitroglycerine, and lidocaine infusions).

Element 5 for MM.4.40

The hospital consistently uses the same dose packaging system, or if a different system is used, provides education about the use of the dose packaging system to the patients impacted by the change. ____ ____ ____

Authors' Comments, Experiences, and Suggestions

When the organization changes to a different system (e.g., one commercial IV packaging system to another commercial IV packaging system) the organization documents the education provided.

	Yes	NA	No

Standard MM.4.50

The hospital has a system for safely providing medications to meet patient needs when the pharmacy is closed. ___ ___ ___

> *Note:* This standard only applies when a hospital has an on-site pharmacy and patients present in the hospital.

Rationale for MM.4.50

If an urgent or emergent patient need occurs, the hospital must be able to provide medications to the patients in its facility.

Elements of Performance for MM.4.50

Element 1 for MM.4.50

The hospital has a process for providing medications to meet patient needs when the pharmacy is closed. ___ ___ ___

Authors' Comments, Experiences, and Suggestions

The process must be described in writing.

Physicians, nurses, and pharmacists should participate in developing the process.

The process must be in accordance with state laws and regulations and cannot include entry into the pharmacy by nonpharmacy personnel, even if allowed by state laws or regulations.

Element 2 for MM.4.50

When nonpharmacist health care professionals are allowed by law and regulation to obtain medications after the pharmacy is closed, the following safeguards are applied:

- A limited set of medications approved by the hospital is available. ___ ___ ___
- These medications are stored outside of the pharmacy. ___ ___ ___
- These medications are locked. ___ ___ ___
- Only trained, designated prescribers and nurses are permitted access to medications. ___ ___ ___
- Quality control procedures (such as an independent second check by another individual or a secondary verification built into the system, such as bar coding) are in place to prevent medication retrieval errors. ___ ___ ___

Yes **NA** **No**

- The hospital arranges for a qualified pharmacist to be available either on call or at another location (for example, at another organization that has 24-hour pharmacy service) to answer questions or provide medications beyond those accessible to nonpharmacy staff. ___ ___ ___

Authors' Comments, Experiences, and Suggestions

These medications can be stored in a night cabinet/closet or automated medication storage and distribution device.

The P&T committee or its equivalent should approve the limited set of medications.

The list must be limited to medications that are likely to be urgently needed when the pharmacy is closed and should not include any medications that are not safe for storage outside of the pharmacy (e.g., concentrated electrolytes and medications in bulk containers).

Individuals who are permitted access to the medications or perform second checks should be oriented initially and, if needed, periodically (e.g., annually) thereafter. Surveyors may request evidence that these individuals are competent to make removals or perform second checks (e.g., a record that their competence was assessed). (See Example 4-21.)

Most surveyors examine entries in removal records to determine that removals are made by individuals who are permitted access to the medications. (See Example 4-22.)

The organization should have a mechanism to ensure that staff complies with the second check or other quality control requirements (e.g., signature or initials of the individual who performs the second check and/or observation of the process).

Element 3 for MM.4.50

This process is evaluated on an on-going basis to determine the medications accessed routinely and the causes of accessing the pharmacy after hours. ___ ___ ___

Authors' Comments, Experiences, and Suggestions

There must be a record of medications removed from after-hours stocks. (See Example 4-23.)

Pharmacists should document their review of medications removed from after-hours stock (e.g., by initialing the removal record). Their review should include

	Yes	NA	No

determining the appropriateness of the removal (e.g., a clinically urgent situation), if there was an order for the medication, and that the right medication, right dosage form, right strength, and right amount of medication were obtained. (See Element 1 for MM.4.10 in this chapter.)

Ongoing monitoring and analysis should compare medication errors made when a pharmacist is not available to those made when a pharmacist is available.

Element 4 for MM.4.50

Changes are implemented to minimize the number of times nonpharmacist health care professionals obtain medications after the pharmacy is closed. ____ ____ ____

Authors' Comments, Experiences, and Suggestions

Removals from after-hours stocks must be minimized. Medications cannot be removed from the pharmacy when the pharmacy is closed.

Medications that repeatedly require removal by an on-call pharmacist should be made available in after-hours stocks outside the pharmacy with the exception of those not considered safe for storage outside the pharmacy (e.g., concentrated electrolytes).

Standard MM.4.60

Not applicable.

Standard MM.4.70

Medications dispensed by the hospital are retrieved when recalled or discontinued by the manufacturer or the Food and Drug Administration (FDA) for safety reasons. ____ ____ ____

Elements of Performance for MM.4.70

Element 1 for MM.4.70

When the hospital has been informed of a medication recall or discontinuation by the manufacturer or the FDA for safety reasons, medications within the hospital are retrieved* and appropriately handled per hospital policy and law and regulation. ____ ____ ____

Note: Although recalls are generally by lot number, a hospital may retrieve all lots of a recalled medication instead of recording and identifying medications by their lot number.

	Yes	NA	No

Authors' Comments, Experiences, and Suggestions

This policy should also apply to recalled devices.

Policies and procedures should describe a process that addresses recalled medications and devices, including medication samples, and devices stored in the pharmacy and throughout the organization. In addition, the pharmacy's periodic inspection routine should include a check of these areas for recalled medications and devices. (See MM.2.20 in this chapter.)

All medications in stock, including those obtained from other pharmacies, and dispensed to patients must be labeled so that recalls can be performed (e.g., labeled with manufacturer's lot number or pharmacy control number).

There should be a record of the response to the recall (including recalls for medications and devices that are not stocked). (See Example 4-24.) Some organizations keep a file of initialed and dated notices with the response to the recall noted.

Many organizations report recalls and actions taken to an internal safety committee and/or the P&T committee.

Element 2 for MM.4.70

The hospital notifies all those ordering, dispensing, and/or administering active* medications of any manufacturer or FDA recall or discontinuance. ____ ____ ____

Note: Dispensed medications that have not passed expiration date and prescriptions that can be refilled without an additional physician order.

Authors' Comments, Experiences, and Suggestions

Notification may be by memorandum, letter, newsletter, e-mail, copies of committee minutes, or any mechanism that ensures the appropriate individuals are informed of the recall.

A copy of the notification is sufficient evidence of compliance with this element.

Element 3 for MM.4.70

When the hospital has been informed of a medication recall or discontinuation by the manufacturer or the FDA for safety reasons, patients who are actively receiving the medication are identified and informed of the recall or discontinuation. ____ ____ ____

	Yes	NA	No

Authors' Comments, Experiences, and Suggestions

The process should be in writing and staff should be able to describe the process.

The process should be documented if implemented.

Standard MM.4.80

The hospital has a process to address medications that are returned to the pharmacy or the hospital. ____ ____ ____

Rational for MM.4.80

Medications may be returned when allowed under law and regulation and hospital policy. Previously dispensed but unused, expired, or returned medications in the hospital must be accounted for, controlled, and disposed of. The pharmacy is responsible for controlling and accounting for all unused medications returned to the pharmacy.

Elements of Performance for MM.4.80

Element 1 for MM.4.80

The hospital has a process in place that addresses if and when unused, expired, or returned medications will be managed by the pharmacy. ____ ____ ____

Authors' Comments, Experiences, and Suggestions

See Element 7 for MM.2.20 in this chapter.

The process should be described in writing, address accountability, and ensure that the medications are not diverted.

If only a month and year of expiration are provided, the medication may be used until the last day of the month.

Unused medications should be returned to a return bin in automated medication storage and distribution devices. Returning unused medications to a regular storage bin used for distribution is unsafe because they could be placed in the wrong bin.

Unused portions of medications removed from unit-dose containers (e.g., partial tablets and remaining liquid medication) should be disposed of properly and not retained for later use.

Yes NA No

There must be a procedure for making external reports of defective medications (e.g., to the manufacturer and the FDA).

Element 2 for MM.4.80

The hospital has a process in place that addresses how medications are returned to the pharmacy's control, including procedures that address preventing diversion of medications and account for all unused, expired, or returned medications. ____ ____ ____

Authors' Comments, Experiences, and Suggestions

The process should be described in writing.

The process must provide for security of medications while awaiting return to the pharmacy.

The process must describe secure storage for medications after returned to pharmacy control.

Element 3 for MM.4.80

The hospital has a process in place that addresses how outside sources, if any, are used for destruction of medications. ____ ____ ____

Authors' Comments, Experiences, and Suggestions

The process should be described in writing.

The process should describe how outside sources are notified, how medications are stored securely while waiting for destruction, and what destruction records shall be maintained.

Element 4 for MM.4.80

These processes for addressing medications returned to the pharmacy or hospital are implemented. ____ ____ ____

Authors' Comments, Experiences, and Suggestions

There should be evidence that medications returned to the pharmacy are controlled and accounted for according to policy.

Some surveyors inspect patient care areas for the presence of unused medications for discharged patients.

Yes NA No

ADMINISTRATION

Standard MM.5.10

Medications are safely and accurately administered. ___ ___ ___

Elements of Performance for MM.5.10

Element 1 for MM.5.10

Policies and procedures address health care staff who are allowed to administer medications, with or without supervision, consistent with law or regulation and hospital policy. ___ ___ ___

Before administering a medication, the licensed independent practitioner or qualified individual administering the medication does the following:

Element 2 for MM.5.10

Verifies that the medication selected for administration is the correct one based on the medication order and product label. ___ ___ ___

Authors' Comments, Experiences, and Suggestions

Medications should be removed from storage areas (e.g., automated medication storage and distribution devices) for only one patient and one medication pass at a time.

The patient's medication administration record should be taken to the patient's bedside to verify that the correct medication is administered to the correct patient.

Patients must be identified before medications are administered. (See Requirement 1A for NPSG 1 in Chapter 20.)

To the extent possible, a medication should be administered by the individual who prepared the dose (unless the medication was prepared by the pharmacy).

Medications should be removed from the packaging only at the patient's bedside and immediately before administration.

Element 3 for MM.5.10

Verifies that the medication is stable based on visual examination for particulates or discoloration and that the medication has not expired. ___ ___ ___

	Yes	NA	No

Authors' Comments, Experiences, and Suggestions

Medications should be administered as soon as possible after preparation (i.e., within the shorter of the stability range or beyond-use date).

Medications that appear to be deteriorated or otherwise unusable must not be administered.

Element 4 for MM.5.10

Verifies that there is no contraindication for administering the medication. ____ ____ ____

Authors' Comments, Experiences, and Suggestions

Current and appropriate references should be available to those who administer medications.

Those who administer medications should review the patient's record for contraindications.

Element 5 for MM.5.10

Verifies that the medication is being administered at the proper time, in the prescribed dose, and by the correct route. ____ ____ ____

Authors' Comments, Experiences, and Suggestions

Individuals who administer medications must review the medication order and the medication to ensure that medications are administered as ordered.

Each administered dose must be recorded properly in the patient's medical record. This requirement applies to all medications as defined by the Joint Commission's definition of medication (including diagnostic and contrast agents, blood derivatives, and herbal remedies). (See The Joint Commission's Definition of Medication in this chapter.)

Medications dispensed to a discharged patient must be recorded properly in the patient's medical record.

MARs should be checked against the patient's medical record at the organization's defined interval (generally each shift but no less frequent than every 24 hours).

Yes **NA** **No**

Element 6 for MM.5.10

Advises the patient, or if appropriate, the patient's family about any potential clinically significant adverse reaction, or other concerns about administering a new medication. ___ ___ ___

Note: Please refer to PC.6.10, EP 3 for additional information addressing the education of patients regarding medication use.

Authors' Comments, Experiences, and Suggestions

Individuals who administer medications must ensure compliance with the organization's policy as to who is to advise the patient and how the advice is given.

Element 7 for MM.5.10

Discusses any unresolved, significant concerns about the medication with the patient's physician, prescriber (if different from the physician), and/or relevant staff involved with the patient's care, treatment, and service. ___ ___ ___

Authors' Comments, Experiences, and Suggestions

Medications must not be administered until all significant concerns are resolved.

Staff members should be able to describe how they report errors and ADRs to the organization's reporting system.

Element 8 for MM.5.10

Policies and procedures address guidelines for prescriber notification in the event of an adverse drug reaction or medication error. ___ ___ ___

Authors' Comments, Experiences, and Suggestions

Staff should be able to describe how they notify the prescriber if there is an adverse medication reaction or medication error.

Standard MM.5.20

Self-administered medications are safely and accurately administered. ___ ___ ___

	Yes	NA	No

Elements of Performance for MM.5.20

Element 1 for MM.5.20

If self-administration is allowed, procedures guide the safe and accurate self-administration of medications or administration of medications by a person who is not a staff member and address training, supervision, and administration documentation. ____ ____ ____

> ***Note:*** Self-administration includes those instances where a patient independently uses a medication, including medications that may be held by the hospital for the independent use by the patient.

Authors' Comments, Experiences, and Suggestions

Patients may self-administer medications only if there is a specific order in accordance with the organization's policy.

Organizations often limit the medications that may be self-administered.

Policies often address storage, security, and labeling for medications that are self-administered.

Medications stored at the patient's bedside must be stored securely (e.g., locked) so that unauthorized individuals do not have access to them.

Element 2 for MM.5.20

Persons who administer medications but are not staff members (for example, the patient if self-administering) receive information about the following:

- The nature of the medications to be administered ____ ____ ____
- How to administer medications, such as the appropriate frequency, route of administration, and dose ____ ____ ____
- The expected actions and side effects of the medications to be administered ____ ____ ____
- How to monitor the effects of the medications on the patient ____ ____ ____

Authors' Comments, Experiences, and Suggestions

See Chapter 7.

Training and information to be provided should be defined.

Staff members who provide the training (including pharmacy staff) must be competent to do so.

	Yes	NA	No

Patient education should include the safe and effective use of medications. (EP 3 for PC.6.10 in the CAMH.)

Patient education should include the safe and effective use of medical equipment and supplies. (EP 3 for PC.6.10 in the CAMH.)

All patients and their caregivers (e.g., parents, guardians, relatives, friends, home care nurses, and home care aides) should be educated about all medications administered during the patients' hospitalization as well as medications to be taken after discharge. Emphasis should be on educating high-risk patients (e.g., geriatric and pediatric patients), patients with specific diseases (e.g., diabetes and hypertension), and patients receiving specific medications (e.g., anticoagulants and insulin).

Element 3 for MM.5.20

Persons who administer medications but are not staff members (including the patient if self-administering) are determined to be competent at medication administration before being allowed to administer medications. ____ ____ ____

Authors' Comments, Experiences, and Suggestions

There should be evidence that these persons are competent (e.g., a determination that they have the knowledge, an observation of their performance, and a successful demonstration of their skills). Documentation should be in the medical record.

Pharmacy staff who administer medications must be competent to do so and their activities must be within the scope of practice defined by the state and/or the organization's policy.

MONITORING

Standard MM.6.10

The effects of medication(s) on patients are monitored. ____ ____ ____

Rationale for MM.6.10

Monitoring the effects of medications on patients helps to assure that medication therapy is appropriate and minimizes the occurrence of adverse events.

	Yes	NA	No

Elements of Performance for MM.6.10

Element 1 for MM.6.10

Each patient's response to his or her medication is monitored according to the clinical needs of the patient and addresses the patient's response to the prescribed medication and actual or potential medication-related problems. ____ ____ ____

Authors' Comments, Experiences, and Suggestions

Ongoing patient medication monitoring is a collaborative assessment by physicians, nurses, pharmacists, and other individuals responsible for providing care to the patient.

The patient's response to medications administered must be recorded in the patient's medical record.

Element 2 for MM.6.10

Monitoring a medication's effect on a patient includes the following:

- Gathering the patient's own perceptions about side-effects, and when appropriate, perceived efficacy ____ ____ ____
- Referring to information from the patient's medical record, relevant laboratory results, clinical response, and medication profile ____ ____ ____

Authors' Comments, Experiences, and Suggestions

Care providers who monitor patients must alert the prescriber to adverse effects of medications (e.g., adverse reactions).

Care providers should suggest medication therapy modifications when appropriate.

Modifications include changing the medication, modifying the dose, and changing the timing or rate of administration. Suggestions should be documented (e.g., in the medical record).

Element 3 for MM.6.10

The hospital has a process for monitoring the patient's response to the first dose(s) of a medication new to a patient while he or she is under the direct care of the hospital. ____ ____ ____

Yes NA No

Authors' Comments, Experiences, and Suggestions

This element applies to inpatient areas and ambulatory care areas (e.g., ambulatory surgery, clinics, and the emergency department).

The process should be in writing.

When first doses of medications new to a patient are administered to patients in any area of the organization (including the emergency department, imaging, and ambulatory care areas), they are monitored for an appropriate period of time before they are permitted to leave.

The organization should determine if care providers monitor the patient's response in accordance with the written process.

Standard MM.6.20

The hospital responds to actual or potential adverse drug events and medication errors. ___ ___ ___

Elements of Performance for MM.6.20

Element 1 for MM.6.20

The hospital has a process to respond to actual or potential adverse drug events and medication errors. ___ ___ ___

Authors' Comments, Experiences, and Suggestions

There should be a written description of the process.

The process should include clinics and other ambulatory patient areas.

Staff should be able to describe how they respond to an actual or potential adverse medication event.

Data should be aggregated and analyzed and information provided to the appropriate committee.

Example 4-25 is a form for reporting medication errors internally.

Examples 4-26 and 4-27 are forms for reporting adverse drug reactions internally.

Yes NA No

Element 2 for MM.6.20

Action is taken when an actual or potential adverse drug event is identified (depending on the hospital's services, this may be limited to calling for outside assistance, for example, community-sponsored 911 services). ___ ___ ___

Authors' Comments, Experiences, and Suggestions

The action taken should be documented.

The appropriateness of the action taken and the outcome should be evaluated.

Data should be aggregated and analyzed and information reported to the appropriate committee. (See Examples 4-28 and 4-29.)

Element 3 for MM.6.20

The hospital or responsible individual complies with internal and external reporting requirements for actual or potential adverse drug events (for example, to the United States Pharmacopeia [USP], the FDA, and the Institute for Safe Medication Practices [ISMP]). ___ ___ ___

Authors' Comments, Experiences, and Suggestions

Serious adverse events should be reported to the FDA's MedWatch Program. (See Chapter 23.) (See Example 4-30.)

Vaccine-related adverse events must be reported to the Vaccine Adverse Event Reporting System. (See Chapter 23.) (See Example 4-31.)

Organizations, at their discretion, may report medication errors to an external agency (e.g., ISMP and the USP Medication Errors Reporting Program). (See Chapter 21.)

Example 4-32 is a form for voluntary reporting of medication errors to the USP Medication Errors Reporting Program (MERP). (See Chapter 21.)

Device-related adverse events must be reported to the FDA MedWatch program. (See Chapter 23.) (See Example 4-33.)

	Yes	NA	No

HIGH-RISK MEDICATIONS

High-risk or high-alert drugs are those drugs involved in a high percentage of medication errors and/or sentinel events and medications that carry a higher risk for abuse, errors, or other adverse outcomes. Lists of high-risk or high-alert drugs are available from such organizations as the ISMP, the USP, and so forth, based on national data about medication use. However, the hospital needs to develop its own list of high-risk or high-alert drugs based on its unique utilization patterns or drugs, and its own internal data about medication errors and sentinel events. Examples of high-risk drugs include investigational drugs, controlled medications, medications not on the approved FDA list, medications with a narrow therapeutic range, psychotherapeutic medications, and look-alike/sound-alike medications. Hospitals determine whether medications that are new to the market or new to the hospital are high risk.

Standard MM.7.10

The hospital develops processes for managing high-risk or high-alert medications. ____ ____ ____

Elements of Performance for MM.7.10

Element 1 for MM.7.10

The hospital identifies the high-risk or high-alert medications used within the hospital, if any. ____ ____ ____

Authors' Comments, Experiences, and Suggestions

Medications often designated as high-risk or high-alert include concentrated electrolytes (e.g., potassium chloride, potassium phosphate, and sodium chloride greater than 0.9%, magnesium sulfate, calcium chloride, and calcium gluconate), insulin, opiates and narcotics, intravenous anticoagulants (e.g., heparin), oncology medications, neonatal and pediatric medications, epidural medications, patient controlled analgesia medications, neuromuscular blocking agents, and medications with look-alike and sound-alike names.

Element 2 for MM.7.10

Based on the services provided, the hospital develops processes for procuring, storing, ordering, transcribing, preparing, dispensing, administering, and/or monitoring high-risk or high-alert medications. ____ ____ ____

Authors' Comments, Experiences, and Suggestions

Staff should be able to discuss the high-risk or high-alert medications identified by the organization and the safeguards in place to prevent errors with them.

	Yes	NA	No

Many medications have a potential for an error with a serious outcome if staff is not trained adequately, patients are not informed, and information is not readily available.

To the extent possible, preparations of high-risk or high-alert medications should be compounded in the pharmacy.

High-risk or high-alert medications that are easily confused (e.g., heparin vials and insulin vials) must be clearly labeled.

Staff should always double-check doses before administering high-risk or high-alert medications.

Many organizations require documentation of the double check of a few medications. These often include insulin (including infusions and the doses on infusion pumps) and heparin.

Element 3 for MM.7.10

The processes for managing high-risk or high-alert medications are implemented. ____ ____ ____

Standard MM.7.20

Not applicable.

Standard MM.7.30

Not applicable.

Standard MM.7.40

Investigational medications are safely controlled and administered. ____ ____ ____

Rationale for MM.7.40

The hospital protects the safety of patients participating in investigational or clinical medication studies by controlling and monitoring the use of these mediations. In addition, the hospital addresses the use of specific populations for experimentation and research, and reviews all investigational medications to evaluate safety. (*See* Standard RI.2.180).

	Yes	NA	No

Elements of Performance for MM.7.40

Element 1 for MM.7.40

Procedures for the use of investigational medications specify a written process for reviewing, approving, supervising, and monitoring investigational medications use. ____ ____ ____

Element 2 for MM.7.40

When the hospital operates a pharmacy, procedures specify the pharmacy controls the storage, dispensing, labeling, and distribution of the investigational medication. ____ ____ ____

Element 3 for MM.7.40

Procedures specify that when a patient is involved in an investigational protocol that is independent of the hospital, the hospital will review and accommodate the patient's continued participation in the protocol. (*See* Standard RI.2.180.) ____ ____ ____

Element 4 for MM.7.40

The procedures for the use of investigational mediations are implemented. ____ ____ ____

Authors' Comments, Experiences, and Suggestions

See Orders for Investigational Medications under Element 6 for MM.3.20 in this chapter.

Protocols for investigational medications must be approved by the appropriate group (e.g., the institutional review board or the P&T committee).

The pharmacy may dispense investigational medications only pursuant to the prescription of an authorized investigator or prescriber.

Administration of investigational medications may only be by those approved to do so, and only after they have been educated regarding their actions and possible adverse effects.

An accurate record of doses received, dispensed, administered, and destroyed must be maintained.

See EPs 1 through 7 for Standard RI.2.180 in the Ethics, Rights, and Responsibilities chapter of the CAMH for information on the rights of patients who participate or refuse to participate in research, investigations, and clinical trials.

	Yes	NA	No

EVALUATION

Standard MM.8.10

The hospital evaluates its medication management system. ____ ____ ____

Elements of Performance for MM.8.10

Element 1 for MM.8.10

The hospital evaluates its medication management system for risk points and identifies areas to improve safety. ____ ____ ____

Authors' Comments, Experiences, and Suggestions

See Failure Mode and Effects Analysis in Chapter 14.

This is often a medication safety committee function.

Element 2 for MM.8.10

The hospital identifies opportunities for improvement by routinely evaluating the literature for new technologies or successful practices that have been demonstrated to enhance safety in other organizations to determine if it can improve its own medication management system. ____ ____ ____

Authors' Comments, Experiences, and Suggestions

Literature evaluations may be P&T committee and/or medication safety committee topics.

There should be evidence that the organization evaluates the literature (e.g., documentation in P&T committee minutes).

Element 3 for MM.8.10

The hospital reviews internally generated reports to identify trends or issues in its medication management system. (*See* Standards PI.2.10 and PI.2.20.) ____ ____ ____

Authors' Comments, Experiences, and Suggestions

See Chapter 8, Sentinel Events and Failure Mode and Effects Analysis (FMEA) in Chapter 14, and Requirement 7B for NPSG-7 in Chapter 20.

	Yes	NA	No

Internally generated reports include reports of medication errors and adverse drug events, performance monitors, medication-use evaluations, FMEA findings and recommendations, reports of hazardous conditions, and sentinel event review findings.

Information from the organization's review of internally generated reports is used to improve medication management processes.

The organization may ask the pharmacy to collect and aggregate data related to pharmacy services (e.g., clarifications of medication orders, requests for nonformulary medications, and numbers of dispensing errors that were caught before the medication left the control of the pharmacy).

Element 4 for MM.8.10

The hospital acts to implement improvements based on the following:

	Yes	NA	No
• Evaluation of its medication management system	____	____	____
• Review of new technologies	____	____	____
• External data	____	____	____
• Successful practices that have been demonstrated to enhance safety	____	____	____

Authors' Comments, Experiences, and Suggestions

New technologies (e.g., automated delivery systems, bar coding, and infusion devices) should be reviewed and, if deemed appropriate for the organization, implemented.

Examples of external data include data from ISMP, Core Measure Data, ORYX Data, and MedMarx. (See Chapters 1, 15, and 21.)

"Best practices" that have proved successful in other organizations (including ISMP, ASHP, and other health care facilities) should be considered and, if deemed appropriate for the organization, implemented.

Element 5 for MM.8.10

	Yes	NA	No
The performance of new and modified medication management processes is measured.	____	____	____

Authors' Comments, Experiences, and Suggestions

When new medication processes are implemented, the organization must develop a method to measure the success of the process.

Yes **NA** **No**

The organization may choose to conduct a FMEA to identify potential problems with new medication processes.

The organization should establish a baseline and develop measurement metrics that can be used to document improvement.

Measurement methods include performance indicators and observation of processes.

Element 6 for MM.8.10

The hospital uses information from data analysis to identify subsequent changes to improve its medication management system. ____ ____ ____

Authors' Comments, Experiences, and Suggestions

Data gathered through adverse event reporting processes (e.g., adverse drug reaction and medication error reporting) must be used to identify opportunities for improvement within the organization.

Information gathered through the organization's Root Cause Analysis (RCA) or FMEA may be useful in identifying opportunities for improvement.

The organization should apply process improvement techniques to drive and sustain improvements.

CHAPTER 5

Individual-Based System Tracer: Medication Management

Joint Commission™ surveys include visits to patient care and service areas where surveyors use tracers to assess compliance with relevant standards and how well the organization provides care, treatment, and services. This chapter provides an overview of the individual-based system tracer: medication management (MM tracer). (*See* Tracer Activities in Chapter 2.) It focuses on survey specifics (i.e., what to expect during the MM tracer), strategy (i.e., how to prepare for and participate in the MM tracer), and example surveyors' questions (i.e., questions that surveyors have asked during the MM tracer).

Survey Specifics

The organization should ensure that staff understands what to expect during the MM tracer. The descriptions that follow may be helpful.

Surveyors—One or more

Session Length—60 minutes

Participants—Participants include personnel who have a role in managing medications for the individual patient chosen for the Medication Management Tracer. In addition to the director of pharmacy, clinical pharmacist(s), and other pharmacists, participants often include physicians, nurses, therapists, dietitians, personnel responsible for educating staff and patients about medications, clinical personnel with a special knowledge or perspective on medication use (e.g., pediatrics or geriatrics), performance improvement personnel who focus on improving the MM system, laboratory clinicians, and biomedical engineers involved in managing medications (e.g., maintaining infusion pumps).

Purpose—The purpose of this activity is to review the organization's MM system, determine if the organization complies with MM standards, identify MM issues that require further review, discuss relevant standards related to USP <797> (*see* Chapter 18), and assess how the organization complies with National Patient Safety Goals (NPSGs) relating to medications. (*See* Chapter 19.)

Location—Organizations may choose the location for the group discussion. Although many organizations designate a conference room, surveyors often expand the discussion to other areas of the organization that play a role in the individual patient's medication care (e.g., pharmacy, nursing units, diagnostic and procedural areas, laboratory, dietary department, and materials management).

Occurs—This activity occurs toward the end of the survey.

Materials/Documents—The following materials and documents may be helpful:

- MM system description/flowchart (*see* Medication Management System Description in this chapter)
- List of high-risk or high-alert medications
- List of look-alike, sound-alike combinations of medications
- List of prohibited abbreviations
- List of medication use improvement activities
- List of actions taken in response to medication errors and other adverse drug events (ADEs)
- List of medication safety education activities

Format—The MM tracer includes a review of medication records to identify a patient on a high-risk or high-alert medication. A focused tracer activity traces the path of medications through the organization and addresses medication management processes (i.e., selection and procurement, storage, ordering and transcribing, preparing and dispensing, administering, and monitoring). It includes area visits and an evaluation of the organization's MM process; processes for reporting medication errors and other adverse drug events, system breakdowns, near misses; other issues related to safe and effective use of medications; and implementation of NPSGs related to MM. In surveys of small facilities, the MM tracer may be combined with other tracers (i.e., data use and infection control).

Strategy

The organization should ensure that staff are educated and understand how it complies continuously with the standards. The suggestions that follow may help staff prepare for and participate in the MM tracer.

Medication Management System Description

- Prepare a description and/or flowchart of the MM system. (*See* Table 5-1.)
- Include all six MM system processes (i.e., selection and procurement, storage, ordering and transcribing, preparing and dispensing, administering, and monitoring).
- Ensure that all medications from all sources are included. For example, parenteral solutions; surgical kits with medications; other medications that are purchased, stored, or distributed by the materials management department; contrast agents; albumin and other blood derivatives; radiopharmaceuticals; and medications from compounding pharmacies and other outside sources.
- Be able to discuss how the organization ensures that medications from sources other than the pharmacy (e.g., materials management and imaging) meet the same standards of quality and integrity as those from the pharmacy. For example, these medications must be evaluated for inclusion in the formulary, stored and labeled properly, and included in adverse drug event reporting. Areas where these medications are stored must be inspected periodically (e.g., monthly).
- Be able to discuss how medications brought into the organization by patients and, if allowed, by practitioners are handled. The process should include a visual check for integrity of the medications.
- Be able to discuss all components of the MM system description or flowchart.

Medication Use Improvement Activities

- Prepare a summary of medication use improvement activities for the past 12 months.
- Prepare a medication management plan listing future medication use improvement activities.
- List improvements in each of the six MM processes.

High-Risk or High-Alert Medications

- List the high-risk or high-alert medications identified by the organization.
- For each high-risk or high-alert medication, list the safeguards in place to reduce the potential for errors for the six MM processes.
- Ensure that staff who use high-risk or high-alert medications can discuss these medications and safeguards in place to prevent errors.

Look-Alike, Sound-Alike Medications

- List the look-alike, sound-alike combinations chosen by the organization. Ensure that the list includes at least ten combinations chosen from current tables provided by the Joint Commission.
- For each combination, list the safeguards in place throughout the organization (e.g., Tall-Man letters, separate storage areas, and spell-out requirements) to reduce the potential for errors for the six MM processes.
- Ensure that appropriate staff can discuss the look-alike, sound-alike medications and safeguards in place to prevent errors.

Medication Errors and Adverse Drug Events

- Be able to discuss how medication errors and ADEs are detected, reported, and assessed.
- List examples of how medication error and ADE data are used to improve patient care (i.e., actions taken).
- List ongoing medication safety education activities provided for medical staff (including licensed independent practitioners), nursing staff, pharmacy staff, and other personnel who provide patient care.
- Be able to provide a root cause analysis (RCA) for each sentinel event or serious incident. (*See* Chapter 14.)
- If conducted, be able to provide a failure mode and effects analysis (FMEA) for each sentinel event or serious incident. (*See* Chapter 14.)

Formulary

- Be able to discuss how medications are evaluated (including specific criteria) for addition to the formulary.
- Be able to discuss the process for procurement and use of nonformulary medications.
- Be able to discuss the processes used to address medication shortages/outages and recalls.

Evaluation of the Medication Management System

- Be prepared to discuss how you evaluate your MM system to identify risk points and areas to be improved (e.g., the ISMP Medication Safety Self-Assessment, any failure mode and effects analysis [FMEA] of medication use processes, and performance improvement indicators.)

SURVEYOR'S QUESTIONS

The following questions are examples that surveyors have asked during the MM tracer. Discussing the questions with participants is educational and should foster an understanding of how the organization complies continuously with the standards.

Surveyors may ask participants to introduce themselves and identify their positions or roles. Surveyors may direct some questions to specific individuals and other questions to the group. Questions often focus on potential problems identified during the survey, other areas of concern, medication safety, NPSGs, and the six MM processes. Participants should be prepared to respond to the questions and describe processes that are in place to provide a safe medication management system.

National Patient Safety Goals

Patient Identifiers

- How do you identify patients?
- How do you ensure that patient identifiers are checked?

Communication

- What abbreviations are prohibited in your organization?
- What do you do when a prescriber uses a prohibited abbreviation?
- What departments read-back verbal orders to prescribers?
- How has the process improved over the last few years?

Look-Alike/Sound-Alike Medications

- What is your process for identifying and reviewing a list of look-alike/sound-alike medications used in your organization?
- What actions have you taken to prevent errors involving the interchange of these medications?

Anticoagulation Therapy

- What is the status of the organization's anticoagulant management program?
- Is all intravenous heparin administered using a programmable infusion pump?
- What safeguards are in place for patients using oral anticoagulants (e.g. warfarin)?
- What is the organization's procedure for monitoring patients on warfarin therapy?
- How does the organization provide education to patients who are receiving anticoagulants?

Health Care–Associated Infections

- How do you monitor compliance with guidelines for hand hygiene?

Reconciliation of Medications

- How do you obtain and document a complete list of the patient's current medications upon the patient's admission to the organization?
- How do you involve the patient in this process?
- How do you communicate a complete list of a patient's medications to the next provider when a patient is referred or transferred?
- How do you provide a current list of medications to patients who are discharged?

Fall Prevention

- What medications that contribute to patient falls have you identified?
- What actions have you taken to prevent falls due to medications?

Patient-Specific Information

Availability of Patient-Specific Information

- What information about the patient is available to you?
- How do you obtain laboratory results?
- How are you notified about panic values?

Required Information

- How does the pharmacy obtain information about patient allergies?
- Who enters allergy information into the system?

Maintaining Patient Medical Records

- How do you document the administration of respiratory care medications in the patient's medical records?
- How do you document the administration of contrast agents in the patient's medical record?
- How do you reconcile patients' medication administration records?
- How is the pharmacy informed of medications administered in the emergency department?

Selection and Procurement

Formulary

- What is the process for adding medications to the formulary?
- What criteria do you use to evaluate medications for inclusion in the formulary?
- How do you evaluate medication safety?
- What medications have been removed from the formulary in the last 12 months and why were they removed?

Shortages and Outages

- How do you address shortages and outages of medications?
- How do you communicate shortages and outages to the medical staff?

Storage

Ensuring Stability of Medications

- How do you ensure that medications are stored to maintain their stability (inside the pharmacy and outside the pharmacy)?

Security

- How do you prevent unauthorized individuals from having access to medications?
- How do you ensure the security of anesthesia medications?
- What do you do if there is an unexplained loss of a controlled substance?

Emergency Medications

- How do you decide what emergency medications will be available?
- What do you do when an emergency medication must be replaced?

Medications Brought In by Patients or Their Families

- What do you do with medications brought in by patients or their families?
- How does the pharmacy indicate that it has visually examined a patient's own medications?
- When is it acceptable for patients to use their own medications?

Medications Brought In by Practitioners

- Do you allow practitioners to bring in their own medications for patient use?
- How does the pharmacy indicate that it has visually examined medications brought in by practitioners?

Ordering and Transcribing

Ordering

- What medication orders require an indication for use?
- What orders or types of orders are restricted to specific prescribers?

Look-Alike and Sound-Alike Medications

- What look-alike and sound-alike medications are problems in this organization?
- How do you prevent errors with look-alike and sound-alike medications?

Illegible Orders

- Are there prescribers whose orders are often illegible?
- How do you handle this issue?

Verbal and Telephone Orders

- How do you handle verbal and telephone orders?
- What limitations are placed on verbal and telephone orders?

Preprinted Orders

- How do you review, approve, and update preprinted orders?
- What roles do physicians have in developing preprinted orders?
- Do you use protocols for oral contrast?
- How do you choose samples of preprinted orders for retrospective review?

Standing Orders

- What is your process for ensuring that standing orders are current?
- Where do you keep copies of standing orders?

Weight-Based Dosing for Pediatric Patients

- When is weight-based dosing for pediatric patients required?

As Needed PRN Orders

- How do you qualify as needed (prn) orders?

Hold Orders

- What must be included in a hold order in your organization?
- How do you know when a hold order ends?

Automatic Stop Orders

- How do you notify a prescriber when a medication order is to be cancelled?
- What medications are subject to your automatic stop order policy?

Resume Orders

- What must a prescriber do to order the resumption of previous medications?

Titrating Orders

- What must be included in a titrating order in your organization?

Taper Orders

- How do you express taper orders in your organization?

Range Orders

- Do you allow range orders?
- How do you express range orders in your organization?
- What limits are placed on range orders?

Orders for Compounded Medications or Medication Mixtures

- Where do you keep formulas for compounded medications or medication mixtures?
- What is your process for reviewing and approving formulas for compounded medications or medication mixtures?

Orders for Medication-Related Devices

- What must be included in an order for a medication-related device?

Orders for Investigational Medications

- What prescribers are permitted to order investigational medications?
- What do you do if a patient who is taking an investigational medication is admitted to the organization?

Off-Label Use of Medications

- How do you monitor medications used for non-FDA approved indications?

Orders for Herbal Medications

- Must herbal medications be included in your formulary?
- Must orders for herbal medications include an indication or reason for use?

Orders for Medications at Discharge

- What is your process for ordering medications at discharge?
- Under what circumstances, if any, are patients permitted to take the remainder of their inpatient medications home?

Preparing and Dispensing

Appropriateness of Medication Orders

- How do you review medication orders for appropriateness?

Review of Orders in the Absence of a Pharmacist

- How do you ensure that orders are reviewed by a qualified health care professional in the absence of a pharmacist?

- What qualified health care professionals are permitted to review medication orders in the absence of a pharmacist?

After-Hours Pharmacy Services

- How are medications obtained when the pharmacy is closed?
- What do nurses do at night if a medication is not in the automated medication storage and distribution device?
- How often does this occur?
- How do you review orders when the pharmacy is closed?

Clarifying Medication Orders

- What do you do if a medication order is unclear?
- How do you ensure that medication orders are clarified?
- How do you document clarification of medication orders?

Preparing Medications Safely

- What safeguards are in place to ensure that medications are prepared safely?

Preparing Hazardous Medications

- How do you ensure that the preparation of hazardous medications presents no risk of harm to staff?
- Where do you store spill kits?

Accuracy of Medication Preparation

- What techniques do you use to ensure that medications are prepared accurately?

Compounding Sterile Preparations

- Do nurses prepare intravenous admixtures?
- What medications do nurses prepare?
- How do you handle USP <797> issues?
- What progress have you made toward compliance with USP <797> requirements?
- What are the USP risk levels for the sterile preparations that you compound?

Dispensing Medications in a Timely Manner

- What is the time period between when an order is written and when the medication is administered?
- Do you have specific time expectations for "stat" or "now" medication orders?

Dispensing Medications in a Ready-to-Administer Form

- What medications are not dispensed in a ready-to-administer form or unit-dose package?

Labeling of Medications

- How do you ensure that medications are labeled in a standardized manner?
- How does the anesthesia department label medication syringes?
- How are medications labeled on the sterile field?

Recalled Medications

- What is do you do when a medication is recalled or discontinued?
- How do you communicate medication recalls or discontinuations to prescribers and staff?

Medications Returned to the Pharmacy

- How do you handle medications that are returned to the pharmacy?
- Where do you store medications that are returned to the pharmacy?

Administering

Safe Administration

- How do you ensure that medications are safely and accurately administered?
- How do you ensure the competence of staff who administer medications?
- What role does the dietary department have in the safe administration of medications?

Notifying Prescribers

- What is your process for notifying prescribers if there is an adverse event or a medication error?
- How do you document that you have notified prescribers if there is an adverse event or medication error?

Infusion Pumps

- What types of infusion pumps are used in the organization?

- How do you know that your infusion pumps are protected against free-flow?
- Can infusion pump alarms be heard from the nurses' station?
- How does pharmacy collaborate with nursing to ensure that infusion pumps are used in a safe manner?
- How does the organization plan to provide safer infusion devices?
- Does the organization use smart pumps?
- Do infusion pumps have a mechanism (e.g., software) that provides minimum/maximum levels for high-risk or high-alert dangerous medications?

Self-Administration of Medications

- Do patients use or administer their own medications?
- How do you assess the patient's competence to self-administer medications?
- How do you document the patient's competence to self-administer medications?
- Where do you store patients' own medications?

Education

- What education have you provided relating to high-risk or high-alert medications?
- What education have you provided relating to new medications?
- What education have you provided relating to new medication-related devices?
- How do you provide medication information to patients?

References

- What medication references are available to staff?
- How do you ensure that medication references are current?

Monitoring

Monitoring the Effects of Medications

- How do you monitor the effects of medications on patients?
- What role does the laboratory have in monitoring the effects of medications?

Medication Errors

- How do you detect, report, and assess medication errors?
- What is your process for reporting errors, near misses, and system breakdowns?
- How do you collect, aggregate, and analyze data?
- What steps are in place to prevent medication errors?

Adverse Drug Events

- How do you detect, report, and assess adverse drug events?

High-Risk or High-Alert Medications

- What high-risk or high-alert medications have you identified?
- What safety measures are in place to prevent errors with high-risk or high-alert medications?

Evaluation

Medication Management System Evaluation

- Where are the risk points in your MM system?
- Have you conducted any medication-related FMEAs?
- How do you identify MM system problems?
- What improvements did you make when you identified problems?

Literature Evaluation

- How do you evaluate the literature for new technologies or successful practices that can be used to improve your MM system?
- What new technologies or successful practices have you implemented?

Table 5-1. Medication Management System Processes

Selection and Procurement

P&T or Equivalent	Purchasers	Vendors/Sources	Products
Set formulary criteria Develop formulary Provide for nonformulary drugs Develop policies & procedures Review drug literature Review & revise formulary Address shortages & outages Address recalls/discontinuations Communicate/educate	Pharmacy Ambulatory Care Materials Management Imaging Other departments & services	Wholesalers Manufacturers Investigational drug prescribers Compounding pharmacies Other suppliers & sources	Medications—Joint Commission definition: • Medication samples • IVs (plain & with additives) • Respiratory therapy • Anesthesia gases • Blood derivatives • Contrast media • Investigational drugs • Other medications Drug-related devices/ supplies

Storage—All Department/Areas
Securely: Locked/accountable Safely: High risk/hazardous Properly: Temperature/light
Emergency: Available & controlled Patient & Family: Identified & controlled Outdated/Recalled: Removed & disposed of

Ordering & Transcribing—All Prescribers	
Before Ordering: • Obtain patient information • Record patient information • Assess patient • Choose appropriate medication **Ordering:** • Order accurately, clearly, & legibly (written, verbal, or telephone)	**After Ordering:** • Verify order • Transcribe order to MAR properly • Verify transcription • Send/deliver/transmit order

Preparing & Dispensing—Pharmacy		
Pharmacist	**Pharmacist or Staff**	**Pharmacist**
Review, evaluate, & clarify/change order	Prepare or compound safely, properly, & accurately	Perform final check & dispense medication
Maintain patient profile	Package/label properly	Deliver to patient area

Distributing—Pharmacy
Distribute floor stock drugs & supplies to the following: • Patient care & other storage areas • Automated drug storage & distribution devices Provide for after-hours pharmacy services

Table 5-1. Medication Management System Processes (cont'd)

Administering Prescribers, Nurses, Respiratory Therapists, Radiology Technologists, Patients, & Others			
Obtain & prepare right drug for right patient	Identify patient correctly Verify no contraindication Advise patient about medication	Administer right drug & right dose to right patient at right time	Document completely, accurately, & correctly
Perform double checks & take other precautions	Perform double checks & take other precautions	Perform double checks & take other precautions	Comply with policy

Monitoring—All Services
Observe/assess. Monitor effect/response. Intervene as needed. Document effect/response. Document action. Report internally/externally.

MEDICATION MANAGEMENT SYSTEM SUPPORT PROCESSES

Patient & Family Education—All Services
Provide verbal teaching. Provide printed instructions. Evaluate comprehension & competence. Follow-up. Document education.

Surveillance & Process/Performance Improvement Activities—All Services				
Evaluate staff education Evaluate patient education	Evaluate medication use Review literature Review NPSG compliance	Review and analyze adverse drug reactions (ADRs)	Review and analyze medication errors	Conduct FMEA & RCA Perform inspections Do ISMP Self-Assessment Evaluate the medication management system
Outcome: Improve education	Outcome: Improve medication use	Outcome: Reduce ADRs	Outcome: Reduce errors	Outcome: Reduce risks

CHAPTER 6

Human Resources Standards Checklist

The Joint Commission™ in its management of human resources (HR) standards addresses planning (including licensure and staffing); qualifications relating to job responsibilities; roles in minimizing risks; performance evaluations; job descriptions; competence assessment; orientation, education, and training; personnel records; and other topics relating to personnel who provide services in the organization.

> ***Note:*** The Provision of Care, Treatment, and Services (PC) chapter of the *Comprehensive Accreditation Manual for Hospitals (CAMH)* (PC.6.10 through PC.6.30) addresses patient and family education and training relating to the care, treatment, and services provided. (*See* Chapter 7.)

Organization of the Checklist

This chapter presents selected Joint Commission HR standards, rationales, and elements of performance (EPs) for hospitals in a checklist format. Their sequence in the checklist may sometimes differ from the *CAMH.* Requirements that are quoted or paraphrased are clearly indicated (e.g., HR.1.20 or EP3 for HR.1.20).

> ***Note:*** Although this checklist does not address the HR standards completely, it should be sufficient to ensure compliance with standards pertaining to pharmacy personnel. Health care organizations should check for new and updated requirements on the Joint Commission's Internet Web site. (*See* Appendix A.)

A few items are not explicit in the HR standards but are consistent with Joint Commission expectations and/or professional practice standards. These items are not referenced to Joint Commission standards.

The notes are compliance expectations and suggestions that are based on the authors' personal experiences, reports from surveyed organizations, and surveyors' statements. Some notes reflect legal requirements, previous Joint Commission standards, or commonly accepted standards of practice. Others note variations in interpretation of the standards. The notes are not referenced to Joint Commission standards.

Using the Checklist

To assess compliance, use the checklist and proceed systematically. Mark the item "Yes" if you are currently compliant and are sure you will continue to be compliant. Mark the item"No" if you are currently not compliant (even if you are sure you will be compliant later). If you are not sure of your answer, leave a blank response. A few items may be not applicable ("NA"). Answer honestly, use a pencil (so you can change your answers), and make notes on the pages (e.g., reasons for noncompliance). Concentrate your efforts on resolving all "No" and blank responses.

Checklist

Yes NA No

Staffing

The types and numbers of qualified staff are sufficient "to furnish the care, treatment, and services offered by the organization." (Rationale for HR.1.10.) ____ ____ ____

> ***Note:*** The rationale for HR.1.10 states that "staff may be either employees of the organization or employees of a contractor that is employed by the organization."

> ***Note:*** In a footnote to the Overview of the Management of Human Resources chapter in the *CAMH* the Joint Commission defines staff as follows: "As appropriate to their roles and responsibilities, all people who provide care, treatment, and services in the organization, including those receiving pay (e.g., permanent, temporary, and part-time personnel, as well as contract employees), volunteers and health profession students. The definition of staff does not include licensed independent practitioners who are not paid staff or who are not contract employees."

The number and mix of qualified and competent pharmacists and support staff are consistent with the organization's staffing plan and meet the care, treatment, and service needs of the organization's patients. (HR.1.10, EP 1 for HR.1.10.) ____ ____ ____

> ***Note:*** Staffing to provide sufficient pharmacy services in a 600-bed, tertiary care, urban medical center might require several pharmacists and support personnel on duty 24 hours a day. However, a rural facility with 30 beds or fewer might fully meet the requirements with only one pharmacist and part-time support personnel on duty 8 hours a day. An on-call or consultant pharmacist might adequately staff other facilities that provide less acute care and have a low patient census.

> ***Note:*** Surveyors may ask to see a staffing schedule for the pharmacy. The pharmacy should be able to show that there is adequate staff on duty during peak hours and that staffing is sufficient to handle increases in patient census and intensity of care, and changes in types of patients.

> ***Note:*** During a survey, surveyors may compare the organization's staffing plan with actual staffing patterns. Although the organization's leaders must meet these standards, the pharmacy may be called upon to supply pharmacy-staffing data for analysis.

Qualifications of Staff

The organization ensures that "staff qualifications are consistent with his or her job responsibilities." (HR.1.20.) ____ ____ ____

The director of pharmacy defines "the required competence and qualifications of" pharmacy staff. (EP 1 for HR.1.20.) ____ ____ ____

	Yes	NA	No
Pharmacy staff members for whom the organization (but not law or regulation) "requires current licensure, certification, or registration," have had their credentials verified "at the time of hire and upon expiration of the credentials." (EP 2 for HR.1.20.)	____	____	____
Pharmacy staff members for whom "current licensure, certification, or registration are required by law or regulation to practice a profession," have had their credentials verified "with the primary source at the time of hire and upon expiration of the credentials." (EP 3 for HR.1.20.)	____	____	____

> ***Note:*** The primary source may delegate authority to verify credentials to another agency. An electronic or telephone verification is acceptable if it is documented. (Notes for EP 3 for HR.1.20.) (*See* HR.1.20 in the *CAMH* for a more on verification requirements.)

	Yes	NA	No
Pharmacy staff have the "education, experience, and competence appropriate for assigned responsibilities." (EP 4 for HR.1.20.)	____	____	____
The pharmacy verifies "information on criminal background if required by law and regulation or" the organization's policies. (EP 5 for HR.1.20.)	____	____	____
The pharmacy "verifies compliance with applicable health screening requirements if required by law and regulation or established by the" organization. (EP 6 for HR.1.20.)	____	____	____
"The information obtained from EPs 2–6 is used in making decisions regarding staff job responsibilities." (EP 7 for HR.1.20.)	____	____	____
Pharmacy "staff that provide patient care, treatment, and services possess a license, certification, or registration as required by law and regulation." (EP 8 for HR.1.20.)	____	____	____
Pharmacy "staff supervises students when they provide patient care, treatment, and services as part of their training." (EP 14 for HR.1.20.)	____	____	____

Assessing Staff Effectiveness

	Yes	NA	No
Organizations use data from clinical/service and human resource screening indicators to assess and improve staffing effectiveness. (*See* HR.1.30 in the *CAMH.*)	____	____	____

> ***Note:*** The organization may require the director of pharmacy to assist in this activity.

	Yes	NA	No
The pharmacy participates in assessing and continuously improving staffing effectiveness as required by the organization.	____	____	____

> ***Note:*** Organizations must use choose at least two clinical/service and at least two human resource screening indicators from the Joint Commission's list of approved subjects for screening indicators. They may choose additional screening indicators from their own list. The Joint Commission has approved the following list of approved subjects:
>
> 1. "Patient/family complaints/satisfaction (Clinical/Service)
> 2. Adverse drug events (Clinical/Service)
> 3. Injuries to patients (Clinical/Service)

Yes **NA** **No**

4. Skin breakdown (Clinical/Service)
5. Pneumonia (Clinical/Service)
6. Post operative infections (Clinical/Service)
7. Urinary tract infections (Clinical/Service)
8. Upper gastrointestinal bleeding (Clinical/Service)
9. Shock/cardiac arrest (Clinical/Service)
10. Length of stay (Clinical/Service)
11. Death among surgical inpatients with treatable serious complications (failure to rescue) (Clinical/Service) (National Quality Forum measure)
12. Pressure ulcer prevalence (Clinical/Service) (National Quality Forum measure)
13. Falls prevalence (Clinical Service) (National Quality Forum measure)
14. Falls with injury (Clinical Service) (National Quality Forum measure)
15. Restraint prevalence (vest and limb only) (Clinical/Service) (National Quality Forum measure)
16. Urinary catheter–associated urinary tract infection for intensive care unit patients (Clinical/Service) (National Quality Forum measure)
17. Central line catheter–associated blood stream infection rate for intensive care unit and high risk nursery patients (Clinical/Service) (National Quality Forum measure)
18. Ventilator-associated pneumonia for intensive care unit and high-risk nursery patients. (Clinical/Service) (National Quality Forum measure)
19. Smoking cessation counseling for acute myocardial infarction (Clinical/Service) (National Quality Forum measure)
20. Smoking cessation counseling for heart failure (Clinical/Service) (National Quality Forum measure)
21. Smoking cessation counseling for pneumonia (Clinical/Service) (National Quality Forum measure)
22. Overtime (Human Resource)
23. Staff vacancy rate (Human Resource)
24. Staff satisfaction (Human Resource)
25. Staff turnover rate (Human Resource)
26. Understaffing as compared to organization's staffing plan (Human Resource)
27. Staff injuries on the job (Human Resource)
28. On-call or per diem use (Human Resource)
29. Sick time (Human Resource)
30. Agency staff use (Human Resource)

	Yes	NA	No
31. Skill mix (registered nurse, licensed vocational nurse/licensed practical nurse, and unlicensed assistive personnel, and contract) (Human Resource) (National Quality Forum measure)			
32. Nursing care hours per patient day (registered nurse, licensed practical nurse, and unlicensed assistive personnel) (Human Resource) (National Quality Forum measure)			
33. Practice Environment Scale-Nursing Work Index (PES-NWI) composite and five subscales (Human Resource) (National Quality Forum measure)			
34. Voluntary turnover (Human Resource) (National Quality Forum measure)"[1]			

Orientation of Pharmacy Staff

Orientation includes "initial job training and information." (HR.2.10 and Rationale for HR.2.10.)	____	____	____

Note: Orientation to the organization and the pharmacy should start as soon after employment as practical to ensure that personnel are provided with essential information before they perform their activities. Orientation may take only a few hours or may extend over several weeks or months.

Note: Individuals new to the organization must be oriented to inform them of their responsibilities and how to fulfill them. The pharmacy should ensure that all pharmacy staff members receive this orientation.

Note: Individuals new to the pharmacy (including contract and temporary personnel) must be oriented to inform them of their responsibilities and how to fulfill them. Individuals new to the pharmacy but not the organization must be oriented to the pharmacy and their role within it. Individuals who frequently work in more than one department must be appropriately oriented to each department and their corresponding responsibilities. Surveyors sometimes ask to see the orientation record of a recently hired employee.

Note: When needed, orientation must be provided "before providing care, treatment, and services." (Rationale for HR.2.10.)

Orientation to the organization includes, at a minimum, the following:

• Key elements determined by the organization that are to occur before providing "care, treatment, and services." (EP 1 and EP 2 for HR.2.10.)	____	____	____
• The organization's "mission and goals." (EP 3 for HR.2.10.)	____	____	____
• Organization-wide "policies and procedures (including safety and infection control)." (EP 4 for HR.2.10.)	____	____	____

Note: Organization-wide policies and procedures also include work schedules, holidays, vacations, sick leave, and related topics.

• A general orientation to employee health.	____	____	____

	Yes	NA	No
Orientation to the pharmacy includes, at a minimum, the following:			
• Pharmacy policies and procedures. (EP 5 for HR.2.10.)	___	___	___
• "Specific job duties and responsibilities." (EP 5 for HR.2.10.)	___	___	___
Note: Specific job duties and responsibilities include individual performance expectations (e.g., performance and competence standards), educational expectations (e.g., attendance at in-service education programs), and applicable pharmacy law and professional standards of pharmacy practice.			
• "Specific job duties and responsibilities related to safety and infection control." (EP 4 for HR.2.10.)	___	___	___
Note: Safety duties and responsibilities include fire safety, internal and external disaster procedures, management of hazardous materials and wastes, appropriate precautions for handling hazardous medications, and emergency procedures. Safety orientation should also include pharmacy safety plans, Material Safety Data Sheets (MSDSs), location of fire alarms and fire extinguishers, and emergency exit routes.			
Note: Safety policies should include disaster procedures and precautions for safe storage, lifting, and transport of materials. Infection control duties and responsibilities should include prevention of infection (e.g., adherence to standard precautions, hand washing techniques, and appropriate techniques for preparing sterile medications).			
• Processes for minimizing security risks (including emergency procedures to follow during a security incident).	___	___	___
• "Cultural diversity and sensitivity." (EP 7 for HR.2.10.)	___	___	___
"Staff orientation includes education about the rights of patients and ethical aspects of care, treatment, and services and the process used to address ethical issues." (EP 8 for HR.2.10.)	___	___	___
Orientation is documented.	___	___	___
Note: Orientation records should include, at a minimum, the name of the individual undergoing orientation, topics covered, date orientation was completed, and signature of the individual who confirmed the completion of orientation. (*See* Example 6-1.)			
The pharmacy assesses the effectiveness of orientation (e.g., gives pre- and post-tests, observes performance, and assesses competence in critical areas).	___	___	___
The pharmacy assesses the appropriateness of orientation to individual needs.	___	___	___

	Yes	NA	No

Qualifications Relating to Improving Patient and Employee Safety

The organization emphasizes patient and employee safety.	____	____	____

> ***Note:*** Pharmacy staff must be able to assess safety risks and suggest how to improve safety within the organization.

Pharmacy staff members "can describe or demonstrate" the following: (HR.2.20.)

• "Risks within the hospital's environment." (EP 1 for HR.2.20.)	____	____	____
• "Actions to eliminate, minimize, or report risks." (EP 2 for HR.2.20.)	____	____	____
• "Procedures to follow in the event of an incident." (EP 3 for HR.2.20.)	____	____	____
• "Reporting processes for common problems, failures, and user errors." (EP 4 for HR.2.20.)	____	____	____

Education and Training of Pharmacy Staff

Education and training of pharmacy staff aims to maintain and improve their competence (i.e., their knowledge, skills, and ability to do a job). (HR.2.30.)	____	____	____

> ***Note:*** Staff education and training can be accomplished through any method (e.g., off-site seminars and conferences, in-service education programs, self-study materials, correspondence courses, newsletters, and audio and video recordings). On-the-job training may be sufficient. The standards do not require the pharmacy to provide all of the education and training programs for pharmacy staff (i.e., the organization and/or other departments might provide some of them).

> ***Note:*** Some surveyors expect pharmacy staff to receive education and training at least once a month. The time required for education and training sessions can vary from a few minutes to several hours.

> ***Note:*** Although not specifically required by the standards, some surveyors state that the pharmacy and other departments should hold staff meetings regularly (e.g., monthly). Either combined or separate meetings of pharmacists and support personnel should satisfy most surveyors. Many pharmacies combine educational programs and staff meetings. Minutes of meetings or similar records are adequate documentation.

Education and training to improve competence is provided for pharmacy staff. (HR.2.30.)	____	____	____
"Training occurs when job responsibilities or duties change." (EP 1 for HR.2.30.)	____	____	____
"Staff participate in ongoing in-services, training, or other activities to increase knowledge of work-related issues." (EP 2 for HR.2.30.)	____	____	____
Education and training address individual staff member needs.	____	____	____

	Yes	NA	No

> *Note:* Staff member needs may include dispensing procedures; controlled substance handling; prepackaging; compounding of sterile preparations; laws, rules and regulations pertaining to medications and the practice of pharmacy; professional standards; equipment (including computers); bar coding of medications; automated medication storage and dispensing devices; and performing medication area inspections.

> *Note:* Educational topics should ensure the professional competence of pharmacists and the technical expertise of support personnel. However, you need not limit their education to topics that are related to their work. Any educational topic that increases staff effectiveness is acceptable (e.g., planning, time management, and personnel relations). Also, staff should be encouraged to participate in professional activities that are educational in nature (e.g., writing professional articles and joining professional societies).

Education includes CPR and other lifesaving interventions (as required by the organization). ____ ____ ____

> *Note:* The Joint Commission does not require pharmacy staff to receive CPR training. However, if the organization requires CPR training for pharmacy staff, some surveyors may look for documented evidence that they have been trained.

"Ongoing in-services and other education and training of staff are appropriate to the needs of the population(s) served and comply with law and regulation." (EP 3 for HR.2.30.) ____ ____ ____

Education and training address care of patient age groups served by the organization (e.g., neonatal, pediatric, adolescent, adult, and geriatric populations). (Implied by EP 3 for HR.2.30.) ____ ____ ____

Education and training address the type and nature of care provided by the organization and the department (e.g., skilled nursing, psychiatric, substance abuse, and rehabilitation care). (Implied by EP 3 for HR.2.30.) ____ ____ ____

"Ongoing in-services, training, or other staff activities emphasize specific job-related aspects of safety and infection prevention and control." (EP 4 for HR.2.30.) ____ ____ ____

> *Note:* Job-related aspects of safety include basic approaches to patient safety; medication safety; security measures; response to aggressive behavior and hostile situations (e.g., robbery, riot, or hostage situations); reporting of accidents, injuries, damages, and safety and security incidents involving patients, staff, visitors, and property; and processes for minimizing security risks.

> *Note:* Job-related aspects of infection prevention and control include techniques for controlling infection (e.g., hand hygiene and aseptic technique) and findings from the organization's infection control activities.

> *Note:* Pharmacy staff meetings and educational programs should address safety and infection-control-related topics (e.g., findings from the safety management program and the infection control program, general safety measures and measures for preventing infection, fire prevention, methods of containing smoke and fires, hazardous materials, hazards associated with specific jobs [e.g., preparation

	Yes	NA	No
of antineoplastic agents], and emergency preparedness). Staff members who are involved in safety and infection control incidents should be given additional training.			
"Ongoing in-services, training, or other staff education incorporate methods of team training, when appropriate." (EP 5 for HR.2.30.)	___	___	___
"Ongoing in-services, training, or other staff education reinforce the need and ways to report unanticipated adverse events." (EP 6 for HR.2.30.)	___	___	___
Note: Reinforcement should include the need to report and the means available to report adverse drug reactions and medical errors.			
"Ongoing in-services or other staff education are offered in response to learning needs identified through performance improvement findings and other data analysis (that is, data from staff surveys, performance evaluations, or other needs assessments)." (EP 7 for HR.2.30.)	___	___	___
Note: The pharmacy must assess the appropriateness of education and training to individual needs. Sources of information relating to learning needs include findings and actions of drug use improvement teams, findings from individual competence assessments, and findings from peer review activities.			
Note: Appropriate education and training should be developed as new types of therapies emerge (e.g., gene therapy). The pharmacy should also assess the effectiveness of education and training (e.g., give pre- and post-tests and observe performance).			
"Ongoing staff education is documented." (EP 8 for HR.2.30.)	___	___	___
Note: Education and training records include at least a summary of the topic; date of education and training session, program, or meeting; provider (e.g., instructor or lecturer); names of attendees; and continuing education (CE) credit (number of hours), if any.			
Note: Records should show that all shifts were included. Surveyors sometimes ask for lesson plans, training manuals, outlines, handouts, and audiovisual materials. These materials give credence to the documentation. Examples 6-2 and 6-3 are forms for recording attendance at education programs and meetings. Example 6-4 is an individual record of education completed.			
Pharmacy staff members have met the mandatory CE requirements to maintain their licenses and permits.	___	___	___
Note: Some pharmacies keep a log of staff CE credits or keep copies of CE certificates in personnel files. You may need to require staff to provide evidence that they met their CE requirements.			

Yes **NA** **No**

Orientation, Education, and Training for Medical Staff, Nursing Service, and Other Professional Staff

The pharmacy participates in the orientation of medical staff, nursing service, and other professional staff. ___ ___ ___

Note: An orientation program for medical staff, nursing service, and other professional staff (e.g., respiratory therapists, emergency medical service personnel, and nutrition service personnel) can improve medication use, prevent problems, avoid misunderstandings, and provide for safer medication processes. The Joint Commission has no specific requirements relating to pharmacy participation in this program.

Note: Examples of orientation topics include recommendations for the safe prescribing and administration of medications, formulary (e.g., generic and therapeutic drug substitution policies), adverse drug event monitoring and reporting, and automated medication storage and distribution devices.

The pharmacy participates in the education and training of medical staff, nursing service, and other professional staff. ___ ___ ___

Note: Education and training may consist of presentations at medical and nursing staff meetings and at pharmacy-sponsored programs. Pharmaceutical manufacturers will often provide expert speakers. However, pharmacists should make sure that their presentations are consistent with the organization's medication use and cost-containment goals.

Note: Examples of education and training topics include information on drug incompatibilities, interactions, contraindications, and adverse reactions; compounding of sterile preparations; automated medication distribution and storage devices; media fill testing; processes that improve the safe use of medications (i.e., ensure legibility, eliminate trailing zeros, etc.); medication error reporting and prevention; and findings relating to adverse drug reactions.

Competence Assessment

"Competence to perform job responsibilities" is "assessed, demonstrated, and maintained." (HR.3.10.) ___ ___ ___

Note: Competence assessments determine if the individual has the knowledge, skills, and ability to do a job and actually performs the job according to defined expectations. (*See* Chapter 13.)

Note: The Joint Commission requires organizations to assess the competence of staff members who assess, treat, and otherwise work directly with patients. Many organizations extend this requirement to all staff, including staff whose duties are not directly related to patient care (e.g., administrative assistants).

	Yes	NA	No

Note: Pharmacy staff must have access to current and authoritative knowledge-based information resources to help them acquire, maintain, and improve their competence.

Note: The pharmacy must define the specific tasks needed to perform a job and identify competence requirements for the job (e.g., in a job description or other document). Competence requirements must be updated periodically (e.g., annually).

Competence assessment of staff includes the following:

- "Populations served" (EP 1 for HR.3.10*)* by the organization (e.g., skilled nursing, psychiatric, substance abuse, and rehabilitation). ___ ___ ___
- Special needs and behaviors of patient age groups served by the organization (e.g., neonatal, pediatric, adolescent, adult, and geriatric patients). (Implied by EP 1 for HR.3.10.) ___ ___ ___

  Note: Staff members who prepare medications must be familiar with dosages and dosage forms for these age groups and demonstrate their competence before they prepare medications for these patients. Furthermore, staff members who assess, treat, or care for these age groups must be able to understand and react effectively to their unique needs. For example, individuals who educate patients must be aware that pediatric patients might not have the ability to understand the material, adolescent patients may resent an authoritative educational style, and geriatric patients may be hearing impaired. They can gain this awareness through education, training, and/or experience. However, competence assessments must determine if they address these limitations effectively when working with patients in these age groups.

- "Defined competencies to be required" (EP 2 for HR.3.10) (e.g., knowledge, skills, and ability needed to perform jobs, dispense medications, compound sterile preparations, and provide pharmacokinetic consultations). ___ ___ ___

  Note: For example, assessing the competence of pharmacists who provide pharmacokinetic consultations should be based on the completion of education and training and by demonstration of their ability to make appropriate dosing recommendations (e.g., by written tests). In addition, there should be a period during which an experienced pharmacist reviews all of the pharmacist's work prior to making dosing recommendations. Thereafter, the pharmacist's competence should be reassessed periodically.

- Security and safety (including ability to use equipment safely and effectively). ___ ___ ___

  Note: Equipment includes hoods for compounding sterile preparations, medication repackaging equipment, automated compounding and dispensing equipment, and computers. Equipment management procedures must address operator competence. Individuals must be trained to operate the equipment effectively and safely (i.e., without harm to patient or operator) and detect malfunctions (e.g., inaccurate measurements) and signs of impending malfunction (e.g., damage due to dropping or abuse). If necessary, training should be repeated periodically to ensure continued competence of the operator.

Yes **NA** **No**

- Prevention of contamination and transfer of infection (infection control) (e.g., appropriate hand hygiene and appropriate techniques in preparing sterile medications). ___ ___ ___
- Cardiopulmonary resuscitation (CPR) and other lifesaving interventions (as required by the organization). ___ ___ ___

  Note: The Joint Commission does not require pharmacy staff to be competent in CPR. However, if the organization requires CPR competence for pharmacy staff, surveyors may look for documented evidence that they are competent.

- "Defined competencies to be assessed during orientation." (EP 3 for HR.3.10.) ___ ___ ___

  Note: Competence must be assessed before individuals are allowed to perform their duties.

The organization "assesses and documents each person's ability to carry out assigned responsibilities safely, competently, and in a timely manner upon completion of orientation." (EP 8 for HR.3.10.) ___ ___ ___

Competence assessment addresses "defined competencies that need to be assessed and reassessed on an ongoing basis, based on techniques, procedures, technology, equipment, or skills needed to provide care, treatment, and services." (EP 4 for HR.3.10.) ___ ___ ___

Note: Competence assessment should be included in ongoing education and training, introduction of new procedures, assignment of new duties, and training associated with new or updated equipment. Continued competence can be ensured through periodic (e.g., quarterly) testing and frequent (e.g., daily or weekly) observation of work techniques.

Competence assessments "are performed for each person" within the organization's defined time frame, "minimally, once in the three-year accreditation cycle and in accordance with law and regulation." (EP 5 for HR.3.10.) (*See* Chapter 18 for <USP 797> competence requirements.) (Example 6-5 is a list of competencies relating to sterile preparations.) ___ ___ ___

"Assessment methods" are "appropriate to determine the skill being assessed." (EP 6 for HR.3.10.) ___ ___ ___

Note: Competence can be assessed through written or verbal tests, skills checklists, random direct observations, or any combination of these. Reviewing pharmacy and patient records may reveal information relating to an individual's competence. Actual, on-the-job assessments of daily work are preferred. However, simulated competence assessment situations may be necessary. Example 6-6 is a skills test and Example 6-7 is a skills checklist.

Qualified individuals assess competence. (EP 7 for HR.3.10.) ___ ___ ___

Note: Qualified individuals are those who are familiar with the organization's competence assessment process and have the education, knowledge, training, and capability to determine if others possess the required competencies.

Yes NA No

Note: EP 7 for HR.3.10 notes that if no individual within the organization is qualified to assess competence:

- Qualified staff from other organizations may assist with the assessment of competence, or
- Appropriate professional organization guidelines relating to competence expectations may be used to assess competence

Each person is assessed according to the organization's competence assessment process. (EP 9 for HR.3.10.) ____ ____ ____

There is documented evidence (e.g., competence assessment and certification of competence) that pharmacy personnel (including students, volunteers, contract service personnel and temporary agency staff) are competent. ____ ____ ____

Note: The organization may ask the pharmacy, contract service, and/or temporary agency to provide an annual summary of the pharmacy staff's competence to the organization's administration and/or governing body (e.g., a letter, memo, or completed certifications of competence). The organization should specify how this should be reported.

"When improvement activities lead to a determination that a person with performance problems is unable or unwilling to improve, the hospital takes appropriate action (which may include modifying the person's job assignment.)." (EP 10 for HR.3.10.) ____ ____ ____

Performance Evaluations

The pharmacy "conducts performance evaluations periodically at time frames identified by the hospital (at a minimum, at least once in the three-year accreditation cycle)." (EP 1 for HR.3.20.) ____ ____ ____

Note: Performance evaluations relate to how well the individual performs a job according to defined expectations. Performance evaluations may also relate to punctuality, attitude, compliance with policies and procedures, completion of education requirements, attendance at meetings, participation in required activities, maintenance of licensure, etc.

Note: Some laws, regulations, or other requirements (e.g., <USP 797> may specify more frequent performance evaluations and describe the performance expectations that must be met. (*See* Chapter 18.)

The pharmacy evaluates performance "based on the performance expectations described in job descriptions." (EP 2 for HR.3.20.) ____ ____ ____

Note: "Formal performance evaluations can be conducted concurrently with competence assessments or can be completed at a separate time." (Rationale for HR.3.20.)

The pharmacy documents performance evaluations. (EP 4 for HR.3.20.) ____ ____ ____

Yes NA No

Job Descriptions

There is a written job description for each employee. (Required by EP 2 for HR.3.20.) ___ ___ ___

> ***Note:*** Managers must provide job descriptions that clearly and accurately define the minimum qualifications for the position, reporting relationships, authority (e.g., right to purchase equipment), and representative responsibilities and duties (tasks, services, and functions associated with the position). Job descriptions such as those described in this section should satisfy most surveyors.

> ***Note:*** Job descriptions should be prepared for the director of pharmacy, staff pharmacists, and support staff. (*See* Example 6-8.) For some positions, such as administrative assistant, a general job description will suffice. In other cases, job descriptions must be tailored to the individual (e.g., describe the special training and responsibilities in oncology pharmacy or pediatric pharmacy).

> ***Note:*** Job descriptions should be provided at the time of hire. Thereafter, individuals should participate in developing their job descriptions.

The qualifications and performance expectations for positions are defined in the job descriptions and stated in measurable terms. ___ ___ ___

> ***Note:*** Qualifications include education, training, experience, skills, and licensure. Performance expectations relate to the tasks, duties, services, and functions associated with the position and are often stated as performance or competence standards.

Performance and/or competence standards are employee-specific and job related. ___ ___ ___

> ***Note:*** Performance and/or competence standards must be realistic, relevant, achievable, and measurable, and must be used in evaluating performance. They should be agreed on by both the manager and the employee.

Job descriptions (or other documents) address the special needs and behaviors of the patient age groups served (e.g., neonatal, pediatric, adolescent, adult, and geriatric patients). ___ ___ ___

> ***Note:*** There must be evidence that the organization has considered age-specific needs when defining the qualifications of individuals who deal directly with patients of various age groups. Although including statements in individual job descriptions is a common way to meet this requirement, other evidence is acceptable (e.g., an organization policy or other document that defines age-related competencies required for all positions).

> ***Note:*** If the staff deals directly with infants, children, adolescents, adults, or geriatric patients, the requirements for dealing effectively with these patients must be defined. Many surveyors, with good reason, extend this requirement to staff who do not deal directly with patients. For example, they expect job descriptions of staff that fill orders for pediatric patients to reflect that these individuals must be able to meet the needs of these patients (e.g., be familiar with pediatric

	Yes	NA	No
dosages). Job descriptions for individuals who deal with patients of all ages must indicate that these individuals must be able to meet the needs of patients of all ages.			
Job descriptions are reviewed and updated periodically (e.g., annually) to reflect current requirements.	___	___	___
Note: Job descriptions should be reviewed, revised, signed, and dated by employees and their supervisors as provided for in the organization's policies.			

Personnel Records

There is a personnel record for each pharmacy staff member (e.g., pharmacists, technicians, and clerks).	___	___	___
Personnel records are stored in the pharmacy and/or centrally in the organization's files.	___	___	___
Each personnel record includes, at a minimum, the following:			
• Employment application	___	___	___
• Evidence that references were checked	___	___	___
Note: Although the Joint Commission does not explicitly require personnel records to include employment applications and evidence that references were checked, these are good hiring practices and are consistent with the Joint Commission's HR requirements.			
• Licensure information	___	___	___
Note: There should be evidence that licensure was verified with the primary source when the person was hired and upon renewal thereafter. (*See* Qualifications of Staff in this chapter.)			
• Evidence of orientation to the organization and the department (signed and dated by the staff member)	___	___	___
• Records of education and training provided by the organization and the department	___	___	___
• Job description	___	___	___
• Performance evaluations	___	___	___
• Evidence of competence assessments	___	___	___
• Records of counseling and disciplinary action	___	___	___
• Health records (e.g., physical examinations, blood tests, chest X-rays, immunizations, and tuberculosis skin tests) required by the organization (including follow-ups as required)	___	___	___
Note: Pharmacy staff (including contract services staff) must comply with the organization's health record requirements. Copies of test results should			

	Yes	NA	No

satisfy the organization. Complete health records for the pharmacy staff need not be maintained in the pharmacy. Many organizations store health records in a central location.

CHAPTER 7

Education and Training of Patients and Family Checklist

The Joint Commission™ in it's provision of care, treatment, and services (PC) standards requires organizations to provide "education and training specific to the patient's needs and as appropriate to the care, treatment, and services provided." (PC.6.10.) Patients and their caregivers (e.g., parents, guardians, relatives, friends, home care nurses, and home care aides) should be educated about medications administered during the patient's hospitalization as well as medications to be taken after discharge.

> ***Note:*** The Management of Human Resources (HR) chapter of the *Comprehensive Accreditation Manual for Hospitals (CAMH)* addresses staff orientation, education, and training. (*See* Chapter 6.)

Organization of the Checklist

This chapter presents selected Joint Commission patient education standards and elements of performance (EPs) for hospitals in a checklist format. Their sequence in the checklist may sometimes differ from the *CAMH*. Requirements that are quoted or paraphrased are clearly indicated (e.g., PC.6.10 or EP 2 for PC.6.30).

> ***Note:*** Although this checklist does not address the patient and family education requirements completely, it should be sufficient to ensure compliance with requirements pertaining to pharmacy. Health care organizations should check for new and updated requirements on the Joint Commission's Internet Web site. (*See* Appendix A.)

A few items are not explicit in the PC standards but are consistent with Joint Commission expectations and/or professional practice standards. These items are not referenced to Joint Commission standards.

The notes are compliance expectations and suggestions that are based on the authors' personal experiences, reports from surveyed organizations, and surveyors' statements. Some notes reflect legal requirements, previous Joint Commission standards, or commonly accepted standards of practice. Others note variations in interpretation of the standards. The notes are not referenced to Joint Commission standards.

Using the Checklist

To assess compliance, use the checklist and proceed systematically. Mark the item "Yes" if you are currently compliant and are sure you will continue to be compliant. Mark the item"No" if you are currently not compliant (even if you are sure you will be compliant later). If you are not sure of your answer, leave a blank response. A few items may be not applicable ("NA"). Answer honestly, use a pencil (so you can change your answers), and make notes on the pages (e.g., reasons for noncompliance). Concentrate your efforts on resolving all "No" and blank responses.

Checklist	Yes	NA	No
The pharmacy provides education that is "appropriate to the patient's needs." (EP 1 for PC.6.10.)	___	___	___

Note: Providing education that is appropriate to the patient's needs may include an assessment of patients' knowledge and skills relating to their medications. Organizations must also ensure that patient education is appropriate to the needs of high-risk patients (e.g., geriatric and pediatric patients), patients with specific diseases (e.g., diabetes and asthma), and patients receiving specific medications (e.g., anticoagulants and insulin). Pharmacy staff must have access to current and authoritative knowledge-based information resources to help them provide appropriate information and education.

The pharmacy provides patient education that "is appropriate to the patient's abilities." (EP 1 for PC.6.30.)	___	___	___

Note: Patients have a right and need for effective communication. (EP 1 for RI.2.100.) Education and instructions must be appropriate to the patient's age and language, mental health state, and ability to comprehend. (EP2 for RI.2.100.) The organization should provide interpreters or translation services as needed. (EP 3 for RI.2.100.) The needs of patients who have "vision, speech, hearing, language, and cognitive impairments" must be met. (EP 4 for RI.2.100.)

The pharmacy, as appropriate, coordinates its patient education with other disciplines. (EP 2 for PC.6.30.)	___	___	___

Note: Patient education is the mutual responsibility of physicians, nurses, pharmacists, dieticians, discharge counselors, and other health care practitioners. Physicians and nurses are in close contact with patients and are in an ideal position to educate patients and families on most aspects of care (e.g., care for a surgical wound). Qualified discharge counselors can do an excellent job of preparing patients for their departure from the facility. However, pharmacists are most knowledgeable about medications and should play a major role in medication-related patient education. Furthermore, some patients may prefer to talk to pharmacists about their medications. When it is not possible for pharmacists to provide medication-related education, they should ensure that current information and appropriate instructional materials are available to health care practitioners who educate patients.

Note: The pharmacy should be able to describe how it collaborates with nursing service, nutrition services, and other services in the education of patients and families. The pharmacy may suggest medications for inclusion in the program, suggest significant medication-food interactions for inclusion in the program, assist in preparing guidelines for patient education, and, when appropriate, provide education and instruction (e.g., diabetic teaching, anticoagulation therapy teaching, and patient-controlled analgesia pump training). The pharmacy should be able to show examples of handouts and other materials that it provides to patients and their families.

Patient education addresses "the safe and effective use of medications." (EP 3 for PC.6.10.)	___	___	___

	Yes	NA	No
Note: Education relating to the safe and effective use of medications might include the name and use of the medication; dosage, administration route, and frequency of administration; expected actions; special directions and precautions; what to do if a wrong dose is taken or a dose is missed; potential interactions with foods and other medications; expected side effects and what to do if a side effect is serious; contraindications; prevention of contamination; proper storage; proper disposal of unused or expired medications; and how to obtain prescription refills.			
The pharmacy complies with OBRA-90 patient education requirements.	____	____	____
Note: The Omnibus Budget Reconciliation Act of 1990 (OBRA-90) requires pharmacists in a retail setting to offer to provide patient counseling to Medicaid patients. Many states extend these requirements to all patients. Some States apply the act to employee prescriptions, discharge prescriptions, and furlough (or pass) medications (i.e., medications supplied to patients who are not discharged but are temporarily on leave from the organization). Health-system pharmacists should ensure that they comply with both federal OBRA-90 requirements, their state requirements, and their organization's policies.			
Note: Some pharmacists contend that health-system organizations do not have to educate patients about medications to be taken after discharge because OBRA-90 requires a retail pharmacist to offer to educate patients when they fill their prescriptions. The Joint Commission's position is that an organization cannot be certain that retail pharmacists will provide the education nor can the organization be certain that the education will be adequate. Therefore, the fact that pharmacists in retail settings may educate patients when they fill their prescriptions does not relieve organizations from their responsibility to educate patients about their medications prior to discharge.			
Note: OBRA-90 specifies patient education requirements that organizations might consider when developing their education program for patients to be discharged. These include name and description of the medication; dose and dosage form, route of administration, and duration of therapy; special directions and precautions for preparation, administration, and use of the medication; techniques for self-administering medications and action to be taken in the case of a missed dose; common and serious (severe) side effects, adverse effects, as well as interactions and therapeutic contraindications that may be encountered including their avoidance and the action required if they occur; proper storage; and prescription refill information.			
Patients are educated about potential medication-food interactions.	____	____	____
Note: At a minimum, the Joint Commission expects organizations to educate patients about medication-food interactions associated with medications to be taken after discharge. Organizations may limit education to the prevention of well-documented, clinically significant interactions that pose a risk of discomfort or harm to the patient. Medication-food interaction education should emphasize foods to avoid, effect of dietary supplements, effect of alcohol consumption, timing of medication administration (e.g., before meals), importance of adequate fluid consumption, and signs of interactions and adverse reactions.			

	Yes	NA	No
The organization provides relevant information to patients who receive specific vaccines. (*See* Chapter 23.)	___	___	___
As appropriate, the pharmacy provides education that addresses the "safe and effective use of medical equipment or supplies when provided by the" organization. (EP 3 for PC.6.10.)	___	___	___

> ***Note:*** Medical equipment and supplies include inhalation devices (e.g., spacers and nebulizers) glucose meters, patient controlled analgesia devices, and infusion pumps. Pharmacies that provide or support these devices should educate patients on their safe and effective use (including how to detect defects and problems and what to do if there are defects and problems).

	Yes	NA	No
The pharmacy provides education "in an understandable manner." (EP 3 for PC.6.30.)	___	___	___

> ***Note:*** There must be a mechanism to ensure that education is understood and effective. Multilingual instructions should be available in those areas that have a significant number of patients who speak languages other than English. Instructions that use pictures rather than words can be used to educate patients who cannot read or who have low literacy and patients who speak languages in which written instructions are unavailable. Instructions for visually impaired and blind patients can be in Braille or recorded.

	Yes	NA	No
The pharmacy uses teaching methods that "accommodate various learning styles." (EP 4 for PC.6.30.)	___	___	___

> ***Note:*** Patient education may be oral or written. The teaching format may be by individual instruction and/or in a group setting. For consistency (and because oral instructions may be forgotten or remembered incorrectly), printed instructions should be provided when possible. Providing instructional cards and leaflets is a popular way to educate patients. These materials may be prepared by the organization or obtained from pharmaceutical companies, government agencies, specialty professional groups (e.g., the American Heart Association and American Diabetes Association), and other outside sources. A copy of printed materials or summary of instructions should be placed in the patient's medical record.

> ***Note:*** ASHP's *Medication Teaching Manual: The Guide to Patient Drug Information*[1] contains easy-to-read medication monographs in nontechnical language. Each monograph is presented in a question-and-answer format. The monographs include medication-food interaction information when applicable. ASHP's monographs may be photocopied and distributed to patients. ASHP also offers *MedTeach*®, a software program with quarterly updates, which allows the user to tailor the content and format of the monographs to meet the facility's and individual patient's needs.

	Yes	NA	No
The pharmacy evaluates patients' comprehension of education provided. (EP 5 for PC.6.30.)	___	___	___

> ***Note***: Techniques for evaluating comprehension include asking specific questions, having patients repeat instructions and demonstrate administration techniques, giving post-tests, and contacting patients after discharge to see if they are having difficulties with their medications.

	Yes	NA	No
The pharmacy documents patient and family education (e.g., in the patient's medical record).	____	____	____
Note: Surveyors encourage the use of a multidisciplinary patient education record in the patient's medical record.			
Pharmacy staff who educate patients and families are competent to do so.	____	____	____
Note: ASHP's *Competence Assessment Tools for Health-System Pharmacies* contains guidelines for assessing the competence of pharmacists and support staff.[2] (*See* Chapters 6 and 13.)			

Infection Control Checklist

The Joint Commission™ in its surveillance, prevention, and control of infection (IC) standards, requires organizations to take precautions to reduce the risk of acquiring and transmitting infections. Organizations must have effective, organization-wide IC programs. All departments and services must participate in the organization's IC efforts.

Organization of the Checklist

This chapter presents infection control precautions for health care personnel in a checklist format. They are consistent with the Joint Commission's IC standards,[1] current Centers for Disease Control and Prevention (CDC) hand-hygiene guidelines[2] (*see* NPSG 7 in Chapter 20) and, to the extent practical, the provisions of USP General Chapter <797>.[3] (*See* Chapter 18.)

> ***Note:*** Although this checklist does not address these precautions completely, it should help to reduce the risk of acquiring and transmitting infections. Health care organizations should check for new and updated standards on the Joint Commission's Internet Web sites. They should check for new and updated hand hygiene guidelines on the CDC's Internet Web site. (*See* Appendix A.) Pharmacies should contact their board of pharmacy and other state agencies to determine how their state integrates USP <797> provisions into its regulations.

The notes are compliance expectations and suggestions that are based on the authors' personal experiences, reports from surveyed organizations, and surveyors' statements. Some notes reflect legal requirements, previous Joint Commission standards, or commonly accepted standards of practice. Others note variations in interpretation of the standards.

Using the Checklist

To assess compliance, use the checklist and proceed systematically. Mark the item "Yes" if you are currently compliant and are sure you will continue to be compliant. Mark the item "No" if you are currently not compliant (even if you are sure you will be compliant later). If you are not sure of your answer, leave a blank response. A few items may be not applicable ("NA"). Answer honestly, use a pencil (so you can change your answers), and make notes on the pages (e.g., reasons for noncompliance). Concentrate your efforts on resolving all "No" and blank responses.

Checklist	Yes	NA	No

Identifying and Reporting

	Yes	NA	No
Accidents, incidents, unsafe practices, and unsanitary conditions that pose a risk of infection for patients, visitors, and staff are identified and reported.	____	____	____

> *Note:* Infection control-related incidents are usually reported to the infection control committee or a designated individual. The organization's infection control plan should contain specific information on how to make these reports.

Surveillance Activities

	Yes	NA	No
Each department or service participates in infection control surveillance activities as required by the organization.	____	____	____

Cleanliness and Orderliness

	Yes	NA	No
Areas where medications are stored, compounded, dispensed, prepared, and administered are clean, neat, and well-organized.	____	____	____

Cleaning

	Yes	NA	No
Staff uses organization-approved cleaning procedures and cleaning agents.	____	____	____
There are an adequate number of sinks and sufficient space and materials for cleaning equipment and washing hands.	____	____	____

> *Note:* Cleaning should be coordinated with housekeeping personnel, and cleaning agents and procedures approved by the infection control committee must be used. Particular attention must be given to repackaging, compounding, and sterile preparation areas, as well as areas likely to harbor microorganisms that could contaminate medications or transmit disease to staff.

	Yes	NA	No
Cleaning agents and supplies are available to staff.	____	____	____
Equipment is kept clean and stored in a clean area.	____	____	____

> *Note:* Areas under sinks are not clean areas. Mortars, pestles, glassware, and other equipment that must be kept clean must be stored in a clean area.

	Yes	NA	No
Drug packaging and dispensing devices (e.g., counting trays, graduated cylinders, unit-dose packaging devices, and balances) are cleaned after each use and disinfected if necessary.	____	____	____
Devices used for crushing or splitting tablets are cleaned immediately after use according to manufacturers' recommendations and instructions.	____	____	____

	Yes	NA	No
Medication carts, drawers, and bins containing individual patient's medications are kept clean.	___	___	___
Automated medication storage and distribution devices are cleaned according to the manufacturer's recommendations and instructions.	___	___	___

> ***Note:*** Many organizations develop a schedule for cleaning equipment and devices.

Boxes and Cartons

Cardboard boxes are stored off the floor.	___	___	___

> ***Note:*** This is not specifically required by the standards. However, some organizations and surveyors insist that they be stored off the floor.

Shipping containers are not stored or opened (i.e., torn or cut) in any area reserved for repackaging medications or compounding sterile preparations.	___	___	___

> ***Note:*** Handling and storing shipping containers (e.g., cardboard boxes) must be done with minimal air disturbances and dissemination of dust particles. Intravenous (IV) bags and bottles must be removed from cartons and wiped with an approved disinfecting agent prior to moving them to the buffer area/IV preparation room.

Trash and Infectious Waste Disposal

Staff disposes of trash and infectious waste in accordance with the organization's infection control policies and procedures.	___	___	___
Trash and infectious waste do not create a nuisance or a breeding place for insects, rodents, and vermin or otherwise permit the transmission of disease.	___	___	___
Disposal containers are close to the area of use.	___	___	___
Infectious waste is placed in specially marked containers (e.g., red bags) and disposed of separately from routine trash.	___	___	___

> ***Note:*** Check the organization's policies on disposal of trash and infectious waste.

Attire and Personal Hygiene

Personnel wear appropriate attire in nonsterile areas and are attentive to personal cleanliness and hygienic practices.	___	___	___
Attire worn in the sterile compounding area is clean and minimizes the potential for shedding and contamination (e.g., a clean gown or laboratory coat).	___	___	___
Attire worn in the sterile compounding area meets the organization's policy and state regulations.	___	___	___

Yes NA No

Note: USP <797> has specific requirements. (*See* Chapter 18.)

Personnel remove jewelry, fingernail polish, and makeup (i.e., cosmetics) when compounding sterile preparations. ___ ___ ___

Fingernail length complies with the organization's policies and procedures. ___ ___ ___

The use of artificial fingernails complies with the organization's policies and procedures. ___ ___ ___

Note: Organizations often prohibit the wearing of artificial fingernails by individuals who compound sterile preparations and who have contact with patients.

Personnel wear a face mask when compounding sterile preparations. ___ ___ ___

Appropriate, powder-free protective gloves are worn when compounding sterile preparations. ___ ___ ___

Gloves are changed when penetrated or torn and are disposed of properly. ___ ___ ___

Personnel with upper respiratory tract infections, skin rashes, open lesions, and communicable diseases do not prepare sterile preparations. ___ ___ ___

Employee Health

Pharmacy staff participates in the organization's annual influenza vaccination program. (EP.1 for IC.4.15.) ___ ___ ___

Note: The organization must offer immunization against influenza to staff and licensed independent practitioners. (IC.4.15.) The organization must provide access to influenza vaccination on site. (EP 2 for IC.4.15.)

Note: The organization must annually evaluate vaccination rates and reasons for nonparticipation in the immunization program. The organization must implement "enhancements to the program to increase participation. (EP 4 and EP 5 for IC.4.15.)

Education about the following is provided to pharmacy staff:

- "Flu vaccination ___ ___ ___
- Nonvaccine control measures (such as the use of appropriate precautions) ___ ___ ___
- The diagnosis, transmission, and potential impact of influenza" (EP 3 for IC.4.15) ___ ___ ___

Staff participates in the organization's employee health program as required (e.g., tuberculin skin testing and chest x-rays). ___ ___ ___

Note: Most organizations provide an employee health program. This program often includes pre-employment physical examinations, blood tests, chest x-rays, and tuberculin skin tests (and annual follow-ups as required) as a condition of employment to ensure that employees are free from communicable diseases.

Note: The employee health program may restrict the activities of employees and

	Yes	NA	No
visitors. For example, persons with communicable diseases may be prohibited from contact with patients.			

Note: All staff must participate in the organization's employee health program and comply with the organization's employee health policies and procedures. Furthermore, they must be examined, treated, and immunized as required by the organization.

Hand Washing (Routine)

	Yes	NA	No
Hand washing may be the single most important procedure for preventing health–care–associated (nosocomial) infections. The organization's infection control policies and procedures must address hand washing and require staff to comply with CDC or World Health Organization (WHO) hand-hygiene guidelines.[2,4]	___	___	___
Routine hand washing is performed at the beginning of the shift, after visiting the restroom, before and after eating, and when the hands are obviously soiled. (The areas under the fingernails must be kept clean.)	___	___	___
Personnel who have contact with infected or potentially infected patients, body fluids, and contaminated or potentially contaminated objects wash their hands promptly after such contact.	___	___	___
Staff uses a hand washing technique and cleaning agent that are approved by the organization.	___	___	___
Staff uses alcohol-based hand rubs as permitted by CDC hand-hygiene guidelines, organization policy, and manufacturers' recommendations.[2]	___	___	___

Note: The following routine hand washing technique is typical of most organization-approved techniques:

- Use liquid soap and cool or lukewarm (not hot) water. (Cool or lukewarm water removes less oil from the skin and is less drying.)
- Rub all surfaces of lathered hands together vigorously for at least 15 seconds.
- Rinse hands thoroughly under a stream of water.
- Dry the hands with a disposable (e.g., paper) towel or air dryer.
- Use a towel to turn off the water.

Hand Washing (Sterile Preparation Compounding)

	Yes	NA	No
Personnel wash their hands thoroughly prior to compounding sterile preparations.	___	___	___
Personnel who leave the sterile preparations compounding area rewash their hands prior to resuming compounding.	___	___	___

Note: Staff must use a hand washing technique and cleaning agent that are approved by the organization. The following technique for washing hands prior to

	Yes	NA	No

compounding sterile preparations is typical of most organization-approved techniques:

- Moisten hands with water and apply a heavy lather of a cleaning agent approved by the organization. The lather must extend to the wrists and forearms (i.e., up to the elbow).
- Wash hands under running water for at least one minute. Use a rotary motion with friction.
- Be particularly attentive to the nail beds and space under the nails and between the fingers. Nails should be no longer than ¼ inch.
- Rinse hands thoroughly under running water. Hold hands so that the direction of water flow is from the fingertips to the wrists.
- Dry the hands with a disposable, nonshedding towel or air dryer.
- Use a towel to turn off the water.

Standard (or Universal) Precautions

Staff observes standard precautions to reduce the risk of transmission of infection.[5] ____ ____ ____

> ***Note:*** Standard (formerly known as universal) precautions apply to all patients receiving care in hospitals, regardless of their diagnosis or presumed infection status. Standard precautions apply to 1) blood; 2) all body fluids, secretions, and excretions except sweat, regardless of whether or not they contain visible blood; 3) nonintact skin; and 4) mucous membranes. Standard precautions are designed to reduce the risk of transmission of microorganisms from both recognized and unrecognized sources of infection in hospitals.

> ***Note:*** OSHA rules and regulations (Title 29 C.F.R. §1910.1030) require employers to implement plans to dispose of blood and contaminated waste, provide warnings on such waste, and keep records that account for the disposal of the waste. Employers must ensure that health care workers take special precautions to reduce the risk of contracting and transmitting AIDS, hepatitis B, and other diseases from exposure to blood and other body fluids.

> ***Note:*** Standard precautions must be included in the employer's Exposure Control Plan. Health care organizations must regularly educate employees about their Exposure Control Plan and standard precautions. Organizations must offer medical attention, evaluation, testing, and treatment in accordance with their Exposure Control Plan.

Isolation

Staff understands the organization's isolation policies and procedures. ____ ____ ____

Only medications needed for the patient's immediate use are taken into an isolation room. ____ ____ ____

	Yes	NA	No
Gowning, masking, and gloving are done as specified in the organization's isolation policies.	___	___	___
All items taken into an isolation room are placed in a designated receptacle after use.	___	___	___
Hands are washed as specified in the organization's isolation policies after leaving the isolation room.	___	___	___

Sterile Preparation Compounding Area

	Yes	NA	No
Areas for compounding sterile preparations minimize opportunities for particulate and microbial contamination of the preparations.	___	___	___

> ***Note:*** Areas for compounding sterile preparations must meet the requirements of USP <797> and/or state regulations. (*See* Chapter 18.)

> ***Note:*** A laminar airflow hood (sometimes called a laminar airflow workbench) is the accepted standard of practice for compounding sterile preparations. The Joint Commission requires pharmacies that compound sterile preparations to compound them in a laminar airflow hood.

> ***Note:*** Staff must be aware that a laminar airflow hood does not provide a sterile area. It simply provides a clean area that is suitable for compounding parenteral and sterile preparations that will not be used immediately.

> ***Note:*** Organizations may use an alternative technology to a laminar airflow hood if it achieves the same or better level of environmental air quality. An example is a compounding aseptic isolator.

Laminar Air-Flow Hood Cleaning

	Yes	NA	No
Hood surfaces are cleaned at the beginning of each shift with a cleaning agent approved by the infection control committee.	___	___	___

> ***Note:*** Most organizations clean hood surfaces first with purified water to remove water-soluble residues and follow immediately by cleaning the surfaces with 70% isopropyl alcohol. Other cleaning agents may be used if approved by the organization.

	Yes	NA	No
All items (including syringes, vials, and other extraneous items) are removed from the hood before cleaning it.	___	___	___

> ***Note:*** Infection-control policies and procedures should include a schedule and technique (including cleaning agent) for cleaning laminar airflow hoods. Surfaces within the hood must be cleaned with an approved cleaning agent when spills occur. Clean the work surface, side panels, and other accessible surfaces, starting at the top and rear and working downward and toward the front. Be careful to avoid getting the cleaning agent on the high-efficiency particulate air (HEPA) filter. Document the cleaning. Surveyors frequently look at documentation of cleaning (e.g., a monthly hood cleaning log). (*See* Example 8-1.)

	Yes	NA	No

Laminar Air-Flow Hood Maintenance and Certification

	Yes	NA	No
Routine maintenance, such as cleaning or replacing prefilters, is performed regularly and according to manufacturers' specifications (e.g., monthly or quarterly).	___	___	___

Note: These activities must be documented.

	Yes	NA	No
HEPA filters are replaced or repaired when recommended by a qualified inspector.	___	___	___
Evaluations of airborne pathogens are performed as required (e.g., by USP <797> and/ or state regulations). (*See* Chapter 18.)	___	___	___
Checks and certification for operational efficiency are performed at least once every six months by a qualified inspector.	___	___	___

Note: Certification is usually documented by placing a sticker on the hood and keeping inspection records on file. Surveyors frequently check these stickers.

	Yes	NA	No
Hoods are checked and certified when they are moved to a new location.	___	___	___

Cleaning Floors in the Laminar Airflow Hood Area

	Yes	NA	No
Floors in the laminar airflow hood area are cleaned by mopping in accordance with USP <797> requirements.	___	___	___

Note: USP <797> contains requirements for mopping floors in buffer and clean areas. The housekeeping department must be familiar with these requirements.

Compounding Sterile Preparations

	Yes	NA	No
Parenteral and sterile preparations are compounded in a properly maintained laminar airflow hood or acceptable alternative system (e.g., a compounding aseptic isolator).	___	___	___

Note: Some organizations are concerned that preparing sterile medications outside of a laminar airflow hood (e.g., in the emergency room and other patient care areas) is failure to provide a uniform level of care. However, surveyors consider preparing medications with a short stability period or expiration date in patient care areas for immediate use to be acceptable if done in a clean, well-lighted, functionally separate area that is free from clutter, trash, and waste. There must be no intervening steps in the process. In this case, the issue is not where they are prepared but the competence of individuals who prepare them.

Note: Parenteral nutrition, chemotherapeutic, and other preparations that require specialized knowledge or equipment usually found only in the pharmacy must be compounded in the pharmacy by specially trained staff.

	Yes	NA	No

Laminar Air Flow Hood Techniques and Precautions

Proper techniques and precautions are observed when using laminar airflow hoods or an acceptable alternative system (e.g., a compounding aseptic isolator). ____ ____ ____

Note: The following precautions when using laminar airflow hoods are suggested:

- Ensure that laminar airflow hoods run continuously or for the period required by policy (e.g., 30 minutes) prior to compounding sterile preparations. The manufacturers' recommendations must be followed.
- Assemble and organize all necessary materials in or near the hood before beginning work, and keep unnecessary items (e.g., labels, worksheets, notepads, and pencils) out of the hood.
- Work at least 15 centimeters (6 inches) within the hood.
- Keep a clear path between the HEPA filter and sterile objects (i.e., avoid blocking airflow with vials and equipment).
- Do not allow objects (especially sharp or pointed objects) or liquids to contact the HEPA filter.
- Avoid excessive talking and do not cough or sneeze into the hood.

Aseptic Technique

Proper aseptic technique is used in preparing sterile preparations. ____ ____ ____

Note: Touch is the primary source of contamination. Thus, strict adherence to aseptic technique that prevents contamination is more important than the use of a laminar airflow hood. Individuals with open lesions or communicable diseases must not prepare sterile preparations.

Note: The following aspects of aseptic technique are emphasized:

- Prepare the drugs in a clean area away from heavy traffic areas. Compounding in the pharmacy must be in a laminar airflow hood or acceptable alternative (e.g., a compounding aseptic isolator).
- Wash hands before handling drugs and as needed during the procedure.
- Work with moderate speed to minimize errors.
- Inspect containers for cracks, holes, leaks, and evidence of contamination before and after preparation.
- Remove outer metal lids or protective covers but do not remove rubber closures or diaphragms.
- Do not touch sterile areas of containers or allow nonsterile objects to come in contact with sterile areas.
- Clean diaphragms, injection ports, ampul necks, and vial tops with 70% isopropyl alcohol and allow to dry for at least 30 seconds.

Yes NA No

Note: Some organizations require the exteriors of all containers to be sprayed or swabbed with isopropyl alcohol before placing them in the hood.

- Cover ampul necks with a sterile pad and break ampuls by snapping away from the body (for safety purposes).
- Ensure that seals on syringe and needle packages are intact. Do not use items whose sterility is questionable.
- Ensure that touch contamination does not occur when attaching needles to syringes and when mixing drugs and diluents.
- Dispose of used syringes, needles, and other waste in accordance with the organization's policies and procedures.

Beyond-Use Dates for Compounded Sterile Preparations

All compounded sterile preparations are labeled with beyond-use dates. ____ ____ ____

Beyond-use dates for compounded sterile preparations do not exceed the periods specified in USP <797>. (*See* Chapter 18.) ____ ____ ____

Inspection of Compounded Sterile Preparations

Compounded sterile preparations are quarantined and inspected by a pharmacist prior to release from the pharmacy. ____ ____ ____

Note: The inspection must include checking for defective containers, cloudiness, turbidity, leaks, precipitates, particulate matter, evidence of contamination, and evidence of incompatibility. Labels must be checked for completeness and accuracy. When possible, the individual who performs the inspection should not be the individual who compounded the preparation. Defective and doubtful preparations must be destroyed.

Note: The individual who checks the final preparation must verify that the preparation has passed a final examination and is suitable for administration (i.e., compounded accurately and free from incompatibilities and particulate matter). An individual's written signature or initials on the label is a common means of indicating that the preparation has been checked.

Storage of Compounded Sterile Preparations

Compounded sterile preparations are properly stored. ____ ____ ____

Note: Compounded sterile preparations should be administered as soon after preparation as possible. Storage time limits and storage conditions must maximize stability, minimize microbial growth, and be consistent with the requirements of USP <797>. (*See* Chapter 18.)

Yes NA No

Note: Protection from light may be necessary if the preparation is light-sensitive. Check manufacturer and other literature carefully for stability data and storage guidelines.

Automated Compounding Devices

Automated compounding devices are cleaned regularly and checked to verify accurate delivery. ___ ___ ___

Note: Personnel must be knowledgeable about the safe and proper operation of these devices. USP <797> provides information relating to the use of these devices. In addition, personnel should consult the manufacturer's information for specific instructions. (*See* Chapter 18.)

Needles and Syringes

A sterile needle and syringe is used for each medication withdrawn. ___ ___ ___

Syringes are used on one patient only and then disposed of properly. ___ ___ ___

Note: Organizations must be especially attentive to syringes used in anesthetizing areas and other areas where special procedures are performed.

Containers for disposal of used needles and other sharp objects are available, used properly, and not overfilled. ___ ___ ___

Other infection control devices and supplies are available to staff. ___ ___ ___

Single-Use Containers

Single-use containers are not reused. ___ ___ ___

Note: Single use containers should be used whenever feasible. The organization's infection control policies should prohibit the reuse of single-use containers.

Single-use containers are discarded immediately after use in accordance with the organization's policies. ___ ___ ___

Multiple-Dose Containers

Multiple-dose containers are signed or initialed when first used (if required by the organization's policies). ___ ___ ___

Multiple-dose containers are labeled with the date first entered (if required by the organization's policies). ___ ___ ___

Multiple-dose containers are not used beyond the time specified by the organization's policies. ___ ___ ___

Yes **NA** **No**

Note: The length of time a multiple-dose container may be used safely after the initial entry is a controversial topic. The issues relate to adherence to aseptic technique, effectiveness of the preservative, potential for patient-to-patient contamination, storage conditions (e.g., room temperature versus refrigeration) after entry, and stability of the contents. Although Joint Commission standards do not address this issue, the Joint Commission expects organization infection control policies to address it. The Joint Commission accepts any reasonable policy that meets regulatory requirements and surveyors determine if organizations comply with their policy.

Note: A few organizations require dating containers when first entered and discarding them after a short time period (e.g., end of the shift or 24 hours). Other organizations specify a longer time period. The time period should not exceed 28 days unless a longer time period is specifically referenced in the package insert for the product.[6] Whatever the policy, the period must not conflict with the manufacturer's recommendations nor extend beyond the manufacturer's expiration date.

Note: Other practices include the following:

- Limiting the number of times a container may be entered with a needle
- Prohibiting the use of a container on more than one individual
- Requiring containers to be refrigerated after initial use (providing that stability and effectiveness of the preservative is not adversely affected at refrigerator temperatures)

Bulk packages (e.g., vials) of electrolytes and other products are used in the pharmacy for no more than four hours after the initial entry into the container unless the manufacturers' product information provides for another time period. Any unused portions are discarded. ___ ___ ___

Note: This requirement is stated in the package insert of many bulk packages of electrolytes and other products intended for dilution in intravenous infusions (i.e., not for direct infusion).

CHAPTER 9

Safety, Security, and Storage Checklist

The Joint Commission™ in its management of the environment of care (EC) standards requires organizations to provide an environment that minimizes hazardous conditions; prevents accidents; reduces the risk of injury; and provides for the safety and security of patients, visitors, and staff. (EC.1.10 through EC.9.30.) The Joint Commission's medication management (MM) standards require organizations to ensure that "medications are properly and safely stored." (*See* MM.2.20 in Chapter 4.)

Coordination of Safety Management Activities—The Joint Commission requires organizations to identify one or more individuals to coordinate safety management activities. Many organizations designate a safety officer and appoint a safety committee. A pharmacist is often a member of the safety committee.

Building Construction and Safety Codes—Buildings must comply with federal, state, and local safety codes, which specify the construction requirements and the types of materials permitted. Safety codes may differ because of the types of patients in the area (e.g., codes for long-term care areas are more stringent than codes for ambulatory care areas). Also, some equivalencies (i.e., equivalent ways to meet the intent of the codes) are permitted. The pharmacy should check with the safety officer or safety committee to ascertain the organization's safety and security policies and procedures, applicable codes, and permitted equivalencies.

Inspections—The director of pharmacy should ensure that the pharmacy and medication areas are inspected regularly (e.g., monthly or quarterly) for safety, security, and storage violations. This checklist and the medication area inspection form may be used as a guide. (*See* Examples 4-14 and 4-15)

Organization of the Checklist

This chapter presents safety, security, and storage precautions for health care personnel in a checklist format. They are consistent with current Joint Commission standards relating to these topics.

> ***Note:*** Although this checklist does not address safety, security, and storage completely, it should be sufficient to ensure compliance with requirements pertaining to pharmacy. Health care organizations should check for new and updated requirements on the Joint Commission's Internet Web site. (*See* Appendix A.)

The notes are compliance expectations and suggestions that are based on the authors' personal experiences, reports from surveyed organizations, and surveyors' statements. Some notes reflect legal requirements, previous Joint Commission standards, or commonly accepted standards of practice. Others note variations in interpretation of the standards.

Using the Checklist

To assess compliance, use the checklist and proceed systematically. Mark the item "Yes" if you are currently compliant and will continue to be compliant. Mark the item "No" if you are currently not compliant (even if you are sure you will be compliant later). If you are not sure of your answer, leave a blank response. A few items may be not applicable ("NA"). Answer honestly, use a pencil (so you can change your answers), and make notes on the pages (e.g., reasons for noncompliance). Concentrate your efforts on resolving all "No" and blank responses.

Checklist	Yes	NA	No

Environmental Tours

The pharmacy "conducts environmental tours' at least every six months "to identify environmental deficiencies, hazards, and unsafe practices." (EP 1 and EP 2 for EC.1.20.)	___	___	___

Note: EP 3 for EC.1.20 states that environmental tours are conducted "at least annually in areas where individuals are not served."

Identifying and Reporting Accidents, Injuries, and Hazardous Conditions

Pharmacy personnel identify and report accidents, injuries, conditions, and practices that pose a safety hazard to patients, visitors, and staff.	___	___	___

Note: Safety-related incidents are usually reported to the safety committee or safety officer. The organization's safety plan should contain specific information on how to make these reports.

SECURITY

The organization identifies and manages its security risks. (EC.2.10.)	___	___	___

Note: The organization should communicate its security risks to the pharmacy.

Staff Security

Pharmacy personnel are clearly identified (e.g., by visible name badges or other means of identification).	___	___	___
Unauthorized and unidentified individuals are not allowed in the pharmacy or medication preparation and storage areas.	___	___	___

Area Security

The pharmacy door is locked.	___	___	___

Note: Although not specifically required by the standards, surveyors insist that the pharmacy door be locked (even if not required by law). Surveyors often issue a citation if the pharmacy door is unlocked or a Dutch door is locked but the inside locking mechanism can be accessed from the outside. Surveyors determine if security is adequate to keep unauthorized personnel from entering the pharmacy.

	Yes	NA	No
Keys are controlled and knowledge of access codes is limited.	___	___	___
Pharmacy windows are locked.	___	___	___
Other security measures are provided as necessary (e.g., alarms, bulletproof glass, peepholes, video cameras, and security guards).	___	___	___

Note: Many organizations do not post directions to the pharmacy or identify the pharmacy with a sign.

	Yes	NA	No
Prescription pads are in locked storage or stored so only unauthorized personnel have access to them.	___	___	___
Security alarms and equipment, if used, are tested regularly.	___	___	___
Personnel understand the actions to be taken if there is a security incident (e.g., robbery or hostile situation). (EP 7 for EC.2.10.)	___	___	___

Medication Security

	Yes	NA	No
Medications are secured in accordance with legal requirements and the organization's written policies. (*See* EP 3 for MM.2.20 in Chapter 4.)	___	___	___

Mechanical Transport Devices

	Yes	NA	No
All mechanical transport devices (e.g., dumbwaiters and pneumatic tubes) are secure and deliver medications to secure areas.	___	___	___

Detecting Loss or Theft of Medications

	Yes	NA	No
There is a process for detecting loss or theft of medications kept in floor stock and automated medication dispensing and storage devices.	___	___	___

Note: This process often includes establishing stock levels and making periodic comparisons of quantity of floor stocks with medication administration and dispensing records.

Note: Surveyors often look for lists of the kind and quantity of medications kept in each area, along with evidence that these medications are monitored regularly to detect tampering and theft.

Anesthesia Medications

	Yes	NA	No
Anesthesia medications are stored securely and access to them is limited.	___	___	___

Note: Special attention should be given to paralytics, inhalation gasses, and other medications considered dangerous.

	Yes	NA	No
Anesthesia syringes are labeled appropriately.	____	____	____

Note: Empty syringes should not have a preattached label. Syringes containing medications are for immediate use and are destroyed after each case or, at a minimum, by the end of the workday.

Controlled Substances

See EP 4 for MM.2.20 in Chapter 4.

	Yes	NA	No
Controlled substances are stored securely to prevent diversion and according to legal requirements and the organization's policies.	____	____	____

EMERGENCY MANAGEMENT

	Yes	NA	No
The organization has an emergency management plan.	____	____	____

Note: Organizations must have an emergency management plan that addresses internal and external disasters and other emergencies in the organization and the community. (EC.4.10.) Emergency management plans must address the types of emergencies that the organization might reasonably expect to encounter (e.g., catastrophic accidents, fires, explosions, hurricanes, tornadoes, and earthquakes).

Note: Acts of terrorism (e.g., biological or chemical) may also create conditions in which an organization will implement its emergency management program.

Note: Some organizations (e.g., drug abuse and behavioral health facilities) do not need to be prepared to treat victims of accidents, natural disasters, or acts of terrorism.

Note: Organizations must test their emergency management plan at least semiannually, either in an actual emergency or a drill. (EC.4.20.) At a minimum, the pharmacy can expect to participate in emergency drills about twice a year. However, fire drills will be conducted at least quarterly. (EP 1 for EC.5.30.)

	Yes	NA	No
The organization's written emergency management plan is available to pharmacy staff.	____	____	____
The pharmacy's written plan for preparing for and reacting to severe weather situations (e.g., hurricanes, floods, earthquakes and tornadoes) is available to pharmacy staff.	____	____	____

Note: Some severe weather situations (e.g., hurricanes) may be predictable and provide an opportunity to prepare for them. Other situations may be unpredictable and occur suddenly (e.g., earthquakes, tornadoes, and floods). A severe weather plan should address both situations, be proactive, anticipate the worst scenario, and prepare staff to expect the unexpected.

	Yes	NA	No
Note: The pharmacy's severe weather plan should address providing emergency telephone service, dealing with prolonged loss of electric power (including the use of battery backups), ensuring adequate supplies of routine medications when deliveries are delayed, obtaining additional stocks of emergency medications, and moving the pharmacy to another location.			
Note: The pharmacy's plan should also address using manual systems when computers and automated systems are inoperative, operating with reduced and tired staff, providing sleeping and eating accommodations for staff (and their families and pets if needed), and dealing with personal issues (e.g., sick or injured family members).			
The pharmacy's written plan for preparing for and reacting to other emergencies (e.g., fires, catastrophic accidents, and acts of terrorism) is available to pharmacy staff.	___	___	___
Note: This plan will include most of the topics addressed in the pharmacy's severe weather plan.			
Pharmacy personnel are oriented, educated, and trained in emergency management (including assistance in moving and evacuating patients).	___	___	___
Pharmacy personnel understand how to notify other staff members if there is an emergency.	___	___	___
Pharmacy personnel are familiar with their duties in case of an emergency.	___	___	___
Pharmacy personnel participate in emergency drills.	___	___	___

Emergency Codes

	Yes	NA	No
Pharmacy personnel know the organization's emergency codes.	___	___	___
Note: Organizations often have emergency codes for internal and external disasters, security, chemical and hazardous materials spills, cardiac/respiratory arrest, bomb threat, infant or child abduction, and severe weather.			

Emergency Power

	Yes	NA	No
Pharmacy equipment that is designated to be connected to the emergency power system is connected to the system. (EC.7.20.)	___	___	___
Note: Organizations may designate some pharmacy equipment to be connected to the emergency power system. Many organizations connect medication refrigerators, pharmacy computers, automated medication storage and distribution devices, and laminar airflow hoods to the system. Emergency lighting is often supplied to the pharmacy and medication preparation areas.			

	Yes	NA	No

SPACE AND WORK ENVIRONMENT

	Yes	NA	No
Sufficient space and equipment are provided for storing, preparing (compounding, packaging, and labeling), and dispensing medications (including, if appropriate, parenteral products and radiopharmaceuticals).	____	____	____

> ***Note:*** The standards do not specify minimum requirements for pharmacy space, equipment, and supplies. However, the Joint Commission requires health care organization pharmacies to meet state board of pharmacy requirements. Because state requirements are sometimes nonexistent or vague, surveyors seldom check for compliance. Some surveyors look at state board of pharmacy inspection reports to determine if the pharmacy has failed to meet space, equipment, and supply requirements.

	Yes	NA	No
Medication preparation areas are well-lighted.	____	____	____
Medication preparation areas are located where personnel are not interrupted. (Traffic in the pharmacy and other medication preparation areas should be minimized.)	____	____	____
Work surfaces are uncluttered and free of equipment, supplies, records, and labels unrelated to the preparation of medications.	____	____	____
Facilities are available for cleaning and hand washing.	____	____	____

Shelving

	Yes	NA	No
Shelves are sealed to the floor or have sufficient space underneath to permit cleaning and the removal of materials that might present a fire or infection control hazard.	____	____	____

> ***Note:*** Organizations that are located in earthquake prone areas may be required to meet more stringent regulations (e.g., provide each shelf with a lip so that bottles will not slide off and screw shelving to a wall so that it will not topple).

Store Rooms

	Yes	NA	No
Store rooms near the pharmacy and medication areas (e.g., linen rooms, utility rooms, closets, and attics) contain no safety policy violations.	____	____	____

Cleanliness and Orderliness

	Yes	NA	No
The pharmacy and medication areas are clean, neat, and well-organized.	____	____	____
Only authorized medications and supplies are present.	____	____	____
There are no medications and supplies stored in unauthorized places (e.g., closets, cabinets, drawers, and under sinks).	____	____	____
Discontinued medications and medications dispensed to patients who have been discharged are returned to the pharmacy.	____	____	____
Mortars, pestles, graduated cylinders, pill crushers, pill splitters, and other medication preparation devices are cleaned after use.	____	____	____

	Yes	NA	No

Pharmacy Equipment

Pharmacy equipment is inspected and/or tested periodically for operational effectiveness and to assure safety for patients, visitors, and staff.	___	___	___
Cleaning and preventive maintenance of equipment is performed if required and as scheduled.	___	___	___
Operation and maintenance instructions are kept with individual pieces of equipment or in a designated, readily accessible place.	___	___	___
Exit devices on walk-in refrigerators and freezers work properly.	___	___	___
There are no sharp projections or moving parts on equipment that pose a risk to patients, visitors, and staff.	___	___	___
Insulation or other protection is provided to prevent contact with hot and cold water pipes, water heaters, refrigerator compressors, condensing units, and heat-producing equipment.	___	___	___
Defective equipment is marked and stored so that it cannot be used.	___	___	___

Patient Care Equipment

Patient care equipment functions properly and safely.	___	___	___

> ***Note:*** More stringent electrical safety codes apply to patient care equipment. Patient care equipment is usually identified as equipment used in diagnosing, treating, and monitoring patients (e.g., infusion control devices, mechanical ventilators, and electrocardiograph monitors). However, some organizations broadly interpret patient care equipment to include laminar airflow hoods, prescription balances, and equipment used in repackaging and reconstituting medications.

> ***Note:*** Many organizations maintain lists of all patient-care equipment and require an initial inspection prior to use as well as periodic (often semiannual or annual) safety and performance testing thereafter. In addition, some equipment may require preventive maintenance.

Records are kept for the period specified by law.	___	___	___

> ***Note:*** Testing and preventive maintenance records are often kept by the safety officer or in the biomedical engineering department.

Biological Safety Cabinets and Containment Isolators

See Chapter 17.

Hazardous medications are prepared in a Class II Type B2 or Class III biological safety cabinet (BSC) or a containment isolator designed for asepsis and containment of hazardous materials to minimize the exposure of workers to the medications.	___	___	___

	Yes	NA	No
Note: Cytotoxic and other hazardous medications must not be prepared in a clean air work station (e.g., a horizontal laminar airflow hood designed for preparing sterile products). A clean air workstation protects products but not the environment and personnel. Cytotoxic and hazardous materials must be prepared in a vertical airflow BSC or a compounding aseptic containment isolator (CACI).			
Exhaust from the BSC or CACI is HEPA-filtered (if applicable) and vented to the outside environment away from air intake locations.	___	___	___
The BSC or CACI is located in an area separate from the laminar airflow hoods used to compound nonhazardous sterile preparations.	___	___	___

Mechanical Transport Systems

Dumbwaiters and pneumatic tubes used to deliver medications pose no harm to patients, visitors, and staff.	___	___	___
There are provisions for delivery of medications if mechanical systems become unsafe or fail.	___	___	___

Note: The pharmacy should have a policy that limits the types of medications that will be transported through a mechanical system. For example, antineoplastic agents and controlled substances must not be delivered by a mechanical transport system.

ELECTRICAL SAFETY

Electrical Equipment Safety Checks

Electrical equipment has been tested for safety.	___	___	___

Note: A safety plan must identify types of equipment that may pose an electrical hazard. At a minimum, the plan must include high-risk equipment. Faulty electrical systems are a leading cause of fire and injuries in organizations. Some organizations consider all electrical equipment an electrical hazard and apply this requirement to electric typewriters, computers, etc.

Note: In developing the safety plan, the environment of use, maintenance, safety features, and the type of service the equipment provides must all be considered.

Note: Equipment identified by the policy must be inspected prior to initial use and at defined intervals thereafter. Only qualified persons should inspect, repair, or alter electrical equipment and electrical power distribution systems. The organization's inspectors may require periodic access to pharmacy equipment to perform inspections. Inspectors often "tag" equipment that meets the inspection requirements.

	Yes	NA	No

Extension Cords and Adapters

Extension cords and adapters meet safety requirements, are authorized by the organization, and are not overloaded. ____ ____ ____

Note: Most organizations have policies on the use of extension cords and adapters. Some organizations prohibit their use completely. Others permit extension cords and adapters that are approved by the safety committee.

Extension cords and adapters are checked regularly as part of the organization's hazard surveillance program. ____ ____ ____

Electrical Panels

Electrical panels are properly labeled and free from lint and grease. ____ ____ ____

Personal Electrical Equipment

Personal electrical equipment is used in accordance with the organization's safety plans or policies. ____ ____ ____

Note: The organization's safety plans or policies must address the use of personal electrical equipment. For the pharmacy, this often applies to coffee makers, radios, and similar equipment. Some organizations authorize the use of this equipment by policy, but others require an inspection of each item prior to authorizing its use.

HAZARDOUS MATERIALS AND WASTES

Hazard Materials and Waste Plan

A written plan for preventing and dealing with exposures to hazardous materials and waste is available to all individuals who handle them. ____ ____ ____

Note: Organizations must have a plan for safe management of hazardous materials and wastes, such as toxic materials, chemicals, chemotherapeutic materials, radioactive materials, infectious and regulated medical wastes, and sharp items (e.g., needles, razor blades, and broken ampuls). (EC.3.10.) The plan must cover the safe management of hazardous materials and wastes from receipt or generation at the organization through the final disposition at the organization or other site.

Note: Persons who handle hazardous materials and wastes must be informed of the risks and properly oriented, educated, and trained.

Note: The Joint Commission does not provide explicit guidelines for handling hazardous materials and waste. However, surveyors look for compliance with the Occupational Safety and Health Administration (OSHA) Hazard Communication Standard and National Institute for Occupational Safety and Health (NIOSH) rec-

	Yes	NA	No
ommendations. (*See* Chapters 16 and 17.) Compliance with this section should be sufficient to demonstrate compliance.			

Note: Pharmacy personnel must know the location of the hazard communication plan.

Hazardous Materials Storage and Handling Areas

The pharmacy has identified all areas where hazardous materials are stored or handled. ___ ___ ___

Identification of Hazardous Materials

Hazardous materials are identified so that personnel are not unknowingly and unnecessarily exposed or harmed. ___ ___ ___

Note: Hazardous materials can be identified by posting lists of the materials and/or by affixing special warning labels to the materials, storage bins, and shelves.

A list of hazardous materials stored or used routinely in the pharmacy and other areas is readily available to personnel who work in those areas. ___ ___ ___

Note: Pharmacy personnel must know the location of the list. Many organizations post the lists in the appropriate areas. Pharmacy personnel must also know the location of the organization's master list of hazardous materials. The master list is often in the emergency department or office of the safety officer.

Material Safety Data Sheets (MSDSs)

Material Safety Data Sheets (MSDSs) for all hazardous materials on the list are readily available to personnel in the pharmacy and other areas where hazardous materials are stored or handled. ___ ___ ___

Note: Pharmacy personnel must know the location of MSDSs. MSDSs may be made available electronically. There should be a paper backup up for electronic MSDSs. (*See* Chapter 16.)

Personal Protective Apparel

Personal protective apparel (e.g., gowns, gloves, eyewear, and face protection) and equipment is readily available to personnel who handle and prepare hazardous materials. ___ ___ ___

Note: Pharmacy personnel must know the location of personal protective apparel and equipment.

	Yes	NA	No
Eyewash Fountains			
An eyewash fountain is readily available to personnel in the pharmacy and other areas where chemicals, cytotoxic medications, and medications that pose a similar risk to the eyes are stored or handled.	___	___	___
Note: Bottles of eye flush solutions are not adequate. The eyewash fountain must operate with a continuous flow (e.g., from a faucet or fountain).			
Spill Kits			
Clearly labeled spill kits are readily available to personnel in the pharmacy and other areas where hazardous materials are stored or handled.	___	___	___
Note: Pharmacy personnel must know the location of spill kits.			
Disposal of Hazardous Materials and Waste			
Pharmacy personnel collect and dispose of needles, sharps, and other hazardous materials and waste in accordance with the organization's plan.	___	___	___
Hazardous materials and waste are placed in specially marked containers (e.g., yellow chemotherapy waste containers) and disposed of separately from routine trash.	___	___	___
Appropriate containers for the disposal of hazardous materials and waste, contaminated apparel, and contaminated work equipment (e.g., vials, ampuls, syringes, and needles) are close to the area of use and readily available to personnel.	___	___	___
Note: Some states have stringent disposal regulations. Check state regulations and the organization's plan for specific disposal requirements.			
Reporting Hazardous Materials Spills and Exposures			
Pharmacy personnel report hazardous materials spills and exposures.	___	___	___
Note: OSHA requires organizations to keep records of personnel who are exposed to hazardous materials. The organization should have a mechanism for meeting this requirement.			
FIRE SAFETY			
The organization has a plan for managing its fire safety risks. (EC.5.10.)	___	___	___
Note: Fires in health care facilities can be more dangerous than fires in other types of facilities because patients are often not able to provide for their own safety. The organization must have a fire plan that minimizes the risk of fires and maximizes detecting and extinguishing of fires.			

	Yes	NA	No
Combustible Materials			
Combustible materials (i.e., cardboard, paper, and other materials capable of burning) are not stored near sources of ignition (e.g., heat, sparks, and flames).	___	___	___
Flammable Substances			
Flammable substances (i.e., easily set on fire) are not stored with combustible materials (i.e., cardboard, paper, and other materials capable of burning). (Check with the safety officer or safety department.)	___	___	___
Flammable substances are stored in a room, vault, cabinet, or container specially designed for such storage, or away from sources of ignition (e.g., heat, sparks, and flames).	___	___	___

> ***Note:*** Most surveyors allow small quantities of flammable substances (e.g., a one- or two-day working supply) in the pharmacy. Fans, lights, alarms, and other electrical equipment in the vicinity of flammable substances must be spark and explosion proof. (Check with the safety officer or safety department.)

> ***Note:*** There is seldom a reason to keep acetone in the pharmacy. Individual acetone wipes can replace liquid acetone. If the pharmacy needs liquid acetone, it can often be obtained from the laboratory (which usually has special containers or facilities for acetone storage).

> ***Note:*** Flexible collodion contains about 67% ether. It is extremely flammable and should be stored only in a cabinet designed for the storage of flammable substances.

Ether

	Yes	NA	No
Ether is not stored in the organization.	___	___	___

> ***Note:*** Ether is extremely flammable, and upon exposure to oxygen it may form peroxides and become highly explosive. If ether is found, the pharmacy should contact appropriate personnel (as specified in the organization's safety plan), a local fire department, or the Environmental Protection Agency (EPA). The EPA may require disposal by a licensed hazardous waste disposal contractor.

Refrigeration of Flammable Liquids and Gases

	Yes	NA	No
Flammable liquids and gases are not stored in a refrigerator (unless it is a specially constructed, explosion-proof refrigerator).	___	___	___
Refrigerators are labeled as safe or unsafe for the storage of flammable liquids and gases.	___	___	___

	Yes	NA	No
Disposal of Flammable Liquids			
Flammable liquids are disposed of properly (i.e., not poured into the sewage system, poured or placed in the trash, or incinerated).	___	___	___

Note: Flammable liquids must be disposed of properly. If disposal of flammable liquids is required, the pharmacy should contact appropriate personnel (as specified in the organization's safety plan), a local fire department, or the Environmental Protection Agency (EPA). The EPA may require disposal by a licensed hazardous waste disposal contractor.

Oxygen and Other Flammable Gases

	Yes	NA	No
Tanks of oxygen and other flammable gases are stored in an appropriate location (which usually means storage outside the building or in special rooms). (Check with the safety officer.)	___	___	___
Oxygen and other flammable gases are not stored with combustible materials.	___	___	___

Note: More stringent electrical safety codes apply to anesthetizing areas (i.e., areas where inhalation anesthetic gases are administered).

Aerosol Containers

	Yes	NA	No
Aerosol containers (including medication inhalers) are not punctured or stored or used near a fire or open flame.	___	___	___
Aerosol containers are not incinerated.	___	___	___

Alcohol

	Yes	NA	No
Bulk containers of alcohol are stored upright (not on their sides) in a location suitable for storage of flammable substances (e.g., a flammables storage vault).	___	___	___
Only an approved hand-operated pump (not a power-driven pump) is used for withdrawal of alcohol from bulk containers.	___	___	___
Alcohol (including bottles of rubbing alcohol) is not stored with combustible materials.	___	___	___
Alcohol-based hand rubs are stored according to the manufacturers' recommendations.	___	___	___

Smoking

	Yes	NA	No
There is no evidence of smoking in areas where smoking is prohibited. (EC.1.30.)	___	___	___

Note: Although health care organizations are "smoke free" facilities, the organization may make exceptions for specific patients (e.g., a terminally ill patient). However, fire safety precautions for these patients must be observed (e.g., smoking is allowed only in designated, properly ventilated smoking areas). The types of patients excepted and fire safety precautions must be in writing.

	Yes	NA	No
Pharmacy personnel know the locations of smoking areas outside the building.	___	___	___

Space Heaters

The use of portable space heaters is in accordance with the organization's policies.	___	___	___

Note: Organizations must control the use of portable space heating devices. Some organizations permit portable space heaters in nonsleeping areas for staff and employees. Others prohibit the use of both fuel-burning and portable electric space heaters completely.

Trash Containers

Trash containers are made of noncombustible materials approved by the organization.	___	___	___

Note: Cardboard boxes and other combustible containers must not be used for trash containers.

Fire Walls

There are no holes in smoke and fire walls, ceilings, and floors (including around pipes, wires, and cables).	___	___	___

Note: Openings for pipes, wires, and cables must be sealed to prevent passage of smoke and fire. Do not cut holes in walls unless approved by the organization.

Floor and Window Coverings

Floor coverings (e.g., carpet) and window coverings (e.g., draperies) comply with fire safety codes.	___	___	___

Note: The pharmacy should ensure there is safety committee and infection control committee approval prior to replacing or installing floor and window coverings in pharmacy areas. The types of floor coverings used must promote cleanliness, must not present unusual problems for the handicapped, and must have flame-spread and smoke-development ratings appropriate to the area's use (e.g., patient room or exit corridor).

Fire Alarms

Fire alarms are unobstructed, visible, accessible, and tested regularly.	___	___	___

Note: Shelving, equipment, and cartons must not be placed where they will obstruct fire alarms.

	Yes	NA	No
Pharmacy personnel know the location of the nearest fire alarm.			
Pharmacy personnel know how to use a fire alarm.			
Pharmacy personnel know how to report a fire.			

Fire Responsibilities

	Yes	NA	No
Pharmacy personnel know how to respond to a fire alarm.			

> ***Note:*** The acronym RACE (Rescue, Alarm, Control/Contain, and Extinguish/Evacuate) is often used to describe an individual's duties in case of a fire. The exact meaning of the acronym varies from organization to organization.

Fire Extinguishers

	Yes	NA	No
Fire extinguishers are unobstructed, visible, accessible, and kept in their designated places.			

> ***Note:*** Shelving, equipment, and cartons must not be placed where they will obstruct fire extinguishers.

> ***Note:*** There must be a sufficient number of fire extinguishers, appropriate for the type of fire likely to occur in the area, for the contents of the area. Fire extinguishers must be readily available (e.g., no more than 75 feet away) and must not be removed from their designated location except during a drill or actual fire.

	Yes	NA	No
Tags on fire extinguishers reflect up-to-date maintenance (usually monthly).			
Fire extinguishers are appropriate for the type of fire likely to occur in the area.			
Pharmacy personnel know the location of the nearest fire extinguisher.			
Pharmacy personnel know how to use fire extinguishers.			

> ***Note:*** The acronym PASS is often used to describe how to use a fire extinguisher (**P**ull the pin, **A**im the nozzle, **S**queeze the handle, and **S**weep from side to side at the base of the fire).

Fire Detectors

	Yes	NA	No
Fire, heat, and smoke detectors, where required, are unobstructed and tested regularly (e.g., semiannually).			

Fire Sprinklers

	Yes	NA	No
Fire sprinkler heads have at least an 18-inch clearance in all directions (to avoid obstruction of the sprinklers).			

	Yes	NA	No
Note: There must be at least 18 inches from items on top of the shelves to the ceiling. A 36-inch clearance is recommended.			

Shutoff Valves and Switches

	Yes	NA	No
Pharmacy personnel can identify the location of shutoff valves and switches for oxygen, water, natural gas, electricity, and other utilities.	___	___	___

Exit Signs

	Yes	NA	No
Exit signs are illuminated (if applicable) and are not combustible (e.g., made of paper).	___	___	___
A "This is Not an Exit" (or a similar sign) is posted on courtyard doors and other doors that might be confused with exits.	___	___	___

Evacuation Routes

	Yes	NA	No
Pharmacy personnel know the evacuation route from the pharmacy or work area and the evacuation procedures to follow.	___	___	___
Pharmacy personnel know they must not use an elevator in case of a fire.	___	___	___
Evacuation routes are posted.	___	___	___
Exit and evacuation route doors are neither locked nor blocked.	___	___	___
Evacuation routes and corridors are free from obstructions (i.e., boxes, carts, clutter, and other traffic obstacles).	___	___	___
Storage of medications and supplies does not interfere with evacuation routes and access by fire-fighting and other emergency equipment.	___	___	___

Doors

	Yes	NA	No
Fire resistance ratings of doors meet current codes. (Check with the safety officer or safety committee.)	___	___	___
Note: There are specific construction requirements for doors, door frames, and latches (including type of material, thickness, and windows or peepholes). Check with the safety officer before altering or removing doors.			
Fire resistance ratings of Dutch doors meet current codes. (Check with the safety officer.)	___	___	___
Undercuts of doors (i.e., the area between the bottom of the door and the floor) do not exceed current codes. (Check with the safety officer.)	___	___	___
The gap between fire doors does not exceed current codes. (Check with the safety officer.)	___	___	___
Self-closing fire doors are not blocked from closing.	___	___	___

	Yes	NA	No
Doors that must be kept closed are closed.	___	___	___
Door stops are prohibited by the organization and are not available.	___	___	___
Latches on doors meet current codes. (Check with the safety officer.)	___	___	___

Stairwells

Stairwell doors are closed and equipped with positive latches (i.e., the doors do not open when pressure is applied to the doors).	___	___	___
Nothing is stored in stairwells.	___	___	___

STORAGE

Medications are stored in accordance with current standards (e.g., United States Pharmacopeia/National Formulary) so that their integrity, stability, and effectiveness are maintained.	___	___	___

External and Internal Agents

Agents for external use (e.g., antiseptics and disinfectants) and agents for internal use (e.g., injectable medications and oral formulations) are stored separately.	___	___	___

> ***Note:*** Joint Commission standards do not explicitly require separation of external and internal medications. Ideally, however, medications for external use and those intended for internal use should be stored separately and external use products should be clearly labeled as such (e.g., For External Use Only).

> ***Note:*** In practice, most creams and ointments are not likely to be mistaken for internal medications, and there is little risk if they are stored with internal medications. Most surveyors permit the storage of creams, ointments, and similar topical medications (e.g., eye and ear preparations) with internal medications if the risk of an administration error is minimal. However, opened rectal, vaginal, and topical medications that might contaminate internal medications should be isolated from other medications.

Acids and Caustic Substances

Bulk containers of concentrated acids and caustic substances are stored on lower shelves near floor level (to minimize the risk of breakage by falling from shelves).	___	___	___

> ***Note:*** These containers must be stored in an upright position. They must not be stored on their side.

	Yes	NA	No
Large or Heavy Containers			
Large or heavy containers are stored on lower shelves.	___	___	___
Storage of Unusable Medications			
There are no expired, recalled, deteriorated, broken, contaminated, unlabeled, or mislabeled medications.	___	___	___
Medications that cannot be returned for credit are stored properly while awaiting disposition.	___	___	___
Respiratory Care and Irrigation Solutions			
Vials and ampuls of respiratory care medications and medications used to prepare irrigation solutions are separate from injectable medications (to minimize the possibility of accidental injection).	___	___	___
Poisons and Lethal Concentrations of Medications			
Poisons and lethal concentrations of medications (e.g., concentrated potassium chloride) are clearly designated as such and stored securely.	___	___	___
Note: Concentrated electrolytes (potassium chloride, potassium phosphate, sodium chloride greater than 0.9%, and others defined by the organization) must be stored in the pharmacy.			
Similar Names and Packaging			
Medications with similar names and packaging are stored to minimize confusion.	___	___	___
Note: Some surveyors suggest separate trays in the refrigerator for different insulins, antibiotics, and other similarly packaged medications. (*See* Chapter 20.)			
Special Storage Conditions			
Medications requiring special storage conditions are stored properly (e.g., protected from light or at proper temperature).	___	___	___
Storage Temperatures			
Medications are stored at the appropriate temperatures.	___	___	___

	Yes	NA	No

Work Area Temperatures and Ventilation

Temperature levels and ventilation in the work area ensure the integrity of medications and the comfort of personnel. ___ ___ ___

If required, medications are protected from freezing, moisture, light (amber and opaque containers and light-resistant coverings should be available) and excessive heat (above 104°F). ___ ___ ___

Warmer Temperatures

Medications (e.g., intravenous solutions, irrigating solutions, contrast media, and mannitol) stored in warmers are stored at appropriate temperatures. ___ ___ ___

Refrigeration of Medications with Food

Food or other nonmedication items are stored in separate refrigerators and freezers from medications, or stored in a separate compartment from refrigerated medications. ___ ___ ___

> ***Note:*** Joint Commission standards do not prohibit the storage of food and other nonmedication items in the same refrigerator as medications. Nevertheless, surveyors often issue a citation if they find food, reagents, and laboratory specimens in medication storage refrigerators.

> ***Note:*** If medications are stored in a refrigerator that contains food and other items (especially items that could contaminate medications or be administered in error), the medications must be segregated (e.g., in a separate compartment or container). If necessary, access to the compartment should be limited (e.g., locked) while permitting access to food and other items in the refrigerator.

Refrigeration of Flammable Liquids

A notice "NOT FOR THE STORAGE OF FLAMMABLE LIQUIDS" is on refrigerators that are not specially constructed and vented for the storage of flammable liquids. ___ ___ ___

Thermometers

Thermometers are accurate and reliable. ___ ___ ___

> ***Note:*** An accurate and functional thermometer should be kept in refrigerators, freezers, warmers, and areas subject to temperature extremes (e.g., indoor bulk storage areas and outside receiving areas). Mechanical dial-type thermometers may not give an accurate temperature measurement when damaged, and damage to mechanical thermometers is difficult to detect. Digital and liquid-filled thermometers are more reliable than mechanical dial-type thermometers. Damage to a liquid-filled thermometer is usually apparent.

	Yes	NA	No
Note: Some surveyors suggest comparing pharmacy thermometers with a known standard thermometer (e.g., a reference thermometer in the laboratory) periodically. If the pharmacy must refrigerate high-cost medications or medications with narrow temperature requirements (e.g., Factor VIII), consider refrigerators that sound an alarm when temperatures are outside the required range.			

Refrigerators

Medications requiring refrigeration are stored in a refrigerator that maintains the appropriate range. (*See* Examples 4-5 and 4-6.)	___	___	___

Refrigerator Temperature Checks

Refrigerators have thermometers that work properly.	___	___	___
Refrigerators located in areas that are not open every day (e.g., a weekend) have a thermometer that can record temperature fluctuations.	___	___	___
Note: Staff must check the thermometer to ensure that the temperature did not exceed the limits. Some surveyors suggest alarms and other mechanisms that will indicate if refrigerators failed or that temperatures exceeded the limits.			
Refrigerator temperatures are in the acceptable range.	___	___	___
Note: Refrigerator temperatures should be checked regularly. Daily refrigerator temperature checks in the pharmacy and patient care areas are reasonable and should be sufficient.			
All medications requiring refrigeration are stored in a refrigerator with a temperature that maintains the acceptable range.	___	___	___
Refrigerator temperature logs are maintained unless a central monitoring system (e.g., automated system with an alarm) is in place and the system is observed constantly.	___	___	___
Note: Although the standards do not require temperature logs, most surveyors indicate that daily logs or equivalents are needed. (*See* Examples 4-5 and 4-6.)			
Actions are documented if refrigerator temperatures are out of range.	___	___	___
Note: Actions include notifying the pharmacy to check the integrity of the medications and, if necessary, moving the medications to a refrigerator that functions properly.			
Refrigerators are clean and free of excessive frost.	___	___	___

Freezers

Medications that must be frozen are stored in a freezer that maintains the appropriate range. (*See* Examples 4-5 and 4-7.)	___	___	___

	Yes	NA	No
Note: Some medications require freezing at lower temperatures; always consult the manufacturers' product literature or specific United States Pharmacopeia/National Formulary monographs. For example, commercially available dinoprostone vaginal suppositories should be stored at temperatures not exceeding 4°F. A special freezer may be needed, as some refrigerator freezers do not reach these temperatures.			

Freezer Temperature Checks

	Yes	NA	No
Freezers have thermometers that work properly.	___	___	___
Freezers located in areas that are not open every day (e.g., a weekend) have a thermometer that can record temperature fluctuations.	___	___	___
Note: Staff must check the thermometer to ensure that the temperature did not exceed the limits. Some surveyors suggest alarms and other mechanisms that will indicate if freezers failed or that temperatures exceeded the limits.			
Freezer temperatures are in the acceptable range.	___	___	___
Note: Freezer temperatures should be checked regularly. Daily checks in the pharmacy and patient care areas are reasonable and should be sufficient.			
Freezer temperature logs are maintained unless a central monitoring system (e.g., automated system with alarm that is under constant observation) is in place.	___	___	___
Note: Although temperature logs are not required by the standards, most surveyors indicate that daily logs or equivalents are needed. (*See* Examples 4-5 and 4-7.)			
Actions are documented if freezer temperatures are out of range.	___	___	___
Note: Actions include notifying the pharmacy to check the integrity of the medications and, if necessary, moving the medications to a freezer that functions properly.			
Freezers are clean and free of excessive frost.	___	___	___

CHAPTER 10

Policies and Procedures Checklist

The Joint Commission™ in its leadership (LD) standards, requires leaders to "develop and implement policies and procedures for care, treatment, and services." (LD.3.90.) These include policies and procedures that support safe medication management. The pharmacy must ensure that its medication management and other policies and procedures do not conflict with each other or with policies and procedures of other departments; with bylaws, rules, regulations, and policies of the medical staff; with bylaws of the governing body; and with local, state, and federal laws, rules and regulations.

Format for Policies and Procedures—The Joint Commission does not specify a format for policies and procedures and there is no standard or legally required format. Furthermore, surveyors seldom question formats. Although many organizations have adopted a uniform format, other organizations use a variety of formats within the same facility. Example 10-1 is a sample policy and procedure for processing requests for nonformulary medications. The example provides a format that should meet the requirements of most organizations.

Outdated Policies and Procedures—The Joint Commission does not address the disposition of outdated policies and procedures. However, good management practices call for their retention. For legal or other reasons, you may need to refer to them to establish the policies and procedures in effect on a specific date. A separate manual or file of outdated policies and procedures, including those with seemingly minor changes, is suggested.

Organization of the Checklist

This chapter presents suggested policies and procedures in a checklist format. Most of the items in the checklist reflect Joint Commission standards and elements of performance (EPs). The numbers of the standards and EPs follow many of the items. Although the relationships are not always explicit, the items are consistent with the standards and EPs. Some laws and regulations may require policies and procedures for topics not in this checklist.

> ***Note:*** Although this checklist cannot address all pharmacy policies and procedures, it should ensure compliance with most requirements pertaining to the pharmacy.

The notes are compliance expectations and suggestions that are based on the authors' personal experiences, reports from surveyed organizations, and surveyors' statements. Some notes reflect legal requirements, previous Joint Commission standards, or commonly accepted standards of practice. Others note variations in interpretation of the standards.

Using the Checklist

Pharmacy policies and procedures should clearly address the suggested topics and contain the suggested statements in the checklist. It might be helpful to paraphrase or quote standards and underline key words and statements.

To assess compliance, use the checklist and proceed systematically. Mark the item "Yes" if you are currently compliant and will continue to be compliant. Mark the item "No" if you are currently not compliant (even if you are sure you will be compliant later). If you are not sure of your answer, leave a blank response. A few items may be not applicable ("NA"). Answer honestly, use a pencil (so you can change your answers), and make notes on the pages (e.g., reasons for noncompliance) It might be helpful to place the page number, policy and procedure number, or other key to locating the policy or procedure beside the item. Concentrate your efforts on resolving all "No" and blank responses.

Checklist	Yes	NA	No

DEVELOPMENT, ORGANIZATION, REVIEW, REVISION, AND APPROVAL OF POLICIES AND PROCEDURES

Development of Policies and Procedures

The pharmacy collaborates with other departments and services in developing policies and procedures for patient care, treatment and services. (LD.3.90.) ___ ___ ___

> *Note:* Some organizations have moved from departmental policies and procedures to interdepartmental or organization-wide policies and procedures developed by interdisciplinary groups.

Physicians, nurses, pharmacists, and other appropriate staff have developed written policies and procedures that support effective and safe medication management. (MM.1.10 through MM.8.10.) ___ ___ ___

Organization of Policies and Procedures

Pharmacy policies and procedures are organized in a manner that assures their ready availability to pharmacy staff. ___ ___ ___

> *Note:* Many organizations use an electronic format to help ensure only current documents are accessible. There is no requirement for policies and procedures to be kept in a manual. However, a manual is recommended because it allows personnel to review policies and procedures easily and is readily available if they cannot be accessed in the computer.

Pharmacy Review and Revision of Policies and Procedures

The director of pharmacy has reviewed and, if necessary, revised all pharmacy policies and procedures within the last year to ensure consistency with the organization's current practices. ___ ___ ___

> *Note:* The Joint Commission does not specify a review frequency. Some state or federal entities and some health care organizations may require annual reviews. An annual frequency should ensure that policies and procedures are current and ready for unannounced surveys. Although all policies and procedures need not be reviewed and revised at the same time, each one should be reviewed and revised at least once during the year.

To document the pharmacy's review and revision, the director of pharmacy has done one or both (preferably both) of the following within the last year:

	Yes	NA	No
• Signed and dated each policy and procedure.	___	___	___
• Signed and dated a page that documents review and revision of all policies and procedures.	___	___	___

Note: The Joint Commission does not specify how to document the pharmacy's review and revision.

Medical Staff Approval of Policies and Procedures

	Yes	NA	No
The medical staff has approved all medication-related policies and procedures within the last year.	___	___	___

Note: The Joint Commission does not specify an approval frequency. Some state or federal regulations or expectations may specify annual approvals. An annual frequency should ensure that policies and procedures are current and ready for unannounced surveys. Although all policies and procedures need not be approved at the same time, each one should be approved at least once during the year.

To document the medical staff's review and approval, a medical staff representative (e.g., chair of the P&T committee, chief of the medical staff, or other authorized individual) has done one or both (preferably both) of the following within the last year:

	Yes	NA	No
• Signed and dated each policy and procedure.	___	___	___
• Signed and dated a page that documents approval of all policies and procedures.	___	___	___

Note: The Joint Commission does not specify how to document medical staff approval.

Infection Control and Safety Committee Approval of Policies and Procedures

	Yes	NA	No
The infection control committee has approved the pharmacy's infection control policies and procedures within the last year.	___	___	___
The safety committee has approved the pharmacy's safety policies and procedures within the last year.	___	___	___

Leadership Approval of Policies and Procedures

	Yes	NA	No
If required by the organization, the chief executive officer and/or other persons or committees have reviewed and approved (in writing) pharmacy and medication-related policies and procedures.	___	___	___

Yes NA No

SUGGESTED POLICIES AND PROCEDURES

Scope of Pharmacy Services

A policy describing the scope of patient care services provided by the pharmacy. ____ ____ ____

Note: The scope of services typically includes maintaining an adequate stock of medications; preparing, labeling, dispensing and distributing medications, chemicals, sterile products, and parenteral solutions; supervising all medication storage and preparation areas within the pharmacy and throughout the organization; orienting, educating, and training staff; and monitoring medication therapy. Other services typically include medication safety improvement, adverse event reduction, investigational medication studies, patient and family education, clinical pharmacokinetics services, home health care services, and drug information services.

Note: The scope of pharmacy services varies with the type and size of the organization and the acuity of care. For example, a large teaching hospital might have a fully staffed drug information center. Smaller hospitals, however, might have only basic reference materials available.

A policy stating the age groups and other populations that the pharmacy serves. ____ ____ ____

A policy stating goals for the pharmacy's patient care services. ____ ____ ____

Note: At a minimum, the goals should reflect the scope of the pharmacy's patient care services and how the pharmacy assesses and meets the needs of all age groups and other populations that the pharmacy serves.

Absence of Pharmacy Services

Policies and procedures for procuring, storing, controlling, and distributing medications from an outside source when the organization does not have a pharmacy. (LD.3.50.) ____ ____ ____

Obtaining Medications after the Pharmacy Is Closed

Policies and procedures for obtaining medications from after-hours supplies when the pharmacy is closed. (EP 1 for MM.4.50.) ____ ____ ____

A policy designating individuals who are permitted to remove medications from after-hours supplies when the pharmacy is closed. (EP 2 for MM.4.50.) ____ ____ ____

A policy requiring a licensed pharmacist, within a specified time period, to review all orders for medications obtained from after-hours supplies when the pharmacy is closed. (EP 1 and EP 4 for MM.4.10.) ____ ____ ____

Policies and procedures for obtaining medications when the pharmacy is closed and medications are not available from after-hours supplies. (EP 2 for MM.4.50.) ____ ____ ____

Policies and procedures for evaluating medications obtained from after-hours supplies, assessing why they were obtained, minimizing the need for nonpharmacists to

	Yes	NA	No
obtain them, and determining how to improve the process for obtaining them. (EP 3 and EP 4 for MM.4.50.)	___	___	___

Obtaining Medications from Other Organizations

Policies and procedures for obtaining medications from hospitals, community pharmacies, and other organizations in routine or emergency situations. (EP 7 for MM.2.10.)	___	___	___

Emergency Pharmacy Services

Policies and procedures for providing medications and pharmacy services in case of a disaster. (EP 7 for MM.2.10.)	___	___	___

Job Descriptions, Performance Evaluations, and Competence Assessment

Policies and procedures relating to job descriptions, performance evaluations, and competence assessments of pharmacy staff. (HR.3.10; HR.3.20.)	___	___	___

Orientation, Education, and Training

Policies and procedures relating to orienting, educating, and training pharmacy staff. (HR.2.10 and HR.2.30.)	___	___	___
Policies and procedures relating to the pharmacy's role in orienting, educating, and training other health care personnel. (HR.2.30.)	___	___	___

Education of Patients and Family

Policies and procedures relating to the roles of the pharmacy and pharmacists in developing and/or providing patient and family education. (EP 1 through EP 3 for PC.6.10; EP 1 through EP 5 for PC.6.30.)	___	___	___

Patient Information

A policy stating the minimum amount of patient information "to be available to those involved in medication management." (EP 1 for MM.1.10.)	___	___	___

> ***Note:*** Patient information must include at least the patient's age; sex; current medications; diagnosis, comorbidities, and currently-occurring conditions; relevant laboratory values; and past allergies and sensitivities. The patient's height, weight, pregnancy or lactation status and other elements defined by the organization must be available if appropriate. (EP 2 for MM.1.10.)

> ***Note:*** The organization must define who has access to the information (IM.2.10) and the information must be available when and where needed. (EP 3 for MM.1.10.)

	Yes	NA	No
Policies and procedures for maintaining the confidentiality of patient and medical staff information. (IM.2.10.)	___	___	___

Formulary

	Yes	NA	No
Policies and procedures for developing and maintaining the formulary. (EP 1 through EP 3 for MM.2.10.)	___	___	___

> ***Note:*** The policy should include the "criteria for determining what medications are available for dispensing or administration." (EP 1 for MM.2.10.) "At a minimum the criteria must include the indication for use, effectiveness, risks (including propensity for medication errors, abuse potential, and sentinel events), and costs." (EP 2 for MM.2.10.)

	Yes	NA	No
Policies and procedures for reviewing medications "at least annually based on emerging safety and efficacy information." (EP 5 for MM.2.10.)	___	___	___
A policy stating that only approved medications shall be stocked or stored. (EP 1 for MM.2.20.)	___	___	___
A policy stating the standardized medication concentrations available in the organization. (EP 10 for MM.2.20.)	___	___	___
Policies and procedures for using herbal products and other alternative medications. (EP 6 for MM.3.20.)	___	___	___
Policies and procedures for monitoring patients' responses to newly added medications before they are available for dispensing or administering. (EP 4 for MM.2.10.)	___	___	___
Policies and procedures for procuring medications that are not on the formulary. (EP 6 for MM.2.10.)	___	___	___

Medication Quality

	Yes	NA	No
A policy stating the quality specifications for all medications, chemicals, and biologicals relating to the practice of pharmacy. (EP 1 and EP 2 for MM.2.10.)	___	___	___
Policies and procedures for procuring all medications, chemicals, and biologicals relating to the practice of pharmacy. (EP 1 and EP 2 for MM.2.10.)	___	___	___

Medications Acquired by Practitioners from Sources Other Than the Organization

	Yes	NA	No
Policies and procedures that address the safety and use of medications acquired by a practitioner from sources other than the organization for use in patient care in the organization.	___	___	___
At a minimum, these policies and procedures address the following:			
• Whether such medications are allowed to be used.	___	___	___
• If allowed, a process to evaluate the integrity of the medications brought in by a practitioner prior to use in patient care.	___	___	___

	Yes	NA	No
Note: There must be evidence that these policies and procedures are implemented.			

Generic and Therapeutic Equivalents

Policies and procedures for dispensing generic and therapeutic equivalents, if permitted by the organization.	___	___	___

Recalled Medications

Policies and procedures for handling recalled medications. (EP 1 through EP 3 for MM.4.70.)	___	___	___

Defective Medications and Devices

A policy requiring defective medications and devices to be reported to the proper authorities (e.g., the Food and Drug Administration and Nuclear Regulatory Commission). (EP 7 for EC.6.10.)	___	___	___
Policies and procedures for reporting defective medications and devices to the proper authorities (e.g., the Food and Drug Administration and Nuclear Regulatory Commission). (EP 7 for EC.6.10.)	___	___	___

Unusable Medications

A policy stating that unusable medications (e.g., expired; defective; damaged; contaminated; recalled; or with worn, illegible, or missing labels) shall not be distributed or administered but be returned to the pharmacy for proper disposition. (EP 1 through EP 4 for MM.4.80.)	___	___	___
Policies and procedures for removing all unusable medications from stock and segregating them until their proper disposition. (EP 7 for MM.2.20.)	___	___	___
Policies and procedures for ensuring the proper disposition of unusable medications.	___	___	___

Emergency Medications

Policies and procedures for ensuring the integrity, ready availability, control, and security of emergency medications. (MM.2.30.)	___	___	___
Policies and procedures for ensuring the security of mobile or readily portable medication containers. (EP 6 for MM.2.30.).	___	___	___

Note: CMS Interpretive Guidelines state: if the container is mobile or readily portable, when not in use, it must be stored in a locked room, monitored location, or secured location that will ensure the security of the medications or biologicals.[1]

Note: When not in use, nursing medication carts, anesthesia carts, and other medication carts containing medications or biologicals must be locked or stored

	Yes	NA	No
in a locked storage room. However, due to the mobility of carts, when not in use, locked carts that contain medications or biologicals must be stored in a locked room or secure location.[1]			
Policies and procedures for controlling sealing devices for emergency medication containers. (EP 6 for MM.2.30.)	___	___	___
Policies and procedures for replacing emergency medications after use. (EP 7 for MM.2.30.)	___	___	___

Controlled Substances

Policies and procedures for distributing, administering, accounting, and securing controlled substances. (EP 6 for MM.2.20.)	___	___	___
Policies and procedures for storing and distributing controlled substances from automated medication storage and distribution devices. (EP 6 for MM.2.20.)	___	___	___
Policies and procedures for disposal of (wasting) unused portions of controlled substances. (EP 6 for MM.2.20.)	___	___	___
Policies and procedures for using controlled substances in controlled substances infusions and in patient-controlled analgesia devices. (EP 6 for MM.2.20.)	___	___	___
Policies and procedures for epidural administration of controlled substances. (EP 6 for MM.2.20.)	___	___	___
Policies and procedures for keeping controlled substances records (e.g., ordering from vendors, taking inventories, reporting theft and loss, receiving and adding medications to the inventory, distributing to floor stock, reconciling, and prepackaging). (EP 6 for MM.2.20.)	___	___	___

Investigational Medications

A policy requiring investigational medications to be used only after approval by the group authorized to grant approval (e.g., institutional review board or P&T committee). (EP 1 for MM.7.40.)	___	___	___
Policies and procedures for developing and approving protocols for the use of investigational medications. (EP 1 for MM.7.40.)	___	___	___
Policies and procedures for maintaining essential information on investigational medications in the pharmacy (or other designated area if there is no organized pharmacy service). (EP 1 for MM.7.40.)	___	___	___
A policy stating that investigational medications shall be prescribed only by those individuals authorized to do so. (EP 1 for MM.7.40.)	___	___	___
Policies and procedures for ensuring proper labeling, storage, distribution, and control of investigational medications. (EP 6 for MM.3.20 and EP 1 for MM.7.40.)	___	___	___
A policy stating that investigational medications shall be dispensed only pursuant to the prescription of an authorized investigator or prescriber. (EP 1 for MM.7.40.)	___	___	___

	Yes	NA	No
A policy specifying the labeling requirements for investigational medications. (EP 1, EP 3, and EP 4 for MM.4.30; EP 1 for MM.7.40.)	___	___	___

Note: Investigational medication labels must clearly indicate that the contents are for investigational use. The label of an investigational medication may not specifically identify the medication (i.e., in the case of a double-blind study). The identity must be obtainable if needed.

	Yes	NA	No
A policy requiring investigational medications to be administered only in accordance with approved policies and procedures or protocols. (EP 1 for MM.7.40.)	___	___	___
A policy designating individuals who are approved to administer investigational medications. (EP 1 for MM.7.40.)	___	___	___
A policy stating that investigational medications shall be administered only by those approved to do so, and only after they have demonstrated an understanding of the medication's action, possible adverse effects, and appropriate response. (EP 1 for MM.7.40.)	___	___	___
Policies and procedures for orienting, educating, and training nurses and others who administer investigational medications. (EP 1 for MM.7.40.)	___	___	___
Policies and procedures for ensuring that individuals who are approved to administer investigational medications understand their pharmacological action, possible adverse effects, and expected response. (EP 1 for MM.7.40.)	___	___	___
Policies and procedures for requesting and obtaining informed consent from the patient prior to administering investigational medications. (EP 2 and EP 4 for RI.2.180.)	___	___	___
A policy requiring the documentation of doses dispensed, administered, and destroyed. (EP 1 for MM.7.40; EP 1 for IM.6.20.)	___	___	___
Policies and procedures for returning and disposing of investigational medications. (EP 1 for MM.7.40.)	___	___	___
Policies and procedures for auditing investigational medication use to ensure that storage, dispensing, administration, and disposal meet federal and state regulations. (EP 1 for MM.7.40.)	___	___	___
Policies and procedures for ensuring appropriate care for patients admitted to the organization who are participating in investigational medication studies or clinical trials. (EP 3 for MM.7.40; RI.2.180.)	___	___	___

High-Risk or High-Alert Medications

	Yes	NA	No
Policies and procedures for controlling and ensuring the safe use of high-risk or high-alert medications (e.g., insulin, anticoagulants, opiates, and potassium chloride and other concentrated electrolytes). (EP 11 for MM.2.20; EP 1 and EP 2 for MM.7.10.)	___	___	___

Radiopharmaceuticals

	Yes	NA	No
Policies and procedures for procuring, storing, controlling, distributing, and administering radiopharmaceuticals whether managed by the pharmacy or by another department. (Joint Commission definition of medication.) (*See* Chapter 4.)	___	___	___

	Yes	NA	No
Contrast Media			
Policies and procedures for procuring, storing, controlling, distributing, administering, and monitoring contrast media whether managed by the pharmacy or by another department. (Joint Commission definition of medication.) (*See* Chapter 4.)	____	____	____
Blood Derivatives			
Policies and procedures for procuring, storing, controlling, distributing, administering, and monitoring blood derivatives (e.g., albumin and immune globulins) whether managed by the pharmacy or by another department. (Joint Commission definition of medication.) (*See* Chapter 4.)	____	____	____
Medication Samples			
Policies and procedures for storing and securing medication samples to prevent access by unauthorized individuals (e.g., staff, visitors, and patients). (MM.2.20.)	____	____	____
Policies and procedures for controlling and documenting the distribution and use of medication samples. (MM.2.20.)	____	____	____
Note: Control of medications must extend to medication samples throughout the organization (including the emergency department, ambulatory clinics, and physician's offices in or associated with the organization). The pharmacy must include medication samples, including those in clinics and off-site locations, in its process for responding to medication recalls and in its monthly inspection routine.			
Medical Sales Representatives			
Policies and procedures relating to the activities of medical sales representatives.	____	____	____
Note: Although Joint Commission standards do not explicitly restrict the activities of medical sales representatives, many organizations do so.			
Medication Storage			
Policies and procedures for storing medications in a manner that maintains their integrity, stability, and effectiveness. (EP 2 for MM.2.20.)	____	____	____
Policies and procedures for storing medications "between receipt of a medication by an individual health care provider and medication administration. At a minimum, the policy addresses the following:			
• Safe storage	____	____	____
• Safe handling	____	____	____
• Security	____	____	____

	Yes	NA	No
• Disposition of these medications (including return to the pharmacy medication storage area) at the end of the individual's shift." (EP 3 for MM.2.20.)	___	___	___
Policies and procedures for storing medications in accordance with laws, regulations, and the organization's requirements so that unauthorized persons cannot obtain access to them. (EP 5 for MM.2.20.)	___	___	___

Note: The Centers for Medicare and Medicaid Services (CMS) definition of "secured" requires (1) that all drugs and biologicals be kept in a secure area, and locked when appropriate (2) drugs listed in Schedules II, III, IV, and V of the Comprehensive Drug Abuse Prevention and Control Act of 1970 must be kept locked within a secure area (3) only authorized personnel may have access to locked areas.[1]

Policies and procedures describing the actions to be taken if the temperatures of medication refrigerators, freezers, and warmers are not within the normal range. (EP 2 for MM.2.20.)	___	___	___
Policies and procedures for segregating easy-to-confuse (e.g. look-alike or sound-alike) medications. (EP 8 for MM.2.20.)	___	___	___
A policy requiring concentrated electrolytes to be stored only in the pharmacy unless the Joint Commission has approved an alternative approach. (EP 11 for MM.2.20.)	___	___	___

Medication Area Inspections

Policies and procedures for the periodic (e.g., monthly) inspection of medication areas (e.g., patient care units and other areas where medications are dispensed, administered, or stored). (EP 15 for MM.2.20.)	___	___	___

Note: Inspections should be performed by the director of pharmacy or the director's qualified designee.

Medication Orders

Policies and procedures reflecting medical staff rules and regulations specifying who may write patient care orders. (EP 1 for IM.6.10.)	___	___	___
A policy stating the required elements of medication orders. (EP 1 for MM.3.20.)	___	___	___
Policies and procedures reflecting medical staff rules and regulations regarding verbal (e.g., telephone) orders for medications. (EP 7 for MM.3.20.)	___	___	___
A policy designating individuals authorized to accept verbal orders for medications. (EP 7 for MM.3.20.)	___	___	___
Policies and procedures reflecting medical staff rules and regulations regarding authentication of verbal orders for medications. (EP 4 for IM.6.10.)	___	___	___
A policy requiring a documented diagnosis, condition, or indication for use to be available in the patient's medical record (EP 1 for MM.3.10) and whether or when indications for use are required on an order. (EP 3 for MM.3.20.)	___	___	___

	Yes	NA	No
Policies and procedures specifying when generic or brand names are acceptable or required. (EP 2 for MM.3.20.)	___	___	___
Policies and procedures specifying the special precautions needed for ordering look-alike or sound-alike medications. (EP 4 for MM.3.20.)	___	___	___
A policy prohibiting the use of dangerous abbreviations and dosage expressions (e.g., U, IU, QD, QOD, MS, MSO_4, $MgSO_4$, a leading decimal point, and a trailing zero after a decimal point). (EP 2 for IM.3.10.)	___	___	___
Policies and procedures defining the use of dosage ranges (if allowed by the organization). (EP 6 for MM.3.20.)	___	___	___
A policy prohibiting the use of "blanket" or "resume" medication orders (e.g., "resume home medications" and "resume medications prior to surgery") and other vague medication orders. (EP 6 and EP 9 for MM.3.20.)	___	___	___
A policy requiring "as needed" (PRN) orders to be qualified (e. g., include the symptom or indication for use) so there is no question about the prescriber's intent. (EP 6 for MM.3.20.)	___	___	___
Policy and procedures for handling "hold" orders. (EP 6 for MM.3.20.)	___	___	___
Policies and procedures defining the parameters needed for "titrate" orders. (EP 6 for MM.3.20.)	___	___	___
Note: Parameters must include objective measurements (e.g., specific blood pressure reading, sedation level, or analgesia level) for measurement. (EP 6 for MM.3.20.)			
Policies and procedures defining the parameters needed for "taper" orders. (EP 6 for MM.3.20.)	___	___	___
Note: Parameters must include objective measurements (e.g., specific blood pressure reading, sedation level, or analgesia level) for measurement. (EP 6 for MM.3.20.)			
Policies and procedures for compounding special formulas in the pharmacy. (EP 6 for MM.3.20.)	___	___	___
Policies and procedures reflecting specifications for preparations compounded by outside pharmacies and leadership's approval for obtaining preparations from those pharmacies. (EP 6 for MM.3.20.)	___	___	___
Policies and procedures for ordering medication-related devices. (EP 6 for MM.3.20.)	___	___	___
A policy stating the organization's standard times for administering medications.	___	___	___
Policies and procedures for reviewing and approving preprinted orders. (EP 8 for MM.3.20.)	___	___	___
Policies and procedures for handling standing orders. (EP 6 for MM.3.20.)	___	___	___
A policy stating when weight-based dosing for pediatric patients is required. (EP 10 for MM.3.20.)	___	___	___
Policies and procedures stating the actions to be taken when medication orders are illegible, incomplete, or unclear. (EP 5 for MM.3.20.)	___	___	___

	Yes	NA	No

Automatic Stop Orders

	Yes	NA	No
Policies and procedures defining situations in which all or some medication orders for a patient must be canceled, and mechanisms for reinstating them. (EP 6 for MM.3.20.)	____	____	____

Medication Dispensing

	Yes	NA	No
Policies and procedures for preparing and dispensing medications consistent with applicable laws or regulations. (EP 2 for MM.4.40.)	____	____	____
Policies and procedures for dispensing medications safely and accurately. (EP 1 through EP 5 for MM.4.40.)	____	____	____
Policies and procedures for assuring that medications are dispensed in a timely manner to meet the needs of patients. (EP 3 for MM.4.40.)	____	____	____
Policies and procedures for assuring that the quantities of medications dispensed minimize diversion but are sufficient to meet the needs of patients. (EP 1 for MM.4.40.)	____	____	____

Preparation or Supervision by a Pharmacist

	Yes	NA	No
A policy requiring a licensed pharmacist to prepare and dispense all medications or monitor medication preparation and dispensing performed by nonpharmacists.	____	____	____
A policy requiring nonpharmacists to work under the direct supervision of a licensed pharmacist who is fully aware of all medication preparation and dispensing activities.	____	____	____
A policy defining the limitations on the duties and responsibilities of nonpharmacists.	____	____	____

Review of Orders

	Yes	NA	No
Policies and procedures for ensuring that all orders are reviewed prior to dispensing.	____	____	____

> ***Note:*** Reviews must include appropriateness of the medication, dose, frequency, and route of administration; therapeutic duplication; real or potential allergies or sensitivities; real or potential interactions between the prescription and other medications, food, and laboratory values; other contraindications; variation from organizational criteria for use; and other relevant medication-related issues or concerns. (EP 1 and EP 5 for MM.4.10.)

> ***Note:*** A licensed independent practitioner (LIP) is not required to be at a patient's bedside when medications are administered in the emergency department or the imaging department. Organizations are encouraged to develop policies that define the role of LIPs within the two departments. When medications are administered, policies must require the LIP to be available within the department to intervine immediately if there is an adverse medication event.

	Yes	NA	No
A requirement that, when not immediately available, a pharmacist reviews medication orders as soon as possible. (EP 1 and EP 4 for MM.4.10.)	____	____	____

	Yes	NA	No
Verification of Orders			
Policies and procedures for verifying prescriber's orders when questions arise. (EP 6 for MM.4.10.)	____	____	____
Unit-Dose or Ready-to-Administer Forms			
A policy requiring medications supplied to care areas or dispensed to be in the most ready-to-administer forms available. (EP 12 for MM.2.20; EP 3 for MM.2.30; EP 4 for MM.4.40.)	____	____	____
Policies and procedures relating to a unit-dose medication distribution system, if applicable.	____	____	____
Policies and procedures for assuring consistent use of the same dose packaging system and providing education when changes are made. (EP 5 for MM.4.40.)	____	____	____
Automated Medication Storage and Distribution Devices			
Policies and procedures for stocking and using automated medication storage and distribution devices.	____	____	____
Labeling of Medications			
Policies and procedures defining a standard method for appropriately and safely labeling medications that meet applicable laws and regulations and standards of practice. (EP 1 through EP 4 for MM.4.30.)	____	____	____
Ambulatory Care and Discharge Medications			
Policies and procedures for dispensing medications to emergency care, ambulatory care, and discharged patients. (EP 6 for MM.3.20.)	____	____	____
Note: Medications may be dispensed to emergency, ambulatory care, and discharged patients only on the order of an authorized prescriber.			
A policy stating that medications administered or dispensed to emergency, ambulatory care, and discharged patients shall be recorded in their medical records. (EP 1 for IM.6.20.)	____	____	____
Policies and procedures ensuring that medications dispensed to emergency, ambulatory care, and discharged patients are labeled for outpatient use. (EP 1 for MM.4.30.)	____	____	____
Sterile Products and Preparations			
Policies and procedures for the safe preparation of parenteral products (including those prepared outside the pharmacy).	____	____	____

	Yes	NA	No
Note: These should include aseptic technique, compounding procedures, and labeling requirements. (EP 1 through EP 6 for MM.4.20.)			
A policy specifying that sterile preparations must be compounded by the pharmacy when the pharmacy is open (except for emergencies or for medications with short stability). (EP 1 for MM.4.20.)	___	___	___
Policies and procedures for labeling intravenous admixtures. (EP 3 and EP 4 for MM.4.30.)	___	___	___
Policies and procedures for avoiding incompatibilities in sterile preparations (e.g., consulting compatibility references). (EP 4 and EP 5 for MM.4.20.)	___	___	___
Policies and procedures for processing orders for sterile products and preparations (e.g., profiling, labeling, and record keeping). (EP 1 and EP 4 through EP 6 for MM.4.10; EP 1 through EP 6 for MM.4.20; EP 1 through EP 4 for MM.4.30.)	___	___	___
Policies and procedures for establishing and assigning beyond-use dates to compounded sterile preparations. (EP 3 for MM.4.30.)	___	___	___

Parenteral Nutrition

Policies and procedures for preparing and dispensing parenteral nutrition products. (EP 1 through EP 6 for MM.4.20.)	___	___	___

Medication Administration

Policies and procedures for administering medications. (EP 2 through EP 8 for MM.5.10.)	___	___	___
A policy stating that medications shall be administered only on the order of an individual with clinical privileges and legal authorization to write such orders. (EP 1 for IM.6.10.)	___	___	___
A policy stating that medications shall be administered only by or under the supervision of individuals who are licensed, competent, and permitted by law or regulation to administer medications. (EP 1 for MM.5.10.)	___	___	___
A policy listing personnel, by title and category, who are permitted to administer medications. (EP 1 for MM.5.10.)	___	___	___
A policy requiring medications to be prepared properly for administration. (EP 2 through EP 4 for MM.5.10.)	___	___	___
A policy requiring medication orders to be verified before administering the medication. (EP 5 for MM.5.10.)	___	___	___
A policy requiring medications, to the extent possible, to be administered by the person who prepared the dose.	___	___	___
Note: Unit-dose or patient-specific medications prepared by the pharmacy are excluded from the requirement.			
A policy requiring a patient to be identified before administering the medication.	___	___	___
Policies and procedures for advising patients about clinically significant adverse events (e.g., adverse drug reactions) or other concerns. (EP 6 for MM.5.10.)	___	___	___

	Yes	NA	No
Policies and procedures for discussing any unresolved significant concerns with the prescriber and other appropriate staff. (EP 7 for MM.5.10.)	___	___	___
Policies and procedures for notifying the prescriber if there is an adverse event. (EP 8 for MM.5.10.)	___	___	___
A policy requiring each administered dose to be recorded properly in the patient's medical record. (EP 1 for IM.6.20.)	___	___	___

Self-Administered Medications

A policy stating that self-administration of medications is allowed only on the written order of the responsible practitioner and in accordance with the organization's policy. (MM.5.20.)	___	___	___
A policy requiring persons who administer medications who are not staff members to receive training and appropriate information and determined to be competent in medication administration. (EP 1 through EP 3 for MM.5.20.)	___	___	___

Patients' Personal Medications

Policies and procedures for handling and storing medications brought into the organization by patients. (EP 1 for MM.2.40.)	___	___	___
A policy prohibiting administration of a patient's personal medications without a written order from the responsible practitioner. (EP 1 for MM.2.40.)	___	___	___
A policy prohibiting administration of a patient's personal medications until the medications are properly identified by the attending physician, another responsible prescribing practitioner, or a pharmacist (preferably the organization's pharmacist). (EP 2 for NN.2.40.)	___	___	___

Note: The identification process must include a visual determination of the integrity of the medications. (EP 2 for MM.2.40.)

Note: The prescriber and the patient must be notified if use of the patient's personal medications is not permitted. (EP 3 for MM.2.40.)

Medication Errors

A policy reflecting the organization's definition of a medication error. (EP 6 for PI.2.20.)	___	___	___
Policies and procedures for identifying, reporting, and reviewing medication errors. (EP 1 and EP 2 for MM.6.20; EP 6 for PI.2.20.)	___	___	___
A policy requiring medication errors to be reported immediately in accordance with written procedures. (EP 2 for MM.6.20.)	___	___	___
A policy requiring the medication administered (or omitted) in error to be properly recorded in the patient's medical record. (EP 1 for IM.6.20.)	___	___	___

	Yes	NA	No
Adverse Drug Events (ADEs)			
A policy reflecting the organization's definition of a significant adverse drug event (ADE). (EP 5 for PI.2.20.)	___	___	___
Policies and procedures for identifying, reporting, and reviewing significant adverse events. (EP 1 and EP 2 for MM.6.20; EP 5 for PI.2.20.)	___	___	___
A policy requiring the event to be properly recorded in the patient's medical record. (EP 8 for IM.6.10.)	___	___	___
Policies and procedures for reporting significant events to the FDA. (EP 3 for MM.6.20.)	___	___	___
Monitoring Medication Therapy			
Policies and procedures for monitoring each patient for the effectiveness of medication use, adverse effects, and toxicity. (EP 1 through EP 3 for MM.6.10.)	___	___	___
Policies and procedures for contacting the prescriber when the pharmacy identifies the potential for an adverse event (e.g., an adverse reaction or a medication-food interaction). (EP 6 for MM.4.10.)	___	___	___
Policies and procedures for contacting prescribers to suggest modifications of orders. (EP 6 for MM.4.10.)	___	___	___
Evaluation of the Medication System			
Policies and procedures for evaluating the medication system to identify risk points, trends, and methods to improve safety. (EP 1 through EP 6 for MM.8.10.)	___	___	___
Policies and procedures for reviewing, considering, and acting on a Joint Commission *Sentinel Event Alert* relating to medication safety.	___	___	___
Infection Control			
Policies and procedures for infection surveillance, prevention, and control for the pharmacy. (EP 5 for IC.1.10.)	___	___	___
Policies and procedures relating to staff participation in the organization's employee health program. (IC.4.15.)	___	___	___
Policies and procedures relating to the shelf life of all sterile products, preparations, and items in storage. (EP 3 for IC.4.10.)	___	___	___
Policies and procedures relating to hand washing technique and personal hygiene requirements. (EP 2 for IC.4.10.) (*See* Checklist in Chapter 20 for NPSG 7A, Hand Hygiene Guideline.)	___	___	___
Policies and procedures relating to attire worn in nonsterile areas and sterile compounding areas.	___	___	___
Policies and procedures for using single-use and multiple-dose containers of sterile medications in the pharmacy and throughout the facility.	___	___	___

	Yes	NA	No
Policies and procedures for compounding sterile preparations (including aseptic technique). (EP 1 through EP 4 for MM.4.20.)	____	____	____
Policies and procedures for compounding of irrigation solutions.	____	____	____
Policies and procedures relating to standard or universal precautions to reduce the risk of contracting and transmitting AIDS, hepatitis B, and other diseases from exposure to blood and other body fluids.	____	____	____
Policies and procedures for assessing the sterile technique of personnel and the frequency of assessment. (*See* Chapter 18.)	____	____	____
Policies and procedures for media-fill testing. (*See* Chapter 18.)	____	____	____
Policies and procedures for storing sterile products, preparations, and items. (EP 3 for IC.4.10.)	____	____	____
Policies and procedures for controlling traffic in sterile preparation compounding areas.	____	____	____
Policies and procedures for ensuring the proper use of laminar airflow hoods or workbenches or alternative system (e.g., compounding aseptic isolators) to include cleaning, maintenance, and checking for operational efficiency. (EP 3 for IC.4.10; EP 5 for EC.6.10.)	____	____	____
Policies and procedures for microbiological monitoring (culturing) of laminar airflow hoods or workbenches (or alternative system) as well as clean/buffer areas. (*See* Chapter 18.)	____	____	____
Policies and procedures for routine cleaning of pharmacy facilities (e.g., cleaning responsibilities, procedures, schedules, and agents approved by the infection control committee).	____	____	____
Policies and procedures for testing (culturing) for microbial contamination of compounded sterile preparations.	____	____	____
Policies and procedures for reporting unsanitary conditions and practices.	____	____	____
Policies and procedures for containing and disposing of trash and infectious waste.	____	____	____

Safety

Policies and procedures relating to a hazard communication program for identifying, managing, packaging, transporting, cleaning up, and disposing of hazardous materials and wastes (e.g., needles, broken ampuls, cytotoxic medications, and radiopharmaceuticals). (EP 1 for EC.3.10.)	____	____	____
Policies and procedures for ensuring the safe storage of medications and supplies. (EP 3 for MM.2.20.)	____	____	____
Policies and procedures for ensuring the safe storage and handling of hazardous substances. (EP 1 for EC.3.10.)	____	____	____
Policies and procedures for ensuring the safe storage and handling of flammable liquids and gases. (EP 8 for EC.3.10.)	____	____	____
Policies and procedures relating to fire safety precautions (e.g., alarms, reporting processes, fire extinguishers, sprinklers, and evacuation routes). (EP 1 through EP 5 for EC.5.10.)	____	____	____

	Yes	NA	No
Policies and procedures relating to electrical safety precautions. (EP 7 for EC.7.10.)	____	____	____
Policies and procedures for ensuring adequate lighting (EP 5 for EC.8.10) and ventilation. (EP 7 for EC.8.10.)	____	____	____
Policies and procedures for handling of medical device recalls and hazard notices from governmental agencies and manufacturers. (EP 7 for EC.6.10.)	____	____	____
Policies and procedures for reporting accidents, injuries, and safety hazards. (EP 1 for EC.9.10.)	____	____	____
Policies and procedures relating to emergency preparedness (including disaster drills). (EC.4.20.)	____	____	____
Policies and procedures relating to latex allergies and sensitivities.	____	____	____
Policies and procedures for ensuring the safe and proper use of patient care equipment, if applicable (EP 9 for EC.1.10; EP 1 for EC.6.10) and intervals for inspection and maintenance. (EP 4 for EC.6.10.)	____	____	____
Policies and procedures for providing backup delivery service when mechanical transport systems (e.g., dumbwaiters and pneumatic tubes) fail.	____	____	____
Policies and procedures relating to the pharmacy safety plans and specific hazards (e.g., hazardous materials and Material Safety Data Sheets).	____	____	____

Security

Policies and procedures for ensuring secure storage of medications. (MM.2.20.)	____	____	____
Policies and procedures for ensuring secure access and egress from the pharmacy. (EP 6 for EC.2.10.)	____	____	____
Policies and procedures for ensuring the security of staff. (EP 1 for EC.2.10.)	____	____	____
Policies and procedures for controlling visitors and unauthorized personnel. (EP 1 for EC.2.10.)	____	____	____
Policies and procedures relating to actions to take if there is a security incident (e.g., robbery or hostile situation). (EP 7 for EC.2.10.)	____	____	____

CHAPTER 11

Frequently Requested Documents Checklist

The Joint Commission™ expects organizations to maintain adequate documentation to demonstrate continuous compliance with standards and legal requirements. Well-organized and well-maintained documentation fosters high quality patient care and enhances pharmacy management. This checklist should help pharmacies improve their documentation and ensure that most documents and records are readily available.

The notes are compliance expectations and suggestions that are based on the authors' personal experiences, reports from surveyed organizations, and surveyors' statements. Some notes reflect legal requirements, previous Joint Commission standards, or commonly accepted standards of practice. Others note variations in interpretation of the standards.

Organization of the Checklist

This chapter presents frequently requested documents in a checklist format. Many of the items in the checklist reflect Joint Commission standards and elements of performance (EPs). The numbers of the standards and EPs follow these items. Some laws and regulations may require documents that are not in this checklist. An asterisk (*) after an item means that the item is one of the most frequently requested documents.

> ***Note:*** Although the checklist cannot list all required documents, it should ensure compliance with most Joint Commission and legal requirements pertaining to the pharmacy. Unless otherwise requested, the most current 12 months of documentation should be adequate.

Using the Checklist

To assess compliance, use the checklist and proceed systematically. Mark the item "Yes" if you are currently compliant and are sure you will continue to be compliant. Mark the item "No" if you are currently not compliant (even if you are sure you will be compliant later). If you are not sure of your answer, leave a blank response. A few items may be not applicable ("NA"). Answer honestly, use a pencil (so you can change your answers), and make notes on the pages (e.g., reasons for noncompliance). It might be helpful to record the locations of the documents on the checklist (especially if they are kept outside the pharmacy). Concentrate your efforts on resolving all "No" and blank responses.

Checklist	Yes	NA	No

Licenses, Registrations, and Permits

Pharmacy license.*	___	___	___

Note: The pharmacy must be appropriately licensed. (EP 2 for HR.1.20.)

Note: Surveyors usually determine whether pharmacy licenses, registrations, and permits are current. Sometimes current licenses are not available (e.g., when the Board of Pharmacy is delayed in furnishing renewal certificates). Copies of renewal applications, letters from the board acknowledging current licensure, or documented evidence of checking the board's Internet Web site will satisfy surveyors.

Retail pharmacy license or dispensing permit, if required.	___	___	___
License and renewal evidence for each full-time pharmacist and evidence of current licensure for part-time pharmacists who practice primarily at another site.*	___	___	___

Note: Pharmacy staff must be appropriately licensed. (EP 2 for HR.1.20.)

Note: Surveyors usually determine whether all pharmacist licenses, registrations, and permits are current. Sometimes current licenses are not available (e.g., for newly licensed pharmacists or when the Board of Pharmacy is delayed in furnishing renewal certificates). Copies of renewal applications, dated letters from the board acknowledging current licensure, or documented evidence of checking the board's Internet Web site will satisfy surveyors.

Note: Surveyors determine whether pharmacists are currently licensed by the state in which the organization is located. Military pharmacists and pharmacists with the Veterans Administration and U.S. Public Health Service must be currently licensed, but licensure need not be in the state where they practice.

Licenses, registrations, and permits are displayed appropriately or filed in the pharmacy.	___	___	___
Evidence that pharmacists' licenses have been verified.*	___	___	___

Note: Joint Commission standards require organizations to verify that staff (including contract services employees) are currently licensed, certified, or registered. (EP 2 and EP 3 for HR.1.20.) The director of pharmacy must verify the licenses of pharmacists and other pharmacy personnel who must be licensed, certified, or registered. Verification should confirm that they can legally practice and that there is nothing in their records that adversely affects their capability to perform their duties.

	Yes	NA	No
Note: Pharmacy staff "for whom a license, certification, or registration is required by the organization and/or law and regulation," must have the currency of their licenses, certifications, or registrations verified by a primary source when hired. (EP 3 for HR.1.20.)			
Note: Pharmacy staff "for whom a license, certification, or registration is required by the organization and/or law and regulation," must have the renewal of their licenses, certifications, or registrations verified by a primary source upon expiration. (EP 3 for HR.1.20.) Some organizations require annual verification.			
Note: The primary source may delegate authority to verify licensure to an agency. An electronic or telephone verification is acceptable if it is documented. (Notes for EP 2 and EP 3 for HR.1.20.) (*See* HR.1.20 in the *Comprehensive Accreditation Manual for Hospitals [CAMH]* for a more on verification requirements.) Making a telephone inquiry to the state board of pharmacy or checking the board's Internet Web site are acceptable ways to verify current licensure, previous suspension or revocation, and pending challenges. (*See* Chapter 6.)			
Note: Verification of licensure, certification, or registration should be documented (e.g., in the individual's personnel record). (*See* Example 11-1.) Some pharmacies keep a master list of names, license numbers, expiration dates, and documentation (signed and dated by the director of pharmacy) indicating that renewal certificates have been checked and are current. Many pharmacies also track completion of continuing education (CE) requirements for employees whose licensure renewal requires it.			
A license, permit, or equivalent for each pharmacy student, technician, intern, extern, and others, if applicable.	___	___	___
Certification evidence (e.g., a certificate) for each certified pharmacy technician.	___	___	___
Federal Drug Enforcement Administration (DEA) controlled substances registration certificate.*	___	___	___
State controlled substances permit, if required.	___	___	___
Other required licenses and permits.	___	___	___
Note: If separate licensing for retail pharmacies, outpatient pharmacies, nuclear pharmacies, etc., is required, surveyors expect to see evidence of such licensure. If the pharmacy provides services to out-of-state patients (e.g., home health care) it might need a pharmacy license for each state in which it provides services. Some states require retail sales licenses. These documents should be current and displayed or filed as appropriate.			

Organization

	Yes	NA	No
An organization chart showing the pharmacy's relationship to the organization and to other departments and services.	___	___	___

	Yes	NA	No
Note: The organization will probably update the chart before its survey. The pharmacy should have the most recent chart.			
Pharmacy organization plan.	___	___	___
Note: The pharmacy's organization plan should delegate responsibility (e.g., for supervising, interviewing, hiring, orienting, teaching, counseling, and terminating). It should clearly indicate to whom the director of pharmacy reports, as well as the person who is responsible in the absence of the director.			
Note: Some plans list the routine reports required (e.g., staffing reports), the persons responsible for preparing them, and the persons to whom they are submitted.			
Pharmacy organization chart.	___	___	___
Note: The pharmacy's organization chart should be consistent with the pharmacy's organization plan and show the lines of authority within the pharmacy and between the pharmacy and the organization's administration. If the pharmacy has standing committees, include them in the plan and on the chart. The policies and procedures manual is a good place to keep the plan and chart.			

Pharmacy Services

	Yes	NA	No
Medication distribution system flowchart or description showing (at a minimum) how the pharmacy processes medication orders, dispenses medications, and distributes medications to patients and floor stocks. (*See* Table 5-1 in Chapter 5.)	___	___	___
Note: Some pharmacies include all of the components of the medication management system in their flowchart or description (i.e., selection and procurement, storage, ordering and transcribing, preparing and dispensing, administering, and monitoring). (*See* Chapter 4.) (*See* Table 5-1 in Chapter 5.)			

Contracted or Outsourced Pharmacy Services

	Yes	NA	No
Evidence that medical staff and leadership have approved the use of a contracted or outsourced pharmacy service.	___	___	___
Evidence that the medical staff and leadership are aware of the use of outside compounding pharmacies (including nuclear pharmacies).	___	___	___
A statement in the contract for pharmacy services that specifies that the provider will ensure that pharmacy services meet Joint Commission standards.*	___	___	___

Staffing

	Yes	NA	No
Description of pharmacy staffing (e.g., a current staffing schedule) that shows that the pharmacy has an adequate number and mix of staff to meet the care, treatment, and service needs of patients. (EP 1 for HR.1.10.)	___	___	___

	Yes	NA	No
Data used to determine that pharmacy staffing meets the care, treatment, and service needs of patients.	____	____	____

After-Hours and Emergency Pharmacy Services

Records of after-hours removal of medications from after-hours stocks and evidence that a pharmacist reviews the records.* (MM.4.50.)	____	____	____
Information relating to emergency pharmacy services (e.g., as pharmacists' telephone numbers or a procedure for contacting an on-call pharmacist).	____	____	____
Emergency telephone numbers for hospitals, community pharmacies, wholesale suppliers and other emergency sources of medications.	____	____	____
Telephone number of a poison control information center.	____	____	____

> ***Note:*** Many pharmacists affix the telephone number to the telephone. Some also indicate the locations of poison treatment information and medications and antidotes used to treat poisonings.

Policies and Procedures

Policies and procedures for managing the pharmacy. (*See* Chapter 10.)*	____	____	____
Policies and procedures for medication management. (*See* Chapter 10.)*	____	____	____

References

Up-to-date pharmacy references.	____	____	____

> ***Note:*** The pharmacy should be able to provide answers to most routine drug information questions. References should be readily available to all pharmacy personnel and to medical, nursing, and other professional staff, as appropriate. Staff should be familiar with the references and know which are the best sources of information for specific needs. Surveyors seldom cite the pharmacy for failure to have the most recent editions. However, references more than three years old are questionable, especially when new editions are available.

> ***Note:*** Computerized data-retrieval systems provide ready access to information that can be printed and edited to meet the pharmacy's needs. This information may be more up-to-date than printed materials. Manufacturers may be the best source of product-specific information. However, although manufacturers' information is free and readily available, it may be biased and incomplete.

Forms and Records

Examples of current forms and records.	____	____	____

	Yes	NA	No

Pharmacy and Therapeutics Activities

	Yes	NA	No
Committee minutes or other records of pharmacy and therapeutics activities for the last 12 months. (*See* Chapter 12.)	____	____	____

Formulary

	Yes	NA	No
Current formulary or list of medications accepted for use in the organization with dated evidence of approval.* (MM.2.10.)	____	____	____

> ***Note:*** At a minimum, the formulary must include medication names, strengths, and dosage forms. (EP 3 for MM.2.10.)

	Yes	NA	No
Evidence that the formulary was "reviewed at least annually based on emerging safety and efficacy information." (EP 5 for MM.2.10.)	____	____	____
Record of special pharmaceutical formulas used in the organization.	____	____	____

Medication Orders

	Yes	NA	No
List of standardized abbreviations, acronyms, symbols, and dose designations if required by laws or regulations or the organization's policy.	____	____	____

> ***Note:*** Although the Joint Commission does not require this list, many organizations have one.

	Yes	NA	No
List of prohibited abbreviations, acronyms, and symbols.* (EP 2 for IM.3.10.) (*See* Checklist in Chapter 20 for NPSG 2B.)	____	____	____
Metric/apothecaries' weight and measure conversion chart.	____	____	____
Signatures of practitioners *currently* authorized to prescribe medications.	____	____	____

> ***Note:*** This record must be readily available to pharmacy staff. Surveyors prefer the record to be kept in the pharmacy to ensure immediate access if there is a question about a prescriber's credentials. The record must be up-to-date and include only current prescribers. If former prescribers are in the record, their status must be clearly noted (e.g., by a notation on the record or by listing them separately from current prescribers). Surveyors sometimes ask to see the record of a newly added and/or a former member of the medical staff. (*Also see* Controlled Substances in this chapter.)

	Yes	NA	No
Copies of routine or standard orders for medications.*	____	____	____

Pharmacy Patient Profiles

	Yes	NA	No
Pharmacy patient profiles (manual or computerized) with patient information (e.g., age; sex; current medications; diagnoses, comorbidities, and currently occurring conditions; relevant laboratory values; and allergies and past sensitivities).* (EP 2 for MM.1.10.)	____	____	____

	Yes	NA	No
Note: Other pertinent information may be included (e.g., height and weight if needed to calculate body surface area). (*See* EP 2 for MM.1.10 in Chapter 4.)			

Medication Reconciliation

Records of medication reconciliation (e.g., medication reconciliation forms) across the continuum of care. (*See* Requirements 8A and 8B for NPSG 8 in Chapter 20.)	____	____	____

Medication Dispensing

Schedule for filling medication carts.	____	____	____
Override and reconciliation records for automated medication storage and distribution devices.	____	____	____

Medication Administration

List of standard medication administration times (e.g., 9 a.m. and 5 p.m. for medications administered twice a day).	____	____	____

Investigational Medications

Minutes or other records of the group that approves the use of investigational medications (e.g., Institutional Review Board or Pharmacy and Therapeutics Committee). (RI.2.180.)	____	____	____
Records of acquiring, dispensing, administering, and disposing of investigational medications.	____	____	____

Adverse Drug Events

Reports of actual and suspected adverse drug events (ADEs) (e.g., adverse drug reactions) if available to the pharmacy.* (MM.6.20.)	____	____	____
Summaries that document an intense review of ADEs.*	____	____	____
Copies of reports submitted to the Food and Drug Administration (FDA) and manufacturers.	____	____	____

Medication Errors

Reports of actual or suspected medication errors if available to the pharmacy. (MM.6.20.)	____	____	____
Evidence that documents an intense review of medication errors.*	____	____	____
Evidence of tracking and trending medication use processes (e.g., errors and variations of performance) to improve safety.	____	____	____

	Yes	NA	No
Evidence of performance of failure mode and effects analysis of pharmacy processes. (*See* Chapter 14.)	___	___	___

Sentinel Events

Completed sentinel event forms (including a root cause analysis), if any (e.g., for medication errors and ADEs). (*See* Sentinel Events in Chapter 14.)	___	___	___

Medication Problems or Defects

Copies of reports of medication problems or defects submitted to the FDA.	___	___	___

Medication Recalls

Medication recall notices with records of pharmacy action. (MM.4.70.)	___	___	___

Inspections

Inspection records for the pharmacy and all medication areas (including offsite clinics and physician offices owned by the organization) for each of the last 12 months.* (EP 15 for MM.2.20.)	___	___	___

> ***Note:*** The records should include evidence that action was taken to correct deficiencies.

State board of pharmacy, department of health, DEA, and other inspection reports and evidence that the deficiencies were corrected.	___	___	___

> ***Note:*** Surveyors may check for correction of deficiencies and may cite the pharmacy if deficiencies have not been corrected.

Performance Improvement

The organization's performance improvement (PI) plan. (*See* Chapter 14.)	___	___	___
A description of the pharmacy's role in the organization's PI program (e.g., a policy and procedure or plan).	___	___	___
Evidence that the pharmacy participates in the organization's PI activities (e.g., on PI teams).	___	___	___

> ***Note:*** Pharmacy participation need not be limited to medication use improvement teams. The pharmacy should summarize its PI activities for the 12–18 months before the survey and identify examples of improved patient care (or improved pharmacy services). Graphs that show measurable improvements are suggested.

	Yes	NA	No
Medication Use Improvement			
Evidence that the pharmacy participates in medication use improvement activities. (*See* Chapter 14.)	___	___	___

> ***Note:*** Examples include determining medication use patterns, participating on medication use improvement teams, participating on medication safety teams, monitoring medication use and reporting variations and problems to the medical staff, participating in developing the medication formulary, and identifying and reporting ADEs and medication errors.*

Emergencies

	Yes	NA	No
List of emergency medications (including crash cart lists) and poison antidotes approved by the medical staff. (MM.2.30.)	___	___	___
Current toxicology reference materials and poison treatment medications (in the emergency department/service and poison treatment areas).	___	___	___
Current edition(s) of the organization's approved emergency management plan(s).	___	___	___

> ***Note:*** The plan should address internal emergencies (e.g., fire, bomb threat or explosion, flood, and civil disturbance) and external emergencies (e.g., hurricanes, tornadoes, accidents, and terrorist attacks).

Hazardous Materials

	Yes	NA	No
Written plan for handling hazardous materials and wastes, medications, and chemicals located in pharmacy areas. (*See* Chapters 9 and 16.)	___	___	___
List of hazardous materials stored or used routinely in the pharmacy and other areas where hazardous medications are handled.	___	___	___
Material safety data sheets (MSDSs).	___	___	___

> ***Note:*** Access to MSDSs must be readily available in the pharmacy and other areas where hazardous materials are stored or handled.

> ***Note:*** Access may by a printed copy in the areas or electronically by the Internet or the organization's intranet. Some surveyors may question whether electronic access is readily available.

Infection Control

	Yes	NA	No
Records of testing for microbial contamination of sterile preparations. (*See* Chapter 18.)	___	___	___
Records of testing for microbial contamination in the area for compounding sterile preparations. (*See* Chapter 18.)	___	___	___

	Yes	NA	No
Records of media-fill challenge testing. (*See* Chapter 18.)	____	____	____

Laminar Airflow Hoods/Biological Safety Cabinets

Inspection and/or certification records. (*See* Chapters 8 and 18.)	____	____	____
Cleaning records (at least once each shift).*	____	____	____
Maintenance records (e.g., prefilter changing or cleaning).	____	____	____
Records of testing for microbial contamination of the laminar airflow hood. (*See* Chapters 8 and 18.)	____	____	____

Equipment

Preventive maintenance program/schedule and records for pharmacy equipment. (*See* Chapter 9.)	____	____	____

Repackaging

Quality control records for medications that are repackaged by the pharmacy.	____	____	____

Storage

Records of refrigerator, freezer, and warmer temperature monitoring (including actions taken if temperatures were out of range).* (EP 2 for MM.2.20.)	____	____	____

Floor Stock

List of the kinds and quantities of all medications in floor stocks (including medications in automated medication storage and distribution devices).	____	____	____

Controlled Substances (Manual or Automated Systems)

> ***Note:*** The DEA requires all controlled substances records to be readily available. The DEA provides additional information on accountability for controlled substances in its DEA Pharmacists Manual.[1]

Power of attorney, if granted, giving authority to obtain and execute official order forms (DEA Form 222a) for controlled substances.* (*See* Example 11-2.)	____	____	____

> ***Note:*** DEA Form 222a must be signed by an individual authorized to sign the form. Surveyors sometimes check to see if individuals who sign these forms have a power of attorney to do so. The receipt of controlled substances must be entered on the form.

	Yes	NA	No
Invoices showing the receipt of controlled substances.	____	____	____

Note: The DEA requires Schedule I and II records be separate from all other records. Some surveyors check this.

An up-to-date perpetual inventory of Schedule II controlled substances.*	____	____	____

Note: Many states require a perpetual inventory for all Schedule II substances; some states also require it for Schedules III-V substances. Expired, recalled, and other unusable controlled substances must be included on the perpetual inventory. Surveyors sometimes spot-check to determine if the amounts on hand agree with the perpetual inventory.

An annual or biennial inventory of all controlled substances (whichever is required by the state). (*See* Examples 4-9 and 4-10.)	____	____	____

Note: The inventory must include expired, recalled, and other unusable controlled substances.

Records of dispensing and administering controlled substances.*	____	____	____

Note: Proof-of use records must document the administration and use of all controlled substances. Surveyors sometimes spot-check to determine if the amounts on hand agree with the proof-of-use records.

Records documenting the administration of controlled substances in anesthetizing areas.	____	____	____

Note: Surveyors focus on controlled substances used in anesthetizing areas. They understand that accounting for the use of controlled substances in these areas is difficult. They insist that controlled substances in anesthetizing areas be stored securely and that the amounts on hand be checked regularly. Surveyors often determine if staff complies with state and federal requirements as well as the organization's policies and procedures for handling controlled substances in anesthetizing areas.

Note: Anesthesia personnel should be able to account for each dose of a controlled substance at all times. Single-dose ampuls should not be used on more than one patient. Surveyors like to see control systems that have a high degree of accountability (e.g., a tray exchange system or an automated storage and distribution device).

Note: The amounts of controlled substances administered must be recorded accurately (e.g., on a proof of use record) and must agree with the amounts recorded in patients' medical records. Many surveyors ask to see evidence of reconciling anesthesia controlled substances proof-of-use records with patients' anesthesia records. The reconciling process must ensure that records are correct and complete. Wastage must be recorded and should be witnessed by another individual.

	Yes	NA	No
Records of dispensing controlled substances to out-patients and employees.	____	____	____

> *Note:* Outpatient prescriptions for controlled substances must have prescribers' DEA numbers and, if applicable, be marked with a red "C."

	Yes	NA	No
Records of withdrawals from automated medication storage and distribution devices.	____	____	____

> *Note:* These records must show that an authorized individual withdrew the medications.

	Yes	NA	No
Records of periodic inventories (e.g., per shift, daily, weekly, or monthly) as required by the organization or legal requirements.	____	____	____
Records of controlled substance reconciliation processes.*	____	____	____
Records documenting controlled substance wastage.*	____	____	____

> *Note:* A single-use ampul or vial of medication must be administered to only one patient. If the patient does not receive the entire contents of the ampul, the medication remaining in the ampul must be wasted (i.e., destroyed) and the wastage documented appropriately. Nursing proof-of-use records must account for the wastage of unused portions of unit-dose injections and of spilled, contaminated, and refused doses.

> *Note:* The DEA interprets federal regulations to require a witness to the wastage of all controlled substances. The witness must sign the record of wastage.

	Yes	NA	No
Records of theft or loss of controlled substances.	____	____	____

> *Note:* The theft or loss of controlled substances must be documented and reported to the appropriate authorities. (*See* Example 4-12.)

	Yes	NA	No
Signatures and DEA numbers of practitioners *currently* authorized to prescribe controlled substances.	____	____	____

> *Note:* This record must be readily available to pharmacy staff. Surveyors prefer the record to be kept in the pharmacy to ensure immediate access if there is a question about a prescriber's credentials. The record must be up-to-date and include only current prescribers. If former prescribers are in the record, their status must be clearly noted (e.g., by a notation on the record or by listing them separately from current prescribers). Surveyors sometimes ask to see the record of a newly added and/or a former member of the medical staff. (*See* Example 11-3.)

	Yes	NA	No
Records of the disposal of unused and unneeded controlled substances.	____	____	____

> *Note:* Disposal procedures vary from state to state. Some states permit appropriately witnessed, onsite disposal of unusable or unneeded controlled substances. (*See* Example 4-11.) The area DEA office or the Board of Pharmacy can provide advice on how to comply with the disposal requirements.

Personnel Records

	Yes	NA	No
Personnel records or files (including job descriptions, performance evaluations, and competence assessments) for each employee.* (*See* Chapter 6.)	___	___	___

> ***Note:*** These may be stored centrally in the organization instead of in the pharmacy.

	Yes	NA	No
Evidence that performance evaluations are based on standards of performance in job descriptions.	___	___	___
Evidence that performance evaluations were conducted in a timely manner consistent with written policies.	___	___	___

Orientation

	Yes	NA	No
Evidence that pharmacy personnel have been oriented to the organization and to the pharmacy.* (*See* Chapter 6.)	___	___	___
Evidence that the pharmacy orientation includes medication safety, environmental safety, security, and infection control.	___	___	___

Education and Training

	Yes	NA	No
Records (e.g., minutes) of pharmacy staff meetings.	___	___	___
Evidence of education and training for pharmacy personnel.*	___	___	___
Evidence of annual education and training on medication safety, environmental safety, security, and infection control.*	___	___	___
Records of completion of mandatory continuing education for all personnel.	___	___	___
Evidence of education and training for individuals who compound sterile preparations.*	___	___	___
Evidence of education and training for individuals who compound chemotherapeutic preparations.*	___	___	___
Evidence that nurses are educated and trained in the use of investigational medications.	___	___	___
Evidence that pharmacy personnel have received education and training specific to relevant patient age groups.*	___	___	___
Evidence that the pharmacy provides or participates in educational programs (especially for relevant medication safety topics) for medical staff and nursing service.	___	___	___
Evidence that nurses who obtain medications from after-hours stocks have been adequately oriented and trained.	___	___	___
Evidence that the pharmacy provides ADE-related education and training to nurses and others who monitor, detect, and report ADEs.*	___	___	___
Evidence that pharmacy participates in orienting, educating, and training nurses and others who prepare sterile medications.*	___	___	___

	Yes	NA	No
Written guidelines for compounding parenteral medications (e.g., information relating to compatibility, contraindications, dilution, stability, and flow rates).*	___	___	___

CHAPTER 12

Pharmacy and Therapeutics Activities

The Joint Commission's medication management (MM) standards require organizations to develop policies and procedures for selecting and procuring, storing, ordering and transcribing, preparing and dispensing, administering, and monitoring medications. Organizations must develop a formulary or list of medications for dispensing or administration (MM.2.10), respond to actual or potential adverse drug events and medication errors (MM.6.20), and evaluate their medication management system for risk points and identify areas to improve safety. (MM.8.10.) Although the Joint Commission™ does not require organizations to have a pharmacy and therapeutics (P&T) committee, most organizations use a P&T committee to perform many of these activities.

This chapter discusses how to organize an effective P&T committee and provides guidelines for developing policies and procedures and a formulary. (*See* Chapters 4 and 10.) Evaluating the medication management system, responding to medication errors, and responding to adverse drug events are addressed in Chapters 14, 21, and 22, respectively. The approach and suggestions in this chapter can be applied to a P&T committee or other mechanisms for performing the required activities.

The P&T committee also provides a forum for educating and advising the medical staff. Pharmacies should use the committee to their advantage; it may be their best opportunity to meet with the medical staff to discuss matters pertaining to medication management.

Organization of the P&T Committee

The *ASHP Statement on the Pharmacy and Therapeutics Committee* recommends that organizations have a P&T committee, *or its equivalent.*[1] The organization's mechanism for performing the P&T function should be described in the medical staff's bylaws, rules, and regulations. This description should include the composition of the committee, assignment of responsibilities, meeting frequency, reporting requirements, and topics to be addressed. In small organizations, the entire medical staff may participate in P&T activities (sometimes called a "committee of the whole"). In other organizations, the medical staff assigns P&T responsibilities to individuals or divides them among existing committees.

Composition of the P&T Committee—There should be sufficient medical staff representation on the committee to develop policies and procedures, develop a formulary, evaluate and improve the medication management system, and participate in other P&T activities. In small organizations, one physician member might be adequate. Larger organizations might need representation from each medical staff department/service. The *ASHP Statement on the Pharmacy and Therapeutics Committee* recommends that the committee consist of at least the following voting members: physicians, pharmacists, nurses, administrators, quality assurance coordinators, and others as appropriate.[1] It is advisable to have physician members from at least three different services, if possible. Representatives from leadership, respiratory care, imaging, and laboratory often complete the committee.

The ASHP statement specifies that a physician member should be appointed chairperson and that a pharmacist should be designated as secretary.[1] Many organizations also furnish a medical staff secretary, medical records representative, or other individual to help the secretary record minutes.

Persons within or outside the organization with specialized or unique knowledge, skills, and judgments should be invited to meetings.[1] Performance improvement personnel, infection-control personnel, and dietetics services personnel, as well as other pharmacists and nurses, are often invited. ASHP also recommends that the P&T committee establish and maintain liaison with other committees in the organization concerned with medication use (e.g., the infection control committee).[1]

Meeting Frequency—The *ASHP Statement on the Pharmacy and Therapeutics Committee* states that "the committee should meet regularly, at least six times per year, and more often when necessary.[1] Quarterly meetings are often considered to be the minimum. The Joint Commission does not specify a frequency requirement.

Meeting Agendas—The *ASHP Statement on the Pharmacy and Therapeutics Committee* states that "an agenda and supplementary materials (including minutes of the previous meeting) should be prepared by the secretary and submitted to committee members in sufficient time before each meeting for them to review the material properly."[1]

Meeting agendas often include the following:

- Routine topics:
  - Status of previous P&T committee issues (e.g., approval by the medical staff executive committee)
  - Formulary additions, deletions, and changes (including therapeutic interchanges)
  - Nonformulary medication usage
  - Marketplace status (e.g., medication recalls, shortages, and FDA updates and black box warnings)
  - Review of newsletters and other communications
  - Policies and procedures update
  - Medication safety issues (e.g., problems that are reported nationally)
  - Medication use evaluations
- Quarterly topics:
  - Adverse drug reactions reported
  - Medication error summary and analysis
  - Review of failure mode and effects analyses and root cause analyses
  - Summary of pharmacists' interventions
- Annual topics:
  - Review of the entire formulary (including an assessment of emerging safety information)
  - Review, discussion, and approval of the organization's microbial resistance and sensitivity data
  - Review and approval of medication-related policies and procedures

Documentation (Minutes)—"The minutes of committee meetings should be prepared by the secretary and maintained in the permanent records of the organization."[1] P&T committee minutes should include the following:

- Location of meeting
- Date and time of meeting
- Persons present and absent
- Acceptance of minutes of previous meeting
- Old (unresolved) business
- New business
- Problems identified
- Actions taken
- Follow-up activities
- Time of adjournment
- Signature of committee chairperson

Some committees format their minutes in columns that summarize their findings/discussion, conclusions/recommendations, and actions/follow-up. Others use a traditional format for their minutes. Whatever the format, the minutes should summarize the discussion of the various topics in sufficient detail to determine the findings and the actions taken. Supporting data and documents should be attached to the minutes and filed in the permanent records of the organization. Copies of P&T minutes should also be filed in the pharmacy (if permitted by the organization). Example 12-1 contains guidelines for preparing P&T minutes.

The medical staff must review the P&T committee's findings, recommendations, and actions. A medical staff executive committee often performs the review. Acceptance or rejection of the P&T committee's activities must be noted in medical staff records (e.g., minutes of the medical staff executive committee).

Ensuring an Effective P&T Committee—Although most organizations view the P&T committee as a medical staff responsibility, the medical staff and the organization's leadership usually expect the pharmacy to ensure the success of the committee. The following may help to ensure an effective P&T committee meeting:

- Contact the chairperson, key committee members, and essential guests and speakers to determine a suitable date and time. Choose dates that have minimal conflict with other events.
- Reserve a room for the meeting and arrange for meals or other special needs, if necessary.
- Arrange for visual aids, projectors, flip charts, and other necessary equipment.
- Prepare the agenda and confirm it with the committee chairperson.
- Notify all committee members and attendees in writ-

ing or by e-mail of the date, time, and location of the meeting. Include the meeting agenda.

- Discuss any controversial topics with the chairperson and key committee members before the meeting.
- Remind the attendees by e-mail or telephone the day before the meeting. Send additional copies of the agenda and minutes if necessary. Determine if speakers will need additional equipment or materials.
- Follow-up to ensure that the meeting room, meals, and equipment will be ready.

Policies and Procedures

Adherence to comprehensive, explicit policies and procedures is an important factor in managing medications and assuring quality pharmacy services. ASHP's professional policy positions, statements, and guidelines provide a wealth of information on which to base policies and procedures. This section provides guidelines for developing policies and procedures. (*See* Chapter 10.)

Conformance with Bylaws, Rules, and Regulations—Pharmacy policies and procedures should not conflict with each other or with policies and procedures of other departments; with bylaws, rules, regulations, and policies of the medical staff; with bylaws of the governing body; or with local, state, and federal laws and regulations. The organization's medical records department, medical staff, and leadership can supply current documents. Examine them carefully and ensure that pharmacy policies and procedures do not conflict with them.

Generic Policies and Procedures—"Generic" or model policies and procedures and policies and procedures from other organizations can be excellent models. However, they should be reviewed carefully. Many of them may not apply to your processes and they may need numerous revisions to ensure that they reflect the organization's actual practices. Furthermore, poorly written examples may perpetuate unacceptable practices.

Outdated Policies and Procedures—The Joint Commission does not address the disposition of outdated policies and procedures. However, good management practices call for their retention. For legal or other reasons, you may need to refer to them to establish the policies and procedures in effect on a specific date. A separate manual or file of outdated policies and procedures, including those with seemingly minor changes, is suggested.

Policy and Procedure Formats—The Joint Commission does not specify a format for policies and procedures and there is no standard or legally required format. Furthermore, surveyors seldom question formats. Although many organizations have adopted a uniform format, other organizations use a variety of formats within the same facility. Example 10-1 is a sample policy and procedure for processing requests for nonformulary medications. The example provides a format that should meet the requirements of most organizations.

Many organizations require every document to begin with a policy statement. When applicable, the policy must be followed by a procedure for ensuring compliance with the policy. In addition, they may require any or all of the following to be included in the document:

- Name of the organization and department
- Number of the policy and procedure
- Page number (e.g., 1 of 3)
- Date of original approval
- Dates of subsequent review and revision
- Director of pharmacy's signature or initials confirming review and revision
- Signature(s) indicating approval by the medical staff and others required by the organization's policy
- Title or subject of the policy and procedure
- Background information
- Purpose of the policy and procedure
- Paragraph numbers
- References

Organizing the Policy and Procedure Manual—Many organizations use an electronic format to help ensure that only current documents are accessible. There is no requirement for policies and procedures to be kept in a manual. However, a manual is recommended because it allows personnel to review policies and procedures easily and is readily available if they cannot be accessed in the computer.

The following sections and topics are often addressed in a pharmacy policy and procedure manual:

- Table of Contents and/or Index
- Introduction or Organization of the Manual
- Patient Rights and Organization Ethics
- Performance Improvement
- Leadership or Administrative
- Emergency Preparedness
- Human Resources or Personnel
- Education of Staff
- Education of Patients and Family
- Information Management
- Safety
- Hazardous Materials
- Storage
- Security
- Controlled Substances
- Selection and Procurement of Medications
- Formulary
- Prepackaging
- Patient Care Areas
- Automated Medication Storage and Distribution Devices
- Assessment of Patients
- Ordering and Prescribing
- Computerized Prescriber Order Entry
- Dispensing
- Medication Administration
- Bar coding and Scanning
- Monitoring the Effects of Medications
- Continuum of Care
- Infection Control
- Compounding Sterile Preparations
- Emergency Services
- Ambulatory Care
- Other Services
- Forms
- Resources

Review and Revision of Policies and Procedures—The director of pharmacy must review and revise all pharmacy policies and procedures regularly (e.g., at least annually). Although not all policies and procedures need to be reviewed and revised at the same time, each one should be reviewed and revised at least once during the period. In large pharmacies, a pharmacy committee sometimes performs the review. In other organizations, an interdepartmental committee coordinates the review and revision of policies and procedures that cross departmental lines (e.g., nursing and pharmacy policies and procedures on medication distribution). The director of pharmacy's signature and date on each policy and procedure, as well as on a page that documents a review of all policies and procedures, is suggested.

Medical Staff Review and Approval of Policies and Procedures—The medical staff must review and approve pharmacy policies and procedures relating to medication management. As with pharmacy's review and revision, approval of all policies and procedures need not be done at the same time.

Ideally, medical staff review and approval would be conducted and documented in a manner similar to pharmacy review and revision (i.e., on each policy and procedure as well as on each page). However, in practice, it is difficult to get a medical staff representative to sign each document. The signature of a medical staff representative (e.g., chief of staff or chairperson of the P&T committee) on a page that documents approval of all policies and procedures should be sufficient. Medical staff approval should also be documented in P&T and/or medical staff minutes.

Formularies

According to the *ASHP Statement on the Pharmacy and Therapeutics Committee,* the P&T committee should "develop a formulary of drugs accepted for use in the organization and provide for its constant revision."[1] This section provides guidelines for developing and maintaining a formulary.

Joint Commission Requirements—The Joint Commission's medication management standards require organizations to use criteria to develop and maintain a formulary of medications to be available for dispensing and administration. The formulary must list all medications used in the organization including those that are not handled by the pharmacy (e.g., contrast media, anesthetic gases, and blood derivatives). (*See* the Joint Commission's definition of medication in Chapter 4.) Medication samples need not be included in the list.

There must be a mechanism for obtaining medications that are not on the formulary. The formulary must be readily available (in electronic or print format) and include the medication's name, strength, and dosage form. A print version should be available when staff members do not have access to an electronic version (e.g., when computers are inoperative). The organization must review the formulary at least annually. (*See* Chapter 4.)

ASHP Statement on the Formulary System—The *ASHP Statement on the Formulary System* provides broad guidelines for the development of an effective formulary. The following ASHP guidelines are especially important[2]:

- Policies and procedures governing the formulary system and developed by the P&T committee should provide guidelines for the objective evaluation, selection, procurement, storage, distribution, and safe use of medications.
- Medications should be included in the formulary by generic (nonproprietary) names, even though brand (proprietary) names may be used commonly in the organization. Prescribers should be encouraged to prescribe medications by their generic names.
- The number of medication entities and products routinely available from the pharmacy should be limited.
- The formulary system should provide for the use of generic equivalents and therapeutic interchanges in accordance with policies and procedures developed by the P&T committee.

ASHP Technical Assistance Bulletin on Drug Formularies—The *ASHP Technical Assistance Bulletin on Drug Formularies* provides detailed assistance in developing a formulary.[3] The following ASHP recommendations are especially important:

- Medications should be listed alphabetically within therapeutic class or by generic name, or a combination of the two systems.
- There should be a provision for "between revision" additions and deletions and other changes to the current formulary.
- Formularies should be revised annually.

Contents of the Formulary—To facilitate ready access to information, the formulary should include a generic name/brand name cross index.[3] The cross index should not be limited to brand names stocked by the pharmacy.

Other useful information often found in formularies includes the following[3]:

- Dosage forms and strengths
- Formulation (active ingredients) of combination products
- Packaging and sizes available
- Dosage guidelines
- Culture and sensitivity patterns of microbes (reported by the organization's laboratory)
- Policies on the use of investigational medications
- Policies and procedures relating to maintaining and revising the formulary
- Special information (e.g., sodium content of medications)
- List of nutritional products
- List of sugar-free medication
- List of medications that should not be crushed
- Special formulas used in the organization (e.g., active ingredients, compounding information, and ordering information)
- Poison control information
- Electrolyte content of large volume parenterals
- List of prohibited abbreviations, acronyms, and symbols
- List of look-alike and sound-alike medications

Size and Format of the Formulary—The optimal size and format for the formulary should be considered carefully. Pocket-sized editions are far more practical that large versions that are limited to use in areas with sufficient storage space. Using a different color paper for each section and bold-face type for headings improves the ease of use. The *ASHP Technical Assistance Bulletin on Drug Formularies* provides additional information on format and appearance of the formulary.[3]

Additions and Deletions to the Formulary—Additions to the formulary are best handled by the P&T committee through a formal written request system. This system usually requires the submission of a Request for Formulary Addition. (*See* Example 4-2.) The P&T committee should compare the proposed addition with other medications currently in the formulary for therapeutic equivalency and delete any therapeutic duplications that offer no advantages in efficacy, safety, convenience, or cost. The P&T committee should also handle other deletions from the formulary.

Support for Formulary Additions—Requests for formulary additions should be supported by the literature. As the formulary system is intended to ensure the appropriate use of medications, consideration of requests for additions to the formulary should include reviews of clinical research results and the findings of experts. Formulary selections must be evidence-based. Manufacturer's promotional material should be clearly indicated as such. The P&T committee should not be swayed by in vitro test results, misleading advertising, and anecdotal reports. For further information on formulary additions and deletions, see the *ASHP Technical Assistance Bulletin on the Evaluation of Drugs for Formularies*.[4]

Nonformulary Medications—Formularies must provide for the use of nonformulary medications. There should be a process for ensuring that nonformulary medications are obtained expeditiously. Some organizations require a nonformulary medication request form for ordering nonformulary medications. (*See* Example 4-3.) There should be a process for reviewing the use of nonformulary medications to determine if they should be added to the formulary. Example 4-4 is a form for listing nonformulary medications in stock that are awaiting evaluation and approval by the medical staff.

CHAPTER 13

Competence Assessment

The Joint Commission™ considers a competent individual to be one who has the essential knowledge and skills necessary to perform a job and actually performs the job according to defined expectations. It is important to note that competence is the ability to use *essential* rather than *advanced* knowledge and skills. Assessing competence does not necessarily determine if an individual has a high level of knowledge and proficiency. (*See* HR.3.10 in Chapter 6.)

Importance of Assessing Competence

In the past, organizations have hired staff and assigned tasks on the basis of education, experience, and, if applicable, licensure. However, these criteria do not assure organizations that the individual is competent. Therefore, many organizations, including health care organizations, assess competence before hiring staff and assigning responsibilities. Health care organizations realize that good competence assessment programs increase the likelihood that staff will provide effective, appropriate, and safe patient care.

Requiring pharmacy staff to be competent is in the best interest of patients, visitors, and staff. For example, competent personnel can be expected to do the following:

- Prepare medications accurately
- Counsel patients and their families on medications effectively
- Understand the unique needs of various patient types and age groups
- Operate equipment properly
- Handle hazardous materials safely
- Minimize opportunities for contamination and transfer of infection
- Respond promptly and properly to medical emergencies and disasters
- Monitor medication therapy for inappropriate prescribing, allergies, interactions, contraindications and, when necessary, act accordingly
- Be attentive to patient safety and meet management and public expectations

Components of Professional Competence

For the health care professional, competence can be thought of as encompassing three components:

1. Skill (i.e., either psychomotor or intellectual problem-solving). Compounding sterile preparations requires psychomotor skills. Determining the correct dosage of medication for a pediatric patient requires knowledge (e.g., medication distribution, metabolism, and excretion) and intellectual problem-solving (e.g., calculation) skills.
2. Professional socialization (i.e., the attitudes and values of the profession). Maintaining an appropriate relationship with patients, accepting responsibility, and resolving ethical issues require professional socialization.
3. Judgment (i.e., the capacity to successfully apply context to decisions). Applying clinical knowledge and experience to a situation with several solutions requires judgment to select the best choice (e.g., dosage adjustments for anticoagulant or aminoglycoside therapy).

Methods for Assessing Competence

Competence assessment is a measurement of an individual's capability to use the three components to perform up to defined expectations. There are three methods for assessing competence: cognitive tests, simulations, and direct observation of a process or product. Each method has strengths and weaknesses when compared with accepted standards for measuring clinical competence.[1]

Cognitive Tests—Cognitive tests are often multiple-choice, paper-and-pencil tests. Their strengths are accuracy of measurement and generalization to similar tasks, provided enough questions are asked. However, cognitive tests do not indicate what the individual will do in practice, because multiple-choice questions rarely test beyond the recall of facts, understanding of concepts, or straightforward application of rules.

Simulations—Simulations generally take the form of a patient case. The simulations may provide a good indication of how an individual would handle similar cases. However, accuracy of measurement is variable because there may be more than one solution and the best solution may not be clear. Furthermore, extrapolation to what the individual will do in practice is weak because simulations are rarely as complete as real practice.

Direct Observation—The third assessment option, direct observation, involves evaluating the process or product in real practice against a set of objective criteria. Process observations include watching a patient counseling session to assess the individual's patient education skills or monitoring renal dosing adjustments and pharmacokinetic dosing recommendations to assure accuracy and appropriateness. Product observations include reviewing a pharmacist's care plan documentation and examining media-fill tests of compounded sterile preparations. Extrapolation to routine practice is the strength of this method. However, as with simulations, accuracy of measurement is a problem because there may be several solutions. In addition, the time required for direct observation limits the number of observations that can be performed.

Combining Methods for Assessing Competence

Because no one method provides a valid and reliable assessment of clinical competence, the best approach is a combination of two or three methods, with careful attention to choice of assessment measures. For example, for an initial assessment of basic competence, any combination of the methods (i.e., cognitive tests, simulations, and direct observations) may be used to test the individual on the essential knowledge and skills expected for the position. After evaluating the completed assessments, the manager will have a good idea of the individual's strengths and weaknesses and can design education and training programs to address the weaknesses.

Competence Assessment Versus Performance Evaluation

The distinction between competence assessment and performance evaluation is not always clear. Competence assessments determine if the individual has the knowledge, skills, and ability to do a job and actually performs the job according to defined expectations. Performance evaluations determine *how well* the individual performs according to defined expectations. Performance evaluations may also relate to punctuality, attitude, compliance with policies and procedures, management skills, completion of education requirements, attendance at meetings, participation in required activities, maintenance of licensure, etc.

Documenting Competence

Competence should be documented on an ongoing basis beginning with the pre-employment period (if possible) and continuing throughout the duration of employment. Competence should be documented for new employees following orientation as well as for all employees when they are oriented to new patient care areas and new services, procedures, or equipment. Documentation of competence should include, at a minimum, the following information:

- Date
- Reason for assessment
- Method(s) of assessment (e.g., tests, demonstrations, and observations)
- Outcome of assessment
- Recommendations based on assessment (e.g., areas for improvement)
- Date of re-evaluation or next assessment

Pharmacies may use any method to maintain records related to an individual staff member's competence. Some maintain separate records (e.g., in a file or binder). Others keep the records in the individual's personnel file. Still others use combined job descriptions and competence assessment summaries.

Meeting the Joint Commission's Competence Assessment Standards

The Joint Commission's management of human resources (HR) standards requires an individual's competence to perform job responsibilities to be "assessed, demonstrated, and maintained." (HR.3.10.) The elements of the standard include requirements for the organization to define the competencies required, the frequency of assessments, and how assessments will be performed. The Joint Commission's standards relating to competence assessment are in Chapter 6.

Competence Assessment Frequency

The Joint Commission expects competence to be assessed during orientation and at intervals defined in the organization's policies. EP 5 for HR.3.10 requires competence assessments to be performed "minimally, once in the three-year accreditation cycle and in accordance with law and regulation." Many organizations perform assessments at least annually. Some may require more frequent (e.g., semi-annual) assessments of competence relating to high-risk processes.

Competence Assessment Tools for Health-System Pharmacies

ASHP's *Competence Assessment Tools for Health-System Pharmacies*[2] provides practical tools for assessing, maintaining, and improving the competence of pharmacy staff and complying with Joint Commission standards. The book contains five types of tools:

1. Job description templates (to develop customized job descriptions)
2. Pre-employment/initial skills assessments (to assess the initial level of competence of pharmacists and support staff)
3. Competence assessment checklists (to document the assessment of the specific elements of competence through tests, simulation, and direct observation)
4. Written tests (to assess the basic knowledge that is expected of the individual)
5. Study guides (to provide a general overview of topics)

CHAPTER 14

Performance Improvement Activities

This chapter describes activities relating to improving performance. It includes an overview of the Joint Commission's performance improvement (PI) requirements, basic process improvement tools, the Joint Commission's sentinel event policy, proactive assessment of high-risk or high-alert processes, and benchmarking.

Joint Commission's Improving Organization Performance Standards

The Joint Commission's improving organization performance (PI) standards require organizations to have an organization-wide program for improving performance. The program should be described in a separate plan or within other planning documents. All departments and services (e.g., pharmacy and nursing) must participate in the program.

The Joint Commission™ does not specify a term for the program; organizations may call their program PI, quality improvement (QI), quality management (QM), continuous quality improvement (CQI), etc. Whatever the term, the organization must show that its program meets the intent of the standards (i.e., improves performance).

The Joint Commission does not require organizations to follow a specific PI approach nor adhere to a specific stepwise process for improving performance. Nevertheless, organizations must collect data to measure current performance, assess current performance, and improve performance. The PI standards, as they relate to pharmacy, require organizations to do the following:

- Collect data to measure the performance of medication management and other high-risk processes. (PI.1.10 and EP 4 for PI.1.10.)
- Systematically aggregate and analyze data at an appropriate frequency using statistical tools and techniques. (PI.2.10, EP 2 for PI.2.10, and EP 3 for PI.1.10.) (*See* Process Improvement Tools in this chapter.)
- Analyze undesirable patterns and trends relating to serious adverse drug events and significant medication errors. (PI.2.20, EP 5 and EP 6 for PI.2.20.) (*See* Process Improvement Tools in this chapter.)
- Compare data internally and with external information sources to determine if the data vary excessively or performance is at an unacceptable level. (EP 4 for PI.2.10.) (*See* Benchmarking in this chapter.)
- Identify and manage sentinel events. (PI.2.30.) (*See* Sentinel Events in this chapter.)
- Use information from data analysis "to make changes that improve performance and patient safety and reduce the risk of sentinel events." (PI.3.10.)
- Have "an ongoing, proactive program for identifying and reducing unanticipated adverse events and safety risks to patients." (PI.3.20.)
- Include the use of failure mode and effects analysis in its proactive activities. (EPs 1 through 9 for PI.3.20.) (*See* Failure Mode and Effects Analysis in this chapter.)

Focus on Improving Processes—PI programs must focus on improving processes. Over time, organizations must evaluate the processes that compose their medication management system (i.e., how they select and procure, store, order and prescribe, prepare and dispense, administer, and monitor medications). The Joint Commission's medication management (MM) standards require organizations to do the following relating to evaluating their medication management system. (MM.8.10.)

- Evaluate their medication management system to identify risk points and areas to improve patient safety. (EP 1 for MM.8.10.)
- Evaluate literature for new technologies or successful practices that have been shown to enhance safety in other organizations and determine if they can improve their own medication management system. (EP 2 for MM.8.10.)
- Review their internal reports to identify trends or issues in their own medication management system. (EP 3 for MM.8.10.) (*See* standards PI.2.10 and PI .2.20.)

- Act to implement improvements in the medication management system based on the following:
  - Evaluation of the system
  - Review of new technologies
  - External data
  - Successful practices that have enhanced safety in other organizations (EP 4 for MM.8.10)
- Measure the performance of the new and modified processes. (EP 5 for MM.8.10.)
- Use information for data analysis to identify subsequent changes that will improve the medication management system. (EP 6 for MM.8.10.)

Methods for Improving Processes—All processes can and must be improved to reduce the likelihood of undesirable outcomes (e.g., sentinel events) and increase the likelihood of desirable outcomes. Process improvements may be achieved by better training, acquiring better equipment, changing or simplifying procedures, and other actions. Although some actions may produce only small improvements, numerous small improvements add up to significant overall improvements.

Setting Priorities for Improving Processes—The Joint Commission understands that lack of resources may prevent organizations from addressing all of their processes at the same time. Therefore, organizations must set priorities for addressing processes and concentrate their efforts on improving processes having the highest priority. Organizations should be able to explain the reasoning behind their priorities and have a plan for addressing other processes.

Improvement Expectations—The Joint Commission does not expect every improvement effort to be successful. However, over a period of time, a well-planned PI program should result in well-designed processes and measurable improvements in one or more of the key dimensions of performance. (*See* PI Team Focus in this chapter.)

PI Coordinating Group—Organizations must have a mechanism for coordinating PI activities. Most organizations have a coordinating group (e.g., a PI committee). The coordinating group is responsible for designing, measuring, assessing, and improving the organization's overall PI approach, allocating resources to the PI effort, setting PI priorities, and assessing the effectiveness of PI activities. There should be a mechanism for the group to oversee or coordinate other groups involved in PI activities.

PI Teams—The Joint Commission does not require PI teams. However, it does require staff (including the medical staff) to participate in multidisciplinary activities to assess and improve performance. Many organizations meet this requirement by forming teams of the organization's leaders, department directors and managers, physicians, other clinicians, trustees, and support staff. In this book, the term *PI team* refers to any multidisciplinary group that uses a planned approach to improve performance.

PI Team Focus—PI teams should focus on processes that make up a function. The team should look at the function from a global perspective and identify key processes of that function. Once key processes have been identified, the team should identify processes that are weak, set priorities, and develop a plan to improve one or more of the following key dimensions of performance:

- Efficacy — Achieves the desired patient outcome
- Appropriateness — Is relevant to a patient's needs
- Availability — Can be provided if necessary
- Timeliness — Is provided at the optimal time
- Effectiveness — Is provided correctly to achieve the desired outcome
- Continuity — Is coordinated between services, practitioners, and locations over time
- Safety — Reduces risks to the patient and employees
- Efficiency — Makes good use of resources
- Respect and caring — Is sensitive to a patient's needs and expectations

Process Improvement Tools

When possible, PI teams should use tools to help them assess processes, set priorities, determine patterns and trends, and monitor performance. Some of these tools are listed below. It is important that tools be used properly; poorly designed studies, bad data, and decisions based on worthless analysis can be misleading and are a waste of time and resources. Some organizations use consultants to help design sophisticated studies, provide training in using the tools, and assist in the analysis of data.

Flow Chart—A flow chart (or diagram) shows all of the steps and stages of a process (e.g., dispensing process) and sometimes includes the equipment needed and the individuals or departments responsible for each step. Flow charts use standard symbols that represent a start and finish, intermediate steps, decision points, and the direction of workflow. A flow chart is an essential first step in process analysis and can be used to identify areas of a process that might be sources of problems and candidates for improvement.

Check Sheet—A check sheet is a form for gathering data. For example, a check sheet can be used to record the numbers of each kind of dispensing error made (e.g., wrong drug and wrong dose). Data from check sheets are used in Pareto diagrams. (*See* Pareto Diagram in this chapter.)

Cause-and-Effect Diagram—A cause-and-effect diagram (sometimes called a fishbone or Ishikawa diagram) organizes findings from brainstorming sessions (i.e., facts, opinions, ideas, and guesses from a group [e.g., pharmacists, technicians, nurses, and physicians]). Brainstorming data can be used to identify possible causes of problems in processes (e.g., causes of dispensing errors).

Pareto Diagram—A Pareto diagram is a bar graph representing the types of problems (e.g., causes of dispensing errors) and the total number of occurrences (e.g., number of dispensing errors) for each type of problem. Pareto diagrams are based on the Pareto principle or 80:20 rule: only a few causes (about 20% or less) account for 80% or more of an effect. For example, about 20% of the causes of dispensing errors may account for 80% of the errors. A Pareto diagram helps to establish priorities for resolution of problems (e.g., causes of dispensing errors that merit the most attention) and helps to keep the costs of improving processes affordable.

Scatter Plot—A scatter plot is a tool for plotting two variables to show whether and how they relate (e.g., number of dispensing errors and number of orders filled).

Histogram—A histogram is a bar graph that shows how many times each of various events (e.g., different kinds of dispensing errors) occurred.

Run Chart—A run chart tracks patterns and trends over a period of time. For example, a run chart may be used to track the number of dispensing errors made per day during a quarter, year, etc.

Control Chart—A control chart sets upper and lower limits expected in a process (e.g., the expected highs and lows of dispensing errors). Performance that is above or below these limits warrants further study.

Sentinel Events

The Joint Commission's sentinel event policy encourages organizations to respond to serious adverse events, focus on the underlying causes of the events, and take actions that will reduce the frequency of their occurrence. This chapter describes some elements of the sentinel event policy. The policy is described fully in the Sentinel Events (SE) section of the *Comprehensive Accreditation Manual for Hospitals: The Official Handbook (CAMH).*[1]

Joint Commission Definition of a Sentinel Event—The Joint Commission defines a sentinel event as "an unexpected occurrence involving death or serious physical or psychological injury, or the risk thereof. Serious injury specifically includes loss of limb or function. The phrase 'or the risk thereof,' includes any process variation for which a recurrence would carry a significant chance of a serious adverse outcome."[1]

Organization-Specific Definition of a Sentinel Event—The Joint Commission requires every organization to establish an organization-specific definition of a sentinel event. Although the Joint Commission allows some latitude, the organization's definition must be consistent with the Joint Commission's definition and must include occurrences that the Joint Commission defines as reviewable sentinel events.

Reviewable Sentinel Events—Reviewable sentinel events include those that meet the following criteria:

- "The event has resulted in an unanticipated death or major permanent loss of function, not related to the natural course of the patient's illness or underlying condition, or
- The event is one of the following (even if the outcome was not death or major permanent loss of function, unrelated to the natural course of the patient's illness or underlying condition):
  - Suicide of any patient receiving care, treatment and services in a staffed around-the-clock care setting or within 72 hours of discharge
  - Unanticipated death of a full-term infant
  - Abduction of any patient receiving care, treatment, and services
  - Discharge of an infant to the wrong family
  - Rape
  - Hemolytic transfusion reaction involving administration of blood or blood products having major blood group incompatibilities
  - Surgery on the wrong patient or wrong body part
  - Unintended retention of a foreign object in a patient after surgery or other procedure
  - Severe neonatal hyperbilirubinemia (bilirubin >30 milligrams/deciliter)
  - Prolonged fluoroscopy with cumulative dose >1500 rads to a single field or any delivery of radiotherapy to the wrong body region or >25% above the planned radiotherapy dose"[1]

The Joint Commission may revise the definition of a reviewable sentinel event. Revisions will be published in *Joint Commission Perspectives®* and included in updates to the *CAMH*.

Organization Response to a Sentinel Event—The Joint Commission requires organizations to identify and respond to *all* sentinel events *as defined by the organization*. These include significant "near misses" (e.g., potentially lethal medication errors) even though there was no harm to the patient. Completion of an acceptable (i.e., thorough and credible) root cause analysis (RCA) after the event or after becoming aware of the event is a mandatory component of the response.

The RCA Process—An RCA is a process for identifying the underlying causes or reasons why an event (e.g., a sentinel event) occurred. Identifying the underlying causes is more than simply determining who or what caused the event or noting a failure to follow policies and procedures. The underlying causes may include lack of leadership, misplaced priorities, and failure to provide adequate equipment, funding, education, and resources. The elements of the RCA process include the following:

- Identifying causes and analyzing processes and systems related to the causes
- Identifying ways to improve processes and systems and reduce the likelihood of a recurrence of the event
- Creating an action plan for implementing the improvements to the processes and systems
- Implementing the improvements and evaluating the effectiveness of the improvements (i.e., measuring the results of the action)

Help in Conducting an RCA—The Joint Commission provides organizations with written guidelines, templates, and forms to help them conduct an RCA of a sentinel event, and on-site technical help by the Joint Commission is available. Although these materials are not required and do not need to be followed strictly, they provide a good framework for conducting an acceptable RCA. Organizations that need to conduct an RCA should obtain up-to-date materials and publications from the Joint Commission. The *CAMH* describes the minimum scope of an RCA for specific types of sentinel events.[1]

Reporting Sentinel Events to the Joint Commission—Organizations are encouraged, *but not required*, to voluntarily self-report to the Joint Commission *actual* occurrences that meet the Joint Commission's reviewable sentinel event definition. "Near misses" (e.g., medication errors that almost occurred and other events that could have resulted in serious consequences) and actual medication errors that do not result in death or major permanent loss of function are examples of events that should *not* be reported to the Joint Commission.

Organizations that do not voluntarily self-report a sentinel event must nevertheless complete an acceptable RCA. Organizations do not have to send their RCA to the Joint Commission or allow the Joint Commission to review it. Organizations must, however, permit the Joint Commission to review relevant documents (e.g., policies, procedures, and action plans) related to the RCA. Although organizations must perform an RCA on sentinel events that are *not* reviewable by the Joint Commission, they are not required to make the RCA-related documents available to the Joint Commission.

Joint Commission Response to a Sentinel Event—The Joint Commission's options in response to a sentinel event include acceptance of the organization's RCA and action plan, consultation and additional time to resubmit a response, placing an organization on accreditation watch, on-site visits, and issuing an accreditation decision (e.g., preliminary denial of accreditation). These are described in greater detail in the *CAMH*. The *CAMH* also contains information relating to follow-up activity and handling sentinel event-related documents.

Assessing Compliance with the Sentinel Event Policy—Surveyors expect organizations to have processes in place that relate to identifying and managing sentinel events. During a survey, surveyors will do the following:

- Review minutes and other documents that describe how the organization responds to a sentinel event.
- Conduct interviews relating to identifying, reporting, and responding to sentinel events.
- Review at least one example of an RCA that demonstrates the organization's process for responding to a sentinel event.

Failure Mode and Effects Analysis

Joint Commission standard PI.3.20 states "An ongoing, proactive program for identifying and reducing unanticipated adverse events and safety risks to patients is defined and implemented." The elements of performance for PI.3.20 describe a method for conducting a proactive assessment of high-risk processes. Organizations can meet standard PI.3.20 by performing a failure mode and effects analysis (FMEA) of processes that are likely to be associated with sentinel events.

Description of FMEA—FMEA is the systematic analysis of a process to identify the possible ways it might fail, the effects of failures, and the possible causes of failures. This technique has been used extensively in the aerospace and automobile industries. FMEA aims to proactively identify how and where systems might fail. If the potential effects of a failure are intolerable, actions are taken to eliminate or minimize the possibility of the error occurring, or minimize the consequences of the error when the potential for error cannot be eliminated.

FMEA vs. Root Cause Analysis—FMEA is a proactive technique that is used to identify and address problems *before* they occur. In comparison, RCA is used retrospectively to address problems *after* they occur. FMEA is also an ongoing process of quality improvement. Even when improvement is made, efforts to improve processes should continue.

How to Conduct an FMEA—Organizations may use the following steps to conduct an FMEA:

1. ***Choose a Process***

   When utilized as a tool in a medication error prevention program, FMEA should be used to analyze specific medications or drug classes, medication use procedures, medication-related equipment, and other aspects of the medication use system. Good items for analysis include the following:

   - *High-Risk Medications*—Examples include heparin, insulin, concentrated injectable electrolytes, opiates and narcotics.
   - *Error-Prone Procedures*—Examples include dose calculations and measurements, telephone and oral transmission of orders, handwritten and preprinted orders, and the use of infusion control devices.
   - *Errors or Incidents Reported in the Medical Literature*—Examples of publications that regularly publish information about medication errors include *ISMP Medication Safety Alert*, *Hospital Pharmacy*, and *American Journal of Health-System Pharmacy*.
   - *Errors or Incidents Reported by Health Care Organizations and Regulatory Agencies*—Example organizations and agencies include the Joint Commission (in *Sentinel Event Alerts*) (*see* Chapter 1), American Society of Health-System Pharmacists (ASHP), the United States Pharmacopeia (USP), and the Food and Drug Administration (FDA).
   - *Errors or Incidents Reported within the Facility*—Items for analysis may be identified through the medication error reporting program or other quality improvement processes.

2. ***Form a Team***

   FMEA is most effective when conducted by a multidisciplinary team. When forming the team, include representatives of all disciplines involved in the process being analyzed. Members should include pharmacists, nurses, physicians, and risk managers. Other potential members include pharmacy technicians, dieticians, nursing unit secretaries, and materials management personnel.

3. ***Analyze the Process***

   All team members should understand the process. The following steps should be useful in analyzing the process:

   - Prepare a flow chart or diagram that tracks the process from the point of initiation until completion.
   - Evaluate each step in the flow chart to determine what could go wrong with the process (i.e., potential failure modes).
   - List the effects of the identified failures.
   - List the root causes that can produce the failure mode or error.
   - Estimate the probability of each failure occurring using a ranking scale.
   - Estimate the severity of the effects of each failure using a ranking scale.
   - Estimate the probability of each failure being detected using a ranking scale.
   - Calculate the criticality index (CI) for each failure mode by multiplying the scores for frequency of occurrence, severity of effects, and probability of detection for each failure mode.
   - Assign a priority ranking for each failure mode by listing them in decreasing order of CI value (i.e., highest to lowest).

4. ***Identify Strategies for Improvement***

   Begin with the failure modes that have the highest CI values and identify actions or strategies that could reduce the CI. Include actions that decrease the likelihood of occurrence, decrease the severity of effects, and increase the probability of detection of failures. Example strategies include warning signs and labels, special packaging, limiting access to medications, implementing protocols for high-risk medications or procedures, double-checking calculations, and using technology (e.g., bar coding).

5. ***Implement Strategies for Improvement***

   Develop an action plan to implement the improvement strategies. Implement the action plan.

6. ***Evaluate the Effectiveness of Actions Taken***

   Evaluate the effectiveness of each action taken. Recalculate the CI of the failure modes to determine if the actions have had an effect. If the CI is not reduced, continue with the FMEA process to identify and implement new improvement strategies. The team should continuously improve the process.

Benchmarking

A benchmark is a standard by which something can be measured or judged. Benchmark standards are commonly considered to be the best performance achievable. To benchmark is to compare performance with benchmark standards. By comparing performance with benchmark standards, organizations can do the following:

- Identify deficiencies in their performance or opportunities to dramatically improve their performance.
- Determine how the best performance was achieved (i.e., learn from others).
- Determine what they can do to improve their performance (i.e., adopt better methods or practices).

What Organizations Should Benchmark—Organizations should benchmark key processes that are essential to serving patients (e.g., clinical pathways, patient assessment, transferring patients to other organizations, and medication management). Key medication management processes include selection and procurement, storage, ordering and transcribing, preparing and dispensing, administering, and monitoring. (*See* Chapter 4.)

National Benchmarks—There are currently few, if any, nationally recognized medication-use benchmarks. For example, there are no nationally recognized medication error and adverse drug reaction rates.

Self-Comparison and Comparison with Other Organizations—Health care organizations should, over a period of time, compare their current performance with their best historical performance (internal benchmarking) and, if available, with the best performance of other health care organizations that have similar processes (external benchmarking). When possible, they should compare their performance with organizations that rank among the best in their class.

Health care organizations can also compare their performance with organizations outside the health care industry that have similar processes. For example, many organizations have outstanding processes for maintaining records (similar to patient profiles), training staff (similar to pharmacy orientation and education), educating customers (similar to patient education), and assuring accuracy in filling orders for products (similar to medication dispensing).

Joint Commission Benchmarking Requirements—The Joint Commission does not explicitly require organizations to compare their performance with the best performance achievable. However, benchmarking is consistent with Joint Commission requirements that organizations compare data internally and with external information sources. (*See* EP 4 for PI.2.10.)

CHAPTER 15

Overview of the Joint Commission's ORYX Initiative

The Joint Commission's ORYX initiative integrates performance measures into the accreditation process and aims to provide health care organizations with an ongoing evaluation of their performance. Organizations can use their findings from the ORYX initiative to focus their performance improvement activities.

Hospitals must comply with the ORYX requirements in this chapter and the *Comprehensive Accreditation Manual for Hospitals: The Official Handbook (CAMH)*.[1] ORYX requirements for long-term care, behavioral health care, and home care organizations are similar but not the same as for hospitals. These organizations should consult the accreditation manual applicable to their organization for specific ORYX requirements.

Core Measures

The Joint Commission™ has identified standardized core measures for measuring the performance of hospitals in critical focus areas. Each of the core measures contains data elements, calculation algorithms, and standardized protocols for collecting data.

Core Measure Sets—The Joint Commission organizes related core measures into groups called *core measure sets*. The Joint Commission currently utilizes six core measure sets:

1. Acute myocardial infarction (AMI)
2. Heart failure (HF)
3. Pneumonia (PN)
4. Surgical care improvement project (SCIP)
5. Pregnancy and related conditions (PR)
6. Children's asthma care (CAC)

Details (e.g., data elements) for the core measures in the Joint Commission's core measure sets are available on the Joint Commission's Internet Web site. (*See* Appendix A.) The Joint Commission will develop and implement additional core measure sets and publish them on the site.

Pharmacy Participation Relating to Core Measures—The pharmacy often participates in performance improvement, medication use evaluation, and other activities relating to the core measures (e.g., collecting and evaluating data on the use of medications associated with the core measures or participating in advice/counseling activities). Table 15-1 lists core measures associated with the medications and advice counseling. Table 15-2 lists reliever medications associated with children's asthma care. Table 15-3 lists systemic corticosteroid medications associated with children's asthma care.

Noncore Measures and Performance Measures—Some hospitals may not be able to use the Joint Commission's core measure sets. (*See* ORYX Requirements for Hospitals in this chapter.) These hospitals may need to use noncore measures or performance measures to satisfy ORYX requirements.

Many performance measurement systems can help hospitals identify and select suitable noncore measures or performance measures. If noncore measures or performance measures focus on medication use, pharmacy services involvement may be significant. (*See* Performance Measurement Systems in this chapter.)

Hospital Quality Measures—The Joint Commission is working with the Centers for Medicare and Medicaid Services (CMS) to identify measures that are common to both organizations. When completed, these Hospital Quality Measures will satisfy both Joint Commission and CMS requirements.[2]

Performance Measurement Systems

Organizations must contract with an acceptable performance measurement system to submit ORYX data. They cannot submit ORYX data directly to the Joint Commission. A list of performance measurement systems that the Joint Commission considers acceptable is available on the Joint Commission's Internet Web site. (*See* Appendix A.) Many performance measurement systems can accept data related to both core measures and noncore measures.

Initial Accreditation—Organizations seeking their initial accreditation must contract with a performance measurement system and participate in the ORYX initiative. The *CAMH* contains additional information relating to initial surveys. Organizations seeking initial accreditation should contact the Joint Commission for current requirements.

ORYX Requirements for Hospitals

The Joint Commission's ORYX requirements for hospitals surveyed under the *CAMH* follow:

- If four applicable core measure sets can be identified, then no noncore measures are required.
- If three applicable core measure sets can be identified, then three noncore measures are required.
- If only two applicable core measure sets can be identified, then six noncore measures must also be collected.
- If only one applicable core measure set can be identified, then nine noncore measures must also be collected.
- If no core measure sets are applicable, then nine noncore measures must be collected.

The Joint Commission is capping the noncore measure requirement at nine measures through 2009.[3]

Organizations should check the Joint Commission's Internet Web site for changes to the core measure sets and any modified requirements (e.g., for smaller organizations or psychiatric organizations). (*See* Appendix A.)

Surveying the ORYX Initiative

Prior to a survey, the Joint Commission provides surveyors with information submitted by the organization. If the organization submits ORYX data to the Joint Commission, it will receive an ORYX Performance Measure Report. The *CAMH* contains additional information on the contents of the Performance Measure Report, sample reports, and sample charts.[4] The Joint Commission uses this information to plan for a survey. (*See* Chapter 2.) During the survey, surveyors assess an organization's use of its selected core measure sets in its performance improvement activities (including the organization's processes for collecting and analyzing data and disseminating the findings).

Obtaining More Information

Organizations and other health care organizations can obtain current information about the ORYX initiative through the Joint Commission's special ORYX information line, by e-mail, or by accessing the Joint Commission's Internet Web site and selecting "Performance Measurement." (*See* Appendix A.)

Table 15-1. Core Measures Associated with Medications and Advice/Counseling

Acute Myocardial Infarction (AMI)

Core Measure Set Measure ID #	*Core Measure Name*
AMI-1	Aspirin at arrival
AMI-2	Aspirin prescribed at discharge
AMI-3	ACEI or ARB for LVSD[a]
AMI-4	Adult smoking cessation advice/counseling[b]
AMI-5	Beta-blocker prescribed at discharge
AMI-6	Beta-blocker at arrival
AMI-7a	Fibrinolytic therapy received within 30 minutes of hospital arrival

[a]ACEI—Angiotensin converting enzyme inhibitor; ARB—Angiotensin receptor inhibitor; LVSD—Left ventricular systolic dysfunction.
[b]Pharmacists may offer advice on the use of medications associated with smoking cessation programs or counseling relating to smoking cessation.

Heart Failure Measures (HF)

Core Measure Set Measure ID #	*Core Measure Name*
HF-3	ACEI or ARB for LVSD[a]
HF-4	Adult smoking cessation advice/counseling[b]

[a]ACEI—Angiotensin converting enzyme inhibitor; ARB—Angiotensin receptor inhibitor; LVSD—Left ventricular systolic dysfunction.
[b]Pharmacists may offer advice on the use of medications associated with smoking cessation programs or counseling relating to smoking cessation.

Pneumonia Measure (PN)

Core Measure Set Measure ID #	*Core Measure Name*
PN-2	Pneumococcal vaccination
PN-3b	Blood cultures preformed in the emergency department prior to initial antibiotic received in hospital
PN-4	Adult smoking cessation advice/counseling[a]
PN-5	Antibiotic timing
PN-5a	Initial antibiotic received within 8 hours of hospital arrival
PN-5b	Initial antibiotic received within 4 hours of hospital arrival
PN-6a	Initial antibiotic selection for CAP in immunocompetent—–ICU patient
PN-6b	Initial antibiotic selection for CAP in immunocompetent— non-ICU patient
PN-7	Influenza vaccination

[a]Pharmacists may offer advice on the use of medications associated with smoking cessation programs or counseling relating to smoking cessation.

Pregnancy and Related Conditions (PR)

Core Measure Set Measure ID #	*Core Measure Name*
None	None

Table 15-1. Core Measures Associated with Medications and Advice/Counseling (cont'd)

Surgical Care Improvement Project (SCIP)	
Core Measure Set Measure ID #	*Core Measure Name*
SCIP-Inf-1a	Prophylactic antibiotic received within 1 hour prior to surgical incision—overall rate
SCIP-Inf-1b	Prophylactic antibiotic received within 1 hour prior to surgical incision—CABG
SCIP-Inf-1c	Prophylactic antibiotic received within 1 hour prior to surgical incision—other cardiac surgery
SCIP-Inf-1d	Prophylactic antibiotic received within 1 hour prior to surgical incision—hip arthroplasty
SCIP-Inf-1e	Prophylactic antibiotic received within 1 hour prior to surgical incision—knee arthroplasty
SCIP-Inf-1f	Prophylactic antibiotic received within 1 hour prior to surgical incision—colon surgery
SCIP-Inf-1g	Prophylactic antibiotic received within 1 hour prior to surgical incision—hysterectomy
SCIP-Inf-1h	Prophylactic antibiotic received within 1 hour prior to surgical incision—vascular surgery
SCIP-Inf-2a	Prophylactic antibiotic selection for surgical patients—overall rate
SCIP-Inf-2b	Prophylactic antibiotic selection for surgical patients—CABG
SCIP-Inf-2c	Prophylactic antibiotic selection for surgical patients— other cardiac surgery
SCIP-Inf-2d	Prophylactic antibiotic selection for surgical patients—hip arthroplasty
SCIP-Inf-2e	Prophylactic antibiotic selection for surgical patients—knee arthroplasty
SCIP-Inf-2f	Prophylactic antibiotic selection for surgical patients—colon surgery
SCIP-Inf-2g	Prophylactic antibiotic selection for surgical patients—hysterectomy
SCIP-Inf-2h	Prophylactic antibiotic selection for surgical patients—vascular surgery
SCIP-Inf-3a	Prophylactic antibiotic discontinued within 24 hours after surgery end time—overall rate
SCIP-Inf-3b	Prophylactic antibiotic discontinued within 48 hours after surgery end time—CABG
SCIP-Inf-3c	Prophylactic antibiotic discontinued within 48 hours after surgery end time—other cardiac surgery
SCIP-Inf-3d	Prophylactic antibiotic discontinued within 24 hours after surgery end time—hip arthroplasty
SCIP-Inf-3e	Prophylactic antibiotic discontinued within 24 hours after surgery end time—knee arthroplasty
SCIP-Inf-3f	Prophylactic antibiotic discontinued within 24 hours after surgery end time—colon surgery
SCIP-Inf-3g	Prophylactic antibiotic discontinued within 24 hours after surgery end time—hysterectomy
SCIP-Inf-3h	Prophylactic antibiotic discontinued within 24 hours after surgery end time—vascular surgery

Table 15-1. Core Measures Associated with Medications and Advice/Counseling (cont'd)

Surgical Care Improvement Project (SCIP) (cont'd)	
Core Measure Set Measure ID #	*Core Measure Name*
Cardiac	
SCIP-Card-2	Surgery patients on beta-blocker therapy prior to admission who received a beta-blocker during the perioperative period
VTE	
SCIP-VTE-1	Surgery patients with recommended venous thromboembolism prophylaxis ordered
SCIP-VTE-2	Surgery patients who received appropriate venous thromboembolism prophylaxis within 24 hours prior to surgery to 24 hours after surgery

Children's Asthma Care (CAC)	
Core Measure Set Measure ID #	*Core Measure Name*
CAC-1a	Relievers[a] for inpatient asthma (age 2 years through 17 years)—overall rate
CAC-1b	Relievers[a] for inpatient asthma (age 2 years through 4 years)
CAC-1c	Relievers[a] for inpatient asthma (age 5 years through 12 years)
CAC-1d	Relievers[a] for inpatient asthma (age 13 years through 17 years)
CAC-2a	Systemic corticosteroids[b] for inpatient asthma (age 2 years through 17 years)—overall rate
CAC-2b	Systemic corticosteroids[b] for inpatient asthma (age 2 years through 4 years)
CAC-2c	Systemic corticosteroids[b] for inpatient asthma (age 5 years through 12 years)
CAC-2d	Systemic corticosteroids[b] for inpatient asthma (age 13 years through 17 years)

[a]See Table 15-2 for list of reliever medications.

[b]See Table 15-3 for list of corticosteroid medications.

Table 15-2. Children's Asthma Care (CAC-1)

Reliever Medication	
Reliever Medications Selection Options (Trade Names)	*Reliever Medications Selection Options (Generic Name Crosswalk)*
Accuneb	Albuterol sulfate
Adrenaline	Epinephrine
Alupent	Metaproterenol
Atrovent	Ipratropium bromide
Brethine	Terbutaline
Combivent	Albuterol/ipratropium
Epi-Pen	Epinephrine
Maxair Autoinhaler	Pirbuterol acetate
Maxair	Pirbuterol acetate
Proventil	Albuterol sulfate
Proventil HFA	Albuterol sulfate
Proventil Repetabs	Albuterol sulfate
Sus-phrine Injection	Epinephrine
Tornalate	Bitolterol
Ventolin	Albuterol sulfate
Ventolin HFA	Albuterol sulfate
Ventolin Rotacaps	Albuterol sulfate
Volmax	Albuterol sulfate
Vospire	Albuterol sulfate
Xopenex	Levalbuterol hydrochloride

Table 15-3. Children's Asthma Care (CAC-2)

Systemic Corticosteroids Medication Table	
Systemic Corticosteroids Selection Options (Trade Names)	*Systemic Corticosteroids Selection Options (Generic Name Crosswalk)*
Adlone 80/40	Methlyprednisolone
Adrenocort	Prednisolone
Colone	Prednisolone
Cortastat	Prednisolone
Cortef	Hydrocortisone
Dalalone	Dexamethasone
Decadron	Dexamethasone
Deltasone	Prednisone
Depmedalone	Methylprednisolone
DepMedalone 80	Methylprednisolone
Depo Medrol	Methylprednisolone
Depopred	Methylprednisolone
Depo-Predate	Prednisolone
De-Sone LA	Dexamethasone
Dexacren	Dexamethasone
Dexamethasone Intensol	Dexamethasone
Dexasone LA	Dexamethasone
Dexapak Taperpak	Dexamethasone
Hexadrol	Dexamethasone
Hydeltrasol	Prednisone
Liquid Pred	Prednisone
Medralone 80	Methylprednisolone
Medrol	Methylprednisolone
Medrol Dosepak	Methylprednisolone
Methacort 40/80	Methylprednisolone
Methylcotol	Methylprednisolone
Methylpred DP	Methylprednisolone
Meticorten	Prednisone
Orapred	Prednisolone
Pediapred	Prednisolone
Predacort 50	Prednisolone
Predaject 50	Prednisolone
Predalone	Prednisolone
Predate 50	Prednisolone
Pred-Ject 50	Prednisolone
Prednicen–M	Prednisone
Prednicot	Prednisone
Prelone	Prednisolone

Table 15-3. Children's Asthma Care (CAC-2) (cont'd)

Systemic Corticosteroids Medication Table	
Systemic Corticosteroids Selection Options (Trade Names)	*Systemic Corticosteroids Selection Options (Generic Name Crosswalk)*
Solu-Cortef	Hydrocortisone
Solu-Medrol	Methylprednisolone
Solurex	Prednisone
Sterapred	Prednisone

CHAPTER 16

Overview of the Occupational Safety and Health Administration's Hazard Communication Standard

The Joint Commission™ requires health care organizations to manage their hazardous materials and wastes risks. (EP 1 through EP 13 for EC.3.10.) They must also comply with the Hazard Communication Standard (HCS) of the Occupational Safety and Health Administration (OSHA).[1]

This chapter summarizes the application of the HCS to pharmacies in health care organizations. More information about the HCS (including the standard, frequently asked questions, interpretation letters, compliance directives, and compliance guides) is available on OSHA's Internet Web site. (*See* Appendix A.) OSHA's eTool pharmacy module provides information specific to pharmacies in health care organizations.[2] (*See* Chapters 9 and 17.)

Materials Covered by the HCS—The HCS covers the following materials:

- Materials that the manufacturer has determined to be hazardous and are known to be present in the workplace in such a manner that employees are exposed under normal conditions of use or in a foreseeable emergency
- Chemicals that are carcinogens, corrosive, toxic or highly toxic, irritating, sensitizing, or target organ effecting
- Liquid drugs that contain hazardous chemicals (e.g., chemotherapeutic medications) and other drugs (e.g., powdered drugs) that contain hazardous chemicals and are *intended* to be mixed before administration
- Tablets, capsules, pills, and other solid drugs that contain hazardous chemicals and are *intended* to be dissolved or crushed before administration. Products that are *on occasion* dissolved or crushed to facilitate administration are exempt

Note: There is no complete list of hazardous materials (including drugs). Manufacturers must determine if a material is hazardous. OSHA provides an incomplete list of common drugs that are considered to be hazardous.[3]

Note: The National Institute for Occupational Safety and Health (NIOSH) provides a sample list of drugs that should be handled as hazardous. The NIOSH list is on its Internet Web site. (*See* Appendix A.) (*See* Table 17-1 in Chapter 17.)[4]

Materials Exempt from the HCS—The following materials are exempt from the HCS:

- Chemicals and drugs that do not contain hazardous materials (including solids and liquids)
- Chemicals and drugs in a retail establishment (e.g., in an outpatient pharmacy) that are packaged for sale to consumers
- Personal food, drugs, and cosmetics intended for use or consumption while in the workplace
- Hazardous drug-containing products in a solid, final form for direct administration to a patient (e.g., tablets, pills, suppositories, and pellet-, powder-, and liquid-filled capsules)
- Hazardous drug-containing products in a solid, final form that are *on occasion* dissolved or crushed to facilitate administration

Manufacturers' Responsibilities—The HCS requires manufacturers to do the following:

- Determine if a material is hazardous.
- Label hazardous materials with the chemical identity, appropriate hazard warnings, and name and address of the manufacturer, importer, or responsible party.

  Note: Pharmaceuticals labeled to meet FDA requirements are exempt from the hazard warning label requirements.
- Provide Material Safety Data Sheets (MSDSs) for hazardous materials to distributors, wholesalers, and pharmacies.

Note: MSDSs must inform workers of the hazards, protective measures, and actions to take if exposed to hazardous materials. Package inserts and publications such as the *Physician's Desk Reference* cannot be used instead of MSDSs.

Distributors' and Wholesalers' Responsibilities—The HCS requires distributors and wholesalers to do the following:

- Provide MSDSs for hazardous materials to pharmacies.

Organization Responsibilities—The health care organization must comply with the HCS requirements. Pharmacies may need to help the organization do the following:

- Post a notice of employee rights under the act.
- Have a written hazard communication program that includes policies and procedures for preventing and dealing with exposure to hazardous materials.
- Identify areas in which hazardous materials are stored or handled.
- Provide (e.g., post) a list of hazardous materials stored and handled in those areas.
- Provide protective apparel (e.g., gowns, gloves, eyewear, and face protection) and supplies for cleanup and disposal of hazardous materials (e.g., spill kits).
- Maintain a readily accessible file (e.g., electronically or in a distinctly labeled binder) of MSDSs in areas in which hazardous materials are stored or handled.
- Document an attempt to obtain an MSDS for a hazardous material if the manufacturer, distributor, or wholesaler will not or cannot provide it.
- Keep records of personnel who are exposed to hazardous materials.

Orienting, Educating, and Training Staff—The organization must orient, educate, and train staff on handling hazardous materials and procedures to follow if exposed to hazardous materials. Staff must be reeducated as necessary and when a new hazard is introduced into the work area. Orienting, educating, and training staff should include the following topics:

- Selection, storage, handling, use, and disposal of hazardous materials
- Prevention of exposure to hazardous materials
- Health risks associated with mishandling hazardous materials
- Emergency spill and exposure procedures (e.g., what to do if a hazardous material splashes in the eyes or contacts the skin)
- How to report spills, exposures, and other incidents with hazardous materials and wastes

Hazardous materials orientation, education, and training records should include the following information:

- Dates of orientation, education, or training
- Summary of orientation, education, or training
- Name(s) of instructor(s)
- Names and titles of attendees

Note: ASHP's *Competence Assessment Tools for Health-System Pharmacies* contains materials that will help document pharmacy staff competence in handling hazardous materials.[5]

Pharmacy Staff Responsibilities—Pharmacy staff must comply with the HCS requirements. The HCS requires health care organizations to ensure that pharmacy staff members know the following:

- The location of
  - the pharmacy's hazard communication program
  - a list of hazardous materials in pharmacy areas
  - a master list of all hazardous materials in the organization
  - MSDSs in pharmacy work areas
  - protective apparel
  - spill kits (for cleanup and disposal of hazardous materials)
- How to use the information on labels and MSDSs
- How to use protective apparel and spill kits
- How to report a spill of a hazardous material
- What to do if a hazardous material splashes in the eyes or contacts the skin
- How to report an exposure to hazardous materials

CHAPTER 17

Overview of the National Institute for Occupational Safety and Health (NIOSH) Recommendations for Handling Hazardous Drugs

The National Institute for Occupational Safety and Health (NIOSH) in its *NIOSH Alert* "Preventing Occupational Exposure to Antineoplastic and Other Hazardous Drugs in Health Care Settings" warns that "Working with or near hazardous drugs in health care settings may cause skin rashes, infertility, miscarriage, birth defects, and possible leukemia or other cancers."[1] The *NIOSH Alert* recommends methods and equipment for protecting worker's health. This chapter provides an overview of selected NIOSH recommendations. The overview is not complete and must not be relied on solely. The complete, detailed recommendations are in the *NIOSH Alert*.[1] They must be read carefully.

Regulations and Additional Guidelines Associated with Handling Hazardous Drugs—The NIOSH recommendations are consistent with practice guidelines of the American Society of Health-System Pharmacists (ASHP).[2] They are also consistent with Occupational Safety and Health Administration (OSHA) guidelines for the handling of hazardous drugs in the workplace. (*See* Chapter 16.) Some of the drugs are covered under the Hazard Communication Standard in the Code of Federal Regulations. Individual state and local entities may have regulations that must be followed by pharmacies within that state or locality.

Applicability of the NIOSH Recommendations—The NIOSH recommendations apply to all personnel in health care settings who may be involved in any phase of hazardous drug handling including receipt, storage, preparation, dispensing, transporting, administering, housekeeping, and cleanup and disposal of unused drugs, spills, and patient wastes.

Enforcement of the NIOSH Recommendations—NIOSH does *not* have regulatory authority. Its recommendations are advisory. NIOSH requests that employers (e.g., health care organizations) bring the recommendations to the attention of all workers who are at risk.

Joint Commission Expectations—Joint Commission standards require staff to use safety materials and equipment while preparing hazardous medications. (EP 4 for MM.4.20.) The Joint Commission™ also requires organizations to manage "its hazardous materials and waste risks." (EC.3.10.) The Joint Commission expects an organization's practices for preparing and managing hazardous drugs to be consistent with NIOSH recommendations.

Drugs That Should Be Handled as Hazardous—The *NIOSH Alert* provides guidance and criteria for determining whether a drug is hazardous. If a drug meets one or more of the criteria or is known or suspected to be associated with carcinogenicity, genotoxicity, teratogenicity, or reproductive or developmental toxicity it should be handled as hazardous.

The *NIOSH Alert* includes a sample list of major hazardous drugs.[3] (*See* Table 17-1.) The list was compiled from several sources. However, it is not complete. This list is available on the NIOSH Internet Web site. (*See* Appendix A.) Organizations should check the NIOSH site periodically for an updated list. NIOSH encourages organizations to develop their own list of hazardous drugs that workers might encounter within the organization. Organizations may want to use the NIOSH list as the basis for creating their own list.

Summary of NIOSH Worker Employer Recommendations

The NIOSH Internet Web site provides the following summary of worker employer recommendations for preventing exposures to antineoplastic and other hazardous drugs in health care settings. (*See* Appendix A.) The summary is not complete. The complete, detailed recommendations are in the *NIOSH Alert*.[1]

Health care workers should take the following steps to protect themselves from hazardous drugs:

- Read all information and material safety data sheets (MSDSs) your employer provides to you for the hazardous drugs you handle.
- Participate in any training your employer provides on the hazards of the drugs you handle and the equipment and procedures you should use to prevent exposure.
- Be familiar with and able to recognize sources of exposure to hazardous drugs. Sources of exposure include
  - all procedures involving hazardous drugs (including preparation, administration, and cleaning)
  - all materials that come into contact with hazardous drugs (including work surfaces, equipment, personal protective equipment [PPE], intravenous [IV] bags and tubing, patient waste, and soiled linens)
- Prepare hazardous drugs in an area that is devoted to that purpose alone and is restricted to authorized personnel.
- Prepare hazardous drugs inside a ventilated cabinet designed to protect workers and others from exposure and to protect all drugs that require sterile handling.
- Use two pairs of powder-free, disposable chemotherapy gloves, with the outer one covering the gown cuff whenever there is risk of exposure to hazardous drugs.
- Avoid skin contact by using a disposable gown made of polyethylene-coated polypropylene material (which is nonlinting and nonabsorbent). Make sure the gown has a closed front, long sleeves, and elastic or knit closed cuffs. Do not reuse gowns.
- Wear a face shield when splashes to the eyes, nose, or mouth may occur and when adequate engineering controls (such as the sash or window on a ventilated cabinet) are not available.
- Wash hands with soap and water immediately *before* using personal protective clothing (such as disposable gloves and gowns) and *after* removing it.
- Use syringes and IV sets with Luer-Lok™ fittings for preparing and administering hazardous drugs.
- Place drug-contaminated syringes and needles in chemotherapy sharps containers for disposal.
- When supplemental protection is needed, use closed-system drug transfer devices, glove bags, and needleless systems inside the ventilated cabinet.
- Handle hazardous wastes and contaminated materials separately from other trash.
- Clean and decontaminate work areas before and after each activity involving hazardous drugs and at the end of each shift.
- Clean up small spills of hazardous drugs immediately, using proper safety precautions and PPE.
- Clean up large spills of hazardous drugs with the help of an environmental services specialist.

Employers of health care workers should take the following steps to protect their workers from exposure to hazardous drugs:

- Make sure you have written policies about the medical surveillance of health care workers and all phases of hazardous drug handling—including receipt and storage, preparation, administration, housekeeping, decontamination and cleanup, and disposal of unused drugs, contaminated spills, and patient wastes.
- Seek input from workers who handle hazardous drugs when developing these policies and other programs to prevent exposure.
- Prepare a written inventory of all hazardous drugs used in the workplace, and establish a procedure for regular review and updating of this inventory.
- Train workers to recognize and evaluate hazardous drugs and to control exposure to them.
- Provide workers who handle or work near hazardous drugs with appropriate information and MSDSs.
- Provide a work area that is devoted solely to preparing hazardous drugs and is limited to authorized personnel.
- Do not permit workers to prepare hazardous drugs using laminar-flow work stations that move air from the drug toward the worker.
- Provide and maintain ventilated cabinets designed to protect workers and others from exposure to hazardous drugs and to protect all drugs that re-

quire sterile handling. Examples of ventilated cabinets include biological safety cabinets (BSCs) and containment isolators designed to prevent hazardous drugs from escaping into the work environment.

- Filter the exhaust from ventilated cabinets with high-efficiency particulate air filters (HEPA filters). Make sure these cabinets are exhausted to the outdoors whenever feasible—well away from windows, doors, and other air-intake locations.
- Consider providing supplemental equipment to protect workers further (e.g., glove bags, needleless systems, and closed-system drug-transfer devices).
- Establish and oversee appropriate work practices for handling hazardous drugs, patient wastes, and contaminated materials.
- Provide workers with proper PPE on the basis of a risk assessment and train workers how to use it—as required by the Occupational Safety and Health Administration (OSHA) PPE standard [29 CFR* 1910.132]. PPE may include chemotherapy gloves, nonlinting and nonabsorbent disposable gowns and sleeve covers, and eye and face protections. (*Code of Federal Regulations.)
- Ensure the proper use of PPE by workers.
- Use NIOSH-certified respirators [42 CFR 84]. Note: Surgical masks do not provide adequate respiratory protection.
- Provide syringes and IV sets with Luer-Lok™ fittings for preparing and administering hazardous drugs. Also provide containers for their disposal.
- Consider using closed-system drug transfer devices and needleless systems to protect nursing personnel during drug administration.
- Periodically evaluate hazardous drugs, equipment, training effectiveness, policies, and procedures in your workplace to reduce exposures as much as possible.
- Comply with all relevant U.S. Environmental Protection Agency/Resource Conservation and Recovery Act (EPA/RCRA) regulations related to the handling, storage, and transportation of hazardous waste.

Table 17-1. Sample List of Drugs That Should Be Handled as Hazardous[a]

This list is available on the NIOSH Web site [www.cdc.gov/niosh]. It will be updated periodically.

Drug	Source	AHFS Pharmacologic-Therapeutic Classification
Aldesleukin	4,5	10:00 Antineoplastic agents
Alemtuzumab	1,3,4,5	10:00 Antineoplastic agents
Alitretinoin	3,4,5	84:36 Miscellaneous skin and mucous membrane agents (Retinoid)
Altretamine	1,2,3,4,5	Not in AHFS (Antineoplastic agent)
Amsacrine	3,5	Not in AHFS (Antineoplastic agent)
Anastrozole	1,5	10:00 Antineoplastic agents
Arsenic trioxide	1,2,3,4,5	10:00 Antineoplastic agents
Asparaginase	1,2,3,4,5	10:00 Antineoplastic agents
Azacitidine	3,5	Not in AHFS (antineoplastic agent)
Azathioprine	2,3,5	92:00 Unclassified therapeutic agents (immunosuppressant)
Bacillus Calmette-Guerin	1,2,4	80:12 Vaccines
Bexarotene	2,3,4,5	10:00 Antineoplastic agents
Bicalutamide	1,5	10:00 Antineoplastic agents
Bleomycin	1,2,3,4,5	10:00 Antineoplastic agents
Busulfan	1,2,3,4,5	10:00 Antineoplastic agents
Capecitabine	1,2,3,4,5	10:00 Antineoplastic agents
Carboplatin	1,2,3,4,5	10:00 Antineoplastic agents
Carmustine	1,2,3,4,5	10:00 Antineoplastic agents
Cetrorelix acetate	5	92:00 Unclassified therapeutic agents (GnRH antagonist)
Chlorambucil	1,2,3,4,5	10:00 Antineoplastic agents
Chloramphenicol	1,5	8:12 Antibiotics
Choriogonadotropin alfa	5	68:18 Gonadotropins
Cidofovir	3,5	8:18 Antivirals
Cisplatin	1,2,3,4,5	10:00 Antineoplastic agents
Cladribine	1,2,3,4,5	10:00 Antineoplastic agents
Colchicine	5	92:00 Unclassified therapeutic agents (mitotic inhibitor)
Cyclophosphamide	1,2,3,4,5	10:00 Antineoplastic agents
Cytarabine	1,2,3,4,5	10:00 Antineoplastic agents
Cyclosporin	1	92:00 Immunosuppressive agents
Dacarbazine	1,2,3,4,5	10:00 Antineoplastic agents
Dactinomycin	1,2,3,4,5	10:00 Antineoplastic agents
Daunorubicin HCl	1,2,3,4,5	10:00 Antineoplastic agents
Denileukin	3,4,5	10:00 Antineoplastic agents
Dienestrol	5	68:16.04 Estrogens
Diethylstilbestrol	5	Not in AHFS (nonsteroidal synthetic estrogen)
Dinoprostone	5	76:00 Oxytocics

Table 17-1. Sample List of Drugs That Should Be Handled as Hazardous[a] (cont'd)

Drug	Source	AHFS Pharmacologic-Therapeutic Classification
Docetaxel	1,2,3,4,5	10:00 Antineoplastic agents
Doxorubicin	1,2,3,4,5	10:00 Antineoplastic agents
Dutasteride	5	92:00 Unclassified therapeutic agents (5-alpha reductase inhibitor)
Epirubicin	1,2,3,4,5	10:00 Antineoplastic agents
Ergonovine/methylergonovine	5	76:00 Oxytocics
Estradiol	1,5	68:16.04 Estrogens
Estramustine phosphate sodium	1,2,3,4,5	10:00 Antineoplastic agents
Estrogen-progestin combinations	5	68:12 Contraceptives
Estrogens, conjugated	5	68:16.04 Estrogens
Estrogens, esterified	5	68:16.04 Estrogens
Estrone	5	68:16.04 Estrogens
Estropipate	5	68:16.04 Estrogens
Etoposide	1,2,3,4,5	10:00 Antineoplastic agents
Exemestane	1,5	10:00 Antineoplastic agents
Finasteride	1,3,5	92:00 Unclassified therapeutic Agents (5-alpha reductase inhibitor)
Floxuridine	1,2,3,4,5	10:00 Antineoplastic agents
Fludarabine	1,2,3,4,5	10:00 Antineoplastic agents
Fluorouracil	1,2,3,4,5	10:00 Antineoplastic agents
Fluoxymesterone	5	68:08 Androgens
Flutamide	1,2,5	10:00 Antineoplastic agents
Fulvestrant	5	10:00 Antineoplastic agents
Ganciclovir	1,2,3,4,5	8:18 Antiviral
Ganirelix acetate	5	92:00 Unclassified therapeutic agents (GnRH antagonist)
Gemcitabine	1,2,3,4,5	10:00 Antineoplastic agents
Gemtuzumab ozogamicin	1,3,4,5	10:00 Antineoplastic agents
Gonadotropin, chorionic	5	68:18 Gonadotropins
Goserelin	1,2,5	10:00 Antineoplastic agents
Hydroxyurea	1,2,3,4,5	10:00 Antineoplastic agents
Ibritumomab tiuxetan	3	10:00 Antineoplastic agents
Idarubicin	1,2,3,4,5	Not in AHFS (antineoplastic agent)
Ifosfamide	1,2,3,4,5	10:00 Antineoplastic agents
Imatinib mesylate	1,3,4,5	10:00 Antineoplastic agents
Interferon alfa-2a	1,2,4,5	10:00 Antineoplastic agents
Interferon alfa-2b	1,2,4,5	10:00 Antineoplastic agents
Interferon alfa-n1	1,5	10:00 Antineoplastic agents
Interferon alfa-n3	1,5	10:00 Antineoplastic agents
Irinotecan HCl	1,2,3,4,5	10:00 Antineoplastic agents
Leflunomide	3,5	92:00 Unclassified therapeutic agents (antineoplastic agent)
Letrozole	1,5	10:00 Antineoplastic agents

Table 17-1. Sample List of Drugs That Should Be Handled as Hazardous[a] (cont'd)

Drug	Source	AHFS Pharmacologic-Therapeutic Classification
Leuprolide acetate	1,2,5	10:00 Antineoplastic agents
Lomustine	1,2,3,4,5	10:00 Antineoplastic agents
Mechlorethamine	1,2,3,4,5	10:00 Antineoplastic agents
Megestrol	1,5	10:00 Antineoplastic agents
Melphalan	1,2,3,4,5	10:00 Antineoplastic agents
Menotropins	5	68:18 Gonadotropins
Mercaptopurine	1,2,3,4,5	10:00 Antineoplastic agents
Methotrexate	1,2,3,4,5	10:00 Antineoplastic agents
Methyltestosterone	5	68:08 Androgens
Mifepristone	5	76:00 Oxytocics
Mitomycin	1,2,3,4,5	10:00 Antineoplastic agents
Mitotane	1,4,5	10:00 Antineoplastic agents
Mitoxantrone HCl	1,2,3,4,5	10:00 Antineoplastic agents
Mycophenolate mofetil	1,3,5	92:00 Immunosuppressive agents
Nafarelin	5	68:18 Gonadotropins
Nilutamide	1,5	10:00 Antineoplastic agents
Oxaliplatin	1,3,4,5	10:00 Antineoplastic agents
Oxytocin	5	76:00 Oxytocics
Paclitaxel	1,2,3,4,5	10:00 Antineoplastic agents
Pegaspargase	1,2,3,4,5	10:00 Antineoplastic agents
Pentamidine isethionate	1,2,3,5	8:40 Miscellaneous anti-infectives
Pentostatin	1,2,3,4,5	10:00 Antineoplastic agents
Perphosphamide	3,5	Not in AHFS (antineoplastic agent)
Pipobroman	3,5	Not in AHFS (antineoplastic agent)
Piritrexim isethionate	3,5	Not in AHFS (antineoplastic agent)
Plicamycin	1,2,3,5	Not in AHFS (antineoplastic agent)
Podoflilox	5	84:36 Miscellaneous skin and mucous membrane agents (mitotic inhibitor)
Podophyllum resin	5	84:36 Miscellaneous skin and mucousmembrane agents (mitotic inhibitor)
Prednimustine	3,5	Not in AHFS (antineoplastic agent)
Procarbazine	1,2,3,4,5	10:00 Antineoplastic agents
Progesterone	5	68:32 Progestins
Progestins	5	68:12 Contraceptives
Raloxifene	5	68:16.12 Estrogen agonists-antagonists
Raltitrexed	5	Not in AHFS (antineoplastic agent)
Ribavirin	1,2,5	8:18 Antiviral
Streptozocin	1,2,3,4,5	10:00 Antineoplastic agents
Tacrolimus	1,5	92:00 Unclassified therapeutic agents (immunosuppressant)
Tamoxifen	1,2,5	10:00 Antineoplastic agents
Temozolomide	3,4,5	10:00 Antineoplastic agents

Table 17-1. Sample List of Drugs That Should Be Handled as Hazardous[a] (cont'd)

Drug	Source	AHFS Pharmacologic-Therapeutic Classification
Teniposide	1,2,3,4,5	10:00 Antineoplastic agents
Testolactone	1,2,3,4,5	10:00 Antineoplastic agents
Testosterone	5	68:08 Androgens
Thalidomide	1,3,5	92:00 Unclassified therapeutic agents (immunomodulator)
Thioguanine	1,2,3,4,5	10:00 Antineoplastic agents
Thiotepa	1,2,3,4,5	10:00 Antineoplastic agents
Topotecan	1,2,3,4,5	10:00 Antineoplastic agents
Toremifene citrate	1,5	10:00 Antineoplastic agents
Tositumomab	3,5	Not in AHFS (antineoplastic agent)
Tretinoin	1,2,3,5	84:16 Cell stimulants and proliferants (retinoid)
Trifluridine	1,2,5	52:04.06 antivirals
Trimetrexate glucuronate	5	8:40 Miscellaneous anti-infectives (folate antagonist)
Triptorelin	5	10:00 Antineoplastic agents
Uracil mustard	3,5	Not in AHFS (antineoplastic agent)
Valganciclovir	1,3,5	8:18 Antiviral
Valrubicin	1,2,3,5	10:00 Antineoplastic agents
Vidarabine	1,2,5	52:04.06 Antivirals
Vinblastine sulfate	1,2,3,4,5	10:00 Antineoplastic agents
Vincristine sulfate	1,2,3,4,5	10:00 Antineoplastic agents
Vindesine	1,5	Not in AHFS (antineoplastic agent)
Vinorelbine tartrate	1,2,3,4,5	10:00 Antineoplastic agents
Zidovudine	1,2,5	8:18:08 Antiretroviral agents

Source: www.cdc.gov/niosh/docs/2004-165/2004-165d.html#o. Accessed August 2, 2007.

[a]These lists of hazardous drugs were used with the permission of the institutions that provided them and were adapted for use by NIOSH. The sample lists are intended to guide health care providers in diverse practice settings and should not be construed as complete representations of all of the hazardous drugs used at the referenced institutions. Some drugs defined as hazardous may not pose a significant risk of direct occupational exposure because of their dosage formulation (for example, intact medications such as coated tablets or capsules that are administered to patients without modifying the formulation). However, they may pose a risk if solid drug formulations are altered outside a ventilated cabinet (for example, if tablets are crushed or dissolved, or if capsules are pierced or opened).

[1]The NIH Clinical Center, Bethesda, MD. Revised August 2002.

The NIH Health Clinical Center Hazardous Drug (HD) List is part of the NIH Clinical Center's hazard communication program. It was developed in compliance with the OSHA hazard communication standard [29 CFR 1910.1200] as it applies to hazardous drugs used in the workplace. The list is continually revised and represents the diversity of medical practice at the NIH Clinical Center; however, its content does not reflect an exhaustive review of all FDA-approved medications that may be considered hazardous, and it is not intended for use outside the NIH.

[2]The Johns Hopkins Hospital, Baltimore, MD. Revised September 2002.

[3]The Northside Hospital, Atlanta, GA. Revised August 2002.

[4]The University of Michigan Hospitals and Health Centers, Ann Arbor, MI. Revised February 2003.

[5]This sample listing of hazardous drugs was compiled by the Pharmaceutical Research and Manufacturers of America (PhRMA) using information from the AHFS DI monographs published by ASHP in selected AHFS Pharmacologic-Therapeutic Classification categories [ASHP/AHFS DI 2003] and applying the definition for hazardous drugs. The list also includes drugs from other sources that satisfy the definition for hazardous drugs [PDR 2004; Sweetman 2002; Shepard 2001; Schardein 2000; REPROTOX 2003]. Newly approved drugs that have structures or toxicological profiles that mimic the drugs on this list should also be included. This list was revised in June 2004.

CHAPTER 18

Overview of United States Pharmacopeia (USP) Chapter <797>: Pharmaceutical Compounding—Sterile Preparations

Chapter <797> of the United States Pharmacopeia (USP) provides procedures and requirements for the safe preparation of compounded sterile preparations (CSPs).[1] The overview in this chapter addresses Chapter <797> requirements. It is not complete and must not be relied on solely. The complete, detailed procedures and requirements in Chapter <797> must be read carefully and thoroughly. (*Also see* Chapters 16 and 17 in this book.)

Revisions to Chapter <797>—USP Chapters are subject to revisions, based on practice changes. Proposed changes are published in *Pharmacopeia Forum*, a public comment period is announced, and the revision becomes official on the stated date. Revisions to Chapter <797> are likely to be announced. This overview is based on information that was effective at the time it was written and reflects requirements that were expected to be announced in the next revision. The USP will publish information relating to revisions on its Internet Web site. (*See* Appendix A.) The most recent revision of the chapter must be used.

Application and Enforcement of Chapter <797>—Chapter <797> applies to all persons associated with compounding sterile preparations and all places in the United States where CSPs are prepared, stored, and dispensed. The Food and Drug Administration (FDA) and other federal agencies can cite Chapter <797> in their visits to facilities. Furthermore, state boards of pharmacy can enforce all or parts of Chapter <797> if they stipulate so in their regulations. Pharmacies in these states must comply with Chapter <797> provisions as well as other state requirements relating to CSPs.

The Joint Commission™ Expectations—The Joint Commission expects organizations to comply with Chapter <797>. The Joint Commission will survey for compliance with provisions of Chapter <797> that overlap with Joint Commission standards (e.g., standard MM.8.10 relating to evaluation of the medication management system and standard EC.6.10 relating to medical equipment risks).

USP Contamination Risk Levels

Chapter <797> defines USP risk levels as low-, medium-, and high-risk according to the probability of contamination. Requirements differ for each level and must be read carefully. Table 18-1 lists the USP risk levels and selected requirements for each level. There are specific requirements for some CSPs (e.g., those mixed in satellite pharmacies, allergy extracts, hazardous drugs, and radiopharmaceuticals). There is also a provision for CSPs that are to be used immediately. Additional information about risk levels are in Chapter <797>.

Facilities and Equipment

Chapter <797> provides guidelines for facilities and equipment for compounding sterile preparations. Organizations should review the USP guidelines if they plan to redesign their compounding area or obtain new equipment.

Cleanrooms—A cleanroom contains specific design elements (e.g., ISO 7 air quality and HEPA filtered air).

Anteroom (or Antearea)—An anteroom adjacent to the cleanroom provides an area for storing supplies, locating sinks and other equipment, and donning garb. A separate anteroom is required for preparing high-risk agents. For low- and medium-risk agents, either a separate anteroom or delineated area within the cleanroom can be used.

Storage Area—A storage area should be adjacent to the anteroom. This area is used for storing supplies, preparing supplies for transfer into the anteroom and cleanroom, and other activities that require minimizing particles in the anteroom and cleanroom.

Hoods—Primary engineering controls are generally referred to as *hoods*, and include laminar air flow workbenches (LAFWs), biological safety cabinets (BSCs), compounding aseptic isolators (CAIs), and compounding aseptic containment isolators (CACIs). Ideally, these are located in a cleanroom, but in some cases they are in buffer areas that do not meet cleanroom specifications. CAIs and CACIs may be located outside of a cleanroom if the manufacturer certifies that a cleanroom is not required. Hoods must be inspected and certified every six months or when moved. The air quality (i.e., particle count) of the cleanroom (or buffer area) and anteroom must also be checked when hoods are inspected and certified.

Certification of Sterile Compounding Facilities—Hoods, cleanrooms/buffer areas, and anterooms should be certified by an independent organization. The Controlled Environment Testing Association (CETA) provides guidelines for testing primary engineering controls and cleanrooms.[2-4]

Other Equipment—Automated compounding devices, repeater pumps, and other devices should be maintained as recommended by the manufacturers. The biomedical engineering department (or equivalent) should be aware of these devices and include them in their preventive maintenance plan.

Other Facility Issues—Appropriate temperature, ventilation, humidity, and pressure gradients are essential to the proper and efficient operation of sterile compounding facilities. The temperature of the cleanroom should be 19ºC ± 1º (66ºF ± 2º) and relative humidity should be between 30% and 65%.

International Organization of Standards (ISO) Air Quality Standards

The International Organization of Standardization (ISO) sets standards for particulate matter in air. Selected ISO air quality standards for work areas follow:

- LAFWs, BSCs, CAIs, and CACIs (i.e., the primary engineering controls where manipulations are performed) must meet ISO Class 5 air quality standards. ISO Class 5 is equivalent to a US Class 100 environment.
- Cleanrooms (i.e., where the primary engineering controls are located) must meet ISO Class 7 air quality standards. ISO Class 7 is equivalent to a US Class 10,000 environment.
- Anterooms must meet ISO Class 8 air quality standards. ISO Class 8 is equivalent to a US Class 100,000 environment.

Responsibilities of Compounding Personnel

Chapter <797> requires personnel who compound sterile preparations to possess the skills, education, and training needed to compound sterile preparations. They must disinfect nonsterile compounding surfaces, use devices to control contamination, use aseptic technique to prepare CSPs, sterilize high-risk level CSPs, and ensure that CSPs are labeled properly. In-process quality control checks, and postcompounding inspections and testing must ensure that final preparations meet specifications of quality. The pharmacy and pharmacy compounding personnel are clearly responsible for the entire sterile compounding process and meeting the requirements contained in Chapter <797>.

> ***Note:*** Pharmacy personnel compound sterile *preparations*. Manufacturers make or produce sterile *products*.

Education and Training of Personnel Who Compound Sterile Preparations—Chapter <797> requires personnel who compound sterile preparations to be adequately skilled, educated, and trained in appropriate techniques and procedures. All compounding personnel must receive didactic instruction and pass written tests in aseptic techniques.

Competence of Personnel Who Compound Sterile Preparations—Initial and annual assessment of the competence of personnel who compound sterile preparations is required. Competence must be documented. *Competence Assessment Tools for Health-System Pharmacies* includes documents to help comply with this requirement.[5]

Use of Media-Fill Challenge Testing—Chapter <797> requires each person who compounds sterile preparations to complete a successful media-fill challenge test initially and periodically thereafter (at least annually for low- and medium-risk levels and semiannually for high-risk levels). Chapter <797> chapter describes methods for media-fill challenge testing.

Requirements for Cleaning and Disinfecting Workspaces

Chapter <797> specifies requirements for cleaning and sanitizing workspaces. Selected, abbreviated requirements are listed below. Complete, detailed requirements are in the chapter.

- Select cleaning and disinfecting agents that have been approved by the infection control committee.

  Note: Many facilities use 70% isopropyl alcohol. Other agents can be used if approved by the organization.

- Remove all items from the sterile compounding areas and clean all surfaces at the beginning of each shift.
- Mop floors once daily.
- Use nonshedding cleaning tools.
- Clean and sanitize storage shelving at least weekly.
- Ensure that there are no extraneous items (e.g., syringes, vials, and paper) inside the hoods.
- Collect trash in suitable plastic bags.

- Clean and sanitize the anteroom floors daily and the full anteroom (e.g., walls, shelves, and counters) at least weekly.

Personnel Cleansing and Garb

Chapter <797> specifies requirements for personnel cleansing and garb. The chapter addresses outerwear, makeup, jewelry, handwashing, hair and shoe covers, gloves, and other issues pertaining to cleansing and garb. The requirements should be read completely and thoroughly.

Standard Operating Procedures

Chapter <797> suggests that organizations have standard operating procedures (SOPs) to ensure the quality of the environment in the compounding area. USP's recommendations for SOPs address access to compounding areas, handling of cartons, storage and handling of supplies, use of transportation carts, traffic flow, and procedures for compounding sterile preparations.

Environmental Monitoring

Chapter <797> requires organizations to monitor and evaluate the quality of the environment in the compounding area (i.e., for particulate matter and microbes). Air quality can be certified by testing the primary engineering controls, cleanroom or buffer area, and anteroom. Microbial monitoring must be completed as described in the chapter

Processing CSPs

Chapter <797> states that compounding personnel must be appropriately trained and qualified in the use of aseptic techniques. They must ensure that sterile ingredients and components are truly sterile as well as defect-free. The chapter specifies that if nonsterile ingredients and components are used, compounding must meet high-risk level requirements. Equipment used in preparing CSPs must operate properly and personnel must be trained to operate the equipment.

Verification of Automated Compounding Devices for Compounding Parenteral Nutrition Preparations—Pharmacies that use automated compounding devices should review USP <797> in its entirety. Specific requirements for accuracy and precision of these devices are in the chapter.

Physical Inspection of CSPs—Chapter <797> requires that each finished CSP be inspected after compounding. Inspection must include observation for visible particulates, other foreign matter, and other evidence of defects. The chapter contains complete and detailed requirements that must be read completely and thoroughly.

Verifying Compounding Accuracy—Chapter <797> requires every CSP to be double-checked for compounding accuracy. Double checks must verify the accuracy of the ingredients and the label. If necessary, CSP samples must be assayed to determine if the identities and concentrations of ingredients are correct and accurate. Chapter <797> suggests procedures for checking and verifying compounding accuracy.

Sterility Testing—Chapter <797> requires sterility testing for specified high-risk CSPs. The chapter provides guidelines for selecting appropriate sterilization methods and describes methods for sterilization by filtration and by steam. If high-risk preparations are compounded, other USP chapters that should be read in detail include the following:

- Chapter <71> Sterility tests
- Chapter <85> Bacterial endotoxin tests
- Chapter <788> Particulate matter in injections
- Chapter <1075> Good compounding practices
- Chapter <1116> Microbiological evaluation of cleanrooms and other controlled environments
- Chapter <1191> Stability considerations

Verifying the Identity and Strength of Ingredients—Chapter <797> requires organizations to have procedures for verifying the identity and strength of ingredients. The correct names and amounts or concentrations of the ingredients must be listed on the label. Other labeling requirements include a beyond-use date, route of administration, appropriate storage conditions, and information that assures the preparation is used safely.

Storage of CSPs

Chapter <797> requires CSPs to be stored under conditions that will assure their stability. CSPs that have not been stored properly must be discarded. The chapter contains complete and detailed storage requirements that must be read completely and thoroughly.

Monitoring Controlled Storage Area Temperatures—Chapter <797> requires temperatures in storage areas for CSPs to be monitored at least once daily. The results must be documented. The chapter includes additional guidelines for monitoring temperatures in these storage areas.

Beyond-Use Dates and Times

Beyond-use dates and times must reflect manufacturers' product labeling or sources in the literature. Otherwise, beyond-use dates and times must be assigned according to USP guidelines, which are dependent on risk level of the preparation. The *shorter* of stability time (such as from manufacturers' information or the *Handbook on Injectable Drugs*[6] or USP limits of sterility time must be used. Chapter <797> contains complete and detailed guidelines for assigning beyond-use dates and times. These guidelines must be read completely and thoroughly.

Beyond-Use Time for Preparations for Immediate Use—Preparations of nonhazardous drugs that need to be compounded outside of a hood for immediate patient use may be used if the following conditions are met:

- The preparation contains no more than three sterile products (including the IV solution, drug, and diluent).
- There is no direct contact contamination when preparing the solution.
- Administration begins within one hour of preparation.

Chapter <797> provides additional information.

Beyond-Use Times of Single-Dose Containers—Single-dose containers are intended to be used immediately. The beyond-use times vary depending on the type of container and air quality in which it is opened. Unless the manufacturer states differently, the maximum beyond-use times for open or needle-punctured containers are the following:

- Single-dose ampules cannot be stored for any time period.
- Single-dose bags, bottles, syringes, and vials opened in worse that ISO 5 air quality can be stored no longer than one hour.
- Single-dose bags, bottles, syringes, and vials opening in ISO 5 or better air quality can be stored no longer than six hours.

Chapter <797> provides additional information.

Beyond-Use Time of Multiple-Dose Vials—Multiple-dose vials intended for multiple entries have a beyond-use time of 28 days unless otherwise specified by the manufacturer. Chapter <797> provides additional information.

Maintaining Product Quality and Control after the CSP Leaves the Pharmacy

Chapter <797> clearly indicates that the pharmacy is responsible for the quality and the control of CSPs in the pharmacy and throughout the organization. The pharmacy must educate and train nonpharmacy personnel in maintaining the quality and control of CSPs. Chapter <797> also provides guidelines that address how CSPs should be packaged, handled, and transported; used and stored in patient-care areas; administered; and redispensed if not used on the patient for whom originally intended. These guidelines must be read completely and thoroughly.

Packing and Transporting CSPs

Chapter <797> provides guidelines for delivering CSPs to locations that are off the premises of the organization. These guidelines address how CSPs should be packed for transit and transported to the off-premises locations. They must be read completely and thoroughly.

Patient or Caregiver Training

Chapter <797> specifies that organizations must have a formal training program to ensure that patients or caregivers know how to store, handle, and administer CSPs. The chapter specifies the desired outcomes of the training program.

Patient Monitoring and Adverse Events Reporting

Chapter <797> requires organizations to monitor patients who receive CSPs and report adverse events. The chapter contains guidelines for establishing a system for patient monitoring and adverse event reporting.

Quality Assurance Program

Chapter <797> requires organizations to have written quality assurance (QA) policies and procedures. QA procedures must be in place and followed. QA activities should include monitoring and evaluating all components of the sterile compounding process. Organizations should review USP's QA requirements and include them in their QA program.

Table 18-1. USP Risk Levels and Selected Requirements (*See* USP Chapter <797> for complete requirements)

Low-Risk	Medium-Risk	High-Risk
***All* of the following conditions are present:** • Only sterile ingredients, products, components, and devices are used (e.g., those that are commercially available). • Aseptic manipulations are used. • Manipulations are entirely within an ISO Class 5 or better air-quality environment. • Compounding involves only transferring, measuring, and mixing with closed or sealed packages. • Manipulations are performed promptly and attentively. • Manipulations are basic (e.g., aseptically opening ampuls and withdrawing and transferring sterile liquids from a sterile vial with a sterile needle and syringe).	**Aseptic compounding meets low-risk conditions but *one or more* of the following are present:** • Multiple doses of sterile products are combined and the CSP is to be administered to multiple patients or to one patient on multiple occasions. • Aseptic manipulations are numerous or complex. • The compounding process requires a long time to complete (e.g., to ensure complete dissolution). • The CSP does not contain a broad-spectrum bacteriostatic substance and it is to be administered over several days.	***Any* of the following are present:** • Nonsterile ingredients are used. • Nonsterile devices are used before terminal sterilization. • The compounding procedure exposes ingredients, components, devices, and mixtures to less than ISO Class 5 air-quality conditions. • Nonsterile preparations are exposed for 6 or more hours before being sterilized. • The chemical purity and content strength of ingredients is not verified or cannot be verified.
Examples—*See* USP Chapter <797> for Additional Examples		
• Reconstitute a vial of medication and transfer the contents to a single container of sterile fluid for administration to one patient.	• Reconstitute a vial of medication and transfer the contents to multiple containers of sterile fluids for administration to one or more patients.	• Compound an irrigation solution from nonsterile ingredients. • Prepare morphine from powder.
Storage—CSPs Must Be Stored Properly and Storage Periods Must Not Exceed the Following Times unless They Pass a Sterility/Stability Test		
Controlled Room Temperature: 48 hours Cold Temperature/Refrigerator (2–8°C): 14 days Freezer (–20°C or colder): 45 days	Controlled Room Temperature: 30 hours Cold Temperature/Refrigerator (2–8°C): 9 days Freezer (–20°C or colder): 45 days	Controlled Room Temperature: 24 hours Cold Temperature/Refrigerator (2–8°C): 3 days Freezer (–20°C or colder): 45 days

Quality Assurance—*See* USP Chapter <797> for Specific Quality Assurance Practices for Each Risk Level

Quality assurance practices include routine disinfecting and air quality testing, confirmation that personnel wear appropriate protective garments and goggles, review to assure correct ingredients and amounts were used, visual inspection of CSPs, and media-fill testing for compounding personnel.

CHAPTER 19

National Patient Safety Goals

The Joint Commission™ has an ongoing commitment to improving patient safety. To support its commitment, the Joint Commission develops National Patient Safety Goals (NPSGs) and integrates them into the accreditation process. This chapter reviews the development of the NPSGs, provides a general discussion of the Joint Commission's expectations for the goals, and describes how organizations can pursue alternative approaches to meeting the requirements. The 2008 NPSGs for hospitals are included in this chapter. Chapter 20 presents each NPSG applicable to hospitals in a checklist format and provides suggestions on how to implement them.

Development of NPSGs

The Joint Commission's Sentinel Event Advisory Group recommends potential NPSGs to the Joint Commission's Board of Commissioners. The Board of Commissioners reviews the group's recommendations and announces a final set of approved NPSGs during the year before they become effective.[1] Some NPSGs and their related requirements may be carried over from year to year; others may be retired or modified. The 2008 NPSGs were published in July of 2007 and are effective from January 1, 2008.[2]

NPSGs for each accreditation program are published in *Joint Commission Perspectives*® and the accreditation manual for each program. (*See* Chapter 1.) They are also available at the Joint Commission's Internet Web site. (*See* Appendix A.)

Sentinel Event Alert—Many of the NPSGs stem from the Joint Commission's publication *Sentinel Event Alert.* (*See* Chapter 2.) *Sentinel Event Alert* identifies high-risk patient safety concerns and offers recommendations for minimizing risks to patients. The first *Sentinel Event Alert*, published in 1998, addressed dangers associated with concentrated potassium chloride. Subsequent issues addressed medication errors, blood transfusions, high-alert medications, wrong-site surgery, dangerous abbreviations, infection control, infusion pumps, medication reconciliation, and other patient safety concerns. (*See* Table 19-1 for a list of *Sentinel Event Alerts.*)

Format of NPSGs—The NPSGs are formatted to be similar to formatting of the standards in the accreditation manuals. Each goal has one or more requirements and rationales are included for some requirements. Each requirement has one or more implementation expectations. The implementation expectations are numbered consecutively for each requirement. Notes and footnotes clarify some of the requirements and implementation expectations.

Frequently Asked Questions about NPSGs—Organizations can direct specific questions about NPSGs to the Joint Commission at its Internet Web site. (*See* Appendix A.) The Joint Commission publishes frequently asked questions (FAQs) about the NPSGs and their requirements on the site.

Evaluating Compliance with Requirements for the NPSGs

The Joint Commission evaluates compliance with requirements for the NPSGs during all types of surveys (e.g., full surveys and for cause surveys). (*See* Chapter 2.) Organizations must evaluate their compliance with the goals during their self-assessments (i.e., Periodic Performance Reviews). (*See* Chapter 2.) All accredited health care organizations that provide care relevant to the goals must show continuous compliance with carry over goals *for at least 12 months.* They must show continuous compliance with new goals from the date they became effective. Some requirements may have a phase-in period after the goals become effective.

Scoring the NPSGs—Each NPSG includes one or more clearly-stated requirements. Organizations are either compliant or not compliant with the requirements or the requirements are not applicable to the organization. Noncompliant requirements are scored as 0. The Joint Commission assigns the organization a Requirement for Improvement for each goal with noncompliant requirements. Organizations must address each Requirement for Improvement. (*See* Chapter 2.)

Documentation and Evidence of Compliance—Surveyors evaluate compliance with NPSGs throughout the survey (e.g., through tracer methodology). (*See* Chapter 2.) Organizations do not need extra documentation, new processes, and additional evidence of compliance. Nevertheless, some organizations might find it difficult to demonstrate compliance unless they modify their current documentation to reflect evidence of compliance.

Surveyors are instructed to look at current processes and relevant documentation, observe performance, and discuss with leaders and caregivers how the organization implemented the requirements. Surveyors state that a policy and procedure that describes how the organization will comply with an NPSG is not, by itself, sufficient.

Alternative Approaches to an NPSG Requirement

The Joint Commission must approve alternative approaches to an NPSG requirement.[3] Organizations may request the Joint Commission to consider an alternative approach to a requirement by submitting a form, Request for Review of an Alternative Approach to a National Patient Safety Goal (NPSG) Requirement. (*See* Example 19-1.) The most current version of the form is available on the Joint Commission's Internet Web site. (*See* Appendix A.) Complete instructions for completing and submitting the form are on the Web site and on the form itself. Organizations are not required to submit a Request for Review form if they implement an approved acceptable alternative (i.e., one that the Joint Commission has approved and published).[3]

Submitting the Form—Organizations may submit the form electronically, by fax, or by mail. However, the Joint Commission prefers forms to be filled out and transmitted electronically as an e-mail attachment. A separate form must be submitted for each proposed alternative approach. Organizations must submit the form to their account representatives, if known. The Joint Commission will not consider forms submitted by consultants. Organizations must submit forms no less than 60 days before their next survey.[3]

Joint Commission Review of the Request—The Joint Commission's Sentinel Event Advisory Group reviews each request and advises the Joint Commission on whether the alternative is acceptable (i.e., meets or exceeds the published requirements) or unacceptable. The Joint Commission advises organizations if their alternative is acceptable or unacceptable.[3]

If Requests Are Not Accepted—If a request is not accepted, the Joint Commission provides the rationale for nonacceptance to the organization. The organization must implement the Joint Commission's published requirement or revise the proposed alternative until approved by the Joint Commission.[3]

If Requests Are Accepted—The Joint Commission publishes acceptable alternatives to NPSG requirements in *Joint Commission Perspectives®* and on its Internet Web site. (*See* Appendix A.) Organizations should determine if the Joint Commission has published acceptable alternatives to the requirements. If an organization implements an acceptable alternative, surveyors will evaluate the organization's implementation of the requirements.[3]

If the Organization Implements an Alternative That Has Not Been Reviewed and Accepted—If a surveyed organization implements an alternative approach that has not been reviewed and accepted, surveyors will score the requirement as noncompliant. Surveyors will describe the organization's alternative in their report and note that it must be reviewed. The Joint Commission will review the alternative and either accept or reject it. If, after review, the Joint Commission rejects the alternative, it will issue a special Requirement for Improvement for the goal. The organization must address the Requirement for Improvement and submit evidence of compliance with the published requirements for the goal.[3]

Joint Commission Leadership Standards Relating to Patient Safety

The Joint Commission clearly places the responsibility for patient safety on the organization's leaders. The complete requirements are addressed in the Leadership (LD) standards in the *Comprehensive Accreditation Manual for Hospitals (CAMH)*.

2008 NPSGs for Hospitals and Their Requirements

The Joint Commission's 2008 NPSGs for hospitals are listed below.[2]

Goal 1: Improve the accuracy of patient identification.

Requirement 1A

Use at least two patient identifiers when providing care, treatment, or services.

Rationale for Requirement 1A

Wrong-patient errors occur in virtually all aspects of diagnosis and treatment. The intent for this goal is twofold; first, to reliably identify the individual as the person for whom the service or treatment is intended; second to match the service or treatment to that individual.

Implementation Expectations for Requirement 1A

1. Two patient identifiers are used when administering medications or blood products.
2. Two patient identifiers are used when collecting blood sample and other specimens for clinical testing.
3. Two patient identifiers are used when providing other treatments or procedures.
4. The patient's room number or physical location is not used as an identifier.
5. Containers used for blood and other specimens are labeled in the presence of the patient.

Goal 2: Improve the effectiveness of communication among caregivers.

Requirement 2A

For verbal or telephone orders or for telephonic reporting of critical test results, verify the complete order or test result by having the person receiving the information record and "read-back" the complete order or test result.

Rationale for Requirement 2A

Ineffective communication is the most frequently cited category of root causes of sentinel events. Effective communication, which is timely, accurate, complete, unambiguous, and understood by the recipient, reduces error and results in improved patient safety.

Implementation Expectation for Requirement 2A

1. The receiver of the information **writes** down the complete order or test result or enters it into a computer.
2. The receiver of the information **reads** back the order or test result.
3. The receiver of the information **receives** confirmation from the individual who gave the order or test result.

Requirement 2B

Standardize a list of abbreviations, acronyms, symbols, and dose designations that are not to be used throughout the organization.

Implementation Expectations for Requirement 2B

1. The organization develops a standardized a list of abbreviations, acronyms, symbols, and dose designations that are not to be used throughout the organization.
2. The list of abbreviations not to be used includes the following:
   - U,u
   - IU
   - Q.D., QD, q.d., qd
   - Q.O.D., QOD, q.o.d., qod
   - Trailing zero (X.0 mg)*
   - Lack of leading zero (.X mg)
   - MS
   - MSO4
   - MgSO4

   ***Exception:** A "trailing zero" may be used only where required to demonstrate the level of precision of the value being reported, such as for laboratory results, imaging studies that report size of lesions, or catheter/tube sizes. It may not be used in medication orders or other medication-related documentation.
3. The organization implements the "do not use" list and applies this list to all orders and all medication-related documentation when handwritten or entered as free text into a computer.
4. Preprinted forms do not include any abbreviations identified as not to be used.

Requirement 2C

Measure, assess, and if appropriate, take action to improve the timeliness of reporting, and the timeliness of receipt by the responsible licensed caregiver, of critical tests and critical results and values.

Implementation Expectations for Requirement 2C

1. The organization defines critical tests and critical results and values.
2. The organization defines the acceptable length of time between the ordering of critical tests and reporting the critical tests and critical results and values.
3. The organization defines the acceptable length of time between the availability of critical tests and critical results and values and receipt by the responsible licensed caregiver.
4. The organization collects data on the timeliness of reporting critical tests and critical results and values.
5. The organization assesses the data and determines whether there is a need for improvement.
6. The organization takes appropriate action to improve and measure the effectiveness of those actions.

Requirement 2D

Not applicable.

Requirement 2E

Implement a standardized approach to "hand-off" communications, including an opportunity to ask and respond to questions.

Rationale for Requirement 2E

The primary objective of a "hand off" is to provide accurate information about a patient's care, treatment, services, current condition, and any recent or anticipated changes. The information communicated during a hand off must be accurate in order to meet patient safety goals.

In health care there are numerous types of patient hand offs, including but not limited to nursing shift changes; physicians transferring complete responsibility for a patient; physicians transferring on-call responsibility; temporary responsibility for staff leaving the unit for a short time; anesthesiologist report to postanesthesia recovery room nurse; nursing and physician hand off from the emergency department to inpatient units, different hospitals, nursing homes, and home health care; and critical laboratory and radiology results sent to physician offices.

Implementation Expectations for Requirement 2E

1. The organization's process for effective "hand-off" communication include: interactive communications allowing for the opportunity for questioning between the giver and receiver of patient information.
2. The organization's process for effective "hand-off" communication include: up-to-date information regarding the patient's care, treatment, services, condition, and any recent or anticipated changes.
3. The organization's process for effective "hand-off" communication include: a process for verification of the received information, including repeat-back or read-back, as appropriate.
4. The organization's process for effective "hand-off" communication include: an opportunity for the receiver of the hand-off information to review relevant patient historical data, which may include previous care, treatment, and services.
5. Interruptions during hand offs are limited to minimize the possibility that information would fail to be conveyed or would be forgotten.

Goal 3: Improve the safety of using medications.

Requirement 3A

Retired in 2006.

Requirement 3B

Retired in 2007.

Requirement 3C

Identify and, at a minimum, annually review a list of look-alike/sound-alike drugs used by the organization, and take action to prevent errors involving the interchange of these drugs.

Implementation Expectations for Requirement 3C

1. Identify a list of look-alike/sound-alike (LASA) drugs used by the organization (the list must include a minimum of 10 look-alike/sound-alike drug combinations selected from the tables of LASA drugs posted on the Joint Commission Web site).
2. Review the list of look-alike/sound-alike drugs used by the organization at least annually.

3. The organization takes action to prevent errors involving the interchange of these drugs.

Requirement 3D

Label all medications, medication containers (for example, syringes, medicine cups, basins), or other solutions on and off the sterile field.

Rationale for Requirement 3D

This risk reduction activity is consistent with safe medication practices and addresses a recognized risk point in the safe administration of medications in perioperative and other procedural settings.

Errors, sometimes tragic, have resulted from medications and other solutions removed from their original containers and placed into unlabeled containers. Medications or other solutions in unlabeled containers are unidentifiable. This unsafe practice neglects basic principles of medication management safety yet has been routine in many organizations with respect to medications transferred to the sterile field.

Implementation Expectations for Requirement 3D

1. Medications and solutions both on and off the sterile field are labeled even if there is only one medication being used.
2. Labeling occurs when any medication or solution is transferred from the original packaging to another container.
3. Labels include the drug name, strength, amount (if not apparent from the container), expiration date when not used within 24 hours, and expiration time when expiration occurs in less than 24 hours.
4. All labels are verified both verbally and visually by two qualified individuals when the person preparing the medication is not the person administering the medication.
5. No more than one medication or solution is labeled at one time.
6. Any medications or solutions found unlabeled are immediately discarded.
7. All original containers from medications or solutions remain available for reference in the perioperative/procedural area until the conclusion of the procedure.
8. All labeled containers on the sterile field are discarded at the conclusion of the procedure.
9. At shift change or break relief, all medications and solutions both on and off the sterile field and their labels are reviewed by entering and exiting personnel.

Requirement 3E

Reduce the likelihood of patient harm associated with the use of anticoagulation therapy.

> ***Note:*** This requirement applies only to organizations that provide anticoagulation therapy.

Rationale for Requirement 3E

Anticoagulation is a high-risk treatment, which commonly leads to adverse drug events due to the complexity of dosing these medications, monitoring their effects, and ensuring patient compliance with outpatient therapy. The use of standardized practices that include patient involvement can reduce the risk of adverse drug events associated with the use of heparin (unfractionated), low molecular weight heparin (LMWH), warfarin, and other anticoagulants.

> ***Note:*** This requirement has a one-year phase-in period that includes defined expectations for planning, development, and testing ("milestones") at 3, 6, and 9 months in 2008, with the expectation of full implementation by January 1, 2009.

1. As of April 1, 2008, the organization's leadership has assigned responsibility for oversight and coordination of the development, testing, and implementation of NPSG Requirement 3E.
2. As of July 1, 2008, an implementation work plan is in place that identifies adequate resources, assigned accountabilities, and a time line for full implementation of NPSG Requirement 3E by January 1, 2009.
3. As of October 1, 2008, pilot testing in at least one clinical unit is under way.
4. As of January 1, 2009, the process is fully implemented across the organization.

The Implementation Expectations that will apply beginning January 1, 2009, are provided below.

Implementation Expectations for 3E

1. The organization implements a defined anticoagulant management program to individualize the care provided to each patient receiving anticoagulant therapy.
2. To reduce compounding and labeling errors, the organization uses ONLY oral unit-dose products and premixed infusions, when these products are available.
3. When pharmacy services are provided by the organization, warfarin is dispensed for each patient in accordance with established monitoring procedures.
4. The organization uses approved protocols for the initiation and maintenance of anticoagulation therapy appropriate to the medication used, to the condition being treated, and to the potential for drug interactions.
5. For patients being started on warfarin, a baseline International Normalized Ratio (INR) is available, and for all patients receiving warfarin therapy, a current INR is available and is used to monitor and adjust therapy.
6. When dietary services are provided by the organization, the service is notified of all patients receiving warfarin and responds according to its established food/drug interaction program.
7. When heparin is administered intravenously and continuously, the organization uses programmable infusion pumps.
8. The organization has a policy that addresses baseline and ongoing laboratory tests that are required for heparin and low molecular weight heparin therapies.
9. The organization provides education regarding anticoagulation therapy to prescribers, staff, patients, and families.
10. Patient/family education includes the importance of follow-up monitoring, compliance issues, dietary restrictions, and potential for adverse drug reactions and interactions.
11. The organization evaluates anticoagulation safety practices (see MM.8.10).

Goal 4: Not applicable.

Goal 5: Not applicable.

Goal 6: Not applicable.

Goal 7: Reduce the risk of health care–associated infections.

Requirement 7A

Comply with current World Health Organization (WHO) Hand Hygiene Guidelines or Centers for Disease Control and Prevention (CDC) hand-hygiene guidelines.

Rationale for Requirement 7A

Compliance with the WHO Hand Hygiene Guidelines or CDC hand-hygiene guidelines will reduce the transmission of infectious agents by staff to patients, thereby decreasing the incidence of health care–associated infections.

Implementation Expectation for Requirement 7A

Comply with current WHO Hand Hygiene Guidelines or Centers for Disease Control and Prevention (CDC) hand-hygiene guidelines.

> *Note:* Organizations are required to comply with all 1A, 1B, 1C, CDC, or WHO guidelines.

Requirement 7B

Manage as sentinel events all identified cases of unanticipated death or major permanent loss of function associated with a health care–associated infection.

Rationale for Requirement 7B

A significant percentage of patients who unexpectedly die or suffer major permanent loss of function have health care–associated infections. These unanticipated deaths and injuries meet the definition of a sentinel event and, therefore, are required to undergo a root cause analysis. The root cause analysis should attempt to answer the questions (1) why did the patient acquire an infection and, (2) given the fact of the infection, why did the patient die or suffer permanent loss of function?

Implementation Expectations Requirement 7B

1. The organization manages all identified cases of unanticipated death or major permanent loss of function associated with a health care–associated infection as sentinel events (that is, conducts a root cause analysis).
2. The root cause analysis addresses the management of the patient before and after the identification of infection.

Goal 8: Accurately and completely reconcile medications across the continuum of care.

Requirement 8A

There is a process for comparing the patient's current medications with those ordered for the patient while under the care of the organization.

Rationale for Requirement 8A

Patients are most at risk during transitions in care (hand-offs) across settings, services, providers, or levels of care. The development, reconciliation, and communication of an accurate medication list throughout the continuum of care is essential in the reduction of transition-related adverse drug events.

Implementation Expectations for Requirement 8A

1. The organization, with the patient's involvement, creates a complete list of the patient's current medications at admission/entry.
2. The medications ordered for, administered to, or dispensed to the patient while under the care of the organization are compared to those on the list and any discrepancies (e.g., omissions, duplications, potential interactions) are resolved.

Requirement 8B

A complete list of the patient's medications is communicated to the next provider of service when a patient is referred or transferred to another setting, service, practitioner or level of care within or outside the organization. The complete list of medications is also provided to the patient on discharge from the organization.

Implementation Expectations for Requirement 8B

1. The patient's accurate medication reconciliation list (complete with medications prescribed by the first provider of service) is communicated to the next provider of service, whether it be within or outside the organization.
2. The next provider of service checks the medication reconciliation list again to make sure it is accurate and in concert with any new medications to be ordered/prescribed.
3. The complete list of medications is also provided to the patient on discharge from the organization.

Goal 9: Reduce the risk of patient harm resulting from falls.

Requirement 9B

Implement a fall reduction program including an evaluation of the effectiveness of the program.

Rationale for Requirement 9B

Falls account for a significant portion of injuries in hospitalized patients, long-term care residents, and home care recipients. In the context of the population it serves, the services it provides, and its environment of care, the organization should evaluate its patients' risk for falls and take action to reduce the risk of falling and to reduce the risk of injury, should a fall occur. The evaluation could include fall history, medications and alcohol consumption review, gait and balance screening, walking aids, assistive technologies, protective devices assessment and environmental assessments.

Implementation Expectations for Requirement 9B

1. The organization establishes a fall reduction program.
2. The fall reduction program includes an evaluation as appropriate to the patient population, settings and services provided.
3. The fall reduction program includes interventions to reduce the patient's fall risk factors.
4. Staff receive education and training for the fall reduction program.
5. The patient and patient's family is educated on the fall reduction program and any individualized fall reduction strategies.
6. The fall reduction program is evaluated to determine the effectiveness of the program. (Outcome indicators such as decreased number of falls and decreased number and severity of fall-related injuries could be used.)

Goal 10: Not applicable.

Goal 11: Not applicable.

Goal 12: Not applicable

Goal 13: Encourage patients' active involvement in their own care as a patient safety strategy.

Requirement 13A

Define and communicate the means for patients and their families to report concerns about safety and encourage them to do so.

Rationale for Requirement 13A

Communication with patients and families about all aspects of their care, treatment, or services is an important characteristic of a culture of safety. When patients know what to expect, they are more aware of possible errors and choices. Patients can be an important source of information about potential adverse events and hazardous conditions.

Implementation Expectation for Requirement 13A

1. Patients and families are educated on methods available to report concerns related to care, treatment, services, and patient safety issues.
2. The organization encourages patients and their families to report concerns about safety.

Goal 14: Not applicable.

Goal 15: The organization identifies safety risks inherent in its patient population.

Rationale for Goal 15

Probabilistic risk assessment has been used to assess the designs of high hazard systems such as chemical engineering plants and space initiatives. Probabilistic risk assessment looks at events that contributed to adverse outcomes. Health care has the ability to identify those areas of high risk potential based on previous sentinel events and other data.

Requirement 15A

The organization identifies patients at risk for suicide.

> *Note*: This requirement only applies to psychiatric hospitals and patients being treated for emotional or behavioral disorders in general hospitals.

Rationale for Requirement 15A

Suicide ranks as the eleventh most frequent cause of death (third most frequent in young people) in the United States, with one person dying from suicide every 16.6 minutes. Suicide of a care recipient while in a staffed, round-the-clock care setting has been the #1 most frequently reported type of sentinel event since the inception of the Joint Commission's Sentinel Event Policy in 1996. Identification of individuals at risk for suicide while under the care of or following discharge from a health care organization is an important first step in protecting and planning the care of these at-risk individuals.

Implementation Expectations for Requirement 15A

1. The risk assessment includes identification of specific factors and features that may increase or decrease risk for suicide.
2. The patient's immediate safety needs and most appropriate setting for treatment are addressed.
3. The organization provides information such as a crisis hotline to individuals and their family members for crisis situations.

Goal 16: Improve recognition and response to changes in a patient's condition.

Requirement 16A

The organization selects a suitable method that enables health care staff members to directly request additional assistance from a specially trained individual(s) when the patient's condition appears to be worsening.

Rationale for Requirement 16A

A significant number of critical inpatient events are preceded by warning signs for an average of 6 to 8 hours. Critical events such as cardiopulmonary and respiratory arrests or changes in patient's vital signs are estimated to occur in 4% to 17% of inpatient admissions. Early response by a specially trained individual(s) to changes in a patient's condition may reduce cardiopulmonary arrests and patient mortality.

Note: This requirement has a one-year phase-in period that includes defined expectations for planning, development, and testing ("milestones") at 3, 6, and 9 months in 2008, with the expectation of full implementation by January 1, 2009.

1. As of April 1, 2008, the organization's leadership has assigned responsibility for oversight and coordination of the development, testing, and implementation of NPSG Requirement 16A.
2. As of July 1, 2008, an implementation work plan is in place that identifies adequate resources, assigned accountabilities, and a time line for full implementation of NPSG Requirement 16A by January 1, 2009.
3. As of October 1, 2008, pilot testing in at least one clinical unit is under way.
4. As of January 1, 2009, the process is fully implemented across the organization.

The Implementation Expectations that will apply beginning January 1, 2009, are provided below.

Implementation Expectations for Requirement 16A

1. The organization selects an early recognition and response method most suitable for its needs and resources.
2. The organization develops criteria for calling additional assistance to respond to a change in patient's condition or perception of change by the staff, patients, and/or families.
3. The organization empowers staff, patients, and/or families to request additional assistance when they have a concern about the patient's condition.
4. Formal education for urgent response policies and practices is conducted with the people who may request assistance and the people who may respond to those requests.
5. The organization measures the utility and effectiveness of the intervention(s) employed.
6. The organization measures cardiopulmonary arrest, respiratory arrest, and mortality rates before and after implementation of an early intervention plan.

Table 19-1. Sentinel Event Alerts

Issue	Date	Topic
1	Feb 27, 1998	Medication Error Prevention—Potassium Chloride
2	Mar 20, 1998	Board to Review Modifications to Sentinel Event Procedures
3	May 1, 1998	Board Approves Changes to Sentinel Event Policy and Procedures
4	May 11, 1998	Accreditation Committee Approves Examples of Voluntarily Reportable Sentinel Events
5	Jul 24, 1998	Board Approves Changes to Sentinel Event Policy and Procedures
6	Aug 28, 1998	Lessons Learned: Wrong-Site Surgery
7	Nov 6, 1998	Inpatient Suicides: Recommendations for Prevention
8	Nov 18, 1998	Preventing Restraint Deaths
9	Apr 9, 1999	Infant Abductions: Preventing Future Occurrences
10	Aug 30, 1999	Blood Transfusion Errors: Preventing Future Occurrences
11	Nov 19, 1999	High-Alert Medications and Patient Safety
12	Feb 4, 2000	Operative and Postoperative Complications: Lessons for the Future
13	Apr 21, 2000	Making an Impact on Health Care
14	Jul 12, 2000	Fatal Falls: Lessons for the Future
15	Nov 30, 2000	Infusion Pumps: Preventing Future Adverse Events
16	Feb 27, 2001	Mix-Up Leads to a Medication Error
17	Mar 20, 2001	Lessons Learned: Fires in the Home Care Setting
18	Apr 2001	Kernicterus Threatens Healthy Newborns
19	May 2001	Look-Alike, Sound-Alike Drug Names
20	Jun 2001	Exposure to Creutzfeldt-Jakob Disease
21	Jul 2001	Medical Gas Mix-Ups
22	Aug 2001	Preventing Needlestick and Sharps Injuries
23	Sep 2001	Medication Errors Related to Potentially Dangerous Abbreviations
24	Dec 5, 2001	A Follow-Up Review of Wrong-Site Surgery
25	Feb 26, 2002	Preventing Ventilator-Related Deaths and Injuries
26	Jun 17, 2002	Delays in Treatment
27	Sep 6, 2002	Bed Rail–Related Entrapment Deaths
28	Jan 22, 2003	Infection Control Related Sentinel Events
29	Jun 24, 2003	Preventing Surgical Fires
30	Jul 21, 2004	Preventing Infant Death and Injury During Delivery
31	Aug 31, 2004	Revised Guidance to Help Prevent Kernicterus
32	Oct 6, 2004	Preventing, and Managing the Impact of, Anesthesia Awareness
33	Dec 20, 2004	Patient Controlled Analgesia by Proxy
34	Jul 14, 2005	Preventing Vincristine Administration Errors
35	Jan 15, 2006	Using Medication Reconciliation to Prevent Errors
36	Apr 3, 2006	Tubing Misconnections—A Persistent and Potentially Dangerous Occurrence
37	Sep 6, 2006	Preventing Adverse Events Caused by Emergency Electrical Power Failures

Source: Adapted from www.jointcommission.org/SentinelEvents/SentinelEventAlert/. Accessed August 2, 2007.

National Patient Safety Goals Checklists

Health care professionals who understand the Joint Commission's National Patient Safety Goals (NPSGs) and the accreditation process should be able to achieve continuous compliance with the goals if they use a well-organized approach. The checklists in this chapter present the 2008 goals and requirements for hospitals in a format that promotes understanding, provides an organized approach to implementing the goals, and helps foster continuous compliance. This chapter contains the following checklists:

2008 NPSG 1	Improve the accuracy of patient identification
2008 NPSG 2	Improve the effectiveness of communication among caregivers
2008 NPSG 3	Improve the safety of using medications
2008 NPSG 7	Reduce the risk of health care–associated infections
2008 NPSG 8	Accurately and completely reconcile medications across the continuum of care
2008 NPSG 9	Reduce the risk of patient harm resulting from falls
2008 NPSG 13	Encourage patients' active involvement in their own care as a patient safety strategy
2008 NPSG 15	The organization identifies safety risks inherent in its patient population
2008 NPSG 16	Improve recognition and response to changes in a patient's condition

The checklists address only the goals and requirements that are applicable to hospitals. They do not address goals and requirements that are only applicable to other accreditation programs and goals that have been retired. For example:

- Requirement 3A (for NPSG 3) relating to the storage of concentrated electrolytes on patient care units was retired effective January 1, 2006 and is no longer an NPSG. (*See* EP 9 for MM.2.20 in Chapter 4.)
- Requirement 3B (for NPSG 3) relating to standardizing and limiting the number of drug concentrations used by the organization was retired effective January 1, 2008 and is no longer an NPSG. (*See* EP 10 for MM.2.20 in Chapter 4.)
- NPSGs 10 thorough 14 are not applicable to hospitals.

NPSGs for other accreditation programs are available in the accreditation manual for each program and on the Joint Commission's Internet Web site. (*See* Appendix A.)

Checklist items that reflect the authors' comments, experiences, and suggestions; reports from surveyed organizations; and surveyors' statements are noted with an asterisk. References and resources are in the References and Resources section of this book.

Because the NPSG requirements and survey expectations may change, organizations should check regularly for updates. NPSGs for 2009 and subsequent years are expected to be announced during the year before they become effective. (*See* Chapter 19.) The Joint Commission's Internet Web site (*see* Appendix A), *Joint Commission Perspectives*®, and *Joint Commission Perspectives on Patient Safety*™ are the best sources for updates on NPSG requirements and survey expectations.

> ***Note:*** Organizations should determine if the Joint Commission has published acceptable alternatives to the requirements in the checklists. (*See* Chapter 19.)

> ***Note:*** Organizations should refer to the Joint Commission's Internet Web site for answers to frequently asked questions (FAQs) about the requirements. (*See* Appendix A.)

Using the Checklist

To assess compliance, use the checklist and proceed systematically. Mark the item "Yes" if you are currently compliant and will continue to be compliant. Mark the item "No" if you are currently not compliant (even if you are sure you will be compliant later). If you are not sure of your answer, leave a blank response. A few items may be not applicable ("NA"). Answer honestly, use a pencil (so you can change your answers), and make notes on the pages (e.g., reasons for noncompliance). Concentrate your efforts on resolving all "No" and blank responses.

CHECKLIST FOR 2008 NPSG 1

Goal 1. Improve the Accuracy of Patient Identification

Requirement 1A

Use at least two patient identifiers when providing care, treatment, or services.

Rationale for Requirement 1A

Wrong-patient errors occur in virtually all aspects of diagnosis and treatment. The intent for this goal is twofold; first, to reliably identify the individual as the person for whom the service or treatment is intended; second to match the service or treatment to that individual.

Implementation Expectations for Requirement 1A

1. Two patient identifiers are used when administering medications or blood products.
2. Two patient identifiers are used when collecting blood samples and other specimens for clinical testing.
3. Two patient identifiers are used when providing other treatments or procedures.
4. The patient's room number or physical location is not used as an identifier.
5. Containers used for blood and other specimens are labeled in the presence of the patient.

Note: Organizations should refer to the Joint Commission's Internet Web site for answers to frequently asked questions (FAQs) about this requirement. (*See* Appendix A.)

Note: Organizations should determine if the Joint Commission has published acceptable alternatives to the requirements for this goal. (*See* Chapter 19.)

Source: Joint Commission. *Perspectives.* Oakbrook Terrace, IL; Joint Commission: 2007;27(7):10–9.

Checklist items that reflect the authors' comments, experiences, and suggestions; reports from surveyed organizations; and surveyors' statements are noted with an asterisk. References and resources are in the References and Resources section of this book.

Authors' Comments, Experiences, and Suggestions

	Yes	NA	No
The organization uses at least two patient identifiers whenever			
• administering medications[1]	____	____	____
• administering blood products[1]	____	____	____
• collecting blood samples[1]	____	____	____
• collecting other specimens for clinical testing[1]	____	____	____
• providing other treatments or procedures[1]	____	____	____

Note: For the purpose of its standards, the Joint Commission states that the term "*medication* includes prescription medications, sample medications, herbal remedies, vitamins, nutraceuticals, over-the-counter drugs, vaccines, diagnostic and contrast agents used on or administered to persons to diagnose, treat, or prevent disease or other abnormal conditions; radioactive

	Yes	NA	No

medications; respiratory therapy treatments; parenteral nutrition; blood derivatives; intravenous solutions (plain, with electrolytes and/or drugs); and any product designated by the Food and Drug Administration (FDA) as a drug. The definition of *medication* does not include enteral nutrition solutions (which are considered food products), oxygen, and other medical gases."[2]

Note: The Joint Commission states that the two identifier requirement also applies to delivering special diets and snacks associated with special diets.[3]

Note: The Joint Commission states that the two identifier requirement also applies to reporting critical test results.[3]

Note: The Joint Commission states that the two identifier requirement also applies to writing orders for treatment (including computerized prescriber order entry).[3]

	Yes	NA	No
Neither identifier is the patient's room number.[1]	____	____	____
Neither identifier is the patient's physical location.[1]	____	____	____
The two patient identifiers are patient-specific (i.e., directly associated with the patient).[3]	____	____	____
If the organization uses more than two identifiers, at least two of the identifiers are patient-specific.*	____	____	____
Staff can state the organization's two patient-specific identifiers.*	____	____	____

Note: Organizations frequently use the patient's name, an identification number that is specific to the patient (e.g., billing or medical record number), and the patient's date of birth. Surveyors have suggested that other acceptable patient-specific identifiers might include the patient's social security number, driver's license number, telephone number, and home address (although the latter two are not always specific to the patient). Organizations should consider using biometric recognition techniques (e.g., fingerprint and retinal scans) as technology develops, reliability improves, and the cost of equipment and implementation becomes affordable.*

Note: Surveyors also point out that identifiers may be in the same place (e.g., written on the patient's wristband and/or contained in a bar code on the patient's wristband). For example, a single bar code that contains two or more patient-specific identifiers (e.g., name, identification number, and date of birth) meets the requirement.[3]

Note: The Joint Commission does not require the use of wristbands for identification. If wristbands are used, they must be attached to the patient at all times. Wristbands must not be attached to the bed or lie at the bedside.[3]

	Yes	NA	No
The two patient identifiers are directly associated with the medication, blood product, blood sample, specimen, treatment, or procedure (e.g., on the medication administration record or on an attached label).[3]	____	____	____

Note: The requirement states that the *patient* must be identified using two patient-specific identifiers. The Joint Commission does not require *medications* to

	Yes	NA	No
be labeled with two patient identifiers. However, the authors suggest that medication labels, IV labels, and medication bin/drawer labels include the two identifiers to the extent practical. However, labeling unit-dose packaged medications and medications in automated medication storage and distribution devices with two identifiers might not be possible.*			
Note: Many organizations enter the two patient identifiers on the medication administration record (MAR). Some surveyors expect this. Before administering the medication, nurses (1) match the two identifiers on the MAR with the two identifiers on the patient's wristband and then (2) match the order on the MAR with the medication to be administered.*			
The *same* two patient identifiers are used throughout the *same* setting (i.e., not necessarily throughout the organization).[3]	____	____	____
If *different* patient identifiers are used in *different* settings within the organization,			
• The identifiers are consistent in each setting.[3]	____	____	____
• Use of the identifiers meets the intent of the requirement.[3]	____	____	____
If *different* patient identifiers are used for different *processes* (e.g., name and birth date for the laboratory and name and patient number for medication administration), all of the following should be in place:			
• Their use is specified in the organization's policy.	____	____	____
• Their use is followed consistently for each process.	____	____	____
• Identifiers are not switched on a patient-by-patient basis for the same process.	____	____	____
• Different individuals do not use different identifiers for the same process.	____	____	____
• Patients display all of the identifiers used for all processes (e.g., name, birth date, and patient identification number).[4]	____	____	____
Containers used for blood are labeled in the presence of the patient.[1]	____	____	____
Containers used for other specimens are labeled in the presence of the patient.[1]	____	____	____
Note: The Joint Commission states that the most reliable way to match the patient to the blood or other specimen is to label the containers at the time of collection in the presence of the patient. Prelabeling and batch processing can lead to misidentification errors.[3]			

Visual Identification of Patients

Home care surveyors state that visual identification of the patient may be allowed in some home care settings. However, the surveyors insist that two patient-specific identifiers be used when caregivers first meet the patient. After the patient is well-known to the caregivers, they may use visual identification in place of *one* of the patient-specific identifiers. Caregivers in home care settings should contact the Joint Commission to confirm that visual identification, as described here, is permitted in their practice.[3]

	Yes	NA	No
Behavioral health surveyors state that visual identification of the patient may be allowed in some behavioral health care settings (e.g., those with low turnover of patients and staff). Surveyors caution that two patient-specific identifiers must be used when administering high-risk medications (i.e., visual identification can not be one of the identifiers). Organizations should contact the Joint Commission to confirm that visual identification, as described here, is permitted in their organization.[3]			
Some surveyors recommend that the patient's photo be readily available to help staff recognize the patient.*			
The organization should specify which medications are high risk and state in their policies that high-risk medications require the use of two patient-specific identifiers.*			

Emergency Identification of Patients

In emergencies and other situations when patients are not able to communicate with their caregivers, some organizations assign emergency patient-specific identifiers. One or both of the identifiers may be temporary (e.g., a temporary name if the patient is unknown and a temporary number if there is no medical record or emergency department number).[3]

Education and Competence

	Yes	NA	No
The organization provides education and training relating to using patient identifiers.*	____	____	____
The organization assesses the competence of individuals who use patient identifiers.*	____	____	____

Monitoring and Enforcement

	Yes	NA	No
The organization monitors compliance with policies and procedures relating to using patient identifiers.*	____	____	____
The organization enforces policies and procedures relating to using patient identifiers.*	____	____	____

Process Improvement

	Yes	NA	No
The organization identifies ways to improve the patient identification process.*	____	____	____
The organization acts as necessary to improve the patient identification process.*	____	____	____

Required Documentation

No specific form or document is required. No required documentation has been published.*

Suggested Documentation or Evidence of Compliance

	Yes	NA	No
Two patient identifiers on the medication administration record match the two identifiers used to identify the patient (e.g., on the patient's wristband).*	____	____	____
Medications and patient medication drawers are labeled with the two organization-required identifiers.*	____	____	____
Blood products, blood samples, and other specimens for clinical testing are labeled with the two organization-required identifiers.*	____	____	____

	Yes	NA	No
Suggested Measurement Indicators (Performance Trackers)			
Number of patients with appropriate identifiers on wristbands *divided by* number of patients audited during the period.*	___	___	___
Number of patients who confirm that staff checked their wristbands and asked them to state their name and date of birth (or other organization-approved patient identifiers) before administering medications or blood products, taking blood samples or other specimens for clinical testing, or providing any other treatments or procedures *divided by* number of patients audited during the period.*	___	___	___
Surveyor Expectations			
Surveyors may do the following:			
• Look for a 12-month history of continuous compliance.*	___	___	___
• Review policies and procedures relating to patient identification and the use of patient identifiers.*	___	___	___
• Review how the organization chose its two patient identifiers.*	___	___	___
• Determine if the two patient identifiers are patient-specific.*	___	___	___
• Determine if staff complies with policies and procedures relating to the use of two patient identifiers.*	___	___	___
• Observe medication administration in nursing and other patient care areas. (Surveyors expect staff to take MARs to the bedside to verify the patient's identity and the medication to be administered.)*	___	___	___
• Look for consistent application of the two identifiers in non-nursing units where medications are administered (e.g., respiratory, imaging, and nuclear medicine).*	___	___	___
• Talk with staff about the patient identifier process.*	___	___	___

Example Surveyors' Questions

What two patient identifiers do you use?*

Do other areas in the organization use different identifiers?*

What is your procedure for checking identifiers?*

What do you do when a patient is unresponsive?*

Do you take the MAR with you when you administer medications?*

What is your process for labeling containers used for blood and other specimens?*

CHECKLIST FOR 2008 NPSG 2

Goal 2. Improve the Effectiveness of Communication among Caregivers

Requirement 2A

For verbal or telephone orders or for telephonic reporting of critical test results, verify the complete order or test result by having the person receiving the information record and "read-back" the complete order or test result.

Rationale for Requirement 2A

Ineffective communication is the most frequently cited category of root causes of sentinel events. Effective communication, which is timely, accurate, complete, unambiguous, and understood by the recipient, reduces error and results in improved patient safety.

Implementation Expectations for Requirement 2A

1. The receiver of the information **writes** down the complete order or test result or enters it into a computer.
2. The receiver of the information **reads** back the order or test result.
3. The receiver of the information **receives** confirmation from the individual who gave the order or test result.

Note: Organizations should refer to the Joint Commission's Internet Web site for answers to frequently asked questions (FAQs) about this requirement. (*See* Appendix A.)

Note: Organizations should determine if the Joint Commission has published acceptable alternatives to the requirements for this goal. (*See* Chapter 19.)

Source: Joint Commission. *Perspectives.* Oakbrook Terrace, IL; Joint Commission: 2007;27(7):10–9.

Checklist items that reflect the authors' comments, experiences, and suggestions; reports from surveyed organizations; and surveyors' statements are noted with an asterisk. References and resources are in the References and Resources section of this book.

Authors' Comments, Experiences, and Suggestions	Yes	NA	No
See EP 4 for IM.6.50.			
For verbal orders the person receiving the order writes the order on the final document (e.g., an order form) and verifies the complete order by reading back the complete order.[1]	___	___	___
For telephone orders the person receiving the order writes the order on the final document (e.g., an order form) and verifies the complete order by reading back the complete order.[1]	___	___	___
For telephonic reporting of critical test results the person receiving the test result writes the test result on the final document and verifies the test result by reading back the complete test result.[1]	___	___	___
The organization has a written process for taking verbal or telephone orders or critical test results.*	___	___	___

	Yes	NA	No
The organization's policies and procedures *discourage* the use of verbal and telephone orders. (Joint Commission standards do not *prohibit* the use of verbal and telephone orders.)*	___	___	___
The process applies to *all* verbal and telephone orders. (The requirement is not limited to orders for medications.)*	___	___	___
Note: Surveyors state that critical test results are those requiring immediate action (e.g., stat tests and reports of panic values). They include results from laboratory, imaging, and all services that conduct tests. Many organizations extend the requirement to include *all* test results (i.e., not just critical results). Surveyors also say they are expected to consider all test results critical if the organization has not defined critical results in writing.*			
Note: The readback requirement applies to the food service department when taking verbal or telephone orders from nursing service.[2]			
The organization's process requires the person who receives the order or test result to read it back verbatim (i.e., exactly as written) to the person who gave it to verify that the order or test result was received *and written* correctly.[2]	___	___	___
Note: A repeat back is not the same as a read back. To read back an order or test result, it must first be written on paper or entered into a computer. Reading the order back while it is being written is a repeat back and does not meet the requirement.[2]			
Note: The use of *well-designed*, preprinted order forms or forms for taking verbal or telephone orders or critical test results makes it easier to write the order or test result on paper and can reduce errors. The same format for all preprinted order forms should be used throughout the organization.*			
The person who gives the verbal or telephone order or test result confirms the correctness of the read-back and clarifies the order or test result if necessary.[2]	___	___	___
Note: Although this is not explicit in the requirement, some surveyors state that the organization's process must specify that confirmation of the read-back is required. Staff who give orders or test results should request a read back.*			
Note: The use of voice mail does not meet the intent of the requirement. When orders or test results are left on a voice mail message, the person who receives it must (1) call the person who gave it, (2) receive the order directly, (3) read it back to the person who gave it, and (4) receive verbal confirmation that the order or test result was written correctly.[2]			
When a verbal or telephone order or test result cannot be written directly into a medical record or entered into a computer, it is written on a separate piece of paper and read back to the prescriber. (Orders and test results transcribed from this paper must be verified against what is written on the paper. Orders and test results should be written directly into a medical record or entered into a computer when possible.)[3]	___	___	___

	Yes	NA	No
Note: Organizations should eliminate transcription of orders and test results to the extent possible. Order forms should be available to pharmacists and pharmacists should enter orders directly on the order form. After reading an order back to the prescriber, the pharmacist should take the order form to the patient care area, place it in the patient's medical record, and ensure that appropriate patient care staff in the area are aware of the new order.*			
The organization specifies persons who are permitted to give and receive verbal or telephone orders or test results and requires that they be qualified. (The number of persons should be limited and the persons must be educated, trained, and deemed competent.)*	____	____	____
Note: The person receiving the order must be a designated, qualified individual who is authorized to accept verbal or telephone orders.[2]			
Note: Persons who are allowed to give and receive verbal or telephone orders or test results are often specified in medical staff bylaws, rules, and regulations. Pharmacists and other health care personnel should review these documents to determine if they are authorized to give and receive verbal or telephone orders or test results.*			
Persons who receive verbal or telephone orders or test results sign them and note the time and date received. (*See* Centers for Medicare and Medicaid Services requirements in §482.23(c)(2) in Chapter 24.)*	____	____	____
Note: The Joint Commission does not require persons who receive a verbal or telephone order or test result to document their read-back to the prescriber. If an organization requires a read-back to be documented, the Joint Commission expects individuals to comply with their organization's requirements.[2]			
Persons who give verbal or telephone orders verify them with their signature and date of verification. (The organization's policies must set the time period for verifying the order. The time period must be consistent with state and other regulations.)*	____	____	____
The organization has a process for ensuring that persons who give verbal or telephone orders verify, sign, and date them. (This process often includes flagging orders that require verification and informing these persons that orders are awaiting their verification.)*	____	____	____
Note: Organizations can improve the accuracy of verbal and telephone orders and help ensure their accuracy and clarity by following the recommendations of the National Coordinating Council for Medication Error Reporting and Prevention (NCCMERP). (*See* Table 20-1.)[4]			
Note: If necessary, words should be spelled using a phonetic alphabet (e.g., alpha for a, bravo for b, charlie for c, etc.) and numbers should be pronounced individually (e.g., one five for 15). Many military organizations, airlines, pilots, telecommunications organizations, and businesses have adopted the North Atlantic Treaty Organization (NATO) Phonetic Alphabet and Phonetic Numbers in Table 20-2. Health care organizations should consider standardizing their phonetic alphabet and numbers. They may adopt the NATO version or use it to help them develop a standard phonetic alphabet and numbers of their own. A number of phonetic alphabets are available on the Internet by searching for "Phonetic Alphabet."*			

	Yes	NA	No

Read Back in Emergency Situations

Surveyors state that writing orders or test results on paper or entering them in a computer may not be practical in emergency situations where time is of essence (e.g., during a code or when performing sterile surgical procedures) . Nevertheless, accuracy is essential in these situations. Surveyors suggest that if a read-back is not practical or impossible, persons who receive orders or test results may *repeat* them back instead of *reading* them back to the person who gave the order. When possible, the person who gave the order or test result should verbally confirm the repeat back.[2]

Education and Competence

	Yes	NA	No
The organization provides education and training relating to taking verbal or telephone orders or critical test results.*			
The organization assesses the competence of individuals who take verbal or telephone orders or critical test results.*			

Monitoring and Enforcement

	Yes	NA	No
The organization monitors compliance with policies and procedures relating to taking verbal or telephone orders or critical test results. (The Joint Commission does not require a specific monitoring method.)*			
The organization enforces policies and procedures relating to taking verbal or telephone orders or critical test results.*			

Process Improvement

	Yes	NA	No
The organization identifies ways to improve the process for taking verbal or telephone orders or critical test results.*			
The organization acts as necessary to improve the process for taking verbal or telephone orders or critical test results.*			

Required Documentation

No specific form or document is required. No required documentation has been published.*

Suggested Documentation or Evidence of Compliance

	Yes	NA	No
A record that tracks the organization's compliance with the requirement.*			
If the organization's policies require specific documentation that verbal or telephone orders or critical test results were read back (e.g., by noting RBV on patient records for read back of verbal orders), such documentation is available.*			

Suggested Measurement Indicators (Performance Trackers)

	Yes	NA	No
Number of staff responding appropriately to questions about verbal orders (including read back) *divided by* number of staff audited.*			
Number of patient records documenting compliance with the read-back requirement *divided by* number of patient records audited.*			

	Yes	NA	No
Surveyor Expectations			
Surveyors may do the following:			
• Look for a 12-month history of continuous compliance.*	___	___	___
• Review policies and procedures relating to verbal or telephone orders or critical test results.*	___	___	___
• Determine how policies and procedures limit verbal or telephone orders or critical test results.*	___	___	___
• Review how the organization developed its policies and procedures relating to verbal or telephone orders or critical test results.*	___	___	___
• Review how the organization monitors the read-back process.*	___	___	___
• Review how the organization ensures compliance with the read-back process.*	___	___	___
• Observe staff taking verbal and telephone orders.*	___	___	___
• Determine if staff complies with the read-back process.*	___	___	___
• Talk with staff about processes for verbal or telephone orders or critical test results.*	___	___	___

Example Surveyors' Questions

How often do you take verbal or telephone orders or critical test results?*

What happens when a physician is on the unit and gives a verbal order?*

Do you document the read-back of verbal or telephone orders or critical test results?*

Who takes phones calls from the laboratory concerning panic values?*

How do you record and verify verbal orders during a code or emergency situation?*

CHECKLIST FOR 2008 NPSG 2

Goal 2. Improve the Effectiveness of Communication among Caregivers

Requirement 2B

Standardize a list of abbreviations, acronyms, symbols, and dose designations that are not to be used throughout the organization.

Implementation Expectations for Requirement 2B

1. The organization develops a standardized a list of abbreviations, acronyms, symbols, and dose designations that are not to be used throughout the organization.
2. The list of abbreviations not to be used includes the following:
   - U,u
   - IU
   - Q.D., QD, q.d., qd
   - Q.O.D., QOD, q.o.d., qod
   - Trailing zero (X.0 mg)*
   - Lack of leading zero (.X mg)
   - MS
   - MSO4
   - MgSO4

   ***Exception:** A "trailing zero" may be used only where required to demonstrate the level of precision of the value being reported, such as for laboratory results, imaging studies that report size of lesions, or catheter/tube sizes. It may not be used in medication orders or other medication-related documentation.
3. The organization implements the "do not use" list and applies this list to all orders and all medication-related documentation when handwritten or entered as free text into a computer.
4. Preprinted forms do not include any abbreviations identified as not to be used.

Note: Organizations should refer to the Joint Commission's Internet Web site for answers to frequently asked questions (FAQs) about this requirement. (*See* Appendix A.)

Note: Organizations should determine if the Joint Commission has published acceptable alternatives to the requirements for this goal. (*See* Chapter 19.)

Source: Joint Commission. *Perspectives.* Oakbrook Terrace, IL; Joint Commission: 2007;27(7):10–9.

Checklist items that reflect the authors' comments, experiences, and suggestions; reports from surveyed organizations; and surveyors' statements are noted with an asterisk. References and resources are in the References and Resources section of this book.

	Yes	NA	No
Authors' Comments, Experiences, and Suggestions			
The organization has standardized a list of abbreviations, acronyms, symbols, and dose designations that are not to be used throughout the organization (i.e., a "Do Not Use" list).[1] *(See* EP 2 for IM.3.10.)	___	___	___

	Yes	NA	No
Note: The term *dose designations* refers to units of measurement (e.g., "unit" or "International Unit") and frequency of dose administration (e.g., "daily" or "every 4 hours").[2]			
Note: Some organizations also develop a list of approved or acceptable abbreviations and other items (i.e., a "May Use" list). The Joint Commission does not require such a list. Organizations that chose to develop a "May Use" list must also develop a "Do Not Use" list.[2]			
Note: The development of the "Do Not Use" list should be interdisciplinary (i.e., have participation of pharmacists, nurses, physicians, and other health care providers). (An interdisciplinary effort fosters greater acceptance of the items on the list.)*			
The organization's "Do Not Use" list includes the items listed in the implementation requirements.[1]	___	___	___
Note: The abbreviations on the "Do Not Use" list cannot be used in any of their forms (e.g., upper case, lower case, and with or without periods).[2]			
Note: The organization's "Do Not Use" list may include additional items of the organization's own choosing.*			
Note: The Joint Commission publishes a list of additional abbreviations, acronyms, and symbols for *possible* future inclusion in the Official "Do Not Use" List. (*See* Table 20-4.) The Institute for Safe Medication Practices (ISMP) publishes a list of error-prone abbreviations, symbols, and dose designations that should be prohibited. This list is available on the ISMP Internet Web site. (*See* Appendix A.)*			
The "Do Not Use" list is consistent throughout the organization.*	___	___	___
The organization implements the "do not use" list and applies this list to all orders and all medication-related documentation when handwritten or entered as free text into a computer.[1]	___	___	___
Note: This includes progress notes, consultation reports, and discharge summaries that contain medication-related documentation.[2]			
Preprinted forms do not include any items that are on the "Do Not Use" list.[1]	___	___	___
Note: Organizations must work with their print and electronic suppliers/providers to ensure they eliminate items on the "Do Not Use" list. Organizations should review their printed orders (including protocols, standing orders, and routine orders) and eliminate *all* abbreviations. Abbreviations are seldom, if ever, necessary on printed orders.*			
The organization has an aggressive program for eliminating the use of items on its "Do Not Use" list (e.g., posting the list, printing the list on order forms, educating and training staff, rewards for staff who do not use items on the list, and inclusion in the organization's competence assessment program). (*See* Examples 20-1, 20-2, and 20-3.)*	___	___	___

	Yes	NA	No
Note: The Joint Commission states that it is not the responsibility of nurses and pharmacists to manage the behavior of prescribers. The Joint Commission's standards assign that responsibility to the medical staff.[2]			
Note: Contracted services must not use the terms on the organization's "Do Not Use" list.[2]			
Pharmacists, nurses, and others who receive orders containing items on the "Do Not Use" list must contact the prescriber for clarification and confirmation of the item (if clarification and confirmation is necessary).[2]	___	___	___
Note: Surveyors state that if an order containing an item on the "Do Not Use" list is clear and complete but any delay in confirming the item increases the risk to the patient, staff should carry out the order and confirm the unacceptable item as soon as possible. Before carrying out the order, staff should consult with pharmacists, nurses, and others who can help clarify the order.*			
The organization tracks its performance in eliminating the use of items on its "Do Not Use" list.*	___	___	___
Education and Competence			
The organization provides education and training relating to standardization of abbreviations, acronyms, and symbols and avoiding the use of items on the organization's "Do Not Use" list.*	___	___	___
The organization assesses the competence of individuals relating to the use of items on the organization's "Do Not Use" list.*	___	___	___
Monitoring and Enforcement			
The organization monitors compliance with policies and procedures relating to the use of items on the "Do Not Use" list.*	___	___	___
The organization enforces policies and procedures relating to the use of items on the "Do Not Use" list.*	___	___	___
The organization monitors its process for responding to unclear orders.[2]	___	___	___
Process Improvement			
The organization identifies ways to improve performance relating to the use of items on the "Do Not Use" list.*	___	___	___
The organization acts as necessary to improve performance relating to the use of items on the "Do Not Use" list.*	___	___	___

Required Documentation

No specific form or document is required. No required documentation has been published.*

	Yes	NA	No
Suggested Documentation or Evidence of Compliance			
A "Do Not Use" list that includes items required by the Joint Commission*	___	___	___
Performance tracking records showing no use of items on the "Do Not Use" list.*	___	___	___
Records showing that when orders are not clear, prescribers confirmed the meaning of items on the "Do Not Use" list (either in the original order or pursuant to a call-back from the person who received the order.)*	___	___	___
Suggested Measurement Indicators (Performance Trackers)			
Number and percentage of unacceptable occurrences. (Example 20-4 is a monitoring form that includes measurement indicators that surveyors have used in the past.)*	___	___	___
Surveyor Expectations			
Surveyors may do the following:			
• Look for a 12-month history of continuous compliance.*	___	___	___
• Review policies and procedures relating to the "Do Not Use" list.*	___	___	___
• Review the organization's "Do Not Use" list.*	___	___	___
• Review orders and other documents to determine if staff complies with the "Do Not Use" list.*	___	___	___
• Talk with staff about the "Do Not Use" list.*	___	___	___
• Review how the organization monitors compliance with its "Do Not Use" list.*	___	___	___

Example Surveyors' Questions

What abbreviations and other items are prohibited?*

How did you determine the additional items that must not be used?*

What do you do when you receive an order with an unacceptable items?*

How do you clarify emergency orders that must be carried out prior to confirmation by the prescriber?*

What other abbreviations and items are problems in your organization?*

CHECKLIST FOR 2008 NPSG 2

Goal 2. Improve the Effectiveness of Communication among Caregivers

Requirement 2C

Measure, assess, and if appropriate, take action to improve the timeliness of reporting, and the timeliness of receipt by the responsible licensed caregiver, of critical tests and critical results and values.

Implementation Expectations for Requirement 2C

1. The organization defines critical tests and critical results and values.
2. The organization defines the acceptable length of time between the ordering of critical tests and reporting the critical tests and critical results and values.
3. The organization defines the acceptable length of time between the availability of critical tests and critical results and values and receipt by the responsible licensed care giver.
4. The organization collects data on the timeliness of reporting critical tests and critical results and values.
5. The organization assesses the data and determines whether there is a need for improvement.
6. The organization takes appropriate action to improve and measure the effectiveness of those actions.

Note: Organizations should refer to the Joint Commission's Internet Web site for answers to frequently asked questions (FAQs) about this requirement. (*See* Appendix A.)

Note: Organizations should determine if the Joint Commission has published acceptable alternatives to the requirements for this goal. (*See* Chapter 19.)

Source: Joint Commission. *Perspectives.* Oakbrook Terrace, IL; Joint Commission: 2007;27(7):10–9.

Checklist items that reflect the authors' comments, experiences, and suggestions; reports from surveyed organizations; and surveyors' statements are noted with an asterisk. References and resources are in the References and Resources section of this book.

Authors' Comments, Experiences, and Suggestions	Yes	NA	No
The organization defines critical tests and critical results and values.[1]	____	____	____

Note: This requirement addresses both critical tests and the results of critical tests. Critical tests are those for which the results always require rapid communication. Critical results are findings for which rapid communication is warranted. Organizations need to make these distinctions.[2]

Note: The term *critical test results* applies to all diagnostic tests including imaging studies, electrocardiograms, laboratory tests and other diagnostic tests defined by the organization as "critical."[2]

	Yes	NA	No
The organization defines the acceptable length of time between the ordering of critical tests and reporting the critical tests and critical results and values.[1]	___	___	___

Note: The organization must establish by policy what the expected turn-around time is from the time ordered until the time reported.[2]

The organization defines the acceptable length of time between the availability of critical tests and critical results and values and receipt by the responsible licensed care giver.[1]	___	___	___

Note: The organization must establish by policy what the expected turn-around time is from the time available until the time received.[2]

Note: Reports may be made to an authorized agent of the responsible licensed caregiver provided "the organization can demonstrate that there will be no significant additional delays in getting the test result to the responsible licensed caregiver so that the patient can be promptly treated."[2]

The organization collects data on the timeliness of reporting critical tests and critical results and values.[1]	___	___	___

Note: The organization must collect data that can be compared with its defined turn-around times.*

The organization assesses the data and determines whether there is a need for improvement.[1]	___	___	___

Note: The organization must compare the collected data with its defined turn-around times.*

The organization takes appropriate action to improve and measure the effectiveness of those actions.[1]	___	___	___

Note: The organization does not need to collect data, measure, assess, and improve all critical tests and all critical results at all times. The organization may focus on selected tests and categories and then shift its focus to other tests and categories.[2]

Education and Competence

The organization provides education and training relating to improving the timeliness of reporting of critical test results and values.*	___	___	___
The organization provides education and training relating to improving the timeliness of receipt by the responsible licensed caregiver of critical test results and values.*	___	___	___
The organization assesses the competence of individuals who report critical test results and values.*	___	___	___
The organization assesses the competence of individuals who receive critical test results and values.*	___	___	___

	Yes	NA	No
Monitoring and Enforcement			
The organization monitors compliance with policies and procedures relating to the timeliness of reporting and receipt of critical test results and values.*	____	____	____
The organization enforces policies and procedures relating to the timeliness of reporting and receipt of critical test results and values.*	____	____	____
Process Improvement			
The organization identifies ways to improve the timeliness of reporting and receipt of critical test results and values.*	____	____	____
The organization acts as necessary to improve the timeliness of reporting and receipt of critical test results and values.*	____	____	____
Required Documentation			
No specific form or document is required. No required documentation has been published.*	____	____	____
Suggested Documentation or Evidence of Compliance			
Time of reporting of critical test results and values is documented and within the acceptable limits.*	____	____	____
Time of receipt of critical test results and values is documented and within the acceptable limits.*	____	____	____
Suggested Measurement Indicators (Performance Trackers)			
Number of records documenting compliance with the requirements for reporting critical test results and values *divided by* number of records audited during the period.*	____	____	____
Number of records documenting compliance with the requirements for receiving critical test results and values *divided by* number of records audited during the period.*	____	____	____
Surveyor Expectations			
Surveyors may do the following:			
• Look for a 12-month history of continuous compliance.*	____	____	____
• Review policies and procedures relating to the timeliness of reporting and receipt of critical test results and values.*	____	____	____
• Determine if the organization has defined critical test results and values.*	____	____	____
• Determine if staff complies with policies and procedures relating to the timeliness of reporting and receipt of critical test results and values.*	____	____	____
• Review how the staff monitors its processes relating to the timeliness of reporting and receipt of critical test results and values.*	____	____	____
• Determine if the organization has taken action to improve the timeliness of reporting of critical test results and values.*	____	____	____

	Yes	NA	No
• Determine if the organization has taken action to improve the timeliness of receipt of critical test results and values.*	___	___	___
• Talk with staff about the timeliness of reporting and receipt of critical test results and values.*	___	___	___

Example Surveyors' Questions

How do you ensure the timeliness of reporting of critical test results and values?*

How do you ensure the timeliness of receipt of critical test results and values?*

How do you document the reporting of critical test results and values?*

How do you document the receipt of critical test results and values?*

What have you done to improve the timeliness of reporting of critical test results and values?*

What have you done to improve the timeliness of receipt of critical test results and values?*

CHECKLIST FOR 2008 NPSG 2

Goal 2. Improve the Effectiveness of Communication among Caregivers

Requirement 2E

Implement a standardized approach to "hand-off" communications, including an opportunity to ask and respond to questions.

Rationale for Requirement 2E

The primary objective of a "hand off" is to provide accurate information about a patient's care, treatment, and services, current condition and any recent or anticipated changes. The information communicated during a hand off must be accurate in order to meet patient safety goals.

In health care there are numerous types of patient hand offs, including but not limited to nursing shift changes, physicians transferring complete responsibility for a patient, physicians transferring on-call responsibility, temporary responsibility for staff leaving the unit for a short time, anesthesiologist report to postanesthesia recovery room nurse, nursing and physician hand off from the emergency department to inpatient units, different hospitals, nursing homes and home health care, critical laboratory and radiology results sent to physician offices.

Implementation Expectations for Requirement 2E

1. The organization's process for effective "hand-off" communication includes: Interactive communications allowing for the opportunity for questioning between the giver and receiver of patient information.
2. The organization's process for effective "hand-off" communication includes: Up-to-date information regarding the patient's care, treatment and services, condition and any recent or anticipated changes.
3. The organization's process for effective "hand-off" communication includes: A process for verification of the received information, including repeat-back or read-back, as appropriate.
4. The organization's process for effective "hand-off" communication includes: An opportunity for the receiver of the hand off information to review relevant patient historical data, which may include previous care, treatment and services.
5. Interruptions during hand offs are limited to minimize the possibility that information would fail to be conveyed or would be forgotten.

Note: Organizations should refer to the Joint Commission's Internet Web site for answers to frequently asked questions (FAQs) about this requirement. (*See* Appendix A.)

Note: Organizations should determine if the Joint Commission has published acceptable alternatives to the requirements for this goal. (*See* Chapter 19.)

Source: Joint Commission. *Perspectives.* Oakbrook Terrace, IL; Joint Commission: 2007;27(7):10–9.

Checklist items that reflect the authors' comments, experiences, and suggestions; reports from surveyed organizations; and surveyors' statements are noted with an asterisk. References and resources are in the References and Resources section of this book.

	Yes	NA	No

Authors' Comments, Experiences, and Suggestions

The organization has implemented a standardized approach to hand-off communications.[1] ___ ___ ___

> ***Note:*** A standardized approach is one that is defined, communicated to staff, and implemented to ensure that information about a patient is communicated in a consistent manner. Staff must be educated about the standardized process.[2]

> ***Note:*** The standardized approach should be defined in writing and include what to communicate and how to communicate effectively, accurately, and adequately.*

> ***Note:*** The Joint Commission states that the "process may differ from one setting to another but not from unit to unit when the unit functions are essentially the same."[2]

> ***Note:*** The Joint Commission states the hand-off communication requirement applies to physician-to-physician handoffs. The process must be standardized and it must be "communicated to and understood by all those physicians who will be involved in hand-off communication." The Joint Commission provides answers to other physician-to-physician hand-off communications questions.[2]

> ***Note:*** Hand offs relating to pharmacy include from pharmacists to pharmacists, pharmacists to nurses, nurses to pharmacists, pharmacies to remote order entry facilities when pharmacies close, and remote order entry facilities to pharmacies when pharmacies reopen. (*Also see* the rationale for this requirement.)*

> ***Note:*** Hand-off communication is "required when a patient moves from an inpatient unit to radiology or other diagnostic unit."[2]

The organization's process for effective "hand-off" communication includes interactive communications allowing for the opportunity for questioning between the giver and receiver of patient information.[1] ___ ___ ___

> ***Note:*** Taped reports would not be acceptable unless there is "an opportunity to ask clarifying questions and to receive answers in a time frame that is consistent with having complete and accurate information available to the patient's caregivers when they are providing the care." The process must be interactive.[2]

> ***Note:*** Physician to physician hand-offs must include an opportunity to ask and respond to questions.[2]

> ***Note:*** Taped reports would not be acceptable unless there is "an opportunity to ask clarifying questions and to receive answers in a time frame that is consistent with having complete and accurate information available to the patient's caregivers when they are providing the care." The process must be interactive.[2]

	Yes	NA	No
Note: Hand-off communication applies to services such as "physical therapy where patients are seen only on the day shift." The Joint Commission states that the time frames may be expanded. "However, whatever method is used, there must still be an opportunity to ask and get responses to questions."[2]			
The organization's process for effective "hand-off" communication includes up-to-date information regarding the patient's care, treatment and services, condition, and any recent or anticipated changes.[1]	___	___	___
Note: The information communicated during a hand off is accurate.[1]			
The organization's process for effective "hand-off" communication includes a process for verification of the received information, including repeat-back or read-back, as appropriate.[1]	___	___	___
The organization's process for effective "hand-off" communication includes an opportunity for the receiver of the hand-off information to review relevant patient historical data, which may include previous care, treatment and services.[1]	___	___	___
Interruptions during hand offs are limited to minimize the possibility that information would fail to be conveyed or would be forgotten.[1]	___	___	___

Education and Competence

	Yes	NA	No
The organization provides education and training relating to hand-off communications.*	___	___	___
The organization assesses the competence of individuals who are involved in hand-off communications.*	___	___	___

Monitoring and Enforcement

	Yes	NA	No
The organization monitors compliance with policies and procedures relating to hand-off communications.*	___	___	___
The organization enforces policies and procedures relating to hand-off communications.*	___	___	___

Process Improvement

	Yes	NA	No
The organization identifies ways to improve the hand-off communication process.*	___	___	___
The organization acts as necessary to improve the hand-off communication process.*	___	___	___

Required Documentation

No specific form or document is required. No required documentation has been published.*

Suggested Documentation or Evidence of Compliance

	Yes	NA	No
Records reflect compliance with the hand-off communication process and include evidence that there was an opportunity to ask and respond to questions. *	___	___	___

	Yes	NA	No
Suggested Measurement Indicators (Performance Trackers)			
Number of hand-off communications that met requirements *divided by* number of hand-off communications during the period.*	___	___	___
Surveyor Expectations			
Surveyors may do the following:			
• Look for a 12-month history of continuous compliance.*	___	___	___
• Review policies and procedures relating to hand-off communications.*	___	___	___
• Determine if there is a standardized approach to hand-off communications.*	___	___	___
• Determine if the standardized approach to hand-off communications includes an opportunity to ask questions.*	___	___	___
• Determine if the standardized approach to hand-off communications includes an opportunity to respond to questions.*	___	___	___
• Determine if staff complies with policies and procedures relating to hand-off communications.*	___	___	___
• Review how the organization monitors hand-off communications.*	___	___	___
• Determine if there are opportunities to ask and respond to questions during hand-off communications.*	___	___	___
• Talk with staff about the hand-off communication process.*	___	___	___

Example Surveyors' Questions

How do you ensure that you use a standardized approach to hand-off communications?*

How do you ensure there is an opportunity to ask and respond to questions during hand-off communications?*

How do you document hand-off communications?*

CHECKLIST FOR 2008 NPSG 3

Goal 3. Improve the Safety of Using Medications

Requirement 3C

Identify and, at a minimum, annually review a list of look-alike/sound-alike drugs used by the organization, and take action to prevent errors involving the interchange of these drugs.

Implementation Expectations for Requirement 3C

1. Identify a list of look-alike/sound-alike (LASA) drugs used by the organization (the list must include a minimum of 10 look-alike/sound-alike drug combinations selected from the tables of LASA drugs posted on the Joint Commission website).
2. Review the list of look-alike/sound-alike drugs used by the organization at least annually.
3. The organization takes action to prevent errors involving the interchange of these drugs.

Note: Organizations should refer to the Joint Commission's Internet Web site for answers to frequently asked questions (FAQs) about this requirement. (*See* Appendix A.)

Note: Organizations should determine if the Joint Commission has published acceptable alternatives to the requirements for this goal. (*See* Chapter 19.)

Source: Joint Commission. *Perspectives.* Oakbrook Terrace, IL; Joint Commission: 2007;27(7):10–9.

Checklist items that reflect the authors' comments, experiences, and suggestions; reports from surveyed organizations; and surveyors' statements are noted with an asterisk. References and resources are in the References and Resources section of this book.

Authors' Comments, Experiences, and Suggestions	Yes	NA	No
The organization has identified a list of look-alike/sound-alike (LASA) drugs used by the organization.[1]	___	___	___
Note: The term *used* applies "to any component of the medication management process: selection and procurement, storage, order and transcribing, preparing and dispensing, administration or monitoring."[2]			
At a minimum, the organization annually reviews the list of LASA drugs used by the organization.[1]	___	___	___
Note: The review should include updating the list if needed.*			
The organization includes on its list a *minimum* of 10 look-alike/sound-alike drug combinations from tables posted on the Joint Commission's Internet Web site. (*See* Appendix A.)[1]	___	___	___

	Yes	NA	No

Note: The organization must ensure that its list of LASA drugs reflects the most recent tables posted on the Joint Commission's Internet Web site.[2]

Note: Tables I, II, and III list the potential problematic drug names and, for most combinations, potential errors and consequences and specific safety strategies. Hospitals must select at least five combinations from Table I. They must select an additional five combinations from any of Tables I, II, and/or III.[3]

Note: Some organizations may have difficulty identifying 10 pairs of drugs from the tables. These organizations must select pairs of dangerous or easily confused drugs that are not in the tables or submit a Request for Review of an Alternative Approach to a National Patient Safety Goal. (*See* Chapter 19.)[2]

The organization takes action to prevent errors involving the interchange of LASA drugs that are on the list.[1] ____ ____ ____

Note: The specific actions are up to the organization and should be based on an analysis of the medication systems, recognized best practices, and specific strategies and general recommendations provided in the literature. Actions may include one or more of the suggested specific safety strategies (i.e., prevention measures) included in the Joint Commission's tables.[2]

Note: The Joint Commission states that different concentrations of the same medication should be treated as LASA drugs.[2]

Note: This requirement applies to medication storage areas throughout the organization—not just in the pharmacy.*

Note: Some organizations require orders for medications with look-alike and sound-alike names to include an indication for use and/or to contain both brand and generic names.*

Note: Some organizations require individuals who give verbal or telephone orders for medications with sound-alike names to spell-out the name of the medication.*

Note: Many organizations do not store drugs in alphabetical order and require look-alike drugs to be physically separated.*

Note: Some organizations determine if drugs have the potential for errors due to look-alike/sound-alike names when adding them to their formulary.*

Note: Organizations should use distinctive packaging and labeling to the extent practical. The use of combinations of upper and lower case (e.g., "Tall Man") letters on medication labels can reduce errors due to look-alike names. For example, labeling medications as HydrOXYzine or HydrALAzine can help prevent mistaking one medication for the other. Some manufacturers include these combinations on their labels. Organizations may also use these combinations on their internally created labels.*

	Yes	NA	No
Education and Competence			
The organization provides education and training relating to look-alike/sound-alike drugs used in the organization.*	___	___	___
The organization assesses the competence of individuals relating to look-alike/sound-alike drugs.*	___	___	___
Monitoring and Enforcement			
The organization monitors compliance with policies and procedures relating to look-alike/sound-alike drugs.*	___	___	___
The organization enforces policies and procedures relating to look-alike/sound-alike drugs.*	___	___	___
Process Improvement			
The organization identifies ways to reduce errors associated with look-alike/sound-alike drugs.*	___	___	___
The organization acts to improve the process for reducing errors associated with look-alike/sound-alike drugs.*	___	___	___
Required Documentation			
No specific form or document is required. No required documentation has been published.*			
Suggested Documentation or Evidence of Compliance			
Evidence of annual review and update or revision*	___	___	___
Patient records reflect compliance with policies and procedures relating to look-alike/sound-alike drugs.*	___	___	___
Suggested Measurement Indicators (Performance Trackers)			
Number of look-alike/sound-alike drugs reflecting compliance with applicable safety strategies *divided by* number of look-alike/sound-alike drugs audited during the period. (Some organizations may incorporate this into their monthly medication area inspections.)*	___	___	___
Surveyor Expectations			
Surveyors may do the following:			
• Look for a 12-month history of continuous compliance.*	___	___	___
• Review policies and procedures relating to look-alike/sound-alike drugs. *	___	___	___
• Review the list of look-alike/sound-alike drugs.*	___	___	___
• Determine if the list contains a minimum of ten look-alike/sound-alike drugs from tables issued by the Joint Commission.*	___	___	___
• Determine if the list of look-alike/sound-alike drugs is reviewed at least annually.*	___	___	___

	Yes	NA	No
• Determine if the organization has updated the list of look-alike/sound-alike drugs if needed.*	____	____	____
• Determine if staff complies with policies and procedures relating to look-alike/sound-alike drugs.*	____	____	____
• Determine if look-alike/sound-alike drugs are physically separated.*	____	____	____
• Review how the organization monitors look-alike/sound-alike drugs.*	____	____	____
• Determine if the organization has taken action to prevent errors involving the interchange of look-alike/sound-alike drugs on the list (i.e., put specific safety strategies in place).*	____	____	____
• Talk with staff about the look-alike/sound-alike drugs used in the organization. *	____	____	____

Example Surveyors' Questions

What look-alike/sound-alike drugs are used in the organization?*

How do you identify look-alike/sound-alike drugs? *

What is your procedure when a look-alike/sound-alike drug is ordered?*

What action have you taken to prevent errors involving the interchange of look-alike/sound-alike drugs on the list?*

How do you store and separate insulin products in patient care areas?*

How do you document the action taken relating to orders for look-alike/sound-alike drugs?*

CHECKLIST FOR 2008 NPSG 3

Goal 3. Improve the Safety of Using Medications

Requirement 3D

Label all medications, medication containers (for example, syringes, medicine cups, basins), or other solutions on and off the sterile field.

Rationale for Requirement 3D

This risk reduction activity is consistent with safe medication practices and addresses a recognized risk point in the safe administration of medications in perioperative and other procedural settings.

Errors, sometimes tragic, have resulted from medications and other solutions removed from their original containers and placed into unlabeled containers. Medications or other solutions in unlabeled containers are unidentifiable. This unsafe practice neglects basic principles of medication management safety yet has been routine in many organizations with respect to medications transferred to the sterile field.

Implementation Expectations for Requirement 3D

1. Medications and solutions both on and off the sterile field are labeled even if there is only one medication being used.
2. Labeling occurs when any medication or solution is transferred from the original packaging to another container.
3. Labels include the drug name, strength, amount (if not apparent from the container), expiration date when not used within 24 hours, and expiration time when expiration occurs in less than 24 hours.
4. All labels are verified both verbally and visually by two qualified individuals when the person preparing the medication is not the person administering the medication.
5. No more than one medication or solution is labeled at one time.
6. Any medications or solutions found unlabeled are immediately discarded.
7. All original containers from medications or solutions remain available for reference in the perioperative/procedural area until the conclusion of the procedure.
8. All labeled containers on the sterile field are discarded at the conclusion of the procedure.
9. At shift change or break relief, all medications and solutions both on and off the sterile field and their labels are reviewed by entering and exiting personnel.

Note: Organizations should refer to the Joint Commission's Internet Web site for answers to frequently asked questions (FAQs) about this requirement. (*See* Appendix A.)

Note: Organizations should determine if the Joint Commission has published acceptable alternatives to the requirements for this goal. (*See* Chapter 19.)

Source: Joint Commission. *Perspectives.* Oakbrook Terrace, IL; Joint Commission: 2007;27(7):10–9.

Checklist items that reflect the authors' comments, experiences, and suggestions; reports from surveyed organizations; and surveyors' statements are noted with an asterisk. References and resources are in the References and Resources section of this book.

	Yes	NA	No

Authors' Comments, Experiences, and Suggestions

Medications and solutions both on and off the sterile field are labeled even if there is only one medication being used.[1] ___ ___ ___

Note: This requirement includes medications, medication containers (for example, syringes, medicine cups, basins), or other solutions.[1]

Note: "Other solutions" referred to in the requirement include, but are not limited to, formalin, povidine iodine, chlorhexidine, tincture of benzoin, ferric subsulfate (Monsel's), and Lugol's.*

Note: The Joint Commission states that this requirement "applies to any surgical other procedural setting and includes pre-, intra-, and post-operative/procedural components. Consequently, it applies not only to the surgical suite but also to prep areas, pre-op holding, and PACU. It also applies to medications used by anesthesia providers." Other settings to which the requirement applies include "all procedural areas that use medications or solutions including, but not limited to, radiology and other imaging services, endoscopy units, dental services, and patient care units were 'bedside' procedures are done."[2]

Note: For the purpose of its standards, the Joint Commission states that the term "*medication* includes prescription medications, sample medications, herbal remedies, vitamins, nutraceuticals, over-the-counter drugs, vaccines, diagnostic and contrast agents used on or administered to persons to diagnose, treat, or prevent disease or other abnormal conditions; radioactive medications; respiratory therapy treatments; parenteral nutrition; blood derivatives; intravenous solutions (plain, with electrolytes and/or drugs); and any product designated by the Food and Drug Administration (FDA) as a drug. The definition of *medication* does not include enteral nutrition solutions (which are considered food products), oxygen, and other medical gases."[3]

Labeling occurs when any medication or solution is transferred from the original packaging to another container.[1] ___ ___ ___

Note: Medications, medication containers or other solutions must be labeled even if there is only one medication, medication container, or solution.*

Note: The only exception to this is when one solution or medication is "removed from its original container and immediately administered or disposed of in some fashion, labeling is not required." This also applies to anesthesia services.[2]

Note: "If the medication is prepared and slowly administered over the course of a procedure, if the medication is prepared by a staff member other than the administering provider, if the medication is prepared in bulk for the day's cases, or if the provider preparing the medication participates in another function prior to administration, the syringe or other container must be labeled."[2]

Note: If an individual draws up two medications into two separate syringes and then administers both medications, both syringes need to be labeled.[2]

	Yes	NA	No
Note: Labeling expectations for contrast media that are loaded into power injectors are the same as for other medications. If the contrast media is administered immediately the injector does not need to be labeled. If the contrast media is not administered immediately, the injector must be labeled.[2]			
Labels include the drug name, strength, amount (if not apparent from the container), expiration date when not used within 24 hours, and expiration time when expiration occurs in less than 24 hours.[1]	___	___	___
Note: The Joint Commission requires the "date prepared and the diluent for all compounded IV admixtures."[2]			
Note: "In most cases of medications and solutions in the procedural setting, only the drug name and strength (concentration) will be needed."[2]			
Note: It is not acceptable to "label" a syringe by taping the vial from which the medication was removed to the syringe.[2]			
All labels are verified both verbally and visually by two qualified individuals when the person preparing the medication is not the person administering the medication.[1]	___	___	___
Note: "If the same person prepares and administers a medication, or pours and uses a solution, a two-person verification is not required."[2]			
Note: Medications prepared and labeled by a pharmacist (e.g., a pharmacist assigned to surgery) do not require a two-person verification.[2]			
No more than one medication or solution is labeled at one time.[1]	___	___	___
Note: Although presterilized, prelabeled syringes are commercially available, "prelabeling medication and solution containers is not acceptable." However, commercially-available or pharmacy-prepared prefilled, prelabeled syringes are acceptable.[2]			
Note: Prelabeling "syringes for anesthesia medications for the anesthesia cart...as a means of reducing the time it takes to prepare needed medications" in an emergency situation is not acceptable.[2]			
Note: Prelabeled or pre-engraved "basins for use only with sterile saline or other routine solutions" are not acceptable.[2]			
Note: Preprinted adhesive labels for application to syringes when medications are drawn up are acceptable. Labels can be prepared by the organization or purchased commercially. Sterile labels are available.[2]			
Any medications or solutions found unlabeled are immediately discarded.[1]	___	___	___
Note: The Joint Commission does not specify a procedure for discarding unlabeled medications or solutions.*			

	Yes	NA	No
All original containers from medications or solutions remain available for reference in the perioperative/procedural area until the conclusion of the procedure.[1]	___	___	___

Note: The Joint Commission does not specify how the containers are to remain in the area. Any safe method that retains the items in the area and that will allow access to the items if the need arises meets the requirement. The method used must allow verification of the drugs and concentrations that were administered.[2]

	Yes	NA	No
All labeled containers on the sterile field are discarded at the conclusion of the procedure.[1]	___	___	___

Note: The Joint Commission does not specify a procedure for discarding containers at the conclusion of a procedure.*

	Yes	NA	No
At shift change or break relief, all medications and solutions both on and off the sterile field and their labels are reviewed by entering and exiting personnel.[1]	___	___	___

Note: The Joint Commission does not specify a procedure for reviewing medications, solutions, and their labels.*

Education and Competence

	Yes	NA	No
The organization provides education and training relating to labeling medications, medication containers, or other solutions in the perioperative and other procedural settings.*	___	___	___
The organization assesses the competence of individuals who label medications, medication containers, or other solutions in the perioperative and other procedural settings.*	___	___	___

Monitoring and Enforcement

	Yes	NA	No
The organization monitors compliance with policies and procedures relating to labeling medications, medication containers, or other solutions in the perioperative and other procedural settings.*	___	___	___
The organization enforces policies and procedures relating to labeling medications, medication containers, or other solutions in the perioperative and other procedural settings.*	___	___	___

Process Improvement

	Yes	NA	No
The organization identifies ways to improve the process for labeling medications, medication containers, or other solutions in the perioperative and other procedural settings.*	___	___	___
The organization acts as necessary to improve the process for labeling medications, medication containers, or other solutions in the perioperative and other procedural settings.*	___	___	___

	Yes	NA	No
Required Documentation			
No specific form or document is required. No required documentation has been published.*			
Suggested Documentation or Evidence of Compliance			
Medications, medication containers, or other solutions in the perioperative and other procedural settings are labeled properly and correctly.*	____	____	____
Suggested Measurement Indicators (Performance Trackers)			
Number of properly and correctly labeled medications, medication containers, or other solutions *divided by* number of medications inspected during the period.*	____	____	____
Surveyor Expectations			
Surveyors may do the following:			
• Look for a 12-month history of continuous compliance.*	____	____	____
• Review policies and procedures relating to labeling medications in the perioperative and other procedural settings.*	____	____	____
• Determine if staff complies with policies and procedures relating to labeling medications, medication containers, or other solutions in the perioperative and other procedural settings.*	____	____	____
• Review how the organization monitors the labeling of medications, medication containers, or other solutions in the perioperative and other procedure settings.*	____	____	____
• Talk with staff about labeling medications, medication containers, or other solutions in the perioperative and other procedural settings.*	____	____	____

Example Surveyors' Questions

What is your procedure for labeling medications, medication containers, or other solutions in the perioperative and other procedural settings?*

What do you do when you find unlabeled/mislabeled medications, medication containers, or other solutions in the perioperative and other procedural settings?*

How do you document your action when you find unlabeled/mislabeled medications, medication containers, or other solutions in the perioperative and other procedural settings?*

Have you found anesthesia syringes (containing medications) that have not been discarded at the end of a surgical procedure?*

Does anesthesia "save time" by prelabeling syringes prior to a surgical procedure?*

How does anesthesia label syringes that contain medications?*

Goal 3. Improve the Safety of Using Medications

Requirement 3E

Reduce the likelihood of patient harm associated with the use of anticoagulation therapy.

Note: This requirement applies only to organizations that provide anticoagulation therapy.

Rationale for Requirement 3E

Anticoagulation is a high risk treatment, which commonly leads to adverse drug events due to the complexity of dosing these medications, monitoring their effects, and ensuring patient compliance with outpatient therapy. The use of standardized practices that include patient involvement can reduce the risk of adverse drug events associated with the use of heparin (unfractionated), low molecular weight heparin (LMWH), warfarin, and other anticoagulants.

Note: This requirement has a one-year phase-in period that includes defined expectations for planning, development, and testing ("milestones") at 3, 6, and 9 months in 2008, with the expectation of full implementation by January 1, 2009.

1. As of April 1, 2008, the organization's leadership has assigned responsibility for oversight and coordination of the development, testing, and implementation of NPSG Requirement 3E.
2. As of July 1, 2008, an implementation work plan is in place that identifies adequate resources, assigned accountabilities, and a time line for full implementation of NPSG Requirement 3E by January 1, 2009.
3. As of October 1, 2008, pilot testing in at least one clinical unit is under way.
4. As of January 1, 2009, the process is fully implemented across the organization.

The Implementation Expectations that will apply beginning January 1, 2009, are provided below.

Implementation Expectations for 3E

1. The organization implements a defined anticoagulant management program to individualize the care provided to each patient receiving anticoagulant therapy.
2. To reduce compounding and labeling errors, the organization uses ONLY oral unit-dose products and premixed infusions, when these products are available.
3. When pharmacy services are provided by the organization, warfarin is dispensed for each patient in accordance with established monitoring procedures.
4. The organization uses approved protocols for the initiation and maintenance of anticoagulation therapy appropriate to the medication used, to the condition being treated, and to the potential for drug interactions.
5. For patients being started on warfarin, a baseline International Normalized Ratio (INR) is available, and for all patients receiving warfarin therapy, a current INR is available and is used to monitor and adjust therapy.
6. When dietary services are provided by the organization, the service is notified of all patients receiving warfarin and responds according to its established food/drug interaction program.
7. When heparin is administered intravenously and continuously, the organization uses programmable infusion pumps.
8. The organization has a policy that addresses baseline and ongoing laboratory tests that are required for heparin and low molecular weight heparin therapies.
9. The organization provides education regarding anticoagulation therapy to prescribers, staff, patients, and families.

10. Patient/family education includes the importance of follow-up monitoring, compliance issues, dietary restrictions, and potential for adverse drug reactions and interactions.
11. The organization evaluates anticoagulation safety practices (see MM.8.10).

Note: Organizations should refer to the Joint Commission's Internet Web site for answers to frequently asked questions (FAQs) about this requirement. (*See* Appendix A.)

Note: Organizations should determine if the Joint Commission has published acceptable alternatives to the requirements for this goal. (*See* Chapter 19.)

Source: Joint Commission. *Perspectives.* Oakbrook Terrace, IL; Joint Commission: 2007;27(7):10–9.

Checklist items that reflect the authors' comments, experiences, and suggestions; reports from surveyed organizations; and surveyors' statements are noted with an asterisk. References and resources are in the References and Resources section of this book.

Authors' Comments, Experiences, and Suggestions	Yes	NA	No
As of April 1, 2008, the organization's leadership has assigned responsibility for oversight and coordination of the development, testing, and implementation of NPSG Requirement 3E.[1]	___	___	___
As of July 1, 2008, an implementation work plan is in place that identifies adequate resources, assigned accountabilities, and a time line for full implementation of NPSG Requirement 3E by January 1, 2009.[1]	___	___	___
As of October 1, 2008, pilot testing in at least one clinical unit is under way.[1]	___	___	___
As of January 1, 2009, the process is fully implemented across the organization.[1]	___	___	___

The Implementation Expectations that will apply beginning January 1, 2009, are provided below.

The organization implements a defined anticoagulant management program to individualize the care provided to each patient receiving anticoagulant therapy.[1]	___	___	___
To reduce compounding and labeling errors, the organization uses ONLY oral unit-dose products and premixed infusions, when these products are available.[1]	___	___	___
When pharmacy services are provided by the organization, warfarin is dispensed for each patient in accordance with established monitoring procedures.[1]	___	___	___
The organization uses approved protocols for the initiation and maintenance of anticoagulation therapy appropriate to the medication used, to the condition being treated, and to the potential for drug interactions.[1]	___	___	___
For patients being started on warfarin, a baseline International Normalized Ratio (INR) is available, and for all patients receiving warfarin therapy, a current INR is available and is used to monitor and adjust therapy.[1]	___	___	___
When dietary services are provided by the organization, the service is notified of all patients receiving warfarin and responds according to its established food/drug interaction program.[1]	___	___	___

	Yes	NA	No
When heparin is administered intravenously and continuously, the organization uses programmable infusion pumps.[1]	___	___	___
The organization has a policy that addresses baseline and ongoing laboratory tests that are required for heparin and low molecular weight heparin therapies.[1]	___	___	___
The organization provides education regarding anticoagulation therapy to prescribers, staff, patients, and families.[1]	___	___	___
Patient/family education includes the importance of follow-up monitoring, compliance issues, dietary restrictions, and potential for adverse drug reactions and interactions.[1]	___	___	___
The organization evaluates anticoagulation safety practices (see MM.8.10).[1]	___	___	___

Note: The safe use of anticoagulants involves *all* medication-use processes. For example:

- Selection and procurement (e.g., reducing the number of strengths of warfarin available)
- Storage (e.g., separating anticoagulants from other medications)
- Ordering and transcribing (e.g., eliminating the use of the abbreviation *U* or *u* and writing the word *unit*)
- Dispensing (e.g., developing anticoagulation clinics)
- Administering (e.g., implementing double checks)
- Monitoring (e.g., using a baseline International Normalized Ratio [INR] when starting patients on warfarin).*

Note: Only heparin infusions that are commercially available or that are prepared by the pharmacy should be used throughout the organization.*

Note: Staff should be aware that many common medications (e.g., lipid-lowering agents, erythromycin, metronidazole, and trimethoprim-sulfa) will enhance the anticoagulant effect of warfarin.*

Note: When using anticoagulants (e.g., heparin and warfarin), independent double checks (i.e., selection of drug, calculations, settings of programmable pumps, etc.) must be implemented.*

Education and Competence

The organization provides education and training relating to anticoagulation therapy to the medical staff.*	___	___	___
The organization provides education and training relating to anticoagulation therapy to nursing service.*	___	___	___
The organization provides education and training relating to anticoagulation therapy to pharmacy staff.*	___	___	___
The organization provides education and training relating to anticoagulation therapy to the dietary staff (including food/drug interactions).*	___	___	___

	Yes	NA	No
Education and training includes the organization's policies and procedures relating to anticoagulation therapy.*	____	____	____
Patient and family education provides patient-oriented educational materials and services (including materials at a 6th grade reading level and, if possible, in the patient's language).*	____	____	____
The organization assesses the competence of staff involved in anticoagulation therapy.*	____	____	____

Monitoring and Enforcement

The organization reviews orders and results outside of expected parameters.*	____	____	____
The organization reviews all reported medication errors and adverse drug reactions relating to anticoagulation therapy.*	____	____	____
The organization reviews the use of programmable pumps to ensure full functionality.*	____	____	____
The organization reviews reports from programmable pumps (e.g., overrides of set limits) and aggregates data to determine trends in timing of doses, variances in practices in patient-care areas, etc.*	____	____	____
The organization enforces policies and procedures relating to anticoagulation therapy.*	____	____	____

Process Improvement

To demonstrate improvement, organizations should determine their baseline parameters and compare them with subsequent measurements.*	____	____	____
The organization evaluates the safety and effectiveness of its anticoagulation therapy program. (*See* MM.8.10.) Examples of evaluation methods include failure mode and effects analysis, medication-use evaluation, analysis of adverse drug reaction and medication error reports, and tracking the percentage of patients who reach specific clinical goals (e.g., therapeutic laboratory values).*	____	____	____

Required Documentation

No specific form or document is required. No required documentation has been published.*

Suggested Documentation or Evidence of Compliance

Tracking of phase-in period during 2008, 2009, and beyond (e.g., a gap analysis and action plan with timelines for implementation).*	____	____	____
A written, defined anticoagulation management program.*	____	____	____
Policies and procedures (e.g., required laboratory tests and protocols) relating to anticoagulation therapy.*	____	____	____

Suggested Measurement Indicators (Performance Trackers)

Number of patients for whom anticoagulants are ordered. Sorted by drug and dose (or dosage range).*	____	____	____
Orders for drugs that are weight-based compared with orders that should be weight-based.*	____	____	____

	Yes	NA	No
Percentage of patients receiving anticoagulants under approved protocols.*	____	____	____
Percentage of patients with required laboratory tests and other monitoring.*	____	____	____
Percentage of patients receiving dietary education.*	____	____	____
Percentage of patients receiving anticoagulant therapy education.*	____	____	____
Percentage of staff receiving education.*	____	____	____

Surveyor Expectations

Surveyors may do the following:

	Yes	NA	No
• Request evidence (e.g., an action plan) that phase-in milestones were achieved in 2008.*	____	____	____
• Request evidence of compliance with each implementation expectation.*	____	____	____
• Review patients' medical records to view availability of dosing parameters and laboratory data.*	____	____	____
• Observe medication administration.*	____	____	____
• Review patient education materials.*	____	____	____
• Review staff education materials.*	____	____	____

Example Surveyors' Questions

Who is in charge of the implementation of the anticoagulant program?*

How is staff educated about drugs and protocols?*

How are patients' weights obtained?*

Are patients' weights used in determining doses?*

What monitoring is required for patients on anticoagulant therapy?*

If a laboratory test is out of range, how is the nurse made aware of the situation?*

When must the prescriber be notified if a laboratory test is out of range?*

Do patients administer their own anticoagulants?*

How is the dietary department made aware of new patients who receive warfarin?*

What food/drug interactions are considered significant?*

Are these interactions reviewed by the medical staff?*

How are the safety and effectiveness of the anticoagulant management program evaluated?*

What safeguards are in place to reduce the potential for errors with anticoagulants?*

How often are programmable pumps inspected and tested?*

What do you do if there is a power failure while a patient is receiving heparin via an infusion pump?*

CHECKLIST FOR 2008 NPSG 7

Goal 7. Reduce the Risk of Health Care–Associated Infections

Requirement 7A

Comply with current World Health Organization (WHO) Hand Hygiene Guidelines or Centers for Disease Control and Prevention (CDC) hand-hygiene guidelines.

Rationale for Requirement 7A

Compliance with the WHO Hand Hygiene Guidelines or CDC hand-hygiene guidelines will reduce the transmission of infectious agents by staff to patients, thereby decreasing the incidence of health care–associated infections.

Implementation Expectation for Requirement 7A

1. Comply with current WHO Hand Hygiene Guidelines or Centers for Disease Control and Prevention (CDC) hand-hygiene guidelines.

Note: Organizations are required to comply with all 1A, 1B, 1C CDC or WHO guidelines.

Note: Organizations should refer to the Joint Commission's Internet Web site for answers to frequently asked questions (FAQs) about this requirement. (*See* Appendix A.)

Note: Organizations should determine if the Joint Commission has published acceptable alternatives to the requirements for this goal. (*See* Chapter 19.)

Source: Joint Commission. *Perspectives.* Oakbrook Terrace, IL; Joint Commission: 2007;27(7):10–9.

Checklist items that reflect the authors' comments, experiences, and suggestions; reports from surveyed organizations; and surveyors' statements are noted with an asterisk. References and resources are in the References and Resources section of this book.

Authors' Comments, Experiences, and Suggestions	**Yes**	**NA**	**No**
The organization complies with current WHO or CDC hand-hygiene guidelines.[1]	____	____	____
Note: The full guidelines are available on the WHO and CDC Internet Web sites. (*See* Appendix A.)*			
The organization implements all Category I WHO or CDC recommendations (i.e., IA, IB, and IC). (*See* Table 20-5.)[1]	____	____	____
Note: The Joint Commission requires organizations to implement all Category IA, IB, and IC recommendations. The organization should consider implementing Category II recommendations.[2]			
The organization's policies and procedures reflect current WHO or CDC hand-hygiene guidelines.*	____	____	____

	Yes	NA	No
The organization enforces policies and procedures relating to the hand-hygiene guidelines.*	____	____	____
Staff can identify patients at high risk for a health care–associated infection. (Immunodeficient, surgical, and elderly patients are among those at high risk.)*	____	____	____
The organization has an active program for reducing the risk of health care–associated infections and promoting compliance with WHO or CDC hand-hygiene guidelines.*	____	____	____
Staff use approved cleaning agents and alcohol-based hand rubs according to the organization's policies and procedures and WHO or CDC hand-hygiene guidelines.*	____	____	____

Note: Staff members are not required to use alcohol-based hand rubs. Staff may use soap and water instead of alcohol-based hand rubs.[2]

Note: The hand-hygiene guidelines specify conditions in which alcohol-based hand rubs may be used instead of an organization-approved cleaning agent.*

	Yes	NA	No
Alcohol-based hand rubs are conveniently located in safe areas and are readily available to staff. (Check local fire codes and the organization's infection control policies for guidance in locating alcohol-based gel hand rubs. Some codes specify that hand-rub dispensers must be in egress corridors outside the patients' rooms. There may be other requirements for foam hand rubs. Some organizations provide staff with pocket-sized containers of the hand rubs.)[2]	____	____	____
Staff use sterile gloves as specified in the organization's policies and procedures. (Some procedures require sterile gloves; others do not.)*	____	____	____
Staff members who are in direct contact with patients comply with hand-hygiene guidelines (e.g., the use of alcohol-based hand rubs). This includes food service personnel and telemedicine providers who are in direct contact with patients.[2]	____	____	____
Staff members who provide direct care to high-risk patients do not wear artificial nails.[2]	____	____	____

Education and Competence

	Yes	NA	No
The organization provides education and training relating to compliance with current WHO or CDC hand-hygiene guidelines and universal precautions for preventing infection.*	____	____	____
The organization assesses the competence of individuals relating to use of current WHO or CDC hand-hygiene guidelines and infection control and prevention.*	____	____	____

Note: Hand-hygiene educational aids, posters, monitoring tools, slide presentations, and other materials are available on the CDC and Hand Hygiene Resource Center Internet Web sites. (*See* Appendix A.)*

Monitoring and Enforcement

	Yes	NA	No
The organization monitors compliance with policies and procedures relating to using WHO or CDC hand-hygiene guidelines.*	____	____	____

Note: A hand-hygiene monitoring tool is available at the Hand Hygiene Resource Center Internet Web site. (See Appendix A.)

	Yes	NA	No
The organization enforces policies and procedures relating to WHO or CDC hand-hygiene guidelines.*	____	____	____

Process Improvement

	Yes	NA	No
The organization identifies ways to improve compliance with WHO or CDC hand-hygiene guidelines.*	____	____	____
The organization acts as necessary to improve compliance with WHO or CDC hand-hygiene guidelines.*	____	____	____

Required Documentation

No specific form or document is required. No required documentation has been published.*

Suggested Documentation or Evidence of Compliance

	Yes	NA	No
Documentation of education, training, and competence assessment of hand hygiene in employee records.*	____	____	____
Evidence that licensed independent practitioners and nonclinical staff are educated and trained in hand hygiene.*	____	____	____

Suggested Measurement Indicators (Performance Trackers)

	Yes	NA	No
Number of staff and physicians observed in compliance with the hand-hygiene guidelines after patient contact *divided by* number of staff and physicians observed.*	____	____	____
Number of staff observed in compliance with policies dealing with length of natural nails *divided by* number of staff observed.*	____	____	____

The CDC recommends the following performance indicators[2]:

	Yes	NA	No
• "Periodically monitor and record adherence as the number of hand-hygiene episodes performed by personnel/number of hand-hygiene opportunities, by ward or by service. Provide feedback to personnel regarding their performance."	____	____	____
• "Monitor the volume of alcohol-based hand rub (or detergent used for handwashing or hand antisepsis) used per 1000 patient days."	____	____	____
• "Monitor adherence to policies dealing with wearing of artificial nails."	____	____	____
• "When outbreaks of infection occur, assess the adequacy of health-care worker hand hygiene." (*See* Table 20-5.)	____	____	____

Surveyor Expectations

Surveyors may do the following:

	Yes	NA	No
• Look for a 12-month history of continuous compliance with the guidelines.*	____	____	____
• Review policies and procedures relating to compliance with current WHO or CDC hand-hygiene guidelines.*	____	____	____
• Review how the organization developed its policies and procedures relating to compliance with WHO or CDC hand-hygiene guidelines.*	____	____	____

	Yes	NA	No
• Review records to determine if staff were educated and trained on WHO or CDC hand-hygiene guidelines.*	____	____	____
• Observe to determine if staff complies with policies and procedures relating to WHO or CDC hand-hygiene guidelines. If surveyors observe 3 or more instances of noncompliance, a Recommendation for Improvement (RFI) will result.[2]*	____	____	____
• Look for documentation of handwashing if documentation is required by the organization.*	____	____	____
• Look for availability of alcohol-based hand rubs.*	____	____	____
• Observe to determine if staff use alcohol-based hand rubs properly.*	____	____	____
• Look for nonapproved hand-hygiene products and lotions.*	____	____	____
• Talk with staff about WHO or CDC hand-hygiene guidelines.*	____	____	____

Example Surveyors' Questions

How often (or when) do you wash your hands?*

When did you last receive education and training on the WHO or CDC hand-hygiene guidelines?*

Do you use alcohol-based hand rubs?*

What is your approved hand washing agent?*

Do you allow clinical staff to wear artificial nails? (Policies should address the wearing of artificial nails.)*

CHECKLIST FOR 2008 NPSG 7

Goal 7. Reduce the Risk of Health Care–Associated Infections

Requirement 7B

Manage as sentinel events all identified cases of unanticipated death or major permanent loss of function associated with a health care–associated infection.

Rationale for Requirement 7B

A significant percentage of patients who unexpectedly die or suffer major permanent loss of function have health care–associated infections. These unanticipated deaths and injuries meet the definition of a sentinel event and, therefore, are required to undergo a root cause analysis. The root cause analysis should attempt to answer the questions (1) why did the patient acquire an infection and, (2) given the fact of the infection, why did the patient die or suffer permanent loss of function?

Implementation Expectations Requirement 7B

1. The organization manages all identified cases of unanticipated death or major permanent loss of function associated with a health care–associated infection as sentinel events (that is, conducts a root cause analysis).
2. The root cause analysis addresses the management of the patient before and after the identification of infection.

Note: Organizations should refer to the Joint Commission's Internet Web site for answers to frequently asked questions (FAQs) about this requirement. (*See* Appendix A.)

Note: Organizations should determine if the Joint Commission has published acceptable alternatives to the requirements for this goal. (*See* Chapter 19.)

Source: Joint Commission. *Perspectives.* Oakbrook Terrace, IL; Joint Commission: 2007;27(7):10–9.

Checklist items that reflect the authors' comments, experiences, and suggestions; reports from surveyed organizations; and surveyors' statements are noted with an asterisk. References and resources are in the References and Resources section of this book.

	Yes	NA	No
Authors' Comments, Experiences, and Suggestions			
The organization manages as sentinel events all identified cases of unanticipated death or major permanent loss of function associated with a health care–associated (nosocomial) infection.[1]	____	____	____
Note: Chapter 14 contains an overview of the Joint Commission's Sentinel Event Policy.*			
The organization performs a root cause analysis (RCA) to identify ways to improve systems and prevent similar events.[1]	____	____	____
Note: Chapter 14 contains an overview of root cause analysis.*			

	Yes	NA	No
The root cause analysis addresses the management of the patient before and after the identification of infection.[1]	___	___	___
Note: The root cause analysis should address the event and not just the infection itself (i.e., "why did the patient die or suffer major permanent loss of function").[2]			
The organization considers reporting sentinel events relating to all identified cases of unanticipated death or major permanent loss of function associated with a health care–acquired (nosocomial) infection to the Joint Commission.*	___	___	___

Education and Competence

The organization provides education and training relating to managing sentinel events associated with health care–acquired infections.*	___	___	___
The organization assesses the competence of individuals relating to managing sentinel events associated with health care–acquired infections.*	___	___	___

Monitoring and Enforcement

The organization monitors compliance with policies and procedures relating to managing sentinel events associated with health care–acquired infections.*	___	___	___
The organization enforces policies and procedures relating to sentinel events associated with health care–acquired infections.*	___	___	___

Process Improvement

The organization identifies ways to improve how it handles sentinel events associated with health care–acquired infections.*	___	___	___
The organization acts as necessary to improve how it handles sentinel events associated with health care–acquired infections.*	___	___	___

Required Documentation

No specific form or document is required. No required documentation has been published.*

Suggested Documentation or Evidence of Compliance

Infection control records and sentinel event records that show that all identified cases of unanticipated death or major loss of function due to a nosocomial infection were managed as sentinel events.*	___	___	___

Suggested Measurement Indicator (Performance Tracker)

Number of incident reports of death or major loss of function due to a nosocomial infection managed as a sentinel event *divided by* number of incident reports of death or major permanent loss of function due to a nosocomial infection.*	___	___	___

	Yes	NA	No
Surveyor Expectations			
Surveyors may do the following:			
• Look for a 12-month history of continuous compliance.*	___	___	___
• Review policies and procedures relating to managing sentinel events associated with health care–acquired infections.*	___	___	___
• Review how the organization developed its policies and procedures relating to managing sentinel events associated with health care–acquired infections.*	___	___	___
• Review records to determine if staff were educated and trained on managing sentinel events associated with health care–acquired infections.*	___	___	___
• Determine if staff complies with policies and procedures relating to sentinel events associated with health care–acquired infections.*	___	___	___
• Talk with staff about managing sentinel events associated with health care–acquired infections.*	___	___	___

Example Surveyors' Questions

What is your policy concerning a patient death from a health care–acquired infection?*

What is your process for follow-up on a patient who died or had a major loss of function due to a health care–acquired infection?*

How would you evaluate a patient death due to a health care–acquired infection?*

How would you decide to do a root cause analysis if a patient died or suffered a major loss of function due to a health care–acquired infection?*

CHECKLIST FOR 2008 NPSG 8

Goal 8. Accurately and Completely Reconcile Medications across the Continuum of Care

Requirement 8A

There is a process for comparing the patient's current medications with those ordered for the patient while under the care of the organization.

Rationale for Requirement 8A

Patients are most at risk during transitions in care (hand-offs) across settings, services, providers, or levels of care. The development, reconciliation, and communication of an accurate medication list throughout the continuum of care are essential in the reduction of transition-related adverse drug events.

Implementation Expectations for Requirement 8A

1. The organization, with the patient's involvement, creates a complete list of the patient's current medications at admission/entry.
2. The medications ordered for, administered to, or dispensed to the patient while under the care of the organization are compared to those on the list and any discrepancies (e.g., omissions, duplications, potential interactions) are resolved.

Note: Organizations should refer to the Joint Commission's Internet Web site for answers to frequently asked questions (FAQs) about this requirement. (*See* Appendix A.)

Note: Organizations should determine if the Joint Commission has published acceptable alternatives to the requirements for this goal. (*See* Chapter 19.)

Source: Joint Commission. *Perspectives.* Oakbrook Terrace, IL; Joint Commission: 2007;27(7):10–9.

Checklist items that reflect the authors' comments, experiences, and suggestions; reports from surveyed organizations; and surveyors' statements are noted with an asterisk. References and resources are in the References and Resources section of this book.

Authors' Comments, Experiences, and Suggestions	Yes	NA	No
The organization has implemented a process for accurately and completely reconciling medications across the continuum of care.[1]	___	___	___

Note: Reconcile means to compare and reach agreement. The purpose is "to avoid errors of transcription, omission, duplication of therapy, drug-drug and drug-disease interactions, etc."[2]

Note: This requirement is not just for inpatients. Across the continuum of care includes admission, discharge, emergency department, ambulatory clinic, home care, and all other settings or services where medications are used.[2]

	Yes	NA	No
Note: When medications are used in outpatient settings (e.g., imaging, physical therapy, respiratory therapy, and clinics) a list of the patient's current medications must be available to check for discrepancies.[2]			
Note: The Joint Commission does not specify who is to do the reconciliation. Physicians, nurses, and pharmacists are often involved in the reconciliation process. The organization must determine the qualifications and competency of those who reconcile medications.[2]			
Note: There must be a single, complete list that is updated as needed and is provided to the patient and all of the patient's care providers.[2]			
The process for obtaining and documenting a complete list of the patient's current medications involves the patient.[1]	___	___	___
Note: Patient involvement means that the organization asks the patient about his/her medications or gets the information by another process (e.g., from a family member, primary care provider, or pharmacist).[2]			
A complete list of the patient's current medications is created at admission/entry.[1]	___	___	___
Note: If no medications are to be used with the patient's care, treatment, or services, a list of medications is not required.[2]			
Note: A complete list of current medications is required. A complete medication history is not required.[2]			
Note: If a complete list of current medications is not obtained, the organization must provide a reasonable patient-related explanation.[2]			
Note: In emergency or urgent situations, immediate care of the patient takes precedence. However, the organization must take steps as soon as possible thereafter to obtain this information and compare it with the medications that the organization provides.[2]			
Note: Pharmacists should identify possible discrepancies in the list and bring them to the attention of the prescriber.[2]			
Note: To ensure that prescribers have the information they need when ordering medications, every effort should be made to obtain a complete list of the patient's current medication as soon as possible.[2]			
The process includes a comparison of the medications the organization provides to those on the list.[1]	___	___	___
Note: The organization is expected to define a timeframe for obtaining and documenting the list. Ideally the information will be available prior to ordering new medications. "At a minimum, the list should be completed within 24 hours." There should be a shorter timeframe for gathering information about high-risk medications.[2]			

	Yes	NA	No

Note: The Joint Commission's FAQs about its NPSGs defines levels of medication reconciliation for the emergency department depending on severity of the patient's condition.[26]

Note: For the purpose of its standards, the Joint Commission states that the term "*medication* includes prescription medications, sample medications, herbal remedies, vitamins, nutraceuticals, over-the-counter drugs, vaccines, diagnostic and contrast agents used on or administered to persons to diagnose, treat, or prevent disease or other abnormal conditions; radioactive medications; respiratory therapy treatments; parenteral nutrition; blood derivatives; intravenous solutions (plain, with electrolytes and/or drugs); and any product designated by the Food and Drug Administration (FDA) as a drug. The definition of *medication* does not include enteral nutrition solutions (which are considered food products), oxygen, and other medical gases."[2]

Note: Although the Joint Commission does not require organizations to have a medication reconciliation form, a standardized form can foster accuracy and prevent errors. Forms are available at the Massachusetts Coalition for the Prevention of Medical Errors Internet Web site. (*See* Appendix A.)*

Education and Competence

	Yes	NA	No
The organization provides education and training relating to obtaining and documenting a complete list of current medications upon admission.*	___	___	___
The organization assesses the competence of individuals who obtain and document a complete list of current medications upon admission.*	___	___	___

Monitoring and Enforcement

	Yes	NA	No
The organization monitors compliance with policies and procedures relating to obtaining and documenting a complete list of current medications upon admission.*	___	___	___
The organization enforces policies and procedures relating to obtaining and documenting a complete list of current medications upon admission.*	___	___	___

Process Improvement

	Yes	NA	No
The organization identifies ways to improve the process for obtaining and documenting a complete list of current medications upon admission.*	___	___	___
The organization acts as necessary to improve the process for obtaining and documenting a complete list of current medications upon admission.*	___	___	___

Required Documentation

No specific form or document is required. No required documentation has been published.*

Suggested Documentation or Evidence of Compliance

	Yes	NA	No
Patient records indicate that a complete list of current medications were obtained and documented upon admission.*	___	___	___

	Yes	NA	No
Records that indicate that the complete list of current medications was reconciled with medications ordered by the prescriber and discrepancies were addressed.*	____	____	____

Suggested Measurement Indicators (Performance Trackers)

Number of patients for whom a complete list of current medications was obtained and documented upon admission *divided by* number of patients audited during the period.*	____	____	____

Surveyor Expectations

Surveyors may do the following:

• Look for a 12-month history of continuous compliance.*	____	____	____
• Review policies and procedures relating to obtaining and documenting a complete list of current medications upon admission.*	____	____	____
• Determine if staff complies with policies and procedures relating to obtaining and documenting a complete list of current medications upon admission.*	____	____	____
• Determine if lists of current medications were reconciled with medications ordered by the prescriber and discrepancies were addressed.*	____	____	____
• Review how the organization monitors obtaining and documenting a complete list of current medications upon admission.*	____	____	____
• Talk with staff about the process for obtaining and documenting a complete list of current medications upon admission.*	____	____	____

Example Surveyors' Questions

What is your procedure for obtaining and documenting a complete list of current medications upon admission?*

Who obtains and documents a complete list of patients' medications upon admission?*

Is the same form for obtaining and documenting a complete list of patients' medications upon admission used throughout the organization?*

CHECKLIST FOR 2008 NPSG 8

Goal 8. Accurately and Completely Reconcile Medications across the Continuum of Care

Requirement 8B

A complete list of the patient's medications is communicated to the next provider of service when a patient is referred or transferred to another setting, service, practitioner or level of care within or outside the organization. The complete list of medications is also provided to the patient on discharge from the organization.

Implementation Expectations for Requirement 8B

1. The patient's accurate medication reconciliation list (complete with medications prescribed by the first provider of service) is communicated to the next provider of service, whether it be within or outside the organization.
2. The next provider of service checks the medication reconciliation list again to make sure it is accurate and in concert with any new medications to be ordered/prescribed.
3. The complete list of medications is also provided to the patient on discharge from the organization.

Note: Organizations should refer to the Joint Commission's Internet Web site for answers to frequently asked questions (FAQs) about this requirement. (*See* Appendix A.)

Note: Organizations should determine if the Joint Commission has published acceptable alternatives to the requirements for this goal. (*See* Chapter 19.)

Source: Joint Commission. *Perspectives.* Oakbrook Terrace, IL; Joint Commission: 2007;27(7):10–9.

Checklist items that reflect the authors' comments, experiences, and suggestions; reports from surveyed organizations; and surveyors' statements are noted with an asterisk. References and resources are in the References and Resources section of this book.

	Yes	NA	No
Authors' Comments, Experiences, and Suggestions			
A complete list of the patient's medications is communicated to the next provider or service when a patient is referred or transferred to another:			
• Setting within or outside the organization[1]	___	___	___
• Service within or outside the organization[1]	___	___	___
• Practitioner within or outside the organization[1]	___	___	___
• Level of care within or outside the organization[1]	___	___	___

Note: For the purpose of its standards, the Joint Commission states that the term "*medication* includes prescription medications, sample medications, herbal remedies, vitamins, nutraceuticals, over-the-counter drugs, vaccines, diagnostic and contrast agents used on or administered to persons to diagnose, treat, or prevent disease or other abnormal conditions; radioactive medications; respiratory therapy treatments; parenteral nutrition; blood derivatives; intravenous solutions (plain,

	Yes	NA	No
with electrolytes and/or drugs); and any product designated by the Food and Drug Administration (FDA) as a drug. The definition of *medication* does not include enteral nutrition solutions (which are considered food products), oxygen, and other medical gases."[2]			
The "next provider of service checks the medication reconciliation list to make sure it is accurate and in concert with any new medications to be ordered/prescribed."[3]	___	___	___
Note: "At a minimum, reconciliation must occur any time the organization requires that orders be rewritten and any time the patient changes service, setting, provider or level of care and new medication orders are written. For transitions not involving new medications or rewriting of orders, the organization should determine whether reconciliation must occur."[3]			
Note: At discharge or transfer, the list must contain medications to be continued.*			
Note: The list may be written or electronic.*			
A complete list of medications is communicated to patients upon discharge.[2]	___	___	___
Note: The terms *admission* and *discharge* are interchangeable with the terms *entry* and *exit* for the purpose of NPSG 8. The requirements apply whenever medication is used in an inpatient or outpatient setting.[2]			
Note: The list of discharge medications is an excellent place to include information about the dose, route, frequency, duration of therapy, indications for the drug and other relevant information about each medication.[2]			
Note: The discharge list should include all medications (e.g., prescription, over-the-counter, and herbal) that the patient will be taking upon discharge.[2]			
Note: "The Joint Commission does not require any signatures as part of the medication reconciliation process." However, if the organization's reconciliation process requires a signature on a medication reconciliation record, surveyors will expect to see a signature.[2]			
Note: If the complete discharge medication list is available electronically (e.g., an electronic medical record) and the next provider of care can access the list, this process will meet the requirement of Goal 8B.[2]			
Note: The patient can refuse to allow information to be sent the next provider of care. However, the organization is obligated to inform the patient of the reason for sending the list and the potential risks of not sharing the information with the next provider of care.[2]			
Note: The discharge list must be communicated directly to the next provider of care. The only exception is when the next provider is unknown. In this case, it is permissible to make the patient responsible for communicating the information. The list must always be communicated to the patient.[2]			

	Yes	NA	No
Education and Competence			
The organization provides education and training relating to communicating a complete list of patients' medications to the next provider of service.*	____	____	____
The organization assesses the competence of individuals who communicate a complete list of patients' medications to the next provider of service.*	____	____	____
The organization provides education and training relating to communicating a complete list of medications to the patient on discharge.*	____	____	____
The organization assesses the competence of individuals who communicate a complete list of medications to the patient on discharge.*	____	____	____
Monitoring and Enforcement			
The organization monitors compliance with policies and procedures relating to communicating a complete list of patients' medications to the next provider of service.*	____	____	____
The organization enforces policies and procedures relating to communicating a complete list of patients' medications to the next provider of service.*	____	____	____
The organization monitors compliance with policies and procedures relating to communicating a complete list of medications to the patient on discharge.*	____	____	____
The organization enforces policies and procedures relating to communicating a complete list of medications to the patient on discharge.*	____	____	____
Process Improvement			
The organization identifies ways to improve the process for communicating a complete list of patients' medications to the next provider of service.*	____	____	____
The organization acts as necessary to improve the process for communicating a complete list of patients' medications to the next provider of service.*	____	____	____
The organization identifies ways to improve the process for communicating a complete list of medications to the patient on discharge.*	____	____	____
The organization acts as necessary to improve the process for communicating a complete list of medications to the patient on discharge.*	____	____	____

Required Documentation

No specific form or document is required. No required documentation has been published.*

	Yes	NA	No
Suggested Documentation or Evidence of Compliance			
Patient's records indicate that complete lists of patients' medications are communicated to the next provider of service.*	____	____	____
Patient's records indicate that complete lists of medications were communicated to the patient on discharge.*	____	____	____

	Yes	NA	No
Suggested Measurement Indicators (Performance Trackers)			
Number of patients with a complete list of medications communicated to the next provider of service *divided by* number of patients audited during the period.*	___	___	___
Number of patients with a complete list of medications communicated on discharge *divided* by number of patients audited during the period.*	___	___	___
Surveyor Expectations			
Surveyors may do the following:			
• Look for a 12-month history of continuous compliance.*	___	___	___
• Review policies and procedures relating to communicating a complete list of patients' medications to the next provider of service.*	___	___	___
• Determine if staff complies with policies and procedures relating to communicating a complete list of patients' medications to the next provider of service.*	___	___	___
• Review how the organization monitors the process for communicating a complete list of patients' medications to the next provider of service.*	___	___	___
• Talk with staff about the process for communicating a complete list of patients' medications to the next provider of service.*	___	___	___
• Review policies and procedures relating to communicating a complete list of medications to patients on discharge.*	___	___	___
• Determine if staff complies with policies and procedures relating to communicating a complete list of medications to patients on discharge.*	___	___	___
• Review how the organization monitors the process for communicating a complete list of medications to patients on discharge.*	___	___	___
• Talk with staff about the process for communicating a complete list of medications to patients on discharge.*	___	___	___

Example Surveyors' Questions

What is your process for communicating a complete list of patients' medications to the next provider of service?*

What is your process for communicating a complete list of medications to patients on discharge?*

Who communicates a complete list of patients'medications to the next provider of service?*

Who communicates a complete list of medications to patients on discharge?*

Is the same form used organization-wide for communicating a complete list of patients' medications to the next provider of service?*

Is the same form used organization-wide for communicating a complete medication list to patients on discharge?*

CHECKLIST FOR 2008 NPSG 9

Goal 9. Reduce the Risk of Patient Harm Resulting from Falls

Requirement 9B

Implement a fall reduction program including an evaluation of the effectiveness of the program.

Rationale for Requirement 9B

Falls account for a significant portion of injuries in hospitalized patients, long-term care residents, and home care recipients. In the context of the population it serves, the services it provides, and its environment of care, the organization should evaluate its patients' risk for falls and take action to reduce the risk of falling and to reduce the risk of injury, should a fall occur. The evaluation could include fall history, medications and alcohol consumption review, gait and balance screening, walking aids, assistive technologies and protective devices assessment and environmental assessments.

Implementation Expectations for Requirement 9B

1. The organization establishes a fall reduction program.
2. The fall reduction program includes an evaluation as appropriate to the patient population, settings and services provided.
3. The fall reduction program includes interventions to reduce the patient's fall risk factors.
4. Staff receive education and training for the fall reduction program.
5. The patient and patient's family is educated on the fall reduction program and any individualized fall reduction strategies.
6. The fall reduction program is evaluated to determine the effectiveness of the program. (Outcome indicators such as decreased number of falls and decreased number and severity of fall-related injuries could be used.)

Note: Organizations should refer to the Joint Commission's Internet Web site for answers to frequently asked questions (FAQs) about this requirement. (*See* Appendix A.)

Note: Organizations should determine if the Joint Commission has published acceptable alternatives to the requirements for this goal. (*See* Chapter 19.)

Source: Joint Commission. *Perspectives.* Oakbrook Terrace, IL; Joint Commission: 2007;27(7):10–9.

Checklist items that reflect the authors' comments, experiences, and suggestions; reports from surveyed organizations; and surveyors' statements are noted with an asterisk. References and resources are in the References and Resources section of this book.

	Yes	NA	No
Authors' Comments, Experiences, and Suggestions			
The organization has established a fall reduction program.[1]	___	___	___

Note: There is no standard definition of a fall. Organizations must define what they consider a fall.[2]

	Yes	NA	No
Note: The National Guideline Clearing House and the Department of Veterans Affairs provide guidelines and materials for designing a fall reduction program.[2] (*See* Appendix A.)			
The fall reduction program includes an evaluation as appropriate to the patient populations, settings and services provided.[1]	___	___	___
Note: The fall reduction program must include all populations served.[2]			
Note: "Criteria should be developed to assist in identifying populations of children at risk for harm from falls. Any child who is in an 'at risk' population should be assessed and protected." [2]			
Note: As appropriate, the "fall reduction program may include risk assessment and periodic reassessment of patients or of the environment of care.[2]			
Note: If the organization's fall reduction program includes a risk assessment, the maximum time frame for completing the assessment is 24 hours.[2]			
Note: Many risk assessment instruments include factors such as recent history of falls, cognitive impairment/dementia, functional or mobility (e.g., gait) problems, and balance impairment. Other factors should be considered.[2]			
The fall reduction program includes interventions to reduce the patient's fall risk factors.[1]	___	___	___
Note: Steps that can be taken to reduce the risk of falls include physical, psychological, and environmental measures as well as education of staff, patients and families. More information on these steps is available in the Joint Commissions frequently asked questions (FAQs) for the NPSGs available on the Joint Commission's Internet Web site.[2] (*See* Appendix A.)			
The fall reduction program includes specific strategies to minimize the risk of falls relating to medications.*	___	___	___
Note: The fall reduction program should identify medications that produce drowsiness, impair motor skills, and otherwise increase the risk of falls. Patients' medications should be reviewed for their potential to cause patients to fall.[2]			
Note: Medications that increase the risk of falls include, but are not limited to, sedatives, hypnotics, anesthesia agents, analgesics, antihypertensive medications, laxatives, diuretics, and psychotropic medications. Staff must be aware that any medication that has an effect on the patient's senses increases the risk of falls.[2]			
Note: Strategies for reducing the risk of falls due to medications include evaluating patient medications, observing patients for signs of drowsiness and impairment, orienting and educating staff, and ensuring staff competence. Some organizations place warnings about the potential for falls associated with specific medications or classes of medications on medication administration records and computer screens.*			

	Yes	NA	No
Staff receive education and training for the fall reduction program.[1]	___	___	___
The patient and patient's family is educated on the fall reduction program and any individualized fall reduction strategies.[1]	___	___	___
The fall reduction program is evaluated to determine the effectiveness of the program. (Outcome indicators such as decreased number of falls and decreased number and severity of fall-related injuries could be used.)[1]	___	___	___

Education and Competence

	Yes	NA	No
The organization provides education and training to staff relating to fall reduction.[1]	___	___	___
The organization provides education and training to patients and families relating to fall reduction.[1]	___	___	___
Education for patients and families includes any individualized fall reduction strategies.[1]	___	___	___
The organization assesses the competence of individuals who are associated with fall reduction.*	___	___	___

Monitoring and Enforcement

	Yes	NA	No
The organization monitors compliance with policies and procedures relating to fall reduction.*	___	___	___
The organization enforces policies and procedures relating to fall reduction.*	___	___	___

Process Improvement

	Yes	NA	No
The organization identifies ways to improve the process for reducing falls.*	___	___	___
The organization acts as necessary to improve the process for reducing falls.*	___	___	___

Required Documentation

No specific form or document is required. No required documentation has been published.*

Suggested Documentation or Evidence of Compliance

	Yes	NA	No
Written evidence of a fall reduction plan.*	___	___	___
Records that indicate that the organization implements procedures for reducing falls.*	___	___	___
Records of the evaluation of the effectiveness of the fall reduction program.*	___	___	___
Evidence that patients were assessed and reassessed for the risk of falls and specific actions taken.*	___	___	___

Suggested Measurement Indicators (Performance Trackers)

	Yes	NA	No
Decreased number of falls.[1]	___	___	___
Decreased number and severity of fall-related injuries.[1]	___	___	___
Number of falls *divided by* number of patients audited during the period.*	___	___	___

	Yes	NA	No
Surveyor Expectations			
Surveyors may do the following:			
• Look for a 12-month history of continuous compliance.*	___	___	___
• Review policies and procedures relating to reducing patient falls.*	___	___	___
• Determine if staff complies with policies and procedures relating to reducing patient falls.*	___	___	___
• Review patient records for documentation of assessment and reassessment of patients for the risk of falls and specific actions taken.*	___	___	___
• Review how the organization monitors patient falls.*	___	___	___
• Determine how the organization evaluates the effectiveness of the fall reduction program.*	___	___	___
• Talk with staff about procedures for reducing patient falls.*	___	___	___

Example Surveyors' Questions

How does your organization define a fall?*

What populations do you include in your fall reduction program?*

How do you assess and reassess patients who are at risk of harm from falls?*

How do you identify children who are at risk of harm from falls?*

What are your procedures for reducing patient falls?*

What medications increase the risk of falls?*

How do you reduce the risk of falls due to medications?*

How do you document patient falls?*

How do you evaluate your fall reduction program?*

How effective is your fall reduction program?*

CHECKLIST FOR 2008 NPSG 13

Goal 13. Encourage Patients' Involvement in Their Own Care as a Patient Safety Strategy

Requirement 13A

Define and communicate the means for patients and their families to report concerns about safety and encourage them to do so.

Rationale for Requirement 13A

Communication with patients and families about all aspects of their care, treatment or services is an important characteristic of a culture of safety. When patients know what to expect, they are more aware of possible errors and choices. Patients can be an important source of information about potential adverse events and hazardous conditions.

Implementation Expectations for Requirement 13A

1. Patients and families are educated on methods available to report concerns related to care, treatment, services, and patient safety issues.
2. The organization encourages patients and their families to report concerns about safety.

Note: Organizations should refer to the Joint Commission's Internet Web site for answers to frequently asked questions (FAQs) about this requirement. (*See* Appendix A.)

Note: Organizations should determine if the Joint Commission has published acceptable alternatives to the requirements for this goal. (*See* Chapter 19.)

Source: Joint Commission. *Perspectives.* Oakbrook Terrace, IL; Joint Commission: 2007;27(7):10–9.

Checklist items that reflect the authors' comments, experiences, and suggestions; reports from surveyed organizations; and surveyors' statements are noted with an asterisk. References and resources are in the References and Resources section of this book.

Authors' Comments, Experiences, and Suggestions	Yes	NA	No
The organization has a defined program for encouraging patients' involvement in their own care as a patient safety strategy.[1]	___	___	___
The organization has defined and communicated a means for patients and their families to report concerns about safety.[1]	___	___	___
Note: The organization must establish processes for reporting concerns about safety and make the processes known throughout the organization.*			
Patients and families are educated on methods available to report concerns relating to care, treatment, services, and patient safety issues.[1]	___	___	___

	Yes	NA	No
The organization encourages patients and their families to report concerns about safety.[1]	___	___	___

Note: The organization must *actively* encourage patients and their families to express concerns and ask questions about their care.[2]

Note: More information about involving patients in their own care is on the Internet Web sites for the Agency for Healthcare Research and Quality, Consumers Advancing Patient Safety, Partnership for Patient Safety, and other organizations. Additional agencies are listed in frequently asked questions (FAQs) for the Joint Commission's National Patient Safety Goals on the Joint Commission's Internet Web site.[2] (*See* Appendix A.)

Education and Competence

	Yes	NA	No
The organization provides education and training to staff relating to involving patients in their own care.*	___	___	___
The organization provides education to patients and families on methods available to report concerns relating to care, treatment, services, and patient safety issues.[1]	___	___	___
Patient and family education encourages patients and their families to report concerns about safety.[1]	___	___	___
The organization assesses the competence of individuals who are provide education to patients and families on methods to report concerns relating to care, treatment, services, and patient safety issues.*	___	___	___

Monitoring and Enforcement

	Yes	NA	No
The organization monitors compliance with policies and procedures relating to involving patients in their own care.*	___	___	___
The organization enforces policies and procedures relating to involving patients in their own care.*	___	___	___

Process Improvement

	Yes	NA	No
The organization identifies ways to improve its process for involving patients in their own care.*	___	___	___
The organization acts as necessary to improve its process for involving patients in their own care.*	___	___	___

Required Documentation

No specific form or document is required. No required documentation has been published.*

Suggested Documentation or Evidence of Compliance

	Yes	NA	No
Written evidence of a program for encouraging patients to be involved in their own care.*	___	___	___

	Yes	NA	No
Records that indicate that the organization provides education to staff members relating to involving patients in their own care.*	____	____	____
Records that indicate that the organization provides education to patients and families on methods available to report concerns related to care, treatment, services, and patient safety issues.*	____	____	____
Records of the evaluation of the effectiveness of the program for involving patients in their own care.*	____	____	____

Suggested Measurement Indicators (Performance Trackers)

Numbers of patients and families educated about methods available to report concerns relating to care, treatment, services, and patient safety issues.*	____	____	____

Surveyor Expectations

Surveyors may do the following:

• Look for a 12-month history of continuous compliance.*	____	____	____
• Review policies and procedures relating to involving patients in their own care.*	____	____	____
• Determine if staff complies with policies and procedures relating to involving patients in their own care.*	____	____	____
• Review patient records for documentation that patients and families have been educated about methods available to report concerns relating to care, treatment, services, and patient safety issues.*	____	____	____
• Review patient records for evidence that family and patient education actively encourages patients and their families to report concerns about safety.*	____	____	____
• Review how the organization monitors its program for involving patients in their own care.*	____	____	____
• Determine how the organization evaluates the effectiveness of its program for involving patients in their own care.*	____	____	____
• Talk with staff members about how they involve patients in their own care.*	____	____	____

Example Surveyors' Questions

How do you actively encourage patients and their families to express concerns about safety?[2]

What educational materials are available for involving patients and their families in their own care?*

How effective is your program for involving patients and their families in their own care?*

What do you do when a patient or the patient's family expresses concerns about patient safety?*

What have you done or what are you doing to improve your processes for involving patients in their own care?*

CHECKLIST FOR 2008 NPSG 15

Goal 15. The Organization Identifies Safety Risks Inherent in Its Patient Population

Rationale for Goal 15

Probabilistic risk assessment has been used to assess the designs of high hazard systems such as chemical engineering plants and space initiatives. Probabilistic risk assessment looks at events that contributed to adverse outcomes. Health care has the ability to identify those areas of high risk potential based on previous sentinel events and other data.

Requirement 15A

The organization identifies patients at risk for suicide.

***Note*:** This requirement only applies to psychiatric hospitals and patients being treated for emotional or behavioral disorders in general hospitals.

Rationale for Requirement 15A

Suicide ranks as the eleventh most frequent cause of death (third most frequent in young people) in the United States, with one person dying from suicide every 16.6 minutes. Suicide of a care recipient while in a staffed, round-the-clock care setting has been the #1 most frequently reported type of sentinel event since the inception of the Joint Commission's Sentinel Event Policy in 1996. Identification of individuals at risk for suicide while under the care of or following discharge from a health care organization is an important first step in protecting and planning the care of these at-risk individuals.

Implementation Expectations for Requirement 15A

1. The risk assessment includes identification of specific factors and features that may increase or decrease risk for suicide.
2. The patient's immediate safety needs and most appropriate setting for treatment are addressed.
3. The organization provides information such as a crisis hotline to individuals and their family members for crisis situations.

Note: Organizations should refer to the Joint Commission's Internet Web site for answers to frequently asked questions (FAQs) about this requirement. (*See* Appendix A.)

Note: Organizations should determine if the Joint Commission has published acceptable alternatives to the requirements for this goal. (*See* Chapter 19.)

Source: Joint Commission. *Perspectives*. Oakbrook Terrace, IL; Joint Commission: 2007;27(7):10–9.

Checklist items that reflect the authors' comments, experiences, and suggestions; reports from surveyed organizations; and surveyors' statements are noted with an asterisk. References and resources are in the References and Resources section of this book.

	Yes	NA	No

Authors' Comments, Experiences, and Suggestions

	Yes	NA	No
The organization identifies patients at risk for suicide.[1]	___	___	___

> ***Note:*** This requirement applies to any patient in a general hospital with a primary diagnosis or primary complaint of an emotional or behavioral disorder. These disorders refer to any *Diagnostic and Statistical Manual of Mental Disorders* (DSM) diagnosis or condition, including those related to substance abuse.[2]

> ***Note:*** This is not just an inpatient requirement. Any setting in the organization that is included in a survey is within the scope of this requirement.[2]

	Yes	NA	No
The risk assessment includes identification of specific factors and features that may increase or decrease risk for suicide.[1]	___	___	___

> ***Note:*** Patient's brought to a hospital emergency department for a psychiatric-related condition must be assessed for suicide risk.[2]

	Yes	NA	No
The patient's immediate safety needs and most appropriate setting for treatment are addressed.[1]	___	___	___
The organization provides information such as a crisis hotline to individuals and their family members for crisis situations.[1]	___	___	___

> ***Note:*** The organization does not have to provide its own crisis hotline. However, it must provide information about the availability of a crisis hotline or other resources, and how to access them if needed.[2]

Education and Competence

	Yes	NA	No
The organization provides education and training to staff relating to specific factors and features that may increase or decrease risk for suicide.*	___	___	___
The provides education and training to staff relating to providing information such as a crisis hotline to individuals and their family members for crisis situations.*	___	___	___
The organization assesses the competence of staff who assess patients for risk of suicide*	___	___	___

Monitoring and Enforcement

	Yes	NA	No
The organization monitors compliance with policies and procedures for identifying patients at risk of suicide.*	___	___	___
The organization enforces policies and procedures for identifying patients at risk of suicide.*	___	___	___

Process Improvement

	Yes	NA	No
The organization identifies ways to improve its process for identifying patients at risk of suicide.*	___	___	___
The organization identifies ways to improve its process for providing information to individuals and their family members for crisis situations.*	___	___	___

	Yes	NA	No
The organization acts as necessary to improve its process for identifying patients at risk of suicide.*	____	____	____
The organization acts as necessary to improve its process for providing information to individuals and their family members for crisis situations.*	____	____	____

Required Documentation

No specific form or document is required. No required documentation has been published.*

Suggested Documentation or Evidence of Compliance

	Yes	NA	No
Written evidence that the organization has a process for identifying patients at risk of suicide.*	____	____	____
Records that indicate that the organization provides education to staff members relating to identifying patients at risk of suicide.*	____	____	____
Evidence that the organization has information available for providing information such as a crisis hotline to individuals and their family members for crisis situations.*	____	____	____
Evidence that staff uses the process for identifying patients at risk for suicide.*	____	____	____
Evidence that the organization, when needed, provides information such as a crisis hotline to individuals and their family members for crisis situations.*	____	____	____

Suggested Measurement Indicators (Performance Trackers)

	Yes	NA	No
Numbers of staff members who are educated, trained, and competent relating to identifying patients at risk of suicide.*	____	____	____
Numbers of patients identified as at risk of suicide.*	____	____	____
Numbers of individuals and their family members who have been provided information for crisis situations.*	____	____	____

Surveyor Expectations

Surveyors may do the following:

	Yes	NA	No
• Look for a 12-month history of continuous compliance.*	____	____	____
• Review policies and procedures relating to identifying patients at risk of suicide.*	____	____	____
• Determine if staff complies with policies and procedures relating to identifying patients at risk of suicide.*	____	____	____
• Review information provided to individuals and their family members relating to crisis situations.*	____	____	____
• Review records to determine if staff have been educated, trained, and deemed competent relating to identifying patients at risk of suicide.*	____	____	____
• Review how the organization monitors its program for identifying patients at risk of suicide.*	____	____	____

	Yes	NA	No
• Determine how the organization evaluates the effectiveness of its program for identifying patients at risk of suicide.*	____	____	____
• Talk with staff members about how they identify patients at risk of suicide.*	____	____	____

Example Surveyors' Questions

How do you identify patients at risk of suicide?*

What specific factors and features may increase or decrease risk for suicide?*

What educational materials are available for identifying patients at risk of suicide?*

How effective is your program for identifying patients at risk of suicide?*

What do you do when you identify a patient at risk of suicide?*

What have you done or what are you doing to improve your processes for identifying patients at risk of suicide?*

What information is available, such as a crisis hotline, for providing to individuals and their family members for crisis situations?*

CHECKLIST FOR 2008 NPSG 16

Goal 16. Improve Recognition and Response to Changes in a Patient's Condition

Requirement 16A

The organization selects a suitable method that enables health care staff members to directly request additional assistance from a specially trained individual(s) when the patient's condition appears to be worsening.

Rationale for Requirement 16A

A significant number of critical inpatient events are preceded by warning signs for an average of 6 to 8 hours. Critical events such as cardiopulmonary and respiratory arrests or changes in patient's vital signs are estimated to occur in 4% to 17% of inpatient admissions. Early response by a specially trained individual(s) to changes in a patient's condition may reduce cardiopulmonary arrests and patient mortality.

> ***Note:*** This requirement has a one-year phase-in period that includes defined expectations for planning, development, and testing ("milestones") at 3, 6, and 9 months in 2008, with the expectation of full implementation by January 1, 2009.

1. As of April 1, 2008, the organization's leadership has assigned responsibility for oversight and coordination of the development, testing, and implementation of NPSG Requirement 16A.
2. As of July 1, 2008, an implementation work plan is in place that identifies adequate resources, assigned accountabilities, and a time line for full implementation of NPSG Requirement 16A by January 1, 2009.
3. As of October 1, 2008, pilot testing in at least one clinical unit is under way.
4. As of January 1, 2009, the process is fully implemented across the organization.

The Implementation Expectations that will apply beginning January 1, 2009, are provided below.

Implementation Expectations for Requirement 16A

1. The organization selects an early recognition and response method most suitable for its needs and resources.
2. The organization develops criteria for calling additional assistance to respond to a change in patient's condition or perception of change by the staff, patients and/or families.
3. The organization empowers staff, patients, and/or families to request additional assistance when they have a concern about the patient's condition.
4. Formal education for urgent response policies and practices is conducted with the people who may request assistance and the people who may respond to those requests.
5. The organization measures the utility and effectiveness of the intervention(s) employed.
6. The organization measures cardiopulmonary arrest, respiratory arrest and mortality rates before and after implementation of an early intervention plan.

Note: Organizations should refer to the Joint Commission's Internet Web site for answers to frequently asked questions (FAQs) about this requirement. (*See* Appendix A.)

Note: Organizations should determine if the Joint Commission has published acceptable alternatives to the requirements for this goal. (*See* Chapter 19.)

Source: Joint Commission. *Perspectives.* Oakbrook Terrace, IL; Joint Commission: 2007;27(7):10–9.

Checklist items that reflect the authors' comments, experiences, and suggestions; reports from surveyed organizations; and surveyors' statements are noted with an asterisk. References and resources are in the References and Resources section of this book.

	Yes	NA	No
Authors' Comments, Experiences, and Suggestions			
As of April 1, 2008, the organization's leadership has assigned responsibility for oversight and coordination of the development, testing, and implementation of NPSG Requirement 16A.[1]	___	___	___
As of July 1, 2008, an implementation work plan is in place that identifies adequate resources, assigned accountabilities, and a time line for full implementation of NPSG Requirement 16A by January 1, 2009.[1]	___	___	___
As of October 1, 2008, pilot testing in at least one clinical unit is under way.[1]	___	___	___
As of January 1, 2009, the process is fully implemented across the organization.[1]	___	___	___
The Implementation Expectations that will apply beginning January 1, 2009, are provided below.			
The organization selects an early recognition and response method most suitable for its needs and resources.[1]	___	___	___
The organization develops criteria for calling additional assistance to respond to a change in patient's condition or perception of change by the staff, patients and/or families.[1]	___	___	___
The organization empowers staff, patients, and/or families to request additional assistance when they have a concern about the patient's condition.[1]	___	___	___
Formal education for urgent response policies and practices is conducted with the people who may request assistance and the people who may respond to those requests.[1]	___	___	___
The organization measures cardiopulmonary arrest, respiratory arrest and mortality rates before and after implementation of an early intervention plan.[1]	___	___	___
Education and Competence			
The organization provides education and training to medical staff, other clinical staff, and nonclinical staff relating to its recognition and response to changes in a patient's condition.*	___	___	___
The organization assesses the competence of individuals relating to their recognition and response to changes in a patient's condition.*	___	___	___
The organization provides information to patients and caregivers relating to requesting assistance if needed.*	___	___	___
Monitoring and Enforcement			
The organization monitors compliance with policies and procedures for recognizing and responding to changes in a patient's condition.*	___	___	___

	Yes	NA	No
The organization enforces policies and procedures for recognizing and responding to changes in a patient's condition.*	____	____	____
The organization measures the utility and effectiveness of the intervention(s) employed.[1]	____	____	____
The organization reviews the number and responses for requests for urgent assistance.*	____	____	____

Process Improvement

	Yes	NA	No
The organization identifies ways to improve its process for recognizing and responding to changes in a patient's condition.*	____	____	____
The organization acts as necessary to improve its process for recognizing and responding to changes in a patient's condition.*	____	____	____

Required Documentation

No specific form or document is required. No required documentation has been published.*

Suggested Documentation or Evidence of Compliance

	Yes	NA	No
Evidence that the organization has met its phase-in targets for recognizing and responding to changes in a patient's condition.*	____	____	____
Gap analysis of progress in meeting phase-in targets and action plan with timelines for implementation.*	____	____	____
Written evidence that the organization has a process for recognizing and responding to changes in a patient's condition.*	____	____	____
Records that indicate that the organization provides education to staff members relating to recognizing and responding to changes in a patient's condition.*	____	____	____
Evidence that staff recognizes and responds to changes in a patient's condition.*	____	____	____
Records of cardiopulmonary arrest rates*	____	____	____
Records of respiratory arrest rates*	____	____	____
Records of mortality rates*	____	____	____

Suggested Measurement Indicators (Performance Trackers)

	Yes	NA	No
Numbers of staff members who are educated, trained, and competent relating to recognizing and responding to changes in a patient's condition.*	____	____	____
Baseline measurements against which to compare future performance.*	____	____	____
Number of patients for whom staff have recognized and responded to changes in their condition.*	____	____	____
Number of requests for urgent assistance.*	____	____	____
Number of cardiopulmonary arrests.*	____	____	____
Number of transfers from medical/surgical units to critical care.*	____	____	____

	Yes	NA	No
Surveyor Expectations			
Surveyors may do the following:			
• Look for a 12-month history of continuous compliance.*	___	___	___
• Review records that document meeting phase-in targets during 2008.*	___	___	___
• Review information provided to patients and their families relating to recognizing and responding to changes in a patient's condition.*	___	___	___
• Determine if the organization is complying with each implementation expectation.*	___	___	___
• Review policies and procedures relating to recognizing and responding to changes in a patient's condition.*	___	___	___
• Determine if staff complies with policies and procedures relating to recognizing and responding to changes in a patient's condition.*	___	___	___
• Review records to determine if staff have been educated, trained, and deemed competent to recognize and respond to changes in a patient's condition.*	___	___	___
• Review how the organization monitors its program for recognizing and responding to changes in a patient's condition.*	___	___	___
• Determine how the organization evaluates the effectiveness of its process for recognizing and responding to changes in a patient's condition. *	___	___	___
• Talk with staff members about how they recognize and respond to changes in a patient's condition.*	___	___	___

Example Surveyors' Questions

Who in your organization can request urgent assistance?*

What staff respond to requests?*

How are dietary and housekeeping employees informed about this process?*

How many requests do you get monthly?*

How has this process improved patient care?*

How do you recognize and respond to changes in a patient's condition?*

What education have you received relating to recognizing and responding to changes in a patient's condition?*

How effective is your program for recognizing and responding to changes in a patient's condition?*

What do you do when you recognize a change in a patient's condition?*

What have you done or what are you doing to improve your processes for recognizing and responding to changes in a patient's condition?*

Table 20-1. Recommendations to Reduce Medication Errors Associated with Verbal Medication Orders and Prescriptions

National Coordinating Council for Medication Error Reporting and Prevention

Adopted February 20, 2001

Revised February 24, 2006

Preamble

Confusion over the similarity of drug names accounts for approximately 25% of all reports to the USP Medication Errors Reporting (MER) Program. To reduce confusion pertaining to verbal orders and to further support the Council's mission to minimize medication errors, the following recommendations have been developed.

In these recommendations, verbal orders are prescriptions or medication orders that are communicated as oral, spoken communications between senders and receivers face to face, by telephone, or by other auditory device.

Recommendations

1. Verbal communication of prescription or medication orders should be limited to urgent situations where immediate written or electronic communication is not feasible.
2. Health care organizations[a] should establish policies and procedures that
   - Describe limitations or prohibitions on use of verbal orders
   - Provide a mechanism to ensure validity/authenticity of the prescriber
   - List the elements required for inclusion in a complete verbal order
   - Describe situations in which verbal orders may be used
   - List and define the individuals who may send and receive verbal orders
   - Provide guidelines for clear and effective communication of verbal orders
3. Leaders of health care organizations should promote a culture in which it is acceptable, and strongly encouraged, for staff to question prescribers when there are any questions or disagreements about verbal orders. Questions about verbal orders should be resolved prior to the preparation, or dispensing, or administration of the medication.
4. Verbal orders for antineoplastic agents should **NOT** be permitted under any circumstances. These medications are not administered in emergency or urgent situations, and they have a narrow margin of safety.
5. Elements that should be included in a verbal order:
   - Name of patient
   - Age and weight of patient, when appropriate
   - Drug name
   - Dosage form (e.g., tablets, capsules, inhalants)
   - Exact strength or concentration
   - Dose, frequency, and route
   - Quantity and/or duration
   - Purpose or indication (unless disclosure is considered inappropriate by the prescriber)
   - Specific instructions for use
   - Name of prescriber and telephone number when appropriate
   - Name of individual transmitting the order, if different from the prescriber

Table 20-1. Recommendations to Reduce Medication Errors Associated with Verbal Medication Orders and Prescriptions (cont'd)

6. The content of verbal orders should be clearly communicated:
   - The name of the drug should be confirmed by any of the following:
     - Spelling
     - Providing both the brand and generic names of the medication
     - Providing the indication for use
   - In order to avoid confusion with spoken numbers, a dose such as 50 mg should be dictated as "fifty milligrams...five zero milligrams" to distinguish from "fifteen milligrams...one five milligrams."
   - In order to avoid confusion with drug name modifiers, such as prefixes and suffixes, additional spelling-assistance methods should be used (i.e., S as in Sam, X as in X-ray).
   - Instructions for use should be provided without abbreviations. For example, "1 tab tid" should be communicated as "Take/give one tablet three times daily."
   - Whenever possible, the receiver of the order should **write** down the complete order to enter it into a computer, then **read** it back, and receive confirmation from the individual who gave the order or test result.
7. All verbal orders should be reduced immediately to writing and signed by the individual receiving the order.
8. Verbal orders should be documented in the patient's medical record, reviewed, and countersigned by the prescriber as soon as possible.

Source: ©1998-2005 National Coordinating Council for Medication Error Reporting and Prevention. All Rights Reserved. Permission is hereby granted to reproduce information contained herein provided that such reproduction shall not modify the text and shall include the copyright notice appearing on the pages from which it was copied.

[a]Health care organizations include community pharmacies, physicians' offices, hospitals, nursing homes, home care agencies, etc.

Table 20-2. NATO Phonetic Alphabet and Numbers

Phonetic Alphabet	
A	Alpha
B	Bravo
C	Charlie
D	Delta
E	Echo
F	Foxtrot
G	Golf
H	Hotel
I	Indigo
J	Juliet
K	Kilo
L	Lima (pronounced “lee-ma”)
M	Mike
N	November
O	Oscar
P	Papa
Q	Quebec (pronounced “kay-bec”)
R	Romeo
S	Sierra
T	Tango
U	Uniform
V	Victor
W	Whiskey
X	X-Ray
Y	Yankee
Z	Zulu

Phonetic Numbers	
0	Zero
1	One
2	Two
3	Tree (not three)
4	Fower (pronounced “fo-wer”)
5	Fife (not five)
6	Six
7	Seven
8	Eight
9	Niner (pronounced “nine-er”)

Table 20-3. Abbreviations That Must Be on the Organization's "Do Not Use" List

Abbreviation (Do Not Use)	Potential Problem	Preferred Term
U, u (for unit)	Mistaken for *0* (zero), *4* (four) or *cc*	Write *unit*
IU (for international unit)	Mistaken for IV (intravenous) or *10* (ten)	Write *international unit* or 10 (ten)
Q.D., QD, q.d., qd (for daily) and Q.O.D., QOD, q.o.d., qod (for every other day)	Often mistaken for each other. The period after the Q can be mistaken for *I* and the *O* mistaken for *I*	Write *daily* or *every other day*
Trailing zero (X.0 mg)[a]	Decimal point can be missed.	Write *X mg*
Lack of leading zero (.X mg)	Always use a zero before a decimal point.	Write *0.X mg*
MS, MSO_4, and $MgSO_4$	Can mean morphine sulfate or magnesium sulfate. Often confused for each other.	Write *morphine sulfate* or *magnesium sulfate*

This list applies to all orders and all medication-related documentation that is handwritten (including free-text computer entry) or on preprinted forms.

Source: Adapted from the Joint Commission's Official "Do Not Use" List. Available at: www.jointcommission.org/NR/rdonlyres/2329F8F5-6EC5-4E21-B932-54B2B7D53F00/0/06_dnu_list.pdf. Accessed August 12, 2007.

[a]**Exception:** A "trailing zero" may be used only where required to demonstrate the level of precision of the value being reported, such as for laboratory results, imaging studies that report size of lesions, or catheter/tube sizes. It may not be used in medication orders or other medication-related documentation.

Table 20-4. Additional Abbreviations, Acronyms, and Symbols[a]

Abbreviation (Do Not Use)	Potential Problem	Use Instead
> (greater than) < (less than)	Misinterpreted as the number *7* (seven) or the letter *L* Confused for one another	Write *greater than* Write *less than*
Abbreviations for drug name	Misinterpreted due to similar abbreviations for multiple drugs	Write drug names in full
Apothecary units	Unfamiliar to many practitioners Confused with metric units	Use metric units
@	Mistaken for the number *2* (two)	Write *at*
cc	Mistaken for U (units) when poorly written	Write *mL* or *milliliters*
µg	Mistaken for mg (milligrams) resulting in one thousand-fold overdose	Write *mcg* or *micrograms*

Source: Adapted from the Joint Commission's Official "Do Not Use" List. Available at: www.jointcommission.org/NR/rdonlyres/2329F8F5-6EC5-4E21-B932-54B2B7D53F00/0/06_dnu_list.pdf. Accessed August 12, 2007.

[a]The Joint Commission suggests these abbreviations, acronyms, and symbols for *possible* future inclusion in the Official "Do Not Use" List.

Table 20-5. CDC Hand-Hygiene Guidelines

Centers for Disease Control and Prevention. Guideline for Hand Hygiene in Health-Care Settings. Morbidity and Mortality Weekly Report. 2002; 51(No. RR-16):31–4.

Part II. Recommendations

Categories

These recommendations are designed to improve hand-hygiene practices of HCWs and to reduce transmission of pathogenic microorganisms to patients and personnel in health-care settings. This guideline and its recommendations are not intended for use in food processing or food-service establishments, and are not meant to replace guidance provided by FDA's Model Food Code.

As in previous CDC/HICPAC guidelines, each recommendation is categorized on the basis of existing scientific data, theoretical rationale, applicability, and economic impact. The CDC/HICPAC system for categorizing recommendations is as follows:

Category IA. Strongly recommended for implementation and strongly supported by well-designed experimental, clinical, or epidemiologic studies.

Category IB. Strongly recommended for implementation and supported by certain experimental, clinical, or epidemiologic studies and a strong theoretical rationale.

Category IC. Required for implementation, as mandated by federal or state regulation or standard.

Category II. Suggested for implementation and supported by suggestive clinical or epidemiologic studies or a theoretical rationale.

No recommendation. Unresolved issue. Practices for which insufficient evidence or no consensus regarding efficacy exist.

Recommendations

1. Indications for handwashing and hand antisepsis
   - A. When hands are visibly dirty or contaminated with proteinaceous material or are visibly soiled with blood or other body fluids, wash hands with either a nonantimicrobial soap and water or an antimicrobial soap and water (IA) (*66*).
   - B. If hands are not visibly soiled, use an alcohol-based hand rub for routinely decontaminating hands in all other clinical situations described in items 1C–J (IA) (*74, 93, 166, 169, 283, 294, 312, 398*). Alternatively, wash hands with an antimicrobial soap and water in all clinical situations described in items 1C–J (IB) (*69–71, 74*).
   - C. Decontaminate hands before having direct contact with patients (IB) (*68, 400*).
   - D. Decontaminate hands before donning sterile gloves when inserting a central intravascular catheter (IB) (*401, 402*).
   - E. Decontaminate hands before inserting indwelling urinary catheters, peripheral vascular catheters, or other invasive devices that do not require a surgical procedure (IB) (*25, 403*).
   - F. Decontaminate hands after contact with a patient's intact skin (e.g., when taking a pulse or blood pressure, and lifting a patient) (IB) (*25, 45, 48, 68*).
   - G. Decontaminate hands after contact with body fluids or excretions, mucous membranes, nonintact skin, and wound dressings if hands are not visibly soiled (IA) (*400*).
   - H. Decontaminate hands if moving from a contaminated-body site to a clean-body site during patient care (II) (*25, 53*).
   - I. Decontaminate hands after contact with inanimate objects (including medical equipment) in the immediate vicinity of the patient (II) (*46, 53, 54*).

Table 20-5. CDC Hand-Hygiene Guidelines (cont'd)

J. Decontaminate hands after removing gloves (IB) (*50, 58, 321*).

K. Before eating and after using a restroom, wash hands with a nonantimicrobial soap and water or with an antimicrobial soap and water (IB) (*404–9*).

L. Antimicrobial-impregnated wipes (i.e., towelettes) may be considered as an alternative to washing hands with nonantimicrobial soap and water. Because they are not as effective as alcohol-based hand rubs or washing hands with an antimicrobial soap and water for reducing bacterial counts on the hands of HCWs, they are not a substitute for using an alcohol-based hand rub or antimicrobial soap (IB) (*160, 161*).

M. Wash hands with nonantimicrobial soap and water or with antimicrobial soap and water if exposure to *Bacillus anthracis* is suspected or proven. The physical action of washing and rinsing hands under such circumstances is recommended because alcohols, chlorhexidine, iodophors, and other antiseptic agents have poor activity against spores (II) (*120, 172, 224, 225*).

N. No recommendation can be made regarding the routine use of nonalcohol-based hand rubs for hand hygiene in health-care settings. Unresolved issue.

2. Hand-hygiene technique

A. When decontaminating hands with an alcohol-based hand rub, apply product to palm of one hand and rub hands together, covering all surfaces of hands and fingers, until hands are dry (IB) (*288, 410*). Follow the manufacturer's recommendations regarding the volume of product to use.

B. When washing hands with soap and water, wet hands first with water, apply an amount of product recommended by the manufacturer to hands, and rub hands together vigorously for at least 15 seconds, covering all surfaces of the hands and fingers. Rinse hands with water and dry thoroughly with a disposable towel. Use towel to turn off the faucet (IB) (*90–2, 94, 411*). Avoid using hot water, because repeated exposure to hot water may increase the risk of dermatitis (IB) (254, 255).

C. Liquid, bar, leaflet or powdered forms of plain soap are acceptable when washing hands with a nonantimicrobial soap and water. When bar soap is used, soap racks that facilitate drainage and small bars of soap should be used (II) (*412–415*).

D. Multiple-use cloth towels of the hanging or roll type are not recommended for use in health-care settings (II) (*137, 300*).

3. Surgical hand antisepsis

A. Remove rings, watches, and bracelets before beginning the surgical hand scrub (II) (*375, 378, 416*).

B. Remove debris from underneath fingernails using a nail cleaner under running water (II) (*14, 417*).

C. Surgical hand antisepsis using either an antimicrobial soap or an alcohol-based hand rub with persistent activity is recommended before donning sterile gloves when performing surgical procedures (IB) (*115, 159, 232, 234, 237, 418*).

D. When performing surgical hand antisepsis using an antimicrobial soap, scrub hands and forearms for the length of time recommended by the manufacturer, usually 2–6 minutes. Long scrub times (e.g., 10 minutes) are not necessary (IB) (*117, 156, 205, 207, 238–41*).

E. When using an alcohol-based surgical hand-scrub product with persistent activity, follow the manufacturer's instructions. Before applying the alcohol solution, prewash hands and forearms with a nonantimicrobial soap and dry hands and forearms completely. After application of the alcohol-based product as recommended, allow hands and forearms to dry thoroughly before donning sterile gloves (IB) (*159, 237*).

Table 20-5. CDC Hand-Hygiene Guidelines (cont'd)

4. Selection of hand-hygiene agents
   A. Provide personnel with efficacious hand-hygiene products that have low irritancy potential, particularly when these products are used multiple times per shift (IB) (*90, 92, 98, 166, 249*). This recommendation applies to products used for hand antisepsis before and after patient care in clinical areas and to products used for surgical hand antisepsis by surgical personnel.
   B. To maximize acceptance of hand-hygiene products by HCWs, solicit input from these employees regarding the feel, fragrance, and skin tolerance of any products under consideration. The cost of hand-hygiene products should not be the primary factor influencing product selection (IB) (*92, 93, 166, 274, 276–8*).
   C. When selecting nonantimicrobial soaps, antimicrobial soaps, or alcohol-based hand rubs, solicit information from manufacturers regarding any known interactions between products used to clean hands, skin care products, and the types of gloves used in the institution (II) (*174, 372*).
   D. Before making purchasing decisions, evaluate the dispenser systems of various product manufacturers or distributors to ensure that dispensers function adequately and deliver an appropriate volume of product (II) (*286*).
   E. Do not add soap to a partially empty soap dispenser. This practice of "topping off" dispensers can lead to bacterial contamination of soap (IA) (*187, 419*).

5. Skin care
   A. Provide HCWs with hand lotions or creams to minimize the occurrence of irritant contact dermatitis associated with hand antisepsis or handwashing (IA) (*272, 273*).
   B. Solicit information from manufacturers regarding any effects that hand lotions, creams, or alcohol-based hand antiseptics may have on the persistent effects of antimicrobial soaps being used in the institution (IB) (*174, 420, 421*).

6. Other Aspects of Hand Hygiene
   A. Do not wear artificial fingernails or extenders when having direct contact with patients at high risk (e.g., those in intensive-care units or operating rooms) (IA) (*350–3*).
   B. Keep natural nails tips less than 1/4-inch long (II) (*350*).
   C. Wear gloves when contact with blood or other potentially infectious materials, mucous membranes, and nonintact skin could occur (IC) (*356*).
   D. Remove gloves after caring for a patient. Do not wear the same pair of gloves for the care of more than one patient, and do not wash gloves between uses with different patients (IB) (*50, 58, 321, 373*).
   E. Change gloves during patient care if moving from a contaminated body site to a clean body site (II) (*50, 51, 58*).
   F. No recommendation can be made regarding wearing rings in health-care settings. Unresolved issue.

7. Health-care worker educational and motivational programs
   A. As part of an overall program to improve hand-hygiene practices of HCWs, educate personnel regarding the types of patient-care activities that can result in hand contamination and the advantages and disadvantages of various methods used to clean their hands (II) (*74, 292, 295, 299*).
   B. Monitor HCWs' adherence with recommended hand-hygiene practices and provide personnel with information regarding their performance (IA) (*74, 276, 292, 295, 299, 306, 310*).

Table 20-5. CDC Hand-Hygiene Guidelines (cont'd)

C. Encourage patients and their families to remind HCWs to decontaminate their hands (II) (*394, 422*).

8. Administrative measures

A. Make improved hand-hygiene adherence an institutional priority and provide appropriate administrative support and financial resources (IB) (*74–5*).

B. Implement a multidisciplinary program designed to improve adherence of health personnel to recommended hand-hygiene practices (IB) (*74–5*).

C. As part of a multidisciplinary program to improve hand-hygiene adherence, provide HCWs with a readily accessible alcohol-based hand-rub product (IA) (*74, 166, 283, 294, 312*).

D. To improve hand-hygiene adherence among personnel who work in areas in which high workloads and high intensity of patient care are anticipated, make an alcohol-based hand rub available at the entrance to the patient's room or at the bedside, in other convenient locations, and in individual pocket-sized containers to be carried by HCWs (IA) (*11, 74, 166, 283, 284, 312, 318, 423*).

E. Store supplies of alcohol-based hand rubs in cabinets or areas approved for flammable materials (IC).

Part III. Performance Indicators

1. The following performance indicators are recommended for measuring improvements in HCWs' hand-hygiene adherence:

A. Periodically monitor and record adherence as the number of hand-hygiene episodes performed by personnel/number of hand-hygiene opportunities, by ward or by service. Provide feedback to personnel regarding their performance.

B. Monitor the volume of alcohol-based hand rub (or detergent used for handwashing or hand antisepsis) used per 1000 patient-days.

C. Monitor adherence to policies dealing with wearing of artificial nails.

D. When outbreaks of infection occur, assess the adequacy of health-care worker hand hygiene.

CHAPTER 21

Medication Safety Improvement

Improving medication safety is a significant challenge to health care practitioners. There are no simple answers or quick fixes to this complex problem. To be effective, medication safety improvement programs must be comprehensive and include all of the following elements:

- Support of leadership
- Management by an interdisciplinary group
- A supportive culture that emphasizes cooperation and minimizes discipline
- Analysis to determine the causes of reported errors
- Proactive assessments of the medication system to identify risks
- Medication safety education and competence assessment of staff and patients
- Management of patient and drug information to ensure that it is accurate and readily available
- Safe use of appropriate technology
- Improvement of medication use processes

A review of some of these elements (e.g., the use of technology) is beyond the scope of this chapter and the review of other elements is not covered in detail. However, this chapter will help organizations improve processes for selecting and procuring, storing, ordering and transcribing, preparing and dispensing, administering, and monitoring medications. It emphasizes practices that foster accuracy and reduce the potential for errors. It also provides guidance for detecting, reporting, reviewing, and analyzing medication errors. Chapters 19 and 20 address the Joint Commission's National Patient Safety Goals (NPSGs). Chapter 14 provides an overview of the Joint Commission's Sentinel Event Policy. Chapter 22 addresses adverse drug reactions.

Definitions of Medication Errors

Definitions of medication errors vary and in the past tended to include only errors that reached a patient (i.e., with the exception of errors of omission, a patient had to receive the medication for the incident to be classified as a medication error). Some examples of current definitions follow:

National Coordinating Council for Medication Error Reporting and Prevention—The National Coordinating Council for Medication Error Reporting and Prevention (NCC MERP) defines a medication error as "any preventable event that may cause or lead to inappropriate medication use or patient harm while the medication is in the control of the health care professional, patient, or consumer. Such events may be related to professional practice, health care products, procedures, and systems, including prescribing; order communication; product labeling, packaging, and nomenclature; compounding; dispensing; distribution; administration; education; monitoring; and use."[1]

ASHP and The Joint Commission™ are member organizations of NCCMERP. Both organizations endorse the NCCMERP definition.

The Joint Commission—In the glossary to the *CAMH*, the Joint Commission defines medication errors, sentinel events, and near misses:

- A *medication error* is "Any preventable event that may cause inappropriate medication use or jeopardize patient safety."
- A *sentinel event* is an "unexpected occurrence involving death or serious physical or psychological injury, or the risk thereof. Serious injury specifically includes loss of limb or function. The phrase 'or the risk thereof' includes any process variation for which a recurrence would carry a significant chance of a serious adverse outcome."
- A *near miss* is "any process variation, which did not affect an outcome, but for which a recurrence carries a significant chance of a serious adverse outcome."

The Joint Commission states that these "near misses" are "within the scope of the definition of a sentinel event, but outside the scope of those sentinel events that are subject to review by the Joint Commission under its Sentinel Event Policy." (Chapter 14 provides an overview of the Joint Commission's Sentinel Event Policy and guidelines for responding to a sentinel event.)

ASHP—ASHP does not define medication errors. However, ASHP categorizes 12 specific types of medication errors, which are described in Table 21-1.[2]

Organization Definitions—The Joint Commission expects organizations to develop and approve a medication error definition that includes near misses that cause no harm as well as sentinel events that result in serious adverse outcomes. The NCCMERP definition provides an excellent foundation for an organization medication error definition. (*See* Reviewing and Analyzing Medication Errors in this chapter.)

Causes of Medication Errors

Although human error is often associated with medication errors, most medication errors are caused by problems in the medication use system (i.e., the processes for selecting and procuring, ordering and transcribing, preparing and dispensing, administering, and monitoring the effects of medications on patients). Since human errors cannot be eliminated, organizations should focus on identifying and eliminating root causes related to faulty processes.

Many errors may be due to multiple problems with the system. For example, failure to administer a medication on time may occur because the medication was not available for administration. Reasons for nonavailability of the medication could include the following:

- Order was not sent to the pharmacy promptly.
- Order was not written legibly or clearly (e.g., unclear abbreviations used) and filling was delayed until clarified.
- Order was written for a nonformulary agent.
- Order was not entered correctly in the pharmacy patient profiles.
- Drug product was not available from the supplier.
- Order was not filled promptly.
- Filled order was not delivered to the patient-care unit or was misplaced at the patient care unit.

The Institute for Safe Medication Practices (ISMP) has identified several common causes of medication errors. Some of these are listed in Table 21-2.[3]

High-Risk or High-Alert Medications

Some medications pose a high risk for serious errors that may lead to sentinel events. Medications often designated as high-risk or high-alert include concentrated electrolytes (e.g., potassium chloride, potassium phosphate, and sodium chloride greater than 0.9%, magnesium sulfate, calcium chloride, and calcium gluconate), insulin, opiates and narcotics, intravenous anticoagulants (e.g., heparin), chemotherapeutic medications, neonatal and pediatric medications, epidural medications, patient controlled analgesia medications, neuromuscular blocking agents, and medications with look-alike and sound-alike names. ISMP has identified the high-risk or high-alert medications listed in Table 21-3. (*See* MM.7.10 in Chapter 4.) (Example 21-1 is a list of selected high-risk/high-alert medications and precautions for administering them.)

There are other medications that pose a risk for errors with serious outcomes. Furthermore, other factors that are unrelated to specific medications may increase the potential for errors with any medication. These factors relate to the environment (e.g., poor lighting), patient education (e.g., failure to educate patients about their medications adequately), and information management (e.g., failure to communicate patient and drug information clearly).

Proactive Risk Assessment

Organizations should assess their medication use system proactively to identify risk points in the processes. At a minimum, organizations should assess high-risk processes that are often associated with sentinel events (e.g., processes relating to the use of the high-risk medications listed in Table 21-3).

Data Analysis—Pharmacies should aggregate and analyze data and report the findings through their performance improvement process. Examples of such data include the following:

- Clarifications of questionable medication orders
- Usage patterns of after-hours access to medications
- Administering first doses of medications prior to review by a pharmacist

- Unusual removals of controlled substances from stock

Organizations should review the data and act as necessary (e.g., by using process improvement tools) to improve their medication use processes. (*See* Chapter 14.)

Failure Mode and Effects Analysis—Failure mode and effects analysis (FMEA) (sometimes called failure mode, effects, and criticality analysis) is a proactive method for identifying possible ways that a process might fail (failure modes), the likelihood of the failure, the capability of detecting a failure, and the criticality of the effect. Although FMEA has been used principally by engineers, health care facilities are adapting it to identify failure modes in their medication use processes that occur frequently and/or pose a high risk of serious adverse outcomes. They then focus on redesigning the processes to minimize the probability of failure or to protect patients from the effects of the failure. This chapter suggests measures for preventing medication errors. An example of applying FMEA to a medication use process is available on the Joint Commission's Web site. (*See* Chapter 14 and Appendix A.)

Improving Processes

Measures for preventing medication errors should focus on improving processes. Processes for selecting and procuring, storing, ordering and transcribing, preparing and dispensing, administering, and monitoring the effects of medications on patients should be reviewed to identify ways to improve them and reduce the potential for medication errors. To improve processes, organizations should do the following:

Develop Policies and Procedures—All departments involved in the process (e.g., medical staff, nursing service, imaging, emergency department, ambulatory surgery, clinics, and pharmacy services) should cooperate in developing policies and procedures that will prevent medication errors. Policies and procedures should describe the medication distribution process in detail and should promote consistency and accuracy. There should be an emphasis on points in the process that are most prone to cause errors. For example:

- Transcription of orders
- Labeling
- Calculations

Policies and procedures for compounding medications should emphasize the following:

- Double checks of critical steps prone to error (e.g., calculations)
- Order (sequence) of preparation
- Compounding technique (e.g., sterile or nonsterile)

Policies and procedures for selecting and procuring, storing, ordering and transcribing, preparing and dispensing, administering, and monitoring the effects of medications on patients should be reviewed and updated regularly. Adherence to policies and procedures must be emphasized.

Standardize—Standardization can greatly reduce the potential for medication errors. Standard dosage charts and standard concentrations of medications can minimize the need for calculations (a major source of errors). Standard medication administration times can reduce confusion.

Avoid Dangerous and Confusing Abbreviations and Expressions—All abbreviations pose a risk of misinterpretation and the use of abbreviations should be minimized throughout the medication use process (e.g., ordering, labeling, and maintaining pharmacy patient profiles). However some abbreviations and expressions are especially dangerous and a list of standard abbreviations can reduce confusion. (The Joint Commission requires organizations to have a list of "Do not use" or prohibited abbreviations.) The NCCMERP has identified the abbreviations and expressions in Table 21-4 that are commonly misinterpreted and should not be used.[1]

Other examples of dangerous and confusing abbreviations and expressions include the following:

- *Roman Numerals and Apothecaries' Symbols*—Use Arabic numerals (e.g., 6) instead of Roman numerals (e.g., VI or vi).
- *Apothecaries' System and Symbols*—Express quantities in the metric system. The apothecaries' system and symbols are confusing and should be avoided. For example:
    - The dram symbol is easily confused with the number 3.
    - The minim symbol is sometimes confused with the abbreviations for milliliter (mL).
    - The grain abbreviation (gr) is sometimes confused with the abbreviation for gram (g).

- *Latin*—Limit the use of Latin to common expressions and abbreviations whose meanings are clear and universally understood (e.g., *stat* and *prn*).
- *Decimal Points*—Avoid the use of decimals (e.g., write 500 mg instead of 0.5 g). Decimal points may not reproduce on a copy of the order or may be hidden by lines or imperfections in the copy.
- *Leading and Trailing Zeros*—Place a zero in front of a leading decimal point (e.g., write 0.5 mg rather than .5 mg) and do not use unnecessary decimal points or zeros after a decimal point (e.g., write 25 mg rather than 25.0 mg).
- *Dosage Units*—Express dosage in strengths (e.g., 50 mg) rather than dosage units (e.g., 2 tablets).
- *Vague Directions*—Do not use vague directions for use (e.g., "take as directed").
- *Chemical Symbols*—Avoid using chemical symbols to abbreviate drug names. For example: MgSO4 (magnesium sulfate) has been misinterpreted as morphine sulfate.
- *Acronyms and Other Coined or Abbreviated Names*—Avoid using acronyms and other coined or abbreviated names. As the numbers of drugs with similar names increases, the risks associated with the use of acronyms and other coined or abbreviated drug names increases. For example:
    - AZT could stand for zidovudine, azathioprine, or aztreonam.
    - HCTZ (for hydrochlorothiazide) has been misinterpreted as hydrocortisone.
    - DPT could stand for Diptheria, Pertussis, and Tetanus or Demerol, Phenergan, and Thorazine.
    - A-pen (for ampicillin) may be quite clear to the prescriber's staff but can be confusing to those who are unfamiliar with the prescriber's personal abbreviations.
    - Coined names (e.g., clafagyl) for a combination of Claforan™ and Flagyl™ are unlikely to be found in drug information sources and could be confusing to those who are not familiar with them.
    - MOM (for milk of magnesia) could be an acronym for another product in some organizations.
    - Nonstandard names (e.g., "half-and-half," "asthma cocktail," "GI cocktail," and "magic mouthwash") are nonspecific and the drug ingredients and strengths may vary from organization to organization. Furthermore, half-and-half could refer to combinations of medications (e.g., laxatives) or a combination of milk and cream. Nonstandard names are confusing when practitioners move from organization to organization.
- *Computer Mnemonics*—Computer mnemonics can sometimes result in the wrong drug being displayed on the computer screen. Increasing the number of characters can minimize the opportunity for entering a drug with a similarly spelled name. Mneumonics should never be used for high-risk or high-alert medications (e.g., cancer chemotherapeutic agents).

Ensure That Personnel Are Qualified—Care should be taken to ensure that personnel are qualified to dispense and administer medications. You should select personnel who demonstrate their ability to give attention to detail, perform accurate work, and follow procedures.

Educate Staff—Ensuring that personnel are qualified also includes orientation, education, and training for prescribers, persons who dispense medications (pharmacists and pharmacy technicians), and persons who administer medications (e.g., nurses, respiratory therapists, and imaging technologists). These individuals must stay informed of current knowledge on the appropriate and safe use of medications (e.g., through reading the literature, participating in educational programs, or by consulting with other health care professionals). Pharmacists should provide educational programs for prescribers and persons who administer medications (e.g., programs on medication actions, indications, precautions, appropriate dosages, and administration techniques). Education for personnel who dispense medications should include the following:

- Weights, measures, and calculations
- Incompatibilities
- Nomenclature and abbreviations
- Compounding procedures (including procedures to promote compounding accuracy)
- Labeling
- Maintaining dispensing records
- Administration routes, devices, and techniques

Assess Staff Competence—Personnel, especially new personnel, must demonstrate their competence through competence assessment before dispensing and administering medications. Competence assessment will assure that the person's education has been successful and should emphasize correct interpretation of orders and accurate calculations. Competence testing for persons who administer medications should include an assessment of administration technique. Testing for persons who dispense medications should include compounding procedures. Continued competence can be assured through periodic (e.g., quarterly or annual) testing and frequent (e.g., daily or weekly) observation of techniques. Records should document education, training, and competence assessment of personnel.

Educate Patients and Involve Them in Their Care—Education should extend to patients and their caregivers (i.e., those who provide postdischarge care for patients). Patients who are knowledgeable about medication use (including drug-drug and drug-food interactions) may be more aware of the need for communicating their medication allergies, sensitivities, and adverse drug reactions. In addition, knowledgeable patients can prevent medication errors by questioning unusual dosages and routes of administration and unfamiliar medications. Education efforts should encourage patients and caregivers to communicate their questions and concerns to physicians, nurses, and pharmacists responsible for the patient's care.

Assess Patient Competence—Assessing patient competence may not be easy. Techniques for assessing patient competence include the following:

- Stop frequently during education and ask questions to see if the patient understands instructions up to that point.
- Ask the patient to repeat instructions or demonstrate a technique.
- Ask questions that test the patient's understanding of signs of events that pose a risk of harm (e.g., signs of toxicity, and adverse reactions) and actions to be taken.

Minimize Discipline—Some organizations require specific educational actions when specified types or numbers of errors occur. For example, an excessive number of omitted doses in a period may result in mandatory attendance at error-prevention educational programs. Punitive actions are likely to be counter-productive (e.g., deter error reporting and delaying process improvements).

When process problems have been ruled out and personnel continue to make errors consistently, they should be reassigned to duties that do not require them to dispense or administer medications. Discipline, such as probation, demotion, suspension, and termination, should be the last resort and reserved for specified, serious errors (e.g., overdose of a medication due to gross negligence and a disregard for established policies and procedures).

Preventing Selecting, Storing, Securing, and Procuring Medication Errors

Measures to prevent errors should start before orders are written or medications are dispensed and administered. Error prevention measures should be in place in all medication storage areas (including pharmacy storerooms and dispensing areas, automated medication storage and distribution devices, and nonautomated storage areas). Organizations that have both automated and nonautomated storage should ensure that error prevention measures are equally effective (although the process may be different). Adherence to the following practices can prevent errors relating to selecting, storing, securing, and procuring medications:

- Organize medication storage and work areas to minimize the potential for dispensing errors (i.e., uncluttered and free from distractions and interruptions).
- Review floor stock and night stock lists to ensure that they are limited to urgently needed medications.
- Ensure that a pharmacist is available when the pharmacy is closed and is readily accessible to nursing and medical personnel.
- Ensure that medications are available in the most ready-to-use form(s).
- Ensure that medications are clearly and completely labeled (including name, strength, dosage form, and expiration date) and that the information is displayed prominently.
- Ensure that medications with look-alike and sound-alike names are stored to minimize the potential for confusion.
- Label high-risk or high-alert medications distinctly (e.g., with different colors or bright stickers).
- Store dangerous medications in isolated areas or segregate them from other medications.
- Do not store injections of concentrated potassium chloride, potassium phosphate, or sodium chloride greater than 0.9% in patient care areas.

- Ensure that other concentrated electrolytes (e.g., magnesium sulfate and calcium chloride) are stored only in areas where the concentrated forms are needed.
- Eliminate multiple-dose vials of medications when possible.
- Provide cautionary warnings for medications with a narrow margin of safety.
- Inspect areas regularly to ensure that medications are labeled properly and stored to minimize the likelihood of a medication error. Remove deteriorated, expired, and otherwise unusable medications immediately.
- Adhere to the following precautions for automated medication storage and distribution devices:
  - Place medications in the devices carefully with particular attention to look-alike and sound-alike medications.
  - Store all high-alert or high-risk medications in single-access pockets.
- Adhere to the following precautions for nonautomated medication storage:
  - Assess the storage of all items that are not distributed by the pharmacy (e.g., bulk items, IV products distributed by the materials management department, contrast media, and patients' personal medications).
  - Deliver filled orders promptly to predesignated, secure points in patient care areas.
  - Arrange medications to minimize errors in retrieving them (e.g., by storing ampuls and vials of medications intended for irrigation and respiratory therapy separately from ampuls and vials for parenteral use, by storing ophthalmic and otic medications separately, and by storing medications and products intended for external use separately from injectable medications and medications intended for internal use).

Preventing Ordering/Prescribing Errors

Measures for preventing errors in the ordering/prescribing process must focus on standardization of prescribing practices, clarity, and accuracy. Policies and procedures should address these issues. Adherence to the following practices can prevent errors relating to ordering/prescribing medications:

- Review the patient's status, current medication regimen, and laboratory reports prior to ordering medications.
- Order medications that are listed in the organization's formulary. Personnel are probably more familiar with formulary than nonformulary medications and are therefore less likely to make medication errors if formulary medications are prescribed.
- Avoid verbal orders except in emergency situations. Some organizations adopt policies that prohibit verbal orders when the prescriber is able to provide written orders.
- When a verbal order is received, write the order on the order sheet and read back the written order to the prescriber. Many organizations require the read back of the order to be documented.
- Authenticate verbal orders promptly.
- Eliminate the need for transcription of orders (and the possibility of transcription errors) by using computer prescriber order entry, or scan or facsimile transmissions.
- Write (preferably print) legibly, use an approved preprinted order form, or use a computerized order-entry system.
- Ensure that the order includes the patient's name, location, required identifiers, age, and, if appropriate, weight and height.
- Write complete orders (i.e., medication name, dosage form, dose, strength, route, frequency, rate, method, and site of administration).
- Do not use vague expressions (e.g., "resume orders" or "continue medications").
- Indicate the reason for ordering the medication (e.g., prochlorperazine 5 mg IM every 4 hours as needed for nausea).
- Prescribe medications to be administered orally (rather than parenterally) when possible.
- Double-check orders to ensure that they are clear and complete.

Preventing Dispensing Errors

Measures for preventing errors in the dispensing process must focus on accuracy. Although dispensing errors may not result in medication administration errors, they increase the potential for making medication errors. Examples of dispensing errors include the following:

- Dispensing the wrong medication
- Dispensing the wrong dosage form
- Dispensing the wrong dose
- Dispensing a medication that is contraindicated because of the patient's diagnosis or physical condition (unless the prescriber authorizes the administration on the basis that the benefits outweigh the risks)
- Dispensing a medication that interacts with another medication the patient is taking (unless the prescriber authorizes the administration on the basis that the benefits outweigh the risks)
- Dispensing a medication to which the patient has a known or stated allergy (unless the prescriber authorizes the administration on the basis that the benefits outweigh the risks or if the prescriber is attempting to desensitize the patient)
- Errors in labeling medications (e.g., wrong medication, wrong strength, and wrong concentration)
- Errors in preparing medications (e.g., compounding errors, wrong ingredients, and wrong amounts or ratios of ingredients)
- Unavailability of doses for administration at the scheduled time (e.g., orders not filled or orders filled but not delivered to the patient-care or procedural unit)

Most dispensing errors are caused by problems in the dispensing process. Simply "trying" for zero dispensing errors is rarely sufficient to reduce errors significantly over the long term. Therefore, managers must improve the dispensing process and educate staff continuously. Adherence to the following practices can prevent dispensing errors:

- Provide all doses in a ready-to-use format. Solid oral medications, including most ½ tablet doses, should be in unit-dose packages. Liquid medications should be in unit-dose packages (e.g., oral syringes or cups) if possible. IV medications should be in ready to administer forms (e.g., manufacturers' premixed solutions, manufacturers' vial/bag systems, and pharmacy-prepared IV solutions with additives).
- Ensure that a pharmacist reviews all medication orders before administering the first dose of medication except in the following situations:
    - The urgency of the patient's condition requires administration before the review.
    - A physician is present to oversee the review, administration of the medication, and monitoring of the patient.
- Ensure that a pharmacist's review includes comparing orders with patient medication profiles (e.g., for allergies, potential interactions, laboratory results, and duplicate therapies).
- Ensure that the pharmacy computer system is enabled to check for interactions, duplicate therapy, and dose ranges.
- Question all orders that call for an unusual number of dosage units (e.g., orders for more than two tablets, vials, or ampuls).
- If technicians enter orders, ensure that a pharmacist checks the entries and reviews all warnings (including warnings that the technicians may have bypassed).
- Identify medications, therapies, patient types (e.g., pediatric), and patient conditions (e.g., oncology) that require a second person to check the order. Ensure that the second checks are performed and documented.
- Ensure that the organization's policies address how pharmacists are to retrospectively review orders when a prospective review is not possible. Ensure that the policies include the time frame for the review. The organization should monitor compliance with the policies, gather data (e.g., types and numbers of errors) relating to compliance, and target processes for improvement. The organization should review and communicate the results of its process improvement efforts.
- Ensure that policies clearly define when a nurse is permitted to administer the first dose of a medication before a pharmacist reviews the order. The policies should address removing medications from automated medication storage and distribution devices and from nonautomated floor stock. A limited list of medications for which this "override" is permitted should be defined by policy. In all cases, administering medications without a pharmacist's review of the order must be warranted by the urgency of the patient's condition or the availability of a physician to oversee the process.
- Review orders carefully. Clarify ambiguous and incomplete orders and inappropriate doses with the prescriber prior to dispensing. Document efforts

to resolve questionable medication orders (e.g., by telephone communication with the prescriber).

- Keep the process simple to minimize the chance for errors.
- Ensure that all personnel are familiar with policies and procedures and understand the importance of following them.
- Require a double check of all calculations by another qualified individual (especially for compounding medications and for pediatric, oncology, and other high-risk dosage calculations). Incorrect calculations may result in significant underdosing or serious overdosing of patients. All calculations should be documented in writing.
- Use standardized concentrations of medications to minimize the need for calculations and necessity to compound medications.
- Triple-check labels on medication containers (i.e., when removing from shelf, before dispensing, and when returning to the shelf).
- Prepare one order at a time.
- Compound medications carefully and correctly. The compounding process must ensure the following:
  - All entries in compounding records are correct.
  - Products (medications, excipients, etc.) are used as ordered.
  - Amounts used are correct.
  - Compounding equipment is used correctly.
  - In-process checks (e.g., inspection of products and checks of calculations) are performed.
- Label medications clearly and accurately. All medications must be labeled with a minimum of the following:
  - Medication name, strength, and amount
  - Patient name, location, and other identifiers, if applicable
  - Expiration date (and time if applicable)
  - Lot number and manufacturer (if applicable)
  - Ancillary precaution labels that will decrease the risk of medication administration errors (e.g., "For the Ear" and "Not for Injection")
  - Initials of preparer
  - For compounded sterile preparations, the diluent and date prepared
- Dispense outpatient prescriptions in containers that meet the requirements of the Poison Prevention Packaging Act of 1970. Label outpatient prescriptions in accordance with State Board of Pharmacy and Federal regulations.
- Require a final check for accuracy on every order filled. Review the order if there are apparent discrepancies. Compounding errors may be difficult to detect, so compounded preparations should be discarded if errors are suspected. The final check should include the following:
  - Appearance and labeling of the finished preparation
  - Inspection of containers of ingredients used in preparing the medication
  - Accuracy of written calculations relating to the preparation
- Ensure that technicians have their work checked by a pharmacist. Pharmacists *should* have their work checked by another person (preferably a pharmacist), but if a nonpharmacist checks a pharmacist's work (e.g., in organizations with only one pharmacist on duty), the pharmacist retains legal responsibility for the accuracy of the orders filled.
- Provide drug information references (including standard dosage charts and standard flow rate charts) to personnel who dispense and administer medications.

Preventing Sterile Preparation Errors—Adherence to the following can prevent errors in compounding sterile preparations:

- Avoid compounding sterile preparations when premixed products are available. This also eliminates the risk of contamination during compounding.
- Use premixed solutions with standardized concentrations (e.g., heparin 25,000 units in D5W 500 mL) when possible. The use of standardized concentrations can also minimize the risk of administration errors if flow rate charts are used to eliminate the need for flow rate calculations.
- Inspect stock regularly for expiration dates and package integrity. Remove all expired or damaged stock from the preparation area.
- Avoid stocking concentrated injectable medications that can be lethal if administered without dilution.

- Minimize the use of multiple-dose containers. Limit the use of multiple-dose containers to nonlethal medications and limit the size of multiple-dose containers to nonlethal amounts of medications.
- Store potentially lethal additives (e.g., concentrated potassium chloride) only in the pharmacy (not in floor stock or crash carts). Prepare all solutions containing potentially lethal additives in the pharmacy.
- Eliminate after-hours access to concentrated potassium chloride and potassium phosphate throughout the organization.
- Prepare only one sterile preparation at a time.
- Leave containers of all additives and diluents in the work area (to facilitate checking by a second party). Use a different syringe for each additive and diluent, and leave syringes with their respective containers. Leave the plungers of syringes at the position marking the volume of solution withdrawn.
- Label preparations at the time they are prepared.
- Ensure that another individual checks the labeled final preparation prior to dispensing.

Preventing Incompatibilities and Particulate Matter in Sterile Preparations—Care must be taken to prevent incompatibilities and particulate matter in sterile preparations. The following measures should be observed:

- Consult compatibility references (e.g., ASHP's *Handbook on Injectable Drugs*[4] to establish the compatibility of compounded sterile preparations.
- Avoid adding more than one drug to a solution unless the compatibility of the mixture is established.
- Use a separate syringe and needle for each additive.
- Mix powdered ingredients thoroughly with diluents and ensure that they dissolve completely.
- To avoid coring (cutting of rubber pieces as a needle is inserted into a vial), make entries into vials with the bevel of the needle (slanted portion of needle tip) facing up and use a slight downward and lateral (toward the bevel) pressure.
- Use a filter to reduce the number of glass particles from ampuls. Some organizations require the use of a filter for drugs in ampuls even though the drug may be administered through an IV set with an inline filter. However, filters may adsorb some drugs and result in a subtherapeutic final preparation. Use of a filter is not a substitute for good technique.
- Inspect solutions for turbidity, discoloration, evidence of incompatibilities, and particulate matter before and after preparation. A haze or a precipitate may be evidence of a physical incompatibility, although some incompatibilities may be chemical or therapeutic and may not be visible. Viewing solutions against both light and dark backgrounds can help to identify particulate matter.

Preventing Medication Administration Errors

Medications should be administered only by persons who are qualified and authorized to administer them. Policies and procedures often restrict the persons who are authorized to administer specific medications or types of medications, and they usually list those persons by position or title (such as registered nurse, licensed practical nurse, and critical care registered nurse) as well as by the routes by which they are authorized to administer medications. If special training is required (e.g., for oncology agents or moderate sedation), it should be indicated in the organization's policies and procedures. Adherence to the following practices can prevent medication administration errors:

- Ensure that verbal orders are written in the patient's medical record promptly and authenticated by the prescriber.
- Ensure that orders are communicated promptly to the pharmacy.
- Double-check the accuracy of orders transcribed onto medication administration records (MARs) by comparing transcriptions with original orders. Have a second individual make the comparison when possible.
- Check that the pharmacy has interpreted and filled the order correctly. Check the label and appearance of the product provided by the pharmacy, and contact the pharmacy if there are apparent discrepancies.
- Ensure that nurses reconcile MARs with patient medical records every shift (or a minimum of every 24 hours). Ensure that the reconciliation is documented.
- Clarify ambiguous medication orders or questionable administration routes with the prescriber before administering the medication. Document the clarification and all changes made in the order.

- Question all orders that call for an unusual number of dosage units (e.g., more than two tablets or more than one ampul or vial).
- Consult current drug information and administration references as needed.
- Contact the pharmacy when medications are unavailable for administration. The order may have been discontinued without the discontinuation being noted on nursing records.
- Do not permit borrowing medication from one patient to administer to another patient.
- Prepare medications for administration in an area that is free from distractions and interruptions.
- Prepare doses for one patient for one medication pass at a time.
- Check mathematical calculations (e.g., dosage and flow rates) with another qualified individual (e.g., a pharmacist or a nurse). Using standard concentrations of medications and standard flow rate charts can reduce the need for mathematical calculations.
- Ensure that patients are identified accurately (using the organization's two selected patient identifiers) immediately prior to medication administration.
- Double-check the name of the medication and strength on the label with the medication and dose prescribed.
- Check the medication, original order, and MAR if the patient questions the administration of the medication. This reduces the likelihood of administering a wrong medication or administering a duplicate dose of a medication.
- Use the proper administration equipment (e.g., infusion control device) and technique.
- Use infusion control devices properly and safely. Use only devices that protect against allowing uncontrolled flow into a patient. Ensure that those who use these devices understand how to use them. Require two individuals to compare the settings with the order and verify that the drug, concentration, and flow-rate are correct.
- Minimize the types of devices used. A single type of device reduces the potential for confusion associated with multiple types of devices.
- Ensure that devices that are rented or leased are configured consistently with the organization's own devices and are protected from free-flow.
- Use standardized IV administration rate charts to determine the flow rate of critical care medications dosed in mcg per kg per min (e.g., dobutamine).
- Observe the patient after administering oral medications to ensure that he or she swallows the medications.
- Record the administration of medications soon after their administration. Prompt recording fosters complete and accurate documentation and reduces the likelihood of omitted and duplicate doses.
- If required by the organization's policies, return all discontinued and unneeded medications and medications for discharged patients to the pharmacy.

Preventing Errors When Medications Are Self-Administered—Self-administration of medications should be minimized because it decreases accountability (accurate administration records are not kept), creates the potential for medication errors, may lead to misuse of medications, and increases the organization's potential liability. However, in some organizations and drug rehabilitation facilities, self-administration of medications is part of the patient's therapy (e.g., for cardiac and transplant patients).

Organizations should have a process to ensure that patients who self-medicate do so correctly. Policies and procedures should emphasize the following:

- Only patients deemed competent are permitted to self-administer medications.
- A member of the professional staff must supervise self-administration.
- Amounts of medications supplied to the patient must be limited.
- Types of medications supplied must be limited to those that can be self-administered with little risk of harm.
- The patient must be instructed in the proper use of the medications. When possible, pharmacists should instruct patients who self-administer medications.

Preventing Errors Relating to Monitoring Patients

A complete medication use system includes processes for monitoring the effects of medications on patients. Adherence to the following practices can prevent errors relating to monitoring patients:

- Monitor patients for the desired therapeutic effect. Failure to monitor can lead to prescribing errors.
- Monitor patients for signs and symptoms of adverse drug reactions, toxic doses, and change in status. Failure to respond appropriately can lead to overdoses or inappropriate medication selection. (*See* Chapter 22.)
- Ensure that laboratory tests are performed and the results provided promptly to physicians , nurses, pharmacists and others who need the information. Failure to monitor laboratory results can result in inappropriate drug use or drug dosing.

Detecting Medication Errors

Some medication errors are detected by the persons who make the errors, whereas others are detected by chance observation (e.g., observation of administration by the wrong route). However, many errors are undetected because there is no reliable mechanism for detecting them. Methods for improving detection of actual and potential errors include direct observation of persons who prepare and administer medications, evaluation of missing doses, and evaluation of excess doses.

Direct Observation of Persons Who Prepare and Administer Medications—Direct observation of persons who prepare and administer medications may be the most effective method to detect medication errors and may be the only method to detect certain types of errors (e.g., incorrect preparation and administration techniques). Although direct observation may require additional personnel, time, and funds, the potential for improvement outweighs these disadvantages. To reduce costs and the demands on personnel, observation may be conducted randomly.

Review of Patient Medical Records—A review of patient medical records may reveal indications that a medication error occurred. For example, bleeding problems might signal an overdose of an anticoagulant and the administration of drugs used to treat adverse drug reactions might indicate the misuse of a drug to which a patient has a known allergy.

Evaluation of Missing Doses—Evaluation of the reasons for doses missing from the patient's medication supply may reveal medication errors (e.g., administration of duplicate doses). However, some missing doses may be justified. For example, a missing dose may be justified because the first dose was administered earlier than expected. Missing doses should be recorded as they are identified (e.g., on a log). Unjustified and unexplained missing doses should be brought to the nursing staff's attention.

Evaluation of Excess Doses—Frequent (e.g., daily) reconciliation of pharmacy dispensing records with nursing MARs and the patient's medication supply (e.g., unit-dose cassette drawers) can help identify excess doses. Excess doses may be caused by omissions or partial administration of medications or by administration of another patient's medication. However, accountability for excess doses is difficult if nurses fail to record administration of doses accurately or if pharmacists dispense extra doses routinely (a practice that is strongly discouraged). Unjustified and unexplained excess doses should be brought to the nursing staff's attention.

Some excess doses may be justified. Justified reasons for excess doses include the following:

- Pharmacy dispensed extra doses (e.g., *prn* medications).
- Pharmacy dispensed enough doses to start administration at once, while nursing waited until the next scheduled administration time before administering the first dose.
- Doses were contraindicated.
- Patient was not to take anything (including medications) by mouth.
- Patient was temporarily absent from the patient care area or organization (e.g., off the floor for a scheduled procedure or on pass).
- Patient was transferred to another unit (e.g., an intensive care unit) and a new supply of medications was dispensed.
- Order was discontinued after delivery of medications.
- Patient refused doses.

Organizations should have a policy and procedure to address administration of medication doses when patients are away from the patient care area. Refused doses are not necessarily justified reasons for omission and should be evaluated carefully. Another equally effective medication or the same medication by a different route or in a different vehicle may be acceptable to the patient.

Reporting Medication Errors

Prompt attention to the patient and providing appropriate supportive treatment are paramount when medication errors are made. After attending to the patient's immediate needs, medication errors must be reported.

Individuals who have the greatest knowledge of the errors should report them. This is usually the person who discovers the error and may not be the person who made the error. Organizations often rely on voluntary reporting of errors but individuals who make errors may be unaware that they made them or reluctant to report them because of the stigma associated with errors and fear of disciplinary action. Reporting by individuals who make errors may be improved if the organization does not require them to identify themselves. To further minimize the reluctance to report errors, the beneficial rather than punitive aspects of an error-prevention program should be stressed.

Reports to the Physician Responsible for the Patient—Medication errors should be reported immediately to the physician responsible for the patient. Reports may be oral, although oral reports must be supplemented with written reports. The physician responsible for the patient should assess the patient for evidence of harm and document the findings in the patient's medical record.

Entries in Patient's Medical Record—The medication administered in error should be noted in the patient's medical record. The organization's risk management department should determine how this information is to be recorded. Often entries are limited to the same information recorded for doses administered correctly (e.g., name of medication administered, dose administered, site, route, date, and time). Patient medical records (e.g., MARs and nurses' notes) should *not* refer to "wrong" doses of medications or "errors," and should not indicate that a medication error report was filed.

Written Medication Error Reports—In addition to prompt notification of the physician responsible for the patient and documentation in the patient's medical record, written reports of medication errors should be prepared as soon as the error is recognized. Some organizations report medication errors on an incident report form (sometimes called a variance or occurrence report form). ("Incidents" are occurrences that result or could result in harm to patients, staff, or visitors.) Other organizations provide a special form for reporting medication errors. (*See* Example 4-25.) Medication error reports should be reviewed by individuals or committees as defined by the organization's policy. Furthermore, they should be kept confidential and not be filed in the medical record. The organization uses the reports to evaluate errors, minimize further occurrences, report to outside agencies, and to help defend the organization in a lawsuit.

Reporting Medication Errors to the USP/ISMP—The USP, in cooperation with the ISMP, provides the USP Medication Errors Reporting Program (MERP). Organizations may voluntarily report actual or potential medication errors to MERP. The USP and ISMP use the information in the reports to reduce occurrence of similar errors (e.g., by recommending changes in packaging and labeling and by promoting safe medication practices). MERP reports are routinely forwarded to the manufacturer. Organizations may request that their identity not be released. Example 4-32 is a form for reporting medication errors to the MERP. Information is available on the USP and ISMP Web sites. (*See* Appendix A.)

Reporting Medication Errors to the USP MedMARx℠ Program—The USP MedMARx℠ program is an internet-based, confidential, subscription service that can be used for both internal and external reporting. MedMARx enables a health care facility to anonymously report, track, and compare medication error data in a nationally standardized format. More information on subscribing to the USP MedMARx program is available on the USP Web site. (*See* Appendix A.)

Reporting Medication Errors to the Joint Commission—Organizations are not required to report medication errors (including sentinel events) to the Joint Commission. However, voluntarily submitting reports of sentinel events to the Joint Commission adds to the Joint Commission's database. Organizations that do not voluntarily submit a report of a sentinel event must nevertheless complete an acceptable root cause analysis. (*See* Chapter 14.)

Reviewing and Analyzing Medication Errors

Organization policy should define the types of medication errors that must be reviewed and analyzed. The organization's procedures should provide for prompt review of medication errors by physicians, nurses, pharmacists, risk managers, performance improvement personnel, and other qualified individuals who can act to improve processes and minimize their recurrence. The review should include meeting with persons associated with the errors (e.g., persons who reported the errors, persons who made the errors, and witnesses). The analysis should focus on determining the causes of errors and how the errors could have been prevented. The following can be helpful in reviewing medication errors:

- Use forms for tabulating, summarizing, tracking, and evaluating medication errors. Display the data graphically if possible. Some organizations use Pareto diagrams and other statistical analysis tools described in Chapter 14. Errors may be summarized by one or more of the following:
    - Type of error
    - Cause of error
    - Type of medication
    - Type of patient (e.g., geriatric)
    - Area where error occurred (e.g., nursing unit or emergency department)
    - Shift
    - Time
    - Service (e.g., infectious disease)
    - Department (e.g., anesthesia)
    - Categories of personnel involved (e.g., registered nurses, licensed practical nurses, agency or temporary staff, prescribers, and pharmacists)
- Review and evaluate medication error data monthly or quarterly to identify patterns and trends (e.g., changes in frequency, types of incidents, causes of errors, and personnel involved). Reviews for patterns and trends should cover at least the past 12 months.

Determining the Seriousness of Errors—The clinical effects of many medication errors are minimal. However, other medication errors are disabling or life threatening, and some result in patient mortality. Some organizations evaluate errors for seriousness (one or two serious errors may be worse than numerous minor errors) and focus their efforts on preventing the most serious ones. The NCCMERP has an index on its internet web site to categorize the severity of medication errors based on patient outcomes. (*See* Appendix A.)

Evaluating Action Taken and Patient Care Provided—It is often not possible to determine if an error caused a change in the patient's condition or an increased length of stay in the organization. However, reviews of medication errors should include an evaluation of the appropriateness of action taken by staff, emergency preparedness, and quality of care provided to patients. Pharmacists should participate in this evaluation, which should include the following:

- Action taken by a physician when notified
- Observation of the patient for signs of adverse effects
- Appropriateness and timeliness of supportive treatment, if needed
- Availability of emergency medications and antidotes
- Observation of the patient after treatment

Conducting a Root Cause Analysis—Organizations should conduct a root cause analysis (RCA) when such an analysis is indicated. (*See* Chapter 14 for a description of the RCA process and where to obtain help in conducting an RCA.)

Improving Processes When Errors Are Made

Medication use processes should be reviewed when medication errors are made. If necessary, processes must be improved and education relating to the improved processes must be provided. The measures for preventing medication errors listed in this chapter may be helpful in redesigning and improving processes. Leadership support, cultural changes, and the use of appropriate technology may be needed to significantly improve some processes.

Medication Error Rates

Organizations often determine their medication error rates and use their findings to judge the safety of their medication use system or measure their progress in reducing medication errors. However, such measurements and comparisons are of questionable value. High rates can mean that many medication errors occurred—or that the organization has an excellent process for detecting and reporting errors; low rates can mean that only a few medication errors occurred—or that medication errors were not detected and reported. Nevertheless, organizations find comfort in knowing their error rates. If determined accurately and used responsibly in conjunction with other measurements, error rates may be a helpful tool in a medication safety improvement program.

Calculating Medication Error Rates—Medication error rates can be calculated a number of ways. Two examples follow:

1. Divide the number of errors by the number of doses administered during a specified period and multiply by 100 to express the error rate as a percentage.
2. Divide the number of errors by the number of admissions or patient days for the period (e.g., monthly or quarterly). (Number of patient days is the sum of the census for each day in the period.) It may be necessary to multiply the quotient by 100 or 1000 to yield a rate that can be easily compared with previous or subsequent periods.

"Standard" Medication Error Rates—There are no "national," "standard," or "acceptable" medication error rates against which an organization can compare its error rate. Comparison of error rates between organizations is meaningless because there are too many variables (e.g., organization size, type, patient mix, types of medications used, frequency of use, and medication error definition). An organization's rate may be significantly higher or lower than rates reported by other organizations.

As there are no standard error rates, an organization should establish its own benchmark rate. This can best be done after a one- or two-year trend analysis (i.e., an evaluation of the type and seriousness of the errors). The error rate in an organization should reflect its patient characteristics, types of medications used, and the organization's definition of medication errors that must be reported. Organizations should periodically review their error detection process to ensure effective detection and reliable reporting (e.g., by determining if low rates are due to failure to report errors).

Thresholds for Evaluation—An organization can use its benchmark rates as thresholds for evaluating medication errors. (*See* Benchmarking in Chapter 14.) When errors exceed the thresholds, the medication distribution process should be evaluated. Thresholds for medications for which accurate administration is critical should be set at zero (i.e., all occurrences with these medications will be evaluated to determine if problems are present in the process).

Table 21-1. Types of Medication Errors[a]

Type	Definition
Prescribing error	Incorrect drug selection (based on indications, contraindications, known allergies, existing drug therapy, and other factors), dose, dosage form, quantity, route, concentration, rate of administration, or instructions for use of a drug product ordered or authorized by physician (or other legitimate prescriber); illegible prescriptions or medication orders that lead to errors that reach the patient
Omission error[b]	The failure to administer an ordered dose to a patient before the next scheduled dose, if any
Wrong time error	Administration of medication outside a predefined time interval from its scheduled administration time (this interval should be established by each individual health care facility)
Unauthorized drug error[c]	Administration to the patient of medication not authorized by a legitimate prescriber for the patient
Improper dose error[d]	Administration to the patient of a dose that is greater than or less than the amount ordered by the prescriber or administration of duplicate doses to the patient, i.e., one or more dosage units in addition to those that were ordered
Wrong dosage-form error[e]	Administration to the patient of a drug product in a different dosage form than ordered by the prescriber
Wrong drug-preparation error[f]	Drug product incorrectly formulated or manipulated before administration
Wrong administration-technique error[g]	Inappropriate procedure or improper technique in the administration of a drug
Deteriorated drug error[h]	Administration of a drug that has expired or for which the physical or chemical dosage-form integrity has been compromised
Monitoring error	Failure to review a prescribed regimen for appropriateness and detection of problems, or failure to use appropriate clinical or laboratory data for adequate assessment of patient response to prescribed therapy
Compliance error	Inappropriate patient behavior regarding adherence to a prescribed medication regimen
Other medication error	Any medication error that does not fall into one of the above predefined categories

[a]The categories may not be mutually exclusive because of the multidisciplinary and multifactorial nature of medication errors.

[b]Assumes no prescribing error. Excluded would be (1) a patient's refusal to take the medication or (2) a decision not to administer the dose because of recognized contraindications. If an explanation for the omission is apparent (e.g., patient was away from nursing unit for tests or medication was not available), the reason should be documented in the appropriate records.

[c]This would include, for example, a wrong drug, a dose given to the wrong patient, unordered drugs, and doses given outside a stated set of clinical guidelines or protocols.

[d]Excluded would be (1) allowable deviations based on preset ranges established by individual health care organizations in consideration of measuring devices routinely provided to those who administer drugs to patients (e.g., not administering a dose based on a patients's measured temperature or blood glucose level) or other factors such as conversion of doses expressed in the apothecary system to the metric system and (2) topical dosage forms for which medication orders are not expressed quantitatively.

[e]Excluded would be accepted protocols (established by the pharmacy and therapeutics committee or its equivalent) that authorize pharmacists to dispense alternate dosage forms for patients with special needs (e.g., liquid formulations for patients with nasogastric tubes or those who have difficulty swallowing), as allowed by state regulations

[f]This would include, for example, incorrect dilution or reconstitution, mixing drugs that are physically or chemically incompatible, and inadequate product packaging.

[g]This would include doses administered (1) via the wrong route (different from the route prescribed), (2) via the correct route but at the wrong site (e.g., left eye instead of right), and (3) at the wrong rate of administration.

[h]This would include, for example, administration of expired drugs and improperly stored drugs.

Table 21-2. Common Causes of Medication Errors

Common Causes of Errors	Examples
Failed communication	Poor handwriting Inaccurate transcription of orders Drugs with similar names Inappropriate use of zeroes and decimal points Use of metric and apothecary systems Use of inappropriate abbreviations Ambiguous or incomplete orders
Poor drug distribution practices	Unlabeled and mislabeled drugs Improper storage practices Unlimited access to drugs and pharmacy Improper use of dispensing equipment
Dose miscalculations	Failure to stock standardized concentrations and commercially premixed products
Problems related to drugs and drug devices	Labeling and packaging problems Device design issues
Incorrect administration of drug	Failure to check or improper patient identification Wrong route administration
Lack of patient education	Patients not involved Patients do not understand their medications
Little or no knowledge about the drug	Nursing and/or pharmacy staff are unaware of common dose Staff unaware of side effects or drug interactions Staff is unaware of the need for special monitoring or warnings for the drug
Little or no knowledge of the patient's identity, physical state, past or current drug therapy	Staff unaware of liver or kidney function No patient allergies Little or no physical data on patient (e.g., height, weight, pregnancy or lactation status)

Table 21-3. ISMP List of High-Alert Medications

Classes/Categories of Medications
adrenergic agonists, IV (e.g., epinephrine. phenylephrine, norepinephrine)
adrenergic antagonists, IV (e.g., propranolol, metoprolol, labetalol)
anesthetic agents, general, inhaled and IV (e.g., propofol, ketamine)
antiarrhytmics, IV (e.g., lidocaine, amiodarone)
antithrombotic agents (anticoagulants), including warfarin, low-molecular-weight heparin, IV unfractionated heparin, Factor Xa inhibitors (fondaparinux), direct thrombin inhibitors (e.g., argatroban, lepirudin, bivalirudin), thromolytics (e.g., alteplase, reteplase, tenecteplase), and glycoprotein IIb/IIIa inhibitors (e.g., eptifibatide)
cardioplegic solutions
chemotherapeutic agents, parenteral and oral
dextrose, hypertonic, 20% or greater
dialysis solutions, peritoneal and hemodialysis
epidural or intrathecal medications
hypoglycemics, oral
inotropic medications, IV (e.g., digoxin, milrinone)
liposomal forms of drugs (e.g., liposomal amphotericin B)
moderate sedation agents, IV (e.g., midazolam)
moderate sedation agents, oral, for children (e.g., chloral hydrate)
narcotic/opiates, IV, transdermal, and oral (including liquid concentrates, immediate and sustained-released formulations)
neuromuscular blocking agents (e.g., succinylcholine, rocuronium, vecuronium)
radiocontrast agents, IV
total parenteral nutrition solutions

Specific Medications
colchicine injection
epoprostenol (Flolan), IV
insulin, subcutaneous and IV
magnesium sulfate injection
methotrexate, oral, non-oncologic use
oxytocin, IV
nitroprusside sodium for injection
potassium chloride for injection concentrate
potassium phosphate injection
promethazine, IV
sodium chloride injection, hypertonic (greater than 0.9% concentration)
sterile water for injection, inhalation, and irrigation (excluding pour bottles) in containers of 100 mL or more

Source: *ISMP Medication Safety Alert! Acute Care Edition.* 2007 Aug 9; 12(16).

Table 21-4. Dangerous and Confusing Abbreviations

Abbreviation	Intended Meaning	Common Error	Recommendations
U	Units	Mistaken as a zero or a four (4) or six (6) resulting in overdose. Also mistaken for cc (cubic centimeters) when poorly written.	Write out *units.*
μg	Micrograms	Mistaken for mg (milligrams) resulting in an overdose.	Use *mcg* or write out *micrograms.*
Q.D.	Latin abbreviation for *every day*	The period after the Q has sometimes been mistaken for an I, and the drug has been given QID (four times daily) rather than daily. Also, QD can be misinterpreted to mean OD (right eye).	Write out *daily.*
Q.O.D.	Latin abbreviation for *every other day*	Misinterpreted as QD (daily) or QID (four times daily). If the O is poorly written, it looks like a period or an I.	Use *q other day* or write out *every other day.*
SC or SQ	Subcutaneous	Mistaken as SL (sublingual) when poorly written.	Write out *subcutane-ous.*
TIW	Three times a week	Misinterpreted as *three times a day* or *twice a week.*	Write out *three times a week.*
D/C	Discharge; also discontinue	Patient's medications have been prematurely discontinued when D/C, (intended to mean *discharge*) was misinterpreted as *discontinue,* because it was followed by a list of drugs.	Write out *discontinue* and *discharge.*
HS	Half strength	Misinterpreted as the Latin abbreviation HS (hour of sleep).	Write out the strength of the medication. Writing out *at bedtime* is preferred over using *hs.*
CC or cc	Cubic centimeters	Mistaken as U (units) when written poorly; also, can be read as two zeros.	Use *mL* or write out *milliliters.*
AU, AS, AD	Latin abbreviation for both ears; left ear; right ear	Misinterpreted as the Latin abbreviation OU (both eyes); OS (left eye); OD (right eye).	Write out the intended meaning in full (i.e., *both eyes, both ears, left eye,* and *right eye*).
IU	International unit	Mistaken as IV (intravenous) or 10 (ten).	Write out *international units.*
MS, MSO4, MgSO4	Confused for one another	Can mean morphine sulfate or magnesium sulfate.	Write out *morphine, morphine sulfate,* or *magnesium sulfate.*

Source: Adapted from the National Coordinating Council for Medication Error Reporting and Prevention. Rockville, MD.

CHAPTER 22

Adverse Drug Reactions

Improving medication safety includes preventing and reducing adverse drug events (ADEs). ADEs include medication errors and adverse drug reactions (ADRs). Chapter 21 focuses on medication errors. This chapter focuses on ADRs.

The Joint Commission™ requires organizations to respond to actual or potential ADRs. Responding to ADRs improves medication safety by

- preventing or minimizing the occurrence of ADRs
- improving the understanding of side effects associated with the use of specific drugs
- identifying previously unreported side-effects of newly-approved drugs
- reducing the severity of ADRs
- improving the detection and reporting of ADRs
- providing for appropriate care when ADRs occur

Definitions of ADRs

Definitions of ADRs vary. Examples of current definitions follow:

FDA—The Food and Drug Administration (FDA) MedWatch program defines a serious adverse event as any event when the patient outcome is any of the following:

- Is death
- Is life threatening (i.e., presents a real risk of dying)
- Results in initial hospitalization or prolongs hospitalization
- Is a disability or permanent damage
- Results in a congenital anomaly or birth defect
- Requires medical or surgical intervention to prevent permanent impairment or damage
- Other serious important medical events[1]

(*Also see* Chapter 23.)

ASHP—*ASHP Guidelines on Adverse Drug Reaction Monitoring and Reporting* defines a significant ADR as "any unexpected, unintended, undesired, or excessive response to a drug that

1. requires discontinuing the drug,
2. requires changing the drug therapy,
3. requires modifying the dose (except for minor dosage adjustments),
4. necessitates admission to a hospital,
5. prolongs stay in a health care facility,
6. necessitates supportive treatment,
7. significantly complicates diagnosis,
8. negatively affects prognosis,
9. results in temporary or permanent harm, disability, or death."[2]

Joint Commission—In the glossary to the *Comprehensive Accreditation Manual for Hospitals (CAMH)*, the Joint Commission defines ADRs as[3]:

"Unintended, undesirable, or unexpected effects of prescribed medications or of medication errors that require discontinuing a medication or modifying the dose; require initial or prolonged hospitalization; result in disability; require treatment with a prescription medication; result in cognitive deterioration or impairment; are life threatening; result in death; or result in congenital anomalies."

Organization Definitions—The Joint Commission expects organizations to develop and approve an ADR definition to use in their ADR programs. To clarify their definition, organizations might consider the following effects:

- Life threatening (e.g., anaphylaxis, arrhythmias, and gastrointestinal hemorrhage)
- Temporarily or permanently disables the patient (e.g., renal failure, ototoxicity, shortness of breath, nausea, vomiting, or diarrhea)
- Otherwise poses a risk of harm to the patient, (e.g., convulsions)

- Complicates treatment (e.g., hallucinations)
- Results in readmission or prolonged stay in the organization (e.g., severe rashes)
- Necessitates supportive treatment (e.g., treatment with drugs or assisted respiration)
- Requires reducing the dose (except for small reductions to improve tolerance)
- Requires stopping or changing the drug (except when the drug is stopped because of minor discomfort and an equally effective alternative drug is ordered)
- Allergic or hypersensitivity reactions (fever, rash, etc.)
- Reactions that are not listed in the manufacturer's product information
- Reactions that occur when drugs are not used in accordance with the manufacturer's product information
- Reactions that have not been reported in the literature

Side Effects

Some ADRs (e.g., nausea, vomiting, diarrhea, headache, and rashes) are expected side effects of therapy and are often accepted because the benefits of therapy outweigh the risk. These "acceptable ADRs" have been reported in the literature, occur with a predictable frequency, and may be related to the size of the dose. Some organization ADR definitions exclude specific side effects associated with specific medications that occur repeatedly and require little or no change in patient management (e.g., drowsiness or dry mouth due to an antihistamine). Although side effects may be excluded from ADR reporting, they should be documented in the patient's record and care should be taken to minimize the patient's distress.

Approval of the ADR Definition

In many organizations, the medical staff, in collaboration with other departments through the P&T committee, approves the organization's ADR definition. However, other options that retain the collaborative nature of this function can also be used. A periodic review and confirmation of the definition is suggested. Initial approval and periodic reviews and confirmations of the definition should be documented.

Incidence of ADRs

Estimates of the incidence of adverse reactions to drugs administered in organizations vary greatly. Early studies showed incidences ranging up to 20 percent of hospitalized patients. However, rates of this magnitude may reflect the reporting of intentional overdoses, overdoses due to drug administration errors, or side effects that require no treatment or change in therapy. Unfortunately, some individuals (including surveyors) cite these rates as typical of the rates that should be identified in institutional ADR reporting programs. Although the true incidence of adverse reactions is in question, many ADRs require treatment or discontinuation of the drug, and some contribute to patient mortality.

Predicting and Preventing ADRs

ADRs occur frequently in susceptible patients (e.g., patients with a history of allergies) and may be dose related. Geriatric patients have more reactions and more severe reactions than younger patients. Therefore, it is possible to predict and prevent some ADRs or minimize their severity by

- interviewing patients for a past history of allergies, ADRs, and intolerance to drugs
- administering test doses and conducting skin testing to identify patients at risk for allergic reactions to selected drugs
- identifying high-risk patients (e.g., with a symbol on the patient's chart, bed, or name band)
- clearly indicating sensitivities or known allergies on the medical record and the pharmacy patient profile
- administering drugs within recommended dosage ranges
- administering drugs by an appropriate technique (e.g., at the appropriate infusion rate)
- reducing doses of drugs known to be associated with ADRs in susceptible patients
- reducing doses in geriatric patients, underweight patients, patients with impaired renal or hepatic function, and patients with congestive heart failure, as appropriate
- monitoring to ensure that serum drug concentrations remain within an acceptable therapeutic (yet nontoxic) range

Detecting ADRs

Because ADRs can be associated with any drug and any patient, some cannot be predicted or prevented. All drugs should be suspect; early detection can minimize the effects of ADRs.

ADR Signs and Symptoms—Signs and symptoms of reactions that may be due to a drug include the following:

- Changes in a patient's physical and mental condition (e.g., elevated temperature, confusion, depression, loss of appetite, or other unexplained discomfort)
- Bleeding problems
- Blood dyscrasias (e.g., leukopenia)
- Liver enzyme elevations
- Cardiac arrhythmias
- Skin rashes and hives
- Anaphylactic type reactions
- Convulsions
- Hallucinations
- Renal failure

Passive ADR Detection Programs—Nurses, physicians, respiratory therapists, imaging technologists, and nuclear medicine personnel are in the best position to observe ADRs. However, passive programs that rely only on nonpharmacists to detect ADRs and complete ADR reports are minimally effective. Nonpharmacists are often unaware that ADRs must be reported and do not know the procedures for reporting them. Some may find the completion of ADR reports too time consuming.

Another problem with passive detection programs is that nurses and physicians may consider ADRs to be drug administration errors and be reluctant to report them. Furthermore, physicians sometimes believe that ADRs make them look bad and increase their liability. Pharmacists should emphasize that ADRs are not necessarily errors and do not necessarily reflect poor patient care: No one is at fault. In addition, pharmacists should point out that litigation is more likely to result if ADRs go undetected or unreported and patient care suffers.

Retrospective Reviews of Medical Records—Retrospective reviews of patient medical records may identify some previously undetected (or detected but unreported) ADRs. However, this information may be difficult to evaluate and may not be helpful in determining if the patient was cared for appropriately.

Active ADR Detection Programs—Detection and reporting of ADRs is increased when pharmacists take an active role. An active ADR detection program encourages nurses, physicians, and other health care personnel to notify (orally, electronically, or in writing) the pharmacy of suspected ADRs for subsequent investigation and reporting by a pharmacist. Other active detection methods include targeting specific patients or specific drugs for monitoring.

Targeting Patients to Detect ADRs—Although ADRs can occur in any patient, the following "target" patients can be selected for close observation:

- Patients who have experienced an ADR
- Patients who receive *stat* doses of drugs that are often used for managing ADRs (e.g., parenteral diphenhydramine, epinephrine, aminophylline, corticosteroids, phenytoin, vitamin K, diazepam, phenobarbital, topical steroids, and sodium polystyrene sulfonate)
- Patients who have *stat* serum drug concentrations ordered
- Patients with serum drug concentrations above the therapeutic range
- Patients who receive only one or two doses of a drug that is usually administered on a regular schedule for a long period
- Patients who have an abrupt dosage reduction or discontinuation of long-term maintenance drugs (e.g., antihypertensives)
- Patients with impaired renal function (e.g., serum creatinine above a specified level or a noticeable change in serum creatinine) or impaired liver function
- Patients older than a specified age
- Pediatric patients or patients younger than a specified age
- Patients under a specified weight
- Patients taking more than a specified number of drugs
- Patients whose condition worsens after a dose is increased or a new drug is administered

Targeting Drugs to Detect ADRs—Monitoring of patients receiving selected target drugs can also improve ADR detection. Although any drug may cause an adverse reaction, targeted drugs can include the following:

- Drugs frequently associated with ADRs (e.g., analgesics, antibiotics, anti-inflammatory drugs, anticoagulants, cardiovascular agents, diuretics, antineoplastics, antihyperglycemic agents, and central nervous system agents)
- Radiology and nuclear medicine preparations
- Respiratory therapy drugs
- Recently released drugs (e.g., drugs approved by the FDA during the preceding 3 years)

Use of Computers to Detect ADRs—A computerized monitoring program can facilitate detection and evaluation of ADRs and can be used to identify trends. For example, a computer can identify "stat" or one-time doses of drugs used to treat ADRs and compile a report in a format that can be used by the pharmacy to investigate and record the reasons for the doses. In addition, computerized scanning of medical records information can identify patients whose diagnostic and treatment codes indicate a drug reaction.

Other Methods to Improve ADR Detection—Other methods to improve detection of ADRs include

- informing physicians and nurses of target patients, target drugs, and symptoms of common ADRs
- questioning nurses about target patients and target drugs
- reviewing nurses' notes for evidence of ADRs
- rounding with physicians
- attending nursing "end-of-shift reports" and listening for clues to possible ADRs
- providing incentives for detecting and reporting (e.g., recognition, awards, or monetary rewards)
- interviewing patients who claim that their condition or symptoms are drug related
- reviewing records of clinical trials of investigational drugs for possible ADRs
- reviewing incident reports to identify potential drug-related incidents (e.g., patient falls due to vertigo associated with hypnotic therapy)

Care for Patients Who Experience ADRs

If an ADR is detected early (i.e., before serious consequences develop), the drug can be stopped or the dosage reduced and appropriate care provided. Appropriate patient care includes

- taking the patient's vital signs before and after administering a new drug
- ensuring that emergency drugs and antidotes used to treat ADRs are readily available (e.g., parenteral diphenhydramine, epinephrine, and corticosteroids)
- notifying the prescriber or the attending physician immediately if an ADR is suspected
- discontinuing the drug if the reaction poses a risk to the patient
- substituting a less toxic drug
- providing the patient with written notice stating the drug or type of drug responsible for the reaction and precautions to prevent or minimize further reactions (*see* Example 4-27)

Documenting and Reporting ADRs

ADRs should be reported immediately by persons who have the greatest knowledge of the reaction (usually a physician, nurse, or pharmacist). The reporter may or may not be the person who first observed the reaction. The reaction should be reported to the prescriber. If the prescribing practitioner is not available, the reaction should be reported to the attending physician or house officer. The person who reports the reaction should record a description of the reaction, action taken, and outcome in the patient's medical record.

Written Reports—In addition to the initial, immediate report to the prescriber (which is usually oral), ADRs should be reported to the pharmacy in writing. Some pharmacies simply ask to be notified of a suspected reaction, name and location of the patient, and name of the person reporting. Pharmacy personnel then assist the reporter or observer in completing an ADR report. Information reported to the pharmacy should include the following:

- Patient's name
- Patient's medical and drug history (including all drugs administered to the patient)
- Description of the suspected ADR (including the name of the drug suspected of causing the reaction)

- Temporal sequence of the event (including date and time of the reaction)
- Relevant laboratory tests or diagnostic findings
- Comments relating to the severity of the reaction
- Any remedial treatment required
- Outcome of the event and patient prognosis

In addition to the above, written reports of ADRs often include the following:

- Patient's age, sex, and race
- Name and title of the person making the report
- A notation that the reaction is *suspected* if a drug is not clearly the cause

ADR report forms should provide areas to be completed by the observer or reporter, pharmacist reviewer, prescriber, physician responsible for the patient, and reviewing committee. (*See* Example 4-26.)

Improving Reporting—To improve ADR reporting, ADR monitoring and reporting procedures should be included in orientation and ongoing education programs for pharmacists, nurses, physicians, and others who are in a position to detect and report ADRs. At a minimum, ADR education should include the following:

- The organization's ADR definition
- Detecting and reporting procedures for ADRs
- Care for the patient
- Review by the pharmacy and medical staff

Other methods of improving ADR reporting include the following:

- Ensuring that ADR report forms are available at nursing units and other areas where drugs are used (e.g., diagnostic, procedural, and ambulatory areas) and in the pharmacy
- Ensuring that personnel know when and how to complete ADR report forms (e.g., by describing the forms in detail during ADR educational programs)
- Offering rewards for reporting ADRs, installing an ADR telephone recorder and/or hotline, and posting ADR-related posters and reminders at nursing stations and other appropriate areas

Review and Evaluation of ADRs

ADRs should be reviewed and evaluated by the prescriber and/or the physician responsible for the patient, a pharmacist, and the medical staff. These are described below.

Review by the Prescriber and/or the Physician Responsible for the Patient—The physician responsible for the patient should review and evaluate the reported reaction and comment in the appropriate area of the report form. Physician comments should include the following:

- The physician's assessment of the reported reaction (e.g., likely or unlikely to be associated with a drug)
- Treatment ordered, if any
- An assessment of the patient's condition

Review by a Pharmacist—A pharmacist should review all ADR reports and record comments in the pharmacist section of the report form. Pharmacist comments should include the following:

- A review of the literature and the package insert for the suspected drug
- A note if the reaction has been previously reported (e.g., in the literature or package insert)
- A statement on the likelihood of the drug being responsible for the reaction
- A recommendation relating to reporting the reaction to the FDA or the manufacturer

If recurrences appear likely and pose a significant risk to patients, the pharmacist should notify the medical staff and nursing service immediately.

Review and Assessment by the Medical Staff—The pharmacy should submit ADR reports to the medical staff (usually through the P&T committee) at least quarterly. Some medical staffs prefer that pharmacists screen ADR reports and withhold reports of reactions that are (in the pharmacy's opinion) insignificant or unlikely to be due to a drug. However, many organizations assess all ADRs (including minor ADRs and common side effects). The rationale for assessing all ADRs is that many of them can be prevented and preventing them minimizes patient discomfort. Organizations should consider assessing all ADRs and common side effects but place the highest priority on significant ADRs.

At a minimum, all serious ADRs (e.g., potentially life-threatening or harmful or contributed to death or disability) should be intensively assessed (e.g., studying the process, determining the cause, and conducting a root cause analysis). The ADR assessment should determine the severity of the reaction (*see* Ranking ADRs) and determine whether

- the reaction was due to a drug (*see* Estimating the Probability of ADRs)
- the ADR was listed in the package insert
- the ADR was reported in the literature
- the ADR was predictable
- the ADR could have been prevented (*see* Assessing Preventability of ADRs)
- the administration of another drug would have been more appropriate
- the dosage of the drug was appropriate
- appropriate care was provided (e.g., appropriateness of the response to the ADR and the choice of drugs for treatment)
- the care was effective
- documentation in the patient's medical record was appropriate
- the patient was informed (or is to be informed) of potential reactions to the drug (or similar drugs) and precautions to take

The ADR should be reported to the FDA and manufacturer. To ensure prompt reporting, some organizations permit the pharmacist and prescriber to determine if the ADR should be reported to the FDA and manufacturer prior to P&T review. The communication with the FDA and manufacturer is reported later to the P&T committee.

Medical Staff Action on ADR Reports—The medical staff (through the P&T committee) should take action to reduce the incidence and severity of ADRs. Examples of effective action include the following:

- Education that promotes appropriate dosing, administration, monitoring (e.g., serum drug concentrations), and early detection of symptoms of toxicity or adverse reaction
- Restricting use of the drug
- Administering test doses, identifying high-risk patients, and reducing the dose of medications associated with ADRs
- Requiring another physician to agree that the drug is indicated, (e.g., a countersignature on a drug order)
- Ensuring that drugs needed to treat ADRs are readily available in emergency stocks
- Including the drug in the medication use improvement program or targeting the drug for close monitoring

Estimating the Probability of ADRs

Careful evaluation of ADR reports may prevent incrimination of a useful drug. There are several methods for estimating the probability of ADRs. The Naranjo algorithm, a well-known method, is described in Table 22-1.

Ranking ADRs by Severity

Ranking ADRs by severity can be helpful in evaluating patterns and trends. A simple 0–5 scale for ranking ADRs follows:

0—The reaction required little or no treatment, no change in therapy, did not require significant reduction in dosage or discontinuation of the drug, and did not cause harm or extend the stay in the facility.

1—The reaction caused no harm to the patient but required a significant reduction in dosage, or discontinuation of the drug, and required treatment or caused an extension of stay in the facility.

2—The reaction contributed to or resulted in temporary harm to the patient and required initial or prolonged hospitalization.

3—The reaction contributed to or resulted in permanent patient harm or disability.

4—The reaction required intervention necessary to sustain life.

5—The reaction contributed to or resulted in the patient's death.

Assessing the Preventability of ADRs

Although many ADRs are unexpected and unavoidable, some may be preventable. The questions in Table 22-2 may be helpful in assessing the preventability of ADRs. If the answer is "Yes" to any question, the reaction may have been preventable or avoidable.

Summarizing Reported ADRs

Summarizing reported ADRs by drug, description of reaction, classification, severity, preventability, and action taken can be helpful in identifying trends (e.g., drugs most often associated with ADRs and the numbers and severity of specific reactions). Examples 4-28 and 4-29 are forms for summarizing ADRs.

Calculating and Comparing ADR Rates

Although it is difficult to compare ADR rates across organizations (because of variability in ADR definitions, types of patients, and types of drugs used), a comparison of rates over time within one organization can be valuable. Rates are often expressed as a percentage of total admissions and may reflect one or more of the following:

- Reported (including suspected) reactions
- Confirmed reactions
- Serious reactions
- Reactions involving selected drugs (i.e., those responsible for the highest percentages of confirmed reactions in the organization such as morphine and cytotoxic agents)

Some organizations measure the success of their ADR-reporting program by the number of ADRs detected and reported. However, numbers alone are not reliable indicators of quality. Furthermore, there are no "national," "standard," or "acceptable" ADR rates against which an organization can compare its ADR rate. Comparison of ADR rates between organizations is meaningless because there are too many variables (e.g., organization size, type, patient mix, types of drugs used, frequency of use, and ADR definition). For example, some organizations may have a high census of patients who are hypersensitive to drugs; other organizations may have a high use of drugs that are associated frequently with ADRs. Furthermore, high rates can mean that many ADRs occurred—or that the organization has an excellent process for detecting and reporting ADRs; low rates can mean that only a few ADRs occurred—or that ADRs were not detected and reported. An organization's rate may be significantly higher or lower than rates reported by other organizations.

As there are no standard ADR rates, an organization should establish its own benchmark rate. This can best be done after a one- or two-year trend analysis (i.e., an evaluation of the type and seriousness of the ADRs). The rate in an organization should reflect the organization's patient characteristics, types of drugs used, and the organization's definition of reactions that must be reported.

An analysis of changes in rates should consider variables that can influence the number of occurrences and distort the ADR rate. These might include changes in patient mix, changes in services offered, numbers of new drugs used, numbers of drugs in clinical trials, and different emphases on reporting. Example 4-29 can be used to compare ADR rates and the numbers and types of ADRs. An organization should periodically review its ADR program to ensure effective detection and reliable reporting (e.g., by determining if low rates are due to failure to report ADRs).

Reporting ADRs to the FDA

The FDA has established MedWatch for the reporting of serious adverse events. (*See* Chapter 23 for an overview of MedWatch and other FDA reporting programs.)

Reporting ADRs to the Manufacturer

ADRs should be reported to the manufacturer as well as the FDA. If the reaction is reported to the manufacturer, this fact should be noted on the report to the FDA so that duplicate reports can be identified.

Publishing ADRs in the Literature

ADRs are often published in the literature before they are published by the FDA or are incorporated into the package insert. Furthermore, many ADRs never appear in FDA material. To ensure widespread dissemination of ADR information, pharmacists and other health care professionals should report serious, unusual, and unexpected reactions to the pharmacy literature.

Table 22-1. Naranjo Algorithm for Estimating the Probability of Adverse Drug Reactions

Drug	Yes	No	Not Known	Score
1. Are there previous *conclusive* reports on this reaction?	+1	0	0	
2. Did the adverse event appear after the suspected drug was administered?	+2	-1	0	
3. Did the adverse reaction improve when the drug was discontinued or a *specific* antagonist was administered?	+1	0	0	
4. Did the adverse reaction reappear when the drug was readministered?	+2	-1	0	
5. Are there alternative causes (other than the drug) that could on their own have caused the reaction?	-1	+2	0	
6. Did the reaction reappear when a placebo was given?	-1	+1	0	
7. Was the drug detected in the blood (or other fluids) in concentrations known to be toxic?	+1	0	0	
8. Was the reaction more severe when the dose was increased, or less severe when the dose was decreased?	+1	0	0	
9. Did the patient have a similar reaction to the same or similar drugs in *any* previous exposure?	+1	0	0	
10. Was the adverse event confirmed by any objective evidence?	+1	0	0	

Total Score

≥9 = Definite 5–8 = Probable 1–4 = Possible ≤0 = Doubtful

Source: Naranjo CA, Busto U, Sellers EM, et al. A method for estimating the probability of adverse drug reactions. *Clin Pharmacol Ther.* 1981;30:239–45.

Table 22-2. Assessing the Preventability of Adverse Drug Reactions

1.	Yes____	No____	Was the drug(s) involved appropriate for the patient's condition?
2.	Yes____	No____	Was the dose, route, or frequency of administration appropriate for the patient's age, weight, or disease?
3.	Yes____	No____	Was required therapeutic drug monitoring or other necessary laboratory test(s) performed or performed frequently enough?
4.	Yes____	No____	Did the patient have a history of allergy or previous reaction to the drug?
5.	Yes____	No____	Was a known interaction the suspected cause of the reaction?
6.	Yes____	No____	Was the serum drug concentration above the therapeutic range documented?
7.	Yes____	No____	Was noncompliance associated with the reaction (for outpatient only)?
8.	Yes____	No____	Was a medication error associated with the reaction?

Source: Adapted from Winterstein AG, Hatton RC, Gonzalez-Rothi R, et al. Identifying clinically significant preventable adverse drug events through a hospital's database of adverse drug reaction reports. *Am J Health Syst Pharm.* 2002;59:1742–9.

CHAPTER 23

Overview of the Food and Drug Administration's MedWatch Program

The Food and Drug Administration (FDA) requires extensive drug testing (premarketing trials) prior to granting marketing approval. Because these tests are conducted frequently on young, healthy individuals for a short period of time, the nature, severity, and frequency of adverse drug reactions (ADRs) may not be evident during premarketing trials.

Postmarketing Reports

In contrast to premarketing trials, postmarketing use of a drug may involve millions of patients of all ages and states of health. The FDA relies on postmarketing reports from manufacturers and health care professionals to increase its database on ADRs. Well-documented ADR reports lead to the addition of previously unreported or unnoted ADRs to the package insert, publicity to health care professionals (e.g., on the FDA's Internet Web site) (*see* Appendix A), and, if necessary, recall of dangerous drugs. Manufacturers, who are required to report adverse reactions, provide most postmarketing reports. Health care professionals, including pharmacists, physicians, and nurses, may submit reports voluntarily.

MedWatch Program

The FDA has established MedWatch for voluntary reporting by health professionals of serious adverse events (including ADRs) and product problems.[1] The FDA defines a serious adverse event as any event when the patient outcome is any one of the following:

- Death
- Life threatening (i.e., presents a real risk of dying)
- Results in initial hospitalization or prolongs hospitalization
- Results in disability or permanent damage
- Results in a congenital anomaly or birth defect
- Requires medical or surgical intervention to prevent permanent impairment or damage
- Other important medical events

The FDA encourages health care professionals to report their adverse experiences with the following:

- Medications (drugs or biologicals)
- Medical devices (including in vitro diagnostics)
- Combination products (medication and medical devices)
- Special nutritional products (dietary supplements, medical foods, and infant formulas)
- Other products regulated by FDA

Health care professionals are also encouraged to report their quality, performance, or safety concerns related to products. Examples of product problems include, but are not limited to, the following:

- Suspected contamination
- Suspected counterfeit product
- Questionable stability
- Defective components
- Therapeutic failures
- Product confusion (caused by name, labeling, design or packaging)
- Suspected super potent or subpotent medication
- Labeling problems caused by printing errors/omissions

The FDA encourages reports even if it is uncertain that the product caused the event and not all details are known.

Confidentiality of Reports—The FDA holds the patient's identity in strict confidence. The FDA will share the reporter's identity with the manufacturer unless requested otherwise. Reporters can indicate on the report form that their identities are not to be released to the manufacturer. The FDA will not disclose the reporter's identity in response to a request from the public.

Voluntary Reporting of Adverse Events to the FDA—Written reports of serious ADRs and other serious events should be made to the FDA MedWatch program on FDA Form 3500. (*See* Example 4-30.) Reports can be mailed, faxed, telephoned or submitted online to the FDA. (*See* Appendix A.) If ADRs are also reported to the manufacturer, this fact should be noted on FDA Form 3500 so that duplicate reports can be identified.

Mandatory Reporting of Suspected Device-Related Deaths and Serious Injuries to the FDA—Risk managers and other personnel within user facilities (e.g., hospitals and nursing homes) are legally required to report suspected medical device-related deaths to both the FDA and the manufacturer, if known, and serious injuries to the manufacturer, or to the FDA if the manufacturer is unknown. Reports of suspected device-related deaths and serious injuries must be made in writing on FDA Form 3500A. (*See* Example 4-33.)

Pharmacies that provide or support infusion devices for patients must be aware of their proper use and how to detect problems. Where it is probable that a manufacturer's defect or problem has caused or contributed to death or serious illness or injury, the facility must report the information to the manufacturer within 10 days and must annually inform the FDA of all such reports that have been sent. If the manufacturer is unknown, the reports must be made directly to the FDA. Further information is available at the MedWatch Internet Web site. (*See* Appendix A.)

Additional MedWatch Information—You can obtain up-to-date MedWatch information (including FDA Forms 3500 and 3500A) from the MedWatch Internet Web site. (*See* Appendix A.)

Vaccine Adverse Events Reporting System (VAERS)

The FDA requires persons who administer selected vaccines to report specified adverse events. Adverse events that must be reported under the Vaccine Adverse Events Reporting System (VAERS) are those related to administration of diphtheria, tetanus, pertussis, polio, measles, mumps, rubella, hepatitis B, hemophilus influenzae, varicella, rotavirus, pneumococcal, hepatitis A, and influenza vaccines vaccines.[2] A complete list of the vaccines is available on the VAERS Internet Web site. (*See* Appendix A.) The VAERS also accepts all reports of suspected adverse events, in all age groups, after the administration of any U.S. licensed vaccine.

Adverse events and product problems that occur with vaccines should not be reported to the MedWatch program or on the MedWatch form but should be sent to the VAERS. (*See* Appendix A.) Form VAERS-1 is used to report these events. (*See* Example 4-31.)

Additional VAERS Information—Up-to-date VAERS information (including Form VAERS-1) is available on the VAERS Internet Web site and MedWatch Internet Web site. You can also contact VAERS by telephone. (*See* Appendix A.)

Vaccine Information Statements

The Public Health Service (PHS) Centers for Disease Control and Prevention (CDC) requires organizations to provide relevant information to any adult to whom the vaccine is to be administered and to the legal representative of any child to whom the vaccine is to be administered. Your organization may develop its own information materials or obtain them from the PHS or vaccine manufacturers. Information materials developed by the organization must meet PHS requirements. The CDC provides Vaccine Information Statements (VIS) on its Internet Web site. (*See* Chapter 7 and Appendix A.)

CHAPTER 24

Centers for Medicare and Medicaid Services Surveys

Organizations that are not accredited by the Joint Commission™ or the Healthcare Facilities Accreditation Program (HFAP) of the American Osteopathic Association (AOA) must meet federal Conditions of Participation of the Centers for Medicare and Medicaid Services (CMS) to be certified to participate in the federal Medicare program.[1] This chapter provides information and suggestions for meeting each Condition of Participation (CoP) relating to pharmaceutical services and the use of medications.

> ***Note:*** CMS CoPs and related information are found in the Federal Register at the CMS Internet Website. (*See* Appendix A.)

Conditions of Participation and Standards

Each CoP consists of one or more standards that define the requirements for compliance. Organizations do not need to comply with all standards to comply with a CoP. However, they must comply with all CoPs to be certified. Certification of a facility's compliance with each CoP is accomplished through observations, interviews, and document/record reviews.

> ***Note:*** CMS *certifies*; the Joint Commission and HFAP *accredit*. Either CMS certification or Joint Commission or HFAP accreditation qualifies the organization to participate in the Medicare program. (*See* Chapter 1.)

The standards take into consideration that health care organizations and departments within organizations are subject to state and federal laws and undergo substantial state inspection through licensure programs (hospital, pharmacy, fire and safety, health department, etc.). Therefore, CMS standards encourage practices in accordance with generally recognized principles and avoid conflict with state and federal laws, state licensure requirements, and Joint Commission and HFAP standards.

Although CMS CoPs and standards are uniform throughout the country, interpretation and stringency of application vary considerably from state to state. However, if the pharmacy meets state board of pharmacy rules and regulations and practices are generally in accordance with Joint Commission standards, it should be compliant with CMS CoPs in most states.

Interpretive Guidelines

Each CoP contains general requirements and expectations. In most cases, interpretive guidelines immediately follow each CoP. The guidelines contain additional information and in many instances state what is required to demonstrate compliance with the CoPs.

Survey Procedures—In most cases, survey procedures follow the interpretive guidelines for each CoP. Survey procedures give surveyors information on how to conduct that portion of the survey and how to measure compliance with a CoP and its standards. When preparing for a survey, the pharmacy should review the interpretive guidelines and survey procedures to determine the surveyors' expectations.

CMS Surveys

Regular CMS surveys are conducted periodically (e.g., annually) and are unannounced. Surveys are usually conducted Monday through Friday during normal (daytime) working hours. Surveyors may conduct portions of the survey outside normal working hours and will modify the survey agenda to fit staffs' schedules and patients' activities.

Validation Surveys—CMS selects a small percentage (usually about 5%) of Joint Commission and HFAP-accredited organizations to undergo validation surveys. Validation surveys are conducted to ensure that Joint Commission and HFAP surveys are equivalent to CMS surveys and CoPs are met. A validation survey is usually conducted shortly after a Joint Commission or HFAP survey.

Surveyors

CMS surveys are conducted by a state agency (often the state health department) under contract to CMS. The size and composition of survey teams and the length of surveys vary from state to state. The survey is conducted under the leadership of a team coordinator. Each survey team includes at least one registered nurse with survey experience, as well as other surveyors (e.g., physician, administrator, pharmacist, and laboratory technologist) who have the expertise needed to determine whether an organization is in compliance.

Note: A typical survey team for a full survey of a mid-sized organization would include two to four surveyors who would be onsite at the facility for three or more days.

Documents

The following documents are often requested on the first morning of most surveys:

- A list of department heads, their locations, and telephone numbers
- A copy of the facility's organizational chart
- Names and addresses of all off-site locations
- The organization's infection control plan
- A list of employees
- Medical staff bylaws and rules and regulations
- Policy and procedure manuals
- A list of contracted services
- A copy of the organization's floor plan, including location of patient care and treatment areas
- A current list of inpatients, including patient's names, room numbers, diagnosis(es), admission date, age, attending physician, and other significant information

Note: Whenever possible surveyors will review the records of patients who are in the facility during the survey (i.e., open records). Open records allow surveyors to conduct a patient-focused survey and enable surveyors to validate information obtained through record reviews with observations and patient and staff interviews.

Note: Surveyors base the sample size of patient records on the organization's average daily census (ADC). The sample size is at least 10% of the ADC but not less than 30 inpatient records. In hospitals with an ADC of less than 20 patients, the sample size should not be less than 20 inpatient records. The sample will include at least one patient selected from each patient care area (e.g., emergency department, ICU, OB, pediatrics, medical/surgical, and specialty units).

Compliance with CMS Conditions and Standards

The following information is adapted from pharmacy CoPs that were in effect in 2007. Also included are pharmacy-related CoPs (e.g., nursing services—preparation and administration of drugs), standards, and interpretive guidelines that specifically apply to pharmacy (e.g., Quality Assessment and Performance Improvement, Physical Environment, Infection Control, and Nuclear Medicine). Conditions, standards, and interpretive guidelines are subject to change. The pharmacy should obtain a current edition of the CoPs prior to the survey.

Numbers with uppercase letters are data tag numbers (i.e., A-0247 is the tag number for the condition for pharmaceutical services). Each condition and standard has a unique tag number. Numbers without letters in the suffix are conditions (i.e., §482.25 is the condition of participation for pharmaceutical services). Numbers with lowercase letters in the suffix are standards (i.e., §482.25.a and §482.25.a.1 are standards for condition §482.25). Authors' comments are in italics and reflect their suggestions and experiences or provide clarification.

A-0247

§482.25 Condition of Participation: Pharmaceutical Services

The hospital must have pharmaceutical services that meet the needs of the patients. The institution must have a pharmacy directed by a registered pharmacist or a drug storage area under competent supervision. The medical staff is responsible for developing policies and procedures that minimize drug errors. This function may be delegated to the hospital's organized pharmaceutical service.

Authors' Comment: *Although the standards stress the need for pharmaceutical services, they do not require an organized pharmacy supervised on a day-to-day basis by a registered pharmacist. CMS continues to allow a drug storage area in lieu of a pharmacy, be-*

cause that is the only way pharmacy services can be furnished in some small organizations. CMS does not believe that prescriptive federal regulations should be imposed on organizations that can meet this requirement in other ways that are consistent with federal and state laws and patient needs.

Authors' Comment: *If the organization does not have an organized pharmacy service, surveyors look for medical staff policies and procedures that address the management of pharmaceuticals.*

Interpretive Guidelines §482.25

Provision of pharmaceutical services must meet the needs of the patients' therapeutic goal by promoting a safe medication use process that ensures optimal selection of medications, dose, dosage form, frequency, route, duration of therapy and that substantially reduces or eliminates adverse drug events and duplication of treatment.

The hospital's pharmacy must be directed by a registered pharmacist. If a drug storage area is used instead of a pharmacy at any location providing pharmacy services, that storage area must be under competent supervision in accordance with State and Federal law.

Pharmaceutical Services would include:

- The procuring, manufacturing, compounding, packaging, dispensing, ordering, distributing, disposition, use, and administering of all medications, biologicals, chemicals and the use of medication related devices
- Provision of medication-related information to hospital health care professionals and patients necessary to optimize therapeutic outcomes
- Provision of pharmaceutical care. Pharmaceutical care is defined as the direct, responsible provision of medication-related care for the purpose of achieving definite outcomes that improve a patient's quality of life while minimizing patient risk.

Functions of Pharmaceutical Care are the:

- Collection and organization of patient-specific information
- Determination of the presence of medication-therapy problems, both potential and actual
- Summary of the patient's medication related health care needs
- Identification and specification of pharmacotherapeutic goals
- Development of a pharmacotherapeutic regimen
- Implementation of a monitoring plan in collaboration with the patient, if applicable, and other health care professionals
- Monitoring the effects of the pharmacotherapeutic regimen
- Redesigning the regimen and monitoring plan as indicated

Medication errors are a substantial source of morbidity and mortality in the hospitalized setting. Therefore, the development of policies and procedures to minimize medication errors should be based on accepted professional principles; external alerts and proactive review of facility reported and reviewed adverse drug events. It is important to flag new types of mistakes and continually improve and refine things, based on what went wrong.

The hospital's medical staff must develop policies and procedures to minimize drug errors, but may delegate this function to the hospital's organized pharmaceutical service.

Policies and procedures to minimize drug errors should include:

- High-alert medications—dosing limits, administration guidelines, packaging, labeling and storage
- Limiting the variety of medication-related devices and equipment; for example, limit the types of general-purpose infusion pumps to one or two
- Availability of up-to-date medication information
- Availability of pharmacy expertise. Pharmacist available on-call when pharmacy does not operate 24 hours a day
- Standardization of prescribing and communication practices to include:
  - avoidance of dangerous abbreviations
  - all elements of the order—dose, strength, units (metric), route, frequency, and rate
  - alert systems for look-like and sound-alike drug names
  - use of facility-approved preprinted order sheets whenever possible
- That orders to "resume previous orders" are prohibited

- A voluntary, nonpunitive, reporting system to monitor and report adverse drug events (including medication errors and adverse drug reactions)
- The preparation, distribution, administration and proper disposal of hazardous medications
- Drug recalls
- That patient-specific information is readily accessible to all individuals involved in provision of pharmaceutical care. The patient information must be sufficient to properly order, prepare, dispense, administer and monitor medications as appropriate.
- Identification of when weight-based dosing for pediatric populations is required
- Requirements for review and revision based on facility-generated reports of adverse drug events and QAPI activities

Authors' Comment: *See CoP §482.21 in this chapter.*

The hospital should have policies and procedures to actively identify potential and actual adverse drug events. Proactive identification could include; direct observation of medication administration, review of patient's clinical records, identification of patient signals that would warrant immediate review of patient's medication therapy and implementation of medication use evaluation studies.

The hospital should have a means to incorporate external alerts and/or recommendations from national associations and governmental agencies for review and facility policy and procedure revision consideration. National associations could include Institute for Safe Medications Practice, National Coordinating Council for Medication Error Reporting and Prevention, and Joint Commission *Sentinel Event Alerts*. Governmental agencies may include: Food and Drug Administration, MedWatch Program, and Agency for Health Care Research and Quality.

The hospital's pharmacy services must be integrated into its hospital-wide QAPI program.

Authors' Comment: *It is critical to demonstrate to surveyors that the facility has procedures in place that promote the safe use of medications. Throughout the survey, surveyors look for written policies that establish safeguards for the use of medications and evidence of compliance with those policies.*

Survey Procedures §482.25

- Interview the chief pharmacist or the individual delegated to fulfill the chief pharmacist's functions. Determine that either the medical staff has developed policies and procedures regarding the management of pharmaceuticals or that this function is fulfilled by the pharmacy service.
- Verify that the purpose of pharmaceutical policies and procedures is to minimize drug errors. Review the pharmaceutical policies and procedures, the hospital's formulary and, if there is a pharmacy and therapeutic committee, the minutes of the committee meetings.
- Does a multidisciplinary committee composed of representatives from nursing, pharmacy, administration and medicine develop policies and procedures?
- Are there policies and procedures to minimize drug errors?
- Are policies and procedures reviewed and amended based on:
  - Facility-generated reports of adverse drug events
  - Facility QAPI activities pertaining to pharmaceutical care
  - Evaluation of external alerts and/or recommendations from national associations
  - Evaluation of literature for new technologies or successful practices that have demonstrated enhanced medication safety in other organizations
- Is the staff familiar with the medication-related policies and procedures?
- Is there a method to periodically review and evaluate the actual implementation of pharmaceutical policies and procedures by staff?
- Upon review of patient clinical record, are issues with regard to provision of pharmaceutical services identified? Is the facility aware of the issues? Was there a failure to implement a policy and procedure?
- Are pharmacists an integral component of pharmaceutical care?
- Verify that the hospital's pharmacy services are integrated into its hospital-wide QAPI program.

A-0248

§482.25(a) Standard: Pharmacy Management and Administration

The pharmacy or drug storage area must be administered in accordance with accepted professional principles.

Authors' Comment: *Surveyors review policies and procedures and records of drug receipt and dispensing and examine drug storage areas to ensure that practices conform to state law and professional standards. Surveyors specifically look for evidence of inspections of drug storage areas, as well as an established drug recall procedure.*

Interpretive Guidelines §482.25(a)

The hospital may utilize a unit-dose system, individual prescription, floor stock system or a combination of these systems, properly stored.

Pharmaceutical services must be administered in accordance with accepted professional principles. Accepted professional principles includes compliance with applicable Federal and State laws, regulations, and guidelines governing pharmaceutical services, as well as standards or recommendations promoted by nationally recognized professional organizations. Agencies and organizations could include FDA, NIH, American Society of Health-System Pharmacists, etc.

A fundamental purpose of pharmaceutical services is to ensure the safe and appropriate use of medications and medication-related devices. The pharmacy director, with input from appropriate hospital staff and committees, develops, implements, and periodically reviews and revises policies and procedures governing provision of pharmaceutical services.

Methods a hospital may use to maintain professional principles include:

- Policies and procedures have been developed and are being followed.
- Drugs and biologicals are stored in accordance with manufacturer's directions and State and Federal requirements.
- Employees provide pharmaceutical services within their scope of license and education.
- Pharmacy records have sufficient detail to follow the flow of pharmaceuticals from their entry into the hospital through dispensation/administration.
- Maintaining controls over drugs and medications including the floor stock and those of the pharmacy or drug room.
- Maintaining pharmacy and accounting records pertaining to the requisitioning and dispensing of drugs and pharmaceutical supplies.
- Ensuring that drugs are being dispensed only by a licensed pharmacist.
- Only pharmacists or pharmacy-supervised personnel compound, label, and dispense drugs or biologicals.

Survey Procedures §482.25(a)

- Are the policies and procedures consistent with accepted professional principles?
- Determine that professional principles are maintained by verifying that:
    - policies and procedures have been developed and are being followed
    - drugs and biologicals are stored in accordance with manufacturers' directions and State and Federal requirements
    - records have sufficient detail to follow the flow of control from entry through dispensation
    - employees provide pharmaceutical services within their scope of license and education
- Does the hospital have a means to incorporate external alerts and/or recommendations from national associations and governmental agencies for review and facility policy and procedure revision consideration?
- Are policies developed to promote consistent application of pharmaceutical services and care throughout the hospital?
- Is the pharmacy director periodically monitoring implementation of policies and procedures?
- Are policies and procedures reviewed and revised as warranted?
- Are services provided in a manner consistent with accepted professional principles?
- Is the pharmacy responsible for the procurement, distribution and control of all medication products used in the hospital (including medication-related devices) for inpatient and outpatient care?

A-0249

§482.25(a)(1) A full-time, part-time, or consulting pharmacist must be responsible for developing, supervising, and coordinating all the activities of the pharmacy services.

Authors' Comment: *A designated individual must be responsible for the day-to-day operation of the pharmacy. That person does not have to be on the premises; however, surveyors look for evidence (e.g., schedules and time logs) of regularly scheduled visits. Surveyors also review job descriptions or written agreements to ensure that this pharmacist's responsibilities are clearly defined and include development, supervision, and coordination of all pharmacy services.*

Interpretive Guidelines §482.25(a)(1)

Direction of pharmaceutical services may not require continuous on-premise supervision at the hospital's single pharmacy or at any pharmacy location but may be accomplished through regularly scheduled visits, and/or telemedicine in accordance with Federal and State law and regulation and accepted professional principles.

A single pharmacist must be responsible for the overall administration of the pharmacy service and must be responsible for developing, supervising, and coordinating all the activities of the hospitalwide pharmacy service.

The job description or the written agreement for the responsibilities of the pharmacist should be clearly defined and include development, supervision and coordination of all the activities of pharmacy services.

A professional, competent, legally qualified pharmacist must manage the pharmacy. The Director of pharmacy service must be thoroughly knowledgeable about hospital pharmacy practice and management.

Pharmacists and pharmacy technicians must perform their duties within scope of their license and education.

The Pharmacy Director should be actively involved in those committees responsible for establishing medication-related policies and procedures.

Survey Procedures §482.25(a)(1)

- Determine whether the pharmacist is a full-time or part-time employee, or is employed on a consultative basis.
- Review the implementation of the chief pharmacist's responsibilities by:
  - Reviewing written status reports.
  - Reviewing minutes of meetings (if any) with facility staff regarding pharmaceutical services.
  - Reviewing schedules, time logs, etc.
  - Reviewing the job description or the written agreement to see that the responsibilities of the pharmacist are clearly defined and include development supervision and coordination of all the activities of pharmacy services.
  - Determining whether the Pharmacy Director routinely evaluates the performance and competency of pharmacy personnel. Do performance evaluations include high-risk activities such as the compounding of hazardous medications, pharmacy-based prescriptive activities (e.g., aminoglycoside protocols) and pharmaceutical care for high-risk patients (pediatric, ICU, geriatric, etc.)?
- Determine whether the pharmacy director is actively involved in those committees responsible for establishing medication-related policies and procedures.

A-0250

§482.25(a)(2) The pharmaceutical service must have an adequate number of personnel to ensure quality pharmaceutical services, including emergency services.

Authors' Comment: *CMS does not establish minimum staffing levels for pharmaceutical services. Surveyors expect pharmacy staff to be adequate in terms of training, education, and licensure as well as number. Pharmacy services must be available at all times, even when a pharmacist is not present. Policies and procedures should address the provision of pharmaceutical services in the absence of a pharmacist.*

Interpretive Guidelines §482.25(a)(2)

There must be sufficient personnel to respond to the pharmaceutical needs of the patient population being served.

The pharmaceutical services staff must be sufficient in types, numbers, and training to provide quality services, including 24 hour, 7-day emergency coverage, or there is an arrangement for emergency services, as determined by the needs of the patients and as specified by the medical staff.

The number of pharmacists and/or the number of hours of services provided by pharmacists at the hospital, or at each location of the hospital that provides pharmaceutical services, must meet and be in accordance with the needs of its patients and accepted professional principles (as previously defined), and reflect the scope and complexity of the hospital's pharmaceutical services.

There must be sufficient numbers and types of personnel to provide accurate and timely medication delivery, ensure accurate and safe medication administration and to provide appropriate clinical services, as well as the participation in continuous quality improvement programs that meet the needs of the patient population being served.

Survey Procedures §482.25(a)(2)

- Determine that the pharmaceutical services staff is sufficient in number and training to provide quality services, including 24 hour, 7-day emergency coverage, or there is an arrangement for emergency services, as determined by the needs of the patients and as specified by the medical staff.
- Determine if there are sufficient personnel to provide accurate and timely medication delivery, ensure accurate and safe medication administration and to provide appropriate clinical services, as well as the participation in continuous quality improvement programs that meet the needs of the patient population being served.

A-0251

§482.25(a)(3) Current and accurate records must be kept of the receipt and disposition of all scheduled drugs.

Authors' Comment: *A complete audit trail for all controlled substances from receipt to disposition is required. Surveyors spot-check records of drug use and inventory drugs to ensure that they are accounted for. They also interview pharmacy staff to determine their knowledge of policies on handling controlled substances.*

Interpretive Guidelines §482.25(a)(3)

Components of a record system to maintain current and accurate records of the receipt and disposition of scheduled drugs would include:

- Accountability procedures to ensure control of the distribution, use, and disposition of all scheduled drugs.
- Records of the receipt and disposition of all scheduled drugs must be current and must be accurate.
- Records trace the movement of scheduled drugs throughout the service.
- The pharmacist is responsible for determining that all drug records are in order and that an account of all scheduled drugs is maintained and reconciled.
- The record system, delineated in policies and procedures, tracks movement of all scheduled drugs from the point of entry into the hospital to the point of departure either through administration to the patient, destruction or return to the manufacture. This system provides documentation on scheduled drugs in a readily retrievable manner to facilitate reconciliation of the receipt and disposition of all scheduled drugs.
- All drug records are in order and an account of all scheduled drugs is maintained and any discrepancies in count are reconciled promptly.
- The hospital system is capable of readily identifying loss or diversion of all controlled substances in such a manner as to minimize the time frame between the actual loss or diversion to the time of detection and determination of the extent of loss or diversion.
- Facility policies and procedures should minimize scheduled drug diversion.

Survey Procedures §482.25(a)(3)

- Determine if there is a record system in place that provides information on controlled substances in a readily retrievable manner.
- Review the records to determine that they trace the movement of scheduled drugs throughout the service.
- Determine if there is a system, delineated in policies and procedures, that tracks movement of all scheduled drugs from the point of entry into the hospital to the point of departure either through administra-

tion to the patient, destruction or return to the manufacture. Determine if this system provides documentation on scheduled drugs in a readily retrievable manner to facilitate reconciliation of the receipt and disposition of all scheduled drugs.

- Determine if the pharmacist is responsible for determining that all drug records are in order and that an account of all scheduled drugs is maintained and periodically reconciled.
- Is the hospital system capable of readily identifying loss or diversion of all controlled substances in such a manner as to minimize the time frame between the actual losses or diversion to the time of detection and determination of the extent of loss or diversion?
- Determine if facility policy and procedures minimize scheduled drug diversion.

A-0252

§482.25(b) Standard: Delivery of Services

In order to provide patient safety, drugs and biologicals must be controlled and distributed in accordance with applicable standards of practice, consistent with Federal and State law.

Authors' Comment: *Surveyors interview pharmacy staff and the organization's staff, observe dispensing procedures, and review pharmacy records to verify that this standard is met. CMS standards neither require nor prohibit a unit-dose drug-distribution system.*

Interpretive Guidelines §482.25(b)

Drugs and biologicals must be controlled and distributed in accordance with applicable Federal and State laws and regulations, and in accordance with applicable standards of practice. Applicable standards of practice include compliance with all Federal and State laws, regulations, and guidelines, as well as standards and recommendations promoted by nationally recognized professional organizations that apply to pharmaceutical care and the control and distribution of drugs and biologicals.

The procedures established to prevent unauthorized usage and distribution must provide for an accounting of the receipt and disposition of drugs subject to the Comprehensive Drug Abuse Prevention and Control Act of 1970.

The pharmacist, in consultation with appropriate hospital staff and committees, is to develop and implement guidelines, protocols, policies and procedures for the provision of pharmaceutical services that ensure patient safety through the appropriate control and distribution of medications, medication-related devices and biologicals.

For high-risk medications and high-risk patients (pediatric, geriatric or patients with renal or hepatic impairment) there should be systems in place to minimize adverse drug events. Such systems could include, but are not limited to, checklists, dose limits, preprinted orders, special packaging, special labeling, double checks, and written guidelines. "**High-risk medications**" are those medications involved in a high percentage of medication errors and/or sentinel events and medications that carry a higher risk for abuse, errors, or other adverse outcomes. Lists of high-risk or high-alert drugs are available from such organizations as the Institute for Safe Medication Practices (ISMP) and the United States Pharmacopoeia (USP). Examples of high-risk drugs may include investigational drugs, controlled medications, medications not on the approved FDA list, medications with a narrow therapeutic range, psychotherapeutic medications and look-alike/sound-alike medications, and those new to the market or new to the hospital.

All medication orders (except in emergency situations) should be reviewed for appropriateness by a pharmacist before the first dose is dispensed.

Review of medication orders should include:

- Therapeutic appropriateness of a patient's medication regimen
- Therapeutic duplication in the patient's medication regimen
- Appropriateness of the drug, dose, frequency, route, and method of administration
- Real or potential medication-medication, medication-food, medication-laboratory test, and medication-disease interactions
- Real or potential allergies or sensitivities
- Variation from organizational criteria for use
- Other contraindications

The effects of medication(s) on patients are monitored to assure medication therapy is appropriate and minimizes the occurrence of adverse events. That monitoring process includes:

- Clinical and laboratory data to evaluate the efficacy of medication therapy to anticipate or evaluate toxicity and adverse effects
- Physical signs and clinical symptoms relevant to the patient's medication therapy
- Assessing the patient's own perceptions about side effects, and, when appropriate, perceived efficacy

Sterile products should be prepared and labeled in a suitable environment by appropriately trained and qualified personnel.

The pharmacy should participate in hospital decisions about emergency medication kits. The supply and provision of emergency medications stored in the kits must be consistent with standards of practice and appropriate for a specified age group or disease treatment, as well as consistent with applicable Federal and State laws.

The pharmacy should be involved in the evaluation, use and monitoring of drug delivery systems, administration devices and automated drug-dispensing machines. The evaluation and monitoring should include the potential for medication errors.

There must be a process to report serious adverse drug reactions to the FDA in accordance with the MedWatch program.

There is a policy that addresses the use of medications brought into the hospital by patients or their families.

There is a process and policy to ensure that investigational medications are safety controlled and administered. Procedures for the use of investigational medications include the following: A written process for reviewing, approving, supervising and monitoring investigational medications specifying that when pharmacy services are provided, the pharmacy controls the storage, dispensing, labeling, and distribution of the investigational medication.

Medications dispensed by the hospital are retrieved when recalled or discontinued by the manufacturer or the Food and Drug Administration (FDA) for safety reasons.

The hospital pharmacy must ensure that medication orders are accurate and that medications are administered as ordered. The pharmacy should have a system to reconcile medications that are not administered, that remain in the patient's medication drawer, slot, etc., when the pharmacy inventories patient medications or restocks patient medications. The pharmacy should determine the reason the medications were not used. For example, did the patient refuse the medication, was there a clinical or treatment reason the medication was not used, or was the medication not used due to an error?

Survey Procedures §482.25(b)

- Are there limits on the number of possible concentrations for a medication, particularly high-alert drugs like morphine and heparin?
- Is access to concentrated solutions (e.g., potassium chloride, sodium chloride solutions greater than 0.9%) restricted?
- Are questions regarding the order resolved with the prescriber and a written notation of these discussions documented in the patient's medical record or pharmacy copy of the prescriber's order?
- Identify and assess the quality assurance procedures for the preparation of sterile products.
- Is appropriate monitoring of medication therapy being conducted?
- Is the pharmacy involved in the evaluation, use and monitoring of drug delivery systems, administration devices and automated drug dispensing machines? The evaluation and monitoring should include the potential for medication errors.
- Is there a process to report serious adverse drug reactions to the Federal MedWatch program?
- Review the procedures established to prevent unauthorized usage and distribution. These procedures must provide for an accounting of the receipt and disposition of drugs subject to the Comprehensive Drug Abuse Prevention and Control Act of 1970.
- Are medication storage areas periodically inspected to make sure medications are properly stored?
- Does the hospital retrieve and remove medications available for patient use when the hospital has been informed of a drug recall? Does the recall include notification of patients that have been impacted and those that would order, dispense or administer the medication?

A-0253

§482.25(b)(1) All compounding, packaging, and dispensing of drugs and biologicals must be under the supervision of a pharmacist and performed consistent with State and Federal laws.

Interpretive Guidelines §482.25(b)(1)

All compounding, packaging, and dispensing of drugs and biologicals must be conducted by a registered pharmacist or under the supervision of a registered pharmacist and performed consistent with State and Federal laws.

Medications must be prepared safely. Safe preparation procedures could include:

- Only the pharmacy compounds or admixes all sterile medications, intravenous admixtures, or other drugs except in emergencies or when not feasible (for example, when the product's stability is short).
- Whenever medications are prepared, staff uses safety materials and equipment while preparing hazardous medications.
- Wherever medications are prepared, staff uses techniques to assure accuracy in medication preparation.
- Whenever medications are prepared, staff uses appropriate techniques to avoid contamination during medication preparation, which include, but are not limited, to the following:
    - Using clean or sterile technique as appropriate
    - Maintaining clean, uncluttered, and functionally separate areas for product preparation to minimize the possibility of contamination
    - Using a laminar airflow hood or other appropriate environment while preparing any intravenous (IV) admixture in the pharmacy, any sterile product made from nonsterile ingredients, or any sterile product that will not be used with 24 hours
    - Visually inspecting the integrity of the medications

Medications should be dispensed in a manner that is safe and meets the needs of the patient:

- Quantities of medications are dispensed that minimize diversion and potential adverse events while meeting the needs of the patient.
- Medications are dispensed in a timely manner. The hospital must have a system that ensures that medication orders get to the pharmacy and medications get back to patients promptly.
- Whenever possible, medications are dispensed in the most ready to administer form available from the manufacturer or, if feasible, in unit doses that have been repackaged by the pharmacy.
- The hospital consistently uses the same dose packaging system, or, if a different system is used, provides education about the use of the dose packaging system.
- All concerns, issues or questions are clarified with the individual prescriber before dispensing.

Survey Procedures §482.25(b)(1)

- Determine that only pharmacists or pharmacy supervised personnel compound, label and dispense drugs or biologicals in accordance with State and Federal laws and regulations and as accepted national principles by:
    - reviewing policies and procedures
    - interviewing pharmacy and hospital staff to determine how drugs and biologicals are prepared and dispensed
    - observing on site dispensing and compounding operations (if applicable)
    - reviewing records of drugs and biologicals removed from the pharmacy by nonpharmacy personnel
    - inspecting drug storage areas
- Verify through interviews of pharmacy and hospital staff, observation of on-site dispensing operations, inspection, and review of hospital records that compounding, dispensing, and packaging of drugs and biologicals are performed under the supervision of a pharmacist, in accordance with applicable laws and in a manner to promote patient safety.

A-0254

§482.25(b)(2)(i) All drugs and biologicals must be kept in a secure area and locked when appropriate.

§482.25(b)(2)(ii) Drugs listed in Schedules II, III, IV, and V of the Comprehensive Drug Abuse Prevention and Control Act of 1970 must be kept locked within a secure area.

§482.25(b)(2)(iii) Only authorized personnel may have access to locked areas.

Interpretive Guidelines §482.25(b)(2)

All drugs and biologicals must be kept in a locked room or container. If the container is mobile or readily portable, when not in use, it must be stored in a locked room, monitored location, or secured location that will ensure the security of the drugs or biologicals.

All drugs and biologicals must be stored in a manner to prevent access by nonauthorized individuals.

Persons without legal access to drugs and biologicals cannot have unmonitored access to drugs or biologicals.

Persons without legal access to drugs or biologicals cannot have keys to medication storage rooms, carts, cabinets, or containers. Whenever persons without legal access to the drugs or biologicals have unmonitored access to or could gain access to the drugs or biologicals stored in an area, the hospital is not in compliance with the requirement to store all drugs and biologicals in a locked storage area.

Nursing Medication Carts, Anesthesia Carts, and Other Medication Carts

When not in use, nursing medication carts, anesthesia carts, and other medication carts (hereafter referred to as *carts*) containing drugs or biologicals must be locked or stored in a locked storage room. However, due to the mobility of carts, when not in use, locked carts that contain drugs or biologicals must be stored in a locked room or secure location. If a cart containing drugs or biologicals is in use and unlocked, someone with legal access to the drugs and biologicals in the cart must be close by and directly monitoring the cart. That person could be a nurse, a physician, or other individual who in accordance with State and Federal law and hospital policy has legal access to the drugs and biologicals in the cart. That person must monitor the cart and be aware of other people's activities near the cart. He/she is responsible for the security of the drugs and biologicals in the cart.

Survey Procedures §482.25(b)(2)

- Determine that there is a policy for the safeguarding, transferring and availability of keys to the locked storage area.
- Determine by inspection whether all medications are stored in a manner that prevents unauthorized access.
- Determine if the facility identifies what personnel may have access to medications.

> ***Authors' Comment:*** *Surveyors look for a policy addressing the safeguarding, transferring, and availability of keys (or codes to automatic locks) to the locked storage area, particularly where a pharmacist is not on duty full time.*

A-0255

§482.25(b)(3) Outdated, mislabeled, or otherwise unusable drugs and biologicals must not be available for patient use.

> ***Authors' Comment:*** *Surveyors spot-check drug labels to verify that they are consistent with federal and state laws.*

Interpretive Guidelines §482.25(b)(3)

The hospital must have a pharmacy labeling, inspection, and inventory management system that ensures that outdated, mislabeled, or otherwise unusable drugs and biologicals are not available for patient use.

Survey Procedures §482.25(b)(3)

- Spot-check the labels of individual drug containers to verify that they conform to State laws, and/or contain the following minimal information:
  - Each patient's individual drug container bears his/her full name, the prescriber's name, and strength and quantity of the drug dispensed. Appropriate accessory and cautionary statements are included, as well as the expiration date.
  - Each floor stock container bears the name and strength of the drug, lot and control number or equivalent, and expiration date.

- If the unit dose system is utilized, verify that each single unit-dose package bears name and strength of the drug, lot and control number or equivalent, and expiration date.
- Inspect patient-specific and floor stock medications to identify expired, mislabeled, or unusable medications.

A-0256

§482.25(b)(4) When a pharmacist is not available, drugs and biologicals must be removed from the pharmacy or storage area only by personnel designated in the policies of the medical staff and pharmaceutical service, in accordance with Federal and State law.

> ***Authors' Comment:*** *Although CMS does not require that a licensed individual remove drugs, state laws may prohibit their removal by personnel who are not licensed or registered. Designated individuals should be identified by name and qualifications in your pharmacy's policies and procedures, and the amount of drug(s) sufficient for immediate therapeutic needs that may be removed should be specified. Surveyors examine records of drugs removed from the pharmacy by nonpharmacy personnel to verify compliance.*

Interpretive Guidelines §482.25(b)(4)

Routine after-hours access to the pharmacy by nonpharmacists for access to medication should be minimized and eliminated as much as possible. The use of well-designed night cabinets, after-hours medication carts, and other methods may preclude the need for nonpharmacist to enter the pharmacy. Policies and procedures should be consistent with Federal and State Law.

If an urgent or emergent patient need occurs, the hospital must be able to provide medications to the patients in its facility.

The hospital must have a process for providing medications to meet patient needs when the pharmacy is closed.

When nonpharmacist health care professionals are allowed by law and regulation to obtain medications after the pharmacy is closed, the following safeguards are applied:

- Access is limited to a set of medications that has been approved by the hospital. These medications can be stored in a night cabinet, automated storage and distribution device, or a limited section of the pharmacy.
- Only trained, designated prescribers and nurses are permitted access to medications.
- Quality control procedures (such as an independent second check by another individual or a secondary verification built into the system, such as bar coding) are in place to prevent medication retrieval errors.
- The hospital arranges for a qualified pharmacist to be available either on-call or at another location (e.g., at another organization that has 24-hour pharmacy service) to answer questions or provide medications beyond those accessible to nonpharmacy staff.
- This process is evaluated on an ongoing basis to determine the medications accessed routinely and the causes of accessing the pharmacy after hours.
- Changes are implemented as appropriate to reduce the amount of times nonpharmacist health care professionals are obtaining medications after the pharmacy is closed.

Survey Procedures §482.25(b)(4)

- Determine through pharmacy records that when the pharmacist is not available, drugs are removed from the pharmacy (drug storage area) only by a designated individual (in accordance with State law if applicable) and only in amounts sufficient for immediate therapeutic needs.
- Review policies and procedures to determine who is designated to remove drugs and biologicals from the pharmacy or storage area and the amount a nonpharmacist may remove in the absence of a pharmacist. The individual(s) designated should be identified by name and qualifications.
- Determine that a system is in place that accurately documents the removal of medications (type and quantity) from either the pharmacy or the after-hours supply.
- Determine that the pharmacist reviews all medication removal activity and correlates the removal with current medication orders in the patient medication profile.
- Determine if the pharmacist routinely reviews the contents of the after-hours supply to determine if it is adequate to meet the after-hours needs of the hospital.

A-0257

§482.25(b)(5) Drugs and biologicals not specifically prescribed as to time or number of doses must automatically be stopped after a reasonable time that is predetermined by the medical staff.

Authors' Comment: *CMS considers the extended use of any drug a risk to patient safety and thus requires the medical staff to set a reasonable time limit for all drugs.*

Authors' Comment: *Surveyors look for automatic stop order policies and examine medication administration records to determine whether these policies are followed. Some surveyors suggest the following statement in an automatic stop order policy: "All orders for drugs not specifically included in this policy shall be discontinued after (a specific number) days." A period of 10–14 days (no more than 30) is suggested.*

Authors' Comment: *Some states mandate automatic stop orders for specific drugs and types of agents.*

Interpretive Guidelines §482.25(b)(5)

In accordance with accepted standards of practice, the medical staff, in coordination and consultation with the pharmacy service, determines and establishes the reasonable time to automatically stop orders for drugs and biologicals not specifically prescribed as to time or number of doses. The hospital must implement, monitor, and enforce this automatic stop system.

Survey Procedures §482.25(b)(5)

- Review policies and procedures to determine that there is a protocol established by the medical staff to discontinue and review patients' medical records to determine compliance with stop-order policy.

A-0258

§482.25(b)(6) Drug administration errors, adverse drug reactions, and incompatibilities must be immediately reported to the attending physician and, if appropriate, to the hospital-wide quality assurance program.

Interpretive Guidelines §482.25(b)(6)

Drug administration errors, adverse drug reactions, and drug incompatibility must be immediately reported to the patient's attending physician, or when appropriate the covering physician. When the covering physician is notified due to the attending physician not being available, the patient's attending physician must be notified as soon as he/she is available. Additionally in accordance with the regulation and 482.21, the hospital must report drug administrative errors, adverse drug reactions, and drug incompatibilities to its hospital wide QAPI program.

Reduction of medication errors and adverse reactions can be achieved by effective reporting systems that proactively identify causative factors and are used to implement corrective actions to reduce or prevent reoccurrences. To facilitate reporting, the facility should adopt a medication error and adverse drug reaction (ADR) definition that is broad enough in scope to capture "near misses" and suspected ADRs, as well as actual medication errors and ADRs.

An example is the use of the National Coordinating Council Medication Error Reporting and Prevention definition of a medication error.

> "Any preventable event that may cause or lead to inappropriate medication use or patient harm while the medication is in the control of the health care professional, patient, or consumer. Such events may be related to professional practice, health care products, procedures, and systems, including prescribing; order communication; product labeling, packaging, and nomenclature; compounding; dispensing; distribution; administration; education; monitoring; and use."

When compared to the traditional definition of a medication error (right patient, right drug, right route, right time, right dose) all errors secondary to any aspect of medication utilization (including purchasing, ordering, dispensing, administrative, preparation, compounding, etc.) would be reported versus only those that occurred in the administration phase of medication utilization.

In addition to broad scope definitions, the facility must also proactively identify medication errors and adverse drug reactions. Reliance solely on incident reporting fails to identify the majority of adverse drug events. Proactive identification includes observation of medications passes, concurrent and retrospective review of patient's clinical records, ADR surveillance team, implementation of medication usage evaluations for high-alert drugs, and identification of indicator drugs or "patient signals" that, when ordered, or noted automatically generate a drug regimen review for a potential adverse drug event.

The facility must have a method by which to measure the effectiveness of their reporting system so as to identify whether or not their system(s) is identifying as many medication errors and adverse drug reactions that would be expected for the size and scope of services provided by their hospital. Such methods could include use of established benchmarks or studies on reporting rates published in peer-reviewed journals.

To improve incident reporting the facility should adopt a nonpunitive system with the focus on the system and not the involved health care professionals.

Authors' Comment: *See Chapter 21-Medication Safety Improvement and Chapter 22-Adverse Drug Reactions.*

Survey Procedures §482.25(b)(6)

- Determine that the hospital has an effective procedure that ensures drug administration errors, adverse drug reactions, and drug incompatibilities are immediately reported to the attending physician.
- Review records of medication errors and adverse drug reactions to determine that they are reported immediately in accordance with written procedures, and that medications administered and/or drug reactions are promptly recorded in the patient's medical record.
- Is the facility's definition of an adverse drug reaction and medication error based on established benchmarks or studies on report rates published in peer-review journals? Is it identifying as many medication errors and adverse drug reactions as would be expected for the size and scope of services provided by the hospital?
- If upon review of patient's clinical records, a suspected ADR or medication error is identified, determine if it was reported immediately to the attending or on-call physician, in accordance, with written procedures and that it was promptly recorded in the patient's medical record.
- Review QAPI activities for medication errors and adverse reaction reports to determine if upon analyses of the reports that potential corrective actions are identified and implemented, if appropriate.
- Determine if the number of medication errors and adverse drug reactions reported is consistent with the size and scope of services provided by the hospital.
- Interview facility staff (nursing, pharmacy, and medicine) to ascertain awareness of the facility's policy on reporting and documentation of medication errors and adverse drug reactions

A-0259

§482.25(b)(7) Abuses and losses of controlled substances must be reported, in accordance with applicable Federal and State laws, to the individual responsible for the pharmaceutical service, and to the chief executive officer, as appropriate.

Authors' Comment: *Some surveyors review reports of abuses and losses to determine what action was taken to correct the situation.*

Survey Procedures §482.25(b)(7)

- Interview the pharmacists or pharmacy employees to determine their understanding of the controlled drug policies.
- Conduct a spot-check of drug use and other inventory records to ensure that drugs are properly accounted for.
- Review reports of pharmaceutical services to determine if there are reported problems with controlled drugs and what actions have been taken to correct the situation.
- Interview the Pharmacy Director, pharmacist, and pharmacy employees to determine their understanding of the controlled drug policies. Is there a policy and procedure for handling controlled drug discrepancies?
- Review reports of pharmaceutical services to determine if there are reported problems with controlled drugs and what actions have been taken to correct the situation.
- Determine if controlled drug losses were reported to appropriate authorities in accordance with State and Federal laws.

A-0260

§482.25(b)(8) Information relating to drug interactions and information on drug therapy, side effects, toxicology, dosage, indications for use, and routes of administration must be available to the professional staff.

Authors' Comment: *Surveyors determine whether staff development programs on drug therapy and new drugs are offered and check references to be sure that they are current. Surveyors also expect a pharmacist to be readily available (by telephone or other means) to discuss drug therapy with practitioners and assist in selection of medications and identification of adverse drug reactions.*

Interpretive Guidelines §482.25(b)(8)

The facility has immediately available sufficient texts and other resources on drug therapy. The pharmacist also should be readily available by telephone or other means to discuss drug therapy, interactions, side effects, dosage, etc., with practitioners to assist in drug selection and with nursing personnel to assist in the identification of drug-induced problems.

Survey Procedures §482.25(b)(8)

- Examine the sources of drug information available at the nursing station and/or drug storage area and determine if they are current.
- Determine whether staff development programs on drug therapy are available to facility staff to cover such topics as new drugs added to the formulary, how to resolve drug therapy problems, and other general information as the need arises.

A-0261

§482.25(b)(9) A formulary system must be established by the medical staff to assure quality pharmaceuticals at reasonable costs.

Authors' Comment: *To meet this requirement, the formulary system should provide a mechanism for evaluating and selecting products and entities that are most useful and cost effective. A formulary (i.e., a compilation of drugs approved for use in the organization) should be developed and continuously revised. Although CMS no longer requires a pharmacy and therapeutics (P&T) committee, the requirement that the medical staff establish a formulary system is best fulfilled by a P&T committee.*

Interpretive Guidelines §482.25(b)(9)

The medical staff must establish a formulary system. The formulary lists medications for dispensing or administration that the hospital maintains or that are readily available. In accordance with accepted standards of practice, the medical staff, in consultation with the pharmacy service, should develop written criteria for determining what medications are available for dispensing or administration. At a minimum, the criteria include the indication for use, effectiveness, risks (including propensity for medication errors, abuse potential, and sentinel events), and costs.

Processes and mechanisms should be established to monitor patient responses to a newly added medication before the medication is made available for dispensing or administration within the hospital.

Medications designated as available for dispensing or administration are reviewed periodically based on emerging safety and efficacy information.

The hospital should have processes to approve and procure medications that are not on the hospital's medication list.

The hospital should have processes to address medication shortages and outages, including the following:

- Communicating with appropriate prescribers and staff
- Developing approved substitution protocols
- Educating appropriate LIPs, appropriate health care professionals, and staff about these protocols
- Obtaining medications in the event of a disaster

Survey Procedures §482.25(b)(9)

- Interview the pharmacist to determine that the medical staff has established a formulary that lists drugs that actually are available in the hospital.
- Interview the Pharmacy Director to determine that there is a process for creation and periodic review of a formulary system.
- Determine that the formulary lists drugs that are available.

A-0208

§482.23(c) Standard: Preparation and Administration of Drugs

§482.23(c) Drugs and biologicals must be prepared and administered in accordance with Federal and State laws, the orders of the practitioner or practitioners responsible for the patient's care as specified under §482.12(c), and accepted standards of practice.

Interpretive Guidelines §482.23(c)

Drugs and biologicals must be prepared and administered in accordance with Federal and State laws.

Drugs and biologicals must be prepared and administered in accordance with the orders of the practitioner or practitioners responsible for the patient's care as specified under §482.12(c).

Drugs and biologicals must be prepared and administered in accordance with accepted standards of practice.

Accepted standards of practice include maintaining compliance with applicable Federal and State laws, regulations (including all the hospital Conditions of Participation (CoP) such as Pharmacy, Medical Records, Patients' Rights, QAPI), and guidelines governing drug and biological use in hospitals, as well as any standards and recommendations promoted by nationally recognized professional organizations.

Survey Procedures §482.23(c)

- Select patients from the patient sample. Review their medication orders, medication administration records, and appropriate medication documentation in the medical record. Observe the preparation and administration of medications to those patients.
- Are medications prepared and administered in accordance with Federal and State laws, other hospital CoP, accepted national standards of practice, manufacturer's directions, and hospital policy?

A-0209

§482.23(c)(1) All drugs and biologicals must be administered by, or under supervision of, nursing or other personnel in accordance with Federal and State laws and regulations, including applicable licensing requirements, and in accordance with the approved medical staff policies and procedures.

Survey Procedures §482.23(c)(1)

Verify that there is an effective method for the administration of drugs. Use the following indicators for assessing drug administration:

- Verify that there are policies and procedures approved by the medical staff covering who is authorized to administer medications, and that the policies are followed.
- Review a sample of medication administration records to see that they conform to the practitioner's order, that the order is current, and that drug and dosage are correct and administered as ordered.
- Observe the preparation of drugs and their administration to patients in order to verify that procedures are being followed. Are patients addressed by name and/or identiband checked? Does the nurse remain with the patient until medication is taken? Are drugs administered within 30 minutes of the scheduled time for administration?
- Verify that nursing or other personnel authorized by medical staff policy to administer drugs have completed appropriate training courses or are licensed or authorized to do so by State law and function under supervision as necessary.
- Check the QAPI activities to see if the administration of drugs is regularly monitored. The monitoring should include reports of medication irregularities or errors, their nature, frequency, and the corrective action taken.
- Interview supervisory nursing personnel to determine how supervision is provided. Also, interview personnel who administer medication to verify that the supervision is, in fact, provided.
- Are personnel other than nursing personnel administering drugs or biologicals? If yes, determine if those personnel are administering drugs or biologicals in accordance with Federal and State laws and regulations. Use the above procedures to determine compliance.

A-0210

§482.23(c)(2) With the exception of influenza and pneumococcal polysaccharide vaccines, which may be administered per physician-approved hospital policy after an assessment for contraindications, orders for drugs and biologicals must be documented and signed by a practitioner who is authorized to write orders by hospital policy and in accordance with State law, and who is responsible for the care of the patient as specified under §482.12(c).

Authors' Comment: *See CoP §482.23(c)(2)(i), CoP §482.23(c)(2)(ii).*

Authors' Comment: *CMS standards allow acceptance of telephone and verbal orders by registered nurses, licensed practical nurses, pharmacists, respiratory care personnel, and others, provided they are permitted to do so by state and federal law and medical staff policies and procedures. CMS does not set a time limit for prescribers to sign or initial these orders. However, many states require countersigning (authentication) within 24–48 hours.*

Interpretive Guidelines §482.23(c)(2)

All entries in the medical record must be legible, timed, dated, and authenticated. All orders for drugs and biologicals, including verbal orders, must be legible, timed, dated, and authenticated with a signature by the practitioner or practitioners responsible for the care of the patient.

Verbal orders are orders for medications, treatments, interventions, or other patient care that are communicated as oral, spoken communications between senders and receivers face-to-face or by telephone.

Verbal communication of orders should be limited to urgent situations where immediate written or electronic communication is not feasible.

Hospitals should establish policies and procedures that

- describe limitations or prohibitions on use of verbal orders
- provide a mechanism to ensure validity/authenticity of the prescriber
- list the elements required for inclusion in a complete verbal order
- describe situations in which verbal orders may be used
- list and define the individuals who may send and receive verbal orders
- provide guidelines for clear and effective communication of verbal orders

Hospitals should promote a culture in which it is acceptable and strongly encouraged for staff to question prescribers when there are any questions or disagreements about verbal orders. Questions about verbal orders should be resolved prior to the preparation, or dispensing, or administration of the medication.

Elements that should be included in any verbal medication order include:

- name of patient
- age and weight of patient, when appropriate
- date and time of the order
- drug name
- dosage form (e.g., tablets, capsules, inhalants)
- exact strength or concentration
- dose, frequency, and route
- quantity and/or duration
- purpose or indication
- specific instructions for use
- name of prescriber

The content of verbal orders must be clearly communicated. The entire verbal order should be repeated back to the prescriber. All verbal orders must be reduced immediately to writing and signed by the individual receiving the order. Verbal orders must be documented in the patient's medical record, and be reviewed and countersigned by the prescriber as soon as possible.

We recognize that in some instances, the ordering physician may not be able to authenticate his or her verbal order (e.g., the ordering physician gives a verbal order, which is written and transcribed, and then is "off duty" for the weekend or an extended period of time). In such cases, it is acceptable for a covering physician to cosign the verbal order of the ordering physician. The signature indicates that the covering physician assumes responsibility for his/her colleague's order as being complete, accurate, and final. This practice must be addressed in the hospital's policy. However, a qualified practitioner such as a physician assistant or nurse practitioner may not cosign a physician's verbal order or otherwise authenticate a medical record entry for the physician who gave the verbal order.

As noted above, CMS further requires that verbal orders, when used, be used infrequently (§482.23(c)(2)(i). Therefore, it is not acceptable to allow covering physicians to authenticate verbal orders for convenience or to make this common practice. When assessing compliance with this requirement, surveyors review the frequency and practice of using verbal orders within the hospital.

Survey Procedures §482.23(c)(2)

- Determine that all drug orders, including verbal orders, are written in the patient charts and signed by the practitioner caring for the patient.
- Read the hospital's policy for practitioner's orders. Does it require that orders must be in writing and signed by the attending practitioner?
- Verify that the prescriber has reviewed and authenticated the orders in accordance with medical staff policy and/or applicable State laws.

A-0211

§482.23(c)(2)(i) If verbal orders are used, they are to be used infrequently.

Interpretive Guidelines §482.23(c)(2)(i)

Verbal orders, if used, must be used infrequently. This means that the use of verbal orders is not a common practice. Verbal orders pose an increased risk of miscommunication that could result in a patient adverse event (which includes medication errors). Verbal orders should be used only to meet the care needs of the patient when the ordering practitioner is unable to write the order himself/herself. Verbal orders are not to be used for the convenience of the ordering practitioner.

Survey Procedures §482.23(c)(2)(i)

- Review patient medical records for the use of verbal orders.
  - Are verbal orders used infrequently?
  - Is there a pattern to the use of verbal orders?
  - Are verbal orders used frequently for certain situations?
  - Do certain practitioners use verbal orders frequently?

A-0212

§482.23(c)(2)(ii) When verbal orders are used, they must only be accepted by persons who are authorized to do so by hospital policy and procedures consistent with Federal and State law.

Interpretive Guidelines §482.23(c)(2)(ii)

A telephone or verbal order must be written in the medical record by a nurse or other professional who is permitted by State law and hospital policy to accept verbal orders. The written verbal order must be legible and include the date, time, order, name of the ordering practitioner, and the signature of the accepting individual. The ordering practitioner must date and time the order at the time that he or she signs the order.

Survey Procedures §482.23(c)(2)(ii)

- Request to see several patient charts with telephone orders. Check to determine if they are taken by authorized hospital personnel, and are correctly countersigned by the practitioner. Ask several nurses if they are permitted to take telephone and oral orders and how frequently they do so.

A-0214

§482.23(c)(3) Blood transfusions and intravenous medications must be administered in accordance with State law and approved medical staff policies and procedures. If blood transfusions and intravenous medications are administered by personnel other than doctors of medicine or osteopathy, the personnel must have special training for this duty.

Survey Procedures §482.23(c)(3)

- Review the transfusions and intravenous medications practices:
  - Does the hospital have special training for administering blood transfusions and intravenous medications?
  - Are blood transfusions and IVs administered in accordance with State law and approved hospital policies and procedures?
  - Are blood transfusions and IVs administered by personnel who are trained and working within their scope of practice in accordance with State law and hospital policies?
  - Review transfusion records. Determine the identity of practitioners who administered the blood. Do they have documented, special training.
  - Review a sample of medical records to determine that only doctors of medicine or osteopathy or specially trained personnel perform this duty. If the nursing service trains personnel for IV administration, look at the content of the in-service course. It should include:
    - fluid and electrolyte balance,
    - blood components,
    - venipuncture techniques, demonstrations, and supervised practice.

A-0215

§482.23(c)(4) There must be a hospital procedure for reporting transfusion reactions, adverse drug reactions, and errors in administration of drugs.

Survey Procedures §482.23(c)(4)

- Request the hospital procedure for reporting adverse drug reactions and errors and transfusion reactions. Review the incident reports or other documentation that the procedure is being implemented and regularly monitored through hospital's QAPI program.

A-0141

§482.21 Condition of Participation: Quality Assessment and Performance Improvement

The hospital must develop, implement, and maintain an effective, ongoing, hospital-wide, data-driven quality assessment and performance improvement program. The hospital's governing body must ensure that the program reflects the complexity of the hospital's organization and services; involves all hospital departments and services (including those services furnished under contract or arrangement); and focuses on indicators related to improved health outcomes and the prevention and reduction of medical errors.

The hospital must maintain and demonstrate evidence of its QAPI program for review by CMS.

> ***Authors' Comment:*** *Although similar in their intent, CMS QAPI standards are not as detailed as Joint Commission performance improvement (PI) standards. However, a program that is generally in compliance with Joint Commission PI standards should also meet CMS QAPI requirements.*

> ***Authors' Comment:*** *The organization evaluates all organized services related to patient care, including services (e.g., pharmacy) furnished by a contractor.*

A-0154

§482.21(c)(2) Performance improvement activities must track medical errors and adverse patient events.

A-0155

§482.21(c)(2) continued

[Performance improvement activities must track medical errors and adverse patient events,] and analyze their causes, and

A-0156

§482.21(c)(2) continued

[Performance improvement activities must track medical errors and adverse patient events, analyze their causes, and] implement preventive actions and mechanisms that include feedback and learning throughout the hospital.

> ***Authors' Comment:*** *The organization takes and documents appropriate remedial action to address deficiencies found through the QAPI program in regards to medication errors and adverse drug reactions.*

> ***Authors' Comment:*** *Documentation should describe the action taken and the extent to which the problem is resolved or patient care is improved. Surveyors will look at staff meeting minutes, memoranda, and other records to see if problems are addressed and corrected.*

A-0317

§482.41 Condition of Participation: Physical Environment

The hospital must be constructed, arranged, and maintained to ensure the safety of the patient, and to provide facilities for diagnosis and treatment and for special hospital services appropriate to the needs of the community.

A-0318

§482.41(a) Standard: Buildings

The condition of the physical plant and the overall hospital environment must be developed and maintained in such a manner that the safety and well-being of patients are assured.

Interpretive Guidelines §482.41(a)

Assuring the safety and well-being of patients would include developing and implementing appropriate emergency preparedness plans and capabilities. The hospital must develop and implement a comprehensive plan to ensure that the safety and well-being of patients are assured during emergency situations. The hospital must coordinate with federal, state, and local emergency preparedness and health authorities to identify likely risks for their area (e.g., natural disasters, bioterrorism threats, disruption of utilities such as water, sewer, electrical communications, fuel: nuclear accidents, industrial accidents, and other likely mass casualties, etc.) and to develop appropriate responses that will assure the safety and well-being of patients. The following issues should be considered when developing the comprehensive emergency plan(s):

- Pharmaceuticals, food, other supplies and equipment that may be needed during emergency/disaster situations

A-0331

§482.41(c)(2) Facilities, supplies, and equipment must be maintained to ensure an acceptable level of safety and quality.

Interpretive Guidelines §482.41(c)(2)

Equipment must be maintained to ensure an acceptable level of safety and quality.

Equipment includes both facility equipment (e.g., elevators, generators, air handlers, medical gas systems, air compressors and vacuum systems, etc.) and medical equipment (e.g., biomedical equipment, radiological equipment, patient beds, stretchers, IV infusion equipment, ventilators, laboratory equipment, etc.).

A-0333

§482.41(c)(4) There must be proper venti-

lation, light, and temperature controls in pharmaceutical, food preparation, and other appropriate areas.

Interpretive Guidelines §482.41(c)(4)

There must be proper ventilation in at least the following areas:

- Areas using ethylene oxide, nitrous oxide, guteraldehydes, xylene, pentamidine, and other potentially hazardous substances
- Locations where oxygen is transferred from one container to another
- Isolation rooms and reverse isolations rooms (both must be in compliance with Federal and State laws, regulations, and guidelines such as OSHA, CDC, NIH, etc.)
- Pharmaceutical preparation areas (hoods, cabinets, etc.)
- Laboratory locations

There must be adequate lighting in all the patient care areas, and food and medication preparation areas.

The hospital must ensure that an appropriate number of refrigerators and/or heating devices are provided and ensure that food and pharmaceuticals are stored properly and in accordance with nationally accepted guidelines (food) and manufacturer's recommendations (pharmaceuticals).

A-0338

§482.42 Condition of Participation: Infection Control

The hospital must provide a sanitary environment to avoid sources and transmission of infections and communicable diseases. There must be an active program for the prevention, control, and investigation of infections and communicable diseases.

> ***Authors' Comment:*** *The pharmacy must participate in the organization-wide program for the prevention, control, and investigation of infections and communicable diseases.*

A-0428

§482.53 Condition of Participation: Nuclear Medicine

If the hospital provides nuclear medicine services, those services must meet the needs of the patients in accordance with acceptable standards of practice.

A-0433

§482.53(b)(1) In-house preparation of radiopharmaceuticals is by, or under, the direct supervision of an appropriately trained registered pharmacist or doctor of medicine or osteopathy.

> ***Authors' Comment:*** *Preparation of radiopharmaceuticals in the organization is by, or under, the direct supervision of an appropriately trained registered pharmacist or a doctor of medicine or osteopathy.*

Healthcare Facilities Accreditation Program (HFAP) Surveys

The Healthcare Facilities Accreditation Program (HFAP) of the American Osteopathic Association (AOA) is a recognized alternative to certification by the Centers for Medicare & Medicaid Services (CMS) or accreditation by the Joint Commission™. HFAP is recognized nationally by the federal government, state governments, insurance carriers, and managed care organizations. HFAP accreditation is not limited to osteopathic hospitals and some health care organizations are accredited by both HFAP and the Joint Commission.[1]

HFAP Requirements

The HFAP requirements were revised in February 2005 and are published in the HFAP *Accreditation Requirements for Healthcare Facilities* manual.[2] The requirements address all departments and functions including pharmacy and medication use. Several new pharmacy standards have been added since 2005 and others revised.[1] Organizations should access the HFAP Web site for the most current HFAP standards and revisions. (*See* Appendix A.)

Some HFAP standards are more prescriptive than Joint Commission and Centers for Medicare and Medicaid Services (CMS) standards. Therefore, compliance with Joint Commission and CMS standards is not necessarily sufficient to meet HFAP standards and vice versa.

HFAP Surveys

Any health care organization may request an accreditation survey to determine its level of compliance with HFAP requirements. Surveyors review key systems, assess compliance with standards, and determine how well the organization provides care, treatment, and services.

HFAP accreditation surveys are unannounced. Surveys are usually performed by three surveyors consisting of a physician, who heads the team, a hospital administrator, and a registered nurse. Larger organizations may require additional surveyors. The composition of the survey team is dependent on the size and scope of care of the health care organization to be surveyed.

HFAP Accreditation

If HFAP determines an organization is compliant with its requirements, it awards the organization the status of "Accredited." The length of accreditation is three years. HFAP provides hospitals with a written report of any areas of noncompliance after completion of the survey. Organizations are required to demonstrate corrective actions of all deficiencies prior to the awarding of accreditation. Note that HFAP and the Joint Commission accredit health care organizations; Medicare certifies. HFAP accreditation, Joint Commission accreditation, or Medicare certification qualifies an organization to participate in the Medicare program. (*See* Chapters 1 and 24.)

Arrangement of HFAP Standards/Elements

HFAP *Accreditation Requirements for Healthcare Facilities* manual is organized by department, service, or function. Each chapter includes standards that link directly with CMS Conditions of Participation (CoP) or other regulations. Chapter 25, Pharmacy Services and Medication Use, consists of standards 25.00.00 through 25.03.06. CMS standards are italicized. Most standards have an explanation (e.g., rationale) that gives specific information concerning the intent of the standard. All standards are arranged in four columns as described in Table 25-1.

HFAP Standards/Elements for Pharmacy Services/Medication Use

Many of the HFAP standards/elements quote the CMS Conditions of Participation (CoPs), CMS Standards, and CMS Interpretative Guidelines. (*See* Chapters 4 and 24.) The information in those chapters and other chapters of this book may be helpful in complying with HFAP standards.

HFAP standards/elements for Pharmacy Services/Medication Use are listed below. Standards/elements that are also CMS CoPs and Standards are quoted. The quotations are taken from the Federal Register and may differ slightly from the version in *Accreditation Requirements for Healthcare Facilities*. The appropriate CMS number (beginning with 482) follows each HFAP standard/element that is also a CMS CoP or Standard.

HFAP standards/elements that are not CMS CoPs or Standards are, when necessary, paraphrased. They are not followed by a CMS number.

Authors' comments are in italics and include their suggestions and experiences or provide clarification. They often reflect HFAP explanations, scoring procedures, and scoring system.

Pharmacies should obtain a copy of current HFAP requirements prior to the survey. For additional information and compliance guidelines, they should review the actual standards/elements as well as the relevant explanations and scoring procedures. Other chapters in the *Accreditation Requirements for Healthcare Facilities* may also contain requirements for pharmacy services.

HFAP uses several terms for medications (e.g., drugs, biologicals, items, products, and preparations). When the authors have paraphrased the HFAP standards/elements they usually use the term *medications,* which should be considered interchangeable with the terms used by HFAP.

25.00.00 Pharmaceutical Services

The hospital must have pharmaceutical services that meet the needs of the patients. The institution must have a pharmacy directed by a registered pharmacist or a drug storage area under competent supervision. The medical staff is responsible for developing policies and procedures that minimize drug errors. This function may be delegated to the hospital's organized pharmaceutical service. 482.25

> ***Authors' Comment:*** *The explanation for 25.00.00 notes that competent supervision for a drug storage area must be in accordance with state and federal law.*

The pharmacy or drug storage area must be administered in accordance with accepted professional principles. 482.25(a)

The pharmacy or drug storage area must meet all legal requirements.

The medical staff must develop policies and procedures to minimize drug errors. These must address the following:

- Dosing limits, administering guidelines, and guidelines for packaging, labeling, and storing high-alert or high-risk medications
- Placing limits on the variety of medication-related devices and equipment
- Ensuring that current medication information is available
- Ensuring that pharmacy expertise is available when the pharmacy is not staffed 24 hours a day, seven days a week
- Standardizing prescribing and communicating practices to include the following:
  - Avoiding dangerous abbreviations
  - Stating that a complete medication order includes the dose, strength, units, route of administration, and rate of administration
  - Providing a system for alerting staff to medications with look-alike and sound-alike names
  - Using preprinted order sheets, approved by the organization, whenever possible
- Prohibiting the use of the expression "resume previous orders"
- Providing a voluntary, nonpunitive system for monitoring and reporting medication errors, adverse drug reactions, and other adverse drug events
- Ensuring that hazardous medications are prepared, distributed, administered, and disposed of properly
- Handling medication recalls and external alerts
- Ensuring that patient-specific information is readily available to all individuals who provide pharmaceutical care
- Identifying when weight-based dosing for pediatric patients is required
- Stating when review and revision are required based on the organization's reports of adverse drug events and Quality Assurance/Performance Improvement (QAPI) activities

25.00.01 Licensure

The pharmacy (including each separate pharmacy location) must be currently licensed to meet state requirements and the licenses must be prominently displayed if required.

> ***Authors' Comment:*** *The explanation for 25.00.01 states that the pharmacy must be licensed as a retail pharmacy if required by the state.*

25.00.02 Permits and Certifications

Other required permits and certificates must be current and, if required, prominently displayed.

> ***Authors' Comment:*** *The explanation for 25.00.02 states that examples of permits and certificates include the Drug Enforcement Administration registration, state controlled substances permit, tax free alcohol permit, and a permit to be a preceptor for pharmacist interns.*

25.00.03 Scope of Service

Pharmaceutical services must reflect the organization's scope of services.

25.00.04 Management

A full-time, part-time, or consulting pharmacist must be responsible for developing, supervising, and coordinating all the activities of the pharmacy services. 482.25(a)(1)

25.00.05 Staffing

The pharmaceutical service must have an adequate number of personnel to ensure quality pharmaceutical services, including emergency services. 482.25(a)(2)

25.00.06 Scheduled Drugs

Current and accurate records must be kept of the receipt and disposition of all scheduled drugs. 482.25(a)(3)

> ***Authors' Comment:*** *The explanation for 25.00.06 requires the maintenance of a perpetual inventory of scheduled drugs.*

A complete and accurate record system for the receipt and distribution of scheduled drugs must include the following components:

- Procedures that ensure the accountability and control for distributing, using, and disposing of all scheduled medications
- Current and accurate records of the receipt and distribution of all scheduled medications
- Records that trace how scheduled medications move throughout the organization
- A means to ensure that a pharmacist is responsible for keeping orderly medication records and that accounts of all scheduled medications are maintained and reconciled
- A record system, described in policies and procedures, that tracks how scheduled medications move from their point of entry (e.g., receipt) through administration to a patient or their return to the manufacturer. (Documentation relating to scheduled medications is readily retrievable in order to facilitate reconciliation of their receipt and disposition.)
- Records for scheduled medications that are in order. (An account of all scheduled medications must be maintained, and if discrepancies in the count of such medications is discovered, they are reconciled promptly.)
- A means for the organization to readily identify any loss or diversion of scheduled medications. (The time between the actual loss or diversion to the time the loss or diversion is detected and the extent of the loss or diversion determined must be minimized.)
- Policies and procedures that minimize the diversion of scheduled medications

25.00.07 Space Requirements

Pharmacy space must be adequate so that medications can be stored securely.

> ***Authors' Comment:*** *The explanation and scoring procedure for 25.00.07 state that space must permit orderly storage of medications and there must be separate double-locked storage for Schedule II controlled substances.*

25.01.01 Medication Control and Distribution

In order to provide patient safety, drugs and biologicals must be controlled and distributed in accordance with applicable standards of practice, consistent with Federal and State law. 482.25(b)

> ***Authors' Comment:*** *The explanation for 25.01.01 states that examples of high-risk medications include those medications involved in a high percentage of medication errors and/or critical events and medica-*

tions that carry a higher risk for abuse, errors, or other adverse outcomes; additional high-risk drugs are identified as those listed by the Institute for Safe Medication Practices and the United States Pharmacopoeia, which include investigational drugs, controlled medications, medications that are not FDA approved, medications with a narrow therapeutic range, psychotherapeutic medications, medications with look-alike/sound-alike names, and medications that are new to the organization. The scoring procedure lists morphine, heparin, concentrated potassium chloride solutions, and sodium chloride solutions with a concentration greater than 0.9%.

Authors' Comment: *The scoring procedure for 25.01.01 indicates that medication storage areas are to be inspected periodically. The explanation for 25.01.05 states that monthly inspections are required.*

25.01.02 Supervision of Pharmacy Activities

All compounding, packaging, and dispensing of drugs and biologicals must be under the supervision of a pharmacist and performed consistent with State and Federal laws. 482.25(b)(1)

Authors' Comment: *The explanation for 25.01.02 lists safe medication preparation procedures that must be followed. These should be read carefully.*

25.01.03 Security of Medications

All drugs and biologicals must be kept in a secure area, and locked when appropriate. 482.25(b)(2)(i)

Drugs listed in Schedules II, III, IV, and V of the comprehensive Drug Abuse Prevention and Control Act of 1970 must be kept locked within a secure area. 482.25(b)(2)(ii)

Only authorized personnel may have access to locked areas. 482.25(b)(2)(iii)

All controlled substances must be locked within a secure area. Schedule II, III, IV, and V drugs must be locked (e.g., locked storage cabinet, locked cart) within a secure area, regardless of whether the area is staffed.

Schedule II, III, IV, and V drugs cannot be stored on a shelf or unlocked cabinet/container within a locked area (e.g., surgical suite, special procedure area).

Organizations have the flexibility to determine the most effective method to safeguard noncontrolled medications and biologicals when they are not stored in a locked area. Medications in the pharmacy and throughout the organization must be stored in a secure area and locked when appropriate, as required by laws or regulations.

Authors' Comment: *The explanation and scoring procedure for 25.01.03 emphasize the need for security. Unauthorized individuals must not have access to medications. Keys must be safeguarded. Carts containing medications (e.g., nursing carts and anesthesia carts) must be locked or stored in a locked room or secure location.*

Medications are considered to be secure when unauthorized individuals cannot obtain access to them.

Authors' Comment: *Individuals who are not legally permitted access to medications must be monitored. They cannot have keys to medication storage areas or carts containing medications.*

An area would generally be considered secure when staff are actively providing patient care or preparing to receive patients

Organization policies must specifically address

- storage, security, and monitoring of noncontrolled medications and biologicals in all patient care areas
- safeguards in place to prevent tampering and minimize diversion of medications
- identification of "secure" areas
- identification of authorized personnel who have access to locked and secured areas and the degree of supervision needed in carrying out their routine duties and responsibilities (e.g., housekeeping, maintenance)
- security of bedside medications
- assurance of patient competence to self-administer their medications

When the surgical suite is closed or not in use, the organization must lock the entire suite. Within the suite, all noncontrolled medications and biologicals must be locked in a secure area, or locked in nonmobile carts, or stored in mobile carts within a locked room.

Bedside medications must be secured to prevent tampering and access by unauthorized individuals.

25.01.04 Pharmacy Security

The pharmacy has locking entities (i.e., it must be capable of being locked).

> ***Authors' Comment:*** *The explanation and scoring procedure for 25.01.04 states that the pharmacy must be locked when staff is not present. Access codes, security codes, and keys must be strictly controlled and secure.*

25.01.05 Inventory Management System

Outdated, mislabeled, or otherwise unusable drugs and biologicals must not be available for patient use. 482.25(b)(3)

The director of pharmacy must ensure that all medication inventories are reviewed, medications are sequestered if necessary and logged, and recalled and/or unusable medications are destroyed or returned.

> ***Authors' Comment:*** *The explanation and scoring procedure for 21.01.05 states that medications, including those in crash carts, must be inspected at least monthly, for products that are about to expire. Expired Schedules II and III medications must be sequestered separately from nonscheduled medications. Medications for patients must include the patient's full name as well as the prescriber's name. Additional requirements are listed.*

25.01.06 Pharmacy Access

When a pharmacist is not available, drugs and biologicals must be removed from the pharmacy or storage area only by personnel designated in the policies of the medical staff and pharmaceutical services, in accordance with Federal and State law. 482.25(b)(4)

> ***Authors' Comment:*** *The explanation for 25.01.06 permits nonpharmacists to have access to the pharmacy after the pharmacy is closed. Access must be strictly controlled and limited to medications that have been approved by the organization. Access must be limited to trained, designated prescribers and nurses. A pharmacist must review and evaluate the removals and make changes to reduce the frequency of access. Additional requirements are listed.*

25.01.07 Automatic Stop Medication Orders

The medical staff must set time frames for automatically stopping orders for medications and those orders are automatically stopped as required.

Drugs and biologicals not specifically prescribed as to time or number of doses must automatically be stopped after a reasonable time that is predetermined by the medical staff. 482.25(b)(5)

> ***Authors' Comment:*** *The explanation for 25.01.07 lists medications that are usually included in an automatic stop order policy. A maximal time frame of 21 to 30 days is indicated but not specifically required. The practitioner must be notified before stopping the order.*

25.01.08 Drug Reactions and Administration Errors and Incompatibilities

Drug administration errors, adverse drug reactions, and incompatibilities must be immediately reported to the attending physician and, if appropriate, to the hospital-wide quality assurance program. 482.25(b)(6)

> ***Authors' Comment:*** *HFAP adds "performance improvement program" to 482.25(b)(6).*

There must be a hospital procedure for reporting transfusion reactions, adverse drug reactions, and errors in administration of drugs. 482.23(c)(4)

> ***Authors' Comment:*** *The explanation for 25.01.08 states that errors must include "near misses." Adverse drug reactions (ADRs) must be classified by probability, severity, mechanism, and dosing location. The National Coordinating Council for Medication Error Reporting and Prevention (NCCMERP) definition of a medication error is satisfactory to HFAP.*

25.01.09 Reporting of Controlled Drug Loss and/or Abuse

Abuses and losses of controlled substances must be reported, in accordance with applicable Federal and State laws, to the individual responsible for the pharmaceutical service, and to the chief executive officer, as appropriate. 482.25(b)(7)

Authors' Comment: *The explanation for 25.01.09 states that the organization must be able to track abuses and losses.*

25.01.10 Information Resources

Information relating to drug interactions and information on drug therapy, side effects, toxicology, dosage, indications for use, and routes of administration must be available to the professional staff. 482.25(b)(8)

Authors' Comment: *The explanation and scoring procedure for 25.01.10 indicates that the state pharmacy practice act, toxicology reference (including the regional poison control center telephone number), and pharmacy texts must be available. There must be an on call or readily available pharmacist for consultation.*

25.01.11 Formulary System

A formulary system must be established by the medical staff to assure quality pharmaceuticals at reasonable costs. 482.25(b)(9)

Authors' Comment: *The explanation and scoring procedure for 25.01.11 states that a formulary must be available in clinical areas. Surveyors must check the date that the medical staff approved the formulary. The formulary must be reviewed periodically. There must be written criteria for selecting medications included in the formulary.*

25.01.12 Nonformulary Medications

There must be provisions for ordering medications that are not listed in the organization's formulary.

Authors' Comment: *The explanation and scoring procedure for 25.01.12 states that there must be methods for changing or amending the formulary.*

25.01.13 Integrity of Medication

Medications must be stored at the proper temperatures and records of medication refrigerator and freezer temperatures must be maintained.

Authors' Comment: *The explanation and scoring procedure for 25.01.13 states that daily temperature logs are required for all medication refrigerators and freezers. Thermometers must be accurate and their accuracy must be verified against a known standard (e.g., a reference thermometer) semiannually. Medications must be stored within the manufacturer's guidelines.*

25.01.14 Consultations/Resource Availability

The pharmacy must ensure that those who prescribe and administer medications as well as patients and families are provided with pharmaceutical consultation as appropriate.

Authors' Comment: *The explanation for 25.01.14 states that a pharmacist must serve on the medical staff committee that discusses medication therapy (e.g., a pharmacy and therapeutics committee). A pharmacist must provide inservice education programs for nursing staff.*

25.01.15 Medication Protocols

There must be a review and revision of standing, routine, or protocol orders at least annually. (Master copies of these orders are kept in the pharmacy.)

25.01.16 Home Medications

There must be policies and procedures that provide standards for the use of medications that patients bring into the organization.

Authors' Comment: *The explanation for 25.01.16 states that a pharmacist or physician must positively identify patients' home medications that are to be administered to patients. The manufacturer's lot number must be included in the identification.*

25.01.17 Labeling

Labels of medications intended for the use of specific patients must include the patient's full name and the name of the prescriber, identify of the medication, strength, quantity, expiration or beyond-use date, and accessory or cautionary statements as appropriate for the medication.

Authors' Comment: *The explanation for 25.01.17 states that labeling of repackaged medications must meet state and federal requirements. There must be a way to track the manufacturer's lot number. The manufacturer's lot number must be on medications dispensed to outpatients.*

25.01.18 Standardization of Labeling

Medications must be labeled, packaged, and stored in a standardized manner throughout the organization. (The intention of this requirement is to reduce adverse events.)

25.01.19 High-Alert Medications

The organization's actions to ensure the safe use of high-alert or high-risk medications must include identifying such medications that are present in the organization, identifying new high-alert or high-risk medications as they are introduced into the organization, establishing protocols for their safe use and making the protocols available to staff who must use the medications, auditing compliance with the protocols, and using a multidisciplinary team to review the safeguards in place for these medications.

Authors' Comment: *The explanation for 25.01.19 states that examples of high-alert medications are intravenous adrenergic agonists and antagonists, chemotherapeutic agents, anticoagulants and antithrombotics, concentrated parenteral electrolytes, general anesthetics, neuromuscular blockers, insulin and oral hypoglycemics, narcotics and opiates. Compare this list with 25.01.01.*

25.01.20 Dispensing Methods

Whenever possible, the pharmacy must dispense medications in unit-dose, unit-of-use, or ready-to-administer forms. Medications so dispensed must be labeled with the medication name, strength, manufacturer, expiration or beyond-use date, and lot number in machine-readable code. No more than a 24-hour supply is to be provided to patient care areas at any one time. The medication distribution system must be monitored so that performance relating to medication distribution can be improved.

Authors' Comment: *The explanation for 25.01.20 states that medications purchased in bulk must be repackaged into unit-dose aliquots.*

Authors' Comment: *No explanation or clarification is provided for the reference to machine-readable code in the standard/element.*

25.01.21 Preparation of Intravenous Drugs and Fluids

To prevent contamination, the pharmacy must compound sterile preparations (including intravenous medications and fluids) according to pharmacy practice standards and state/federal regulations. The methods used must reduce the potential for contamination by bacteria and drugs.

Authors' Comment: *The explanation and scoring procedure for 25.01.21 states that the expiration date of a reconstituted or admixed preparation must be prominently displayed on the label. Horizontal and vertical laminar airflow hoods must be used for their intended purposes. Maintenance personnel must clean vertical hoods quarterly. Horizontal hoods must be inspected and the filter changed every six months. Spill kits, spill procedures, and personal protective equipment must be immediately available if cytotoxic medications are prepared.*

25.01.22 Sample Drugs

The pharmacy must control the use of medication samples in accordance with state/federal laws.

Authors' Comment: *The explanation for 25.01.22 states that there must be full accountability for the storage, distribution, and use of medication samples and a log must be maintained. Medication samples must be included in the medication recall procedure.*

25.01.23 Patient Medication Profile

There must be a medication profile maintained for each inpatient and outpatient who receives medications. (The profile must include information that will assure that medications are administered safely and accurately.)

Authors' Comment: *The explanation for 25.01.23 states that data to be entered into a patient medication profiles includes diet orders, history of prescribed medications, nonprescribed medications, over-the-counter medications, home remedies, and street drugs.*

25.01.24 Profile Review

A pharmacist must review patient profiles daily and when ever an order is changed. The review must occur before dispensing the medication or providing the medication for administration (unless the delay would be medically unacceptable). Profile reviews must include potential drug-drug and food-drug interactions as well as interferences and incompatibilities. There must be documentation of the reviews in the patient's record. Pharmacists who review patient profiles must maintain a log that documents their interventions. The organization must audit compliance with the patient profile review requirements and use the findings to improve medication safety.

> ***Authors' Comment:*** *The scoring procedure for 25.01.24 states that policies must define when a delay would be medically acceptable.*

25.01.25 Drug Administration

The organization must have mechanisms in place to ensure that medications are safely, accurately, and effectively administered.

> ***Authors' Comment:*** *The explanation for 25.01.25 says that this is self-explanatory. The scoring procedure says that surveyors are to compare physicians' orders against medication administration records for accuracy.*

25.01.26 Label Medications and Solutions on the Sterile Field

The organization must develop and implement policies for labeling medications and solutions used on and off the sterile field in perioperative settings. Policies must include at least the following:

- required labeling of medications and solutions, regardless of container type, used throughout the procedure

  Authors' Comment: *All types of containers including cups, basins, syringes, and specimen cups must be labeled.*

- process for labeling look-alike and sound-alike medications and solutions
- process used to verify and confirm each medication and solution label against the original label

A label is required even if only one solution is involved in the procedure.

Two staff members must verbally and visually confirm each medication and solution with the respective label. At least one of the staff must be a licensed individual participating in the procedure.

Original medication and solution containers must be retained until the procedure is completed in case they are needed for reference.

25.01.27 Investigational Drugs

The organization must have policies that address administration of the following:

- Medications for indications that are not approved by the FDA
- Experimental medications
- Investigational medications when one or more of the primary investigators are members of the organization's medical staff
- Investigational medications brought by patients into the organization that have been prescribed by practitioners who are not members of the organization's medical staff

> ***Authors' Comment:*** *The explanation for 25.01.27 lists seven concepts that must be addressed in investigational drug policies. The scoring procedure for 25.01.27 requires surveyors to verify that each of the seven concepts is addressed.*

25.01.28 Documentation

The effects of therapy (including medication therapy) must be noted in patient medical records. The record must include the following:

- Accurate documentation of all doses administered
- The effects of the medications or products
- Progress notes of prescribing practitioners and medical consultants
- Nursing staff notes relating to the effects of prn dosing and dosing for clinical outcomes

- Record of clinical outcomes
- Record of laboratory, imaging, cardiogram, and other objective testing to determine therapeutic effects

25.01.29 Antithrombotic Therapy

The organization must have policies and procedures that ensure safe and effective antithrombotic (i.e., anticoagulation) therapy is provided by dedicated, antithrombotic services.

> ***Authors' Comment:*** *The explanation and scoring procedure for 25.01.29 states that policies and procedures must define staff training requirements, dose scheduling and tracking mechanisms, patient education materials, and mechanisms for training.*

25.02.01 Preparation and Administration of Drugs

Drugs and biologicals must be prepared and administered in accordance with Federal and State laws, the orders of the practitioner or practitioners responsible for the patient's care as specified under 482.12(c), and accepted standards of practice. 482.23(c)

> ***Authors' Comment:*** *The explanation for 25.02.01 states that policies must identify the categories of personnel who can administer various kinds of medications. Organizations may require compentency testing of these personnel. Personnel are not permitted to administer medications outside their sphere of practice.*

25.02.02 Preparation and Administration of Drugs

The organization's medical staff and pharmacy and therapeutics committee must approve medication preparation and administration policies that address, at a minimum, the following:

- Review of medication orders and patient profiles by a pharmacist, documenting the review, and any exceptions to the requirements for review by a pharmacist
- The pharmacists role in the organization's medication-use process
- On-call availability of a pharmacist when a full-time pharmacist is not available in the organization; the policy must ensure that a pharmacist can be contacted by telephone or can be accessed at a location that provides 24-hour pharmacy services
- Verification of an order by the dispensing pharmacist if the medication is not stocked in the patient care area
- Verification of orders by staff who administer medications
- How to ensure positive identification of patients before administering medications
- Accurate recording of the medication name, route of administration, dose administered, and time(s) of administration. (The record must show that the medication was administered to the correct patient.)
- How to provide a bedside supply of medications for patient's authorized to self-administer medications. (The policy must ensure compliance with the storage requirements of 25.00.03.)

> ***Authors' Comment:*** *The above requirement should probably be 25.01.03 relating to security of medications.*

- How to teach patients and/or their families about medications
- How to identify and respond to medication variances

Authors' Comment: *The scoring procedure for 25.02.02 requires surveyors to observe the preparation and administration of medications to verify that procedures are followed. Patients are to be positively identified (e.g., addressed by name and their wristband checked). Medications should be administered within 30 minutes of the scheduled time. Medications must be identifiable up to the point of administration.*

25.02.03 Drug Orders

With the exception of influenza and pneumococcal polysaccharide vaccines, which may be administered per physician-approved hospital policy, after an assessment for contraindications, orders for drugs and biologicals must be documented and signed by a practitioner who is authorized to write orders by hospital policy and in accordance with State law, and who is responsible for the care of the patient as specified under 482.12(c).

I. If verbal orders are used, they are to be used infrequently. 482.23(c)(2)(i)

II. When verbal orders are used, they must be accepted only by persons who are authorized to do so by hospital policy and procedures consistent with Federal and State law. 482.23(c)(2)(ii)

III. All orders, including verbal orders, must be dated, timed, and authenticated promptly by the ordering practitioner. 482.23(c)(1)(i)

IV. For the 5-year period following January 26, 2007, all orders, including verbal orders, must be dated, timed, and authenticated by the ordering practitioner or another practitioner who is responsible for the care of the patient as specified under 482.12(c) and authorized to write orders by hospital policy in accordance with State law. 482.24(c)(1)(ii)

V. All verbal orders must be authenticated based upon Federal and State law. If there is no State law that designates a specific timeframe for the authentication of verbal orders, verbal orders must be authenticated within 48 hours. 482.24(c)(1)(iii)

If permitted by state and local regulations, electronically transmitted orders (e.g., FAX orders) may be treated as an original document and considered to be an original order.

Telephone orders are a type of verbal orders. All requirements for verbal orders apply to telephone orders.

The organization discourages the use of verbal orders when the ordering practitioner is physically present, except in emergency situations. Verbal orders should be limited to situations when it is impossible or impractical for an ordering practitioner to manually or electronically write the order.

All verbal orders must be

- Used infrequently
- Dated, timed, and signed (authenticated) promptly by the ordering practitioner
- Read back immediately (after transcription) to the ordering practitioner to verify the accuracy of the order received
- Not permitted for orders relating to chemotherapy
- Not permitted for other high-risk medications as defined by the organization

The organization must have policies/rules and regulations that address the following:

- The infrequent use of verbal orders
- Any limitations or prohibitions on verbal orders
- Only duly licensed physicians or other practitioners approved under state law and authorized by the medical staff are permitted to write orders
- The elements that must be included in a complete verbal order
- Protocol for the administration of flu and pneumonia vaccine has been approved by the medical staff
- The time frame for authentication of verbal orders is specified
- A description of the situations in which verbal orders are permitted
- A list of individuals who have been authorized to accept verbal orders
- Guidelines that ensure verbal orders are communicated clearly and effectively

Services must be provided in accordance with the orders of practitioners who the medical staff has authorized to order the services. Orders of these practitioners must be incorporated in the patient's record.

> ***Authors' Comment:*** *The explanation and scoring procedure for 25.02.03 list a number of requirements relating to ordering medications. Some of the requirements address electronically transmitted orders, verbal and telephone orders, who may receive orders, authentication of orders, who can order medications, questioning prescribers and clarifying orders, reading back verbal orders, and co-signing orders. These must be read carefully to ensure compliance.*

25.02.04 Administration of Blood Products and IV Medications

Blood transfusions and intravenous medications must be administered in accordance with State law and approved medical staff policies and procedures. If blood transfusions and intravenous medications are administered by personnel other than doctors of medicine or osteopathy, the personnel must have special training for this duty. 482.23(c)(3)

> ***Authors' Comment:*** *The scoring procedure for 25.02.04 states that surveyors must verify that personnel are trained and working within their scope of practice.*

25.02.05 Medication Preparation Environment

The environment for preparing medications must foster attention to detail and the accurate filling and dispensing of medication orders. Policies and procedures must provide for nursing and pharmacy environments and guidelines that foster medication preparation safety. They must include a means for ongoing monitoring for compliance with the guidelines.

> ***Authors' Comment:*** *The scoring procedure for 25.02.05 states that surveyors must inspect medication preparation areas to ensure they are clean, well-lighted, and free of clutter, distractions, and noise.*

25.02.06 Monitoring of Appropriateness

The organization must use multiple mechanisms to document the monitoring of patients who receive medications.

> ***Authors' Comment:*** *The explanation for 25.02.06 states that this is self-explanatory.*

25.02.07 Medication Reconciliation

The must be an organization-wide process to reconcile medications across the continuum of care. The process must address the reconciliation of medications at key intervals such as the following:

- On admission, prepare a complete list of medications the patient takes at home.
- The patient or family member validates the list when possible.
- Any variance is reconciled when the preadmission list is compared to admitting orders.
- A complete, current list of each patient's medications is available to prescribers when writing medication orders.
- When patients are transferred or discharged, a complete list of medications is provided to the next care provider.
- When patients are discharged, a complete list of medications is provided to the patient.

25.03.01 Performance Improvement

There must be an organization-wide Quality Assessment-Performance Improvement program that includes the findings from adverse drug responses. The program must monitor the desired outcomes of medication use.

> ***Authors' Comment:*** *The explanation for 25.03.01 indicates that priority should be given to high-volume, high-risk, or problem-prone areas.*

25.03.02 Data Collection and Monitoring

Medication-use monitoring must assess the appropriateness of prescribing, preparing and dispensing, administering, and outcomes of medication use.

> ***Authors' Comment:*** *The explanation for 25.03.02 indicates that all four processes must be reviewed.*

25.03.03 Medication-Use Review

The organization's medication-use review program must monitor medications used in all principal populations that the organization serves.

> ***Authors' Comment:*** *The explanation for 25.03.03 states that populations should be age specific (e.g., pediatric to geriatric) and cover inpatient, outpatient, and emergency care patients. The organization should publish and distribute antibiogram studies at least twice a year.*

25.03.04 Data Reporting

The organization must ensure that medication-use review findings are reported to the appropriate medical staff committee and/or departments. The findings must be considered by the organization's Quality Assessment-Performance Improvement (QAPI) program and used to make improvements in the organization's service areas. Reports must be shared with other disciplines so they may be used in their QAPI activities.

25.03.05 Annual Report on Medication Use

The organization must document improvement due to medication-use review in an annual summary.

> ***Authors' Comment:*** *The scoring procedure for 25.03.05 notes that reviews may not always result in improvements and that this is legitimate.*

25.03.06 Performance Improvement in Medication Use

The organization must use the information from its review of medication processes and outcomes to continuously improve the safety of administering medications to patients. To improve its processes, the organization must consider implementing technological advances that are available. If the organization is not able to implement technological advances, the organization must implement alternatives that will resolve medication safety issues and reduce adverse events due to medication associated with medication use.

> ***Authors' Comment:*** *The scoring procedure for 25.03.06 instructs surveyors to determine if the organization has considered new technologies and if new technologies are not feasible, has the organization implemented alternative strategies.*

Table 25-1. Arrangement of HFAP Standards/Elements

Standard/Element	Explanation	Scoring Procedure	Score
HFAP incorporates CMS Conditions of Participation (CoPs) in each chapter. As appropriate, CMS Standards, and relevant CMS Interpretative Guidelines are also included. HFAP requirements also include non-CMS quality standards, which provide focus and continuity to the survey process.	CMS Interpretative Guidelines are often quoted as a source of reference. Specific HFAP explanations of the requirements are also included.	HFAP incorporates CMS regulations. Therefore, the CMS Survey Procedures are reflected in this column. Specific scoring guidelines for HFAP surveyors are also included.	Most HFAP standards are scored on a scale of 1 to 4. A score of 1 usually reflects full compliance (or an equivalent). A score of 4 usually reflects noncompliance (or an equivalent).

EXAMPLE 3-1

Suggested Activity Frequency

Minimum Frequency: S = Each Shift, D = Daily, W = Weekly, M = Monthly, Q = Quarterly, 6M = Every 6 Months, Y = Yearly, 2Y = Every 2 Years, 3Y = Every 3 Years, ON = Ongoing, AR = As Required

Activity	S	D	W	M	Q	6M	Y	2Y	3Y	ON	AR
Licensure verification							X				
Job description updating							X				
Performance evaluations							X				
Competence assessments							1				1
Staff orientation											X
Pharmacy staff meetings			2	2							
Education programs for pharmacy staff				X							
Education programs for nursing staff					X						
Education programs for medical staff						X					
Formulary approval							X				
Formulary additions/deletions (updating)					X						
Emergency medication inspections	3	3		3							
Controlled substances inventories							4	4			
Refrigerator/freezer/warmer temperature checks		X									
Refrigerator/freezer inspections				X							
Medication area inspections				X							
P&T committee meetings				5	5						
Policy and procedure review & revision							X				
Policy and procedure approval							X				
Laminar airflow workbench cleaning	X										
Prefilter cleaning or changing					X	X					
Laminar airflow workbench/barrier isolator certification						X					
Air quality certification for sterile preparation room and anteroom						X					
Microbiology monitoring - laminar airflow work-bench, sterile preparation room, and anteroom						AR					
Performance improvement activity										X	
Medication use improvement activity										X	

1. Before or soon after hiring, before performing new tasks, and yearly.
2. Monthly staff meetings are the suggested minimum. Weekly meetings may be more appropriate.
3. Monthly inspections by the pharmacy. Those who use the medications must inspect them at least daily.
4. DEA requires a biennial inventory. Some states require annual inventories. Time of year varies.
5. Quarterly is the minimum frequency. Some organizations may need more frequent meetings (e.g., monthly).

EXAMPLE 4-1

Confidentiality of Patient Information Agreement

I, ____, understand that patients have a need and right to confidentiality.

I also understand the following:

- Discussions relating to patients must be out of the hearing range of staff, visitors, other patients, and individuals who do not have a need or reason to know the information.
- Medication orders, pharmacy patient profiles, labels, meeting minutes, and other patient-related documents (i.e., those that contain patients' names or identifying numbers, or information related to patients' status, treatment, diagnosis, and medications) must be securely stored and access restricted to those who have a legitimate need or reason to know and use the information therein.
- Disposal of patient-related documents must guarantee confidentiality. Patient-related documents must not be placed in regular trash for disposal.
- E-mail and other electronic communications pose a particular risk of inadvertent dissemination inside and outside the facility. Care must be taken to protect e-mail and electronic communications.
- Patient-related information must not be released to the news media or unauthorized individuals, firms, and agencies. Requests for information must be forwarded to the organization's administration.

I hereby affirm that I will protect the confidentiality of patient-related information.

________________________________ ________________________________

Signature Date

EXAMPLE 4-2

Request for Formulary Addition

This form is to be used by individuals requesting a change in the current formulary. Please complete the form, provide supportive references, and submit to the Pharmacy and Therapeutics Committee. Copies of the request and references will be distributed to the committee. The committee meets monthly. You will be asked to attend the meeting and present the request. The committee will vote on the change to the formulary after it completes its review of all information. Please write legibly.

Requested by (Name) ______________________________

Phone Number ______________________________

Medication Requested

Generic Name ______________________________

FDA Approval Status ______________________________

Black Box Warning ______________________________

Description

Approved Indication(s) ______________________________

Proposed Use(s) ______________________________

____

Is a similar drug currently in the formulary? Yes ____ No____

If yes, are you proposing this drug as a replacement? Yes ____ No ____

Clinical Trials (Brief overview with copies of studies) ______________________________

____

____

____

____

____

Risks (Include propensity for medications errors, abuse potential, and/or sentinel events)______________________________

____

Adverse Effects______________________________

____

Dosage and Administration______________________________

____

____

Cost Analysis (Brief overview with copies of studies)______________________________

____

____

EXAMPLE 4-2 (continued)

Reasons for Using This Medication

What are the reasons for using this medication instead of medications currently in the formulary? (*Circle all that apply.*)

1. The medication is FDA approved for the proposed indication whereas the others are not.
2. The medication is more clinically efficacious.
3. The medication has an improved side effect profile.
4. The medication is more convenient.
5. The medication costs less.
6. The medication is more cost effective.
7. Other:____

Availability

How should the medication be offered?

1. Available to all providers.
2. Restricted to a service.
3. Restricted to an individual.
4. Restricted to a treatment protocol.
5. Not for primary care use.

What is the anticipated usage rate?

1. It is a continuous use product. Yes____ No____
2. It is a seasonal product used during the following month(s).____________________
3. The following amount should be on hand.____________________

Conflict of Interest Disclosure

Has the requester received any grants, current or pending, to support research on this or any product associated with the company manufacturing, repackaging, marketing, or distributing this medication?

Yes____ No____

Has any member of the requester's service/section received any grants, current or pending, to support research on this or any product associated with the company manufacturing, repackaging, marketing, or distributing this medication?

Yes____ No____

Has the requester, any member of his/her family, or any organization in which the requestor serves as an officer, director, trustee, general partner, employee, or consultant received gifts of training, transportation, or honoraria from the company manufacturing, repackaging, marketing, or distributing this medication?

Yes____ No____

Requested by (Signature) ______________________________ **Date** ____________

Signature of Service/Section Chief______________________________ **Date**____________

EXAMPLE 4-3

Nonformulary Medication Request

Completion of this form does *not* constitute a request for adding this medication to the formulary. Proposals for adding medications to the formulary must be made on a Request for Formulary Addition form which is available from the pharmacy.

Patient Name________________________________ **Patient Number**____________________

Location____________________________________ **Date**_____________________________

A separate request must be completed for each patient for whom the following medication is prescribed.

Medication Requested (Generic Name)____

Trade Name(s)/Manufacturer(s)____

Dosage Form____ **Route**_______________________

Dose Prescribed_____________________________________ **Frequency**__________________

Black Box Warnings____

Expected Duration of Therapy with This Medication_________________________________

The pharmacy will obtain an initial supply sufficient to treat this patient for the expected duration of therapy.

Reason for Using This Medication Instead of One Listed in the Formulary

No equivalent formulary medication available____ Alternative medications unacceptable____

Patient failed therapy with alternative medications____ Other____

Patient had an adverse effect from alternative medications____

I understand that the above medication has not been accepted by the medical staff for use in this organization and is not listed in the formulary. I further understand that since this medication must be obtained from outside the organization, its procurement might be delayed. If the expected delay will exceed four hours, I will be so notified.

I anticipate a recurring need for this medication. Yes____ No____

Requested by (Printed Name)________________________________

Requested by (Signature)__________________________________ **Date**_________________________

Pharmacy Use Only

Cost of Nonformulary Medication____

Alternative Medication Suggested by the Pharmacy__________________________________

Suggested by (Pharmacist)__________________________________ **Date/Time**_____________________

Outcome/Comments____

____

____

EXAMPLE 4-4

Nonformulary Medications

Date	Medication	Prescriber	Reason	Date Presented to P&T Committee

EXAMPLE 4-5

Refrigerator, Freezer, or Warmer

Place an "X" in a box to the right to indicate the type of use.

	Refrigerator: 36 to 46°F, 2 to 8°C
	Freezer: –4 to 14°F, –20 to –10°C
	Warmer:

Department______________________________ **Month**____________________

Location ______________________________ **Year**____________________

Note corrective action if temperature is not within the acceptable range (e.g., adjust temperature, replace thermometer, or call Facilities Management [date/time]). Notify pharmacy if out of range.

Date	Time	Name	Action Taken	Clean Date
1				
2				
3				
4				
5				
6				
7				
8				
9				
10				
11				
12				
13				
14				
15				
16				
17				
18				
19				
20				
21				
22				
23				
24				
25				
26				
27				
28				
29				
30				
31				

Comments____

EXAMPLE 4-6

Medication Refrigerator Temperature Log

Department ______________________ **Location** ______________________ **Month** ________ **Year** ________

Log temperatures on the days the department is open.

	1	2	3	4	5	6	7	8	9	10	11	12	13	14	15	16	17	18	19	20	21	22	23	24	25	26	27	28	29	30	31
49°																															
48°																															
47°																															
46°																															
45°																															
44°																															
43°																															
42°																															
41°																															
40°																															
39°																															
38°																															
37°																															
36°																															
35°																															
34°																															
33°																															

Temperature Range: Refrigerator = 36 – 46° F. (Shaded areas = out of range temperatures.)

Note: If not within acceptable range, call the pharmacy and, if applicable, facilities management. Note time the call is made. Corrective action must be noted (e.g., turned temperature down or replaced thermometer).

Date	❑ Pharmacy Notified	❑ Facilities Management Notified (if applicable)	Corrective Action and/or Comments

EXAMPLE 4-7

Medication Freezer Temperature Log

Department ____________________ **Location** ____________________ **Month** ________ **Year** ________

Log temperatures on the days the department is open.

	1	2	3	4	5	6	7	8	9	10	11	12	13	14	15	16	17	18	19	20	21	22	23	24	25	26	27	28	29	30	31
20°																															
18°																															
16°																															
14°																															
12°																															
10°																															
8°																															
6°																															
4°																															
2°																															
0°																															
–2°																															
–4°																															
–8°																															
–10°																															
–12°																															

Temperature Range: Freezer = –4 – 14° F. (Shaded areas = out of range temperatures.)

Note: If not within acceptable range, call the pharmacy and, if applicable, facilities management. Note time the call is made. Corrective action must be noted (e.g., turned temperature down or replaced thermometer).

Date	❑ **Pharmacy Notified**	❑ **Facilities Management Notified (if applicable)**	**Corrective Action and/or Comments**

EXAMPLE 4-8

Medication Sample Receiving or Dispensing Log

Medication and Strength ______________________

Date	Patient Name	Medical Record Number	Prescriber	Manufacturer & Lot Number	Expiration Date	Amount Rec.(+) / Disp.(−)	Balance

EXAMPLE 4-9

Controlled Substances Inventory Cover Sheet

Name of Registrant____

Address____

City__________________________ **State**______ **Zip Code**____________

DEA Registration Number_____________________

Date of Inventory___________________________

Inventory Taken at **Opening of Business**______

Close of Business________

Actual Time Completed_______________________

____ _______________
Signature of Person Taking Inventory **Date**

____ _______________
Signature of Pharmacist-in-Charge **Date**

Note: Do not send this completed inventory to the DEA. Retain this inventory at the above address for at least two years.

EXAMPLE 4-10

Controlled Substances Biennial Inventory Record

Location____________________ Check *one* of the following: Schedule II____ Schedules III, IV, and V____

Drug	Dosage Form	Strength	Unit Size	Manufacturer	Actual Count	RPh Initials	Date Counted

EXAMPLE 4-11

OMB Approval No. 1117 - 0007	U. S. Department of Justice / Drug Enforcement Administration **REGISTRANTS INVENTORY OF DRUGS SURRENDERED**	PACKAGE NO.

The following schedule is an inventory of controlled substances which is hereby surrendered to you for proper disposition.

FROM: *(Include Name, Street, City, State and ZIP Code in space provided below.)*

Signature of applicant or authorized agent
Registrant's DEA Number
Registrant's Telephone Number

NOTE: CERTIFIED MAIL (Return Receipt Requested) IS REQUIRED FOR SHIPMENTS OF DRUGS VIA U.S. POSTAL SERVICE. See instructions on reverse (page 2) of form.

NAME OF DRUG OR PREPARATION Registrants will fill in Columns 1,2,3, and 4 ONLY.	Number of Containers	CONTENTS *(Number of grams, tablets, ounces or other units per container)*	Controlled Substance Content, *(Each Unit)*	FOR DEA USE ONLY		
				DISPOSITION	QUANTITY	
					GMS.	MGS.
1	*2*	*3*	*4*	*5*	*6*	*7*
1						
2						
3						
4						
5						
6						
7						
8						
9						
10						
11						
12						
13						
14						
15						
16						

FORM DEA-41 (9-01) Previous edition dated **6-86** is usable. *See instructions on reverse (page 2) of form.*

EXAMPLE 4-11 (continued)

DEA-41 (6/1986) Pg. 2

NAME OF DRUG OR PREPARATION Registrants will fill in Columns 1,2,3, and 4 ONLY.	Number of Containers	CONTENTS *(Number of grams, tablets, ounces or other units per container)*	Controlled Substance Content, *(Each Unit)*	FOR DEA USE ONLY DISPOSITION	QUANTITY GMS.	 MGS.
1	*2*	*3*	*4*	*5*	*6*	*7*
17						
18						
19						
20						
21						
22						
23						
24						

The controlled substances surrendered in accordance with Title 21 of the Code of Federal Regulations, Section 1307.21, have been received in _______packages purporting to contain the drugs listed on this inventory and have been: ** (1) Forwarded tape-sealed without opening; (2) Destroyed as indicated and the remainder forwarded tape-sealed after verifying contents; (3) Forwarded tape-sealed after verifying contents.

DATE ______________________ DESTROYED BY: ______________________

** *Strike out lines not applicable.*

WITNESSED BY: ______________________

INSTRUCTIONS

1. List the name of the drug in column 1, the number of containers in column 2, the size of each container in column 3, and in column 4 the controlled substance content of each unit described in column 3; e.g., morphine sulfate tabs., 3 pkgs., 100 tabs., 1/4 gr. (16 mg.) or morphine sulfate tabs., 1 pkg., 83 tabs., 1/2 gr. (32mg.), etc.
2. All packages included on a single line should be identical in name, content and controlled substance strength.
3. Prepare this form in quadruplicate. Mail two (2) copies of this form to the Special Agent in Charge, under separate cover. Enclose one additional copy in the shipment with the drugs. Retain one copy for your records. One copy will be returned to you as a receipt. No further receipt will be furnished to you unless specifically requested. Any further inquiries concerning these drugs should be addressed to the DEA District Office which serves your area.
4. There is no provision for payment for drugs surrendered. This is merely a service rendered to registrants enabling them to clear their stocks and records of unwanted items.
5. Drugs should be shipped tape-sealed via prepaid express or certified mail (**return receipt requested**) to Special Agent in Charge, Drug Enforcement Administration, of the DEA District Office which serves your area.

PRIVACY ACT INFORMATION

AUTHORITY: Section 307 of the Controlled Substances Act of 1970 (PL 91-513).
PURPOSE: To document the surrender of controlled substances which have been forwarded by registrants to DEA for disposal.
ROUTINE USES: This form is required by Federal Regulations for the surrender of unwanted Controlled Substances. Disclosures of information from this system are made to the following categories of users for the purposes stated.
A. Other Federal law enforcement and regulatory agencies for law enforcement and regulatory purposes.
B. State and local law enforcement and regulatory agencies for law enforcement and regulatory purposes.
EFFECT: Failure to document the surrender of unwanted Controlled Substances may result in prosecution for violation of the Controlled Substances Act.

Under the Paperwork Reduction Act, a person is not required to respond to a collection of information unless it displays a currently valid OMB control number. Public reporting burden for this collection of information is estimated to average 30 minutes per response, including the time for reviewing instructions, searching existing data sources, gathering and maintaining the data needed, and completing and reviewing the collection of information. Send comments regarding this burden estimate or any other aspect of this collection of information, including suggestions for reducing this burden, to the Drug Enforcement Administration, FOI and Records Management Section, Washington, D.C. 20537; and to the Office of Management and Budget, Paperwork Reduction Project no. 1117-0007, Washington, D.C. 20503.

EXAMPLE 4-12

U.S. Department of Justice
Drug Enforcement Administration

REPORT OF THEFT OR LOSS OF CONTROLLED SUBSTANCES

Federal Regulations require registrants to submit a detailed report of any theft or loss of Controlled Substances to the Drug Enforcement Administration.

Complete the front and back of this form in triplicate. Forward the original and duplicate copies to the nearest DEA Office. Retain the triplicate copy for your records. Some states may also require a copy of this report.

OMB APPROVAL
No. 1117-0001

1. Name and Address of Registrant (include ZIP Code)

ZIP CODE ☐☐☐☐☐

2. Phone No. (Include Area Code)

3. DEA Registration Number
2 ltr. prefix ☐☐ 7 digit suffix ☐☐☐☐☐☐☐

4. Date of Theft or Loss

5. Principal Business of Registrant (Check one)
- 1 ☐ Pharmacy
- 2 ☐ Practitioner
- 3 ☐ Manufacturer
- 4 ☐ Hospital/Clinic
- 5 ☐ Distributor
- 6 ☐ Methadone Program
- 7 ☐ Other (Specify) ______

6. County in which Registrant is located

7. Was Theft reported to Police?
☐ Yes ☐ No

8. Name and Telephone Number of Police Department (Include Area Code)

9. Number of Thefts or Losses Registrant has experienced in the past 24 months

10. Type of Theft or Loss (Check one and complete items below as appropriate)
- 1 ☐ Night break-in
- 2 ☐ Armed robbery
- 3 ☐ Employee pilferage
- 4 ☐ Customer theft
- 5 ☐ Other (Explain)
- 6 ☐ Lost in transit (Complete Item 14)

11. If Armed Robbery, was anyone:
Killed? ☐ No ☐ Yes (How many) ______
Injured? ☐ No ☐ Yes (How many) ______

12. Purchase value to registrant of Controlled Substances taken?
$

13. Were any pharmaceuticals or merchandise taken?
☐ No ☐ Yes (Est. Value)
$

14. IF LOST IN TRANSIT, COMPLETE THE FOLLOWING:

A. Name of Common Carrier

B. Name of Consignee

C. Consignee's DEA Registration Number

D. Was the carton received by the customer?
☐ Yes ☐ No

E. If received, did it appear to be tampered with?
☐ Yes ☐ No

F. Have you experienced losses in transit from this same carrier in the past?
☐ No ☐ Yes (How Many) ______

15. What identifying marks, symbols, or price codes were on the labels of these containers that would assist in identifying the products?

16. If Official Controlled Substance Order Forms (DEA-222) were stolen, give numbers.

17. What security measures have been taken to prevent future thefts or losses?

PRIVACY ACT INFORMATION

AUTHORITY: Section 301 of the Controlled Substances Act of 1970 (PL 91-513).
PURPOSE: Report theft or loss of Controlled Substances.
ROUTINE USES: The Controlled Substances Act authorizes the production of special reports required for statistical and analytical purposes. Disclosures of information from this system are made to the following categories of users for the purposes stated:
A. Other Federal law enforcement and regulatory agencies for law enforcement and regulatory purposes.
B. State and local law enforcement and regulatory agencies for law enforcement and regulatory purposes.
EFFECT: Failure to report theft or loss of controlled substances may result in penalties under Section 402 and 403 of the Controlled Substances Act.

Under the Paperwork Reduction Act, a person is not required to respond to a collection of information unless it displays a currently valid OMB control number.
Public reporting burden for this collection of information is estimated to average 30 minutes per response, including the time for reviewing instructions, searching existing data sources, gathering and maintaining the data needed, and completing and reviewing the collection of information. Send comments regarding this burden estimate or any other aspect of this collection of information, including suggestions for reducing this burden, to the Records Management Section, Drug Enforcement Administration, Washington, D.C. 20537; and to the Office of Information and Regulatory Affairs, Office of Management and Budget, Washington, D.C. 20503.

DEA Form - **106**
(Dec. 1985)

Previous edition dated 03/83 is OBSOLETE

CONTINUE ON REVERSE

EXAMPLE 4-12 (continued)

DEA-106 (Dec. 1985) Pg. 2

LIST OF CONTROLLED SUBSTANCES LOST

Trade Name of Substance or Preparation	Name of Controlled Substance in Preparation	Dosage Strength and Form	Quantity
Examples: **Desoxyn**	**Methamphetamine Hydrochloride**	**5 mg Tablets**	**3 x 100**
Demerol	**Meperidine Hydrochloride**	**50 mg/ml Vial**	**5 x 30 ml**
Robitussin A-C	**Codeine Phosphate**	**2 mg/cc Liquid**	**12 Pints**
1.			
2.			
3.			
4.			
5.			
6.			
7.			
8.			
9.			
10.			
11.			
12.			
13.			
14.			
15.			
16.			
17.			
18.			
19.			
20.			
21.			
22.			
23.			
24.			
25.			
26.			
27.			
28.			
29.			
30.			
31.			
32.			
33.			
34.			
35.			
36.			
37.			
38.			
39.			
40.			
41.			
42.			
43.			
44.			
45.			
46.			
47.			
48.			
49.			
50.			

I certify that the foregoing information is correct to the best of my knowledge and belief.

Signature ______________________ Title ______________________ Date ______________________

EXAMPLE 4-13

Medication Repackaging Log

Instructions: Complete all necessary information. Label must have medication name, strength, dosage form, manufacturer's name, pharmacy lot number, and pharmacy beyond-use date. Pharmacy beyond-use date is 1 year from date packaged unless manufacturer's expiration date is less or packaging material stability data indicates it is less than 1 year.

Label	Date Packaged	Manufacturers'			Amount per Unit	Number of Units Packaged	Packaged by	Checked by RPh
		Name	Lot Number	Beyond-Use Date				

EXAMPLE 4-14

Medication Area Inspection

Location ______________________________ **Month/Year** ____________

	Yes	No	N/A	Remarks
Medication Preparation Area				
Medication preparation area is clean, neat, and well organized.				
Patient and Stock Medications				
Only authorized medications are present. (There are no excess medications, unauthorized storage areas, or unidentified patient medications.)				
All medications are locked.				
Tops of automated storage and distribution devices and medication carts are free of medications.				
Medications to be returned to pharmacy are in the authorized location.				
All medications are within their expiration or beyond-use dates. (Check bulk supplies, refrigerator, etc.)				
Check of two patient records and medications (automated storage and distribution devices, medication drawer, MAR, chart) matched.				
Check of two MARs show nursing reconciliation documentation.				
Check of automated storage and distribution devices for two items reveal correct count and within expiration dates.				
Internal and external bulk stock is separated.				
Controlled Substances				
Automated storage and distribution devices and manual systems are free of discrepancies.				
Refrigerator				
Refrigerator temperature is between 36°F and 46°F. Note temperature:				
Freezer temperature is between –4°F and 14°F. Note temperature:				
Refrigerator is clean.				
Freezer is free from frost.				
Refrigerator and freezer logs are complete for every day this month.				
Only medications are stored in the refrigerator and freezer. (No food, lab reagents or specimens are allowed.)				
Floor-stock insulins are in the appropriate bin(s).				
Sign indicating "Not for storage of flammables" is present.				
Miscellaneous				
Single-dose vials are destroyed after one entry.				
Multiple-dose vials are dated with the date entered and used within 28 days (or shorter period if appropriate).				
The current formulary is present and can be located by a nurse.				
Only current (within 2 years) reference books are present.				
Saline syringes are appropriately stored.				
The necessary changes have been made since the last inspection.				

Corrective Actions for All *No* Responses

____

____

____

____

______________________________ ______________________________

Pharmacy Signature and Date **Care Unit Signature and Date**

EXAMPLE 4-15

Medication Area Inspection — Clinics

Location ______________________________ **Month/Year** ___________

	Yes	No	N/A	Remarks
Stock Medications				
Only authorized medications are present. (There are no excess medications, unauthorized storage areas, or unidentified patient medications.)				
All medications are locked.				
Medications in treatment rooms are locked.				
Medications to be returned to pharmacy are in the authorized location.				
All medications are within their expiration or beyond-use dates. (Check bulk supplies, refrigerator, etc.)				
Internal and external bulk stock is separated.				
Sample Medications				
Sample cabinet/room is locked and accessible only to licensed individuals in the practice.				
Medication sample log is complete (check two items).				
Samples present reflect medications appropriate for type of practice.				
No controlled substances samples are present.				
All medication samples are within their expiration dates.				
Controlled Substances				
Controlled substance records are complete. (Check count for two items.)				
Wastage is appropriately documented.				
Refrigerator				
Refrigerator temperature is between 36°F and 46°F. Note temperature:				
Freezer temperature is between –14°F and 4°F. Note temperature:				
Refrigerator is clean.				
Freezer is free from frost.				
High/low thermometer is properly reset.				
Refrigerator and freezer logs are complete for every day this month.				
Only medications are stored in the refrigerator and freezer. (No food, lab reagents, or specimens are allowed.)				
Sign indicating "Not for storage of flammables" is present.				
Miscellaneous				
Single-dose vials are destroyed after one entry.				
Multiple-dose vials are dated with the date entered and used within 28 days (or shorter period if appropriate).				
Saline syringes are appropriately stored.				
The necessary changes have been made since the last inspection.				

Corrective Actions for All *No* Responses

____

____

____

____

______________________________ ______________________________

Pharmacy Signature and Date **Clinic Signature and Date**

EXAMPLE 4-16

Monthly Medication Area Inspection Assignment Grid

Note completion of inspection in appropriate block. **Year**____________

Area	Assigned to	Jan	Feb	Mar	Apr	May	Jun	Jul	Aug	Sep	Oct	Nov	Dec

EXAMPLE 4-17

Crash Cart or Emergency Tackle Box Log

Location _______________ **Year**______

Complete for each day the department is open. File completed log in the manager's office.

Date (month and day)														
Time														
Supplies														
Electrodes														
Defib Paddles														
2 Adult Ambu Bags														
Pedi Ambu Bag														
Pedi Defib Paddles														
Extra Monitor Paper														
Oxygen Tanks Present-Oxygen Volume														
Monitor/Defibrillator Check														
Monitor/Defibrillator Battery Check														
Defibrillator Charged/Discharged at Full Load (Weekly)														
Cart Locked/Lock Number														
Check/Recheck New Lock Number														
Checked by														

Initials/Signature _______________ Initials/Signature _______________ Initials/Signature _______________

Initials/Signature _______________ Initials/Signature _______________ Initials/Signature _______________

Initials/Signature _______________ Initials/Signature _______________ Initials/Signature _______________

EXAMPLE 4-18

Patient's Personal Medications Storage Record

If the medications are not to be used during the patient's stay in the facility, they should be given to the patient's family. If these medications must be retained in the facility, they shall be inventoried; packaged, sealed, and labeled with the patient's name; and stored until returned to the patient at the time of discharge (provided such action is approved by the practitioner responsible for the patient).

Patient Name______________________________ **Location**__________________

Patient Number____________________________ **Date**______________________

Admitting Physician____

Rx Number	Medication	Quantity	Notes

Medications Identified by__________________________________

EXAMPLE 4-19

Receipt and Disposal of Patient's Personal Medications

Patient____________________ **Patient Number**____________ **Location**____________

Address____

____

Attending Physician____________________ **Date**____________________

Prescription Number	Medication Name	Quantity	Received by (Signature)	Date of Disposal	Disposal Method	Returned or Destroyed by (Signature)	Notes

Patient's personal medications shall be stored securely and the appropriate information recorded above. Medications shall be returned to the patient, patient's family, or other authorized person upon discharge unless otherwise directed by a physician. Medications that are not returned shall be retained for 30 days after discharge. Medications on hand 30 days after discharge shall be destroyed.

Disposal Method: 1 = Returned to Patient 2 = Returned to Family 3 = Returned to Other Authorized Person 4 = Not Returned (Physician's Directive) 5 = Not Returned 6 = Destroyed

I acknowledge receipt of the above medications (with exceptions noted)____________________ Date Returned____________

Signature of Person to Whom Medications Were Returned

EXAMPLE 4-20

Intervention Log

Monitoring Period ______________________ **Page** _____ **of** _____

Reason Codes 1. Medication 2. Dose/Strength 3. Route 4. Change Frequency/Rate 5. Allergy 6. Interaction 7. Diagnosis/Contraindication 8. Incomplete Order 9. Duplicate Order 10. Nonformulary Medication 11. Restricted Medication

Recommendation Codes 1. Change Medication 2. Change Dose/Strength 3. Change Route 4. Change Frequency/Rate 5. Discontinue Medication

Date	Patient Name/Number	Prescriber	Reason for Intervention	Pharmacist Recommendation	Accepted Y/N	Outcome/Comment

EXAMPLE 4-21

Competence Checklist

After-Hours Medication Removal

Name____________________________________ **Title**____________________

Method of Evaluation

☐ Actual Event ☐ Post-Event Discussion ☐ Demonstration

Actual Event:	Reviewer evaluates individual during actual patient care
Post-Event Discussion:	Reviewer debriefs individual after an actual patient care event
Demonstration:	Individual demonstrates knowledge, skill, and judgment to reviewer

Criteria	**Competence Components** *(Check all that apply)*			**Demonstrated Correctly**
	Knowledge	**Skill**	**Judgment**	*Reviewers Initials*
Demonstrates ability to identify and locate the following items and areas: • Primary retrieval area • Tablets/capsules • Oral liquids • Injectables/parenterals • Topicals • Ophthalmics/otics • Refrigerated medications • Outdated medications • Crash cart medications • Controlled substances				
Demonstrates ability to prepare IV products in an aseptic manner and use the following correctly: • Prepares only for immediate use • Incompatibility/stability charts and tables • Completed sterile preparation competency				
Knows the following pharmacy hours of operation: • Weekdays • Weekends • Holidays				

EXAMPLE 4-21 (continued)

Can locate the following phone numbers if after-hours assistance is needed: • Pharmacist on call • Others				
Understands and can state the importance of after-hours medication stock security relating to the following: • Access to after-hours medication stock • Keys/security codes				
Understands regulations and policies relating to the following: • Relabeling medications • Physician dispensing (in emergency room) • Handling patients' personal medications • Medication error report form • ADR report form				
Completes all necessary documentation before removing medications from the after-hours medication stock (e.g., after-hours medication retrieval log).				
Understands and documents the required checks of medications per pharmacy policy. Each medication removed is checked by another authorized individual for • Correct medication • Correct dose • Correct dosage form • Patient allergies				
Understands and demonstrates proper use of the following: • Hospital formulary • Non-formulary request • Therapeutic interchange lists				

Competence Assessed by________________ **Date**____________________

EXAMPLE 4-22

Individuals Who May Remove Medications from After-Hours Stock

When medications are not available after-hours, the following individuals may remove them from after-hours stock. The amount removed should be sufficient to meet immediate therapeutic needs and should not exceed the amount needed to last until a pharmacist is available.

The individual who removes a medication shall enter the following information in the After-Hours Medication Removal Log:

- Patient name (last name and first initial) and location
- Medication name
- Medication strength
- Dosage form removed (e.g., tablet, capsule, suspension, ampul, and injection)
- Dose prescribed (e.g., one three times a day, two at bedtime, and 50 mg every 4 hours)
- Amount removed
- Prescriber name
- Date and time of removal
- Signature and title of individual who removed the medication

Name (Please Print or Type)	Title	Signature	Date of Authorization

EXAMPLE 4-23

After-Hours Medication Removal Log

Date	Time	Patient Name/Location	Drug, Strength, and Form	Dose Ordered	Amount	Removed by	Witness	RPh Signature, Date, and Time	Code

Indicate the Reason for the Removal in the Code Column

Code: 1. New Order 2. Missed Dose 3. Wasted Dose 4. Not in Floor Stock 5. Order Not Received in Pharmacy

All After-Hours Removals Must Be Reviewed and Signed by a Pharmacist

EXAMPLE 4-24

Recalled Medication or Device Record

Medication/Device and Lot Number______________________________ **Recall Date**______

Areas Inspected	Date Inspected	Number Found	Inspected by	Notes

EXAMPLE 4-25

Medication Error Report

Patient Name and Number________________________________ **Location**____________________

Age__________ **Sex** _____ **Physician**____

Medications Involved____

____

____

Description of Error____

____

____

Date and Time of Error____

Date and Time Physician Notified (and how notified)______________________________

Physician's Instructions____

____

____

Action Taken____

____

____

Severity of Error

Category	Result
No Error	
Category A	Circumstances or events that have the capacity to cause error.
Error, No Harm	
Category B	An error occurred but the medication did not reach the patient. (An "error of omission" *does* reach the patient)
Category C	An error occurred that reached the patient but did not cause patient harm.
Category D	An error occurred that reached the patient and required monitoring to confirm that it resulted in no harm to the patient and/or required intervention to preclude harm.
Error, Harm	
Category E	An error occurred that may have contributed to or resulted in temporary harm to the patient and required intervention.
Category F	An error occurred that may have contributed to or resulted in temporary harm to the patient and required initial or prolonged hospitalization.
Category G	An error occurred that may have contributed to or resulted in permanent patient harm.
Category H	An error occurred that required intervention necessary to sustain life.
Error, Death	
Category I	An error occurred that may have contributed to or resulted in the patient's death.

EXAMPLE 4-25 (continued)

Type of Error

Prescribing error____	Improper dose error____	Deteriorated medication error____
Omission error____	Wrong dosage-form error____	Monitoring error____
Wrong time error____	Wrong medication-preparation error____	Compliance error____
Unauthorized medication error____	Wrong administration-technique error____	Other medication error____

Cause(s) of Error

Failed Communication	Poor handwriting Inaccurate transcription of orders Medications with similar names Inappropriate use of zeroes and decimal points Use of metric and apothecary systems Use of inappropriate abbreviations Ambiguous or incomplete orders Other________________________
Poor Medication Distribution Practices	Unlabeled and mislabeled medications Improper storage practices Unlimited access to medications and pharmacy Improper use of dispensing equipment Other________________________
Dose Miscalculations	Failure to stock standardized concentrations and commercially premixed products Other________________________
Problems Related to Medication and Medication Devices	Labeling and packaging problems Device design issues Other________________________
Incorrect Administration of Medication	Failure to check or improper patient identification Wrong route administration Other________________________
Lack of Patient Education	Patients not involved Patients do not understand their medications Other________________________
Other Causes	

How Error Could Have Been Prevented____

____

____

____

Person(s) Having Knowledge of the Error____

____

Name of Person Completing This Form________________________________

Signature of Person Completing This Form________________________________ **Date**__________

This Report Shall *Not* Be Placed in the Patient's Medical Record.

EXAMPLE 4-26

Adverse Drug Reaction Report

Report (Check one) Concurrent____ Retrospective____

Method Identified (Check all that apply): Orders _____ ADR Card _____ MUE _____ MAR _____
Radiology _____ Quality Management _____ Other________________________________

Patient Name and Number____ **Location**____________

Age_____ **Sex**____ **Wt. (lb.)** _____ **Ht.**______ **Admission Date**__________________ **Discharge Date** ______________________

Attending Physician____________________________________ **Medical Service** ______________________________

Reason for Admission/Diagnoses____

Secondary Diagnoses ____

Medical History____

Allergies____

Date of Reaction_____________________________ **Time of Reaction** _________________________

Ordering Physician Aware of ADR? Yes____ No____ (If No, Date Notified) ______________________

Description of Reaction____

Relevant Labs____

____

Treatment (Check all that apply) No treatment____ Discontinue suspect medication(s)____ Adjust dose, route, frequency____

____Treatment with medications (list)____

____Switch to alternative agent (list)____

____Other medical treatment (list)____

Outcome Resolved without sequelae____ Resolving____ Ongoing____
Permanent disability/damage____ Death____ Unknown____

Increased Length of Stay? Yes____ No____

Drug Regimen at Reaction Time (Use Generic Names)

Medication/Dose/Route/Schedule	Date Started	Date Stopped	Time of Last Dose	Manufacturer

Suspected Drugs (Use generic names)
1.________________________________ 2.________________________________
3.________________________________ 4.________________________________

EXAMPLE 4-26 (continued)

Assessment of ADR:

1. Reaction Type (Check one)

____Exaggerated pharmacological action (exaggerated, but otherwise normal pharmacological action of a drug given in the usual therapeutic doses)

____Unpredicted/unexpected reaction (not to be expected from the known pharmacological actions of a drug given in usual therapeutic doses)

2. Reaction Severity (Check one)

____ 0. The reaction required little or no treatment, no change in therapy, did not require significant reduction in dosage or discontinuation of the drug, and did not cause harm or extend the stay in the facility.
____ 1. The reaction caused no harm to the patient but required a significant reduction in dosage or discontinuation of the drug, and required treatment or caused an extension of stay in the facility.
____ 2. The reaction contributed to or resulted in temporary harm to the patient and required initial or prolonged hospitalization.
____ 3. The reaction contributed to or resulted in permanent patient harm or disability.
____ 4. The reaction required intervention necessary to sustain life.
____ 5. The reaction contributed to or resulted in the patient's death.

3. Avoidable/Preventable (Check all that apply)

- Suspected drug(s) were inappropriate for patient's condition? Yes____ No____
- Dose, route, frequency were inappropriate for age, wt, lab tests, and disease state? Yes____ No____
- Necessary monitoring/lab tests were not performed? Yes____ No____
- Patient had a history of allergy to the drug(s)? Yes____ No____
- Drug interaction was involved in the reaction? Yes____ No____
- Toxic serum drug level was documented? Yes____ No____
- Patient was not compliant with drug therapy? Yes____ No____

4. Probability (Complete the Naranjo Algorithm below by answering the questions and giving the corresponding pertinent score.)

Probability Assessment	**Yes**	**No**	**DK/NA**	**Score**
1. Are there previous <u>conclusive</u> reports of this reaction?	+1	0	0	____
2. Did the adverse event appear after the suspected drug was administered?	+2	−1	0	____
3. Did the adverse reaction improve when the drug was discontinued or a <u>specific</u> antagonist administered?	+1	0	0	____
4. Did the adverse reaction reappear when the drug was readministered?	+2	−1	0	____
5. Are there alternative causes (other than the drug) that could on their own have caused the reaction?	−1	+2	0	____
6. Did the reaction reappear when a placebo was given?	−1	+1	0	____
7. Was the drug detected in the blood (or other fluids) in concentrations known to be toxic?	+1	0	0	____
8. Was the reaction more severe when the dose was increased or less severe when the dose was decreased?	+1	0	0	____
9. Did the patient have a similar reaction to the same or similar drugs in <u>any</u> previous exposure?	+1	0	0	____
10. Was the adverse event confirmed by any objective evidence?	+1	0	0	____
(Taken from Naranjo CA, et al. *Clin Pharmacol Ther*. 1981;30:239−45)	**Total Score**			____

Check One ____Definite (Greater than or equal to 9) ____Probable (5−8)
____Possible (1−4) ____Doubtful (Less than or equal to 0)

Reported by____ **Title**______________ **Date**___________

<u>For Administrative Use Only</u>

Reviewed by____ **Date**______________

Report to P&T Committee____ FDA____

EXAMPLE 4-27

Notice of Drug Reaction

Date:____

Dear:____

You had a reaction to ____ when you were a patient in this facility. The signs and symptoms of your reaction included the following:

____

____

____

____

____

____

____

____

____

____

____

____

Other medications are similar to the medication that caused your reaction. You may have a problem with these medications too. Your physician or pharmacist can advise you of the appropriate precautions to take.

You should show this letter to physicians, dentists, and others who treat you; pharmacists who fill your prescriptions; and to persons who admit you to this or other medical facilities. They should note the reaction in your medical record.

Sincerely,

EXAMPLE 4-28

Adverse Drug Reaction Summary

Year____________ **Page** ______ **of** ______

Drug	Date	Reaction	Probability	Severity	Preventability	Action	Recorded	FDA Report

Probability:	(**Def**)inite, (**Pro**)bable, (**Pos**)sible, (**Dou**)btful
Severity:	**0 1 2 3 4 5**
Preventability	(**Y**)es or (**N**)o
Action Taken:	Describe action(s) taken
Recorded:	Reaction recorded on patient's medical record (**Y**)es or (**N**)o
FDA Report:	Report sent to FDA (**Y**)es or (**N**)o, and date sent

EXAMPLE 4-29

Adverse Drug Reaction Rates

Year ______________________ **Page** ____ **of** ____

	Jan	Feb	Mar	Apr	May	Jun	Jul	Aug	Sep	Oct	Nov	Dec	Total
Total Admissions													
Total Suspected Reactions Reported													
Rate per 100 Admissions													
Total Reactions Confirmed													
Rate per 100 Admissions													
Total Serious Reactions													
Rate per 100 Admissions													

Monthly Adverse Drug Reaction Summary

Enter Type of Reaction and Number of Reactions for Each Drug per Month

Drug	Reaction	Jan	Feb	Mar	Apr	May	Jun	Jul	Aug	Sep	Oct	Nov	Dec	Total

EXAMPLE 4-30

U.S. Department of Health and Human Services

MEDWATCH

The FDA Safety Information and Adverse Event Reporting Program

For VOLUNTARY reporting of adverse events, product problems and product use errors

Page ____ of ____

Form Approved: OMB No. 0910-0291, Expires: 10/31/08
See OMB statement on reverse.

FDA USE ONLY

Triage unit sequence #

PLEASE TYPE OR USE BLACK INK

A. PATIENT INFORMATION

1. **Patient Identifier** — In confidence
2. **Age at Time of Event, or Date of Birth:**
3. **Sex** ☐ Female ☐ Male
4. **Weight** ______ lb or ______ kg

B. ADVERSE EVENT, PRODUCT PROBLEM OR ERROR

Check all that apply:

1. ☐ **Adverse Event** ☐ **Product Problem** *(e.g., defects/malfunctions)*
   ☐ **Product Use Error** ☐ **Problem with Different Manufacturer of Same Medicine**

2. **Outcomes Attributed to Adverse Event** *(Check all that apply)*
   - ☐ Death: ____________ *(mm/dd/yyyy)*
   - ☐ Disability or Permanent Damage
   - ☐ Life-threatening
   - ☐ Congenital Anomaly/Birth Defect
   - ☐ Hospitalization - initial or prolonged
   - ☐ Other Serious (Important Medical Events)
   - ☐ Required Intervention to Prevent Permanent Impairment/Damage (Devices)

3. **Date of Event** *(mm/dd/yyyy)*
4. **Date of this Report** *(mm/dd/yyyy)*
5. **Describe Event, Problem or Product Use Error**
6. **Relevant Tests/Laboratory Data, Including Dates**
7. **Other Relevant History, Including Preexisting Medical Conditions** *(e.g., allergies, race, pregnancy, smoking and alcohol use, liver/kidney problems, etc.)*

C. PRODUCT AVAILABILITY

Product Available for Evaluation? *(Do not send product to FDA)*

☐ Yes ☐ No ☐ Returned to Manufacturer on: ____________ *(mm/dd/yyyy)*

D. SUSPECT PRODUCT(S)

1. **Name, Strength, Manufacturer** *(from product label)*
   #1
   #2

2. | | Dose or Amount | Frequency | Route |
   |---|---|---|---|
   | #1 | | | |
   | #2 | | | |

3. **Dates of Use** *(If unknown, give duration) from/to (or best estimate)*
   #1
   #2

4. **Diagnosis or Reason for Use** *(Indication)*
   #1
   #2

5. **Event Abated After Use Stopped or Dose Reduced?**
   #1 ☐ Yes ☐ No ☐ Doesn't Apply
   #2 ☐ Yes ☐ No ☐ Doesn't Apply

6. **Lot #**
   #1
   #2

7. **Expiration Date**
   #1
   #2

8. **Event Reappeared After Reintroduction?**
   #1 ☐ Yes ☐ No ☐ Doesn't Apply
   #2 ☐ Yes ☐ No ☐ Doesn't Apply

9. **NDC # or Unique ID**

E. SUSPECT MEDICAL DEVICE

1. **Brand Name**
2. **Common Device Name**
3. **Manufacturer Name, City and State**
4. **Model #** — **Lot #**
   Catalog # — **Expiration Date** *(mm/dd/yyyy)*
   Serial # — **Other #**
5. **Operator of Device**
   ☐ Health Professional
   ☐ Lay User/Patient
   ☐ Other: ____________
6. **If Implanted, Give Date** *(mm/dd/yyyy)*
7. **If Explanted, Give Date** *(mm/dd/yyyy)*
8. **Is this a Single-use Device that was Reprocessed and Reused on a Patient?**
   ☐ Yes ☐ No
9. **If Yes to Item No. 8, Enter Name and Address of Reprocessor**

F. OTHER (CONCOMITANT) MEDICAL PRODUCTS

Product names and therapy dates *(exclude treatment of event)*

G. REPORTER *(See confidentiality section on back)*

1. **Name and Address**
   Phone # — **E-mail**
2. **Health Professional?** ☐ Yes ☐ No
3. **Occupation**
4. **Also Reported to:**
   ☐ Manufacturer
   ☐ User Facility
   ☐ Distributor/Importer
5. **If you do NOT want your identity disclosed to the manufacturer, place an "X" in this box:** ☐

FORM FDA 3500 (10/05) Submission of a report does not constitute an admission that medical personnel or the product caused or contributed to the event.

EXAMPLE 4-30 (continued)

ADVICE ABOUT VOLUNTARY REPORTING

Detailed instructions available at: http://www.fda.gov/medwatch/report/consumer/instruct.htm

Report adverse events, product problems or product use errors with:

- Medications *(drugs or biologics)*
- Medical devices *(including in-vitro diagnostics)*
- Combination products *(medication & medical devices)*
- Human cells, tissues, and cellular and tissue-based products
- Special nutritional products *(dietary supplements, medical foods, infant formulas)*
- Cosmetics

Report product problems - quality, performance or safety concerns such as:

- Suspected counterfeit product
- Suspected contamination
- Questionable stability
- Defective components
- Poor packaging or labeling
- Therapeutic failures (product didn't work)

-Fold Here-

Report SERIOUS adverse events. An event is serious when the patient outcome is:

- Death
- Life-threatening
- Hospitalization - initial or prolonged
- Disability or permanent damage
- Congenital anomaly/birth defect
- Required intervention to prevent permanent impairment or damage
- Other serious (important medical events)

Report even if:

- You're not certain the product caused the event
- You don't have all the details

How to report:

- Just fill in the sections that apply to your report
- Use section D for all products except medical devices
- Attach additional pages if needed
- Use a separate form for each patient
- Report either to FDA or the manufacturer *(or both)*

Other methods of reporting:

- 1-800-FDA-0178 -- To FAX report
- 1-800-FDA-1088 -- To report by phone
- www.fda.gov/medwatch/report.htm -- To report online

If your report involves a serious adverse event with a device and it occurred in a facility outside a doctor's office, that facility may be legally required to report to FDA and/or the manufacturer. Please notify the person in that facility who would handle such reporting.

-Fold Here-

If your report involves a serious adverse event with a vaccine call 1-800-822-7967 to report.

Confidentiality: The patient's identity is held in strict confidence by FDA and protected to the fullest extent of the law. FDA will not disclose the reporter's identity in response to a request from the public, pursuant to the Freedom of Information Act. The reporter's identity, including the identity of a self-reporter, may be shared with the manufacturer unless requested otherwise.

The public reporting burden for this collection of information has been estimated to average 36 minutes per response, including the time for reviewing instructions, searching existing data sources, gathering and maintaining the data needed, and completing and reviewing the collection of information. Send comments regarding this burden estimate or any other aspect of this collection of information, including suggestions for reducing this burden to:

Department of Health and Human Services
Food and Drug Administration - MedWatch
10903 New Hampshire Avenue
Building 22, Mail Stop 4447
Silver Spring, MD 20993-0002

Please DO NOT RETURN this form to this address.

OMB statement:
"An agency may not conduct or sponsor, and a person is not required to respond to, a collection of information unless it displays a currently valid OMB control number."

U.S. DEPARTMENT OF HEALTH AND HUMAN SERVICES
Food and Drug Administration

FORM FDA 3500 (10/05) (Back) **Please Use Address Provided Below -- Fold in Thirds, Tape and Mail**

DEPARTMENT OF
HEALTH & HUMAN SERVICES

Public Health Service
Food and Drug Administration
Rockville, MD 20857

Official Business
Penalty for Private Use $300

NO POSTAGE NECESSARY IF MAILED IN THE UNITED STATES OR APO/FPO

BUSINESS REPLY MAIL

FIRST CLASS MAIL PERMIT NO. 946 ROCKVILLE MD

MEDWATCH

The FDA Safety Information and Adverse Event Reporting Program
Food and Drug Administration
5600 Fishers Lane
Rockville, MD 20852-9787

EXAMPLE 4-31

WEBSITE: www.vaers.hhs.gov E-MAIL: info@vaers.org FAX: 1-877-721-0366

VAERS

VACCINE ADVERSE EVENT REPORTING SYSTEM
24 Hour Toll-Free Information 1-800-822-7967
P.O. Box 1100, Rockville, MD 20849-1100
PATIENT IDENTITY KEPT CONFIDENTIAL

For CDC/FDA Use Only
VAERS Number ______
Date Received ______

Patient Name: ______
Last First M.I.
Address ______
City State Zip
Telephone no. (____) ______

Vaccine administered by (Name): ______
Responsible Physician ______
Facility Name/Address ______
City State Zip
Telephone no. (____) ______

Form completed by (Name): ______
Relation to Patient ☐ Vaccine Provider ☐ Patient/Parent ☐ Manufacturer ☐ Other
Address *(if different from patient or provider)* ______
City State Zip
Telephone no. (____) ______

1. State
2. County where administered
3. Date of birth __/__/__ mm dd yy
4. Patient age
5. Sex ☐ M ☐ F
6. Date form completed __/__/__ mm dd yy

7. Describe adverse events(s) (symptoms, signs, time course) and treatment, if any

8. Check all appropriate:
☐ Patient died (date __/__/__ mm dd yy)
☐ Life threatening illness
☐ Required emergency room/doctor visit
☐ Required hospitalization (________days)
☐ Resulted in prolongation of hospitalization
☐ Resulted in permanent disability
☐ None of the above

9. Patient recovered ☐ YES ☐ NO ☐ UNKNOWN

10. Date of vaccination __/__/__ mm dd yy
Time ________ AM PM

11. Adverse event onset __/__/__ mm dd yy
Time ________ AM PM

12. Relevant diagnostic tests/laboratory data

13. Enter all vaccines given on date listed in no. 10

	Vaccine (type)	Manufacturer	Lot number	Route/Site	No. Previous Doses
a.					
b.					
c.					
d.					

14. Any other vaccinations within 4 weeks prior to the date listed in no. 10

	Vaccine (type)	Manufacturer	Lot number	Route/Site	No. Previous doses	Date given
a.						
b.						

15. Vaccinated at:
☐ Private doctor's office/hospital
☐ Public health clinic/hospital
☐ Military clinic/hospital
☐ Other/unknown

16. Vaccine purchased with:
☐ Private funds
☐ Public funds
☐ Military funds
☐ Other/unknown

17. Other medications

18. Illness at time of vaccination (specify)

19. Pre-existing physician-diagnosed allergies, birth defects, medical conditions (specify)

20. Have you reported this adverse event previously? ☐ No ☐ To health department ☐ To doctor ☐ To manufacturer

Only for children 5 and under
22. Birth weight ______ lb. ______ oz.
23. No. of brothers and sisters

21. Adverse event following prior vaccination (check all applicable, specify)

	Adverse Event	Onset Age	Type Vaccine	Dose no. in series
☐ In patient				
☐ In brother or sister				

Only for reports submitted by manufacturer/immunization project
24. Mfr./imm. proj. report no.
25. Date received by mfr./imm.proj.
26. 15 day report? ☐ Yes ☐ No
27. Report type ☐ Initial ☐ Follow-Up

Health care providers and manufacturers are required by law (42 USC 300aa-25) to report reactions to vaccines listed in the Table of Reportable Events Following Immunization. Reports for reactions to other vaccines are voluntary except when required as a condition of immunization grant awards.

Form VAERS-1 (FDA)

EXAMPLE 4-31 (continued)

"Fold in thirds, tape & mail — DO NOT STAPLE FORM"

NO POSTAGE
NECESSARY
IF MAILED
IN THE
UNITED STATES
OR APO/FPO

BUSINESS REPLY MAIL
FIRST-CLASS MAIL PERMIT NO. 1895 ROCKVILLE, MD

POSTAGE WILL BE PAID BY ADDRESSEE

VAERS

VAERS
P.O. Box 1100
Rockville MD 20849-1100

DIRECTIONS FOR COMPLETING FORM

(Additional pages may be attached if more space is needed.)

GENERAL

- Use a separate form for each patient. Complete the form to the best of your abilities. Items 3, 4, 7, 8, 10, 11, and 13 are considered essential and should be completed whenever possible. Parents/Guardians may need to consult the facility where the vaccine was administered for some of the information (such as manufacturer, lot number or laboratory data.)
- Refer to the Reportable Events Table (RET) for events mandated for reporting by law. Reporting for other serious events felt to be related but not on the RET is encouraged.
- Health care providers other than the vaccine administrator (VA) treating a patient for a suspected adverse event should notify the VA and provide the information about the adverse event to allow the VA to complete the form to meet the VA's legal responsibility.
- These data will be used to increase understanding of adverse events following vaccination and will become part of CDC Privacy Act System 09-20-0136, "Epidemiologic Studies and Surveillance of Disease Problems". Information identifying the person who received the vaccine or that person's legal representative will not be made available to the public, but may be available to the vaccinee or legal representative.
- Postage will be paid by addressee. Forms may be photocopied (must be front & back on same sheet).

SPECIFIC INSTRUCTIONS

Form Completed By: To be used by parents/guardians, vaccine manufacturers/distributors, vaccine administrators, and/or the person completing the form on behalf of the patient or the health professional who administered the vaccine.

Item 7: Describe the suspected adverse event. Such things as temperature, local and general signs and symptoms, time course, duration of symptoms, diagnosis, treatment and recovery should be noted.

Item 9: Check "YES" if the patient's health condition is the same as it was prior to the vaccine, "NO" if the patient has not returned to the pre-vaccination state of health, or "UNKNOWN" if the patient's condition is not known.

Item 10: and 11: Give dates and times as specifically as you can remember. If you do not know the exact time, please indicate "AM" or "PM" when possible if this information is known. If more than one adverse event, give the onset date and time for the most serious event.

Item 12: Include "negative" or "normal" results of any relevant tests performed as well as abnormal findings.

Item 13: List ONLY those vaccines given on the day listed in Item 10.

Item 14: List any other vaccines that the patient received within 4 weeks prior to the date listed in Item 10.

Item 16: This section refers to how the person who gave the vaccine purchased it, not to the patient's insurance.

Item 17: List any prescription or non-prescription medications the patient was taking when the vaccine(s) was given.

Item 18: List any short term illnesses the patient had on the date the vaccine(s) was given (i.e., cold, flu, ear infection).

Item 19: List any pre-existing physician-diagnosed allergies, birth defects, medical conditions (including developmental and/or neurologic disorders) for the patient.

Item 21: List any suspected adverse events the patient, or the patient's brothers or sisters, may have had to previous vaccinations. If more than one brother or sister, or if the patient has reacted to more than one prior vaccine, use additional pages to explain completely. For the onset age of a patient, provide the age in months if less than two years old.

Item 26: This space is for manufacturers' use only.

EXAMPLE 4-32

MEDICATION ERRORS REPORTING PROGRAM

USP MEDICATION ERRORS REPORTING PROGRAM

Presented in cooperation with the Institute for Safe Medication Practices

USP is an FDA MEDWATCH partner

Reporters should not provide any individually identifiable health information, including names of practitioners, names of patients, names of healthcare facilities, or dates of birth (age is acceptable).

Date and time of event:

Please describe the error. Include description/sequence of events, type of staff involved, and work environment (e.g., code situation, change of shift, short staffing, no 24-hr. pharmacy, floor stock). If more space is needed, please attach a separate page.

Did the error reach the patient? ☐ Yes ☐ No

Was the incorrect medication, dose, or dosage form administered to or taken by the patient? ☐ Yes ☐ No

Circle the appropriate Error Outcome Category (select one—see back for details): A B C D E F G H I

Describe the direct result of the error on the patient (e.g., death, type of harm, additional patient monitoring).

Indicate the possible error cause(s) and contributing factor(s) (e.g., abbreviation, similar names, distractions, etc.).

Indicate the location of the error (e.g., hospital, outpatient or community pharmacy, clinic, nursing home, patient's home, etc.).

What type of staff or healthcare practitioner made the initial error?

Indicate if other practitioner(s) were also involved in the error (type of staff perpetuating error).

What type of staff or healthcare practitioner discovered the error or recognized the potential for error?

How was the error (or potential for error) discovered/intercepted?

If available, provide patient age, gender, diagnosis. Do not provide any patient identifiers.

Please complete the following for the product(s) involved. (If more space is needed for additional products, please attach a separate page.)

	Product #1	Product #2
Brand/Product Name (If Applicable)		
Generic Name		
Manufacturer		
Labeler		
Dosage Form		
Strength/Concentration		
Type and Size of Container		

Reports are most useful when relevant materials such as product label, copy of prescription/order, etc., can be reviewed.

Can these materials be provided? ☐ Yes ☐ No Please specify:

Suggest any recommendations to prevent recurrence of this error, or describe policies or procedures you instituted or plan to institute to prevent future similar errors.

Name and Title/Profession | ( ) Telephone Number | ( ) Fax Number

Facility/Address and Zip | E-mail

Address/Zip (where correspondence should be sent)

Your name, contact information, and a copy of this report are routinely shared with the Institute for Safe Medication Practices (ISMP). Copies of reports will be sent to third parties such as the manufacturer/labeler, and to the Food and Drug Administration (FDA). You have the option of including your name on these copies.

In addition to releasing my name and contact information to ISMP, USP may release my identity to these third parties as follows (check boxes that apply):

☐ The manufacturer and/or labeler as listed above ☐ FDA ☐ Other persons requesting a copy of this report ☐ Anonymous to all third parties

Signature | Date

Return to:
USP CAPS
12601 Twinbrook Parkway
Rockville, MD 20852-1790

Submit via the Web at www.usp.org/mer
Call Toll Free: 800-23-ERROR (800-233-7767)
or FAX: 301-816-8532

Date Received by USP | File Access Number

PSF116G

WEPDF

©USPC 2003

EXAMPLE 4-32 (continued)

NCC MERP Index for Categorizing Medication Errors

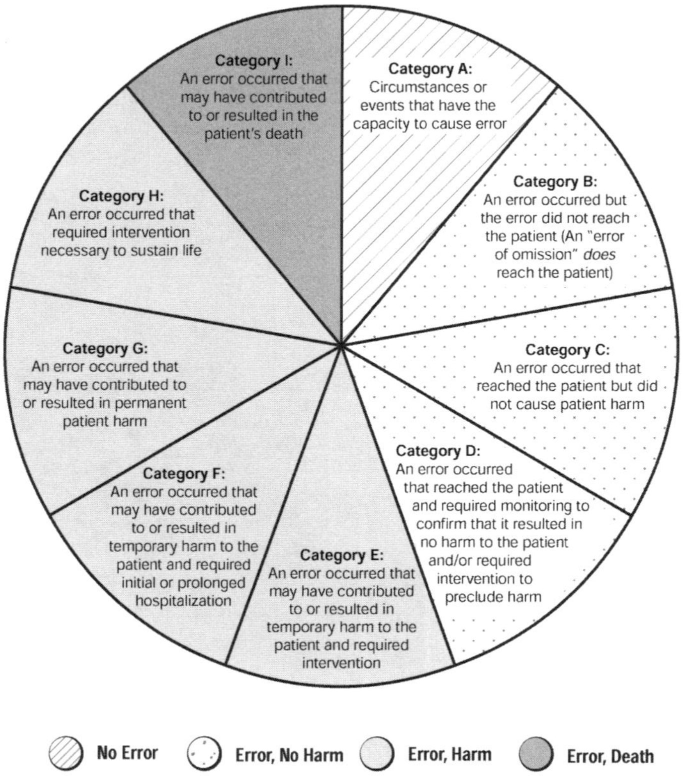

NCC MERP Index for Categorizing Medication Errors Algorithm

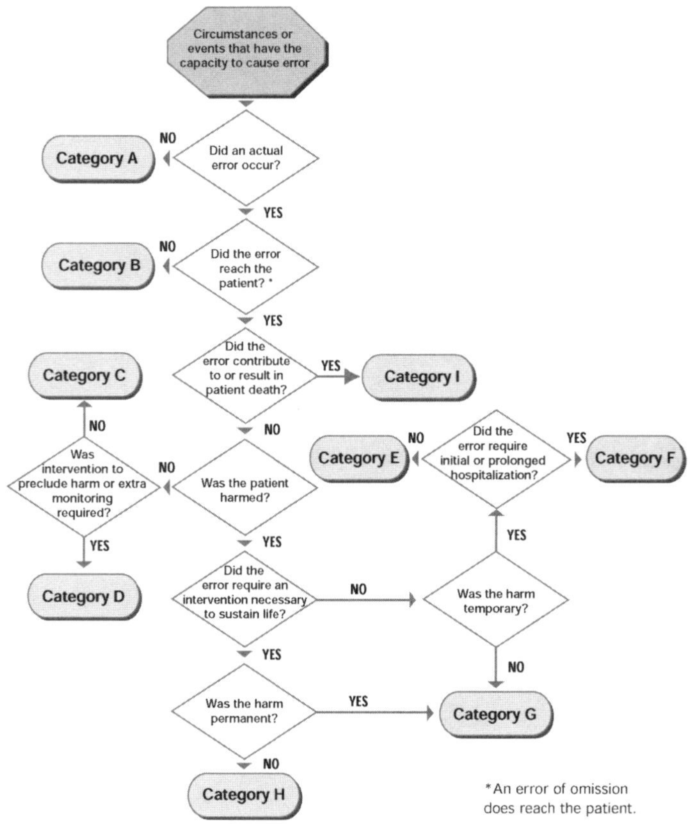

© 2003 National Coordinating Council for Medication Error Reporting and Prevention

Full-size copies are available: **INDEX**—www.nccmerp.org/010612_color_index.pdf; **ALGORITHM**—www.nccmerp.org/010612_color_algo.pdf

National Coordinating Council for Medication Error Reporting and Prevention Definitions

Harm
Impairment of the physical, emotional, or psychological function or structure of the body and/or pain resulting therefrom.

Monitoring
To observe or record relevant physiological or psychological signs.

Intervention
May include change in therapy or active medical/surgical treatment.

Intervention Necessary to Sustain Life
Includes cardiovascular and respiratory support (e.g., CPR, defibrillation, intubation, etc.).

U.S. Pharmacopeia
12601 Twinbrook Parkway
Rockville, MD 20852-1790

NO POSTAGE NECESSARY IF MAILED IN THE UNITED STATES

BUSINESS REPLY MAIL
FIRST-CLASS MAIL PERMIT NO 39 ROCKVILLE MD

POSTAGE WILL BE PAID BY ADDRESSEE:
DIANE D COUSINS RPh
THE USP CENTER FOR THE ADVANCEMENT OF PATIENT SAFETY
12601 TWINBROOK PARKWAY
ROCKVILLE MD 20897-5211

EXAMPLE 4-33

Form Approved: OMB No. 0910-0291, Expires: 10/31/08
See OMB statement on reverse.

U.S. Department of Health and Human Services
Food and Drug Administration

For use by user-facilities, importers, distributors and manufacturers for MANDATORY reporting

Mfr Report #

UF/Importer Report #

FDA Use Only

MEDWATCH

FORM FDA 3500A (10/05)

Page ____ of ____

PLEASE TYPE OR USE BLACK INK

A. PATIENT INFORMATION

1. **Patient Identifier** — In confidence
2. **Age at Time of Event:** or ______ **Date of Birth:**
3. **Sex** — ☐ Female ☐ Male
4. **Weight** — ____ lbs or ____ kgs

B. ADVERSE EVENT OR PRODUCT PROBLEM

1. ☐ **Adverse Event** and/or ☐ **Product Problem** *(e.g., defects/malfunctions)*
2. **Outcomes Attributed to Adverse Event** *(Check all that apply)*
   - ☐ Death: ______ *(mm/dd/yyyy)*
   - ☐ Disability or Permanent Damage
   - ☐ Life-threatening
   - ☐ Congenital Anomaly/Birth Defect
   - ☐ Hospitalization - initial or prolonged
   - ☐ Other Serious (Important Medical Events)
   - ☐ Required Intervention to Prevent Permanent Impairment/Damage (Devices)
3. **Date of Event** *(mm/dd/yyyy)*
4. **Date of This Report** *(mm/dd/yyyy)*
5. **Describe Event or Problem**
6. **Relevant Tests/Laboratory Data, Including Dates**
7. **Other Relevant History, Including Preexisting Medical Conditions** *(e.g., allergies, race, pregnancy, smoking and alcohol use, hepatic/renal dysfunction, etc.)*

Submission of a report does not constitute an admission that medical personnel, user facility, importer, distributor, manufacturer or product caused or contributed to the event.

C. SUSPECT PRODUCT(S)

1. **Name** *(Give labeled strength & mfr/labeler)*
   #1
   #2
2. **Dose, Frequency & Route Used**
   #1
   #2
3. **Therapy Dates** *(If unknown, give duration) from/to (or best estimate)*
   #1
   #2
4. **Diagnosis for Use** *(Indication)*
   #1
   #2
5. **Event Abated After Use Stopped or Dose Reduced?**
   #1 ☐ Yes ☐ No ☐ Doesn't Apply
   #2 ☐ Yes ☐ No ☐ Doesn't Apply
6. **Lot #**
   #1
   #2
7. **Exp. Date**
   #1
   #2
8. **Event Reappeared After Reintroduction?**
   #1 ☐ Yes ☐ No ☐ Doesn't Apply
   #2 ☐ Yes ☐ No ☐ Doesn't Apply
9. **NDC# or Unique ID**
10. **Concomitant Medical Products and Therapy Dates** *(Exclude treatment of event)*

D. SUSPECT MEDICAL DEVICE

1. **Brand Name**
2. **Common Device Name**
3. **Manufacturer Name, City and State**
4. **Model #** — **Lot #**
   Catalog # — **Expiration Date** *(mm/dd/yyyy)*
   Serial # — **Other #**
5. **Operator of Device**
   - ☐ Health Professional
   - ☐ Lay User/Patient
   - ☐ Other:
6. **If Implanted, Give Date** *(mm/dd/yyyy)*
7. **If Explanted, Give Date** *(mm/dd/yyyy)*
8. **Is this a Single-use Device that was Reprocessed and Reused on a Patient?**
   ☐ Yes ☐ No
9. **If Yes to Item No. 8, Enter Name and Address of Reprocessor**
10. **Device Available for Evaluation?** *(Do not send to FDA)*
    ☐ Yes ☐ No ☐ Returned to Manufacturer on: ______ *(mm/dd/yyyy)*
11. **Concomitant Medical Products and Therapy Dates** *(Exclude treatment of event)*

E. INITIAL REPORTER

1. **Name and Address** — **Phone #**
2. **Health Professional?** ☐ Yes ☐ No
3. **Occupation**
4. **Initial Reporter Also Sent Report to FDA** ☐ Yes ☐ No ☐ Unk.

EXAMPLE 4-33 (continued)

FDA USE ONLY

MEDWATCH

FORM FDA 3500A (10/05) *(continued)*

Page ____ of ____

F. FOR USE BY USER FACILITY/IMPORTER *(Devices Only)*

1. **Check One**
☐ User Facility ☐ Importer

2. **UF/Importer Report Number**

3. **User Facility or Importer Name/Address**

4. **Contact Person**

5. **Phone Number**

6. **Date User Facility or Importer Became Aware of Event** *(mm/dd/yyyy)*

7. **Type of Report**
☐ Initial
☐ Follow-up # ________

8. **Date of This Report** *(mm/dd/yyyy)*

9. **Approximate Age of Device**

10. **Event Problem Codes** *(Refer to coding manual)*
Patient Code ____ - ____ - ____
Device Code ____ - ____ - ____

11. **Report Sent to FDA?**
☐ Yes ________ *(mm/dd/yyyy)*
☐ No

12. **Location Where Event Occurred**
☐ Hospital
☐ Home
☐ Nursing Home
☐ Outpatient Treatment Facility
☐ Outpatient Diagnostic Facility
☐ Ambulatory Surgical Facility
☐ Other: ________ *(Specify)*

13. **Report Sent to Manufacturer?**
☐ Yes ________ *(mm/dd/yyyy)*
☐ No

14. **Manufacturer Name/Address**

G. ALL MANUFACTURERS

1. **Contact Office - Name/Address** ***(and Manufacturing Site for Devices)***

2. **Phone Number**

3. **Report Source** *(Check all that apply)*
☐ Foreign
☐ Study
☐ Literature
☐ Consumer
☐ Health Professional
☐ User Facility
☐ Company Representative
☐ Distributor
☐ Other:

4. **Date Received by Manufacturer** *(mm/dd/yyyy)*

5.
(A)NDA # ________
IND # ________
STN # ________
PMA/ 510(k) # ________
Combination Product ☐ Yes
Pre-1938 ☐ Yes
OTC Product ☐ Yes

6. **If IND, Give Protocol #**

7. **Type of Report** *(Check all that apply)*
☐ 5-day ☐ 30-day
☐ 7-day ☐ Periodic
☐ 10-day ☐ Initial
☐ 15-day ☐ Follow-up # ____

8. **Adverse Event Term(s)**

9. **Manufacturer Report Number**

H. DEVICE MANUFACTURERS ONLY

1. **Type of Reportable Event**
☐ Death
☐ Serious Injury
☐ Malfunction
☐ Other: ________

2. **If Follow-up, What Type?**
☐ Correction
☐ Additional Information
☐ Response to FDA Request
☐ Device Evaluation

3. **Device Evaluated by Manufacturer?**
☐ Not Returned to Manufacturer
☐ Yes ☐ Evaluation Summary Attached
☐ No *(Attach page to explain why not)* or provide code: ________

4. **Device Manufacture Date** *(mm/yyyy)*

5. **Labeled for Single Use?**
☐ Yes ☐ No

6. **Evaluation Codes** *(Refer to coding manual)*
Method ____ - ____ - ____ - ____
Results ____ - ____ - ____ - ____
Conclusions ____ - ____ - ____ - ____

7. **If Remedial Action Initiated, Check Type**
☐ Recall ☐ Notification
☐ Repair ☐ Inspection
☐ Replace ☐ Patient Monitoring
☐ Relabeling ☐ Modification/ Adjustment
☐ Other: ________

8. **Usage of Device**
☐ Initial Use of Device
☐ Reuse
☐ Unknown

9. **If action reported to FDA under 21 USC 360i(f), list correction/ removal reporting number:**

10. ☐ **Additional Manufacturer Narrative** and / or 11. ☐ **Corrected Data**

The public reporting burden for this collection of information has been estimated to average 66 minutes per response, including the time for reviewing instructions, searching existing data sources, gathering and maintaining the data needed, and completing and reviewing the collection of information. Send comments regarding this burden estimate or any other aspect of this collection of information, including suggestions for reducing this burden to:

Department of Health and Human Services
Food and Drug Administration - MedWatch
10903 New Hampshire Avenue
Building 22, Mail Stop 4447
Silver Spring, MD 20993-0002
Please DO NOT RETURN this form to this address.

OMB Statement:
"An agency may not conduct or sponsor, and a person is not required to respond to, a collection of information unless it displays a currently valid OMB control number."

EXAMPLE 6-1

Orientation Record

Employee____

The Facility

Review of Facility Organization .... ________

Administration	________	Nursing	________
Medical Staff	________	Department Heads	________
Pharmacy	________		

Facility Policies and Procedures .... ________

Confidentiality of Patient Information	________
Patient Safety Program	________
Employee Health Examination Policy	________
Other Applicable Policies and Procedures	________
Disaster Plan	________
Fire Plan	________

Tour of Facility (to include at least the areas listed below) .... ________

Surgery	________	Emergency Department	________
Eating Areas	________	Central Supply	________
Lounges	________	Restrooms	________
Patient Care Areas	________	Fire Extinguishers	________
Fire Alarms	________		

The Pharmacy

Pharmacy Hours. .... ________

Weekday	________	Holiday	________
Weekend	________	Breaks (meals, rest)	________

After-Hours Services. .... ________

Personnel Information .... ________

Work Schedule	________	Lockers	________
Pay Rate	________	Absenteeism	________
Overtime	________	Tardiness	________
Timecards	________	Holidays	________
Benefits	________	Vacation	________
Insurance	________	Sick Leave	________
Smoking	________	Personal Phone Calls	________
Dress Code	________	Pay Rate Changes	________

Review of Job Description .... ________

Employee Is Enrolled in Benefit Program .... ________

Payroll Documents Are Complete. .... ________

Pharmacy Personnel

Introduction to the Pharmacy Staff .... ________

Director of Pharmacy	________	Pharmacists	________
Support Staff	________	Part-Time Staff	________

Pharmacy Areas

Pharmacy Responsibility for the Following Areas .... ________

Main Pharmacy	________	Office Area	________
Sterile Preparation	________	Storage	________
Emergency Drugs	________	Refrigerators	________
Outdated Drugs	________	Other Areas	________

EXAMPLE 6-1 (continued)

Pharmacy Services

Brief Description of Basic Pharmacy Services . . . . ______

Dispensing	______	Sterile Preparations	______
Emergency Drugs	______	Inventory Control	______
Formulary	______	Drug Therapy Monitoring	______
Drug Information	______	Education Programs	______
Pharmacokinetics	______	E-mail	______

Security

Basic Security Requirements . . . . ______

- Controlled Substances ______
- Other Drugs ______
- Pharmacy Areas ______
- Confidential Materials ______

Medication Safety

Basic Medication Safety Requirements . . . . ______

- Medication Error Reports ______
- Adverse Drug Reaction Reports ______

Continuing Education

Scope of Continuing Education . . . . ______

- Initial Orientation ______
- Subsequent Training ______
- Responsibility of Professional Staff to Conduct Educational Programs (i.e., make presentations) ______
- Attendance at Meetings and/or In-Service Education Programs ______
- Medical/Nursing In-Service Education Provided by Pharmacy ______
- Records/Documentation of Attendance (number of meetings or hours required per year) ______

Pharmacy Policies and Procedures

Pharmacy Policy and Procedure Manual . . . . ______

(Read the following policies or sections now—others later)

- Personnel ______
- Infection Control ______
- Safety ______
- Hazardous Materials (handling) ______
- Incident Reports ______
- Responsibilities and Duties in a Medical Emergency ("Code") ______

Employee Acknowledgment

I have completed the above orientation and am aware of my responsibilities and duties. I understand that pharmacy and facility policies are established to promote quality patient care and to ensure the health and safety of patients and staff.

I further understand that there are potential occupational health and safety risks associated with my duties. I have read and fully understand the pharmacy policies and procedures relating to infection control, safety, and handling of hazardous materials and agree to comply with these policies and procedures as well as all other applicable policies and procedures of the facility.

Completed by________________________________ Date________________________
Employee Signature

Certified by________________________________ Date________________________
Signature

EXAMPLE 6-2

Education Program or Meeting Record

Organization______________________________ **Date(s)**____________________

Length (Hours/Minutes)____________________ **Time(s)**____________________

For Medical Staff_____ Nursing_____ Pharmacy_____ Other____________________

Summary of Program and/or Meeting Topic____________________

____

____

____

Speaker/Chairperson, and/or Instructors____________________

____

Continuing Education Credit ________ **Attach Handouts or Meeting Materials**

Attendees

Name and Title or Department	Name and Title or Department

Use reverse side and/or attach additional information, if necessary.

For the Pharmacy____________________ **Date**____________________

EXAMPLE 6-3

Pharmacy Education or Training Program

Name of Program____

Objective(s)____

____

Relationship to Job Performance______________________________

Date(s) of Program____________________ **Length of Program—Hours**__________

Name of Presenter(s)____________________ **Company Sponsor**____________

Method(s) of Presentation___________________________________

Group(s) Attending (Check all that apply) **Pharmacists** ____ **Technicians**____ **Support Staff**____

Attendees

Name	Identification Number

EXAMPLE 6-4

Continuing Education Record

Source Codes

Inservice Education (pharmacy)............ 1
Inservice Education (medical staff)......... 2
Inservice Education (other department).... 3
Home Study.. 4
Journal Articles....................................... 5
Seminars, Conferences, etc. (outside)............. 6

Name________________________________ **Position** ______________________________

Date	Subject or Title	Source Code	Number of Credits*

*Contact Hours or CEUs if applicable.

EXAMPLE 6-5

Sterile Preparations Competence List

The following appropriately trained or experienced individuals are knowledgeable and competent in the following:

1. Proper attire and gowning technique
2. Aseptic technique
3. Recognizing incompatibilities and determining stability and beyond use dating
4. Sterile preparation compounding techniques
5. Labeling of intravenous admixture preparations, supplies, materials, and equipment
6. Storage of intravenous admixture preparations, supplies, materials, and equipment

They have met the organization's training, education, and experience requirements; demonstrated their competence; completed an annual media fill test; and are qualified and permitted to compound sterile preparations.

Name	Certified by	Date Certified

EXAMPLE 6-6

Competence Assessment Test for Pediatric and Adolescent Patients

Name:____**Date:**____________________________

Use the following case report to answer questions 1 through 5.

D.M. is a 3-year-old, 23-lb. male brought to the outpatient pediatric clinic this morning. His mother indicates that he developed a cold with nasal congestion, fever, and cough 3 days ago. In the last 24 hours, D.M. has become increasingly irritable with episodes of crying and pulling on his right ear and was unable to sleep last night. His mother has been administering acetaminophen for his fever.

Upon examination of D.M.'s right ear, he begins crying loudly and resists examination. The tympanic membrane is bulging and opaque with some inflammation. Nasal congestion and rhinorrhea are also present. D.M.'s temperature is 101°F. There are also crusted erythematous lesions on his face and neck. His mother says the areas have been present about a week and that D.M. constantly scratches them. D.M. has no known allergies.

D.M.'s physician diagnoses acute otitis media and atopic dermatitis and prescribes the following medications:
Augmentin ES-600 90 mg (amoxicillin component)/kg/day PO given in divided doses every 12 hr for 10 days
Antipyrine/benzocaine otic drops two to four drops in right ear every 2 hr prn ear pain
Hydrocortisone 0.5% cream bid to rash on face and neck

1. How many milligrams of amoxicillin clavulanate (amoxicillin component rounded to the nearest 10 milligrams) are needed for one dose?

2. Augmentin ES-600 is available in a 600 mg (amoxicillin component) per 5 mL suspension. How many milliliters are needed for one dose?

____3. Which of the following medications is appropriate for treating fever in this patient?
a. ibuprofen
b. acetaminophen
c. aspirin
d. a and b
e. b and c

____4. D.M.'s physician orders acetaminophen 160 mg PO every 4 to 6 hr as needed for fever or pain. Which of the following dosage forms of acetaminophen would be appropriate for this patient's age group?
a. chewable tablets
b. oral liquid
c. capsules
d. rectal suppository
e. a, b, and d

5. The physician gives instructions to D.M.'s mother to apply the hydrocortisone cream sparingly and as directed to the areas of dermatitis. Explain why this precaution is necessary.

EXAMPLE 6-6 (continued)

Use the following case report to answer questions 6 through 10.

C.L. is an 8-year-old, 55-lb. male brought to the emergency room after suffering a seizure at school. During the seizure he lost consciousness and fell, hitting his head on a desk. He had a second seizure while being transported to the hospital. He has a history of attention deficit hyperactivity disorder (ADHD), depression, and headaches. There is a family history of depression. His current medications include methylphenidate, imipramine, and ibuprofen. C.L. is admitted for observation and evaluation of his seizure.

____6. C.L. is unable to swallow solid oral dosage forms such as tablets and capsules. Which of the following formulations of methylphenidate may be safely administered by crushing and mixing with food or beverages?
a. Ritalin tablets
b. Ritalin SR tablets
c. Concerta tablets
d. Metadate ER tablets
e. a and c

7. The attending physician wishes C.L. to continue his home medications. C.L.'s depression was stabilized with imipramine 3 mg/kg/day administered in divided doses three times a day. How many milligrams of imipramine are needed for one dose?

____8. C.L.'s physician wishes to begin anticonvulsant therapy with carbamazepine. Which of the following methods of drug dosing in pediatric patients is the <u>least</u> dependable?
a. dosage calculations based on Young's Rule
b. dosages based on pharmacokinetic data
c. dosages based on body surface area
d. dosing information found in pediatric dosage publications

____9. C.L.'s physician orders carbamazepine 100 mg PO bid. Which of the following formulations are appropriate for this patient?
a. 100 mg chewable tablets
b. 100 mg/5 mL suspension
c. 200 mg tablets divided in half
d. a and b
e. a, b, and c

10. If C.L. remains on carbamazepine therapy long term, explain why it may be necessary to adjust the dose as he ages through childhood and adolescence.

Use the following case report to answer questions 11 through 18.

G.B. is a 6-year-old (height: 45 inches, weight: 42 lb.) female diagnosed with acute lymphocytic leukemia (ALL). She is currently entering the third week of remission induction therapy. Current medications include
Allopurinol 78 mg bid
Prednisone 30 mg PO daily
Docusate 50 mg PO daily

IV fluids with sodium bicarbonate have been started for adequate hydration and alkalinization of the urine. G.B.'s oncologist orders the following antineoplastic agents:
Vincristine 1.5 mg/m^2 IV times one dose today
Daunorubicin 25 mg/m^2 IV times one dose today

11. How many milligrams of vincristine are needed for today's dose?

12. How many milligrams of daunorubicin are needed for today's dose?

EXAMPLE 6-6 (continued)

____13. Which of the following IV delivery systems are appropriate for this patient's age group?
a. IV push
b. syringe pumps
c. IV infusion pumps
d. b and c
e. a, b, and c

____14. Which of the following are important factors to consider when preparing and administering medications to pediatric patients?
a. selection of correct syringe size
b. fluid volume
c. accuracy of dilutions
d. a and c
e. a, b, and c

15. What are the implications for pediatric patients associate with medication retention in administration devices?

16. What special precaution is required when dispensing vincristine?

17. Allopurinol is available as 100-mg tablets, 300-mg tablets, and 500-mg injection (lyophilized powder for reconstitution). What methods may be used to administer the dose needed for this patient?

____18. Which of the following precautions can minimize the potential for drug-related problems in pediatric patients?
a. including the dose per weight on medication orders
b. dispensing oral liquid medications in unit-dose oral syringes
c. ordering oral liquid medications by volume
d. a and b
e. a, b, and c

Use the following case report to answer questions 19 and 20.

J.P. is a 14-year-old, 90-lb. female who has been admitted to the intensive care unit following a motor vehicle accident. Her physician has ordered a dopamine drip to be administered at a rate of 5 mcg/kg/min.

19. At what rate (mL/hr) should a dopamine infusion of 200 mg in 250 mL be infused?

20. List three medications that are potentially lethal in adolescent patients if prepared or administered inappropriately.

Competence certified by:____________________ **Date:** ____________

EXAMPLE 6-6 (continued)

Competence Assessment Test for Pediatric and Adolescent Patients

Answer Key

1. 470 mg
2. 3.9 mL
3. d. Aspirin would not be an appropriate choice because the patient has a viral illness (i.e., a cold). Salicylate use in children during viral illnesses is associated with Reye's syndrome.
4. e
5. Systemic absorption of medications through the skin is increased in young children compared to adults and may result in adverse effects.
6. a. Ritalin SR, Concerta, and Metadate ER are extended release formulations that must not be crushed or chewed.
7. 25 mg
8. a
9. d
10. It may be necessary to adjust the dose of carbamazepine because biological functions such as metabolism change and mature throughout childhood and adolescence.
11. 1.2 mg
12. 19.5 mg
13. e
14. e
15. The patient may be underdosed due to a significant amount of the medication retained in the administration device. Medication delivery to the patient may also be delayed.
16. Vincristine is required to be dispensed in a labeled overwrap with the statement "Do not remove covering until the moment of injection. Fatal if given intrathecally. For IV use only."
17. Allopurinol may be administered intravenously using the IV formulation or as an extemporaneous oral suspension compounded using allopurinol tablets.
18. d
19. 15 mL/hr
20. Examples include potassium chloride, atropine, lidocaine, digoxin, opiates, local anesthetics, barbiturates, epinephrine, and phenytoin.

EXAMPLE 6-7

Competence Assessment Checklist for Pediatric and Adolescent Patients

Name: ______________________________ **Date:** ______________

KNOWLEDGE AND SKILLS	YES	NO
Explains the differences in drug absorption, distribution, metabolism, and elimination for pediatric and adolescent patients compared to adult patients. Describes how these processes mature.		
Explains how disease processes impact medication therapy.		
Lists medications that are potentially lethal in pediatric and adolescent patients if prepared or administered inappropriately. Describes precautions to prevent errors. Does not store adult-only concentrations and multiple-dose vials containing lethal amounts of medications in pediatric and adolescent patient care areas.		
Explains why younger children have an increased potential for ADRs. Identifies potential sources of ADRs and implements precautions to reduce the incidence and severity of ADRs.		
Accurately prepares extemporaneous formulations and dilutions of commercially available products. Uses appropriate procedures.		
Calculates drug dosages using information in the product information and pediatric dosage publications (when available). Uses body surface area rather than dosing rules when calculating doses for pediatric patients.		
Uses appropriate medication formulations, dosage forms, and routes and methods of administration for pediatric and adolescent patients. Explains how medications may be retained in administration devices and the implications for the patient. Makes recommendations to prevent retention.		
Explains the potential for fluid overload from IV administration. Makes recommendations to prevent fluid overload.		
Demonstrates knowledge of the following IV delivery systems: IV push, IV piggyback, IV infusion, and syringe pumps.		
Takes necessary steps to prevent drug-drug, food-drug, drug-laboratory test, and drug-disease interactions and monitors for evidence of ADRs, overdosage, and other drug-related problems in pediatric and adolescent patients.		
Monitors medication therapy and makes recommendations to manage medication-related problems, ensuring positive therapeutic outcomes for pediatric and adolescent patients.		

Competence certified by: ______________________________ **Date:** ______________

EXAMPLE 6-8

Criteria-Based Job Description/Competence Assessment Summary/Performance Evaluation

Staff Pharmacist

Employee Name: ________________________________ **Date:** ____________________

Type of Evaluation _____ New Employee Evaluation _____ Annual Evaluation _____ Self-Assessment

Job Title/Position: Staff Pharmacist

Job Summary: Staff pharmacists fill orders for medications, monitor patient medication therapies, and provide drug information. Staff pharmacists supervise and direct support personnel. In the absence of the pharmacy manager, a staff pharmacist may be required to assume the essential responsibilities and perform the duties of the pharmacy manager.

Reports to: Director of Pharmacy

Supervises: All pharmacy support personnel

Education: Graduate of an ACPE-accredited School of Pharmacy with a BS Pharmacy degree.

Licenses: Currently licensed to practice pharmacy in the state of ________________.

Experience: Health system experience preferred, but not required.

Work Schedule: Minimum of 40 hours per week, but hours may be long and irregular; includes evenings, weekends, and holidays as necessary.

Physical Requirements: Repetitive use of hands and fingers (e.g., preparing IV admixtures, use of a computer keyboard). May require lifting and carrying light loads (up to 40 lb.), including boxes, equipment, unit-dose cassettes, and IV solutions and stooping or kneeling (e.g., to pick up items from the floor, to remove and replace items on lower shelves, and to file documents in lower file drawers). Sitting, walking, or standing for long periods of time (4–8 hours) is often necessary. Must be able to physically operate the equipment used for the job.

Critical Demands: Ability to work independently with minimal direct supervision. Ability to work cooperatively with health-system and pharmacy staff. Ability to handle frequent interruptions and adapt to changes in workload and work schedule. Ability to set priorities, make critical decisions, and respond quickly to emergency requests. Ability to exercise sound professional judgment. Ability to communicate effectively (orally and in writing). Ability to meet the pharmaceutical care needs of neonatal, pediatric, adolescent, adult, geriatric, psychiatric, oncology, obstetric, rehabilitation, and skilled nursing patients.

Occupational Hazards: Potential for exposure to infectious patients or materials. Potential for exposure to hazardous and toxic substances (including chemotherapy, cytotoxic drugs, and cleaning solutions). Potential for sticks or cuts by needles and other sharp items. Potential for musculoskeletal injuries if proper lifting and carrying techniques are not used.

EXAMPLE 6-8 (continued)

Principal Duties/Responsibilities

Scoring Guide: 2 = Meets Standards 0 = Does Not Meet Standards

Performance Criteria/Standards	*Rating*	*Comments*
A. Prepares and dispenses medication orders per physician request according to established policies, procedures, and protocols.		
1. Interprets medication orders (verbal and written) and transcribes to computerized patient medication profiles accurately. Maintains accurate, complete patient medication profiles.		
2. Prepares and dispenses medications, including sterile, chemotherapy, and parenteral nutrition preparations safely and accurately using appropriate techniques.		
3. Issues controlled substances to patient care areas and maintains records as required by law.		
B. Ensures safe, appropriate, cost-effective medication therapies for patients according to established policies, procedures, and protocols.		
1. Monitors medication therapy regimens for contraindications, drug-drug interactions, drug-food interactions, drug-laboratory test interactions, allergies, appropriateness of drug and dose, and therapeutic duplications.		
2. Assists with pharmacokinetics consult service and drug dosing per organizational protocol.		
3. Reviews/interprets culture and susceptibility data for antibiotic appropriateness and recommends changes, as needed.		
4. Reads, extracts, and interprets information in patient charts accurately.		
5. Detects and reports suspected adverse drug reactions and medication errors accurately and in a timely manner.		
6. Sustains the formulary by minimizing nonformulary procurements, utilizing therapeutic substitution protocols, and promoting rational medication therapy selection.		
7. Provides clinical consultation and clarification to practitioners. Recommends evidence-based medication therapy regimens and monitoring plans. Suggests appropriate, cost-effective therapeutic alternatives to medical staff, as needed.		
8. Provides accurate, adequate, and timely drug information to the professional staff.		
9. Provides drug information to patients and their families.		
10. Documents all clinical activities and interventions accurately and completely.		
11. Participates in the quality improvement and medication use review activities of the department. Collects data; conducts quality monitors and inspections; and maintains logs, records, and other documentation as assigned.		
12. Participates in the development and presentation of orientation, education, and training programs to the pharmacy, medical, nursing, and other staffs.		
C. Contributes to the quality and effective operation of the department.		
1. Supervises and directs pharmacy support personnel. Verifies the daily activities of pharmacy technicians. Participates in the performance appraisal of pharmacy support personnel.		
2. Works independently with minimal supervision. Organizes and prioritizes work assignments. Ensures pharmacy services are provided in a timely manner.		
3. Completes and documents inspections of all assigned medication storage areas at least monthly. Identifies and replaces outdated and unusable medications.		

EXAMPLE 6-8 (continued)

Performance Criteria/Standards	*Rating*	*Comments*
4. Answers the telephone, identifying self and department. Directs calls to appropriate personnel. Answers requests at the window.		
5. Keeps pharmacy areas and equipment clean, neat, and well-organized.		
6. Performs essential duties of the pharmacy director in his/her absence.		
D. Maintains competence required for current job title/position.		
1. Maintains current pharmacist licensure.		
2. Attends pharmacy staff meetings.		
3. Attends orientation, education, and training programs. Reviews literature and other materials pertinent to the practice of pharmacy.		
4. Completes all competence/skills assessment requirements (see attached competence assessment/skills list).		
E. Performs other duties as assigned by supervisor.		
TOTAL POINTS (maximum available points = 52)		

Departmental Standards

Scoring Guide: 2 = Meets Standards 0 = Does Not Meet Standards

Performance Criteria/Standards	*Rating*	*Comments*
1. Is punctual and dependable; reports to work as scheduled. Fulfills on-call obligations per prearranged schedule. Absenteeism and tardiness are within policy guidelines.		
2. Maintains a neat, professional, well-groomed appearance. Observes pharmacy dress code. Wears identification badge at all times.		
3. Performs work within specified time frames. Adapts positively to frequent interruptions and changes in workload and/or work schedule.		
4. Provides courteous, cooperative, and timely service to patients, visitors, and staff. Demonstrates good oral and written communication.		
5. Works cooperatively with all staff. Voices concerns and suggestions to appropriate persons in a positive manner.		
6. Demonstrates sound professional judgment consistent with clinical/academic background.		
7. Maintains strict confidentiality of patient, visitor, and employee information. Complies with the HIPAA Privacy Rule standards.		
8. Fosters a team environment by providing orientation and training to new team members. Assists coworkers in tasks, as time permits.		
9. Adheres to health system and departmental policies and procedures. Complies with all requirements related to risk management, safety, medication use safety, security, fire safety, and infection control. Complies with all applicable federal, state, and local laws, rules, and regulations.		
TOTAL POINTS (maximum available points = 18)		

EXAMPLE 6-8 (continued)

Organizational Standards

Scoring Guide: 2 = Meets Standards 0 = Does Not Meet Standards

Performance Criteria/Standards	*Rating*	*Comments*
1. Performance demonstrates efforts to improve patient satisfaction, lower costs, and improve quality.		
2. Understands and meets customers' needs and expectations. The patient and family members always come first.		
3. Demonstrates the ability to address problems in a group setting using tools and techniques for identification and resolution of problems.		
4. Demonstrates the values and behaviors of the organization.		
TOTAL POINTS (maximum available points = 8)		

Goals and Accomplishments

Scoring Guide: 4 = Goals met *and* special accomplishments achieved 2 = Goals met 0 = Did not achieve set goals

A. Describe status of goals set at previous evaluation.

____

____

B. Describe special accomplishments achieved since previous evaluation.

____

____

TOTAL POINTS (maximum available points = 4)

Scoring

Performance Criteria/Standards	*Total Points Available*	*Employee Score*
Principal Duties/Responsibilities	52	
Departmental Standards	18	
Organizational Standards	8	
Goals and Accomplishments	4	
TOTAL SCORE	**82**	

SCORING GUIDELINES:

____ points Exceptional performance

____ points Exceeds standards

____ points Consistently meets standards

____ points Improvement required*

____ points Does not meet standards*

*Requires action plan.

EXAMPLE 6-8 (continued)

ACTION TAKEN:

1. None at this time ____
2. Extended probation ____ days.
3. Corrective action ____

Type: ____

Action: ____

PERFORMANCE GOALS AND OBJECTIVES:

Provide assessment of own needs for growth and development. Develop a plan to meet educational and professional growth within the next 12 months.

COMMENTS:

A. Supervisor's Comments:

B. Employee's Comments:

Employee's Signature	**Date**
Supervisor's Signature	**Date**

EXAMPLE 8-1

Laminar Airflow Workbench Cleaning Record

Workbench Location/Number________________ Month______ Year________

Clean the workbench each shift and as necessary with purified water followed by 70% isopropyl alcohol.

Initial the appropriate box after cleaning the workbench.

Date	Day Shift	Evening Shift	Night Shift
1			
2			
3			
4			
5			
6			
7			
8			
9			
10			
11			
12			
13			
14			
15			
16			
17			
18			
19			
20			
21			
22			
23			
24			
25			
26			
27			
28			
29			
30			
31			

Prefilter Changed ❑ **Date** ____________________

EXAMPLE 10-1

Policy and Procedure for Nonformulary Medication Requests

Page Number _____ of ____
Policy Number __________

Department Pharmacy

Subject Nonformulary Medication Requests

Issued by Pharmacy and Therapeutics Committee

Reviewed ______________________ ______________________
Director of Pharmacy Date

Approved ______________________ ______________________
For the Medical Staff Date

Purpose

The purpose of this policy and procedure is to provide for the procurement of medications that are not in the organization's formulary.

Background

The formulary lists medications that have been approved by the medical staff for use in this organization. Prescribers must use formulary medications when possible.

Policy

Nonformulary medications shall be used in this organization only after the prescriber has determined that a formulary medication is not appropriate. However, a prescriber shall NOT use a medication that the medical staff has specifically prohibited from use in this organization.

Procedure

Nonformulary Medication Request Form—A request for a nonformulary medication shall be made on a Nonformulary Medication Request form (available at nursing units and from the pharmacy). A separate request form shall be completed for each nonformulary medication ordered. The completed form(s) shall be forwarded to the pharmacy.

Review by a Pharmacist—A pharmacist shall review the request. If, in the opinion of the pharmacist, there is an appropriate alternative medication on the formulary, the pharmacist shall inform the prescriber of the alternative. The pharmacist shall indicate the following on the request form: the suggested alternative(s) and the action taken by the pharmacy to obtain the medication.

Procurement of a Nonformulary Medication—If an alternative medication is not acceptable, the pharmacy shall obtain the nonformulary medication from another facility, community pharmacy, or other approved source. The pharmacy shall obtain a supply of the medication sufficient to meet the anticipated needs of the patient for whom it is ordered. If the nonformulary medication cannot be obtained within 4 hours, the pharmacy shall notify the prescriber and nursing service.

Requests for Addition to the Formulary—Completion of a Nonformulary Medication Request form does not constitute a request for addition of the medication to the formulary. A request may be made on a Request for Formulary Addition form, which is available from the pharmacy.

EXAMPLE 11-1

Verification of Licensure, Registration, or Certification for Pharmacy Personnel

The primary source (agency issuing the license, registration, or certification) verified that the license, registration, or certification of the individuals listed below are current, valid, and there is no disciplinary action pending. They are authorized to practice as of the date noted below.

Name	Pharmacist or Technician	Primary Source	Date Verified	Verified by	Notes

EXAMPLE 11-2

Power of Attorney for DEA Order Forms

Registrant (Facility)____

Address____

City/State/Zip Code____

DEA Registration Number____

I,______________________________, the undersigned, who is authorized to sign the current application for registration of the above-named registrant under the Controlled Substances Import and Export Act, have made, constituted, and appointed, and by these presents do make, constitute, and appoint, ____________________ my true and lawful attorney for me in my name, place, and stead to execute applications for books of official order forms and to sign such order forms in requisition for Schedule I and II controlled substances, in accordance with Section 303 of the Controlled Substances Act (21 U.S.C. 828) and Part 1305 of Title 21 of the Code of Federal Regulations. I hereby ratify and confirm all that said attorney shall lawfully do or cause to be done by virtue hereof.

Signature of Person Granting Power______________________________

I,______________________________, hereby affirm that I am the person named herein as attorney-in-fact, and that the signature affixed hereto is my signature.

Signature of Person Receiving Power______________________________

Witnesses:

1. ______________________________

2. ______________________________

Signed and dated on the ________day of ______________20__________at________________

Notice of Revocation

The foregoing power of attorney is hereby revoked by the undersigned, who is authorized to sign the current application for registration of the above-named registrant under the Controlled Substances Act or the Controlled Substances Import and Export Act. Written notice of this revocation has been given to the attorney-in-fact ________________________ this same day.

Signature of Person Revoking Power______________________________

Witnesses:

1. ______________________________

2. ______________________________

Signed and dated on the ________day of ______________ 20 __________ at ________________

Keep This Document with Controlled Substances Records

EXAMPLE 11-3

Medical Staff Information

The pharmacy is required to maintain information relating to the medical staff (including a means of identifying the signatures of practitioners and their Drug Enforcement Administration [DEA] numbers).

Please provide the following information and return this form to the pharmacy.

Name____

Address____

____

____

____

Service/Department__________________________________

Telephone

Office________________________________

Home________________________________

Mobile________________________________

Fax________________________________

E-Mail Address__________________________________

State License Number________________________________

DEA Number (or hospital assigned number)________________________

Controlled Substances License Number (state or other)____________________

Schedules Authorized to Prescribe (circle all that apply) 2 2N 3 3N 4 5

Sample Signature (for signing drug orders)________________________

EXAMPLE 12-1

Pharmacy and Therapeutics Committee Minutes

Date of Meeting

Topic	Findings/Discussion	Recommendations/Action
Call to order	The meeting was called to order at *TIME* by *PHYSICIAN*, Chairman. A quorum was present.	
Attendance	The attendance list was signed by those attending and is attached to these minutes.	
Minutes of Last Meeting	The minutes of the MONTH meeting were approved as distributed.	
Medical Executive Committee Action	The Medical Executive Committee approved the following action items from the last P&T Meeting: • *LIST*	
Formulary		
Additions		
Deletions		
Changes		
Emerging safety data	The FDA released a Black Box warning for the following formulary agents: *LIST*. The Committee voted to:	
Annual review	The 200X Formulary was approved.	
Policies and Procedures		
Floor stock		
Emergency medications		
Investigational drugs		
Annual review	The Committee approved the current policies and procedures regarding medication management.	
Medication Safety		
Medication errors	The *QUARTER* medication error summary was presented to the Committee.	

EXAMPLE 12-1 (continued)

ADRs	*NUMBER* ADRs were reported in *QUARTER*. A preventability assessment was performed on each. The pharmacy was directed to send *SPECIFICS* to the FDA.	
Joint Commission *Sentinel Event Alert*		
ISMP Medication Safety Alert!		
Marketplace		
Recalls		
Shortages		
Medication Use		
MUEs		
Protocols		
Review of preprinted orders		
Antibiogram		
Pharmacist interventions		
Other Performance Improvement Activities		
Evaluation of Drug Cost Information		
Items Requiring Further Approval	The following items approved during this meeting will be forwarded to the Medical Executive Committee for final action: • *LIST*	
Next Meeting	The next meeting will be held on *DATE* at *TIME* in *LOCATION*.	
Adjournment	The meeting was adjourned at *TIME*.	

____
Physician — Chairman

____
Pharmacist — Secretary

EXAMPLE 19-1

Request for Review of an Alternative Approach to a 2007 National Patient Safety Goal (NPSG) Requirement

Instructions: Please submit a separate form for each proposed Alternative. For each Alternative request, the organization must submit the following: A comprehensive literature search to identify: 1) support for the proposed alternative process; and 2) any risks and barriers to implementation, which must be addressed in the organization's description of its proposed alternative process.

Forms should be submitted to your account representative. If you do not know your account representative, call (630) 792-3007. **To facilitate the review process, please fill out and transmit the form electronically.** To do this, go to File, Save As, and save the form to a file in your computer system. Fill out the form using the keyboard, and send it via e-mail as an attachment. If possible, please try to send any additional pages or materials in electronic format. Forms and additional materials can also be faxed or mailed; however, this may delay the review process.

E-mail: npsg@jointcommission.org **Fax:** (630) 792-4522 **Mail:** One Renaissance Blvd., Oakbrook Terrace, IL 60181

Organization name		**HCO #**
City, State		
Alternative approach submitted for NPSG Requirement: (Ex: Hospital "Two Identifiers") Submit only one alternative per form. **Please indicate accreditation program and requirement.**		

Describe the proposed alternative in the space provided (additional page may be attached if needed).

Describe why this approach was selected instead of the recommended approach.

Identify references in the literature supporting the efficacy of this approach and any potential risks or barriers.

Describe how you will monitor the effectiveness of this approach.

For Joint Commission use

Acceptability of the approach described above as an alternative to the NPSG Requirement:

Acceptable ____ Acceptable with modification[1] ____ Not acceptable[2] ____

1. Modification required ____________________

2. Reason for not accepting ____________________

EXAMPLE 20-1

Prohibited Abbreviations

The following abbreviations are prohibited on all orders and other medication-related documentation when handwritten, entered as free text into a computer, or on preprinted forms.

Do not use a leading decimal point without a leading 0.
Use 0.2 instead.

Do not use a trailing zero after a decimal point.
Use 2 instead.

Spell out *units.*
Spell out *international units.*

Spell out *magnesium sulfate*.

Spell out *morphine sulfate*.

Use *daily* instead of QD, Q.D., qd, and q.d.
Use *every other day* instead of QOD, Q.O.D., qod, and q.o.d.

EXAMPLE 20-2

Order Form with Prohibited Abbreviations List

Hospital Name

Patient Information	**Allergies**

Prohibited Abbreviations

.X mg	Do not use a leading decimal point.	Write *0.X mg*.
X.0 mg	Do not use a trailing zero after a decimal point.	Write *X mg*.
U	Do not use *U* for *units*.	Write *units*.
IU	Do not use *IU* for *international units*.	Write *international units*.
$MgSO_4$	Do not abbreviate *magnesium sulfate*.	Write *magnesium sulfate*.
MS & MSO_4	Do not abbreviate *morphine sulfate*.	Write *morphine sulfate*.
QD	Do not abbreviate *every day*.	Write *daily*.
QOD	Do not abbreviate *every other day*.	Write *every other day*.

Date	Time	Orders	Indication for Order if Not Elsewhere in the Record

EXAMPLE 20-3

Letter to Prescriber about Prohibited Abbreviations

Hospital Name
Pharmacy and Therapeutics Committee
Telephone Number

Dear ___________________________:

The attachments contain the following unsafe abbreviations that are prohibited in our hospital:

_____ **U for units may be** mistaken for 0 (zero), 4 (four), or cc. Please write *unit.*

_____ **IU for international units** may be mistaken for IV (intravenous) or 10 (ten). Please write *international units.*

_____ **Q.D. for every day** may be mistaken for Q.I.D. (four times a day). Please write *daily.*

_____ **Q.O.D. for every other day** may be mistaken for Q.I.D. (four times a day). Please write *every other day.*

_____ **Trailing Zero (X.0 mg).** The decimal point may be missed. Please do not write a zero following a decimal point.

_____ **No Leading Zero. (.X mg)** The decimal point may be missed. Please write a zero before a decimal point.

_____ **MS, MSO4, for morphine sulfate.** These abbreviations may be confused for magnesium sulfate. Please write *morphine sulfate.*

_____ **$MgSO_4$ for magnesium sulfate.** This abbreviation may be confused for morphine sulfate. Please write *magnesium sulfate.*

Please contact a Pharmacy and Therapeutics Committee representative at the above number if you need to discuss the hospital's prohibited abbreviations policy.

Thank you,

EXAMPLE 20-4

Monitoring Form for Unacceptable Terms

Unacceptable Terms	Total Times Used in an Acceptable and Unacceptable Form	Occurrences in an Unacceptable Form	Percent Unacceptable Use
U			
IU			
QD			
QOD			
MS			
MSO_4			
$MgSO_4$			
Trailing Zero			
Leading Zero			
Total			

*Surveyors review records for the above items and use the following criteria to determine compliance:

- One occurrence equals one or more unacceptable uses per clinician, per record (one or more unacceptable uses by the same clinician in the same record counts as a single occurrence.)
- Clarification of an order prior to implementation is expected but does not eliminate that occurrence from being counted.
- Immediate correction of the order by the clinician (before it is transcribed/transmitted) is not counted as an occurrence. However, correction after the order has been transcribed/transmitted results in that use of the prohibited abbreviation being counted as an occurrence.
- Three occurrences generate a requirement for improvement.
- Surveyors will score *satisfactory compliance* if only two occurrences or fewer are noted.

For tracking and trending the percentage of unacceptable uses of the above terms use the following formula:

> Occurrences in an unacceptable form – *divided by* – total times used in an acceptable and unacceptable form – *times 100* – equals percent unacceptable use.

The Joint Commission expects 100% compliance for preprinted forms.

***Source:** Adapted from *Joint Commission Perspectives on Patient Safety.* August 2005.

EXAMPLE 21-1

Handling High-Risk/High-Alert Medications

Examples

The following medication examples pose a high risk for serious errors:

- Concentrated electrolytes:
  - Potassium chloride
  - Potassium phosphate
  - Sodium chloride greater that 0.9%
  - Magnesium sulfate
  - Calcium chloride
  - Calcium gluconate
- Insulin
- Controlled medications (e.g., opiates and narcotics)
- Intravenous anticoagulants (e.g., heparin)
- Antineoplastic medications
- Neonatal and pediatric medications
- Epidural medications
- Patient controlled analgesia medications
- Neuromuscular blocking agents
- Medications with look-alike/sound-alike names
- Investigational medications
- Medications not approved by the FDA

Precautions

Persons who administer high risk/high-alert medications must do the following:

- Verify the medication name and strength
- Prepare the amount of medication to be administered
- Compare and confirm the medication, the name, strength, and amount to administer with the patient's record
- Ensure that the amount to administer does not exceed the maximum amount permitted for administration
- Contact a pharmacist if the amount to administer exceeds the maximum permitted
- Have a second qualified individual verify the medication name, strength, and amount to administer
- Have a second qualified individual check the calculations used in determining the amount to administer
- Document the double checks in the patient's record

Staff must contact the pharmacy or on-call pharmacist if there are any questions about these medications and calculating the amount to administer.

APPENDIX A

Contact Information

Accreditation Council for Pharmacy Education (ACPE)

20 North Clark Street
Suite 2500
Chicago, IL 60602
Telephone: 312-664-3575
Fax: 312-664-4652 or 312-664-7008
Internet Web site: www.acpe-accred.org

Agency for Healthcare Research and Quality (AHRQ)

Office of Communications and Knowledge Transfer
540 Gaither Road
Suite 2000
Rockville, MD 20850
Telephone: 301-427-1364
Internet Web site: www.ahrq.gov

American Association of Poison Control Centers (AAPCC)

3201 New Mexico Avenue
Suite 300
Washington, DC 20016
Telephone: 202-362-7217
Fax: 202-362-3240
Internet Web site: www.aapcc.org

American College of Clinical Pharmacy (ACCP)

13000 West 87th Street Parkway
Lenexa, KS 66215
Telephone: 913-492-3311
Fax: 913-492-0088
Internet Web site: www.accp.com

American Medical Association (AMA)

515 North State Street
Chicago, IL 60610
Telephone: 800-621-8335
Internet Web site: www.ama-assn.org

American Osteopathic Association (AOA)

142 East Ontario Street
Chicago, IL 60611
Telephone: 312-202-8000 or 800-621-1773
Fax: 312-202-8200
Internet Web site: www.do-online.org

American Pain Society

4700 West Lake Avenue
Glenview, IL 60025
Telephone: 847-375-4715
Fax: 877-734-8758
Internet Web site: www.ampainsoc.org/advocacy/range.htm

American Society of Consultant Pharmacists (ASCP)

1321 Duke Street
Alexandria, VA 22314
Telephone: 703-739-1300 or 800-355-2727
Fax: 703-739-1321
Internet Web site: www.ascp.com

American Society of Health-System Pharmacists (ASHP)

7272 Wisconsin Avenue
Bethesda, MD 20814
Telephone: 301-657-3000
Fax: 301-657-1251
Customer Service: 866-279-0681
Internet Web site: www.ashp.org

American Society for Parenteral and Enteral Nutrition (A.S.P.E.N.)

8630 Fenton Street
Suite 412
Silver Spring, MD 20910
Telephone: 301-587-6315 or 800-727-4567
Fax: 301-587-2365
Internet Web site: www.nutritioncare.org

Association of periOperative Registered Nurses (AORN)

2170 South Parker Road
Suite 300
Denver, CO 80231
Telephone: 303-755-6304 or 800-755-2676
Fax: 303-750-3212
Internet Web site: www.aorn.org/PracticeResources/

Centers for Disease Control and Prevention (CDC)

1600 Clifton Road
Atlanta, GA 30333
Telephone: 404-639-3311
Internet Web site: www.cdc.gov

Centers for Medicare and Medicaid Services (CMS)

7500 Security Boulevard
Baltimore, MD 21244
Telephone: 410-786-3000 or 877-267-2323
Internet Web site: www.cms.gov
Internet Web site for Conditions of Participation (CoPs) and related information: www.cms.hhs.gov/manuals/Downloads/som107ap_a_hospitals.pdf.

Drug Enforcement Administration (DEA)

2401 Jefferson Davis Highway
Alexandria, VA 22301
Telephone: 202-307-5000
Internet Web site: www.dea.gov

Food and Drug Administration

5600 Fishers Lane
Rockville, MD 20852-9787
Telephone: 888-INFO-FDA (888-463-6332)
Fax: 800-FDA-0178
Internet Web site: www.fda.gov

Hand Hygiene Resource Center (HHRC)

Hospital of Saint Raphael
1450 Chapel Street
New Haven, CT 06511
Telephone: 203-789-3000
Internet Web site: www.handhygiene.org

Healthcare Facilities Accreditation Program (HFAP)

American Osteopathic Association
142 East Ontario Street
Chicago, IL 60611-2864
Telephone: 312-202-8060 or 800-621-1773, extension 8060
Fax: 312-202-8360
Internet Web site: www.hfap.org

Hospital Pharmacy

77 Westport Plaza
Suite 450
St. Louis, MO 63146-3098
Telephone (Subscription Information): 800-638-3030
Fax: 314-216-2283
Internet Web site: www.hospitalpharmacyjournal.com

Institute of Medicine (IOM)

500 Fifth Street NW
Washington, DC 20001
Telephone: 202-334-2352
Fax: 202-334-1412
Internet Web site: www.iom.edu

Institute for Safe Medication Practices (ISMP)

1800 Byberry Road
Suite 810
Huntingdon Valley, PA 19006
Telephone: 215-947-7797
Fax: 215-914-1492
Internet Web site: www.ismp.org

Joint Commission (The)

One Renaissance Boulevard
Oakbrook Terrace, IL 60181
Telephone: 630-792-5000
Fax: 630-792-5005
Customer Service: 630-792-5800
Current List of Fixed Components: 630-792-5871
Standards Interpretation Unit: 630-792-5900 (Fax: 630-792-5942)
ORYX Information: 630-792-5085
ORYX e-mail: oryx@jointcommission.org
Internet Web site: www.jointcommission.org

Joint Commission Resources (JCR)

Telephone (Consulting Services): 630-268-7400
Internet Web site: www.jcrinc.com

Massachusetts Coalition for the Prevention of Medical Errors

5 New England Executive Park
Burlington, MA 01803
Telephone: 781-272-8000
Fax: 781-272-0605
Internet Web site: www.macoalition.org

MedWatch

The FDA Safety Information and Adverse Event Reporting Program
Food and Drug Administration
5600 Fishers Lane
Rockville, MD 20852-9787
Telephone: 800-FDA-1088
Fax: 800-FDA-0178
Internet Web site: www.fda.gov/medwatch

National Association of Boards of Pharmacy (NABP)

1600 Feehanville Drive
Mount Prospect, IL 60056
Telephone: 847-391-4406
Fax: 847-391-4502
Internet Web site: www.nabp.net

National Coordinating Council for Medication Error Reporting and Prevention (NCCMERP)

Internet Web site: www.nccmerp.org

National Fire Protection Association (NFPA)

1 Batterymarch Park
Quincy, MA 02169
Telephone: 617-770-3000 or 800-344-3555
Fax: 617-770-0700
Internet Web site: www.nfpa.org

National Institute for Occupational Safety and Health (NIOSH)

395 E Street, SW
Suite 9200
Patriots Plaza Building
Washington, DC 20201
Telephone: 800-35-NIOSH (4674)
Internet Web site: www.cdc.gov/niosh

National Quality Forum (NQF)

601 13th Street NW
Suite 500 North
Washington, DC 20005
Telephone: 202-783-1300
Fax: 202-783-3434
Internet Web site: www.qualityforum.org

Occupational Safety and Health Administration (OSHA)

U.S. Department of Labor
200 Constitution Avenue NW
Washington, DC 20210
Telephone: 800-321-OSHA (6742)
Internet Web site: www.osha.gov

Office for Civil Rights (OCR)

U.S. Department of Health and Human Services
200 Independence Avenue SW
Room 509, HHH Building
Washington, DC 20201
Telephone: 800-368-1019
Internet Web site: www.hhs.gov/ocr
HIPAA Internet Web site: www.hhs.gov/ocr/hipaa

United States Pharmacopeia (USP)

12601 Twinbrook Parkway
Rockville, MD 20852-1790
Telephone: 800-227-8772
USP Medication Errors Reporting Program: 800-23-ERROR
Internet Web site: www.usp.org

Vaccine Adverse Event Reporting System (VAERS)

PO Box 1100
Rockville, MD 20849-1100
Telephone: 800-822-7967
Fax: 877-721-0366
Internet Web site: www.vaers.hhs.gov

World Health Organization (WHO)

Avenue Appia 20
1211 Geneva 27
Switzerland
Telephone: (+-41-22)-791-21-11
Fax: (+-41-22)-791-3111
Internet Web site: www.who.int
Internet Web site (Hand Hygiene Guidelines): www.who.int/patientsafety/information_centre/HH_RSGuidelines_FINAL.pdf

References and Resources

Chapter 1

1. The Joint Commission. About us. Available at: <http://www.jointcommission.org/AboutUS/. Accessed August 12, 2007.
2. The Joint Commission. *Comprehensive Accreditation Manual for Hospitals: The Official Handbook.* Oakbrook Terrace, IL: The Joint Commission; 2007.

Chapter 2

1. The Joint Commission. *Comprehensive Accreditation Manual for Hospitals: The Official Handbook.* Oakbrook Terrace, IL: The Joint Commission; 2007.

Chapter 3

No references.

Chapter 4

1. The Joint Commission. *Comprehensive Accreditation Manual for Hospitals: The Official Handbook.* Oakbrook Terrace, IL: The Joint Commission; 2007.
2. Centers for Medicare and Medicaid Services (CMS), Department of Health and Human Services. *State Operations Manual Appendix A—Survey Protocol, Regulations and Interpretive Guidelines for Hospitals.* 1st rev. Washington, DC: Government Printing Office; 2004. Available at: www.cms.hhs.gov/manuals/downloads/som107ap_a_hospitals.pdf. Accessed August 12, 2007.
3. The United States Pharmacopeial Convention (USPC). Pharmaceutical compounding—sterile preparations. In: *The United States Pharmacopeia,* 30th rev. ed., and the *National Formulary*, 25th ed. Rockville, MD: USPC; 2006 (vol 1):334–51.

Chapter 5

No references.

Chapter 6

1. The Joint Commission. *Comprehensive Accreditation Manual for Hospitals: The Official Handbook.* Oakbrook Terrace, IL. The Joint Commission; 2007; HR-9–10.

Chapter 7

1. American Society of Health-System Pharmacists (ASHP). *Medication Teaching Manual: The Guide to Patient Drug Information.* 8th ed. Bethesda, MD: American Society of Health-System Pharmacists; 2004.
2. Murdaugh LB. *Competence Assessment Tools for Health-System Pharmacies.* 4th ed. Bethesda, MD: American Society of Health-System Pharmacists; 2008.

Chapter 8

1. The Joint Commission. *Comprehensive Accreditation Manual for Hospitals: The Official Handbook.* Oakbrook Terrace, IL: The Joint Commission; 2007.
2. Centers for Disease Control and Prevention (CDC). Guideline for hand hygiene in health-care settings. *MMWR*. 2002:51:31–4. Available at: www.cdc.gov/handhygiene. Accessed August 12, 2007.
3. The United States Pharmacopeial Convention (USPC). Pharmaceutical compounding—sterile preparations. In: *The United States Pharmacopeia*, 30th rev. ed., and the *National Formulary*, 25th ed. Rockville, MD: USPC; 2006 (vol 1):334–51.
4. World Health Organization (WHO). Hand hygiene guidelines. Available at: www.who.int/patientsafety/information_centre/HH_RSGuidelines_FINAL.pdf.

5. Centers for Disease Control and Prevention (CDC). Guidelines for isolation precautions in hospitals. CDC; 2007. Available at: http://www.cdc.gov/ncidod/dhqp/gl_isolation.html. Accessed August 12, 2007.

6. The United States Pharmacopeial Convention (USPC). Antimicrobial effectiveness testing. In: *The United States Pharmacopeia*, 30th rev. ed., and the *National Formulary*, 25th ed. Rockville, MD: USPC; 2006 (vol 1):79–81.

Chapter 9

No references.

Chapter 10

1. Centers for Medicare and Medicaid Services (CMS), Department of Health and Human Services. *State Operations Manual Appendix A—Survey Protocol, Regulations and Interpretive Guidelines for Hospitals.* 1st rev. Washington, DC: Government Printing Office; 2004. Available at: www.cms.hhs.gov/manuals/downloads/som107ap_a_hospitals.pdf. Accessed August 12, 2007.

Chapter 11

1. Drug Enforcement Administration (DEA). Pharmacists Manual. Available at: www.deadiversion.usdoj.gov/pubs/manuals/pharm2/index.htm. Accessed August 12, 2007.

Chapter 12

1. American Society of Health-System Pharmacists. ASHP statement on the pharmacy and therapeutics committee. *Am J Hosp Pharm.* 1992;49:2008–9. Available at: www.ashp.org/s_ashp/bin.asp?CID=6&DID=5391&DOC=FILE.PDF. Accessed August 12, 2007.

2. American Society of Health-System Pharmacists. ASHP statement on the formulary system. *Am J Hosp Pharm.* 1983;40:1384–5. Available at: www.ashp.org/s_ashp/bin.asp?CID=6&DID=5392&DOC=FILE.PDF. Accessed August 12, 2007.

3. American Society of Health-System Pharmacists. ASHP technical assistance bulletin on drug formularies. *Am J Hosp Pharm.* 1991;48:791–3. Available at: www.ashp.org/s_ashp/bin.asp?CID=6&DID=5466&DOC=FILE.PDF. Accessed August 12, 2007.

4. American Society of Health-System Pharmacists. ASHP technical assistance bulletin on the evaluation of drugs for formularies. *Am J Hosp Pharm.* 1988; 45:386–7. Available at: www.ashp.org/s_ashp/bin.asp?CID=6&DID=5467&DOC=FILE.PDF. Accessed August 12, 2007.

Chapter 13

1. Kane MT. The assessment of professional competence. *Eval Health Prof.* 1992;15(2):163–82.

2. Murdaugh LB. *Competence Assessment Tools for Health-System Pharmacies.* 4th ed. Bethesda, MD: American Society of Health-System Pharmacists; 2008.

Chapter 14

1. The Joint Commission. *Comprehensive Accreditation Manual for Hospitals: The Official Handbook.* Oakbrook Terrace, IL: The Joint Commission; 2007:SE 1–11.

Resources for Process Improvement Tools

1. Brassard M, Ritter D. *The Memory Jogger II: A Pocket Guide to Tools for Continuous Quality Improvement and Effective Planning.* 1st ed. Methuen, MA: GOAL/QPC; 1994.

2. The Joint Commission. *Using Performance Improvement Tools in Health Care Settings.* 3rd ed. Oakbrook Terrace, IL: The Joint Commission; 2006.

Resources for FMEA

1. Burkhardt M, DeRosier J, Stalhandske E, et al. Veterans Health Administration approach to failure mode and effects analysis. In: Cohen MR, ed. *Medication Errors.* 2nd ed. Washington, DC: American Pharmacists Association; 2007:576–86.

2. Senders JW, Senders SJ. Introduction to failure mode and effects analysis. In: Cohen MR, ed. *Medication Errors.* 2nd ed. Washington, DC: American Pharmacists Association; 2007:561–5.

3. Smetzer JL, Cohen MR. An application of failure mode and effects analysis. In: Cohen MR, ed. *Medication Errors.* 2nd ed. Washington, DC: American Pharmacists Association; 2007:565–76.

4. The Joint Commission. *Failure Mode and Effects Analysis in Healthcare: Proactive Risk Reduction.* 2nd ed. Oakbrook, IL: The Joint Commission; 2005.

Chapter 15

1. The Joint Commission. *Comprehensive Accreditation Manual for Hospitals: The Official Handbook.* Oakbrook Terrace, IL: The Joint Commission; 2007:PM-1–7.
2. Facts about ORYX for Hospitals, Core Measures, and Hospital Core Measures. Available at: www.jointcommission.org/AccreditationPrograms/Hospitals/ORYX/oryx_facts.htm. Accessed August 12, 2007.
3. Joint Commission. *Perspectives.* Oakbrook Terrace, IL; Joint Commission: 2007; 27(3):1–5.
4. The Joint Commission. *Comprehensive Accreditation Manual for Hospitals: The Official Handbook.* Oakbrook Terrace, IL: The Joint Commission; 2007:PM-3–7.

Chapter 16

1. Occupational Safety and Health Administration. Hazard communication standard. Available at: osha.gov. Accessed August 12, 2007
2. Occupational Safety and Health Administration. Hospital eTool pharmacy module. Available at: www.osha.gov/SLTC/etools/hospital/pharmacy/pharmacy.html#HazardCommunicationStandard. Accessed August 12, 2007.
3. Occupational Safety and Health Administration. Some common drugs considered to be hazardous. Available at: www.osha.gov/dts/osta/otm/otm_vi/otm_vi_2.html#app_vi:2_1. Accessed August 12, 2007.
4. National Institute for Occupational Safety and Health (NIOSH). Sample list of drugs that should be handled as hazardous. Available at: www.cdc.gov/niosh/docs/2004-165/2004-165d.html#o. Accessed August 12, 2007.
5. Murdaugh LB. *Competence Assessment Tools for Health-System Pharmacies.* 4th ed. Bethesda, MD: American Society of Health-System Pharmacists; 2008.

Chapter 17

1. Department of Health and Human Services. Centers for Disease Control and Prevention National Institute for Occupational Safety and Health. *NIOSH Alert: Preventing Occupational Exposures to Antineoplastic and Other Hazardous Drugs in Health Care Settings. 2004.* Available at: www.cdc.gov/niosh/docs/2004-165/. Accessed August 12, 2007.
2. American Society of Hospital Pharmacists. ASHP guidelines on handling hazardous drugs. *Am J Health Syst Pharm.* 2006; 63:1172–93. Available at: www.ashp.org/s_ashp/bin.asp?CID=6&DID= 5420&DOC=FILE.PDF. Accessed August 12, 2007.
3. Department of Health and Human Services. Centers for Disease Control and Prevention National Institute for Occupational Safety and Health. Sample list of drugs that should be handled as dangerous. Available at: www.cdc.gov/niosh/docs/2004-165/2004-165d.html#o. Accessed August 12, 2007.

Chapter 18

1. The United States Pharmacopeial Convention (USPC). Pharmaceutical compounding—sterile preparations. In: *The United States Pharmacopeia*, 30th rev. ed., and the *National Formulary*, 25th ed. Rockville, MD: USPC; 2006 (vol 1):334–51.
2. CETA certification guide for sterile compounding facilities. CAG-003-2006. June 7, 2006. Available at: www.cetainternational.org/reference/CETAAsepticCompoundingCertificationGuide.pdf. Accessed August 12, 2007.
3. CETA compounding isolator testing guide. CAG-002-2006. March 3, 2006. Available at: www.cetainternational.org/reference/CETACompoundingIsolatorTestingGuide2006.pdf. Accessed August 12, 2007.
4. CETA applications guide for the use of compounding isolators in compounding sterile preparations in healthcare facilities. CAG-001-2005. November 8, 2005. Available at: www.cetainternational.org/reference/ApplicationsGuideBarrierIsolator110805.pdf. Accessed August 12, 2007.
5. Murdaugh LB. *Competence Assessment Tools for Health-System Pharmacies.* 4th ed. Bethesda, MD: American Society of Health-System Pharmacists; 2008.

6. Trissel LA. *Handbook on Injectable Drugs*, 14th ed. Bethesda, MD: American Society of Health-System Pharmacists; 2007.

Chapter 19

1. The Joint Commission. *Comprehensive Accreditation Manual for Hospitals: The Official Handbook.* Oakbrook Terrace, IL: The Joint Commission; 2007:NPSG-2.
2. The Joint Commission. *Joint Commission Perspectives.* Oakbrook Terrace, IL: The Joint Commission; 2007:27(7).
3. The Joint Commission. Request for Review of an Alternative Approach to a 2007 National Patient Safety Goal Requirement. Available at: www.jointcommission.org/PatientSafety/NationalPatientSafetyGoals/07_npsg_rfr.htm. Accessed August 12, 2007.

Chapter 20

NPSG-1 Requirement 1A

1. The Joint Commission. *Joint Commission Perspectives.* Oakbrook Terrace, IL: The Joint Commission; 2007;27(7):10–9.
2. The Joint Commission. *Comprehensive Accreditation Manual for Hospitals: The Official Handbook.* Oakbrook Terrace, IL: The Joint Commission; 2007.
3. The Joint Commission. FAQs for The Joint Commission's 2007 national patient safety goals. Available at: www.jointcommission.org. Accessed August 12, 2007.
4. Rich DS. More on the requirements of the medication-related national patient safety goals for 2003–2004. *Hosp Pharm.* 2003;38:977–81.

NPSG-2 Requirement 2A

1. The Joint Commission. *Joint Commission Perspectives.* Oakbrook Terrace, IL: The Joint Commission; 2007;27(7):10–9.
2. The Joint Commission. FAQs for The Joint Commission's 2007 national patient safety goals. Available at: www.jointcommission.org. Accessed August 12, 2007.
3. Rich DS. More on the requirements of the medication-related national patient safety goals for 2003–2004. *Hosp Pharm.* 2003;38:977–81.
4. National Coordinating Council for Medication Error Reporting and Prevention (NCCMERP). Available at: www.nccmerp.org. Accessed August 12, 2007.

NPSG-2 Requirement 2B

1. The Joint Commission. *Joint Commission Perspectives on Patient Safety.* The Joint Commission; 2007;27(7):10–9.
2. The Joint Commission. FAQs for The Joint Commission's 2007 national patient safety goals. Available at: www.jointcommission.org. Accessed August 12, 2007.

NPSG-2 Requirement 2C

1. The Joint Commission. *Joint Commission Perspectives.* Oakbrook Terrace, IL: The Joint Commission; 2007;27(7):10–9.
2. The Joint Commission. FAQs for The Joint Commission's 2007 national patient safety goals. Available at: www.jointcommission.org. Accessed August 12, 2007.

NPSG-2 Requirement 2E

1. The Joint Commission. *Joint Commission Perspectives.* Oakbrook Terrace, IL: The Joint Commission; 2007;27(7):10–9.
2. The Joint Commission. FAQs for The Joint Commission's 2007 national patient safety goals. Available at: www.jointcommission.org. Accessed August 12, 2007.

NPSG-3 Requirement 3C

1. The Joint Commission. *Joint Commission Perspectives.* Oakbrook Terrace, IL: The Joint Commission; 2007;27(7):10–9.
2. The Joint Commission. FAQs for The Joint Commission's 2007 national patient safety goals. Available at: www.jointcommission.org. Accessed August 12, 2007.
3. The Joint Commission. Look-alike/sound-alike drug list. Available at: www.jcaho.org/accredited+organizations/patient+safety/npsg.htm. Accessed August 12, 2007.

NPSG-3 Requirement 3D

1. The Joint Commission. *Joint Commission Perspectives.* Oakbrook Terrace, IL: The Joint Commission; 2007;27(7):10–9.
2. The Joint Commission. FAQs for The Joint Commission's 2007 national patient safety goals. Available at: www.jointcommission.org. Accessed August 12, 2007.
3. The Joint Commission. *Comprehensive Accreditation Manual for Hospitals: The Official Handbook.* Oakbrook Terrace, IL: The Joint Commission; 2007.

NPSG-3 Requirement 3E

Reference

1. The Joint Commission. *Joint Commission Perspectives.* Oakbrook Terrace, IL: The Joint Commission; 2007;27(7):10–9.

Resource

1. Improving Anticoagulant Safety—Perspectives on Patient Safety. August 2007;(7):8, 6–7.

NPSG-7 Requirement 7A

1. The Joint Commission. *Joint Commission Perspectives.* Oakbrook Terrace, IL: The Joint Commission; 2007:27(7):10–9.
2. The Joint Commission. FAQs for The Joint Commission's 2007 national patient safety goals. Available at: www.jointcommission.org. Accessed August 12, 2007.

NPSG-7 Requirement 7B

1. The Joint Commission. *Joint Commission Perspectives.* Oakbrook Terrace, IL: The Joint Commission; 2007;27(7):10–9.
2. The Joint Commission. FAQs for The Joint Commission's 2007 national patient safety goals. Available at: www.jointcommission.org. Accessed August 12, 2007.

NPSG-8 Requirement 8A

1. The Joint Commission. *Joint Commission Perspectives.* Oakbrook Terrace, IL: The Joint Commission; 2007;27(7):10–9.
2. The Joint Commission. FAQs for The Joint Commission's 2007 national patient safety goals. Available at: www.jointcommission.org. Accessed August 12, 2007.

NPSG-8 Requirement 8B

1. The Joint Commission. *Joint Commission Perspectives.* Oakbrook Terrace, IL: The Joint Commission; 2007;27(7):10–9.
2. The Joint Commission. FAQs for The Joint Commission's 2007 national patient safety goals. Available at: www.jointcommission.org. Accessed August 12, 2007.

NPSG-9 Requirement 9B

1. The Joint Commission. *Joint Commission Perspectives.* Oakbrook Terrace, IL: The Joint Commission; 2007;27(7):10–9.
2. The Joint Commission. FAQs for The Joint Commission's 2007 national patient safety goals. Available at: www.jointcommission.org. Accessed August 12, 2007.

NPSG-13 Requirement 13A

1. The Joint Commission. *Joint Commission Perspectives.* Oakbrook Terrace, IL: The Joint Commission; 2007; 27(7):10–9.
2. The Joint Commission. FAQs for The Joint Commission's 2007 national patient safety goals. Available at: www.jointcommission.org. Accessed August 12, 2007.

NPSG-15 Requirement 15A

1. The Joint Commission. *Joint Commission Perspectives.* Oakbrook Terrace, IL: The Joint Commission; 2007;27(7):10–9.
2. The Joint Commission. FAQs for The Joint Commission's 2007 national patient safety goals. Available at: www.jointcommission.org. Accessed August 12, 2007.

NPSG-16 Requirement 16A

1. The Joint Commission. *Joint Commission Perspectives.* Oakbrook Terrace, IL: The Joint Commission; 2007;27(7):10–9.

Chapter 21

1. National Coordinating Council for Medication Error Reporting and Prevention (NCCMERP). Internet Web site. Available at: www.nccmerp.org. Accessed August 12, 2007.
2. American Society of Health-System Pharmacists. ASHP guidelines on preventing medication errors in hospitals. *Am J Health Syst Pharm.* 1993;50:305–14.
3. Cohen MR, ed. *Medication Errors.* 2nd ed. Washington: American Pharmacists Association; 2007.
4. Trissel LA. *Handbook on Injectable Drugs.* 14th ed. Bethesda, MD: American Society of Health-System Pharmacists; 2007.

Chapter 22

1. Food and Drug Administration. MedWatch, The FDA Safety Information and Adverse Event Reporting Program Web site. Available at: www.fda.gov/medwatch. Accessed August 12, 2007.
2. American Society of Health-System Pharmacists (ASHP). ASHP guidelines on adverse drug reaction monitoring and reporting. *Am J Health Syst Pharm.* 1995;52:417–9.
3. The Joint Commission. *Comprehensive Accreditation Manual for Hospitals: The Official Handbook.* Oakbrook Terrace, IL: The Joint Commission; 2007.

Chapter 23

1. Food and Drug Administration. MedWatch, The FDA Safety Information and Adverse Event Reporting Program Web site. Available at: www.fda.gov/medwatch. Accessed August 12, 2007.
2. Centers for Disease Control and Prevention and Food and Drug Administration. Vaccine Adverse Event Reporting System Internet Web site. Available at: www.vaers.org Accessed August 12, 2007.

Chapter 24

1. Centers for Medicare and Medicaid Services (CMS), Department of Health and Human Services. *State Operations Manual Appendix A—Survey Protocol, Regulations and Interpretive Guidelines for Hospitals.* 1st rev. Washington, DC: Government Printing Office; 2004. Available at: www.cms.hhs.gov/manuals/downloads/som107ap_a_hospitals.pdf. Accessed August 12, 2007.

Chapter 25

1. American Osteopathic Association. Internet Website. Available at: www.do-online.org. Accessed August 12, 2007.
2. American Osteopathic Association (AOA). *Accreditation Requirements for Healthcare Facilities.* Chicago, IL: American Osteopathic Association; 2005.

Index

A

D

E

F

G

H

I

N

O

P

Q

R

S